A Concise Dictionary
of Nakoda (Assiniboine)

Studies in the
Native Languages
of the Americas

EDITOR

Tim Thornes

*Recipient of the
Mary R. Haas Award
Presented by
The Society for the
Study of the
Indigenous Languages
of the Americas*

A Concise Dictionary
of Nakoda (Assiniboine)

VINCENT COLLETTE

With Wilma Kennedy

Foreword by Chief Ira McArthur

University of Nebraska Press | Lincoln

In cooperation with the Society for the Study
of the Indigenous Languages of the Americas

The University of Nebraska Press is part of a land-grant institution with campuses and programs on the past, present, and future homelands of the Pawnee, Ponca, Otoe-Missouria, Omaha, Dakota, Lakota, Kaw, Cheyenne, and Arapaho Peoples, as well as those of the relocated Ho-Chunk, Sac and Fox, and Iowa Peoples.

This work received funding from TransCanada Energy, the Mosaic Company, Oakland Industries Ltd., and Team Power Solutions.

Library of Congress Cataloging-in-Publication Data
Names: Collette, Vincent, 1976–, author. | Kennedy, Wilma, writer of foreword. | McArthur, Ira, Chief other.
Title: A concise dictionary of Nakoda (Assiniboine) / Vincent Collette with Wilma Kennedy; foreword by Chief Ira McArthur.
Description: Lincoln: University of Nebraska Press; Bloomington: American Indian Studies Research Institute, 2023.
Series: Studies in the Native languages of the Americas | Includes bibliographical references.
Identifiers: LCCN 2022019649
ISBN 9781496229724 (hardback)
ISBN 9781496232724 (pdf)
Subjects: LCSH: Assiniboine dialect–Dictionaries–English. | English language–Dictionaries–Assiniboine. | BISAC: SOCIAL SCIENCE / Ethnic Studies / American / Native American Studies | LANGUAGE ARTS & DISCIPLINES / Grammar & Punctuation | LCGFT: Dictionaries.
Classification: LCC PM2351.Z5 C65 2023 |
DDC 497/.524–dc23/eng/20220721
LC record available at https://lccn.loc.gov/2022019649

Set in Merope (Charles Ellertson/Tseng Informations Systems) by A. Shahan.

Contents

Illustrations

Foreword

Chief Ira McArthur

A Concise Dictionary of Nakoda (Assiniboine) by Vincent Collette and Wilma Kennedy is the culmination of many hours of selfless dedication and commitment by the authors. Their work herein brings to life the hopes and dreams of Nakoda/Assiniboine Elders from the communities of the Pheasant Rump Nakoda First Nation, Ocean Man First Nation, White Bear First Nations, Carry The Kettle Nakoda Nation, and the Mosquito, Grizzly Bear's Head, and Lean Man First Nations, as well as the Nakoda/Assiniboine tribes of the Fort Peck and Fort Belknap Reservations of Montana, who recognize the state of endangerment of the Nakoda language, and encourage preservation and revitalization through any means necessary.

No amount of words can be written or spoken to truly capture the gratitude we all feel in our hearts for the efforts and contributions of the late Elder Wilma Kennedy. Recognizing that her knowledge was priceless, this work became a legacy that highlights her selfless love and dedication to the preservation of the Nakoda language. We also applaud and honor her family and the relatives of Carry The Kettle for allowing us precious time with her to complete this project. The proverb "when an Elder passes, a library of wisdom/knowledge is lost" is really true when used in the context of the state of our language. In this case, Wilma ensured that a small portion of her knowledge and wisdom would live on through her contributions so that we all may learn to love and cherish the Nakoda language as she had.

The word *koná* describes a person who is a friend, not in the manner in which we understand a friend to be in the viewpoint of today's western or Eurocentric society, but rather from the Indigenous viewpoint, that, from my understanding, regards a friend as someone who is held in high regard, not just by an individual, a family, or a small group of people, but rather by the Nation as a whole. In our Nakoda ways and teachings we address and regard Vincent Collette as *koná*. His personal contributions to this project and the time he spent away from his family speak volumes of the type of man he is and the responsibility and reverence with which he undertook the research, collecting, and validating necessary to document our language. The care and diligence he manifests when working with our Elders and communities lends great credence to the quality of work that this book represents.

As with all things we do, in our everyday lives our Elders teach us to lift up and honor one another through kind expressions and gestures. And at this time, I want to mention the following individuals for their enthusiastic and wholehearted efforts to revitalize the Nakoda language in our communities and for the tribe as a whole: Armand McArthur, Juanita McArthur-BigEagle, and Keegan McArthur of Pheasant Rump; Peter Bigstone and Bronte BigEagle of Ocean Man; Leona Kroeskamp, Robert McArthur, Shay McArthur, and Sarah McArthur of White Bear; Nancy Eashappie, Matthew Spencer, Chad O'Watch, Iris O'Watch, Kyrsten Saulteaux and Theresa O'Watch of Carry The Kettle; Kenneth Armstrong of Mosquito/Grizzly Bear's Head/Lean Man; Michael Turcotte and Roger White of Fort Peck; and Kenneth Hegelson and Tom Shawl of Fort Belknap. We also lift up and honor our relatives who returned home to the Creator and whose legacies continue to inspire this work: Victor Sammy of White Bear, Armand McArthur of Pheasant Rump, Freda O'Watch, and Wilma Kennedy of Carry The Kettle.

I want to say thank you to the Elders, Council, and members of Pheasant Rump for allowing us to prioritize the preservation and revitalization of the Nakoda language not only within our band but also on behalf of all communities of the Nakoda tribe. Thanks also to Karen Buseman from the Summer Institute of Linguistics who provided the professional help in untangling the quirks of the Toolbox program used to compile this dictionary.

We also recognize the financial support provided by Mosaic Company, TransCanada, and Oakland Industries for this initiative. With partnership comes responsibility, and with responsibility arises opportunity.

We dedicate this work to the children, youth, and coming generations of the Nakoda tribe and pray that our language will bless our homes, families, and people for as long as our bloodline remains.

Messages from Funders

TransCanada Energy is honored to support the development of this essential resource to aid in the preservation of the Nakoda language.

Congratulations to Pheasant Rump and the Nakoda Nation for recognizing the need to preserve the language and culture by developing this dictionary of the Nakoda language. We thank Elder Wilma Kennedy (Carry The Kettle) for sharing her knowledge to provide the five thousand words and phrases to make this a reality. This is an important first step to save and revitalize the Nakoda language for future generations. The Mosaic Company is proud to sponsor this project and to support First Nations that surround our operations on projects and initiatives such as these.

Oakland Industries, Ltd. and our industry partner Team Power Solutions are grateful for the opportunity to have provided funding support to the community of Pheasant Rump Nakoda First Nation for preserving its culture through the development of this exciting publication by revitalizing the Nakoda language for future generations.

Pinámayaye no!

Introduction

A Short History of the Nakoda People
The Nakoda are an indigenous people of the Siouan family inhabiting the northern plains of North America, in both Saskatchewan (Canada) and Montana (United States). Before contact the Nakoda practiced a tallgrass prairie/parkland culture. In the winter they hunted moose, deer, and elk as well as small game along with fishing and trapping in the fall when they took coverage in the parklands. In the summer some Nakoda followed a seminomadic way of life and used dog travois to haul their tipi poles and other belongings as they followed the buffalo (killed traditionally with buffalo pounds and later with horses). (The Canadian parklands is a large transitional biome located between the boreal forest and the prairies, and it extends from southwestern Manitoba, cutting diagonally through Saskatchewan and up to central Alberta.)

Warfare and counting coups constituted an important part of their culture since they enabled a man to marry and gain respect and social status (DeMallie & Miller 2001:579). Nakoda culture is typical of the northern Plains and encompasses an impressive diversity of songs, dances, and ceremonies (see Denig 2000[1930]:162–71, 223–26). Still nowadays the Nakoda hold Sundances, a four-day ritual that includes vision quests by young men who search for help and protection from their guardian spirits, in June. The highlight of Sundances is the piercing of the young men's chests with skewers that were then attached to the center pole or "holy tree" (DeMallie & Miller 2001:579).

It is possible to roughly circumscribe Nakoda territorial boundaries prior to contact. Ray (1974:4) proposes that the Nakoda territory extended along the parklands from the western shores of Lake Superior, including a thin fringe of northern Wisconsin and Minnesota, to central Saskatchewan, including south-central Manitoba (Ray 1974:4). The Cree and the Nakoda/Stoney seem to have pushed westward from the Hudson Bay in the course of the late seventeenth century in order to extend their role as trade middlemen, but some authors like Andersen (1970:50) state instead that westward expansion might be a "latephase or surge in an old westward migration of Siouan and Algonquian speakers along the forested edge of the northern Plains." This parallels oral Nakoda history that suggests that their precontact homeland extended from Lake Winnipeg to the Rockies and also archaeological findings, such as Walde (2010), who states that ceramic ware of the terminal Mortlach phase found in southwestern Saskatchewan were produced by prehistoric bands of Nakoda. However, the question is complex, and others have proposed that Mortlach phase was the product of prehistoric Hidatsa (another Siouan group).

The Nakoda, who were more commonly known as the "Assiniboine"—a term that means "Stone warrior" in Ojibwe (spelled variously as "Senipoet," "Assinipoualak," or "Assiniboëls")—are mentioned in the Jesuit Relations as early as 1640. In 1678 French trader Daniel Greyloson Dulhut made the first contact with the Nakoda and located the eastern range of their territory west of Lake Nipigon (Ontario) (Ray 1974:11). At that time French sources systematically placed the Nakoda between Rainy Lake-Lake of the Woods area in western Ontario, but Henry Kelsey reports in his voyage (1690–91; Ray 1974:12) that the Nakoda lived along the Carrot River and the Touchwood uplands in Saskatchewan. They made frequent trips to York Factory in the eighteenth century and had become trade middlemen along with their Cree allies between the Hudson Bay Company and western tribes who were in search of European goods (Ray 1974:6).

In the early 1700s the increased access to firearms and other European goods by Algonquian groups and their Nakoda allies enabled them to expand northwestward along the parkland and up to central Alberta. This may have been triggered by hostilities with the Dakota who had recently gained access to French firearms. By 1720 the Nakoda homeland included Touchwood Hills, the Assiniboine River watershed, the Red River, and likely the Qu'Appelle River in eastern Saskatchewan (Ray 1974:21). They acquired horses in the mid-eighteenth century from the Hidatsa, Mandan, or Crow but later lost access to them.

While in the early eighteenth century movements were done northwestward, in the late 1700s the bulk of the Nakoda bands moved southward out of the parklands and adopted a mounted buffalo-hunting culture. Alexander Henry (1808) reported that two thirds of the Nakoda lived between the Qu'Appelle and Souris Rivers and the remaining third in the Battleford region (DeMallie & Miller 2001:574). Later in the early nineteenth century some groups moved even farther south in actual northern Montana where they still cohabit with speakers of Gros Ventres (also known as Atsina), Yankton, and Yanktonai Dakota.

Two ethnically distinct groups of "Assinipoëts" are mentioned by early Hudson Bay Company traders like Kelsey (1690–91) and Henday (1754–55), who made trips inland from York Factory (Ontario). These are the "Woodland Assiniboine" (or "Northern Assiniboine"), who are the ancestors of modern Stoney, and the "Plains

Assiniboine" (or "Southern Assiniboine"), the ancestors of modern Nakoda. The distinction between Woodland and Plains Assiniboine follows an ecological cycle (Ray 1974). One group resides in the boreal forest and relies on hunting and fishing while the other roams the plains for buffalo, but both exploited the parklands in the winter. As suggested by Ray (1974:21) the Southern Assiniboine further divides into the Plains Assiniboine and an intermediate mixed group of Cree and Assiniboine inhabiting central Saskatchewan. This group is referred to as the "Keskatchewan and Southern Senipoet" (but see Russell 1990:chap.11).

Around the late eighteenth century, travelers and traders also started to note the different Nakoda band names. Many band names are found in the diaries of Alexander Henry the younger (1988), Denig (2000[1930]), Lowie (1910), and Rodnick (1937). The following list likely represents social groupings that are ancestors to the speakers of Western Canadian Nakoda, the dialect reflected in the present dictionary (all data from Rodnick 1937:410–12, with my translations):

Cąȟtáda "Moldy people band," or "Strong woods people" (located in the Battleford area, Saskatchewan);

Wazíyam wįcášta "Northern people band" (groups living in the Battleford area; some members moved to Fort Belknap in the nineteenth century. They were named as such after their migration southward in the United States [Rodnick 1937:411]);

Šahíyeskąbi "Piapot band" (lit. Plains Cree translators; this is an ethnically mixed band of Nakoda and Plains Cree led by Chief Piapot);

Cą́ȟe wįcášta "Wood mountain people";

Įšną́ ų́bis'a "They stay alone people" (formerly known as "Cypress Hills Assiniboine" and formerly allied to the "Wood mountain people");

A'ínina ų́bi or **Inína ų́bi** "Silent people" (living near Cypress Hills, Saskatchewan).

According to Carry The Kettle elders, the last two bands listed are the ancestors of people living in Carry The Kettle (Saskatchewan). More research on this complicated topic could help refine the association of each band with a dialect of Nakoda. However, even a cursory look at the situation indicates that most Nakoda bands still inhabit their historic homeland (Battleford and Moose Mountain) while other bands moved southward or eastward (e.g., Carry The Kettle). As shown in the next section the historical identification and geographical locations of these Nakoda groups in the eighteenth and nineteenth centuries seem

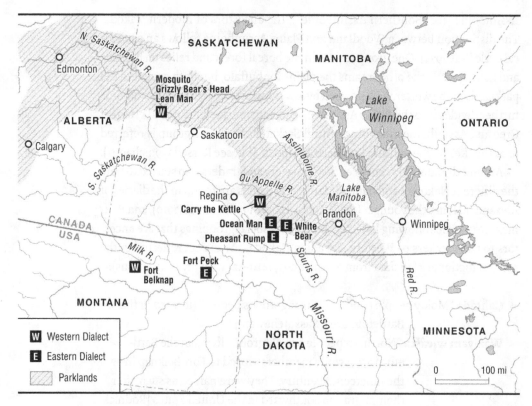

Map 1. Geographical location of the Nakoda People. Cartography by Erin Greb.

to align with contemporary dialectal divisions between the innovative Western Nakoda dialect and the more conservative Eastern Nakoda with an intermediate group (that of Fort Belknap) that shares features of both dialects (see table 2). Map 1 shows the modern distribution of Nakoda communities and dialects (W = Western Nakoda; N = Eastern Nakoda).

From the late eighteenth century on, a series of devastating epidemics of smallpox (1782, 1838, 1856) and influenza, along with a declining bison population, provoked extreme poverty and considerable population decline among the Nakoda who found themselves compelled to abandon their nomadic way of life and forced to amalgamate with their Plains Cree, Saulteaux, and Metis allies, but also with the Dakota. Like other Canadian Indigenous groups in the late nineteenth century, the Nakoda were forced to sign treaties with the encroaching federal governments. In Canada, Chiefs White Bear and Carry The Kettle bands signed adhesion to Treaty 4 in 1877, while Chiefs Mosquito, Grizzly Bear, and Leanman band signed adhesion to Treaty 6 in 1878. The two other bands in the United States signed the Judith River Treaty in 1855. Today the Nakoda People live in Sasktachewan (Canada) in Carry The Kettle and Mosquito/Grizzly Bear

Head/Leanman, White Bear, Pheasant Rump, and Ocean Man reservations, but also in Fort Belknap and Fort Peck reservations located in northeastern Montana.

Dialectal Situation of Nakoda

The Nakoda language, or "Assiniboine," is a language of the Siouan family. All Siouan languages descend from a common ancestor called Proto-Siouan, which was spoken some three thousand years ago. Siouan languages split into four sublevel groupings: 1) Mandan; 2) Crow-Hidatsa; 3) Northern Mississippi Valley Siouan; and, 4) Ohio Valley Siouan. Proto-Northern Mississippi Valley Siouan is the common ancestor of the Dhegihan group (Omaha-Ponca, Kanza†-Osage†, Quapaw), the Chiwerean group (Chiwere†, Hoocąk) and the Dakotan group. The latter comprises Lakȟóta, Western Dakhóta (Yankton-Yanktonai), Eastern Dakhóta (Santee-Sisseton), and Nakhóta, which is the autoethnonym for both Stoney (also known as Stoney Assiniboine, or Stoney Nakoda) and Assiniboine or Nakoda People (Parks & DeMallie 1992). The first three Dakotan subgroups were known as "Sioux" and the last two as "Assiniboine" in colonial history.[1]

Traditionally the classification between the Dakotan groups was done using the distribution of the phonemes *n*, *d*, and *l* (which are reflexes of the Proto-Dakotan phoneme *R) in specific corresponding words like those for "Indigenous person" (e.g., *Nakhóta, Dakhóta, Lakȟóta*) and "friend" but also in the male declarative particle, and the diminutive suffix. However, Parks and DeMallie showed in their seminal article (1992:240) that the *NDL* three-way distinction fails to clearly represent dialectal divisions since it does not explain the *n* in Dakhóta nor does it point to differences between Stoney and Nakhóta, which are now two distinct languages with unilateral mutual intelligibility where Stoney understand Nakhóta but not vice versa. In this section only, comparative data are presented in their phonemic form, so it might not match practical spelling practices.

Table 1. Diagnostic of dialectal differences

	'friend'	'male DECL.'	'diminutive'	'eight'
Stoney	—	no [dno]	-n	šaħnóʔą
Nakhóta	khoná	no [no, ndo]	-na	šaknóǧą
W. Dakhóta	khodá	do	-na	šagdóǧą
E. Dakhóta	khodá	do	-da; -dą; -na	šahdóǧą
Lakȟóta	kȟolá	lo	-la	šaglóǧą

Source: Southern Stoney forms were provided by Corey Telfer from the Language Conservancy and the University of Calgary. Forms for Western Nakoda stem from the present work supplemented by conversations with Tom Shawl from Fort Belknap (Montana). Data from the Mosquito-Grizzly Bear Head were provided by Kenneth Armstrong, and they are identical to the forms collected in Carry The Kettle. Eastern Nakoda forms are from Hollow (1970), Fourstar (1978), and Ryan (1999). We also benefitted from extensive conversations with Michael Turcotte (Fort Peck, Montana), Armand McArthur (Pheasant Rump, Saskatchewan), and Pete Bigstone (Ocean Man, Saskatchewan). All Lakota forms are from Ullrich (2011). Eastern Dakota Santee forms (S) as well as Yankton/Yanktonai (Y) forms are from Riggs (1992[1890]). Finally, Proto-Siouan (PS) and Proto-Dakotan (PD) reconstructions are taken from Rankin et al. (2015).

As shown in table 1 the comparative set for "eight" that contains a consonant cluster with initial ħ, k, g, or h is a much better diagnostic for dialectal differentiation than the *NDL* three-way division since it aligns with the five distinct ethnolinguistic groups.

Parks & DeMallie (1992:238; see also Parks & Rankin 2001:96) state that Nakoda splits into two dialects. This is based on lexical isoglosses and the metathesis of *tk* into *kt*. According to them one dialect (which we label "Western Nakoda") is spoken in Mosquito/Grizzly Bear Head and Carry The Kettle reserves in (Sasktachewan) and to some extent in Fort Belknap (Montana), while the other dialect ("Eastern Nakoda") is spoken in White Bear, Pheasant Rump, and Ocean Man reserves (Saskatchewan), as well as in Fort Peck (Montana). The distinction between these two dialects of Nakoda corresponds roughly to the two historical groups of Plains Assiniboine presented in the preceding section. A list of isoglosses is provided in table 2. Innovations are indicated by shaded boxes and bold characters. The three dashes (—) indicate no forms could be found in the literature. All data are presented in their phonemic form, thus simple stops and the affricate are *p, t, k*, and *č* and aspirated stops and affricate are *ph, th, kh*, and *čh*.

Table 2. Comparative dialectal data

	STONEY	WESTERN NAKODA		EASTERN NAKODA	LAKÓTA
	(South)	*Canada*	*United States*		
1) *tk > kt* 'it is heavy'	**ktá**	**ktá**	tká		tké
2) stem reshaping (a) 'sit'[1]	įgá 'stay'	yįkÁ, (h)įkÁ	yąkÁ	yąkÁ	yąkÁ
(b) 'ask' (PD *iwǫ́ǧA*)	iyúʼa	iyúǧA, iʼúǧA	iwúǧA	iyúǧA, iwúǧA	iyúǧA iwąǧa (S)
(c) 'book'	owábi 'book, paper, writing'	waʼóyapi	wówapi	waʼówapi, wówapi	wówapi

(d) 'camp' (PD *thųwą)	—	othų́ye	othų́we	othų́we	othų́we, othų́wahe
(e) 'and, also'	kho	khóya	khówa	—	kȟóya khóya (S)
(f) 'know'	θnoyá	snokyÁ	snokyÁ	snohyÁ (recent) snonyÁ[2]	slolyÁ
3) he 'interrogative particle'	hų́wo (M) hį́we (F) hį́ (neutral)	male and female speakers		**male speakers only**	male and female speakers
4) 'seven'	šagowį́, šagówį	**iyúšna**	iyúšna (~ šakówį)	šakówį (~ **iyúšna**)	šakówį
5) 'walking cane'	θąhné	sakné		sakyé (WB) sakné (FP)	sagyé
6) 'left-handed'	čhaktá	čhaktá	čhatká	čhatká (~ **swephátahą**)	čhatká
7) 'otter'	θįdé gaphéya	ptą́		šičéčą (PR) škečá ~ ptą́ (FP)	ptą́ 'otter' škéča 'fisher'

1. The historical forms of this entry are Proto-Siouan/Catawba **wų́:ke > Proto-Siouan *rą́:kE > Proto-Dakotan *yąká 'sit.' Rankin et al. (2015) observed that "The sequence *w+u seems to be inherently unstable in Siouan, and the result is always dissimilation of either the vowel to a or the glide to r (or its various reflexes)." This explains why these verbs in y are conjugated as Class 3 (mągá 'I sit') and not Class 2 verbs (Y-stem).

2. Parks and DeMallie (2012b:181n84) state that the verb "to know" evolved as follows: snokyá > snonyá > snohyá. This scenario is unlikely because the ky and hy forms are innovations from the more conservative snonyÁ that is the expected comparative match for Lakȟóta slolyÁ.

Some important landmarks of Nakoda dialectology stem from table 2. First, there is no major phonological, morphological, and lexical differentiation between the Nakoda dialects, which means that it was spoken as a relatively unified language in the recent past. Second, many important innovations like (1, 2a) occur in the western dialect spoken in Carry The Kettle and in Stoney, suggesting that the western dialect is not only different from the conservative eastern dialect but that it has been in contact with Stoney more intensively than the eastern dialect.[2] The innovative western dialect also shows morphological innovation involving a switch of w into y that is not found elsewhere (2c, d). Third, the speech of Fort Belknap (Western Nakoda, United States, in table 2) does not share many phonological or morphological isoglosses with the innovative western dialect (except for 2f) and aligns mostly on the more conservative eastern dialect (for 1a, 2a, b, c, d, f). Although on the basis of lexical differentiation only (4–7) it could be considered as an intermediate dialect more similar to the speech of Carry The Kettle, a suggestion made by Linda Cumberland (2005:36n16). Fourth, Eastern Nakoda has extended the meaning of some words (3, 6, 7) or borrowed some lexical items (5) from their Dakhóta neighbors with whom they have cohabited since the nineteenth century. Fifth and last, in dialectology, isoglosses do not share the same structural significance; as demonstrated by Chambers and Trudgill (1988:112–14) lexical isoglosses are more superficial than phonological ones since the former are "[. . .] subject to self-conscious control or change." For example, isogloss (7) is not a frequent word and is much less relevant than phonological (1) or morphological isoglosses (2) in determining Nakoda dialectal divisions. The reader interested in the comparative and historical dialectology of Nakoda and Stoney is referred to Collette (2022).

Language Vitality
In the late nineteenth and early twentieth centuries Nakoda was still largely spoken in Canadian reservations, but it started losing ground in favor of Plains Cree or English. MacLeod (2000:447) reports that in Mosquito/Grizzly Bear's Head/ Leanman Reserve (located in the Battleford area in Saskatchewan), the migration of three Plains Cree women from the nearby Red Pheasant Reserve at the turn of the twentieth century weakened Nakoda language transmission since the children of these mixed couples learned Plains Cree from their mother despite the fact their fathers spoke Nakoda. Rodnick (1938) provides a good overview of the sociocultural mechanisms of language loss in Fort Belknap at the beginning of the twentieth century.

   Nakoda is now a moribund language spoken by a handful of elderly people of the great-grandparent generation, although some children are exposed to the language through their grandparents. The situation in Canada is even more dire than in the United States, and, according to my estimate, there are less than ten fluent speakers left in Canada and probably a few dozen in Montana. However, in Montana there is a group of partly or nearly fluent speakers in their forties and fifties whose work as language teachers and dedication to language revitalization is crucial for the survival of Nakoda. In Canada the language is used in very restricted contexts such as greetings, introducing oneself, and giving orders but also in highly significant contexts such as singing and praying. This is why the Nakoda language is still considered as the backbone of Nakoda culture and the basis of ethnic identity. The response of the Nakoda language to new domains is minimal. Since in many languages of the Plains there is a tendency to avoid loanwords from European languages, speakers are often prompted to create new and descriptive terms that are often long and difficult to remember. In Carry The Kettle (Canada), which is the reservation that has the highest number of Nakoda band members, some substantial efforts are been deployed to revitalize and teach the language in school to both the staff members and the children through land-based activities. Moreover, a Nakoda language curriculum (reflecting other Canadian indigenous language curricula) has been approved by the Saskatchewan Ministry of Education so that high school teenagers can have their Nakoda language classes credited.

Nineteenth-century material concerning the Nakoda language is scarce since it was considered a dialect of Yanktonai Dakota (Parks & DeMallie 1992:237). Denig (2000[1930]) provides a few words for animals, cultural items, numbers, personal names, dances, and ceremonies in his monograph as well as an extensive wordlist (in Schoolcraft 1854:416–21). The language he wrote down reflects Eastern Nakoda. Prince Maximilian of Wied-Neuwied, a German explorer and ethnologist, also collected a short Nakoda wordlist (in Thwaites 1904–7:215–17) in which he pays special attention to phonetic and accentual details. At the end of the nineteenth century, Edward Griva, who was stationed at St. Paul Catholic Mission in Fort Belknap, compiled a dictionary and translated a catechism (Parks & Rankin 2001:110). Modern linguistic studies on Nakoda include Levin (1964), Hollow (1970), Taylor (1981, 1983), Schudel (1997), West (2003), and, most importantly, Cumberland (2005). Collette, McArthur, and Kennedy (2019) is a pedagogical book based on fieldwork done in Canada. Nakoda texts have been published in Lowie (1910, 1960), Drummond (1976), Farnell (1995), Schudel (1997), and, most importantly, Parks and DeMallie (2002, 2012a, 2012b). There are some short lexicons of Nakoda like that of Fourstar (1978) and one comprehensive dictionary compiled by Douglas Parks (2002), but none of these integrate sentence examples and grammatical explanations. In all, the Nakoda language benefits from high quality (both oral and written) documentation, thanks to the work done by Linda Cumberland, who transcribed oral material collected in the 1980s by anthropologists Douglas Parks and Raymond DeMallie (Parks & DeMallie 2002, 2012a, 2012b). Even though Nakoda is a moribund language, the recording repository and the work done at the American Indian Study and Research Institute (at Indiana University) will hopefully contribute to the revitalization and strengthening of Nakoda in the future.

Methodology

Funding for this project was provided by Pheasant Rump Nakoda First Nations from 2018 to 2020. The fieldwork was carried out with elder Wilma Kennedy, one of the last fluent speakers living in Carry The Kettle (Saskatchewan). The first step was to cross-check and review all the existing sources of the language, especially Ryan (1998) and Parks (2002). Along the way we also collected many valuable stories about the Nakoda People, legends, and colorful expressions as well as archaic words that do not appear in any known sources of the language. The second step consisted of eliciting the derivatives for simple verbs (those marked as *Adv* or *Vrefl*, for example, in verbal entries), many of which do not appear in published sources of the language. During elicitation we also made sure to include one or two textual or seminatural sentences (i.e., sentences volunteered by the speaker) so that the readers would better understand the grammatical structure and word order of the language. Only a few sentence examples stemming from English sentence translation were included since these often fail to reveal the grammatical intricacies of the language. The third step consisted in reviewing four Nakoda readers written in the Western dialect: one from Carry The Kettle published by Valerie Drummond (1976) and three others from Fort Belknap (Parks & DeMallie 2002, 2012a, 2012b). A few hundred sentences stemming from these texts were included in the entries. Finally a few short stories were also obtained from Mrs. Nancy Eashappie from Carry The Kettle, and some of the sentences have been integrated into the dictionary.

Spelling System and Sound Description

The orthography used in this dictionary is known as the "Fort Belknap" orthography (FBO hereafter). It was developed jointly by the Nakoda speakers from Fort Belknap and anthropologists from Indiana University. Nowadays almost all Nakoda material is published in the FBO, so it is slowly becoming the standard spelling. It is based on the APA (American Phonetic Alphabet) and is partly phonemic and indicates primary stress. The major difference between FBO and Lakota orthography is that the former does not indicate aspiration of stops and affricates. As seen in table 3, the phonemes *p, t, k,* and *c* are written either with the letters ⟨b⟩, ⟨d⟩, ⟨g⟩, and ⟨j⟩ (between vowels, or at the beginning of a word) or ⟨p⟩, ⟨t⟩, ⟨k⟩, and ⟨c⟩ (in consonant clusters). The following table displays the orthographic equivalents for different spelling systems (based on Cumberland 2005:448–50). Some of these spelling systems, especially those used in Ryan (1998) and by the Saskatchewan Indian Cultural Center (SICC) are imprecise and do not fully reflect the sounds of the language in that they have variants for a single sound or lack a symbol for specific sounds. In table 3 the Fort Belknap spelling system, as used in this dictionary, is presented in a darker shade. A more keyboard-friendly spelling uses ⟨r⟩ for *ǧ*; ⟨x⟩ for *ȟ*; and ⟨n⟩ for nasal vowels (e.g., *ą* is written ⟨an⟩).

Table 3. Chart of spelling systems for Nakoda

PHONEMES	IPA	APA	CUMBERLAND (2005)	FORT BELKNAP	RYAN (1998)	SICC	INDIANA TEXTS
Unaspirated consonants	p	p	p	**b, p**	b	p̄ ~ b	p
	t	t	t	**d, t**	d	t̄ ~ d	t
	k	k	k	**g, k**	g	c̄	k
	tʃ	č	c	**j, c**	j	k̄ ~ g	c
Aspirated consonants	pʰ	pʰ	pʰ	**p**	p	p	pᶜ
	tʰ	tʰ	tʰ	**t**	t	—	tᶜ
	kʰ	kʰ	kʰ	**k**	k	—	kᶜ
	tʃʰ	čʰ	cʰ	**c**	ch	c̀	cᶜ
Ejective consonants	p'	ṗ	p'	**p'**	p?	p´	p'
	t'	ṫ	t'	**t'**	t?	—	t'
	k'	k̇	k'	**k'**	k?	k´	k'
	tʃ'	č̇	c'	**c'**	—	č´	c'
Fricative consonants	s	s	s	**s**	s	s	s
	ʃ	š	š	**š**	sh	s̀	š
	x	ȟ	ȟ	**ȟ**	x	ħġ	ȟ
	s'	ṡ	s'	**s'**	—	—	s'
	ʃ'	ṧ	š'	**š'**	—	s̀´	š'
	x'	ȟ̇	ȟ'	**ȟ'**	—	ħ´	ȟ'
	z	z	z	**z**	z	z	z
	ʒ	ž	ž	**ž**	zh	j	ž
	ɣ	ǧ	ǧ	**ǧ**	ḡ	ġ	ǧ
Nasal consonants	m	m	m	**m**	m	m	m
	n	n	n	**n**	n	n	n
Glottal consonants	h	h	h	**h**	h	h	h
	ʔ	ʔ	'	**'**	?	—	'
Glides	w	w	w	**w**	w	w	w
	y	y	y	**y**	y	y	y

PHONEMES	IPA	APA	CUMBERLAND (2005)	FORT BELKNAP	RYAN (1998)	SICC	INDIANA TEXTS
Oral vowels	i	i	i	**i**	i	i	i
	e	e	e	**e**	é	e	e
	a	a	a	**a**	a	a	a
	o	o	o	**o**	o	o	o
	u	u	u	**u**	u	u / o	u
Nasal vowels	ĩ	į	į	**į**	ĩ	iŋ	į
	ã	ą	ą	**ą**	ã	aŋ am an	ą
	ũ	ų	ų	**ų**	ũ	uŋ oŋ	ų

CONSONANTS

Nakoda has twenty-seven consonants, displayed in their phonemic transcription (which is based on the American Phonetic Alphabet) in table 4 (taken from Cumberland 2005:15–17).

Table 4. Nakoda consonants

		LABIAL	LAMINO-DENTAL	LAMINO-ALVEOLAR	PALATO-ALVEOLAR	VELAR	LARYNGEAL
Obstruents							
stops	unaspirated	**p**	**t**			**k**	**ʔ**
	aspirated	**pʰ**	**tʰ**			**kʰ**	
	glottalized	**p'**	**t'**			**k'**	
affricates	unaspirated				**č**		
	aspirated				**čʰ**		
	glottalized				**č'**		
fricatives	voiceless			**s**	**š**	**ȟ**	
	glottalized			**s'**	**š'**	**ȟ'**	
	voiced			**z**	**ž**	**ǧ**	
Sonorants							
nasals		**m**	**n**				
glides		**w**		**y**			**h**

Listed in table 5 are all of the Nakoda consonantal phonemes with their spelling in the Fort Belknap orthography along with English equivalents, Nakoda examples, and some phonological information when necessary. The dial # indicates a word boundary, while V and C stand for a vowel and a consonant respectively; the underscore __ indicates the point of insertion of a sound. For example, #__ means "at the beginning of a word."

Table 5. Consonant descriptions

PHONEME	SPELLING	ENGLISH EQUIVALENT	EXAMPLE	ALLOPHONES AND PHONEMIC CONTEXTS
/p/	B b	bat, tab	bahá 'hill'	voiced / #__
	P p	spit	ą́ba 'day'	voiced / V__V
			a'į́kpapsų 'perfume'	unvoiced / C__
			ptą́ 'otter'	unvoiced / __C
/pʰ/	P p	Peter	pahá 'hair'	
			apá 's/he hits sb, smth'	
/p'/	P' p'	(none)	p'ó 'it is steam'	
			cup'ó 'it is foggy'	
/t/	D d	damp	dágu 'what, thing'	voiced / #__
	T t	stick	adé 'my father'	voiced / V__V
			-kta 'potential, future'	unvoiced / C__
			hutką́ 'root'	unvoiced / __C
/tʰ/	T t	team	tanó 'meat'	
			a'úta 's/he shoots at sb'	
/t'/	T' t'	(none)	t'á 'to die'	
			ot'į́ 'it is thundering'	
/k/	G g	gum	gúwa 'Come!'	voiced / #__
	K k	scan	ogíhi 's/he can'	voiced / V__V
			wįtkó 's/he is crazy'	unvoiced / C__
			šų́któgeja 'wolf'	unvoiced / __C
			akták 'running'	unvoiced / __#
/kʰ/	K k	keep	kuwá 'he chases him'	
			įkú 'chin'	
/k'/	K' k'	(none)	k'ú 'he gives it to him'	
			wak'á 'I dig it'	
/č/	J j	jam	júsina 'it is small'	
			cą́šeja 'dead tree'	

PHONEME	SPELLING	ENGLISH EQUIVALENT	EXAMPLE	ALLOPHONES AND PHONEMIC CONTEXTS
/čʰ/	C c	chill	cába 'beaver' néci 'over here' pakcá 's/he combs it' các 'such'	
/čʼ/	Cʼ cʼ	(none)	cicʼú 'I give it to you'	
/s/	S s	sit	sihá 'foot' owádasakyabi 'fridge' agísas 'proudly'	
/sʼ/	Sʼ sʼ	(none)	-sʼa 'habitual'	
/z/	Z z	zipper	zizíbena 'thin cloth'	
/š/	Š š	shadow	šų́ga 'dog' aʼį́tųšį 's/he lies about smth' abáš 'some on the other hand'	
/šʼ/	Šʼ šʼ	(none)	šʼágA 's/he is strong' wašʼáke 'unbearably'	
/ž/	Ž ž	measure	žená 'those' ožúna 'it is full'	
/ȟ/	Ȟ ȟ	(none)	ȟóda 'it is gray' wóȟiyą 's/he pouts'	
/ȟʼ/	Ȟʼ ȟʼ	(none)	ȟʼeyáyana 'grapes' naȟʼų́ 's/he hears sb'	
/ǧ/	Ǧ ǧ	(none)	ǧí 'it is yellow' šaknóǧą 'eight'	
/m/	M m	mine	mína 'knife' smuyá 'it is smooth' sám 'beyond, over'	
/n/	N n	night	nųwą́ 'to swim' aní 's/he steps, climbs' mahén 'inside, in'	
/w/	W w	water	wá 'snow' owá 'all'	

/y/	Y y	yes	yatką́ 'he drinks' áya 's/he/it becomes'
/h/	H h	happy	hiyá 'no' wó'ahope 'respect'
/ʔ/	'	button [bɐʔn̩]	wa'ówabi 'paper' ní' 's/he is living'

The glottal stop [ʔ], written in this dictionary with an apostrophe ⟨ ' ⟩, deserves a few comments since it is both phonemic and nonphonemic. Obviously, glottal stops are indicated in the spelling when they are phonemic, that is when they contribute to a difference in meaning between two words as in *tá* 'moose' versus *t'á* 's/he/it is dead.' However, to ease the reading the Fort Belknap spelling system also marks phonetic glottal stops when they occur between vowels on morpheme boundaries, although this is fully predictable. Thus 'my father' (*mi-* 'my' + *-ade* 'father') is written *mi'áde* 'my father' and not *miáde*. Some speakers also use *y* or *w* as a linker between two vowels, so the reader has to bear this in mind when looking for a word in the Nakoda/English section. Lastly, to find a word that has a glottal stop as *t'* or *k'* inside a word, follow the regular alphabetical order indicated in the preceding list. For example, the verb *wót'į* appears after *wótijağa anówąbi* and before *wotkícuni*.

VOWELS

Nakoda has eight vowels: five oral (*i e a u o*) and three nasal (*ą į ų*), as indicated in table 6. Nasal vowels are indicated by a small hook underneath. A nasal vowel is produced by letting air go through the nasal cavity and the mouth simultaneously. The closest English equivalent of nasal vowels occurs in the words *mean, mango,* and *bingo*. The vowels *e* and *o* do not have a nasalized counterpart in Nakoda.

Table 6. Nakoda vowels

		FRONT	CENTRAL	BACK
Oral	high	i	a	u
	mid	e		o
	low			
Nasal	high	į	ą	ų
	low			

Table 7. Vowel descriptions

PHONEME	SPELLING	ENGLISH EQUIVALENT	EXAMPLE	ALLOPHONES AND PHONEMIC CONTEXTS
/a/	A a	at, hat	aké 'again' waná 'now' tóga 'enemy'	
/ą/	Ą ą	man (nearest equivalent)	ą́ba 'day' tąbá 'birch' wįcą́ 'raccoon'	
/e/	E e	bet	ecágen 'always' dágeyešį 'shut up' šagé 'claw'	[ɛ ~ e ~ i]
/i/	I i	beat	iná nína 'very' wįkni 'fat'	[i ~ ɪ]
/į/	Į į	mean (nearest equivalent)	įȟá 'he laughs' gįza 'it creaks, squeaks' hį 'hair, fur, pelt'	
/o/	O o	open	ómna 'he smells it' hoȟpá 's/he coughs' tó 's/he/it is blue'	[o] or [ɔ]
/u/	U u	two	ubížade 'barn swallow' sudá 'it is hard'	[u] or [ʊ]
/ų/	Ų ų	monk (nearest equivalent)	ų́bi 'they are' matų́bi 'I was born' ecų́ 's/he does it'	

STRESS

In Nakoda stress is phonemic and usually falls on the second syllable, although there are many exceptions where stress falls on the first syllable. This is unpredictable; hence the indication of primary stress in the spelling system. Stress position can make a difference in meaning between two words that would otherwise be spelled alike, as in the following pairs of words:

coná *vt1*   s/he believes sb, smth
cóna *post*   without, lacking, deprived of

oh**Á́** *vi1*	1) s/he cooks by boiling;
	2) s/he wears a shoe
óhạ *post*	among, in the middle, in it

As seen here, the orthography utilized in this dictionary makes use of an acute accent mark on vowels to indicate primary stress (e.g., á, í, ų́, etc.). However, the reader should bear in mind that often words occurring in phrases or sentences bear a different stress than when occurring in their citation form. This process is called "phrase level rhythmic stress pattern" and seeks to produce alternate syllable stress of the type CV́CV CV́CV or CVCV́ CVCV́ (Cumberland 2005:59–60). For example, while the noun *hạwí* 'sun, moon' has its primary stress on the second syllable in its citation form, it shifts to the first syllable in a phrase like *hạhébi hą́wi* 'moon' to keep the alternating syllable stress. Although such a stress pattern seems to be the exception rather than the rule (Cumberland 2005:66), we have kept it in the sentence examples when the speaker produced it.

Key to Entries

General Information

Each entry is ordered on the basis of the first letter of the citation form, printed in boldface. The alphabetical order is the following (note that some glottalized consonants (p') and (s') do not appear initially):

a ą b c d e g ğ h ȟ ȟ' i į j k k' m n o p (p') s (s') š š' t t' u ų w y z ž—affixes

In Nakoda the **citation form** for a verb is the 3rd person singular, which is marked by a zero morpheme (-Ø-). It is the simplest form of any inflected verb, and each verb inflected for "plural," "1st person plural" or the "potential modality" contains, so to speak, the citation form, as with *wóda* 's/he/it eats' and *wówada* 'I eat.' For example, in the following set of verbs the citation form appears in all the inflected forms:

šųkmánų	s/he steals a horse, horses
šųkmáwanų	I steal a horse, horses
šųkmáyanų	you steal a horse, horses
šųkmá'ųnųbi	we steal a horse, horses
šųkmánųbįkta	they will steal a horse, horses
šųkmánųbįkтеšį	they will not steal a horse, horses

As in any dictionary, the number of possible inflected forms for a single verb is enormous, reaching well over one hundred different forms. Normally inflected forms are not listed in a dictionary entry, but rather the principle of forming them is expounded in a grammatical treatise or a verb compendium. However, some inflected forms that cannot be guessed are also included in the entries.

The citation form is followed by an italicized **class** code that indicates the lexical class of the word in question (i.e., *noun, verb, adverb*, etc.) and a **gloss** indicating a possible English translation.

Entries with two or more distinct but related meanings or **subsenses** (which sometimes align with different lexical classes) are indicated by successive numbering: 1), 2), 3), etc., in the entries.

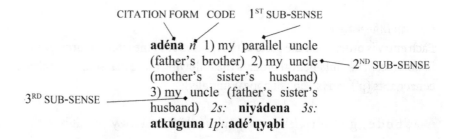

Although this dictionary is based on the speech of Carry The Kettle (Saskatchewan), some Eastern Nakoda variants collected during fieldwork are included and indicated with the codes PR (Pheasant Rump), OM (Ocean Man), WB (White Bear), FP (Fort Peck) or simply listed as *Variant*. Finally, morpheme entries such as -Ø- and -' are listed at the end, after **ž**.

Entries for Verbs in the Nakoda–English Section

Verb entries contain minimally a citation form, a class code, subsenses numbers (if applicable) and gloss(es). Many entries also include **sentence example(s)**, and verbs have the **inflected form** for 1st person singular (*I*), 2nd person singular (*you*), and 1st person plural (*we*) when it was collected. Some verb entries also include derivative forms labeled *collective, contracted, abstract, benefactive, causative(s), collective, dative, ditransitive, possessive, reciprocal, reduplicative*, and *reflexive*. (A complete list of derivatives along with their abbreviations is given in table 8.)

Although the inclusion of all inflected forms may appear superfluous, this is not the case for Nakoda person markers since it is often difficult for second-language learners of Nakoda to figure out the insertion point of the *I* and *you* person markers.

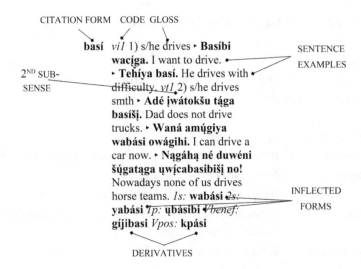

Lastly, some verbs that end in the sounds *a* or *ą* may change to *e* or *į* when followed by certain suffixes, enclitics, demonstratives, or particles that trigger this sound change. This process is known as "ablaut," and it is indicated by the capitalized letters *A* or *Ą* in the citation form of a verb. Two very common ablauting elements include the negative enclitic *-šį* that triggers **e-ablaut** (*wóda > wódešį* 's/he does not eat') and the potential enclitic *-kta* that triggers **į-ablaut** (*wóda > wódįkta* 's/he will/can eat'). The following entry displays both types of ablaut.

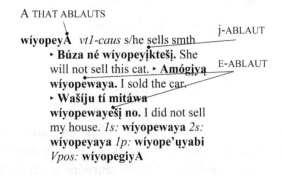

Documenting the process of ablaut is important but also challenging since there are some dialectal or intergenerational differences; some speakers from a community will ablaut a verb's final *a* while speakers in other communities will not do so. Moreover, in direct elicitation some speakers do not ablaut a verb but do so in natural speech, so textual examples were sought in order to properly assign the ablauting process. Derived nouns that ablaut are not indicated in order to limit the use of uppercase symbols.

Entries for Nouns in the Nakoda–English Section

Noun entries are of various types. Common nouns are often simple, but some nouns occur with their possessive inflections for 1st, 2nd, and 3rd person. Ethnonyms, hydronyms, and toponyms as well as surnames and proper names have the first letter capitalized.

common noun	**i̧'íyute** *n* ruler
ethnonym	**Bigána** *nprop* Piegan people, person of Piegan descent
hydronym	**Miníšoše wakpá** *ngeo* Missouri River
toponym	**I̧štágitu̧ tí** *ngeo* Indian Head (Saskatchewan)
surname	**Wówaši** *nprop* O'Watch (surname in Carry The Kettle Saskatchewan)
proper name	**Wi̧cášta hą́ska** *nprop* Tall man (name of Armand McArthur)

Entries of nouns for body parts contain the inflected forms for 1st person singular possessor (*my*) and 2nd person singular possessor (*your*). We did not include the 3rd person singular possessor form (*his/her/its*) simply because it corresponds to the citation form.

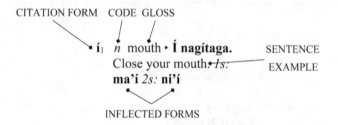

Lastly, since kinship nouns cannot be used without a marker for the possessor, we have listed them as roots and not as inflected nouns. What we label here as roots are not words but uninflected dependent nominal forms . They appear with dashes (e.g., -ROOT-) and no stress. When there are two roots, the first root occurs with 1st and 2nd person markers, while the second root occurs with the 3rd person marker.

As seen in the preceding entry, the 3rd person form has an unpredictable and apparently meaningless element *-gi-* that makes it necessary to list the two roots for many kinship terms as well as the inflected forms including the 3rd person. Of course, another way to avoid this option is to list all the inflected forms as single entries, boosting by a few dozen the number of entries.

CITATION FORMS   CODE   GLOSS

-kuši- ; -kųgiši-   *root*   grandmother
‣ **Mikúši én ų́.** My
grandmother is there. ‣ **Nikúši
iyéwejiska.** I translate for
your grandmother. ‣ **Nikúši
Nakón-i'a jé no!** Your
grandmother always speaks
Nakoda! *1s:* **mikúši** *2s:*
nikúši *3s:* **kų́gišiktu (CTK) ;**
kušícu (PR) *1p:* **ųgíkųšitku**

SENTENCE EXAMPLES

INFLECTED FORMS

DIALECTAL VARIANT

Entries for Morphemes in the Nakoda–English Section

Morphemes (or affixes) are bound forms that bear meaning. They can be lexical or grammatical but cannot occur in isolation and must be added on a stem (or root). Nakoda has **prefixes** that are always added before a stem (although some prefixes occur before or inside the stem). **Infixes** are added inside a stem. **Circumfixes** is a term used here when two independent grammatical morphemes occur together on a stem. **Suffixes** are added after the stem. There are over eighty morpheme entries in this dictionary, all of which include a **morpheme code**, the **underived word** or the **3rd person singular** form onto which the morpheme in question is added (located before the sign >), as well as the **resulting meaning** (located after the sign >). In many cases the *Usage* indicates the verb class and other grammatical (type of verb and verb class) or morphophonemic information (sound changes occurring on morpheme boundaries).

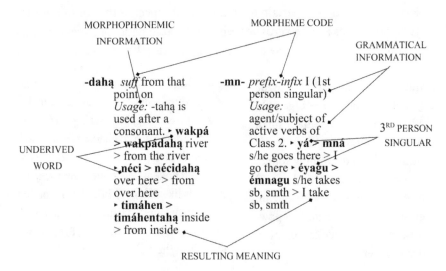

MORPHOPHONEMIC INFORMATION

MORPHEME CODE

GRAMMATICAL INFORMATION

-dahą *suff* from that
point on
Usage: -tahą is
used after a
consonant. ‣ **wakpá**
> **wakpádahą** river
> from the river
‣ **néci > nécidahą**
over here > from
over here
‣ **timáhen >**
timáhentahą inside
> from inside

-mn- *prefix-infix* I (1st
person singular)
Usage:
agent/subject of
active verbs of
Class 2. ‣ **yá > mná**
s/he goes there > I
go there ‣ **éyaǧu >**
émnagu s/he takes
sb, smth > I take
sb, smth

UNDERIVED WORD

3ʳᴰ PERSON SINGULAR

RESULTING MEANING

Entries in the English–Nakoda Section

Entries in the English–Nakoda section (English hereafter) are not a mere reflection of those in the Nakoda-English (Nakoda hereafter). In some respect the English section acts like an index to the Nakoda section. The major difference is that the English section does not contain sentence examples or inflected forms and grammatical information is minimal, so the reader should consult both the English and the Nakoda section to deepen his/her knowledge of a word, its inflections, and usage in a sentence. As shown in the following diagram, many entries in the English–Nakoda section contain derived words so the learner can get familiarized with word construction. Verbal entries in the English section contain an English **key** and its **class code**, a Nakoda translation(s), along with its/their code(s), a gloss, and, in many cases, Nakoda verb **derivatives**.

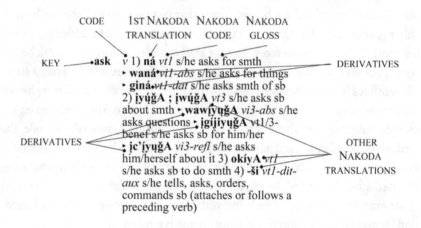

For noun entries that pertain to an important aspect of the culture or lifeways of the Nakoda People, verbs describing related activities or states have also been added to the entries. Here are two examples with the nouns *drum* and *dog*.

drum *n v* 1) **gamúbi** *n* drum ‣ **nąbé gamúbi** *cp* hand drum ‣ **cągámubi** *n* log drum ‣ **gamúbina** *n* small drum; 2) **gamú** *vt1* s/he beats on smth; makes a drumming sound; 3) **muyá** *vs* it is a drumbeat; 4) **ȟ'oká** *vi1* s/he sings with a drum group; beats the drum in a powwow or dance ‣ **ȟ'oká yįgábi** *cp* drum singer

dog *n* 1) **šúga** *n* dog, canine; horse (in possessed forms only) ‣ **šúgagana** n-redup lap dog ‣ **šųk-** *cont* dog, horse, sheep; 2) **šúgawį** n female dog, bitch; 3) **gisúna šúga** *cp* chow dog; 4) **šųkháskusku** n mangy dog, coyote, wolf; unkept dog; 5) **šųgámna** *vs* s/he/it smells like a dog; 6) **šųk'óhąbi** *n* boiled dog, puppy soup; 7) **tašųkkiyA** *vt1-caus* s/he makes smth his/her own dog; 8) **šųgícoco** *vt1-redup* s/he calls his/her own dogs

Glossing and Class Codes

Some English words and abbreviations are overtly used in this work, as we have tried to ease the burden of redundancy and the use of full words like *somebody*, or *something*, etc. This is especially true for verb entries where the following codes are in use:

people	the use of *people* occurs with collective verbs (VI1-COLL) since the subject is not a single person but a group of people.
s/he/it	agent or subject of the verb (*it* is often not included since some verbs do not apply to animals but only to humans);
sb	short form for *somebody* that indicates the animate patient/object of a transitive verb (*sb* obviates the need of either choosing *him* over *her*, or even worse adding *him/her* all over the dictionary in order to indicate the animate patient/object function);
smth	short form for *something* that indicates the inanimate object of a transitive verb;
things	the use of *things* occurs with abstract verbs (VI1-ABS) in order to indicate that the patient/object onto which the action is directed is nonspecific (e.g., *wópetų* s/he buys things).

There are numerous class codes used in this dictionary, and it is essential to know them in order to fully understand the grammatical information contained in an entry. They are all listed and described in table 8.

Table 8. Class codes and abbreviations

CODE	MEANING	DESCRIPTION
abs	abstract verb	derivative with a nonspecified object/patient; wa- or w- is the abstract object prefix (class 1) as in **w**ópetų 's/he buys things'
adv	adverb	modifies the meaning of a following verb as in **Naháȟ** wagáǧikte no. 'I am **still** going to make it.'
art	article	used after a noun to indicate its definiteness (the) or indefiniteness (a, an)

CODE	MEANING	DESCRIPTION
aux	auxiliary verb	occurs after another verb and indicates notions like "suddenly," "become," "can," "order," etc.
benef	benefactive verb	indicates that an action is undertaken for the benefit or honor of somebody else; -giji- is the benefactive affix (class 1) as in ecágiji'ų 's/he does it for sb'
caus	causative verb	derivative where an agent or a thing made a patient do something or made something happen; -yA and -kiyA are causative suffixes (class 1) as in skayá 's/he whitens sb, smth'
circumfix	circumfix	used here when two grammatical elements often appear together in a word as with ų- . . .-bi 'we' in wa'úcibi 'we dance'
coll	collective	collective plural form of some intransitive verbs, as with the prefix e- as in iyódągA 's/he sits down' > éyodąga 'they sit down'
comp	complementizer	functional word that serves to turn a clause into the subject or object of a sentence
conj	conjunction	links two nouns or verbs together such as hį́kna 'and,' duká 'but'
cont	contracted noun	contracted form of a noun, as in pağúda > pağúⁿ 'duck'; máza > mas 'iron, metal; money'
cp	compound	noun comprised of two words (often a noun and a verb, or a noun and a noun, etc.)
dat	dative verb	derivative where an action is directed to or intended for somebody else; gi- or g- is the dative affix (class 1) as in gahí 's/he arrives here bringing sb, smth to him/her'
dem	demonstrative	indicates the location and the distance of an entity in relation to the speaker's point of view as in wįcá né 'this man,' wįkóške gá 'that young woman over there'

dit	ditransitive verb	has two objects which are marked on the verb; one object is the receiver and the other the thing received, as in acáštų 's/he names sb after another person'
encl	enclitic	element that "leans" at the end of the verb and indicates modalities, aspects, number, and negation.
interj	interjection	indicates the mood, feeling, or attitude of the speaker
irr	irregular verb	verb that bears an irregular set of inflections as in eyá 's/he says,' epá 'I say,' ehá 'you say'
Lit	literal meaning	indicates the literal meaning of a word
n	noun	describes a person (košká 'boy'), animal (šų́ga 'dog'), place (Huhúžubina 'Regina'), thing (tába 'ball'), or idea, etc.
ngeo	geographical noun	used for toponyms and hydronyms
np	noun phrase	used here when more than two nouns are put together, as in cą́ą́gan yįgábi wįcášta 'chairman'
n-pl	plural noun	noun that occurs in the plural form only
nprop	proper name	traditional name of a person
num	numeral	used for cardinal numbers (one, two, three, etc.) and ordinal numbers (first, second, third, etc.)
NS	Nakoda Stories	refers to an example taken from: Parks, Douglas R., and Raymond J. DeMallie. eds. 2002. *Nakoda Stories from Fort Belknap Reservation, Montana.* Fort Belknap MT: Hoteja Project and Indiana University American Indian Studies Research Institute.
part	particle	expresses modality, commands, and interrogations; they occur after the verb
pass	passive verb	verbs that have the subject of the verb acting as patient, as in miní abápsųbi 's/he is baptized'

CODE	MEANING	DESCRIPTION
ph	phrase	used here for idiomatic phrases containing more than two words, one of which is a verb, as in hạwí togáhe oyášpe 'quarter moon'
pos	possessive form	derivative where the agent is acting upon his or her relative; the possessive prefix-infix is k- or gi- (class 1) as in ni**gí**ya 's/he heals, saves, rescues his/her own'
post	postposition	specifies a relationship between two words in a sentence; it occurs after a noun, as in mitákona **gicí** 'with my friend'
prefix	prefix	element that occurs before the stem
prefix-infix	prefix-infix	element that occurs either before or inside the stem, like -wa- in **wa**nówą 'I sing' and ma**wá**ni 'I walk'
pro	pronoun	replaces a noun as in Paul is sick > He is sick; The plant is green > It is green; interrogative pronouns are used to form interrogative sentences
quant	quantifier	indicates quantities as with nṹba 'two' and iyúha 'all'
recip	reciprocal verb	derivative where two participants are acting on one another; the reciprocal affix is -gici- (class 1) as in dagú**gici**yabi 'they are related to one another'
redup	reduplication	doubling of one syllable of a word usually to express plurality, iterativity, small size, intensity, etc.
refl	reflexive verb	derivative where the subject of the verb is acting upon himself or herself; the reflexive prefix-affix is -ịc'i- as in **ịc'í**jağA 's/he makes smth for himself/herself'
root	root	used only in entries of kinship terms; they occur with hyphens on both sides
See	cross-reference	indicates another word with a similar meaning

suff	suffix	element that occurs after the stem
Syn	synonym	cross-references a synonym
Usage	usage	indicates information on how to use the word in a sentence; if a word triggers ablaut
v	verb	verb
Variant	dialectal variant	indicates variants found in the eastern subdialects spoken in Pheasant Rump (Saskatchewan), Ocean Man (Saskatchewan), White Bear (Saskatchewan), Fort Peck (Montana), as well as in Fort Belknap (Montana)
voc	vocative	vocative form of a noun as when one calls out one of his/her relatives
vi	intransitive verb	intransitive/active verbs only have a subject marked on the verb
vimp	impersonal verb	verbs that have no definite subject as in dokédu 'it happened as such' or maǧážu 'it rains'
vimper	imperative verb	verbs only used for commands
vt	transitive verb	transitive verbs are marked for an agent and a patient; they are of Classes 1, 2, and 3
vs	stative verb	intransitive/stative verbs of Class 4 only have a subject marked on the verb and require the inflections -ma- 'I' and -ni- 'you'
1	verb of Class 1	verb of Class 1 that requires the person markers -wa- 'I' and -ya- 'you'
1pl	first person plural	person speaking plus one other 'we'
1s	first person singular	person speaking 'I'
2	verb of Class 2	verb of Class 2 that requires the person markers -mn- 'I' and -n- 'you'
2pl	second person plural	two persons spoken to or more 'you all'

CODE	MEANING	DESCRIPTION
2s	second person singular	person spoken to 'you'
3	verb of Class 3	verb of Class 3 that requires the person markers -m- 'I' and -n- 'you'
3pl	third person plural	persons or things spoken about 'they'
3s	third person singular	person or thing spoken about 'she, he, it'
~	variant	indicates idiolectal or dialectal variants of a word
#/#	double inflection	verbs that bear inflections from two different classes of verbs, as in kniyódąga vi1/2 's/he arrives back here and sits' > **wa**kní**mn**odąga '**I** arrive back here and sit'
>	X becomes Y	used in morpheme entries to indicate the change from an underived word to a derived one

Notes

1. Three language families (Algonquian, Siouan, and Caddoan), including Kutenai (an isolate), are represented in the northern Plains. Algonquian languages include Blackfoot, Arapaho, Gros Ventre (also known as Atsina), and Cheyenne (all four forming the Plains Algonquian geographical subgroup), Plains Cree, Saulteaux, and Michif (all belonging to Central Algonquian geographical subgroup). Siouan languages include Dakota, Lakota, Nakoda, and Stoney (Dakotan subgroup), Hidatsa, Crow, and Mandan. Caddoan has only one representative, which is Arikara.
2. To this effect Taylor (1981:10) notes that Stoney is "closest in every way to the dying Assiniboine speech of western Saskatchewan. They differ more from the Assiniboine spoken in eastern Saskatchewan and in Montana, although the Morley dialect of Alberta Assiniboine . . . shows many contacts with the Assiniboine dialect of the Fort Belknap Reservation in north-central Montana."

A Concise Dictionary
of Nakoda (Assiniboine)

Nakoda/English

A

a- *pref* on, onto, over, at *Usage:* adds a participant slot in a verb and turns a stative or intransitive verb into a transitive one, or a transitive verb into a ditransitive one. ‣ **pšá > apšá** s/he sneezes > s/he sneezes on smth ‣ **basísa > abásisa** s/he sews, stitches smth > s/he sews smth on it

á, há *exclamation* ah (expresses surprise, disgust, or when someone has noticed something) ‣ **Á! mitágoža įkšuna žé míja'u'!** Ah! Grandson bring me the beans! ‣ **Á! s'ás'a hįkna hiyákneya gáyabi.** Ah! there was a sound of wings and then suddenly it came down. (NS 2002:14) ‣ **Á! mitágožana yus'íyewicayaye no, eyá.** "Ah! you frightened my grandchildren," he said. (Cumberland 2005:140)

a'á *vs* it is moldy ‣ **Aǧúyabi né a'áši.** The bread is not moldy.

a'ámna *vs* it is a moldy smell ‣ **Hįįį! A'ámna kó!** Oh! They have a moldy smell too!

á'ana *n* crow

á'ana sihá *cp* common water-crowfoot

á'ana sihá iyópsije *ph* crowhop (a style of bucking where the horse's back is arched and all four legs come off the ground) *Lit:* crow foot jump

a'ą́bayabi *vi1-pass* 1) it is a funeral wake after the death of sb ‣ **Cų́guna gicí a'ą́bayabi.** There is a funeral wake for her older sister. *n* 2) funeral wake

abá *quant* some, some of a group *Usage:* used with count and mass nouns. ‣ **Abá giksúyeší.** He does not remember some of it. ‣ **Abáš omą́gipiší.** On the other hand, the other ones do not fit me. ‣ **Wayáhoda nitáwa abá mąk'ú wo.** Give me some of your oats. (Parks et al. 1999:115)

abá'e *Variant:* **abáye** *n* larb (psychoactive plant often mixed with red willow bark and used in ceremonies)

abáha *Variant:* **abáhana** *n* knoll, small hill, mound ‣ **Hokšína žé abáhana iyáni.** That boy climbed up on that knoll. (Fourstar, p. 1)

abáȟnadA *vt1* 1) s/he stitches, pins smth on it ‣ **Niyé abáȟnada!** Pin it on yourself! *1s:* **awábaȟnada** *2s:* **ayábaȟnada** *Vcaus:* **abáȟnadekiyA** *n* 2) ribbon 3) silk, silk cloth *Vcont:* **abáȟnan**

abáȟnadekiyA *vt1-caus* s/he lets sb pin smth on it ‣ **Abáȟnademakiya!** Let me pin it on! *1s:* **abáȟnadewakiya** *2s:* **abáȟnadeyakiya** *1p:* **abáȟnade'ųkiyabi**

abáȟnan *cont* silk, ribbon, smth pinned or stitched

abáȟnan sǫksája *cp* silk dress ‣ **Abáȟnan sǫksája duwé nik'ú he?** Who gave you the silk dress?

abákmįkma *vt1* s/he rolls smth by pushing on it

abámnayA *vt1* s/he irons smth ‣ **Miyé awábamnayįkta.** I will iron it myself. *1s:* **awábamnaya** *2s:* **ayábamnaya** *1p:* **a'úbamnayabi** *Vabs:* **wabámnayA**

abámnǫ *vt1* s/he files smth smooth with a rasp ‣ **Cǫmnáska žé awábamnǫ.** I filed this piece of board.

abámnu *vi1* s/he/it belches, burps ‣ **Ecágen awábamnu.** I often belch. *1s:* **awábamnu** *2s:* **ayábamnu** *1p:* **a'úbamnubi**

abápsų *vt1* s/he pours a liquid on sb, smth; waters smth ‣ **Iyéciga abápsų.** He poured it on his own. *Vredup:* **abápsųpsų**

abápsųpsų *vt1-redup* s/he sprinkles smth (with water)

abási *vt1* s/he drives sb, smth

abásisA *vt1* s/he sews smth on it ‣ **Sǫksája awábasisa.** I sew it on the dress.

abáweǧa *n* cross

abázo *vt1* s/he points at sb, smth ‣ **Hųgá amábazo.** The chief pointed at me. *1s:* **awábazo** *2s:* **ayábazo**

abóǧA *vt1* s/he blows smth (like medicine) on sb, smth *Vrefl:* **a'íkpoǧA**

abúspA *vt1* s/he daubs, glues, tacks smth onto it *1s:* **awábuspa** *2s:* **ayábuspa**

acáštų *vt1-dit* s/he names sb after another person ‣ **Hokšína žé acášwatų.** I named the boy after him. ‣ **Mikúši acášmatųbi.** They named me after my grandmother. *1s:* **acášwatų** *2s:* **acášyatų** *See:* **caštų**

Acáštųbi ecúbi *ph* Naming ceremony

acégicisnibi *vi1-recip* they defecate on one another

acésni *vt1* s/he defecates on sb, smth *1s:* **awácesni** *2s:* **ayácesni** *Vrecip:* **acégicisnibi**

acéti *vt1* s/he builds a fire on smth *1s:* **acéwati** *2s:* **acéyati**

acéžiya úbA *vi1* s/he sticks the tongue at sb ‣ **Adé, né tá né acéžiya úba:gac.** Father, the meat keeps sticking his tongue out at me. (Weasel 215:71)

acóga *Variant:* **acógena** *n* armpit ‣ **Acóga hįšmá.** He has hairy armpits.

acú *vs* it is covered with dew ‣ **Peží žé acú.** The grass is covered with dew.

acúȟewąga *vs* it is frosted, covered with frost; there is hoar frost ‣ **Dágu nówa acúȟewąga.** Everything is covered with hoar frost.

adáka *vi1* s/he tries hard *1s:* **awádąka** *2s:* **ayádąka**

adáyaȟ *adv* thoroughly ‣ **Adáyaȟ akídaga.** He looked at it thoroughly. (Weasel 7:143) *See:* **dąyáȟ**

adé *voc* 1) father *Usage:* term of address. ‣ **Adé! Cémągiya!** Father! Bless me! *n* 2) my father, dad *Usage:* term of reference among younger generations of speakers. ‣ **Adé ya'ówaniya.** I honor my dad. ‣ **adé waná iyáya né** my late father 3) Father, paternal spirit ‣ **Adé wakátąga niyá waká mak'ú no!** Father the Creator, give me the Holy breath of life! *1s:* **mi'áde ; miyáde** *2s:* **mi'áde ; niyáde** *3s:* **aktúgu ; atkúgu** *1p:* **adé'ųyąbi ; ųgíyade**

Adé ába *cp* Father's Day

adéna *n* 1) my parallel uncle (father's brother) 2) my uncle (mother's sister's husband) 3) my uncle (father's sister's husband) *2s:* **niyádena** *3s:* **atkúguna** *1p:* **adé'ųyąbi**

adéyA *vt1-caus* s/he has him as a father ‣ **Duwéni adéwayešį.** I have no father. *1s:* **adéwaya** *2s:* **adéyaya** *1p:* **adé'ųyabi**

adéyabi *n* reservation agent, Indian agent *Lit:* the one that is a father

agábodA *vi* s/he/it floats on smth *Vcont:* **agábon**

agábon *vcont* floating on smth *Vredup:* **agábonbon**

agábonbon *vcont-redup* floating around on smth ▸ **Agábonbon ų́.** He is floating around on it.

agácaǧa *vs* s/he/it is iced, frozen over ▸ **Waktá! Océǧu žé agácaǧa.** Watch out! The roads are icy. *1s:* **amágacaǧa** *2s:* **anígacaǧa**

agáǧA *vt1-dit* s/he makes smth on it

agáǧeǧe *vt1-dit* s/he sews, stitches smth onto it (ribbon, patch) ▸ **Wąhcá né sąksája agáǧeǧe.** Sew this flower on the dress. *1s:* **awágaǧeǧe** *2s:* **ayágaǧeǧe**

agáhi *vt1* s/he buries, covers up smth, sb with mud, earth ▸ **Cahóda awágahikta.** I will cover it with ashes. *1s:* **awágahi** *2s:* **ayágahi** *Vrefl:* **a'į́knahi**

agáȟni *vs* s/he/it is stuck on smth

agáȟpA *vt1* s/he covers sb, smth with it (blanket, lid, roof) ▸ **Iná amą́gaȟpa!** Mom cover me! ▸ **Hináǧa! Acígaȟpįkta.** Wait! I will cover you. ▸ **Amų́giya žé a'ų́gaȟpabi.** We covered the car with a tarp. ▸ **Makóce iyúhana agáȟpac'ehą žehą́ knaptá.** When all the earth was covered [with water], the weather cleared up. (Drummond 1976, The flood) *1s:* **awágaȟpa** *2s:* **ayágaȟpa** *1p:* **a'ų́gaȟpabi** *Vpos:* **aknáȟpA** *Vrefl:* **a'į́knaȟpA**

agáȟpe *n* cover, lid *Syn:* **iyágaȟpa**

agámnas *adv* straddling above ▸ **Miníȟaȟa žé agámnas nážį.** Stand straddling above that flowing water. (Fourstar p. 2)

agámnaza *vt1* s/he/it straddles above smth *Adv:* **agámnas**

agámpadahą *adv* from, on the top of it ▸ **Žécų hį́k agámpadahą įcéti.** He did that and built a fire on top of it. ▸ **Cą'ímaksa žé cą́ agámpadahą yįgá.** The saw is sitting on the wood.

agánA *vt1-dit* s/he pours liquid on sb, smth; spreads, sprinkles smth on it ▸ **Waȟpé awáganeší.** I did not water the plants. ▸ **Opšíja awágana.** I am spreading mud on it. ▸ **Cąpásusuna agána.** He spreads pepper on it. *1s:* **awágana** *2s:* **ayágana** *Vpos:* **aknánA** *Vrefl:* **a'į́knanA**

agá'oȟya *adv* at an angle ▸ **Wí žé agá'oȟya ȟnejáhą.** That tent is torn at an angle.

agápsų *vt1-dit* s/he/it spills a liquid on smth ▸ **Huȟnáȟyabi žé wa'ówabina ayágapsų.** You spilled coffee on that paper. (Fourstar p. 6) *1s:* **awágapsų** *2s:* **ayágapsų** *1p:* **a'ų́gapsųbi**

agásam *adv* across smth (camp, road) ▸ **Océǧu agásam tí.** He lives across the road.

agásampadahą *adv* from there across to here ▸ **"Mniwą́ja agásampadahą ųhíbic'éhą," eyá.** "We came from across the ocean," she said.

Agásam ti'óda *ngeo* Harlem (Montana) *Syn:* **Įdeša ti'óda**

agáské *vt1* s/he gulps a liquid; gets drunk ▸ **Ptewánuwą nína miní agáskabi.** Cattle gulp a lot of water. *1s:* **awágaska** *2s:* **ayágaska**

agásosa *vt1* s/he stirs up smth ▸ **Waȟpé žé agásosa!** Stir up the tea!

agástagA *vt1* s/he daubs, throws, pours out a gooey substance (as to make it stick) ▸ **Paȟní anígastagakta.** He will throw snot on you. *1s:* **awágastaga** *2s:* **ayágastaga**

agášeyA *vt1* s/he blocks smth with a tool (as a cable to hold the door); holds smth open *1s:* **awágašeya** *2s:* **ayágašeya**

agáškibi *n* flat, round stone with a groove used to pound chokecherries

agáštą *vt1* s/he pours smth on it *Vpos:* **aknáštą**

agáwįȟ *vcont* circling ▸ **Hejá agáwįȟ ų́.** A turkey vulture is circling.

agáwįš *vcont* bent over sb, smth; draped over smth; bent under its own weight ▸ **Cuwíknąga žé cą́ agáwįš įȟpéwaya.** I threw my coat over the branch.

agáwįžA *vt1* 1) s/he bends over sb, smth *1s:* **awágawįža** *2s:* **ayágawįža** *1p:* **ųgágawįžabi**

vi 2) it bends over under its own weight *Vcont:* **agáwįš**

agázeze *adv* hanging down from smth, dangling ‣ **Cáǧa agázeze hą́.** The icicles are hanging down.

Agáda *ngeo* Hays (Montana) *Syn:* **Toktí**

agą́n *Variant:* **agám** *post* on top of smth, on it ‣ **Agą́n bóǧa!** Blow on it! ‣ **Awódabi agą́n yúda!** Eat it on the table! ‣ **Agám nážį.** He stands on top. ‣ **íyą agą́n** on the stone ‣ **cą́'ágąn agą́n** on the chair

agą́n iyé'įc'iyA *vi3-refl* s/he mounts on smth (horse) ‣ **Žécen wanáš žén gaškáknoya cén agą́n iyé'c'iya.** Right away he led and mounted it up. (Weasel 17:192) *1s:* **agą́n iyémįc'iya** *2s:* **agą́n iyénįc'iya** *1p:* **agą́n iyé'ųgįc'iyabi**

agą́nayįgakiyA *Variant:* **agą́nyągakiyA** *vt1-caus* s/he makes him/her ride on a horse *1s:* **agą́nyįgawakiya** *2s:* **agą́nyįgayakiya**

agą́nya *adv* on, upon, on the top of smth

agą́nyįgA *Variant:* **agą́nyągA** *vt3* s/he rides a horse *Usage:* short form for šúgataga agą́nyągA 's/he sits on a horse' ‣ **Jim agą́nyągįkta.** Jim will ride a horse. ‣ **Agą́nyąga wo!** Ride the horse! ‣ **Šųkská agą́nmąga.** I ride a white horse. *1s:* **agą́nmąga** *2s:* **agą́nnąga** *1p:* **agą́n'ųyągabi** *Vcaus:* **agą́nayįgakiyA**

agé- *pref* on top of (ten) *Usage:* used with teen numerals from 11 to 19. ‣ **núba > agénųba** two > twelve ‣ **yámni > agéyamni** three > thirteen

agédoba *num* fourteen

agé'iyušna *num* seventeen

agénapcuwąga *num* nineteen

agénųba *num* 1) twelve *n* 2) dozen ‣ **wį́kta agénųba** egg dozen

agéšagowį (PR, OM) *num* seventeen

agéšaknoǧą *num* eighteen

agéšakpe *num* sixteen

agéwąži *num* eleven ‣ **Agéwąži sám hągé ehą́'i.** It is 11:30.

agéyamni *num* thirteen

agézaptą *num* fifteen

agícicipabi *vi1-recip* they meet one another

agícidA *vt1-pos* s/he looks after his/her own ‣ **"Įtó né mąkóce né awécidįktac," eyá cén.** "Well I will look after this earth," he said. (NS 2002:32) *1s:* **awécida** *2s:* **ayécida**

agícida *n* 1) warrior, soldier, police ‣ **Agícida žéca.** He is a soldier. ‣ **Agícida žé nína ohídiga.** That soldier is very brave. ‣ **Agícida mįco.** The police called me. ‣ **Agícida įnáȟmewįcawakiya.** I hid from the police. 2) army ‣ **Agícida owápįkte no!** I will join the army! 3) military uniform *Syn:* **ceskámaza**

agícida įtą́ca *cp* policeman

agícida wacíbi *cp* soldier dance

agícida wi'óti *cp* warrior lodge

agícida wi'óti hųgá *np* chief of the warrior lodge

agíci'i'abi *vi1-recip* they gossip about one another

agíci'įknanabi *vi1-recip* they pour smth (water, sand) on one another *1p:* **a'ųgici'įknanabi**

agícimnezabi *vi1-recip* they examine, observe, scrutinize one another ‣ **Waną́gaš gicíknuzabi dóhądu, nína agícimneząbi.** Long ago when it was time to get married, they really scrutinized one another.

agíciyuptabi *vi1-recip* they answer to one another

agíciyustobi *vi1-recip* they pet one another

agíjida *vt1-benef* s/he looks at sb, smth for him/her *1s:* **awéjida** *2s:* **ayéjida** *1p:* **a'ųgijidabi**

agíjimnezA *vt1-benef* s/he examines smth, sb for him/her

agíjiyuptA *vt1-benef* s/he answers for him/her ‣ **Iná wašín'i'ešį cén awéjimnupta.** Mom does not speak English so I answered for her. *1s:* **awéjimnupta** *2s:* **ayéjinupta**

agíjiyusto *vt1-benef* s/he pets sb, smth for him/her

agíknusto *vt1-pos* s/he pets his/her own *1s:* **awéknusto** *2s:* **ayéknusto**

agíktagA *vt1-dat* 1) s/he runs to sb, smth ‣ **Eyáš šųkšóšona úna néci eyáš iyóptaya agíktaga**

cén. Then the little donkey came over here and he ran toward it. (Weasel 15:141) *vt1-pos* 2) *s/* he runs to his/her own

agíktųža *vt1* s/he forgives sb for smth *1s:* **awéktųža** *2s:* **ayéktųža**

agímnezA *vt1-pos* s/he examines his/her own *1s:* **awágimneza** *2s:* **ayágimneza**

agípša *vt1-pos* s/he sneezes on his/her own (as in his/her handkerchief)

agísas *vcont* proudly ▸ **Agísas mawáni.** I walk proudly. ▸ **Agísas nážį.** He stands proudly.

agísaza *vs* s/he is proud (with negative connotations) ▸ **Nína agísaza otí'įga.** I guess he is very proud. *Vcaus:* **asásya** *Vcont:* **agísas** *Vrefl:* **a'įc'isaza**

agísni *vs-dat* s/he heals, recovers from smth (wound, illness) ▸ **Agísni áya.** He is starting to recover from it. *See:* **asní**

agíš'a *vi1* s/he cheers, emits a war cry

agíto *vs* s/he is tattooed ▸ **Įstó né agíto.** He is tatooed on the arm. *1s:* **amágito** *2s:* **anígito** *Vrefl:* **agíto'įc'iya**

agíto'įc'iya *vi3-refl* s/he tattooed him/herself *1s:* **agítomįc'iya** *2s:* **agítonįc'iya**

agí'ų *vt1-pos* s/he feeds the fire with his/her own

agíwacį *vt1-pos* s/he thinks about his/her own ▸ **Húgu agíwacį.** He thinks about his mother.

agíktųža *vt1* s/he goes crazy over sb, smth ▸ **Nécen agíktųžabi cá.** They go crazy over it in this way.

agú *vt1* s/he brings sb, smth back here ▸ **Mikúši agú cén.** He brought my grandmother back here. ▸ **Ptewánu įjápsįdena ús awícawagu.** I brought the cows back home with the whip. ▸ **Íhiyų aké yá, aké agú.** All right, go there again, bring back more. (Drummond 1976, Įktomi) *1s:* **awágu** *2s:* **ayágu** *Vabs:* **wa'águ** *Vdat:* **gagú**

agúmna *vs* it smells scorched, burnt

agúyabi *n* 1) flour 2) bread, bannock ▸ **Agúyabi né waštémna.** This bread smells good. ▸ **Ağúyabi modábi oyágihi?** Can you slice a loaf of bread? ▸ **Ağúyabi né bųbú.** This bannock is crumbling.

ağúyabi baská *cp* dough

ağúyabi mįmą́ *cp* round bannock

ağúyabi mnúna *cp* flour

ağúyabi océti ągán *ph* bannock baked on top of a stove

ağúyabi skuskúyena *cp-redup* cookie *Syn:* **ağúyabiskuya**

ağúyabi šnoyábi *cp* fried bannock

ağúyabi zipzíbena *cp-pl* pancakes

ağúyabisaga *n* toast, cracker *Lit:* dry bread ▸ **Hąyákena štén ağúyabisaga nagú asábi wacíga.** In the morning I want toast and milk.

ağúyabiskuya (PR) *n* cake, cookie ▸ **Ağuyábiskuya edáhą yúda.** He is eating some cake.

ağúyabisu *n* wheat kernel *Lit:* flour seed

ağúyabisu įjášna *cp* wheat binder

ağúyabiwaką *n* communion bread ▸ **Owácegiye én ağúyabiwaką yúdabi.** They take communion bread in church.

ahíge *adv* 1) last, last one; behind ▸ **Ahíge mawáni.** I walk behind. ▸ **Ába ahíge žén í.** He went there on the last day. ▸ **Ahígeȟ hí.** He arrived the very last. ▸ **Jim ahígeȟ Nakón'i'a.** Jim is the last to speak Nakoda. *vs* 2) s/he/it is the last one ▸ **Todd ejé'enaȟ ahíge.** Todd is the last one left.

ahígeȟ *adv* finally, at last ▸ **Ahígeȟ timáni wa'í.** I finally went for a visit. ▸ **Ahígeȟ cén hí.** He arrived at last. ▸ **Wįcášta t'įkta hąda, ahígeȟ i'ác.** When a person is going to die they say final words. (Weasel 78:356)

ahígeȟtįyA *vs* s/he/it is the very last one ▸ **Ahígeȟtįyą nén wací.** Here is the very last dance.

ahą *vt1* s/he steps on sb, smth ▸ **Šúga cesní awáhą giníja.** I almost stepped on dog poop. ▸ **Ahą híkna naškóba.** He stepped on it and bent it. *1s:* **awáhą** *2s:* **ayáhą**

ahą́tehąga *adv* late at night ‣ **Ahą́tehąga štén waknį́ktac.** I will be back late. (Weasel 150:587) *Syn:* **hątéhą**

ahą́zi *vimp* it is dusk, dark ‣ **ahą́zi áya** it is becoming dusk

ahą́ziga *vimp* it is kind of dark

ahą́zikiyA *vt1* s/he darkens smth

ahé *interj* expression of humility said at the beginning of a prayer or song

ahí *vt1* 1) s/he arrives here bringing sb, smth ‣ **Céǧa žéħ awáhi.** I came with a specific pot. ‣ **Wóyuda awáhi.** I brought food. *Vbenef:* **gíjahi** *vi-coll* 2) they arrive here as a group ‣ **Né hékta nén aškán įħą́ktuwąbi nén ahí no!** Back in recent past the Sioux came here.

ahíduwą *vt1* s/he looks here (in the direction of the speaker) ‣ **Ahíduwąšį céyabi.** They cry without looking here.

ahínąpA *vi* it (plant) sprouts ‣ **Waħcá žé ahínąpa.** The flower sprouted. ‣ **Naháħ ahínąpešį.** It did not sprout yet. ‣ **Žehádu hádahą waħpé įcáǧa nagú pežíto įš ahínąpa cén.** During that time the leaves grow and the grass sprouts as well. (Haywahe 1992:31)

ahíyayA *vi1, vi1/2* s/he sings a song ‣ **Koškábi nówa ahíyayabi.** The young men were all singing. ‣ **Šahíyabi dóken ahíyayabi žécen ecú.** She sang in the Cree style. ‣ **Onówą žé awáhimnįkte no.** I will sing this song. *1s:* **awáhiyaya ; awáhimnamna ; awáhimna** *1p:* **ųgáhiyayabi**

ahíħpayA *vt1* s/he/it falls on sb, smth

ahógijitą'į *vt1-benef* s/he blesses smth for sb ‣ **Wó'iye mitáwa žé ahómijitą'į.** He blessed my sacred cloth for me. ‣ **Mitúgaši, mikúši, wóyude nén éknebi žé ahómijitą'į!** Grandfather, grandmother, bless the food that is placed here for me! *1s:* **ahówejitą'į** *2s:* **ahóyejitą'į**

ahógipA *vt1-pos* s/he has a deep, religious respect for his/her own ‣ **Dóhąni mitáwįju**

ahówagipešį. I never disrespected my wife. *1s:* **ahówagipa** *2s:* **ahóyagipa**

ahópA *vt1* s/he respects, honors, reveres sb ‣ **Makóce ahóyapa bo!** You all respect the land! *1s:* **ahówapa** *2s:* **ahóyapa** *1p:* **ahó'ųpabi** *Vabs:* **wa'áhopA** *Vpos:* **ahógipA**

ahópe'įc'iyA *vi3-refl* s/he has self-respect, honors himself/herself ‣ **Waką́yą ahópe'įc'iya.** He honors, blesses himself spiritually. *1s:* **ahópemįc'iya** *2s:* **ahópenįc'iya**

ahótą'į *vt1* s/he respects, praises sb ‣ **Iná ahówatą'į.** I respect mom. *1s:* **ahówatą'į** *2s:* **ahóyatą'į** *Vbenef:* **ahógijitą'į**

ahúħnaǧa *vt1* s/he burns smth on it

aħcó *n* shoulder (below the shoulder joint)

aħcómaza *n* police constable in a Nakoda reservation *Lit:* iron shoulder (probably refers to the police badge)

aħnó *vt1* s/he/it growls over at sb, smth ‣ **Šúga steħ awáħno:ga.** I growl at him like a dog. *1s:* **awáħno** *2s:* **ayáħno** *See:* **ħnó**

áħunąptą *adv* hillside ‣ **Áħunąptą ųkcékcena ožúna eyáš.** There was cactus all over the hillside. (Weasel 24:29)

a'í *vt1* s/he takes, brings arrives with sb, smth there ‣ **Mihú owáyawa žéci amá'įkta.** My mother will take me to school. ‣ **Micį́kši owáyawa žéci awá'i.** I drove my son to school. ‣ **Wíyąbi níyuhana wón a'íbi cen.** All the women would take food. (Cumberland 2005:354) *1s:* **awá'i** *2s:* **ayá'i**

a'í'A *vt1* s/he gossips about sb, smth ‣ **Ecágen a'í'a.** She is always gossiping about her. ‣ **Wíyą žé amá'i'a.** That woman gossips about me. *1s:* **awá'i'a** *2s:* **ayá'i'a** *Vabs:* **wa'á'i'A** *Vrecip:* **agíci'i'abi**

a'ínina *Variant:* **ánina** ; **inína** *adv* quietly, in silence ‣ **A'ínina yįgá!** Sit quietly! ‣ **Ą́ba né a'ínina yįgá.** It's a quiet day today. ‣ **Áninaħ hą'.** It is really quiet. (Cumberland 2005:236) ‣ **Inína mawánįkte no!** I will walk quietly!

a'íyopsijA *vt1* s/he jumps on, over sb, smth ▸ **Miní žé a'íyowapsiješį.** I did not jump over the water. ▸ **Cą'ágą yįgábi žé a'íyopsija.** He jumped over the chair. *1s:* **a'íyowapsija** *2s:* **a'íyoyapsija**

a'íyopsijac škáda *vi1* s/he is jumping rope

a'įbazija *n* row of hills

a'įc'ibapsųpsų *n-redup* eau de cologne

a'įc'icesni *vi3-refl* s/he defecates on himself/ herself *1s:* **amįc'icesni** *2s:* **anįc'icesni**

a'įc'icidA *vi3-refl* s/he looks at himself/her- self) ▸ **Žécen nína wašté a'įc'icida gá, nína waštégina hųštá, hokšína né.** So then when this boy looked at himself, he looked good and so he was very happy, it is said. (Shields 67:291) *1s:* **amįc'icida** *2s:* **anįc'icida**

a'įc'icidabi *n* mirror

a'įc'iktašį *vi3* s/he neglects himself/herself ▸ **Né, kó a'įc'iktašį nó** This one has just neglected himself. (Shields 61:235) *1s:* **amįc'iktašį** *2s:* **anįc'iktašį**

a'įc'imnezA *vi3-refl* s/he examines himself/her- self *1s:* **amįc'imneza** *2s:* **anįc'imneza**

a'įc'isaza *vi3-refl* s/he is proud of himself/her- self *1s:* **amįc'isaza** *2s:* **anį'c'isaza**

a'įc'iyuptA *vi3-refl* s/he answers a question s/he had *1s:* **amįc'iyupta** *2s:* **anįc'iyupta**

a'įgicitųbįšį *vi1-recip* they lie to one another about smth

a'įȟabi įc'íya *vi3-refl* s/he makes a fool, laughing stock of himself/herself *1s:* **a'įȟabi mįc'íya** *2s:* **a'įȟabi nįc'íya**

a'įjaškA *vt1* s/he ties it on sb, smth

a'įknahi *vi3-refl* s/he covers himself/herself up with smth *1s:* **amįknahi** *2s:* **anįknahi**

a'įknaȟpA *vi3-refl* s/he covers himself/herself with smth *1s:* **amįknaȟpa** *2s:* **anįknaȟpa** *See:* **agáȟpA**

a'įknana *vi3-refl* s/he pours smth over himself/ herself (powder, dirt) ▸ **Mąká amįknana.** I pour dirt on myself. *Vrecip:* **agíci'įknanabi**

a'įknanabi *n* powder, bath powder

a'įknatatabi *n* root, flower (that one chews and blow on oneself)

a'įknuhA *vi3-refl* s/he has, keeps smth for him- self/herself *1s:* **amįknuha** *2s:* **anįknuha**

a'įknutątą *vi3-refl* s/he feels him/herself in search of smth *1s:* **amįknutątą** *2s:* **anįknutątą**

a'įkpapsų *n* perfume ▸ **A'įkpapsų né skúyemna.** This perfume has a sweet smell.

a'įkpapsųpsųbi *n-redup* spray perfume

a'įkpoǧa *vi3-refl* 1) s/he blows smth (medicine, perfume) on himself/herself *n* 2) cedar 3) Indian perfume (sweet pine, cedar)

A'įkpoǧą oyúze *ngeo* Sweet Grass Hills (Mon- tana) *Syn:* **Pežískuya bahá**

a'įktųkiyA *Variant:* **a'įtkųkiyA** *vt1-caus* s/he lights up sb, smth; gives sb a light *1s:* **a'įktųwakiya** ; **a'įtkųwakiya** *2s:* **a'įktųyakiya** ; **a'įtkųyakiya** *1p:* **a'įktų'ųkiyabi** ; **a'įtkų'ųkiyabi**

a'įšį'įyayA *vi2* s/he/it goes out of sight

a'įštimA *vt1* s/he sleeps over at sb's place ▸ **Micíkši kúgišiktu tída a'įštįma.** My son slept at his grandma's place.

a'ítųšį *vt1* s/he lies about smth *1s:* **a'íwatųšį** *2s:* **a'íyatųšį** *1p:* **a'į'ųtųbįšį** *Vredup:* **a'įgicitųbįšį**

akádeja *vs* it is kind of warm

aké *adv* 1) again ▸ **Aké ú!** Come again! ▸ **Aké žécen ecú.** He did the same thing again. ▸ **Aké wącímnagįkte no!** I will see you again! ▸ **Aké koná!** (See you) again friend! 2) another one, one more (usually followed by one); plus ▸ **Aké wąží émnagųkte no!** I will give him one more! ▸ **Dóba aké núba štén šákpe.** Four plus two equals six.

akí- *pref* same, alike, both, joined ▸ **ecén > akí'ecen** in the right, original way; accord- ingly; thus > equally, the same, alike

akídA *vt1* s/he looks at sb, smth ▸ **Né akída!** Look at it! ▸ **Dáguškina žé įštíma akída.** Look if the baby is sleeping. ▸ **Hokšína awícakida hįkna wį'óȟnoǧe žén mahén kiknákta.** The

boy looked at them and went back into the
cave. *1s:* **awákida** *2s:* **ayákida** *Vbenef:* **agíjidA**
Vcont: **akín** *Vpos:* **agícidA** *Vredup:* **akítkidA**
Vrefl: **a'íc'icidA**

akí'ecedu *vs* they are alike ‣ **Núbabina žé
akí'ecedu.** The twins look alike. ‣ **Iyécįgayena
núm akí'ecedu.** Those two cars look alike.
(Fourstar p. 1) *Adv:* **akí'ecen**

akí'ecen *adv-cont* equally, the same, alike ‣
Akí'ecen wįcákuwa. Treat them equally.

akín *vcont* looking, watching ‣ **Gazógic'ų
akín yįgá.** He is watching the hockey game.
‣ **Awįcakin mągá.** I am looking at people. ‣
Optéya awįcakin yįgá. He is watching the
herd. ‣ **Bahá žé agán iyódąga štén awįcakin
yįgá.** He sat down on the hill and watched
them. (Drummond 1976, The boy who made
peace)

akínija *vt1* s/he debates, argues over smth ‣
Ecágen akínijabi. They always argue about
it. *Vabs:* **wa'ákinija**

akínijabi *n* argument, dispute, quarrel ‣
Akínijabi žé dąyą́ knuštą́bi. The argument
was settled peacefully.

akínjjabi *n* candidate

akípa *vt1* 1) s/he meets sb ‣ **Dąyą́ magína acícipa.**
I am pleased to meet you 2) s/he encounters,
experiences smth ‣ **Dágu sijáya ayákipakte no.**
You will encounter something bad. *1s:* **awákipa**
2s: **ayákipa** *1p:* **a'ų́kipabi** *Vabs:* **wa'ákipa** *Vcoll:*
awįcakipa *Vrecip:* **agícicipabi** *See:* **écipabi**

akíšne *n* beau, lover

akíye *adv* same, identical ‣ **Gídą̌h wįcágijaǧa
nupín akíye cén.** Finally he made them for
them, both identical. (Weasel 168:127)

akná *vt1* s/he takes sb, smth back there ‣
Yuwágam aknábi. They took it out, pull-
ing upwards. (Cumberland 2005:233) ‣
Amáyaknabikte no. You are going to take
me back. (NS 2002:17) *1s:* **awákna** *2s:* **ayákna**
Vabs: **wa'ákna**

aknáda *vt1* s/he accompanies sb singing (as in
a chair)

aknáȟpA *vt1-pos* s/he covers his/her own

aknána *vt1-pos* s/he pours smth on his/her own;
powders his/her own ‣ **Mitága awáknana.** I
powdered my little sister. *1s:* **awáknana** *2s:*
ayáknana

aknáštą *vt1-pos* s/he pours smth on his/her own
‣ **Éc pakówa aknáštą cén eyáš įknúžaža kó
eyáš.** So he splashed water over his head, and
even bathed. (Weasel 97:94)

aknáyA *vt2* s/he/it follows sb, smth along ‣ **Hiyá
aknáyįkteší no.** No, he will not follow him
along. *1s:* **aknámna** *2s:* **aknána** *1p:* **akná'ųyabi**

aknák *adv* following, trailing, keeping an eye
on, together, along *Usage:* occurs before
verbs of movement. ‣ **Aknák ú!** Follow (me)!
‣ **Šų́ga žé aknák ú.** The dog is coming along.
‣ **Aknák yábi.** They are following (away from
the speaker). ‣ **Aknák mnį́kta.** I will follow.

aknáya *n* fool

aknáyabi hąwí *cp* April fool

akné *vi1* s/he goes back to smth, somewhere ‣
Wayáwa aknébi. They returned to school.

aknékiyA *vt1-caus* s/he lets, makes sb take sb,
smth back ‣ **Žécen eyáš wįcápaha éyagu
žená kówa aknéwįcakiya hį́kna.** So then he
took those scalps and he made them take all of
them back. (NS 2002:73–74) *1s:* **aknéwakiya**
2s: **aknéyakiya** *1p:* **akné'ųkiyabi**

aknéška *Variant:* **aknéškana** *n* lizard, salamander ‣ **Né Įktómi įwóknagabi hą́da mnogédu
hą́da aknéškana timáhen híbis'a gáyabis'a.**
They used to say that lizards would come to
your tent if you told Įktomi stories in the summertime. (Drummond 1976, Įktomi)

aknéška tą́ga *cp* crocodile

akní *vt1* s/he comes with, brings sb, smth back
home ‣ **Mitáwįju wówaši dahá awákni.** I
picked up my wife at work. ‣ **Wįcá žé šúgatąga
awįcakni.** That man brought the horse back

home. ▸ **Agícida né akní cén yupíbiga.** He honored the returning soldier. *1s:* **awákni** *2s:* **ayákni** *Vabs:* **wa'ákni** *Vbenef:* **gíjakni** *Vcoll:* **awį́cakni** *Vdat:* **gakní**

aknúštą *vt1-pos* s/he loses his/her own thing ▸ **Nąbį́kpa aknúštą.** He lost his gloves. *1s:* **awáknuštą** *2s:* **ayáknuštą**

aktágA *vi1* s/he/it runs ▸ **Wįcíjabina nená aktágabi.** These girls are running. ▸ **Akną́k aktága.** He was jogging along. ▸ **Nús awáktaga.** I run fast. ▸ **Šų́ga žé amų́giya ki'úm aktága.** The dog ran along side the car. *1s:* **awáktaga** *2s:* **ayáktaga** *1p:* **ųgáktagabi** *Vcaus:* **aktákkiyA** *Vcont:* **akták** *Vdat:* **agíktagA**

akták *vcont* running ▸ **Akták iyáyįkta.** He will go running. *Vredup:* **aktáktak**

aktákkiyA *vt1-caus* s/he makes sb, smth run *1s:* **aktákwakiya** *2s:* **aktákyakiya** *1p:* **akták'ųkiyabi**

aktáktak *vcont-redup* running along ▸ **Aktáktak yá.** He is jogging along.

aktášį *vt1* s/he rejects, does not want, disowns sb ▸ **Wįcá žé aktášį.** She does not want that man. ▸ **Tagóžakpagu aktášį.** He disowned his grandchild. *Vrefl:* **aktášį**

aktúgu *Variant:* **atkúgu** (PR, OM) *n* his/her father *1p:* **aktúgu'ųyabi ; atkúgu'ųyabi**

aktúguna *n* 1) his/her uncle (father's brother) 2) stepfather

aktúguya *Variant:* **atkúguya** (PR, WB, OM) *vt1-caus* s/he has him as a father ▸ **Jim aktúgumaya.** I have Jim as a father. ▸ **Žé aktúgušį hųštá.** It is said he was not his real father. *1s:* **aktúgumaya** *2s:* **aktúguniya** *1p:* **aktúgu'ųyabi** *See:* **adéyA**

ak'į́ *n* saddle

ak'į́ha *n* saddlebag

ak'į́maheda *n* saddle blanket

ak'į́pasu *n* saddle horn

ak'į́šų́gatąga *n* pack horse

ak'į́gijitų *vt1-benef* s/he saddles a horse for him/her

ak'į́sų *n* pad saddle

ak'į́tųga *vt1* s/he saddles a horse, harnesses a dog *1s:* **ak'į́watųga** *2s:* **ak'į́yatųga** *1p:* **ak'į́'ųtųgabi**

amádaba *n* ledge

amáǧažu *vs* it rains on smth ▸ **Žécųbi žé ogáȟnoga amáǧažu eštá yužážabi dóȟąni sagéšį sudášį.** By doing this it never dries out and gets hard in rain or washing. (Drummond 1976, Smoking hides)

amáȟpiya *vimp* 1) it is cloudy ▸ **Ába né amáȟpiyašį.** It is not cloudy today. *Syn:* **a'óȟazi** *n* 2) cloud ▸ **Amáȟpiya óda.** There are a lot of clouds.

amáȟpiya naȟnéjA *vimp* there is a cloudburst, a sudden heavy rainfall

amáksA *vt1* s/he cuts smth off with a sharp blade ▸ **Cąmnáska žé awámaksa.** I cut off this plank to make it fit. *1s:* **awámaksa** *2s:* **ayámaksa**

amáni *vt1* s/he walks on smth ▸ **Cąmnáska žé amánišį.** Do not walk on the platform. ▸ **Wanągaš wamákašką wąží makóce amáni** Long ago a creature walked on earth. (BigEagle 2017)

amánibi *n* path

amáštageja *vs* it is kind of warm

amíknąga wacíbi *cp* crow belt dance

amíknągabi *n* dance bustle, Crow belt *Syn:* **mįkną́ge**

amná *n* stench

amnágena *vimp* it is still, peaceful ▸ **Ȟtayédu né amnágena.** The evening is still. ▸ **Ába né dąyą́ amnágena.** Today is a nice day with no breeze. (Fourstar p. 2) ▸ **Žehą́, dáguni naȟ'ų́šį, amnágenahą.** After that he did not hear anything; it stayed really quiet. (Shields 50:94)

amnézA *vt1* s/he examines, scrutinizes sb, smth ▸ **Omákawąži amámneza.** I have my annual check-up. ▸ **Amámneza cíga.** He wants to examine me. ▸ **Amámneza hí.** He came and examined me. *1s:* **awámneza** *2s:* **ayámneza** *1p:* **ųgámnezabi** *Vabs:* **wa'ámnezA** *Vbenef:* **agíjimnezA** *Vcoll:* **awįcamnezA** *Vpos:* **agímnezA** *Vrecip:* **agícimnezabi** *Vrefl:* **a'íc'imnezA**

amnézena *vimp* it is calm, a day without a breeze ▸ **Ába nén nína amnézena'.** It is a very calm day today.

amníjiya *adv* all over, all around ▸ **Owá amníjiya ųbi.** They are all over.

amnó *n* shoulder blade *1s:* **ma'ámno** *2s:* **ni'ámno**

amnóto *Variant:* **amnótona** *n* teal, blue-winged duck *Lit:* blue shoulder blades

amógįyą *Variant:* **amúgiyą ; įmúgiya** *n* car *Usage:* archaic. ▸ **Amógįyą naháň yá.** The car is still running. ▸ **Amógįyą wapíwacįšį.** The car is not clean. ▸ **Amógįyą iyúha mnušnóga.** I dismantled all the cars. ▸ **Amúgiya nuhá he?** Did you have a car? *Syn:* **iyécįgayena ; iyécįga(na) ; iyécįgena ; iyécįgamani**

amógįyą én yįgábi *ph* car seat

amógįyą hú *cp* car tire, wheel ▸ **amógįyą hú napóba** flat tire

amópša *vt1* s/he boils smth over, to a high temperature

amóskijA *vt1* s/he pounds smth smooth with an instrument *1s:* **amówaskija** *2s:* **amóyaskija**

anádą *vt1* s/he raids an enemy ▸ **Nakóda tíbi žéci awícanadąbi.** They raided the Nakoda camped over there. *See:* **nadą**

anágipa *vt1-pos* s/he seeks for his/her own for refuge, protection ▸ **Tugágišiktu anágipa.** He runs to his grandfather for protection. *1s:* **anáwagipa** *2s:* **anáyagipa**

anáğoptą *vt1* s/he listens to sb, smth ▸ **Adé anáwağoptąšį.** I did not listen to dad. ▸ **I'á štén anáğoptą wo.** When he talks you listen to him. ▸ **Nína dąyá i'á duká wįcášta žená anáğoptąbįšį.** She spoke very well but the peo-

ple did not listen to her. *1s:* **anáwağoptą** *2s:* **anáyağoptą** *Vabs:* **wa'ánağoptą**

anáħmA *vt1* s/he keeps a secret ▸ **Dágu omíjiyage anáwaħma.** He told me something I kept as a secret. *1s:* **anáwaħma** *2s:* **anáyaħma** *Adv:* **anáħmaya ; anágiħmą** *See:* **naħmána, onáħmą**

anáħmaya *adv* secretly ▸ **Anáħmaya omíjiyaga.** He told me something in secrecy.

anákokkiyA *vt1-pos* s/he sprains his/her own (foot, thumb) ▸ **Sihá anákokkiya.** She sprained her ankle. *1s:* **anákokwagiya** *2s:* **anákokyagiya** *See:* **nagípšų**

anásnadA *vt1* s/he sneaks up on sb, stalks smth (prey) ▸ **Táňce žé awánasnadįkta.** I will stalk that deer. *1s:* **awánasnada** *2s:* **ayánasnada**

anágiħmą *adv* secretly ▸ **Anágiħmą wóknaga.** He is telling it secretly.

anápomyA *vt1-caus* s/he bombs smth (as a city) *1s:* **anápomwaya** *2s:* **anápomyaya** *1p:* **anápom'ųyabi**

anáptA *vt1* s/he stops, blocks sb, smth ▸ **Šúga anápte wa'í.** I went to stop the horse. *Vabs:* **wa'ánaptA**

anéžA *vt1* s/he urinates on smth ▸ **Cá awáneža.** I urinated on the tree. ▸ **Šúga žé wí anéža.** That dog urinated on the tent. (Fourstar p. 6) *1s:* **awáneža** *2s:* **ayáneža**

aní *vt1* s/he steps, climbs, walks over smth ▸ **Taȟpá agán aní žécen hú né anúk nųbagiya cén hú né yuškom iyáya.** He [Įktomni] stepped on his [diver] back, spreading his legs out and bending them crooked. (Drummond 1976, Įktomi and the ducks) *Vredup:* **aníni**

aníni *vt1-redup* s/he steps, climbs walk over smth here and there

anís'a *n* climber

anósnos mani *vi1* s/he walks staggeringly

anówą *vt1* s/he sings over sb (as a cure)

anówąbi *n* quarterly singing *See:* **wótijağa anówąbi**

anúk *adv* both sides, ways ‣ **Awódabi anúk iyódągabi.** They sat on both sides of the table. ‣ **Yakná štén anúk éduwą!** When you leave look both ways! ‣ **Anúk sųgágu gicíyabi.** They both called each other "younger brother." (Cumberland 2005:353)

anúk éduwą *cp* cross-eyed person

anúkadahą *adv* on each sides, ends, both ways ‣ **Anúkadahą éwaduwą.** I looked both ways.

anúkasą *n* bald eagle *Lit:* off-white on both sides

anúkpesto *n* pickax *Lit:* pointed on both sides

anúk'ope *n* October *Lit:* joins both sides (because the month of October may see both warm and cold days, thus joining together summer and winter)

anúwĄ *vt1* s/he swims after sb, smth; goes after sb, smth while swimming

a'óbazo *n* medal, pin

a'ógadą *vt1* 1) s/he nails smth on it *1s:* **a'ówagadą** *2s:* **a'óyagadą** *1p:* **a'ó'ųgadąbi** *n* 2) nail

a'ógagį *vt1* s/he looks, peeks into smth, at sb

a'ógas'į *vt1* s/he peeks in at sb, smth ‣ **Omnąbi cen ókšadahą a'ógas'į:gabi.** They had smelled them and were peeking in from all around. (Weasel 5:90) *1s:* **awá'ogas'į** *2s:* **ayá'ogas'į**

a'óhązi *vimp* 1) it is cloudy, overcast ‣ **Hąwí tą'įšį a'óhązi no!** The sun is not visible, it is overcast! *n* 2) shade ‣ **A'óhązi én yįgá!** Sit in the shade!

a'ókeyabi *n* shelter

a'ókpazA *vimp* it is a dark night; in the darkness ‣ **A'ókpaza áya.** It is getting dark. ‣ **A'ókpaza hąda tągán yábi kowágipa.** I am afraid to go out in the darkness.

a'ókšą *adv* around smth; around camp *Vcaus:* **a'ókšąyĄ**

a'ókšąyĄ *vt1-caus* s/he encircles, surrounds sb, smth ‣ **Šúktógeja a'ókšą'ųyąbi.** The wolves encircled us. *1s:* **a'ókšąwayą** *2s:* **a'ókšąyayą** *1p:* **a'ókšą'ųyąbi**

a'ómnina *n* place sheltered from the wind

a'ónatagA *vt1-dit* s/he locks sb in, out ‣ **Šúga žé'įš žená a'ónataga cén.** He also closed the dog in with them. (Weasel 10:45)

a'ópekiyA *vt1-caus* s/he adds smth onto it *1s:* **a'ópewakiya** *2s:* **a'ópeyakiya** *1p:* **a'ópe'ųkiyabi**

a'ópeyA *vt1-caus* s/he adds on smth *Vcaus:* **a'ópekiyA**

a'óžąžą *vimp* 1) it is sunny, lightened up ‣ **Tągán a'óžąžą.** It is sunny outside. *n* 2) light ‣ **A'óžąžą né natága!** Shut off the lights!

a'óžąžą yuhá'ųbi *ph* lantern

apÁ *vt1* 1) s/he hits, strikes, knocks sb, smth ‣ **Įknúhana awápa no!** I hit him suddenly! ‣ **Cogáduh awápa.** I hit it right in the center. ‣ **Amápa hį́kna mayúhija.** He hit me and woke me up. ‣ **Šúga žé apá cén howáyaya.** He hit the dog, and it yelped. ‣ **Anípa he eštáš naníhtaga?** Did he hit you or kick you? 2) it is X hour *Lit:* it strikes ‣ **Dóna apá?** What time is it? ‣ **Ecágen záptą apá hąda hí.** He always comes at five. *1s:* **awápa** *2s:* **ayápa** *1p:* **ųgápabi** *Vredup:* **apápA** *See:* **į'ápA**

apáhtA *vt1-dit* s/he ties smth onto it ‣ **Cąbákmįkma žén awápahta.** I tied it up to the wagon. ‣ **Hahúda apáhte žé gapsápsą hą́.** The rope that is tide up onto it is swinging. *1s:* **awápahta** *2s:* **ayápahta**

apápA *vt1-redup* s/he knocks lightly on sb, smth

apéhį ; apéhą *n* mane

apéya *adv* in a waiting manner ‣ **Apéya mągá.** I am sitting waiting.

apšÁ *vt1* s/he sneezes on smth *Vpos:* **agípšA** *See:* **pšÁ**

aptáyĄ *vs* s/he/it turns over, capsizes; is upside down ‣ **Amógiyą aptáyą.** The car turned over. *1s:* **amáptąyą** *2s:* **aníptąyą**

asásya *vt1* s/he is proud of him/her; s/he makes sb proud ‣ **Asásmayaya he?** Are you proud of me? ‣ **Ecágen asásciya.** I am always proud of you. *1s:* **asáswaya** *2s:* **asásyaya** *1p:* **asás'ųyabi**

asábi *n* milk ‣ **Asábi žé sewí.** That milk is sour. ‣ **Wįcíjana gá asábi cįgá.** That girl over there wants milk.

asábi sudá *cp* cheese *Lit:* hard milk

Asábi wakpá *ngeo* Milk River (Montana) *Syn:* **Wakpá juk'ána**

asábi wíkni *cp* butter

askámyA *vt1-caus* s/he sticks smth on it *1s:* **askámwaya** *2s:* **askámyaya** *1p:* **askám'ųyabi** *Vabs:* **wa'áskamyA**

askámyabi *n* glue

asnáyA *vt1-caus* s/he rubs sb, smth with grease

asní₁ *vs* s/he is healed, has recovered from an illness; is well again ‣ **Asní amáya.** I am starting to recover. ‣ **Éstena amásni.** I recovered soon. *1s:* **amásni** *2s:* **anísni** *Vcaus:* **asníyA** *Vdat:* **agísni**

asní₂ *vi1* s/he stops, quits ‣ **Céya asní wo!** Stop crying! *Vpos:* **asnígiya**

asnígiya *vi1-pos* s/he rests, takes a break from his/her activity ‣ **Waná gicúni hík asnígiya.** Quit now and take a rest. (Fourstar p. 3)

asní'įc'iyA *vi3-refl* s/he heals, relieves himself/herself

asníyA *vt1-caus* s/he heals sb *1s:* **asníwaya** *2s:* **asníyaya** *1p:* **asní'ųyabi** *Vrefl:* **asní'įc'iyA**

asnóhĄ *vi1* s/he/it creeps on the belly

astústagA *vs* s/he/it is rather tired ‣ **Midáguye anístustage no.** My relative you look rather tired. *1s:* **amástustaga** *2s:* **anístustaga** *Adv:* **astústagen**

astústagen *adv* kind of tired ‣ **Nén astústagen mągá'.** I am sitting here kind of tired. (Cumberland 2005:339)

as'į *vt1* s/he wishes for sb, smth ‣ **Wįcá žé as'į:ga.** She wishes for that man. *1s:* **awás'į** *2s:* **ayás'į** *Vabs:* **wa'ás'į**

ašínwokcą *vt1* s/he has perverse thoughts about sb, smth ‣ **Gá ašínwokcąbi įšnána én yągá cén.** So they were having perverse thoughts about her as she sat there alone. (Weasel 77:327)

ašítųgeja *vs* s/he/it is kind of fat, chubby

aškáda *vt1* s/he plays on smth

aškádu *vs* s/he/it is late *1s:* **amáškadu** *2s:* **aníškadu** *1p:* **a'úškadubi**

aškáduȟ *adv* lately, recently ‣ **Aškáduȟ žécamų.** I did that recently.

aškán *adv* recently, lately ‣ **Šiyónide aškán žén í.** She arrived there in Pheasant Rump recently. ‣ **Aškán mitákona šųkcíjana né k'ú.** My friend gave her this puppy recently.

aškáyena *adv* close

ašnóya *vt1-caus* s/he solders smth *1s:* **ašnówaya** *2s:* **ašnóyaya** *Vabs:* **wa'ášnoya**

ašón'įc'iyA *vi3-refl* s/he smudges himself/herself *1s:* **ašónmįc'iya** *2s:* **ašónnįc'iya**

ašpáyą *vt1* s/he brands a horse, cattle

atážošA *vt1* s/he spits on smth *1s:* **awátažoša** *2s:* **ayatažoša**

atítoką *Variant:* **titóką** *n* different tent

atkáges'a *Variant:* **aktáges'a** *n* runner ‣ **Micíkši atkáges'a yuką.** My son is a runner. *Syn:* **íyąges'a**

a'ú₁ *vt1* s/he brings, comes here with sb, smth ‣ **Kún a'ú.** Bring it down. ‣ **Pąǧí šáša žé a'ú.** Bring the red potatoes. ‣ **Nitákona a'ú.** Bring your friend. ‣ **Dáguškibina nówa awįcawa'u** I brought all the children here. *1s:* **awá'u** *2s:* **ayá'u** *Vbenef:* **awįca'u**

a'ú₂ *vimp* it flows, comes, oozes out ‣ **Wé a'ú.** Blood was flowing out.

a'úgijitA *vt1-benef* s/he shoots at sb, smth for him/her

a'útA *vt1* s/he shoots at sb, smth ‣ **Ahágeȟ a'ú'ųtabi.** We shot the last one. ‣ **Šúga táwa žé a'úwata.** I shot at his dog. *1s:* **a'úwata** *2s:* **a'úyata** *1p:* **a'ú'ųtabi** *Vbenef:* **a'úgijitA**

a'ú *vt1* s/he feeds the fire with smth *Vpos:* **agí'ų**

a'úyabi *n* blueberry *Syn:* **wíbazuką stéya**

awácegiyA *vt1* s/he prays over, blesses sb, smth
‣ **Mi'áde amáwacegiya.** My father blessed me.
‣ **Wóyuda awácegiya.** He blesses the food. *1s:*
awácewagiya *2s:* **awáceyagiya**

awácį *vt3* 1) s/he feels, thinks about smth; has
smth on the mind ‣ **Dágu síja awácį.** He is
tormented. *vs* 2) it is a purpose ‣ **Né dágu
awácį?** What is the purpose of this? ‣ **Dágu
awácį ecú he?** What is the purpose of doing
that? *1s:* **awáwacį** *2s:* **ayáwacį** *1p:* **ųgáwacįbi**
Vpos: **agíwacį**

awácįyą *adv* 1) for the sake of it, in a contemplative manner ‣ **Awácįyą wahí.** I came for the
sake of it. 2) heading for a place ‣ **A'įkpoǧą
oyúze, žén awácįyą máni.** They were heading for the Sweet Grass Hills on foot. (Shields
79:448)

awáhįhĄ *vs* it snows on it; s/he/it is covered in
deep snow

awákąyA *vt1-caus* s/he blesses, consecrates sb

awánuȟ *adv* unexpectedly, as it happens ‣
Awánuȟ hí. He came unexpectedly.

awánųka *adv* accidentally ‣ **Táȟca awánųka
wakté.** I accidentally killed a deer.

awášpąyą *vii* s/he cooks a feast ‣ **Mikúši
awášpąyą žehą́.** Then grandma cooked a
feast. *1s:* **awášpąwaya** *2s:* **awášpąyaya** *1p:*
awášpą'ųyabi

awáš'ageja *vii* s/he/it is kind of strong

awą́giciyagabi *vii-recip* they watch, care for one
another *1p:* **awą́'ųgiciyagabi**

awą́gijiknagA *vt1-benef* s/he watches, cares for
sb, smth for him/her *1s:* **awą́wejiknaga** *2s:*
awą́yejiknaga

awą́'įc'įknagA *vi3-refl* s/he cares for himself/
herself *1s:* **awą́mįc'įknaga** *2s:* **awą́nįc'įknaga**

awą́knagA *vt1-pos* s/he cares, watches over his/
her own ‣ **Aknúštąbiši, awą́knaga bo!** Do not
lose your own (language), protect it you all!

awą́yagA *vt2* s/he cares, watches, looks after
sb, smth ‣ **Iná awą́mnaga.** I care for mom. ‣

Wáda awą́yageši. He is not looking after the
canoe. ‣ **Wábaȟta awą́yagįkta.** He will look
after the sacred bundles. *1s:* **awą́mnaga** *2s:*
awą́naga *1p:* **awą́'ųyagabi** *Vabs:* **wa'áwąyagA**
Vbenef: **awą́gijiknagA** *Vcoll:* **awį́cawąyagA**
Vpos: **awą́knagA** *Vrecip:* **awą́giciyagabi** *Vrefl:*
awą́'įc'įknagA

awą́yages'a *n* guardian, bodyguard

awédu'įc'iyA *vi3-refl* 1) s/he survives winter
2) s/he stays somewhere during the winter ‣ **Waniyedu žehą́ žén awédumįc'iya.** I
spend the winter there. *1s:* **awédumįc'iya** *2s:*
awédunįc'iya *1p:* awédu'ųgįc'iyabi

awį́ktoktoga *Variant:* **awį́tkotkoga** *vs-redup*
s/he is somehow crazy, retarded ‣ **Wįcá né
awį́tkotkoga.** This man is kind of crazy.

awį́cawąyagA *vt1-coll* s/he watches over people, babysits children *1s:* **awį́cawąmnaga** *2s:*
awį́cawąnaga

awį́hamnA *vt1* s/he dreams about sb, smth ‣
Mikúši awį́wahamna. I dreamed about my
grandmother. ‣ **Šųkská cá awį́wahamna.**
I dreamed about a specific white horse. ‣
Togádagiya awį́wahamna. I dreamed about
the future *1s:* **awį́wahamna** *2s:* **awį́yahamna**

awį́ktogeja *Variant:* **awį́tkogejA** *vs* s/he is slightly
retarded *1s:* **awį́maktogeja** *2s:* **awį́niktogeja**

awódabi *n* table ‣ **Cąšį́ žé awódabi mahén
ayáskama.** The chewing gum is stuck under
the table. ‣ **Awódabi žé ktáši.** That table is not
heavy. ‣ **Awódabi žé yuwą́gan mnúza.** I held
the table upright. ‣ **awódabi ókšą** around the
table ‣ **awódabi gakná** beside the table

awógiciknagabi *vii-recip* they talk, gossip about
one another ‣ **Wíyą žená awógiciknagabis'a.**
Those women habitually gossip about one
another.

awókcą *vt1* s/he has thoughts about sb, smth

awóknagA *vt1* s/he talks, discusses about smth
‣ **Hí ga'éca awóknagabi.** He arrived and then

they talked about it. *Vrecip:* **awógiciknagabi**
See: **wóknaga**

áyA₁ *vs2-aux* s/he becomes, turns into, starts
to *Usage:* used after impersonal and stative
verbs; some speakers inflect only the verbal
complement, while others only the auxiliary.
‣ **Waȟpé šá áya.** The leaves are turning red. ‣
Yazą́ amáya. I am starting to be sick. ‣ **Osní
áya.** It is getting cold. ‣ **Taȟ'įmąt'a áya.** I am
getting out of breath. *1s:* **amáya** *2s:* **aníya** *1p:*
ųgáyabi

áyA₂ *vi2-aux* s/he does it continuously, constantly
‣ **Šúga žé búza žé kuwá áya.** The dog is constantly chasing the cat. ‣ **Cą́ gaksáksa ámna.** I
continuously chop wood. ‣ **Šųkcúk'ana kuwá
awícaya.** The coyote kept coming back at them.
1s: **ámna** *2s:* **ána** *1p:* **ųgáyabi**

áyA₃ *vt2* s/he leaves, takes, goes with sb, smth
there ‣ **Nená ánįkta?** Are you going to take
these? ‣ **Gitézi nų́ba owáyawa ektá awícaya!**
Take these two kids to school! *1s:* **ámna** *2s:* **ána**
Vbenef: **gíjayA**

ayáskaba *Variant:* **ayáskama** *vt1, vs* s/he/it is
stuck on sb, smth; is infatuated with smth ‣
Wamnúška né amáyaskaba. This bug is stuck
on me. ‣ **Wa'óyabi ayáskaba yįgá.** He is infatuated with the newspaper. ‣ **Cąšį́ žé awódabi
mahén ayáskama.** The chewing gum is stuck
under the table. *Vcaus:* **ayáskamyA**

ayáskamyA *vt1-caus* s/he glues, sticks, pastes
smth onto it ‣ **Wa'óyabi žé ayáskamwaya.**
I pasted it in the book. *1s:* **ayáskamwaya** *2s:*
ayáskamyaya

ayáza *vt2* s/he laces beads on smth *Vabs:*
wa'áyaza

ayázabi *vs-pass* it is beaded ‣ **Wįkóške né šiná
ayázabi ų́.** This young woman was wearing a
beaded shawl.

ayúȟuga *n* crust

ayúksA *vt2* s/he cuts smth off with scissors; alters
a piece of clothing *1s:* **amnúksa** *2s:* **anúksa**

ayúmnayA *vt2* s/he spreads smth over it (like a
blanket over a horse, cloth on a table) ‣ **Šiná
žé o'įštime agą́n ayúmnayabi.** The blanket is
spread out on the bed. (Cumberland 2005:256)
1s: **amnúmnaya** *2s:* **anúmnaya**

ayúptA₁ *vt2* s/he plows smth (field, garden) *1s:*
amnúpta *2s:* **anúpta**

ayúptA₂ *vt2* s/he answers sb ‣ **Amáyupta!**
Answer me! ‣ **Dóken amáyanuptįkta?** How
will you answer me? ‣ **Magíbąc'ehą amnúpta.**
When she called me I answered. *1s:* **amnúpta**
2s: **anúpta** *1p:* **ųgáyuptabi** *Vabs:* **wa'áyuptA**
Vbenef: **agíjiyuptA** *Vrecip:* **agíciyuptabi** *Vrefl:*
a'íc'iyuptA

ayúsni *vt1* s/he dims, reduces smth in force; puts
smth out (light, flame) ‣ **Pedį́žaža žé ayúsni!**
Dim the lamp! *1s:* **amnúsni** *2s:* **anúsni**

ayústo *vt2* s/he smooths, pets, pats smth with
the hand (hair, fur of an animal) ‣ **Búza ayústo.**
Pet the cat! ‣ **Mikúši pahá amnústo.** I smooth
down my grandma's hair. *1s:* **amnústo** *2s:*
anústo *Vbenef:* **agíjiyusto** *Vpos:* **agíknusto**
Vrecip: **agíciyustobi** *Vredup:* **ayústosto**

ayústosto *vt2-redup* s/he pets smth repeatedly
‣ **Mitášųga žé ayústosto mągá.** I am sitting
down petting my dog.

ayúštą *vt2* s/he loses sb, smth ‣ **Ayúštąšį!** Do not
lose it! ‣ **Ocą́gu žé amnúštą.** I lost the road. ‣
Dókiyo yá ayúštą. He lost his way. *1s:* **amnúštą**
2s: **anúštą** *1p:* **a'ų́yuštąbi ; ųgáyuštąbi** *Vpos:*
aknúštą

ayútątą *vt2-redup* s/he feels around with the
hands ‣ **Awícayutątą duwé wąží šįtų́ hą́da
éyagu hį́k tahú yubémni.** He felt them over
and when there was a fat one, he took it and
twisted its neck. (Drummond 1976, Įktomi
and the ducks) *1s:* **amnútątą** *2s:* **anútątą** *Vrefl:*
a'į́knutątą

ayútitA *vt2* s/he trims smth (edges of a piece
of cloth); sticks different pieces on smth ‣

Sąksája žé amnútita. I trimmed the dress. *1s:* **amnútita** *2s:* **anútita**

azé *n* breast, udder

azé yazókkiyA *vt1-caus* she breastfeeds a baby ▸ **Naháň azé yazókkiya.** She is still breastfeeding him. *1s:* **azé yazókwakiya** *2s:* **azé yazókyakiya**

azépįkpa *n* nipple, teat

azíngiciyabi *vi1-recip* they smudge one another ritually

azíngijiyA *vt1-benef* s/he smudges sb for him/her ritually *1s:* **azínwejiya** *2s:* **azínyejiya**

azín'įc'iyA *vi3-refl* s/he smudges himself/herself ritually ▸ **"Dágu azínįc'iyam ųspéwįcakiyam,"** **eyá.** "Teach them how to smudge themselves," he said. (Cumberland 2005:331) *1s:* **azínmįc'iya** *2s:* **azínnįc'iya** *1p:* **azín'ųgįc'iyabi**

azínyA *vt1-caus* s/he smudges sb, smth ritually ▸ **Dágu nówa azínya.** He smudges all things. *1s:* **azínwaya** *2s:* **azínyaya** *1p:* **azín'ųyabi** *Vabs:* **wa'ázinyA** *Vbenef:* **azíngijiyA** *Vcoll:* **azínwįcayA** *Vrecip:* **azíngiciyabi** *Vrefl:* **azín'įc'iyA**

azį́ *vi1* s/he sucks on his/her mother's breast

azį́gicuni *vs1* s/he is weaned *Vcaus:* **azį́gicunikiya; azį́kiyagicuni**

azį́gicunikiyA ; azį́kiyagicuni *vt1-caus* she weans a baby *1s:* **azį́kiyawecuni** *2s:* **azį́kiyayecuni**

azį́kiyA *vt1-caus* s/he nurses sb ▸ **Húgu azį́kiya.** His mom nursed him. *1s:* **azį́wakiya** *2s:* **azį́yakiya**

ažų́kta *Variant:* **ažų́tka** *n* kidney ▸ **Ažų́kta mayáza.** My kidneys hurt.

ažų́kta íyą *Variant:* **ažų́tka íyą** *cp* kidney stones

Ą
ç

ąba *n* 1) day, daylight ▸ **Ą́ba káda.** It is a hot day. ▸ **Ą́ba nén owá úbįkta.** They will all come today. ▸ **Ą́ba wąží žé wagášna.** I missed the date. ▸ **Ą́ba núba štén hį́kta.** He will arrive in two days. *vimp* 2) it is day ▸ **Waná ą́bac.** It is day now. *See:* **-cą**

ą́ba įdóba *cp* Thursday *Lit:* fourth day ▸ **Waná ą́ba įdóba ehą́'i.** It is now Thursday.

ą́ba įnúba *cp* Tuesday *Lit:* second day

ą́ba įwą́žį *cp* Monday *Lit:* first day (after the full moon)

ą́ba įyámni *cp* Wednesday *Lit:* third day

ą́ba įzáptą *cp* Friday *Lit:* fifth day ▸ **Huhúžubina wacíbi yuką́ ą́ba įzáptą štén imnámnįkte no!** There is the Regina Powwow on Friday that I will attend.

ą́ba nén *Variant:* **ą́ba né** (PR, OM, WB) *adv* today ▸ **Ą́ba nén nína osní he?** Is it not ever cold today? ▸ **Ą́ba né nína wašté cén hokúwa ųyábi.** It is a nice day today thus we will go fishing. ▸ **Ą́ba né wąží ehą́'i wahíkta.** I will arrive at one o'clock today.

ą́ba ú *vimp* it is dawn, daybreak *Lit:* day is coming

ą́ba ú wįcáȟpi *cp* Morning Star, Venus *Syn:* **wįcáȟpi éstenaȟ**

ą́ba yužáža *Variant:* **ą́ba tiyúžaža** *cp* Saturday *Lit:* laundry day

ąbáhotųna; ąbáhotų *n* chicken *Lit:* it makes its distinctive sound in the morning ▸ **Ąbáhotųna žé pá gaksá.** He beheaded the chicken.

ąbáhotųna cijána *cp* chick

ąbáhotųnamnoga *n* rooster

ąbáhotųwįyena *n* hen

ą́bawaką *n* Sunday *Lit:* Holy day

ą́bawaką gicúni *cp* Monday *Lit:* when Sunday is over

ą́bawaką tą́ga *cp* Christmas *Lit:* great Holy day

ą́bawaką wąží *cp* week

ąbédu *n* day ▸ **Ąbédu wóguga.** It is a beautiful day. ▸ **Ąbédu nén osníšį he?** Is it not cold today? ▸ **Ąbédu nén wówaȟtani cóna mawánįkta.** May I walk with no sins today. *Syn:* **ą́ba,-cą**

ąbédu wéksuya *cp* Remembrance Day *Lit:* I remember day

ạbé'ịštimA *vi3* s/he/it sleeps during daytime; has a catnap ‣ **Mató waníyedu ạbé'ịštima.** The bear sleeps during the winter days. *1s:* **ạbémịštima** *2s:* **ạbénịštima** *1p:* **ạbé'ụgịštimabi**

ạbéyasạ *Variant:* **ạ́baneyasạ** ; **ạm'éyasạ** *adv* 1) all throughout the day, all day ‣ **Ạbéyasạ ịwáȟạcuna.** I kept on laughing all throughout the day. ‣ **Ạbéyasạ cạ́ gaksá.** He chopped wood all day. ‣ **Ạ́baneyasạ céyaga.** He cried all day. ‣ **Ạm'éyasạ mnimózạ.** It drizzled all day. 2) every day ‣ **Ạbéyasạ wówaši ecú.** He works every day.

ạm-; ạp- *cont* day

ạmcógạdu *adv* noon, midday

ạmhạ́ska wí *cp* February *Lit:* long days moon

ạm'ómani *vi1* s/he/it walks around, travels during the day

ạm'ósni *vimp* it is a cold day

ạm'ówaštejagA *vimp* it is a beautiful day

ạmwị́hamna *n* daydream

ạpšíjA *vimp* it is a gloomy day

ạpšíjeja *vimp* it is a stormy day; a day with bad weather

B

ba- *pref* by pushing smth away, poking, sitting on smth to exert pressure ‣ **mnaská > bamnáska** it is flat, plain, smooth > s/he flattens smth by pushing, or with his/her body weight ‣ **hotụ́ > bahótụ** it produces a sound > s/he makes a sound by pushing on smth

babéhạ *vt1* s/he rolls smth up by pushing ‣ **Šiná žé babéhạ éknạga.** Roll the blanket and put it down. *1s:* **wabábehạ** *2s:* **yabábehạ** *1p:* **ụbábehạbi** *Vbenef:* **gíjibabehạ** *Vpos:* **kpabéhạ**

babódA *vt1* s/he wears out a piece of clothing ‣ **Hụskáto babóda.** He wears out his jeans. ‣ **Bibína wị́da cén taȟáge ektá babóda.** The baby crawls so he wears out his knees (pants). *1s:* **wabáboda** *2s:* **yabáboda**

bacáknekne yeyÁ *vt1* s/he to make sb stagger by pushing, shoving ‣ **Wịcá bacáknekne yeyábi.** They pushed that man out. (Fourstar p. 7)

bacácạ *vt1* s/he shakes sb, smth by pushing with the arms ‣ **Sakné né bacácạ ú.** She came tottering on her cane. (Weasel 117:126)

badị́ *vs* s/he/it is stiff ‣ **Téhạ yịgábi né'ụs cuwí mabádị.** My body is stiff after sitting for too long ‣ **Ịstó mabádị míjibawịda.** My arm is stiff, rub it for me. *1s:* **mabádị** *2s:* **nibádị**

badị́da *vt1* s/he pushes, forces smth (with the hands or body) ‣ **Ti'óba wabádịda.** I pushed the door. *1s:* **wabádịda** *2s:* **yabádịda** *Vcont:* **badị́n**

badị́n *vcont* pushing, pressing, forcing ‣ **Badị́n ịȟpéya.** He shove and left him in there.

badị́n iyéyA *vt1* s/he nudges sb, hits sb slightly with the elbow ‣ **I'écuna cén badị́n iyéwaya.** She talks all the time so I nudged her. ‣ **Duká žíyasạ nahạ́ȟ badị́n iyéya:ga [...]** But all that time, the continued to push it out [...] (NS 2002:31) *1s:* **badị́n iyéwaya** *2s:* **badị́n iyéyaya**

ba'éknekiyA *vt1* s/he pushes smth together ‣ **Péda nowá ba'éknekiya cén.** He pushed the fire together (to make it burn better). (Weasel 6:118)

bagạ́ *vt1* s/he respects sb ‣ **Wịcá žé bagạ́bi céyaga.** That man should be respected. (Cumberland 2005:325) *Vabs:* **wóbagạ**

bagị́za *vt1* s/he makes smth squeak by putting pressure, by rubbing

bagé *adv* together, bunched up, as a group ‣ **Bagé paȟtábi.** It is bound together. ‣ **Bagé ụ́bi.** They are as a group. ‣ **Wá bagé éknạga.** He puts the snow in a heap. *Vrefl:* **bagé'ịc'iyabi**

bagé'ịc'iyabi *vi1-refl* they gather themselves

bahá *n* hill, mound ‣ **Bahá sám žéci wa'í.** I went over the hill. ‣ **Hipépena tí bahá žé wabámneja.** I scattered the anthill.

Bahá tága yamní *ngeo* Three Buttes (Montana)

bahádahą *adv* from the hill

bahágan *adv* on a mound, hilltop ‣ **Bahágan yągá wįhámne cá.** He is sitting on a hill having a dream.

Bahásaba *ngeo* Havre (Montana)

bahátakiya *adv* toward the hill ‣ **Bahátakiya maníší.** He did not walk toward the hill.

baháyena ; baháya *quant* plenty of smth, a lot ‣ **Wahíkpe né bahá:yena gága.** He made plenty of arrows. (Weasel 103:223) ‣ **Wįcíjana žé wó'įškade baháya yuhá.** That girl has a lot of toys.

bahí *vt1* s/he gathers, picks up smth ‣ **Cąsága wabáhi.** I gather some twigs. ‣ **Makóce dahą bahí.** He picked it up from the ground. ‣ **Baptús nážį hík cą bahí.** She bent over and picked up wood. *1s:* **wabáhi** *2s:* **yabáhi** *Vbenef:* **gíjibahi**

bahókšu *vt1* s/he wrecks smth by sitting, putting his/her weight on it ‣ **Cą'ágan yįgábi wabáhokšu.** I dismantled the chair. *1s:* **wabáhokšu** *2s:* **yabáhokšu**

bahótų *vt1* s/he makes a sound by pushing on smth; plays a musical instrument (trumpet, accordion) *1s:* **wabáhotų** *2s:* **yabáhotų** *1p:* **ųbáhotųbi**

bahówayA *vt1* s/he makes sb scream in pain by bumping, pushing, sitting on him/her/it; squeals as when bumping onto smth

bahúhųza *vt1* s/he shakes, rocks, moves smth by pushing on it *1s:* **wabáhųhųza** *2s:* **yabáhųhųza** *1p:* **ųbáhųhųzabi**

bahňéjA *vt1* s/he tears, punctures smth with a sharp tool *Vpos:* **kpahňéjA**

bahňógA *vt1* s/he pierces, makes a hole by pressure ‣ **Wi'óti žé bahňóga.** He pierces a hole in the tent. *Vrefl:* **įkpáhňogA**

bahňpÁ *vt1* s/he throws, pushes sb, smth off ‣ **Búza žé bahňpá.** Push that cat off. ‣ [. . .] héya

kóko wįcábahňpa. [. . .] she even combed out all the lice. (Shields 66:286, our translation)

bahňpú *vt1* s/he scrapes smth off by pushing ‣ **Iyógapte ohňní žená bahňpú.** Scrape those dirty plates. (Fourstar p. 8)

bakcá *vt1* s/he combs, brushes sb, smth *Vpos:* **kpakcá**

bakídA *vt1* s/he wipes, brushes sb, smth off; cleans the surface of smth ‣ **Awódabi bakídešį.** He did not wipe off the table. ‣ **Awódabi bakída ócijiyakta.** I will help you clean the table. *1s:* **wabákįda** *2s:* **yabákįda** *1p:* **ųbákįdabi** *Vbenef:* **gíjibakįdA** *Vpos:* **kpakídA**

bakmíkma *vt1* s/he rolls smth by pushing forward ‣ **Ocágu žé wabákmįkma.** I roll it across the street. *1s:* **wabákmįkma** *2s:* **yabákmįkma**

bakpá *vt1* s/he sits on smth and makes it crumble

baksÁ *vt1* s/he breaks, cuts smth off manually or by pressure (as with a chainsaw) ‣ **Cąsága wąží wabáksa.** I broke a twig off. ‣ **Obáwįǧe cogán baksá.** Break the $100 in half. *Vabs:* **wabáksA** *Vbenef:* **gíjibaksA** *Vpos:* **kpaksÁ** *See:* **óbaksa**

bakšíjA *vt1* s/he folds smth over by pushing (blanket, clothes) ‣ **Wa'óyabi bakšíja.** Fold the paper. ‣ **Bakšíja híkna míc'u.** Fold it, and give it back to me. *1s:* **wabákšija** *2s:* **yabákšija** *1p:* **ųbákšijabi**

bakúkA *vt1* s/he crushes smth by sitting on it *1s:* **wabákuka** *2s:* **yabákuka**

bak'éǧA *vt1* s/he scratches smth by pushing, rubbing against smth else *Vrefl:* **įkpák'eǧA**

bamáhen *adv* pushing smth inside

bamáhen iyéyA *vt1* s/he pushes, inserts smth inside ‣ **Cą žé océti én bamáhen iyéya.** Push that wood in the stove. (Fourstar p. 7)

bamíma *vt1* s/he rolls smth forward (dough, snow) ‣ **Aǧúyabi žé bamíma.** He rolled the bannock. *1s:* **wabámima** *2s:* **yabámima** *1p:* **ųbámimabi**

bamnáska *vt1* s/he flattens smth by pushing, or with his/her body weight ‣ **Žécen né bamnáskacuna hį́k nén zizíbenaȟ ecų́.** Then this one kept on flattening it out and he made it thin. (NS 2002:30) *1s:* **wabámnaska** *2s:* **yabámnaska**

bamnáyA *vt1* 1) s/he irons smth 2) s/he presses smth down by pushing ‣ **Aǧúyabi bamnáya!** Press on the dough! *1s:* **wabámnaya** *2s:* **yabámnaya** *1p:* **ųbámnayabi** *Vabs:* **wabámnayA**

bamną́ *vt1* s/he files, rubs smth against it (like a piece of metal) *1s:* **wabámną** *2s:* **yabámną** *1p:* **ųbámnąbi**

bamnéja *vt1* s/he scatters smth by sitting, or putting pressure

bamní *vi1* it (horse, bull) bucks

bamnímni *vi1-redup* it (horse) bucks repetitively ‣ **Bamnímni ų́.** He bucks repatitively.

bamnúǧa *vt1* s/he makes a crunching sound with the hands or a tool

banážį *vt1* s/he pushes smth upwards; makes smth stand by pushing on it ‣ **Cą́ niyúha wabánažį.** I put all of the sticks up. ‣ **Gá écen eyáš húgu žé banážį ye'į́c'iya.** Then his mother got up quickly. (NS 2002:83) *1s:* **wabánažį** *2s:* **yabánažį** *1p:* **ųbánažįbi**

baní *vt1* s/he nudges at sb with the elbow to get his/her attention *1s:* **wabáni** *2s:* **yabáni** *1p:* **ųbánibi**

bapóbA *vt1* s/he explodes, bursts smth by sitting or pressing on it ‣ **Tába bapóba.** He exploded the ball. *1s:* **wabápoda** *2s:* **yabápoda** *1p:* **ųbápodabi**

bapsų́ *vt1* s/he pours, spills, a liquid out; empties a container ‣ **Wį́kni bapsų́.** He spilled oil. ‣ **Waȟpé žé wabápsų.** I spilled the tea. ‣ **Mąká agán bapsų́.** He spilled it on the ground. ‣ **Céǧa žé bapsų́.** Empty the bucket. *1s:* **wabápsų** *2s:* **yabápsų** *1p:* **ųbápsųbi**

bapšų́ka *vt1* s/he rolls smth into a ball by pushing *1s:* **wabápšųka** *2s:* **yabápšųka** *1p:* **ųbápšųkabi**

baptą́yĄ *vt1* s/he overturns sb, smth by pushing, or with a tool

baptús *vcont* bent forward ‣ **Minékši baptús maní.** My uncle walks bent forward. ‣ **Baptús nážį hį́k cą́ bahí.** She bent over and picked up wood.

baptúza *vi1* s/he bends forward, stoops over *1s:* **wabáptuza** *2s:* **yabáptuza** *1p:* **ųbáptuzabi** *Vcont:* **baptús**

baptų́ǧa *vt1* s/he squishes, explodes smth by pushing, or sitting on it

-bas *suff* in that way, manner; of that kind, like that kind ‣ **Žécądu cį́gabas.** And so it was the way he wanted it. (NS 2002:42)

basí *vi1* 1) s/he drives ‣ **Basíbi wacį́ga.** I want to drive. ‣ **Teȟíya basí.** He drives with difficulty. *vt1* 2) s/he drives smth ‣ **Adé įwátokšu tą́ga basíšį.** Dad does not drive trucks. ‣ **Waná amų́giya wabási owágihi.** I can drive a car now. ‣ **Nągáhą né duwéni šų́gatąga ųwį́cabasibišį no!** Nowadays none of us drives horse teams. *1s:* **wabási** *2s:* **yabási** *1p:* **ųbásibi** *Vbenef:* **gíjibasi** *Vcoll:* **wį́cabasi** *Vpos:* **kpási**

basíbi *n* driver

basíjA *vt1* s/he ruins smth by sitting on it *Vbenef:* **gíjibasijA**

basísA *vt1* s/he sews, stitches smth ‣ **Mikúši šiná basísa.** My grandmother sewed the blanket. *1s:* **wabásisa** *2s:* **yabásisa** *1p:* **ųbásisąbi** *Vabs:* **wabásisA** *See:* **abásisA, obásisA, nųbáȟ basísA, owį́ža basísA**

baská *vt1* s/he kneads smth by exerting pressure ‣ **Wįcá aǧúyabi baská kó.** The man is even kneading dough. (Fourstar p. 3)

baská *vt1* s/he melts smth by sitting, pressing smth down ‣ **Wá agán mągá wabáską.** I sat on snow and it melted. *1s:* **wabáską** *2s:* **yabáską**

baskébA *vt1* s/he drains, empties smth out by pushing ‣ **Céǧa žé iyúha wabáskeba.** I emptied all of the pails. *1s:* **wabáskeba** *2s:* **yabáskeba** *1p:* **ųbáskebabi**

baskíjA *vt1* s/he squeezes smth down by pushing, by pressing on it with the hands open

basmíyą *vt1* s/he clears, cleans the surface of smth ‣ **Awódabi wabásmiyą.** I cleared the table. *1s:* **wabásmiyą** *2s:* **yabásmiyą** *1p:* **ųbásmiyąbi**

basnádA *vt1* s/he pushes, plants smth straight into the ground ‣ **Nén cą wąžíȟ basnáda cá wó.** Put a stake in the ground here. (Weasel 150:588) *Vpos:* **kpasnádA**

basní ; bosní *vt1* s/he puts a light, fire out by smothering it, putting smth on it *1s:* **wabásni** *2s:* **yabásni** *1p:* **ųbásnibi**

basníza *vt1* s/he deflates smth by pressing, sitting on it (cushion, ball) *1s:* **wabásniza** *2s:* **yabásniza** *1p:* **ųbásnizabi**

basnóhĄ *vt1* s/he pushes sb, smth along ‣ **Cą'ágąn yįgábi basnóhą iyéwaya.** I pushed the chairs away. *1s:* **wabásnohą** *2s:* **yabásnohą** *1p:* **ųbásnohąbi**

bastó yįgÁ *vi3* s/he/it sits tuckered out, exhausted *1s:* **bastó mągá** *2s:* **bastó nągá** *1p:* **bastó ųyígabi**

bastó yųgÁ *vi3* s/he lies down tuckered out, exhausted ‣ **Wá óhą máni cén nągáhą bastó yųgá.** He walked in the snow, and now he is lying down tuckered out. *1s:* **bastó mųgá** *2s:* **bastó nųgá** *1p:* **bastó ųyúgabi**

bašíba *vt1* s/he breaks smth by putting pressure

bašnógA *vt1* s/he takes smth off

bašpá *vt1* s/he pushes, pries smth open ‣ **Žehą́duȟ cihį́ktu gicí bašpá yá.** Right at that time he burst in with his son. ‣ **Ti'óba wabášpa.** I pushed the door open. *1s:* **wabášpa** *2s:* **yabášpa** *1p:* **ųbášpabi**

bat'Á *vt1* s/he/it kills by pressing on sb, smth

batógam *adv* pushed aside ‣ **Batógam iyéya.** He pushed it aside. (Weasel 64:51)

batúža *vi1* s/he bends over; stoops down ‣ **Ti'óba okná nį́kte žé batúža.** Stoop down to go through that door. (Fourstar p. 8)

bawą́ga *vt1* s/he pushes sb, smth over *1s:* **wabáwąga** *2s:* **yabáwąga** *1p:* **ųbáwągabi** *Vcont:* **bawą́k**

bawą́k *vcont* pushing over ‣ **Bawą́k įȟpéwaya.** I knocked him over.

bawéğa *vt1* s/he breaks smth by pressure *Vpos:* **kpawéğa**

bawíyakpa *vt1* s/he shines, polishes smth ‣ **Kiškána niyúha wabáwiyakpa.** I shine all of the spoons. *1s:* **wabáwiyakpa** *2s:* **yabáwiyakpa** *1p:* **ųbáwiyakpabi**

bawį́da *vt1* s/he rubs smth *Vbenef:* **gíjibawįda**

bawį́žA *vt1* s/he bends smth by pushing, sitting on it ‣ **Cąšáša žé wabáwįža.** I bent the willow branch by sitting on it.

bazó *vt1* s/he shows, points at smth *1s:* **wabázo** *2s:* **yabázo** *1p:* **ųbázobi** *Vdat:* **gibázo** *Vpos:* **kpazó** *Vrefl:* **įkpázo**

bažáža *vt1* s/he washes sb, smth by rubbing *Vrefl:* **įkpážaža**

bažíbA *vt1* s/he pokes, touches sb, smth lightly *1s:* **wabážiba** *2s:* **yabážiba** *1p:* **ųbážibabi** *Vrecip:* **gicíbažibabi** *Vrefl:* **įkpážibA**

bažúžu *vt1* 1) s/he erases smth by pushing ‣ **Wa'ókmabi wabážužu.** I erased the words. ‣ **Wa'óyabi žená wabážužu.** I erased it off the papers. 2) s/he demolishes, make smth fall apart by putting pressure ‣ **Cą'ágąn yągábi agán iyódąga ga'éca bažúžu.** He sat down on the chair, and here he wrecked it. (Fourstar p. 7) *1s:* **wabážužu** *2s:* **yabážužu** *1p:* **ųbážužubi**

bą́ *vi1* s/he shouts, yells ‣ **Hą'éyasą bą́.** She shouted all night long. *1s:* **wabą́** *2s:* **yabą́** *1p:* **ųbą́bi** *Adv:* **bąyą́** *Vbenef:* **gíjibą** *Vdat:* **gibą́**

bąyą́ *adv* loudly, while shouting ‣ **Bąyą́ wa'ų́.** I am yelling.

bemní *vs* s/he/it is twisted, crooked *1s:* **mabémni** *2s:* **nibémni**

-bi *encl* 1) plural marker of nouns *Usage:* used with animate referents (human, animal). ‣ **Misų́gabi įšténwįcawaye no!** I shamed my younger brothers! ▸ **Šų́gabi wapábi.** The dogs are barking. 2) they *Usage:* used with animate referents (human, animal). ▸ **Wašką́škąyabi ektá iyáyabi.** They are going to the movies. ▸ **Ą́bawaką gicúni štén ecúbįkte no.** They will do it on Monday. 3) passive voice *Usage:* indicates that the subject undergoes an action. ▸ **Miní abápsųbi.** She is baptized. ▸ **Šų́ga wówįcak'ubįšį.** The dogs were not fed. ▸ **Ti'óba žé yušpábi?** Is the door open? ▸ **Šiná žé o'įštime agán ayúmnayabi.** The blanket is spread out on the bed. (Cumberland 2005:256) 4) their ▸ **dagúye > dagúyabi** relative > their relative 5) to, that (marker of a subordinate clause) *Usage:* connects two verbs together like 'that' or 'to' in English as in "I like to swim." ▸ **Tíde yįgábi waštéwana.** I like sitting at home. ▸ **Eyábi cįgábišį.** They do not want to say it. 6) nominalizer *Usage:* derives a verb into a noun. ▸ **wací > wacíbi** s/he dances > dance ▸ **basí > basíbi** s/he drives > driver

bibína *n* baby ▸ **Bibína yuhá ų́s iyómagipi.** I am happy because she had a baby. *From:* English baby. *Syn:* **dáguškina**

Bigána *nprop* Piegan people, person of Piegan descent

bis- *cont* 1) rodent (such as gopher, prairie dog, mouse, rat) *vcont* 2) squealing

bisbístąga *n-redup* rat

bisknékneǧa *n-redup* spotted gopher, thirteen-lined ground squirrel *Syn:* **cąkáhuknekneǧa**

biskúwa *vi1* s/he chases, looks for gophers ▸ **Gisápsaba hą́da bis'úkuwabi.** When there are bare patches of ground, we chase gophers.

bispízA *vi1-redup* s/he/it squeals

bispízena *n-redup* mouse

bistą́ga *n* prairie dog

bis'óhnoga *n* gopher hole

bis'óye *n* mouse, gopher tracks

bíško *n* nighthawk

bišpíža *vs-redup* s/he/it is wrinkled ▸ **Įdé bišpíža.** He has a wrinkled face.

bizÁ *vi1* s/he/it squeals *1s:* **wabíza** *2s:* **yabíza** *1p:* **ųbízabi** *Vcont:* **bis-** *Vredup:* **bispízA**

Bízebina *nprop* Gopher people (Nakoda band living near Maple Creek, Saskatchewan)

bízena *n* gopher, ground squirrel

bízena tą́ga *cp* groundhog

bižá *vs* s/he/it is wrinkled ▸ **Šiná bižá yįgá.** The blanket is wrinkled. ▸ **Įté mabíža.** My forehead is wrinkled. *1s:* **mabíža** *2s:* **nibíža** *Vredup:* **bišpíža**

bo *encl* indicates a command made to two or more persons by a male speaker (plural male imperative) ▸ **Ną́žį bo!** You all stand up! ▸ **Midáguyabi néci hiyú bo!** My relatives come over here! ▸ **Šką́šį yįgá bo!** You all sit still!

bó *vs* s/he/it swells ▸ **Sihá mabó.** I have a swollen foot. ▸ **Bóhą cén iyéš yéšį.** It was swelling so he did not go. (NS 2002:49) *1s:* **mabó** *2s:* **nibó** *1p:* **ųbóbi** *Vpos:* **knabó**

bóǧA *vi1* s/he blows on smth (on a candle) ▸ **Agán bóǧa!** Blow on it! ▸ **Péda žé wabóǧa.** I blew out the match. *1s:* **wabóǧa** *2s:* **yabóǧa** *Vcaus:* **boȟkíyA** *Vcont:* **bóȟ** *Vredup:* **boȟpóǧa** *See:* **abóǧA, obóǧA**

bóhiya *vs* it is scattered ▸ [. . .] **hį́žé iyúha bóhiya yągá.** [. . .] all that remained was hair scattered around. (NS 2002:35)

bóȟ- *vcont* blowing on smth ▸ **Žécen dágucen yatáta hį́kna tíbi né agápadahą, bóȟ yeyá.** So then he chewed something or other up and blew it onto the lodge. (Weasel 105:265)

boȟkíyA *vt1-caus* s/he blows, inflates smth *1s:* **boȟwákiya** *2s:* **boȟyákiya**

boȟpóǧa *vt1-redup* s/he blows on smth; cools smth by blowing on it repetitively

bóȟ'iyeyA *vt1* s/he sends smth away by blowing

bu- *pref* by pressure *Usage:* obsolete; occurs only in a handful of verbs. ▸ **skéba > buskébA** it is empty > s/he strains, drains a liquid

bus-₁ *cont* cat, feline

bus-₂ *vcont* dry

buscíjana *n* kitten ▸ **Buscíjabina tągán ódabi.** There a lot of kittens outside. ▸ **Buscíjabina nená duwé táwabi he?** Whose kittens are these? *Syn:* **búzana**

buskébA *vt1* s/he strains, drains a liquid (by pressing) ▸ **Asą́bi žé wabúskeba.** I drained the soup. *1s:* **wabúskeba** *2s:* **yabúskeba**

buskúwa *vi1* s/he chases cats *1s:* **buswákuwa** *2s:* **busyákuwa**

bus'ósni *vimp* it is a dry cold

buspÁ *vt1* s/he daubs, patches smth *1s:* **wabúspa** *2s:* **yabúspa** *1p:* **ųbúspabi** *Vpos:* **kpúspA**

bustágA *vi1* s/he/it hides

bustáges'a *n* unidentified spring bird *Lit:* the hider

bustą́ga *n* bobcat *Syn:* **įkmúna**

busyÁ *vt1-caus* s/he dries smth ▸ **Coníca busyá jé.** He heat dries the meat. *1s:* **buswáya** *2s:* **busyáya** *Vcont:* **bus-**

bus'óye *n* cat, feline tracks

bušpá *vt1* s/he knocks smth open with force, pressure

búza₁ *n* cat *From:* English pussycat. *Cont:* **bus-**

búza₂ *vs* it is dry ▸ **Ptéǧa žé búza.** The slough has dried up. *Vcaus:* **busyÁ** *See:* **ságA**

buzáda *adv* on the shore, away from the water ▸ **Buzáda škádabis'a.** They always play on the shore.

buzádakiya *adv* toward the shore

búzana *n* kitten *Syn:* **buscíjana**

búzatąga *n* cougar *Syn:* **įkmútąga**

bųbú *vs* it crumbles (as rotten wood or dried bannock) ▸ **Aǧúyabi né bųbú.** This bannock is crumbling.

C

-c *encl* exactly, precisely, specific *Usage:* adds specificity to nouns or interrogative pronouns. ▸ **Dónac ehą́'i?** What time is it exactly? ▸ **Šų́gac wakúwa.** I chased a (specific) dog. ▸ **Duwéc yaká?** Who do you mean (specifically)?

c *part* indicates a strong assertion (gender neutral declarative particle) ▸ **Įknúhana oǧų́ǧac.** All of a sudden he woke up. ▸ **Įstókmųs wayácibįktac!** You will dance with your eyes closed. ▸ **Pežúdasije yuhác!** He has bad medicine! ▸ **"Né mak'įkta otá'įgac" ecį.** He thought, "It seems he wants to carry me." (Drummond 1976, A bear story)

ca *part* must, might (deontic and epistemic modality; conveys the idea that an event is likely to occur) ▸ **Yuzípahta ca.** He might have tightened it up. ▸ **Cuwída ca.** He must be cold. ▸ **Nikúwa ca.** He might chase you. ▸ **Wanúh hąyákeji wáhįhą ca.** It might snow tomorrow. ▸ **Wanúh ųgíksuyabiši ca'.** We might not forget about it.

cá₁ *det* such a person, such a kind, at such a time; a, an, the ▸ **Wįcóyazą síja cá Įkcé wįcášta oyáde iyúha ecéyabi.** All of the Indigenous people suffered from a severe epidemic disease. ▸ **Šųkská cá awįwahamna.** I dreamed about such a white horse. ▸ **Wąžína hugá cá.** Only one was chief. ▸ **Nįšnána waníką cá no!** You are the only one as holy! ▸ **Waná cįhįktu cá yuką.** Now they have a son. ▸ **1948 cá žehą hįknáwayatų** I got married in 1948.

cá₂ *det* that *Usage:* complementizer introducing a subordinate clause. ▸ **Paǧúda okíknąge iyúha mniwóhą nųwąbi cá wąwįcayaga.** He saw many ducks of all kinds swimming in the water. (Drummond 1976, Įktomi and the ducks)

cába *n* beaver *Cont:* **cap-**

Cába hé *ngeo* Beaver Hills (Alberta; located east of Edmonton)

Cába wakpá *ngeo* Beaver Creek (Saskatchewan)

cagá *n* palate ▸ **Wahą́bi káda yaktą́ gá cagá špą́.** He drank hot soup and burned his palate. (Fourstar p. 9)

cagípA *vt1-pos* s/he stabs, pierces his/her own

cáǧa *n* ice ▸ **Cáǧa štúnya!** Thaw the ice! ▸ **Cáǧa agázeze hą́.** The icicles are hanging down. ▸ **Hokšína žé cáǧa yamnúǧa.** The boy is crushing ice with his teeth. ▸ **Cáǧa skąwáya, miní mnatką́kta.** I will melt the ice and I drink the water. *Cont:* **caȟ-**

cáǧa amáǧažu *cp* sleet

caǧú *n* lung

caǧú nądáboǧa *cp* pneumonia *Lit:* swollen lungs

caǧúsija *n* tuberculosis ▸ **Waną́ǧaš mitúgaši caǧúsija.** Long ago my grandfather had tuberculosis. *Syn:* **caǧúyazą**

caǧúyazą *n* tuberculosis *Syn:* **caǧúsija**

caȟ- *cont* ice ▸ **caȟšnúšnuda** s/he slips on ice

caȟkáhomni *vi1* s/he spins ice tops

caȟkázo ecúbina *cp* hockey team, game ▸ **Caȟkázo ecúbina owápa.** I am part of a hockey team.

caȟmáhen *adv* under ice ▸ **Caȟmáhen yá.** He goes under ice.

Caȟní wakpá *ngeo* Powder River (Montana)

caȟnísaba *n* gunpowder

caȟnóǧa *n* wild rhubarb

caȟnóȟhu *n* rhubarb stem

caȟóda *n* 1) ashes 2) coal

caȟóda océti *cp* coal stove

caȟpą́ *n* mud hen, American coot

caȟtí *n* house, building to store ice

caȟyúkpąbi *n* ice cream

caȟ'íjahomni *n* game of tops played on ice

caȟ'ópA *vi1* s/he falls in the ice *1s:* **caȟ'ówapa** *2s:* **caȟ'óyapa**

caȟ'ótka hąwí *cp* November *Lit:* ice is hanging

caktá *vs* s/he is left-handed *1s:* **camą́kta** *2s:* **canį́kta**

caktám *Variant:* **catkám** *adv* left side, on the left side

caktápadahą *adv* from the left side ▸ **Caktápadahą awápa.** I hit him from the left.

camką́na *n* old beaver

caná ; caną́ *n* area inside the thigh from hip to the knee; crotch, genital area

canópa *n* crotch ▸ **Canópa naȟtága.** He kicked him in the crotch.

cap- ; cam- *cont* beaver

capÁ *vt1* s/he stabs sb; pricks smth *Vabs:* **wacápA** *Vpos:* **cagípA** *Vredup:* **capápA** *Vrefl:* **cą'íc'ipA**

capápA *vt1-redup* s/he stabs sb, pricks smth repeatedly

capkúwa *vi1* s/he hunts beaver

capúǧa *n* mosquito

Capúǧa-Matópa-Hústaga *ngeo* Mosquito/ Grizzly Bear's Head/Leanman reservation (Saskatchewan)

caš- *cont* name

caštų́ *vt1* s/he names sb, smth ▸ **Šų́ga caštų́šį.** He did not name the dog. ▸ **Minékši cašmátų.** My uncle named me. ▸ **Dáguškina né cašyátų he?** Did you name this baby? *1s:* **cašwátų** *2s:* **cašyátų** *1p:* **caš'ų́tųbi**

catkú *n* honor place

cawį́capabi *n* piercing ritual in ceremonies

cayágagana *n* wren

cažé *n* name ▸ **Nakón-cažé** traditional Nakoda name ▸ **Wįcášta hą́ska žé cažé mitáwa.** Tall Man is my name. ▸ **Tugą́gišiktu cažé yuhá.** He has his grandfather's name. ▸ **Macáže žé ómatągaga.** My name is well known *1s:* **macáže** *2s:* **nicáže** *Cont:* **caš-**

cažé iyóȟpegiyA *vi1-pos* s/he votes *Lit:* s/he drops his/her own name *1s:* **cažé iyóȟpewagiya** *2s:* **cažé iyóȟpeyagiya** *1p:* **cažé iyóȟpe'ųgiyabi**

cažé k'ú *vt1* s/he votes for sb ▸ **Omníjiye žén cažé wak'ú.** I voted there in the meeting. *See:* **cažé ópekiyA, gaȟníǧA**

cažé ópegiyA *vi1-pos* s/he votes, puts his/her name down to become a member; enrolls in an organization *Lit:* s/he joins sb by name *1s:* **cažé ópewagiya** *2s:* **cažé ópeyagiya** *1p:* **cažé ópe'ųgiyabi**

cažé ótągaga *vs-redup* s/he/it has a great, famous name 1s: **cažé ómatągaga** 2s: **cažé ónitągaga**

cažé tą'į́ *vs* s/he is famous; his/her name is famous ▸ **Cažé nitą'į́ yacíga, ócijiyįkta.** You want to make a name for yourself, so I will help you. (NS 2002:76–77) 1s: **cažé matą'į́** 2s: **cažé nitą'į́** 1p: **cažé ųtą'į́bi**

cažé wašté *vs* s/he has a good reputation ▸ **Wíyą né cažé wahtéšį.** This woman does not have a good reputation 1s: **cažé mawášte** 2s: **cažé niwášte**

cažéyadA *vt2* s/he calls sb's name ▸ **Cažémayada amnúptac'ehą.** When she called my name I answered. ▸ **Ųmá né ektáší cažémnada.** I said the wrong name. (Weasel 84:72) 1s: **cažémnada** 2s: **cažénada**

cą- *cont* chokecherry, pin cherry

-cą *vimp* it is a day, 24 hours ▸ **núba > núbacą** it is two > it is two days ▸ **dóna > dónacą** how many > several days; how many days

cą́ *n* 1) tree ▸ **Cą́ iyáni.** Climb up the tree. ▸ **Cą́ waníja.** There are no trees. ▸ **Cą́ né dókiyagen nówa yągá.** This tree is found (sits) every-where. 2) wood ▸ **Cą́ jónana k'ú wo.** Bring a little bit of wood. ▸ **Žécen cą́ a'ú.** Then she brought wood inside. 3) stick ▸ **Cą́ né škóba.** This stick is bent.

cą́ gahómni *np* stick used in a round dance

cą́ océti *cp* woodstove

cą́ ús apábi *ph* bat (baseball bat, hockey stick) *Lit:* stick used to hit

cą'ábaweǧa *n* wooden cross

cą'ágan *Variant:* **cą'ágan yįgábi ; cą'ágan yągábi** *n* chair ▸ **Cą'ágan yągábi né mak'úbi.** They gave me this chair. ▸ **Cą'ágan yįgábi žé a'íyopsija.** He jumped over the chair.

cą'áni *vi1* s/he climbs up a tree 1s: **cą'áwani** 2s: **cą'áyani** 1p: **cą'á'ųnibi** *Syn:* **cą'íyani**

cą'ágan yįgábi wįcášta *np* chairman

cábaǧe *n* pile of wood

cąbáhotųna yucéya *cp* guitar

cąbákmįkma *n* wagon

cąbákmįkma iyóknąga *cp* wagon box

cąbákmįkma okíyabi *cp* covered wagon

cąbásnadabi *n* post

cąbáwįža *n* low-hanging branch bent under its own weight

cąbáza *vi1* s/he puts up a fence 1s: **cąwábaza** 2s: **cąyábaza** *Vpos:* **cą'įkpaza**

cąbázabi ; cąbáza *n* fence

cąbúbu *vs* 1) it is rotten wood ▸ **Nén mahén cąbúbu.** It is rotten wood here inside. *n* 2) rotten wood

cącą́ *vs* s/he/it shivers ▸ **Osní cén cącą́ mągá.** I am sitting shivering because of the cold. 1s: **macącą** 2s: **nicącą** *Syn:* **ȟníyąyą**

cącą́na *n* shiver

cáceǧa *n* wooden pail

cáceǧa awą́yaga *cp* drum keeper

cądé *n* 1) heart ▸ **Cądé įmánaží žehą́.** I had a heart attack then. 2) feelings, emotions, sentiment ▸ **Cądé ksuwágiya.** I hurt my heart (because of her). ▸ **Macą́deskuya cądé mayúksa.** My sweetheart broke my heart. 1s: **macą́de** 2s: **nicą́de** *Cont:* **cąt-**

cądé iyápa *vs* s/he is excited, agitated; his/her heart beats fast 1s: **cądé iyámąpa** 2s: **cądé iyánįpa**

cądé įnáží *vs* s/he has a heart attack ▸ **Cądé įmánaží žehą́** I had a heart attack then. 1s: **cądé įmánaží** 2s: **cądé įnínaží**

cądé kokóna iyápa *vs* s/he is excited; his/her heart beats quickly

cądé ogíhiši *vi1* 1) s/he has a weak heart 2) s/he cannot make it

cądé wanįjA *vs* s/he is heartless 1s: **cądé wamánįja** 2s: **cądé wanínįja**

cądé yasíjA *vt2* s/he makes sb feel bad by speech 1s: **cądé mnasíja** 2s: **cądé nasíja**

cądé yuką́ *vs* s/he is considerate ▸ **Cądé mayúką cén úšiwana.** I pity him because I am considerate. *1s:* **cądé mayúką** *2s:* **cądé niyúką** *1p:* **cądé ųyúkąbi**

cądésijA ; cądéšijA *vs* s/he/it is sad, broken-hearted ▸ **Ecágen cądé'ųsijabi.** We are always sad. ▸ **Cądéšija ecáwakiya.** I think she is sad. ▸ **Onówą né cądéšija.** This song is sad. *1s:* **cądémasija** *2s:* **cądénisija** *1p:* **cądé'ųsijabi** *Vcaus:* **cądéšinyA**

cądéskuya *n* girlfriend, sweetheart ▸ **Macądeskuya tewáȟina cá no!** I really love my sweetheart! ▸ **Macądeskuya cądé mayúksa.** My sweetheart broke my heart.

cądéšinyA *vt1-caus* s/he makes sb sad; breaks sb's heart ▸ **Mnasíja cén cądéšinwaya.** I spoke ill of her and made her feel sad. *1s:* **cądéšinwaya** *2s:* **cądéšinyaya**

cądéwašte *vs* s/he is kind, good-hearted ▸ **Nína cądéniwašte no!** You are very kind! ▸ **Nidáguyabi cądéwašte wo!** Be kind to your relatives! *1s:* **cądémawašte** *2s:* **cądéniwašte** *1p:* **cądé'ųwaštebi** *Adv:* **cądéwašteya** *Vcaus:* **cądéwašteyA**

Cądéwašte ába *cp* Valentine's Day

cądéwašteyA *vt1-caus* s/he satisfies sb *1s:* **cądéwaštewaya** *2s:* **cądéwašteyaya** *1p:* **cądéwašte'ųyabi**

cądéwašteya *adv* with a good heart ▸ **Timáwagini:ga cądéwašteya wa'í.** I went to visit him with a good heart.

cągádodona *n* woodpecker *Lit:* it pecks on wood

cągáǧa *n* log

cągáȟa *n* corral

cągáȟage *n* trailer of a warbonnet

cągáȟni *n* pile of wood

cągáȟtųbi *n* 1) beaver dam 2) bridge

cągákna *adv* along the woods, on the edge of the woods

cągáksaksA *vi1-redup* s/he chops wood into kindling; chops wood ▸ **Cągáksaksa ųkíyabi jé'e.** They always made us chop wood. (Cumberland 2005:323)

cągáksaksąbi *n-redup* splints

cągámnaska *n* board, flat piece of wood

cągámubi *n* log drum

cągáški *vi1* s/he pounds chokecherries

cągážibA *vi1* 1) s/he planes wood (as to make wood shavings for kindling) *n* 2) wood shavings

cągážibe *n* carpenter

cągíjine *vt1-benef* s/he gathers firewood for sb *1s:* **cąwéjine** *2s:* **cąyéjine**

cągú *n* path, trail

Cągúgaǧe *nprop* Trailblazer or Pathmaker (traditional name of Chief Dan Kennedy, father-in-law of Wilma Kennedy)

cągúgaǧe *n* trailblazer

Cągúsam *ngeo* 1) United States of America ▸ **Cągúsam wanągaš žén watí, waná nén wa'ų.** Long ago I lived there in the United States, and now live here. *Syn:* **Tųgášina makóce** 2) Canada *Syn:* **Cąwám**

cągúsam *adv* across the border

Cągúsam wįcášta *nprop* American people, person of American descent *Lit:* across the border person

cągúsampadahą *n* from across the border

cągúwaką *n* US/Canada border

cągúwaką wa'áwąyaga *cp* border patrol

cąhá *n* bark

cáȟaba *n* shoes

cáȟaba hą́ske *cp* cowboy boots

cáȟaba įsámye *cp* shoe polish

cąhą́bi *n* tree sap

cąhúde *n* stump, base of a tree ▸ **Cąhúde žé agą́ mągá.** I sat on a stump.

Cą́ȟe *ngeo* Wood Mountain (Saskatchewan)

Cą́ȟe wįcášta *nprop* Wood Mountain people (band of Nakoda, Saskatchewan)

cąȟéȟe *n* shrub

Cą́ȟnada *nprop* Strong wood people (band of Nakoda)

cąȟóda *n* ash tree

cą'íyani *vi1* s/he/it climbs a tree *Syn:* **cą'áni**

cą'íc'ipA *vi3-refl* s/he stabs himself/herself *Vredup:* **cą'íc'ipapA**

cą'íc'ipapA *vi3-refl-redup* s/he stabs himself/herself repeatedly ‣ **Onówą né waknáštą štén eyáš camíc'ipapa.** When I finish my song, then I would stab myself. (Shields 85:509) *1s:* **camíc'ipapA** *2s:* **caníc'ipapA**

cą'íjaškabi *n* back rest

cą'íjoğą *n* driftwood

cą'íkpa *n* 1) treetop 2) end, tip of a stick ‣ **Cą'íkpa gapéna.** Sharpen the end of the stick.

cą'íkpaza *vt3-pos* s/he fences his/her own field, garden *1s:* **camíkpaza** *2s:* **caníkpaza**

cą'ímaksa *n* wood saw ‣ **Cą'ímaksa žé cą agámpadahą yįgá.** The saw is sitting on the wood. *Syn:* **įcáyukse**

cą'ítku *n* fire, open fire ‣ **Cą'ítku okná éknąga.** He put it in the fire.

cą'ítkuyA *vt1-caus* s/he makes a fire

cą'íyusnohą *n* wooden sleigh, sled *Syn:* **cuwísnohą**

cą'íyutabi *n* cord of wood ‣ **Waníhą cą'íyutabi yámni wagáksa.** Last winter I chopped three cords of wood.

cąkáhu *n* spine, dorsal bone

cąkáhuknekneğa *n-redup* striped gopher

cąkáhuknekneğana *n-redup* striped chipmunk

cąknágiyą *n* 1) neck yoke 2) drying rack made of two poles and a transversal bar ‣ **Cąknágiyą žén tanó oktégiya.** She dried her meat there on the drying rack.

cąkníyaȟpe *n* deadfall ‣ **Žé cąkníyaȟpe kuwá.** He went to check his traps.

cąknúhA *vi1-pos* s/he carries his/her own wood

Cąknúhabi wįcášta *nprop* They carry their own wood people (band of Nakoda)

cąkpé *n* sicą́ shin, *Syn.* **sicą́**

cąkpéhu *n* shin bone

cą́ktam *adv* toward the wood

cąk'ívi1 s/he carries wood on the back ‣ **Wįkóške né nén cąk'íhí.** This young woman arrived here carrying wood. *1s:* **cąwák'į** *2s:* **cąyák'į** *1p:* **cą'úk'įbi**

cąmná *vs* s/he/it smells like wood

cąmnáska *n* wooden board, plank ‣ **Cąmnáska žé awámaksa.** I cut off this plank to make it fit.

cąm'úzįkta *Variant:* **cąm'úzįtka** *n* wild onion, onion

cąm'úzįkta įkcéya *Variant:* **cąm'úzįtka įkcéya** *cp* wild onion *Lit:* common onion

cąné *vi1* s/he looks for wood ‣ **Cąné wa'í.** I went to look for wood. ‣ **Cąné yá!** Go look for wood! *1s:* **cąwáne** *2s:* **cąyáne** *Vbenef:* **cągíjine**

cąní *n* tobacco

cąní o'ópetų *cp* tobacco, smoke shop

cąní sudá *cp* twisted tobacco *Lit:* hard tobacco

cąníhu *n* tobacco plant

cąnípaȟta *n* tobacco tie

cąnísaba *n* cigar *Lit:* black cigarette *Syn:* **cąníska tą́ga**

cąníska *n* cigarette *Lit:* white tobacco ‣ **Cąníska nuhá?** Do you have a smoke?

cąníska tą́ga *cp* cigar *Lit:* big cigarette *Syn:* **cąnísaba**

cąníyatabi *n* chewing tobacco ‣ **Mitúgaši cąníyatabi yatá.** My grandfather chewed tobacco.

cąníyą *Variant:* **cąniya** *vi1* s/he sulks ‣ **Cąníyą mągá.** I am sitting sulking.

cąnúba *n* 1) pipe ‣ **Adé wakátąga cąnúba waká mak'ú wo!** Father the Creator, give me the holy pipe! ‣ **Cąnúba ųgíjukta!** Let us two smoke the pipe. *vi1* 2) s/he smokes pipe ‣ **Šiyónide cąnúba táwa žé gicí cąnúbabįkta.** They will smoke with Pheasant Rump's pipe. *1s:* **cąwánuba** *2s:* **cąyánuba** *1p:* **cą'únubabi**

cąnúba įbáȟage *cp* pipe tamper

cąnúba įȟúcą *cp* pipe stem

Cąnúba oȟpága ecúbi *ph* Pipe ceremony *Lit:* pipe lifting ceremony

cąnúbaha *n* pipe pouch

cą'óda *n* bush

cą'ógapte *n* wooden bowl

cą'óhuhuna *n* wagon spoke

cą'ókpa *n* sawdust

cą'ókšą *Variant:* cąwókšą *adv* around the bush, forest ▸ **Cą'ókšą mawáni.** I walk around the forest.

cą'ómįmą owáci *np* hoop dance

cą'ómįmą yuhá wací *ph* hoop dancer

cą'ónažį (WB) *n* floor *Lit:* stand on wood

cą'ópiya ; cąwópiye *n* box, trunk

cą'ótąga *n* board

cą'óti *n* log cabin

Cą'ótina *nprop* Tree dweller (dwarf that lives in the forest)

cą'ówahązi *n* shade in front of a house, tent

cą'ówą *n* floor ▸ **Mína žé cą'ówą én yįgéšį.** The knife is not on the floor.

cą'ówįža ; cą'ówiža *n* wooden floor, mat ▸ **Cą'ówįža ženáhą wabáhi.** I picked it up from the floor. ▸ **Cą'ówįža žé wapíwacįšį.** The floor is not clean. *Syn:* cą'ówą

cą'ózina *n* forest fire

cąpá *n* chokecherry, pin cherry *Cont:* cą-

cąpá sapsába hąwí ; cąpásaba wí *cp-redup* August *Syn:* cąpá waštéšte hąwí

cąpá waštéšte hąwí *n-redup* August *Syn:* cąpá sapsába hąwí, cąpásaba wí

cąpáhu *n* cherry tree

cąpájuk'a *n* pin cherry

cąpáksa *n* stump

cąpásusuna ; cąpásu *n-redup* pepper *Lit:* choke-cherry pits ▸ **Cąpásu yuká he?** Is there pepper? ▸ **Cąpásusuna agána.** He spreads pepper on it.

cąpépena *n-redup* thistle, prickly plant

cąsága *n* twig ▸ **Cąsága wąží wabáksa.** I broke a twig.

cąságena *n* water willow

cąská *n* white poplar

cąsúda *n* 1) ash tree 2) hardwood

Cąsúska wakpá *ngeo* Maple Creek (Saskatchewan)

cąšáša ; cąšášana *n-redup* red willow

cą́šeja *n* dead tree

cąšíhąba *n* rubber boots ▸ **Cąšíhąba wéc'ųkta.** I will put on my rubber boots.

cąšį́ *n* 1) resin, gum ▸ **cąwába cąšį́** pine resin 2) chewing gum ▸ **Cąšį́žé awódabi mahén ayáskama.** The chewing gum is stuck under the table. 3) rubber

cąšká *n* hawk, chicken hawk

cąškóba *n* curved tree, stick

cąšmúyabi *n* 1) maple syrup 2) sugar, refined sugar ▸ **Huňnáȟyabi cąšmúyabi cóna mak'ú.** Give me coffee without sugar.

cąšmúyabi gigída *cp* syrup

cąšmúyabi pšųkáka *cp* candy

cąšmúyabi yazą́ *vs* s/he has diabetes; is diabetic

cąšúška *n* box elder

cąt- *cont* heart

cą́teja *n* green wood

cątíbi *n* log house

cątkáspeyA *vt1-caus* s/he consoles, tends to sb's heart *Lit:* s/he grasps the heart *1s:* cątkáspewaya *2s:* cątkáspeyaya *1p:* cątkáspe'ųyabi *See:* gaspéya

cątkúša *n* American robin *Lit:* red chest

cątóto *n* green wood *Syn:* cą́teja

Cątų́wąbi *nprop* Forest villagers or Wood villagers people

cąwába *n* evergreen tree, pine

cąwába cąšį́ *cp* pine resin

cąwáką *n* 1) Sun dance tree, center pole 2) wood cross

cąwák'į *n* wood barrel

Cąwám *ngeo* Canada ▸ **Žécen coyote žé'įš cąwám iyáya hųštá.** Then that coyote also went to Canada. (NS 2002:36) *Syn:* Cągúsam

cąwámnuška *n* wood tick *Lit:* wood insect (probable calque from English) *Syn:* taskákpa

cąwą́gan *adv* up in a tree

cąwą́gąduȟ *adv* high up in a tree ▸ **Ziktábina**

né cąwágąduȟ wahóȟpi gáǧabi. These birds made a nest way up there in the tree.

cąwídaga *n* grove of trees

cąwį́šwįžena *n-redup* piece of wood that is flexible

cąwóhą ; cą'óhą *adv* in a wooden area, in the bush, forest ‣ **Gadám cąwóhą yá wo.** Go over there in the woods.

cąwóhocągu *n* trail in the woods

cąwóšma *n* dense bush, forest

cąyága *vi2* s/he moans *Vcont:* **cąyák**

cąyák *vcont* moaning ‣ **Dáguškina né cąyák yįgá** This baby is continuously moaning.

cąyák ų́ *vi1* s/he/it agonizes in pain *1s:* **cąyák wa'ų́** *2s:* **cąyák ya'ų́**

cąyéǧa *n* firefly

cąyúpina *n* squirrel

cąyúpipina *n-redup* chipmunk

cążáda *n* fork in a sacred tree

cé₁ *n* penis *1s:* **macé** *2s:* **nicé**

cé₂ *part* indicates an assertion (declarative female particle) ‣ **"Né adé né šiȟ'ą́ žéca cé, nįco né,"** **eyá.** "My father, the one who called you here, is a monster," she said. (Weasel 65:78)

cedą́ *n* hawk

-cedu *suff* it is thus ‣ né > nécedu this > in this way

cegíjiti *vt1-benef* s/he builds a fire for sb *1s:* **cewéjiti** *2s:* **ceyéjiti**

cegíti *vt1-pos* s/he builds his/her own fire *1s:* **cewágiti** *2s:* **ceyágiti**

cégiyA *vt1-dat* 1) s/he blesses sb, smth ‣ **Adé! Cémągiya!** Father! Bless me! 2) s/he supplicates, prays to sb ‣ **Adé waką́tąga cécigiya, hó namą́ȟ'ų wo!** Holy Father I pray to you, hear my voice! *1s:* **céwagiya** *2s:* **céyagiya** *1p:* **ce'ų́giyabi**

céǧa *n* 1) kettle, pot ‣ **waȟpé céǧa** tea pot 2) pail, bucket *1s:* **mitáceǧa** *2s:* **nitáceǧa** *3s:* **tacéǧa** *Cont:* **ceȟ-**

Céǧa K'ína *nprop* 1) Carry The Kettle (Chief of the Nakoda people from 1891 to 1923) *ngeo 2)* Carry The Kettle reservation (Saskatchewan)

Céǧa K'ína wįcášta *nprop* Carry The Kettle people (band of Nakoda living in Carry The Kettle, Saskatchewan)

céǧa tą́ga *cp* pail

céǧanuǧe yuką́kąna *cp-redup* pot with handles

-c'ehą; -'ehą *suff* back then, in the past, last *Usage:* attaches to adverbs, verbs, and interrogative pronouns. ‣ **Hokšína žé hąhébic'ehą hí.** That boy arrived last night. ‣ **Tanó dóhąc'ehą núda?** When did you eat meat? ‣ **Midáguyebi dóhąc'ehą yahíbi?** My relatives, when did you all arrive here? ‣ **Gįyą́ ųbic'ehą mowį́cawamneja.** I shot and scattered them as they flew.

cehį́ *n* man's pubic hair

cehú *n* jaw

cehúba *n* chin and jaw area ‣ **Miní žé cehúba žén ehą́'i.** The water reached his chin.

cehúbaknakna *vi1-redup* s/he trills

ceȟ- *cont* kettle, pot; bucket, pail

ceȟkúwabi *n* chase the pot dance

ceȟníbi *n* syphilis, sexual disease *Lit:* scabbed penis ‣ **Ceȟníbi ecéyabi.** They have a sexual disease. *Redup:* **ceȟníȟnibi**

ceȟníȟnibi *n-redup* sexual diseases (in the form of viscous spots, rashes) *See:* **ceȟníbi**

ceȟšá *n* copper kettle

ce'į́c'iti *vi3-refl* s/he builds a fire for himself/herself *1s:* **cemį́c'iti** *2s:* **cenį́c'iti**

cejá *n* 1) thigh 2) leg of smth (chair, table) ‣ **awódabi cejá** leg of a table

cekpá *n* navel *1s:* **micékpa** *2s:* **nicékpa** *1p:* **ųgícekpagubi** *3p:* **cekpábi**

cekpá yámni *cp* triplets *Lit:* three umbilical cords

cekpábina *n-pl* twins

cemnóhu *n* clavicle, collarbone

cen *encl* must be, I guess, or what (expresses uncertainty) ‣ **Dónaga cen.** Several I guess.

‣ **Dágu wak'ú cen?** What can I give? ‣ **Úbįkte cen?** Are they coming or what?

cén *conj* then, so, thus, therefore, because, that is why ‣ **Awápa cén įštásaba.** I hit him so he has a black eye. ‣ **Mitúgaši wanągaš i'á cén nawáh'ų jé.** I always heard my grandfather speak it thus long ago. ‣ **Dąyą́ ų́bįkte nówa iyéyabi cén.** They would live well and find everything they needed therefore. ‣ **Ába né nína wašté cén hokúwa ųyábi.** It is a nice day today, therefore we go fishing. ‣ **Šų́ga žená miní cįgábi cén kníbi.** Those dogs came home because they wanted water.

cesní *vs* 1) s/he/it defecates, takes a shit ‣ **Nén nicésnįkta he?** Are you taking a shit here? ‣ **Cesnįkta.** She is going to the bathroom. *1s:* **macésni** *2s:* **nicésni** *1p:* **ųcésnibi** *Vcaus:* **cesníyA** *Vrecip:* **acégicisnibi** *Vrefl:* **a'į́c'icesni** *See:* **acésni, océsni** *n* 2) feces, dung, shit ‣ **Šų́ga cesní awáhą ginįja.** I almost stepped on dog poop. ‣ **Cesní oyátaga.** She is constipated.

cesní hiyáyA *vi2* s/he/it has diarrhea *1s:* **cesní himnámna** *2s:* **cesní hinána** *1p:* **cesní ųhíyayabi** *Syn:* **gažó**

cesní ȟaȟá *vs* s/he/it has diarrhea *Syn:* **gažó**

cesní oyátagA *vs* s/he/it is constipated *1s:* **cesní omáyataga** *2s:* **cesní oníyataga**

cesníyA *vt1-caus* it makes sb defecate *1s:* **cesnímaya** *2s:* **cesníniya**

ceška *n* upper chest

ceškámaza *n* 1) council, alliance (refers to council members to whom a badge was given) 2) police officer *Usage:* used in Carry The Kettle. *Lit:* iron chest (in reference to the badge)

cešnóšno *vi1-redup* s/he has soft stool, diarrhea ‣ **Iná cewášnošno!** Mom, I have soft stool!

cetápą *n* male genitalia (penis and testicles)

cetí *vi1* s/he builds a fire; starts a stove ‣ **Ȟáskeya cetíbi.** They made a fire that burned in a long line. (Drummond 1976, How the woman made pemmican) *1s:* **cewáti** *2s:* **ceyáti** *Vbenef:* **cegíjiti** *Vpos:* **cegíti** *Vrefl:* **ce'į́c'iti**

cetíbi *n* fireplace

cet'ų́'įc'iknA *vi3-refl* s/he doubts himself/herself

cet'ų́knA *vt1* s/he doubt, disbelieves sb, smth ‣ **Wóyaknage né cet'ų́cikna.** I do not believe your story. *1s:* **cewát'ųkna ; cet'ų́wakna** *2s:* **ceyát'ųkna ; cet'ų́yakna** *Vrefl:* **cet'ų́'įc'ikna**

céwą ; céwąna *encl* I wonder, I think (marker of epistemic modality) *Usage:* expresses the likelihood of an event. ‣ **Wįjáka céwą.** I wonder if he is really honest about it! ‣ **Cóȟ céwą.** I wonder if it is true.

céwąna:ga *encl* I wondered, I thought ‣ **Céwąna:ga oká žéceduší.** I thought it was him but it was not.

céyA *vi1* s/he cries ‣ **Dágucen yacéya?** Why are you crying? ‣ **Mitáwįju! Céyeší wo!** My wife! Do not cry! ‣ **Ecágen wacéya.** I always cry. *1s:* **wacéya** *2s:* **yacéya** *1p:* **ųcéyabi** *Vbenef:* **gíjiceyA**

céya ot'át'A *vi1-redup* s/he gasps after crying ‣ **Dáguškina né céya ot'át'a.** The baby is gasping after crying. *1s:* **céya owát'at'a** *2s:* **céya oyát'at'a**

céyagA *part* should, must, ought to, might as well (marker of deontic modality) ‣ **Ú céyaga!** He should come. ‣ **Wanągaš ejíyabi céyaga.** They should have said it to her long ago. ‣ **Ȟeyám mawáni céyaga.** I should walk behind. ‣ **Wanągaš ecámų céyaga.** I should have done that a long ago. ‣ **Iyúha žén ųyábi céyaga.** We must go there together. ‣ **Waná ecámų céyaga.** Now I might as well do it.

ceyágadaga ; cayágadaga *n* wild mint, peppermint *Syn:* **waȟpé ce'ága**

céyageší *part* should not, must not, cannot possibly (negative deontic modality) ‣ **Ú céyageší.** He must not come. ‣ **Cóȟ ecúbi céyageší.** They cannot possibly have done that.

ceyés'a *n* crybaby *See:* **haňníša**

ceží *n* 1) tongue 2) gun trigger

cežížina *n-redup* uvula

-ci- *prefix* I . . . you *Usage:* marker of 1st person singular agent acting on 2nd person patient of transitive verbs. ‣ **teňína > tecíňina** s/he loves, cherishes sb, smth > I love, cherish you ‣ **wąyága > wącímnaga** s/he sees sb, smth > I see you

-ci- . . .-bi *circumfix* I . . . you all *Usage:* marker of 1st person singular agent acting on 2nd— person plural patient of transitive verbs. ‣ **snokyá > snokcíyabi** s/he knows sb, smth > I know you all ‣ **yužąga > cimnúžągabi** s/he picks on sb > I pick on you all

cicá *vs* s/he/it has curly (hair) ‣ **Pahá cicá.** He has curly hair. *See:* **škišká**

cíga *adv* with energy, strenuously ‣ **Cíga wówada.** I ate as fast as I could.

cigÁ ; cígA *vt1* s/he wants, desires smth; is inclined to smth ‣ **Duwé waȟpé cigá?** Who wants tea? ‣ **Dágu yacíga he? —Dáguni wacígeši.** What do you want? —I do not want anything. ‣ **Ȟá, edáȟą wacíga.** Yes, I want some. ‣ **Wócegiya wacíga.** I want to be Christian. ‣ **Wįkóške né wóšpi cigéȟtįyą.** This girl is anxious to pick berries. *1s:* **wacíga** *2s:* **yacíga** *1p:* **ųcígabi** *Vpos:* **gicígA**

cígeši *vt1* s/he objects against, refuses sb, smth ‣ **Úbi cígeši.** He refuses to come. ‣ **Nakóda hikną́bi cíga, duká cígeši.** She wanted to marry a Nakoda, but he refused. *1s:* **wacígeši** *2s:* **yacígeši** *1p:* **ųcígabiši**

ciȟíktuna *n* human offspring

ciȟíktuyA *Variant:* **ciȟítkuyA** *vt1* s/he adopts a son *1s:* **ciȟíktuwaya ; ciȟítkuwaya** *2s:* **ciȟíktuyaya ; ciȟítkuyaya** *1p:* **ciȟíktu'ųyabi ; ciȟítku'ųyabi**

cij- *cont* child

cijá *n* child; one's child; cub ‣ **Cijábi dóna nuhá he?** How many children do you have? *1s:* **micíjana ; micíja** *2s:* **nicíjana ; nicíja** *3s:* **cijá** *1p:* **ųcíjabina ; ųgícijabi** *Cont:* **cij-**

cijána *n* calf, offspring, cub ‣ **Cijána pakóyakyįkta.** He will rope a steer. ‣ **waȟ'ąksija cijábina** bear cubs ‣ **honáǧina cijábina** maggots

cijátų *vi* she gives birth (human and animal) *Syn:* **hokšíyuha**

cijáyA *vt1* s/he adopts a child ‣ **Jan cijáwaya.** I adopted Jan as a child. ‣ **Cijá'ųyąbikte no!** We will have him as our own child. *1s:* **cijáwaya** *2s:* **cijáyaya** *1p:* **cijá'ųyąbi**

cijódA *vs-coll* 1) s/he has many children ‣ **Wanągaš mikúši cijódac'eȟą.** Long ago my grandmother had a lot of kids. *1s:* **cijómada** *2s:* **cijónida** *1p:* **cijó'ųdabi** 2) there are many children

-cįkši-; -ciȟį- *root* son ‣ **Micį́kši iyówapeya no!** I scolded my son! ‣ **Cįȟítku žé hą́ska.** Her son is tall. ‣ **Júsina žé micį́kši.** The small one is my son. ‣ **Žeȟą́duȟ cihį́ktu gicí bašpá yá.** Right at time he burst in with his son. *1s:* **micį́kši** *2s:* **nicį́kši** *3s:* **cįhį́ktu ; cįhį́tku** *1p:* **ųgícįhį́ktubi ; ųgícįhį́tkubi ; ųgícįkši**

-cįkšina-; -cįhį́ktuna- *root* nephew (brother's son for a male speaker; sister's son for a female speaker) *1s:* **micį́kšina** *2s:* **nicį́kšina** *3s:* **cįhį́ktuna** *1p:* **ųgícįkšina**

cį́kta *Variant:* **cį́tka** *n* raisin ‣ **cį́kta oȟnáte co'úbabi** raisin pie

-cįna- *root* 1) older brother (male speaker) ‣ **Micį́na ecúnas'a.** My older brother is a gambler. 2) older male parallel cousin (male speaker) *1s:* **micį́na** *2s:* **nicį́na** *3s:* **cį́cúna** *1p:* **ųgícįna**

có *n* truth, true ‣ **Có iyáya.** It came true.

cogądu *adv* in the middle, center *Cont:* **cogą́n**

cogąduȟ *adv* right in the center, middle ‣ **Cogą́duȟ awápa.** I hit it right in the center.

cogán *adv-cont* in the middle, center ‣ **Cogán yįgá.** He sits in the middle. ‣ **Dóba cogán nųba štén nųbáȟ.** Four divided by two equals two.

cogánwida *n* island in the middle of a lake

cogíjibA *vt1-benef* s/he cooks smth for sb ‣ **Iná tanó edáhą comíjiba wo.** Mom cooked some meat for me. *1s:* **cowéjiba** *2s:* **coyéjiba**

cóǧA *vs* 1) s/he is honest *n* 2) truth, honesty *Adv:* **cóȟ**

coǧážįja *n* diamond willow

cóǧeȟ *adv* honestly, in an honest manner ‣ **Cóǧeȟ ecámųkta.** I will do it honestly.

cóȟ *adv-cont* absolutely, truly, honestly, for sure, really (puts emphasis on the verb) ‣ **Cóȟ wįjáyakeši.** You are not absolutely honest. ‣ **Cóȟ duwé snokwáyešį.** I really do not know him well. ‣ **Cóȟ žeyá?** Did he really say that? ‣ **Cóȟ įwáknįgešį.** I will avoid it for sure.

cóȟtįyĄ *vs* 1) s/he/it is very honest; it is the truth ‣ **Comáȟtįyą wįcášta žemáca.** I am a veeeeery honest man. ‣ **Cóȟtįyą mawáni.** I walk honestly. ‣ **Dágu epá hą́da cóȟtįyą.** When I say something it is the real truth. *1s:* **comáȟtįyą** *2s:* **coníȟtįyą** *n* 2) truth ‣ **Iná cóȟtįyą cíga.** Mom wants the truth.

coȟwíjakA *vi1* s/he tells the real truth *1s:* **coȟwíjawaka** *2s:* **coȟwíjayaka**

coknága *n* breechcloth *Cont:* **coknák**

coknák *cont* breechcloth

coknákkitų *vt1-pos* s/he wears his/her breechcloth *1s:* **coknákwetų** *2s:* **coknákyetų**

coná *vt1* 1) s/he believes sb, smth ‣ **Cowánašįȟtįyą!** I disbelieve it very much! ‣ **Dágu ehé nówa cowána!** I believe everything thing you said. *1s:* **cowána** *2s:* **coyána** *n* 2) belief *Syn:* **wówįjakA**

cóna *post, suff* without, lacking, deprived of ‣ **Huȟnáȟyabi, asą́bi cóna waštéwana.** I like coffee without milk. ‣ **ticóna** s/he is homeless ‣ **hąmcóna** without moccasins, shoeless ‣ **sicócona ; sicóna** barefoot

coníca *n* dried meat *Syn:* **wacónice**

coskíyA *vt1-pos* s/he warms his/her own (feet, hand) ‣ **Péda žén ną́be cos'úgiyabi.** We warmed our hands over the fire. *1s:* **coswágiya** *2s:* **cosyágiya** *1p:* **cos'úgiyabi** *See:* **cóza**

cosyÁ *vt1-caus* s/he warms up smth *1s:* **coswáya** *2s:* **cosyáya** *1p:* **cos'úyabi** *Vpos:* **coskíyA** *Vrefl:* **cos'íc'iyA**

cosyá *adv* warmly ‣ **Cosyá mįknúzįkta.** I will dress myself warmly.

cos'íc'iyA *vi3-refl* s/he warms him/herself ‣ **Cos'íc'iya mągá:ga.** I am sitting warming myself up. *1s:* **cosmíc'iya** *2s:* **cosníc'iya**

cótąga *n* gun *Lit:* big "choo" (onomatopoeia depicting the sound of a gunshot)

cótągawahukeza *n* bayonet

cótąktąga *n-redup* cannon

co'úbA *vt1* 1) s/he roasts smth ‣ **Mihú tanó co'úba híkna wožábi gáǧa.** My mother roasted meat and made gravy. 2) s/he fries smth 3) s/he cooks smth ‣ **Miyé cowá'ųba.** I cook my own dish. *1s:* **cowá'ųba** *2s:* **coyá'ųba** *1p:* **co'úgųbabi** *Vabs:* **wacó'ųbA** *Vbenef:* **cogíjibA** *Vcoll:* **cowįcagijibA**

cówąja *n* forest

coyá *vt1* s/he believes in sb, smth ‣ **Wįcášta toką́ né coyáya he?** Do you believe in aliens? *1s:* **cowáya** *2s:* **coyáya**

cóza *vs* s/he/it is warm ‣ **Nicóza he?** Are you warm? ‣ **Cóza amáya.** I am getting warm. ‣ **Cuwíknąga cóza žéca yaknúhabi he?** Do you all have warm coats with you? *1s:* **macóza** *2s:* **nicóza** *1p:* **ųcózabi** *Adv:* **cosyá** *Vcaus:* **cosyÁ** *Vcont:* **cos**

cucúšte *n* ribs

cudóȟpeya *vi1* s/he has smth slung over the shoulder *Vpos:* **knudóȟpeya**

cuhé *n* ashes

cuȟéwąga *vimp* 1) there is hoar frost *n* 2) hoar frost *See:* **acúȟewąga**

cuȟéwąga wí *cp* November

cuȟpá *vimp* 2) it is a heavy dew ▸ **Hąyákena hąda nína cuȟpą́.** In the morning there is a lot of dew. *n* 2) dew ▸ **Táȟcįjana cuȟpą́ én yasníbabi.** Deer lick the morning dew.

-cųkši-; -cųwį- *root* daughter ▸ **Micų́kši įhágam hí.** My daughter arrived after. ▸ **Nicų́kši wawá'ųšįgina.** Your daughter is kind. ▸ **Micų́kši núǧe įkpáȟnoga.** My daughter pierced her ears. *1s:* **micų́kši** *2s:* **nicų́kši** *3s:* **cųwį́ktu ; cųwį́tku** *1p:* **ųgícųwį́ktubi ; ųgícųwį́tkubi ; ųgícųkši**

-cuna *encl* all the time; keeps on doing; continuously (aspectual marker of repetitive action or event) ▸ **Iná hoȟpácuna.** Mom is coughing all the time. ▸ **Wáhįhącuna.** It keeps on snowing. ▸ **I'écuna!** She is continuously yapping!

cup'ó *vimp* 1) it is foggy ▸ **Duktékten cup'ó.** It is foggy here and there. *n* 2) fog ▸ **Cup'ó šóga.** The fog is thick.

cusní *vimp* it is chilly weather ▸ **Tągán cusní.** It is chilly outside.

cúú *interj* imitation of the sound of a bullet ▸ **Žiyákiyos dágu né "Cúúu," eyábi.** All the while it was going "Choong". (Weasel 58:494)

cuwí *n* 1) waist, chest ▸ **cuwí ókšą** around the waist 2) body (animals and humans) ▸ **Téhą yįgábi né'ųs cuwí mabádį.** My body is stiff after sitting for too long.

cuwíc'iba *n* travois ▸ **Wanągaš šúga cuwíc'iba k'įbis'a.** Long ago dogs carried travois on their back.

cuwícogan *adv* in the middle of the chest, breast ▸ **Cuwícogan cawį́capaga.** He stabbed them in the middle of the breast. (Weasel 4:81)

cuwída *vs* s/he is cold, chilly *Usage:* used with animate referents only. ▸ **Nicúwida cá.** You must be cold. ▸ **Macúwidakte no.** I will be cold. ▸ **Macúwida ga'éca maȟmá.** I am sleepy from being cold. *1s:* **macúwida** *2s:* **nicúwida** *1p:* **ųcúwidabi**

cuwíknagįyą *adv* sideways ▸ **Gá cuwíknagįyą iyéya.** It made it stagger sideways. (Weasel 49:314)

cuwíknąga *n* coat, shirt

cuwíknąga háska *cp* long coat, shirt

cuwíknąga šašábi *cp-pl* Royal Canadian Mounted Police, mounties *Lit:* red coat *Syn:* **ókneša**

Cuwíknąga žé éyagu *nprop* Man who took the coat (Nakoda chief and signatory of Treaty 4)

cuwį́jina *n* curlew

cuwįsnohą *n* sleigh, sled *Syn:* **cą'íyusnohą**

-cųkšina- *root* niece (brother daughter's for a male speaker; sister's daugther for a female speaker) *1s:* **micų́kšina** *2s:* **nicų́kšina** *3s:* **cųkšítkuna** *1p:* **ųgícųkšina**

-cųna- *root* 1) older sister (female speaker) ▸ **Cúguna gicí a'ą́bayabi.** There is a funeral wake for her older sister. 2) older female parallel cousin (female speaker) *1s:* **micų́na** *2s:* **nicų́na** *3s:* **cúguna** *1p:* **ųgícųna**

cútąga *n* thicket

cųwį́ktuya *Variant:* **cųwį́tkuya** *vt1-caus* s/he adopts a daughter *1s:* **cųwį́ktuwaya ; cųwį́tkuwaya** *2s:* **cųwį́ktuyaya ; cųwį́tkuyaya**

D

dágecų *vi3* s/he does smth *1s:* **dágecamų** *2s:* **dágecanų**

dágecųšį *vs* nothing is done; it is a waste of time

dágeyA *vi-irr* s/he says smth ▸ **Iná, adé dágeyabi hąda, wanáȟ'ųbišį.** Whenever mom and dad are saying something, they disobey. ▸ **Duwé dágeya ogíhigen giníhąbi cén.** No one said anything because they were afraid of her. (Weasel 53:406) *1s:* **dágepa** *2s:* **dágeha**

dágeyešį *interj* Shh! Be quiet! Shut up! ▸ **Dágeyešį! Dáguškina žé gídąh̃ įštíma'.** Shh! The baby is finally sleeping.

dágeyešįh̃ *adv* saying nothing ▸ **Dágeyešįh̃ nážį.** He stood up saying nothing.

dágu *pro* 1) thing, something ▸ **Nená dágu i'įjuna.** These are cups. ▸ **Dágu wakạya ecúšį.** He did not do it in a holy way. 2) what ▸ **Dágu yacįga he?** What do you want? ▸ **Mitúgaši dágu nik'ú he?** What did my grandfather give you? *quant* 3) any, none *Usage:* when followed by a negated verb in-šį. ▸ **Mázaska dágu ųk'úbišį.** We did not receive any money. *vs* 4) it is something ▸ **dágugen** it is nothing *Redup:* **dágugu**

dágu giknạga tíbi *ph* warehouse

dágu nówa *pro* everything ▸ **Dágu nówa né yįgá.** Everything is here. ▸ **Dágu nówa wéc'ų.** I gave everything back.

dágucen *pro* why ▸ **Dágucen mázaska yacįga?** Why do you want money? ▸ **Dágucen ecú hún.** I wonder why he did it. ▸ **Dágucen ócijiyįktešį?** Why can't I help you?

dáguga kóšta *pro* anything, just anything, whatever, whichever one ▸ **Dáguga kóšta wíyą žé ewįknagukta.** I will do whatever it takes to get that woman back. ▸ **Dáguga kóšta waštéyana éyagu.** Take whichever one you like.

dágugaš *pro* whatever, whichever one ▸ **Tągán dágugaš.** There is something outside. ▸ **Dágugaš wóyaga.** Tell whatever it is.

dágugen *vs* it is nothing; it is nothing to worry about

dagúgiciyabi *vi1-recip* they are related to one another

dágugu *pro-redup* everything, all things ▸ **Dágugu nówa owáštena yuhá.** Everything is easy to have.

dagúh̃ *pro* something, anything ▸ **Dagúh̃ yawábi wacíga.** I want to read something. ▸ **Dagúh̃ ómna.** He smelled something.

dagúh̃tįyA *vs* 1) it is the real reason, purpose *adv*

2) for a reason, purpose ▸ **Dagúh̃tįyą ecúbi cén?** What is the real purpose of their actions?

dágukiyA *vt1* s/he thinks it is something ▸ **Né dágukiyešį.** He regards this as nothing.

dagúmna *vs* it is the smell of something

dáguni *pro* none, nothing *Usage:* refers to objects and animals only; requires a negated verb. ▸ **Dáguni yuhábišį.** Nothing belongs to them. ▸ **Hiyá, dáguni wacígešį.** No, I do not want anything.

dáguni h̃ *pro* nothing at all ▸ **Dáguni h̃ wacígešį.** I do not want any of it.

dágunišį *vs* 1) it is nothing, there is none ▸ **Dágu dókanų? —Dágunišį!** What are you doing?—Nothing at all! ▸ **Miní dágunišį.** It contains no water. ▸ **Cą né smismí, wah̃pé dágunišį.** This tree is bare, it has no leaves. *1s:* **madágunišį** *2s:* **nidágunišį** *num* 2) zero ▸ **yámni h̃ dágunišį** three zeroes

dágušašana *n-redup* buffalo berry

dáguškina *n* 1) baby, infant, child ▸ **Dáguškina yužáža!** Bathe the baby! ▸ **Dáguškina žé waná wįda.** The baby is now crawling. ▸ **Dáguškina žé įštímabi cįgá.** The baby wants to sleep. *vs* 2) s/he/it is a baby ▸ **Micįkši nidáguškinašį dąyá įknúha céyaga.** My son, you are not a baby, you should take good care of yourself. (BigEagle 2019:8) *1s:* **madáguškina** *2s:* **nidáguškina**

dáguškiškina *n-redup* doll

dáguwiyeknaš *vs* it is numerous, there are many more ▸ **Dáguwiyeknaš óda híbi.** They arrived in great numbers.

dagúyA *vt1* s/he has sb as a relative; s/he is related to sb ▸ **Wįcá žé dagúwaya.** I am related to this man. ▸ **Koná! Dagúciye no.** Friend! I am related to you. *1s:* **dagúwaya** *1p:* **dagú'ųyabi** *Vabs:* **wadáguyA** *Vrecip:* **dagúgiciyabi**

dagúye ; dagúyabi *n* relative, kinsman ▸ **Hą midáguye! Dóken ya'ų he?** Hi my relative! How are you? ▸ **Nidáguyabi cądéwašte wo!** Be kind to your relatives! ▸ **Nená ųdáguyabi.** These

are our people. *1s:* **midáguye ; midáguyabi**
2s: **nidáguye ; nidáguyabi** *1p:* **ųgídaguyebi ;
ųgídaguyabi ; ųdáguyabi**

-dahą *suff* from that point on *Usage:* -tahą is used
after a consonant. ▸ **wakpá > wakpádahą** river
> from the river ▸ **néci > nécidahą** over here
> from over here ▸ **timáhen > timáhentahą**
inside > from inside

daságA *vs* s/he/it is frozen, freezing ▸ **Šų́ga žé
dasága.** That dog is freezing. *1s:* **madásaga**
2s: **nidásaga** *1p:* **ųdásagabi** *Vcaus:* **dasákyA**
See: **odásagA**

dasákyA *vt1-caus* s/he freezes smth *1s:*
dasákwaya *2s:* **dasákyaya** *1p:* **dasák'ųyabi**
Vabs: **wadásakyA**

dąyą́ *Variant:* **dayá** 1) *vs* s/he/it is well, good, all
right; is in good health (after an illness) ▸ **Eyáš
dąyą́.** I guess he is good. ▸ **Tawáci dąyą́ši.** He
is mentally disabled. *1s:* **madą́yą** *2s:* **nidą́yą** *1p:*
ųdą́yąbi 2) *adv* well, properly ▸ **Dąyą́ wa'ú.** I
am fine. ▸ **Iyúhana dąyą́ wódabi.** All ate well.

dąyą́gen *adv* carefully, fairly well, properly,
with ease ▸ **Wįcá žé dąyą́gen ókšą éduwą.** The
man looked around carefully. ▸ **Dąyą́gen ecų́.**
He did it fairly well. ▸ **Dąyą́gen iyútešį.** He did
not measure it properly. ▸ **Dąyą́gen wówaši
ecámų.** I do my work with ease.

dąyą́h̃ *adv* easily; very well, thoroughly ▸ **Dąyą́h̃
né nén wamó'ųsodabikta.** We will easily shoot
many of them here. (Weasel 144:486) ▸ **Dąyą́h̃
yuskábi.** It is very very well kneaded. ▸ **Dąyą́h̃
iyúha špąwícaya.** She burned them thoroughly. (Weasel 51:345)

dąyą́na *vs* s/he/it (small thing, baby, child) is well

dąyą́ši yįgá *cp* death bed

dó *interj* hey ▸ **Há, dó, omá'ųnis.** Ah, hey, let us
go for a walk. (Weasel 45:236)

dóba *num* 1) four *vs* 2) s/he/it is four; there are
four *Cont:* **dóm**

dóbagiya *adv* four by four, in four ways, in four

different directions, locations ▸ **Dóbagiya né
éknąga.** He put them in four different places.

dóbah̃ *adv* four times ▸ **Dóbah̃ yekíye no.** He
sent him out four times.

dóbana *num* only four

dogį́š *adv* poorly, weakly

dogį́š ų́ *vi1* s/he/it is weak from an illness *1s:*
dogį́š wa'ų́ *2s:* **dogį́š ya'ų́**

dogį́š yįgÁ *vi3* s/he is dying; is on his/her death
bed *1s:* **dogį́š mągá** *2s:* **dogį́š nągá** *1p:* **dogį́š
ųyígabi**

dogį́šyagen *adv* poorly ▸ **Dogį́šyagen ų́.** He feels
poorly.

dóhąc'ehą *adv* when *Usage:* used with past events.
▸ **Dóhąc'ehą ya'í?** When did you arrive there?
▸ **Wah̃pé dóhąc'ehą yagága?** When did you
make tea? ▸ **Mikúši dóhąc'ehą hí?** When did
my grandmother arrive?

dóhądu *vimp* it is at such time

dohágeh̃ *adv* after a while ▸ **Žécen dóhągeh̃
žécen gicúni.** Then after awhile she finished.
(NS 2002:81)

dohágeh̃tiyA *vs* it is a while, whenever ▸
Dohágeh̃tiyą štén kníkta. He will be back in
awhile.

dóhągeja *adv* when, at what time *Usage:* used
with future events. ▸ **Dóhągeja yahíkta?**
At what time will you arrive? ▸ **Dóhągeja
yanówąbikta he?** At what time are you all singing? ▸ **Dóhągeja Huhúžubina níktéh̃tiya he?**
At what time do you want to leave for Regina?

dohą́n ; dohą́da *adv* when *Usage:* used with future
and hypothetical events. ▸ **Dohą́n níkta?** When
will you go? ▸ **Tugášina dohą́n timáyanikta
he?** When will you visit grandpa? ▸ **Wayáwa
tíbi dohą́n inánikta he?** When will you go to
school? ▸ **Dohą́n wacíga hą́da iyámne wa'í.**
I go hunting whenever I want. ▸ **Dohą́da
yanówąbikta he?** When will you all sing?

dóhąni *adv* never ▸ **Dóhąni ecámųktešį.** I will
never do it again. ▸ **Búza né dóhąni inážįšį.**

This cat never stops. ‣ **Makóce én dóhani wášį.** In the land where it never snows.

doháya *adv* for a certain time, distance, length ‣ **Doháya žén úbi.** They stayed there a certain time. ‣ **Doháya gúbikta.** They will come back here from far off. ‣ **Ókša doháya makóce né k'ábi.** They would dig a small trench around them. (Drummond 1976, Įktomi)

dókaš *adv* 1) maybe, perhaps ‣ **Dókaš togádagiya amógiya opécijitukta.** Maybe one day I will buy you a car. 2) in time, in awhile, eventually ‣ **Dókaš ecámu cá!** I will do it in awhile! ‣ **Dókaš aké įcímugįkta.** I will ask you another time. ‣ **Owá dókaš daya úbįkta.** All will eventually prosper.

dókedu *vs* 1) s/he/it happened as such; for whatever reason, whatever happens *adv* 2) somehow ‣ **Dókedu wósijeya įȟpéya.** Somehow he got out of trouble. ‣ **Amánibi né anúk įš dokédu omíyejikšu.** Plant both sides of this path over here for me in the same way. (Weasel 12:87)

dókeduš *adv* no matter what, at any rate ‣ **Ogíjiyaga dókeduš!** Tell her that, no matter what!

dókeȟ'a *adv* how it happened ‣ **Žécen dókeȟ'a žé oknáge wįcánabišį.** So they did not believe any of what he told them had happened. (Shields 14:173)

dókeja *vs* it is a matter, way, kind, concern; what is it like? ‣ **Dókeja he?** What is the matter? ‣ **Domákeja!** Something is wrong with me! ‣ **Ába dókeja he?—Amáhpiya!** How is the weather?—It is cloudy! *1s:* **domákeja** *2s:* **donįkeja** *1p:* **do'úkejabi** *Adv:* **dóken**

dókejaga *vs* it is what kind ‣ **Iyécįgayena žé dókejaga he?** What kind is that car?

dókejašį *vs* there is nothing wrong with him/her/it; it is all good; it does not matter ‣ **Dókejašį!** Never mind! ‣ **Domákejašį!** There is nothing wrong with me! ‣ **Dókejašį eyáš wamnágįkta!**

It does not matter, I will see her anyways! *1s:* **domákejašį** *2s:* **donįkejašį** *1p:* **do'úkejabišį**

dóken *adv* 1) how, what ‣ **Dóken ya'ú?—Daya wa'ú!** How are you?—I am fine! ‣ **Dóken yaškáhe?** How are you feeling? ‣ **Dóken eníjiyabi?** What is your name? 2) in some way, whichever way or manner ‣ **Šahíyabi dóken ahíyayabi žécen ecú.** She sang in the Cree style. ‣ **Dóken ecúbi yacíga.** Do it whichever way you want. *Redup:* **dókenken**

dókenken *adv* in no particular fashion or order; any old way ‣ **Dókenken ecú.** He did it in no particular way. ‣ **Eyáš, eyáš dókenken naȟtága:ga, nigé cogán.** So he kept kicking any old way toward the middle of its stomach. (Weasel 9:26)

dóki *adv* 1) where, where to *Usage:* used with dynamic verbs of coming and going. ‣ **Nikúši dóki iyáya?** Where did your grandmother go? ‣ **Timáni wahí duká dóki inánabi žé snohwáyešį.** I came to visit but I do not know where you all went. 2) anywhere, somewhere, to some place *Usage:* often used with negated verbs. ‣ **Dóki ya'íšį he?** You did not go anywhere? *See:* **duktén**

dókikiya *adv-redup* in some direction; toward some places

dokíkiyota *adv-redup* in some direction ‣ **Dokíkiyote yá.** He went in some direction.

dókiya *adv* 1) wherever *Usage:* followed by a positive verb of movement. ‣ **Dókiya wa'í háda watókąwakna.** Wherever I go I feel uneasy with strangers. ‣ **Honágina dókiya cén otápabi.** Flies follow him wherever he goes. (BigEagle 2019:8) 2) anywhere *Usage:* followed by a negated verb of movement. ‣ **Dókiya uyábįkteši.** We are not going anywhere. ‣ **Įknúhana dókiya ta'íšį.** All of a sudden she was gone. 3) where to *Usage:* functions like an interrogative stative verb and occurs in sentence final position. ‣ **Wapáha žé dókiya?** Where is the hat? ‣ **Cąšmúyabi dókiya?** Where is the sugar? ‣ **Ni'áde dókiya?** Where is your dad? ‣ **Céǧa K'ína oyáde tamákoce dókiya he?** Where is Carry The Kettle reserve? *Adv:* **dókikiya**

dókiyadahą *adv* from which direction, where from

dókiyapadahą *adv* from where ‣ **Dókiyapadahą yahí?** Where did you arrive from?

dókiyo *adv* in which direction, direction, course ‣ **Dókiyo iyáya?** In which direction did he go? ‣ **Wakpá žé dókiyo ȟaȟá.** The river is flowing its course. ‣ **Dókiyo mná amnúštą.** I lost my way. ‣ **Eyáš dókiyo yábi yacíge yá!** Just go any which way you want to go!

dokíyo nówaȟ *ph* in every which way ‣ **Dokíyo nówaȟ oȟ'ą:ga gá.** He kept behaving in every which way. (Weasel 114:65)

dóku *vi3-irr* s/he/it does what? ‣ **Šúga gá dágu dóku he?** What is that dog over there doing? ‣ **Dágu dókanu? —Dáguniši!** What are you doing? —Nothing at all! ‣ **Dágu dók'u hún!** I wonder what he is doing! *1s:* **dókamu** *2s:* **dókanu** *1p:* **dóka'ugubi**

dóm *cont* four

dóna *pro* 1) how many, what number ‣ **Waníyedu dóna eháyaki he?** How old are you? ‣ **Dóna ehą'i he?** What time is it? 2) how much ‣ **Mázaska dóna yacígabi he?** How much money will you want? *quant* 3) several ‣ **Žécen waníyedu dóna cén dókiya ta'íšį** And so for several years she had disappeared somewhere. *vs* 4) s/he/it is so many ‣ **Nidónabi he?** How many are you? *1p:* **udónabi** *3p:* **dónabi**

dónacą *adv* several days; how many days ‣ **Hąhébi dónacą žé nįštíma?** How many nights did you sleep there? ‣ **Dónacą nén ú.** He stayed here for several days. ‣ **Dónacą gicí ú.** He stayed with him for a time.

dónągeja *pro* how many, much ‣ **Dónągeja híbi he?** How many arrived?

dónągen *adv* few ‣ **Dónągen híbi.** A few came.

-du *suff* at a particular point in time or space *Usage:* creates impersonal verbs or nouns from adverbs some of which are based on édu 'it is there, it is the place.' ‣ **é > édu** it is there > it is the place ‣ **ȟta-> ȟtayédu** evening > evening, it is evening ‣ **waní > waníyedu** winter > winter, it is winter ‣ **dóhą > dohądu** when > it is at such time ‣ **ába > ąbédu** it is day, day > day ‣ **mahé-> mahédu** inside, in within, under > it is deep inside *Cont:-**n**

duȟáȟa *vs* it is dimpled ‣ **Yaȟúgabi žé duȟáȟa.** The peanuts are dimpled.

duká *Variant:* **oká, uká** *conj* 1) but, although, even though, despite ‣ **Haȟébi duká micíkši nahą kníšį.** It is nighttime, but my son has not come home yet. ‣ **Iyé táwa oká éwejimnagu.** It was hers, but I took it from her. ‣ **Waȟpé wacíga duká huȟnáȟyabi kéš mak'ú.** I wanted tea, but she gave me coffee instead. ‣ **Wahí duká wącímnage wahíšį.** I came but not to see you. ‣ **Nína dąyą i'á duká wįcášta žená anáǧoptąbišį.** She spoke very well although the people did not listen to her. ‣ **Céya:ga uká wéktaší.** Despite her constant crying, I did not get up. ‣ **Ȟtánihą káda oká, nągáhą nína káda.** Even though it was hot yesterday, now it is very hot. *encl* 2) should, obligation to do smth (marker of deontic modality) ‣ **Hą! Waná ukní duká!** We should go home now. ‣ **Žecú duká wo!** You should do that! ‣ **Néci úkta oká.** She should come here. ‣ **Miyé žécen įmnúcą duká ecúbiší.** According to me they did not do it. 3) should have, would have, supposed to *Usage:* following the potential/future enclitic *kta* it expresses counterfactuality. ‣ **Úkteší dukáȟ.** He should not have come. ‣ **Hąyákena úkta oká, nína wówaši ecú.** He was to come this

morning, but he was too busy working. ▸
Tawáci ̧ da ̧yá ̧ u ̧káš waštékta oká. It would be
nice if he had a straight mind. ▸ **Úkteši ̧ u ̧ká.** He
should not have come. ▸ **Táȟca owaní ̧kta u ̧ká.**
I was intending to look for a deer (but none
showed up). ▸ **Žé ecámu ̧kta u ̧ká.** I meant to do
that (but I did not). ▸ **Taníješ žécedukta u ̧ká.** It
almost happened in this way.

duktám *adv* away from a place; to somewhere
▸ **Duktám yá.** He went away from a place.
▸ **Duktám yábi.** They left to somewhere.
▸ **Duktám ináne žehá ̧ pağú ̧da žená
špa ̧wícawaya.** While you were gone I cooked
these geese. (Cumberland 2005:416)

dukté *pro* what, which one (of a set) ▸ **Dukté
okmábi waštéyana?** What color do you like?
▸ **Dukté nitáwa?** Which one is yours? ▸ **Dukté
yací ̧ga, júsina žé eštáš tága žé?** Which one do
you want, a small one or a big one?

duktédaha ̧ *adv* from where, where ▸ **Duktédaha ̧
yahí?** From where did you arrive? ▸ **Duktédaha ̧
šiná né éyagu hú ̧n.** I wonder where he got
this blanket.

duktédu *vimp* it happened somewhere as such ▸
Duktéduȟtiya ̧? Where did it happen exactly?

duktédugaš *adv* wherever, anywhere

duktéduȟ *adv* exactly as such ▸ **Duktéduȟ yi ̧gá
žé wa ̧mnága.** I saw exactly where it was sitting.

dukté'ega kóšta *pro* any which one, whichever
one ▸ **Dukté'ega kóšta mína wací ̧ga.** I want
any knife.

duktéȟ *adv* somewhere ▸ **Duktéȟ wódi ̧kte žéca
oné!** Look for a place to eat! ▸ **Duktéȟ ékna ̧ga!**
Put it somewhere! ▸ **Mini ̧ nén yanú ̧wa ̧ ejé ektá
duktéȟ i ̧š yatí búzakta.** You will only swim in
water, but your home will be dry. (NS 2002:32)

duktékten ; duktékte *adv-redup* here and there;
occasionally ▸ **Duktékten cup'ó.** It is foggy
here and there. ▸ **Omáȟkağe žén í ̧ya ̧ nówa
duktékte ya ̧gá.** The rocks are scattered here
and there in the field. (Cumberland 2005:253)

▸ **Yuká ̧, duktékten.** There are, here and there.
(Cumberland 2005:421)

duktén *adv* where, at what place ▸ **Nikúši duktén
tí?** Where does your grandmother live? ▸
Duktén šú ̧ga žé wa ̧nága he? Where did you
see that dog?

duktén tú ̧bi *cp* place of birth

dukténi *adv* nowhere

dukténiȟ *adv* nowhere at all

dukténiši ̧ *vs* it is nowhere

duktépadaha ̧ *adv* from where

duktéyaš *pro* whichever one

duškế *vs* 1) s/he/it is a runt ▸ **Miši̧c'eši wa ̧ží
duškế.** One of my cousins is a runt. *1s*: **madúške**
2s: **nidúške** *n* 2) runt

duwé *pro* 1) who ▸ **Duwé gicí yahí?** Who did you
come with? ▸ **Duwé wa ̧nága?** Who did you see?
n 2) person ▸ **Né duwé Peter.** This is Peter. ▸
Duwé yazá ̧ há ̧da Jesus yuwáka ̧ When a person was sick Jesus blessed him by imposing
his hands. *quant* 3) nobody *Usage:* followed by
a negated verb. ▸ **Duwé híši ̧.** Nobody came. *vs*
4) s/he is someone ▸ **Madúwe he?** Who am I? ▸
Žé duwé? Who is that? *1s*: **madúwe** *2s*: **nidúwe**
Vrefl: **duwé i ̧c'ína**

duwé i ̧c'ína *vi3-refl* s/he thinks of himself/her-
self as such a person ▸ **Duwé i ̧c'ína?** Who does
he think he is? *1s*: **duwé mi ̧c'ína** *2s*: **duwé
ni ̧c'ína**

duwéga kóšta *pro* anyboby, just anybody, no
matter who ▸ **Duwéga kóšta ú cá.** Anybody
can come. ▸ **Duwéga kóšta ecú ogíhi.** Anybody can do it.

duwégaš *pro* 1) whoever ▸ **Duwégaš nína
wi ̧któkto.** Whoever that was he was very bad.
▸ **Duwégaš i ̧š dóha ̧ni snok'ú ̧yabi ̧kteši ̧.** Whoever that was we will never know *vs* 2) whoever
s/he is ▸ **Nidúwegaš i ̧kpázo.** Whoever you are
show yourself. *1s*: **madúwegaš** *2s*: **nidúwegaš**

duwéȟ *pro* 1) who (presupposed by the speaker)
▸ **Duwéȟ kišnéyaya?** Who do you love specif-

ically? 2) somebody (known to the speaker) ‣ **Duwéȟ toká hí.** Somebody different came. 3) whoever (unknown to the speaker) ‣ **Duwéȟ hí!** Whoever is here!

duwéni *Variant:* **duwéna** *pro* nobody, no one, none *Usage:* followed by a negated verb. ‣ **Duwéni níšį.** No one survived. ‣ **Duwéni híšį.** Nobody came.

duwéni aktúguyešį *cp* illegitimate child *Lit:* s/ he has no father

duwéniȟ *pro* absolutely nobody, no one ‣ **Misúgabi néna duwéniȟ ȟáskešį.** None of my younger brothers is tall.

duwénišį *vs* s/he/it is nobody ‣ **Ókšą akídabi ųká duwénišį.** They looked around but there was nobody. *1s:* **madúwenišį** *2s:* **nidúwenišį**

duwénišį įc'ína *vi3-refl* s/he considers himself/herself as nobody *1s:* **duwénišį mįc'ína** *2s:* **duwénišį nįc'ína**

dųwÁ *vi1* s/he opens his/her eyes ‣ **"Wąžíȟ yadúwąbi štén įštá né nišášabiktac" eyága.** "If one of you opens your eyes, your eyes will be red," he said. (NS 2002:43) *1s:* **wadúwą** *2s:* **yadúwą**

dųwé hí *vi1* s/he arrives scouting *1s:* **dųwé wahí** *2s:* **dųwé yahí** *1p:* **dųwé ųhíbi**

dųwé'i *vi1* s/he went scouting ‣ **Ga'éca žehác'ehą žehádahą, koškábi néca dųwé'ibis'a.** Then at that time some young men were out scouting from there. (Shields 29:108)

dųwé'u *vi1* s/he comes scouting *1s:* **dųwé wa'ú** *2s:* **dųwé ya'ú** *1p:* **dųwé ų'úbi**

dųwéyA *vi2* s/he goes scouting *1s:* **dųwémna** *2s:* **dųwéna** *1p:* **dųwé'ųyabi**

E

é- *pref* 1) to, at, there, toward, in this direction ‣ **bazó > ébazo** s/he shows, points at smth > s/he points his/her finger, gun at smth ‣ **tí > éti** s/ he dwells, lives somewhere > s/he camps there

2) they *Usage:* marks the collective plural form of some intransitive verbs. ‣ **nážį > énažį** s/he stands > they stand ‣ **iyódągA > éyodągA** s/he sits down > they sit down

é *vs* it is *Usage:* used to specify or clarify the identity of something or somebody previously mentioned. ‣ **Wįcášta timáni hí žé minékši é.** The man who came to visit is my uncle. (Cumberland 2005:417) ‣ **Wíyą žé Mary Šúgasaba é'.** That woman is Mary Black Dog. (Parks et al. 1999:39)

ébazo *vt1* s/he points his/her finger, gun at sb, smth

ecá *vs* s/he/it is thus, is of that kind ‣ **Watápabi onówą ecá.** It is a buffalo hunter song. ‣ **Ecá cén wanágaš tatága yúdabi jé.** Because it was like that long ago, they always ate buffalo. *1s:* **emáca** *2s:* **eníca** *Vcaus:* **ecákiyA**

ecábišį *n* invisible spirit, ghost

ecágen *adv* constantly, always, all the time ‣ **Ecágen pamáyazą.** I have a constant headache. ‣ **Ecágen dóki yá.** She is always gone. ‣ **Ecágen asásciya.** I am always proud of you. ‣ **Ecágen yacéya.** You cry all the time.

ecágici'ųbi *vi1-recip* they did smth for one another *1p:* **ecá'ųgici'ųbi**

ecágic'ų *vt3-pos* s/he does his/her own ‣ **Dágu yuhé íš iyúhana wíyeya ecágic'ų.** He prepared everything he had. (Drummond 1976, A bear story)

ecágiji'ų *vt1/3-benef* s/he does smth for sb ‣ **Dágu ecácijimųkte no.** I will do something for you. ‣ **Dágu ecáyejinų?** What did you do for him? ‣ **Wįcášte ecáwįca'ųgiji'ųbi.** We did it for the people. *1s:* **ecáwejimų** *2s:* **ecáyejinų**

ecá'įc'ų *vi3-refl* s/he prepares, does smth to himself/herself ‣ **Áa, yupíya ecá'įc'ų.** Ah, she prepared herself nicely. (Weasel 191:57)

ecákiyA *vt1* s/he considers, thinks sb is as such ‣ **Wíyą žé cądéšija ecáwakiya.** I thought that woman was sad. *1s:* **ecáwakiya** *2s:* **ecáyakiya** *1p:* **ecá'ųkiyabi**

ecámna *vi* it has a smell, odor; it smells ‣ **Asábi žé ecámna.** The milk has an odor. ‣ **Waná ecámna!** Now it is smelly!

ecą́na *adv* during that time, meanwhile ‣ **Ecą́na agípe mągá.** I waited during that time. ‣ **Ecą́naȟ napómyabi.** Right during that time they bombed it.

ecédu *vs* 1) s/he/it is like this, it happens as such, it is the right way ‣ **Mį́š emácedu!** I am like this too! ‣ **Eyáš ecédu.** It is all right. *1s:* **emácedu** *2s:* **enícedu** *adv* 2) equally, the same way, the right way ‣ **Ecédušį ecú́.** He does it in an uncommon way.

ecéduȟ *adv* in this exact way, manner; exactly like this; in the same manner ‣ **Ecéduȟ wóknaga.** She told it exactly the way it is. ‣ **Mį́š ecéduȟ míjağa!** Make me one exactly like this! ‣ **Dágu ecú́ hą́de ecéduȟ ecú́'!** Whenever he does something he does it in the same way!

ecédušį *vs* 1) it is uncommon, wrong, not the way it is supposed to be *adv* 2) in an uncommon way, not the way it is supposed to be ‣ **Ecédušį ecú́.** She does it in an uncommon way.

ecén *adv* 1) in the right, original way; accordingly; thus ‣ **Ecén ecámų.** I do it as I should. ‣ **Ecén ecánų?** In which way are you doing it? ‣ **Ecén įš wacéwagiye no!** That is the way I pray. ‣ **Akí ecén wįcák'u!** Treat them equally! ‣ **Ecén epé no!** I said it thus! *conj* 2) then, and then, so ‣ **Wíyą žé hí, ecén éyagu.** The woman arrived, and then she took it.

ecéya *vs* s/he/it is in such disposition; is affected by smth; happens ‣ **Ceȟníbi ecéyabi.** They have a sexual disease. ‣ **Hąwí žehą́ emáceya.** I have my menses. ‣ **Aké ecéya štén, dóken ecú́kta cén?** If it happens again, how would he react? ‣ **Wanągaš ųgéceyabi.** Long ago it happened to us. ‣ **Wįcóyazą síja cá Įkcé wįcášta**

oyáde iyúha ecéyabi. All of the Indigenous people suffered from a severe epidemic. *1s:* **emáceya** *2s:* **eníciya** *1p:* **ųgéceyabi** *Vbenef:* **egíjiceya**

éceyen *adv* only ‣ **Žé éceyen wacíga.** I want that one only.

ecí *vt1, vt3* s/he thinks, wonders about smth *Usage:* used with a preceding quote. ‣ **"Wanúȟ duwéȟ ú," ecí.** "Maybe there is someone coming," she thought. ‣ **"Dóken waȟ'ą́ štén nahą́n wįcámnuda ų́kaš," ecí.** "What can I do so I can eat them?" he thought. (NS 2002:42) *1s:* **ewáci** ; **ecámį** *2s:* **eyáci** ; **ecáni** *1p:* **ųgécibi** *See:* **gecí**

ecíbağa *vt1* 1) s/he collides with sb, smth 2) s/he joins the two ends together; meets sb

écipa *vi1-recip* they (things, people) meet one another

ecíyadahą *adv* from there ‣ **Ecén napábic'ehą gakíȟ Cągúsam, ecíyadahą í.** And so they fled, over there in the United States, they went from there.

ecú́ *vt3* s/he does smth ‣ **Ecú́šį.** Do not do it. ‣ **Ecú́šį žé wąmnága.** I saw that she did not do it. ‣ **Ecánų oyágihi?** Can you do it? ‣ **Dąyą́ ecánųšį.** You did not do well. ‣ **Dóhąni ecámųktešį no.** I will never do it again. ‣ **Dágu wakáya ecú́šį.** He did not do it in a holy way. ‣ **Dágu ecámųkta.** I have to do something. *1s:* **ecámų** *2s:* **ecánų** *1p:* **ecú́gųbi** *Vabs:* **wa'écų** *Vbenef:* **ecágiji'ų** *Vcaus:* **ecú́kiyA** *Vpos:* **ecágic'ų** *Vrecip:* **ecágici'ųbi** *Vrefl:* **ecá'įc'ų**

ecú́ gabí *vi1* s/he is lazy ‣ **Košká žé ecú́ gabí.** This boy is lazy. *1s:* **ecú́ wagábį** *2s:* **ecú́ yagábį** *3p:* **ecú́ gabį́bi**

ecú́bi *n* ceremony

ecú́bina *n* game, any kind of contest *Syn:* **ecú́na**

ecú́hą *adv* while ‣ **Ecú́hą yá, tída wa'ú́.** While he was gone, I stayed home.

ecú́kiyA *vt1-caus* s/he makes sb do it; s/he allows smth, sb to do smth ‣ **Žécen mikúši**

ecúmakiya. My grandmother let me do that. ▸ Iná ecúmakiyešį. Mom did not let me do that. 1s: ecúwakiya 2s: ecúyakiya 1p: ecú'ųkiyabi

ecúna n 1) game vi3 2) s/he gambles ▸ Mitákona, ecúnašį! My friend, do not gamble! ▸ Iná gicí ecúna. She gambles with my mom.

ecúnas'a n player, gambler ▸ Jim ecúnas'a žecášį. Jim is not a gambler.

ecúpija vs it can be done

edáhą quant 1) some of that Usage: used with mass nouns. ▸ Wahpé edáhą mak'ú! Give me some tea! ▸ Wicíjana né asábi edáhą cįgá. This girl wants some milk. 2) some of a larger group Usage: used with countable nouns. ▸ Tanó edáhą manú. He stole some pieces of meat. ▸ Duwé taspá ğí edáhą nik'ú? Who gave you some oranges? ▸ Cá edáhą nén agú wo! Bring some wood here! vs 3) s/he/it is from (a place or tribe); is a member of a group ▸ Céğa K'ína emádahą. I am from Carry The Kettle. (Cumberland 2005:359) 1s: emádahą 2s: enídahą

édu vimp it is there, it is the place, time ▸ Wédu ába édu én wóknąkmąkiyabi. On this spring day they want me to tell a story. (Shields 44:3) Adv: éduȟ

éduȟ adv where exactly

éduna adv coming close (in space and time)

édunaȟ adv close by, near ▸ Édunaȟ úbi. They stayed close by.

édųwą ; eduwą vt1 s/he looks, faces in a direction ▸ Žedám édųwą. Look that way. ▸ Tągán éduwą wáhįhą. Look outside it is snowing. ▸ Wįcá žé dąyágen ókšą éduwą. The man looked around carefully. ▸ Yakná štén anúk éduwą. When you leave look both ways. 1s: éwaduwą 2s: éyaduwą

é'e vs it is him/her/it/them Usage: only used in the 3rd person. ▸ É'ešį hí. It is the wrong one who came. ▸ Hiyá, é'ešįc. No, that is not it. See: né'e, žé'e

é'ehe interj alas ▸ É'ehe, wagágana mni'ót'a. Alas! the old woman drowned. (Weasel 75:300)

égihųni vt1-pos s/he reaches the end of his/her own (studies, work) 1s: éwagihųni 2s: éyagihųni

egíjiceya vs-benef it happens for sb, to sb 1s: emíjiceya 2s: eníjiceya

égijiknągA vt1-benef s/he puts, places smth down for him/her 1s: éwejiknąga 2s: éyejiknąga

égijikne vt1-benef s/he puts, places smth ready for sb ▸ Miníkta égijikne. He put it in the water for him. (Weasel 38:58) 1s: éwejikne 2s: éyejikne 1p: é'ųgijiknebi

égijiyagu vt1-benef s/he takes, holds sb, smth for/from him/her ▸ Micíkši émijiyagubi. They took my son from me. ▸ Mázaska iyúha é'ųgijiyagubi. They took all of our money. ▸ Iyé táwa duká éwejimnagu. It was hers but I took it from her. 1s: éwejimnagu 2s: éyejimnagu 1p: é'ųgijiyagubi

égiknągA vt1-pos s/he puts, places his/her own thing down (feet, bag) ▸ Sihá kún égiknąga. Put your feet down. ▸ Sąksája žé iyúksa égiknąga. She shortened her dress and put it down.

egíya ; ejíya vt1-dat 1) s/he tells sb smth ▸ Oȟ! Žé ewícayagiya. Oh! You told them that. ▸ Né Įktómi owóknage né wanágaš žé ųgégiyabis'a ųjúsibina žehą. They used to tell us this Įktomi story when were small. (Drummond 1976, Įktomi) 1s: ewágiya 2s: eyájiya 1p: ųgégiyabi Vcaus: ejíyakiyA vs-pass 2) s/he/it is called (by a name) Usage: requires the marker -bi. ▸ Dóken egíyabi he? How is he called? ▸ Dóken eníjiyabi he?—Mary emágiyabi. How are you called?—I am called Mary. ▸ Įktómi ejíyabi húštá. He was called Įktómi, it is said. 1s: emágiya 2s: eníjiya 1p: ųgégiyabi

eháš adv 1) too much, exceedingly ▸ Eháš nína skúya. It is too sweet. ▸ Eháš štušténa óda ecú.

She used too much salt. 2) surely, quite ‣ **Eháš wanáyaȟ'ųšį.** You surely do not listen. ‣ **Eháš onįkte wacį.** He is quite a coward.

ehą *adv* then, as it happened, at a specific point in the past *Usage:* often translates the English past tense. ‣ **Asábi eháš ehą.** There was too much milk. *See:*-**c'ehą**

ehádahą *adv* since *See:* **žehádahą**

ehádu *vs* it was the time when

ehą'i *vi1* 1) s/he/it reaches, arrives at a certain point ‣ **Huhúžubina ektá ehąwa'i.** I reached Regina. ‣ **Miní žé cehúba žén ehą'i.** The water reached his chin. ‣ **Mitáwacį waštéya ehąwa'i.** I reached my goal with a good heart. *1s:* **ehąwa'i** *2s:* **ehąya'i** *1p:* **ehą'ųgibi** *Vpos:* **ehąki** *vs* 2) it is such hour, day of the week, year ‣ **Waná ába įdóba ehą'i.** It is now Thursday. ‣ **Dóna ehą'i he?—Wąží ehą'i.** What time is it?—It is one o'clock.

ehąki *vt1-pos* 1) s/he reaches, arrives at a certain point 2) s/he is of a certain age *Usage:* used after the numbers of winters/years. ‣ **Dóna ehąyaki?—Waníyedu wikcémna núba ehąwaki.** How old are you?—I am twenty years-old. *1s:* **ehąwaki** *2s:* **ehąyaki** *1p:* **ehą'ųkibi**

ehąn *adv* then

e'įc'iya *vi3-refl* s/he talks to himself/herself *1s:* **emįc'iya** *2s:* **enįc'iya**

ejé ; ecé *adv* only, nothing but, exclusively ‣ **Ecé ecú.** Do only that. ‣ **Miní nén yanųwą ejé ektá duktéȟ įš yatí búzakta.** You will only swim in water, but your home will be dry. (NS 2002:32)

ejé'ena ; ejéna *adv* only, simply, alone, just ‣ **Mary šiná ejé'ena gáǧa žé opéwatų.** I bought the only blanket Mary made. ‣ **Yámni ejé'ena yazábišį.** Only three of them were not sick. ‣ **Jim ejé'enaȟ aháge.** Jim is simply the last one left. ‣ **Né miní ejéna wąyák wa'ų né įmástusta.** I am tired of only seeing this water. (NS 2002:28)

ejíyakiyA *vt1-caus* s/he makes sb say it ‣ **Iyé**

ejíyawakiya. I made him say something. *1s:* **ejíyawakiya** *2s:* **ejíyayakiya** *1p:* **ejíya'ųkiyabi**

éknagu *vt1-pos* s/he takes his/her own back ‣ **Ektá yá híkna éknagu!** Go there and take your own back! *1s:* **éwaknagu** *2s:* **éyaknagu**

éknągA *vt1* s/he/it puts, places smth down, away ‣ **Gakí éknąga.** Put it over there. ‣ **Ocábaza éwįcawaknąga.** I put them in the pasture. ‣ **Duktén éwaknąga giksúyįkta šką.** Try to remember where I put them. ‣ **Duwé į'įjuna gá awódabi agąn éknąga he?** Who put that cup over there on the table? *1s:* **éwaknąga** *2s:* **éyaknąga** *1p:* **ųgéknągabi** *Vbenef:* **égijiknągA** *Vpos:* **égiknągA**

ékne *vt1* s/he puts, places smth somewhere ‣ **Amųgiya tí žé ékne.** Put it in the garage. ‣ **Amųgiya žé tí gakná ékne.** Put the car beside the house. ‣ **Mitúgaši, wóyude nén éknebi žé ahómįjitą'į.** Grandfather, bless the food that is placed here for me. *1s:* **éwakne** *2s:* **éyakne** *Vbenef:* **égijikne**

ektá *post* at, in, to a location or destination ‣ **Húgu Céǧa K'įna ektá tí.** Her mother lives at Carry The Kettle. ‣ **Owáyaco ektá mnįkta.** I am going to court. ‣ **Wanągaš Šiyóša ektá wa'í.** I went to Red Pheasant long ago. ‣ **Wanągaš wazíȟe ektá, étibi žén.** Long people were camped there in Cypress Hills. ‣ **Iná tí ektá amáya'i.** Take me to mom's place. *Redup:* **ektáktaš** *See:* **ektám**

ektá ųbi owáyawa *ph* boarding school

ektágiya *adv* toward this direction ‣ **Ektágiya mnákta.** I will go in this direction.

ektáktaš *post-redup* at, in, to various locations or destinations; wherever ‣ **Níyuhana ektáktaš iyúha sna'įc'iya.** He slathered himself everywhere. (Weasel 20:242)

ektám *post* there, in a place *Usage:* often used with cardinal directions. ‣ **Dóhąni o'écųna tíbi ektám né wa'íšį.** I never went to the casino. ‣ **Wiyóȟpeya ektám, Taȟé nén matúbi no!**

There in the West, I was born here in Moose Mountains.

ektáş̌i *adv* wrongly ‣ **Ektáş̌i ecánu.** You did it wrongly. *Redup:* **ektáş̌iş̌i**

ektáş̌iş̌i *adv-redup* mistakenly ‣ **Ektáş̌iş̌i tiyóba né kó gazába [...]** She mistakenly opened the door [...] (NS 2002:20) *See:* **néš**

én *post* 1) in, into, on, onto, at, to ‣ **Įníbi én iyódąga.** They are sitting in the sweatlodge. ‣ **Céǧa K'ína én mątúbi.** I was born in Carry The Kettle. ‣ **Mikúši owókšubi én ú.** My grandmother is in the garden. ‣ **Núǧe én owážiži.** I whispered in her ear. ‣ **Mína žé cą'ówą én yįgéş̌i.** The knife is not on the floor. ‣ **Tiyóba én náž̧i.** He stands at the door. ‣ **Én imá'a.** Talk to me. *adv* 2) here, there ‣ **Én yįgá!** Sit here! ‣ **Gicí én wa'úş̌i.** I was not there with her.

én yągábi *ph* living room

énaž̧i *vi1-coll* they (collectively) stand up ‣ **Žécen waná eyáš, énaž̧i.** So now they were all standing in a line. (Weasel 84–85)

énapA *vi1-coll* they emerge, rise

epcá *vi1* I think, it seems, apparently *Usage:* used with 1st person singular only. *See:* **gepcá, gepcámi̧**

éstena *adv* early, soon, right away ‣ **Éstena giktá.** She wakes up early. ‣ **Éstena yuštą́bįkta.** They will release him soon. ‣ **Éstena amásni.** I recovered right away. *Redup:* **éstestena**

éstestena *adv-redup* very early, soon, quickly ‣ **Įí, né "Éstestena mįksúya. Atą́ga," eciya.** So this one [said], "Quickly remember me. Try hard," she told him. (Weasel 69:152)

éš *vs* it is it; it is indeed *Usage:* expresses a contrast between an expected event and what actually occurs.

eštá *conj* 1) or, either ‣ **Tanó eštá wahą́bi yacíga he?** Do you want meat or soup? ‣ **Hokšína otí'įga, eštáš wįcíjana?** I guess it is a boy, or else a girl? 2) whether it is the case or not

‣ **Įwícamųǧa eštáš ecúbi he?** I asked them whether they did it or not.

éti *vi1* s/he camps there (in a remote place) ‣ **Iyúha žén étibi.** People were camped there. ‣ **Wanągaš Wazíh̊e ektá étibi žén.** Long ago, people were camped there at Cypress Hills.

eyÁ *vt-irr* s/he says smth ‣ **Aké eyá wo!** Say it again! ‣ **Dóken epíkta he?** How could I say this? ‣ **Eyábi wacígiş̌i.** I do not want to say it. ‣ **Nakón'i'ábi dóken eyábi he?** How do they say it in Nakoda? ‣ **Nécen epá jé núš.** That is the way I always say it. ‣ **Nah̊'ú ųkáš, aké epéş̌i cá.** If he had been listening, I would not have to say it again. *1s:* **epá** *2s:* **ehá** *1p:* **ųgéyabi** *Vcaus:* **ejíyakiyA** *Vrecip:* **gicíyabi** *Vrefl:* **e'íc'iyA** *See:* **žeyÁ, gáyA**

éyabaha *n* hilltop announcer

éyagu *vt2* s/he takes, seize, grasps sb, smth ‣ **Pežúda éyagu.** He takes medicine. ‣ **Edáhą énagu? —Hiyá, dágu émnaguş̌i.** Did you take any? —No, I did not take any. ‣ **Wį'íde émayagu.** She took a picture of me. ‣ **Pąǧí šašá žená éyagu.** Take those red potatoes. *1s:* **émnagu** *2s:* **énagu** *1p:* **ųgéyagubi** *Vbenef:* **égijiyagu**

-eyasą; -e'asą ; -(e)są *suff* throughout, during ‣ **ába > ąbéyasą** day > all day ‣ **hą-> hą'éyasą** night > all night long ‣ **omáka > omáka'esą** year > throughout the year, all year

eyáš *adv* 1) sufficient, enough, only, well enough *Usage:* often pronounced as [á:š]. ‣ **Eyáš ožúya.** Fill it up sufficiently. ‣ **Eyáš wįkta óda yúhabi.** They have enough eggs. ‣ **Eyáš snokkíciyabi.** They know one another quite well. 2) any, anyways ‣ **Dókejaş̌i eyáš wąmnágįkta.** I does not matter, I will see her anyways. ‣ **Eyáš dókiyo yábi yacíge yá.** Just go any which way you want to go.

eyaš *conj* but, and yet ‣ **Huh̊náh̊yabi mak'úbi duká miní eyaš wacíga.** They gave me coffee but I just want water.

éyayA *vt2* s/he takes, sets to go with sb, smth there ‣ **Žéci éyaya.** He takes him over there. ‣ **Yuwágan eyáya ecédu dóki kowá eyáya tą'į́šį.** It lifted him up, then it took him out of sight. (NS 2002:15) *1s:* **émnamna** *2s:* **énana**

eyés'a *n* chatterbox, blabbermouth

eyéši *vt1-dit* s/he orders sb to say it

éyodągA *vi1-coll* they sit down

G

ga- *pref* 1) by striking, hitting with an instrument ‣ **céya > gacéya** s/he cries > s/he made sb cry by pushing, hitting 2) by the blowing wind; by the heat of the sun ‣ **busyá > gabúsya** s/he dries smth > s/he dries smth, let smth dry in the wind, sun 3) by itself

-ga *encl* marker of durative aspect *Usage:* marks a repetitive or continuous action or event that occurs within a definite period of time; lengthens a preceeding vowel. ‣ **Gą́na:ga hįníga.** The older she got, the meaner she became. ‣ **Céya:ga ųká wéktašį.** Despite her constant crying, I did not get up. ‣ **Mi'áde įštíma:ga.** My father is fast asleep. ‣ **Šųkcúk'ana né tą́ħca ksu'į́c'iye žé kní:gabi.** The coyotes kept coming back at the injured deer.

gá₁ *dem* that one over there ‣ **Gá dágu?** What is that yonder? ‣ **Šų́ga gá aktága.** That dog over there is running. ‣ **Wįcíjana gá asą́bi cįgá.** That girl over there wants milk.

gá₂ *conj* and *Usage:* links two clauses. ‣ **Wówaši ektá imnámna gá wakní žehą́ waná mayázą.** I went to work and when I came home I was already sick. ‣ **Wahą́bi káda yaktą́ gá cagá špą́.** He drank hot soup and burned his palate. (Fourstar p. 9)

-gA ; a- . . . -gA ;-gejA ;-jA *suff* rather, somewhat, kind of (attenuator of gradable expressions) ‣ **Osníga no!** It is rather cold! ‣ **Wįcá**

né wįtkótkoga. This man is kind of crazy. ‣ **Anístustaga.** You look rather tired. ‣ **Yahį́kta hą́da žehą́duga he?** At about what time will you arrive? ‣ **Nakón'iwa'ageja.** I kind of speak Nakoda.

-ga kóšta *part* any, no matter which/who/what (lack of interest) ‣ **Duwéga kóšta ú cá.** Anybody can come. ‣ **Miyéga kóšta ecámųšį ca.** Even I would not do that.

ga'áktagA *vt1* s/he hits sb, smth while running *Vcont:* **ga'áktak**

ga'áktak *vcont* hitting sb, smth while running

gabé *vt1* s/he spanks sb ‣ **Wįktókto cén wagábe.** He misbehaved, so I spanked him. ‣ **Gitézibina wįcáwagabe.** I spanked the brats. *1s:* **wagábe** *2s:* **yagábe**

gabį́ *vi1-aux* s/he is reluctant, hates doing smth *Usage:* follows a verb. ‣ **Koškáže ecú gabį́** This boy is lazy. ‣ **Ecú wagábį** I am lazy. *1s:* **wagábį** *2s:* **yagábį** *1p:* **ųgábį** *See:* **ecú gabį́**

gabúskiyA *vt1-pos* s/he dries, lets his/her own (clothes, blanket) dry in the wind, sun ‣ **Dágu nówa knužáža hį́k gabúskiya.** She washed all of their things and dried them in the sun. *1s:* **gabúswagiya** *2s:* **gabúsyagiya**

gabúsyA *vt1-caus* s/he dries smth, lets smth dry in the wind, sun ‣ **Oktéya hį́kna gabúsya.** Hang it and let it dry. *1s:* **gabúswaya** *2s:* **gabúsyaya** *1p:* **gabús'ųyabi**

gabúza *vt1* it is dried by the wind, sun ‣ **Tanó gabúza cén.** The meat got dried by the sun. *Vcaus:* **gabúsyA** *Vpos:* **gabúskiyA**

gabúzena *n* dandelion

gaca *encl* as if; something is unlikely to happen (often conveys a sense of ridicule) ‣ **Ecú ogíhi gaca!** As if he was capable of doing it! ‣ **Mázaska nuhé jaca.** As if you had money!

gacédu *vs* s/he/it is in such a way ‣ **Waná gacédu céyaga.** It is about time now. ‣ **Nahą́ħ gacédu céyagešį.** It must not have happened yet.

gacéȟ *adv* about ‣ **Įȟéyam nážįbi cá záptą gacéȟ.** They stood about five feet apart. (NS 2002:64)

gacén *adv* about, approximately ‣ **Wikcémna dóba gacén, né oyáde né wakníšį.** I did not come back in this community for about forty years.

gacéyA *vt1* s/he made sb cry by pushing, hitting ‣ **Wagábe hį́kna wagáceya.** I swatted her and made her cry.

gadáda *vt1* s/he shakes off, clears smth off ‣ **Wá gadáda hį́kna oné!** Clear the snow and look for it!

gadáhą *quant* some (unspecified amount) ‣ **Gadáhą mak'ú!** Give me some! (whatever it is)

gadám *adv* over there, away in that direction ‣ **Gadám yá.** Move away. ‣ **Gadám cąwóhą yá wo.** Go over there in the woods.

gadíyą ; ganíyą *adv* straight, directly; in a beeline, straight line ‣ **Gadíyą máni!** Walk in a straight line! ‣ **Gadíyą néci hí.** He came straight here. ‣ **Gadíyą žéci iyáyabi.** They went straight over there. ‣ **Eyáš gadíyą ektá yá.** Well, he went straight toward them. (NS 2002:78) ‣ **Néci ganíyą híbi.** They came directly here.

gadódo *vt1* 1) s/he shakes, brushes, sweeps, dusts smth off ‣ **Wá žená ųgádodobi.** We swept the snow off. 2) s/he/it pecks sb, smth (tree, ground) *1s:* **wagádodo** *2s:* **yagádodo** *1p:* **ųgádodobi** *Vrefl:* **knadódo**

gadónawąga *vii* it (horse) gallops *Vcaus:* **gadónawąk kíyA** *Vcont:* **gadónawąk**

gadónawąk *vcont* galloping

gadónawąkkiyA *vt1-caus* s/he makes a horse gallop *1s:* **gadónawąkwakiya** *2s:* **gadónawąkyakíya** *1p:* **gadónawąkųkiyabi**

ga'éca *conj* and then ‣ **Hí ga'éca awóknagabi.** He arrived and then they talked about it. ‣ **Ga'éca gakí, gaȟópa ektá, hokšína né wąží škáda:ga.** And then over there, in the deep valley, one little boy was playing along.

gagá *voc* Grandfather! (address form) *Syn:* **ųká**

gagú *vt1-dat* s/he brings sb, smth coming back here *1s:* **wagágu** *2s:* **yagágu** *1p:* **ųgágubi**

gagúda *vt1* s/he makes a groove, notch with an axe *1s:* **wagágųda** *2s:* **yagágųda** *1p:* **ųgágųdabi**

gáǧA *vt1* 1) s/he makes smth ‣ **Waȟpé dóhąc'ehą yagáǧa?** When did you make tea? ‣ **Waȟábi edáhą gáǧa!** Make some soup! ‣ **Mary šiná gáǧa žé, opéwatų no.** I bought the blanket Mary made. ‣ **Įnį́bi wagáǧįkta.** I will make a sweatlodge. *vii* 2) s/he makes money *1s:* **wagáǧa** *2s:* **yagáǧa** *1p:* **ųgáǧabi** *Vabs:* **wagáǧA** *Vbenef:* **gíjaǧA** *Vcaus:* **gaȟkíyA** *Vcont:* **gáȟ** *Vrefl:* **įc'íjaǧA** *See:* **maskáǧA**

gaǧábi *n* clothes *Syn:* **hayábi**

gaǧé *vt1* s/he rakes, gathers, sweeps smth together (leaves, snow) ‣ **Waȟpé žená gaǧé.** Rake the leaves. ‣ **Sihá ų́s gaǧé.** He raked it together using the foot.

gaǧéǧe *vt1-redup* s/he sews smth ‣ **Sąksája žé tahį́špa juk'ána ų́s wagáǧeǧe.** I sewed this dress with a needle. *1s:* **wagáǧeǧe** *2s:* **yagáǧeǧe** *Vabs:* **wagáǧeǧe** *See:* **agáǧeǧe**

gahádu *vs* 1) it will be around that time (in the future) 2) s/he/it is right there *Adv:* **gahán**

gaháduȟ *adv* around that time (not sure exactly when) ‣ **Gaháduȟ mná ca.** I am not sure when I will go.

gaháduȟtįyA *vs* it will be at that time exactly (in the future) ‣ **Gaháduȟtįyą štén wa'ú ca.** I do not know when I will come exactly.

gahágeȟ *adv* that far, not so far off

gahágeja *vs, adv* it is about that long, high, far *Usage:* used with remote objects or when guessing roughly. ‣ **Gahágeja įyútabi.** I am guessing it is about that size.

gahán *adv-cont* around that time *Usage:* used when guessing roughly.

gahí *vt1-dat* s/he arrives here bringing sb, smth to him/her ‣ **Pežíȟoda mągáhi úkta ųká.** He was supposed to bring me sage. *1s:* **wagáhi** *2s:* **yagáhi** *1p:* **ųgáhibi**

gahómni *vt1* s/he knocks, spins sb, smth around

gahóȟpA *vt1* s/he causes sb to cough by hitting

gahókšu *vt1* s/he dismantles smth; the wind blows smth down ‣ **Tí né wagáhokšu.** I dismantled this house. ‣ **Tíbi žé gahókšu.** The house is blown down.

gahómni wacíbi *cp* round dance, courting dance

gahówayA *vt1* s/he makes sb scream, cry by hitting on him/her/it ‣ **Nąbé awáhą wagáhowaya.** I step on her hand and make her scream.

gahų́hųza *vt1* it shakes by itself, or by the force of the wind ‣ **Ganų́za cén cą́ gahų́hųza.** Because it is windy the trees are shaking.

gáȟ *vcont* making smth ‣ **Huȟnáȟayabi gaȟší.** Tell him to make coffee.

gáȟ iyéyA *vt1* s/he makes smth quickly *Vbenef:* **gíjaȟ iyéyA**

gaȟcí *vt1* s/he slits smth; cuts a fringe *Vabs:* **wagáȟci** *Vredup:* **gaȟcíȟci**

gaȟcíȟci *vt1-redup* s/he cuts fringes *1s:* **wagáȟciȟci** *2s:* **yagáȟciȟci** *1p:* **ųgáȟciȟcibi**

gaȟé *n* 1) ravine, coulee, cut bank 2) mountain, hill

Gaȟé nų́ba *ngeo* Zurich (Montana)

gaȟkiyA *vt1-caus* s/he makes sb do it, let sb do it ‣ **Onákoda gaȟwícakiya.** He made them make peace. *1s:* **gaȟwákiya** *2s:* **gaȟyákiya**

gaȟmógA *vs* the wind is blowing smth off ‣ **Ti'ą́gam gaȟmóga.** The wind blew off the roof. ‣ **Nína wá gaȟmóga.** The snow is blowing away hard. ‣ **Waná kúdiyena gaȟmóga.** Now it is blowing close to the ground.

gaȟmógena *n* flag

gaȟná *vt1* s/he makes a rattling sound

gaȟnáda *vs* s/he/it is stained *1s:* **mągáȟnada** *2s:* **nįgáȟnada** *Vpos:* **gijáȟnada**

gaȟnáȟnabina *n-redup* baby rattle

gaȟnéjA *vt1* s/he tears, rips smth open by pressure, or with his/her own weight

gaȟní *vs* s/he/it is stuck *1s:* **magáȟni** *2s:* **nigáȟni**

gaȟníǧA *vt1* s/he selects, chooses sb, smth; elects, votes for sb ‣ **Wíyą žé wagáȟniǧa.** I chose that woman. ‣ **Hųgá gaȟníǧabi.** They elected a chief. *1s:* **wagáȟniǧa** *2s:* **yagáȟniǧa** *1p:* **ųgáȟniǧabi** *See:* **ká**

gaȟnógA *vt1* s/he makes a hole by striking with a tool *Vredup:* **gaȟnóȟnogA**

gaȟnóȟnogA *vt1-redup* s/he makes holes by striking with a tool

gaȟópa *n* canyon, ravine, valley, gully

gaȟpÁ *vt1* s/he takes smth down (as a tent) ‣ **Wí né tóm gaȟpá wó.** Take down four of the lodges. (Weasel 57:482) *Vpos:* **knaȟpÁ**

gaȟpíja *vs* it is possible to make, to do ‣ **Dágu gaȟpíjageší.** This thing is impossible to do.

gaȟší *vt1-dit* s/he orders sb to make it

gaȟtą́yĄ *vt1* s/he rubs smth against it ‣ **Awódabi gaȟtą́yeší.** Do not rub it against the table. *1s:* **gaȟtą́wayą** *2s:* **gaȟtą́yayą**

gaȟúga *vt1* s/he cracks smth; cracks smth open; crushes smth with a tool ‣ **Yahúgabi tą́ga gaȟúga.** He cracked the coconut. ‣ **Íyą žé ús gaȟúga.** He used a stone to crush it.

gaȟ'ú *vt1* s/he scrapes, peels, shaves, chips smth off ‣ **Cą́ žé gaȟ'ú.** Chip that piece of wood. ‣ **ocą́gu gaȟ'ú** grader

ga'íyodągA *vii* s/he/it sits down heavily *Vcont:* **ga'íyodąk**

ga'íyodąk *vcont* sitting down heavily ‣ **Ga'íyodąk įȟpéwaya.** I made him sit down heavily.

ga'íyowas *vcont* in an echo-like manner

ga'íyowaza *vt1* s/he makes an echo by bouncing, hitting smth; it makes an echo *Vcont:* **ga'íyowas**

ga'įdomni *vt1* it (wind) makes him/her dizzy

ga'įš *dem* that one over there ‣ **"Né yewákiya štén įš gá yekíyįkta, ga'įš, ga'įš, ga'įš".** "When I throw it to that one over there, he will throw it to that one over there, to that one over there, to that one over there." (NS 2002:23)

ga'ít'eya *vs* s/he/it died of old age

gáken *adv* in that way ‣ **Gáken ecú.** Do it that way. ‣ **Gáken owáštena įtkúkta.** That way it will burn slowly.

gakí *adv* way over there, yonder, in a distant area ‣ **Gakí dágu he?** What is that yonder? ‣ **Gakí dágu ecúbi hún.** I wonder what is going on over there. ‣ **Gakí iyódąga wo.** Sit over there. ‣ **Gakí wot'á.** It died over there.

gákiya *adv* over there

gákiyadahą *adv* from over there, yonder ‣ **Gá gákiyadahą gúbi.** And they came back from that direction.

gakíyaȟ *adv* at a specific or special place yonder ‣ **Šúga žé gakíyaȟ opáȟta.** Tie the dog over there specifically.

gákiyota *adv* in that direction

gakná *adv* beside, along sb, smth ‣ **Gakná yįgá!** Sit beside him! ‣ **Šųktága gakná nawážį.** I am standing beside the horse. ‣ **Nųpín gakná maníbi.** They both are walking along.

gakní *vt1-dat* s/he brings smth back to sb

gakókyA *vt1-caus* s/he/it makes a sound by hitting things together

gakpá *vt1* s/he crushes, pulverizes, grounds smth fine using a tool ‣ **Cąpá gakpá.** Pound the chokecherries.

gaksÁ *vt1* s/he cuts, chops smth with a tool (axe) ‣ **Hąyákena cą́ gaksá.** He chopped wood in the morning. ‣ **Ąbáhotųna žé pá gaksá.** He beheaded the chicken. ‣ **Waníȟą cą'íyutabi yámni wagáksa.** Last winter I chopped three cords of wood. *1s:* **wagáksa** *2s:* **yagáksa** *1p:* **ųgáksabi** *Vbenef:* **gíjaksA** *Vredup:* **gaksáksA**

gaksáksA *vt1-redup* s/he chops smth into pieces ‣ **Cą́ gaksáksa.** He chops wood. *1s:* **wagáksaksa** *2s:* **yagáksaksa** *1p:* **ųgáksaksabi**

gaksíksį *adv* in a zigzag manner ‣ **Žehą́ žéci**

bába, gaksíksį, aktága híkna įsą́'į iyáya. He was yelling and running back and forth and went out of sight. (Weasel 12:152)

gakšá *vt1* s/he coils, rolls smth up

gaktÁ *vi1* s/he chokes on smth

gaktá *adv* near that yonder

gaktú₁ *vt1* s/he shatters smth with a projectile (like a window) *1s:* **wagáktų** *2s:* **yagáktų** *1p:* **ųgáktųbi**

gaktú₂ *vt1* 1) s/he slices meat for drying *vi1* 2) s/he earns money *See:* **maskámna**

gakúkA *vt1* s/he/it crushes, mashes smth up (with a tool, by hitting, by the action of the wind) *1s:* **wagákuka** *2s:* **yagákuka** *1p:* **ųgákukabi**

gakún *adv* downward ‣ **Įknúhąna gakún yé stéya gá.** All at once it seemed he was heading down. (Weasel 32:119) *See:* **kún**

gak'óȟcąka *n* match

gamímA *vi1* s/he/it forms a circle *Adv:* **gamímeya**

gamímeya *adv* in a circle

gamná *vt1* 1) s/he slices smth (like meat for drying) ‣ **Zipzímneyaȟ gamnábi.** It was sliced up very very thin. (Drummond 1976, How the woman made pemmican) *vi1* 2) s/he earns money *Vabs:* **wagámna**

gamnámnaš *adv-redup* with the legs spread apart ‣ **Gamnámnaš máni.** It waddles.

gamnáska *vt1* s/he flattens smth down by striking, beating, hewing (as a piece of wood) *1s:* **wagámnaska** *2s:* **yagámnaska** *1p:* **ųgámnaskąbi**

gamnáš *adv* with the legs spread apart, open ‣ **Gamnáš įȟpé'įc'iya.** She threw herself on the ground with her legs spread apart. ‣ **Gamnáš yįgé žé ómna.** He smelled the one lying with the legs spread apart. *Redup:* **gamnámnaš**

gamnáyA *vt1* s/he throws, spreads smth out flat (fishnet) ‣ **Įktómi né gamnáya gamnáya:ga hík žécen aké makóce gáǧa.** He [Įktómi] spread it out far and wide and made the earth again (Drummond 1976, The flood)

gamnéja *vt1* 1) s/he/it destroys, shatters smth by hitting 2) the wind scatters, spreads smth out ▸ **Waȟpéȟpe né gamnéja.** The wind scattered the leaves. *1s:* **wagámneja** *2s:* **yagámneja** *1p:* **ųgámnejabi**

gamnézA *vimp* it is morning twilight, dawn ▸ **Mitúgaši, waná gamnéza.** Grandpa, it is now dawn.

gamnúkiyA *vt1-caus* s/he churns, airs out smth ▸ **Šiná gamnúwakiyįkta.** I will air out the blankets. *1s:* **gamnúwakiya** *2s:* **gamnúyakiya**

gamnúyA *vt1-caus* s/he/it (wind) airs out smth *1s:* **gamnúwaya** *2s:* **gamnúyaya**

gamú *vt1* s/he beats on smth; makes a drumming sound

gamúbi *n* 1) drum ▸ **Wakmúhą né minékši gáǧa.** My maternal uncle made this rattle. 2) cattail stem and fuzz

gamúbiha *n* drum case

gamúbina *n* small drum

gamúbipa *n* drum head

gamúyabi *n* drumstick

gán *adv* over there ▸ **Įtó gán tiwícoda tíbi.** Well, many families lived over there. ▸ **Žécen gán éknąga.** Then he put it over there. (NS 2002:30)

ganá *dem* those over there ▸ **Dágu ganá he?** What are those over there?

ganągeja *vs* it is that many; it is such an amount

ganáknana *adv* just a few, less than expected

ganąknanaȟ *adv* very few, way less than expected ▸ **Ganąknanaȟ mak'ú.** She gave me way less than expected.

ganú *vt1* s/he fans sb, smth ▸ **Nína káda! Ganú!** It is too hot! Fan it! ▸ **Péda žé wagánu.** I fanned the fire. *1s:* **wagánu** *2s:* **yagánu** *1p:* **ųgánubi** *Vredup:* **ganúnu**

ganúnu *vt1-redup* s/he fans sb, smth continuously *1s:* **wagánunu** *2s:* **yagánunu** *1p:* **ųgánunubi**

ganúsnuza *vimp* it is breezy *Adv:* **ganúsnuzagen**

ganúsnuzagen *adv* with a breeze ▸ **Ganúsnuzagen hą́'.** It remains breezy.

ganúza *vimp* 1) it is windy ▸ **Nína ganúza.** It is very windy. ▸ **Ȟtánihą nína ganúza híkna maǧážugeja.** Yesterday it was really windy and drizzling. *n* 2) wind ▸ **Ganúza žé yušnóga.** The wind uprooted it.

ganúza tą́ga *vimp* 1) it is a gale wind (between 63–87 km/h) 2) gale wind

gapá *vt1* s/he pounds smth to a pulp *Vredup:* **gapą́pą**

gapą́pą *vt1-redup* s/he pounds smth fine with a tool

gapéna *vt1* s/he sharpens smth ▸ **Cą́íkpa gapéna.** Sharpen the end of the stick. *1s:* **wagápena** *2s:* **yagápena** *Syn:* **yumą́**

gapésto *vt1* s/he shaves, sharpens a point with a tool

gap'óǧena *vs* s/he/it is light ▸ **Cą́ópiye žé gap'óǧena.** The box is light. ▸ **Nągáhąš mągáp'óǧena.** I am lighter now. *1s:* **mągáp'óǧena** *2s:* **nįgáp'óǧena**

gapsága *vt1* 1) s/he/it breaks, cuts smth (rope) by hitting 2) the wind breaks smth 3) it breaks, rips by itself

gapsápsą *vt1* 1) s/he/it swings, shakes smth that is hanging by hitting, pushing 2) it (wind) makes smth swing ▸ **Ȟaȟúda apáȟte žé gapsápsą hą́.** The rope that is tied up is swinging.

gapsídA *vt1* s/he whips sb, smth *1s:* **wagápsįda** *2s:* **yagápsįda** *1p:* **ųgápsįdabi** *Vredup:* **gapsípsįda** *Syn:* **gasága**

gapsíjA *vt1* s/he makes smth bounce, jump by striking; propels by striking

gapsíde *n* whip

gapsípsįdA *vt1-redup* s/he whips sb, smth repeatedly *Vcont:* **gapsípsįn**

gapsípsįn *vcont* whipping sb, smth repeatedly

gapsú *vt1* s/he hits smth accidently and it spills

▸ **Gapsú žé įȟpéya.** He knocked it off and it spilled.

gaptáyA *vt1* 1) s/he/it knocks, hits smth down; the wind knocks, hits smth down *vi1* 2) s/he has a car accident *1s:* **wagáptaya** *2s:* **yagáptaya** *1p:* **ųgáptayabi**

gaptúǧA *vt1* s/he chips, cracks smth with a tool ▸ **Ḷ'íjuna né wagáptuǧa.** I cracked this cup (with a spoon). ▸ **Įyaȟe žé gaptúǧįkta šká aknįkta cén.** He was trying to break up that mountain and bring it back. (Weasel 70:181) *1s:* **wagáptuǧa** *2s:* **yagáptuǧa** *1p:* **ųgátuǧabi**

gasága *vt1* s/he whips sb, smth ▸ **Né'įš šúgataga né, wįcágasagabi écen dóba yuksá'iyayabi huštá.** They whipped the horses and pulled him into four pieces, it is said. (Weasel 210:443) *1s:* **wagásaga** *2s:* **yagásaga** *Syn:* **gapsídA**

gasíjA *vt1* s/he ruins, breaks smth by hitting ▸ **Yá híkna gasíjac'eha.** Then he went over there and broke it. ▸ **Éyagu híkna gasíja.** She picks it all up and ruins it. *1s:* **wagásija** *2s:* **yagásija** *1p:* **ųgásijabi**

gaská *vt1* s/he whitens smth by rubbing

gaskÁ *vi* s/he/it (wind, heat) melts the snow ▸ **Maštá cén wá gaskÁ.** Because it is warm the snow melted.

gaskúyA *vt1* s/he stirs and sweetens smth *1s:* **wagáskuya** *2s:* **yagáskuya**

gasná *vt1* s/he makes smth ring, jingle by striking

gasnéjA *vt1* s/he chops smth in two, splits smth in two by hitting ▸ **Cá žé gasnéja!** Split the wood! *1s:* **wagásneja** *2s:* **yagásneja** *1p:* **ųgásnejabi**

gasní *vt1* 1) s/he smothers, puts out a fire, light ▸ **Há, miyéš wagásni yíkte no.** Ah, I will go myself and put out the fire. (Weasel 77:340) *1s:* **wagásni** *2s:* **yagásni** *1p:* **ųgásnibi** *Vpos:* **knasní** *vi* 2) the rain puts out a fire

gasódA *vi* 1) it (sky) cleared up *vt1* 2) s/he massacres, wipes out sb ▸ **Wįcábi, wíyabi, dáguškibina nówa wįcágasodabi.** They massacred every man, woman, and child. ▸ **Há:di**

bo misúga Įktómi iyúhana ųgásodabįkta. My brothers get out of here! Įktomi is going to wipe us all out. (Drummond 1976, Įktomi and the ducks) ▸ **"Įktómi né iyúhana nįjásodabikte no," eyá.** "Įktómi will do away with all of you," he said. (NS 2002:44) *1s:* **wagásoda** *2s:* **yagásoda** *1p:* **ųgásodabi** *Vcoll:* **wįcágasodA**

gaspá *vii* it (grease, snow, ice) is slushy ▸ **Wédu cén dágu iyúhana gaspá.** In the spring everything is slushy.

gaspéyA *vt1-caus* s/he understands sb, smth *Usage:* archaic. *Lit:* s/he grasps sb, smth ▸ **Gaspéyaya he?** Do you understand it? *1s:* **gaspéwaya** *2s:* **gaspéyaya** *1p:* **gaspé'ųyabi** *See:* **catkáspeya**

gastágA *vt1* s/he daubs, pastes, throws, pours out a gooey substance (as to make it stick); s/he glues smth *Vcont:* **gastástak**

gastástak *vcont-redup* pouring out

gastó *vt1* s/he pets an animal *1s:* **wagásto** *2s:* **yagásto**

gasúda *vimp* the wind compacts the snow

gaškÁ *vt1* s/he ties smth fast as to hold ▸ **Šúga žé gaška éwakne.** I tied up the dog.

gaška ayÁ *vt2* s/he leads an animal with a rope ▸ **Šuȟpéna né gaška anįkta.** You will lead this colt. *1s:* **gaška amná** *2s:* **gaška aná**

gaška yúzA *vt2* s/he leads sb, smth (as a dog, horse) on a rope

gaškí *vt1* s/he crushes, pounds, grinds smth; pulverizes berries using a stone ▸ **Capá gaškíbi.** They are crushing chokecherries. *1s:* **wagáški** *2s:* **yagáški**

gaškóbA *vt1* s/he makes a bent in smth (permanently); bends it with a tool

gašná₁ *vt1* s/he cuts smth short with a tool (hair, grass); mows the lawn ▸ **Pahá gašnábi wacíga.** I want a haircut. ▸ **Įš síyutabi dóba gašná.** It cuts a four feet swath [of wheat]. (Drummond 1976, Early days on Carry The Kettle reserve)

1s: **wagášna** *2s:* **yagášna** *Vbenef:* **gíjijašna** *Vpos:* **gíjašna**

gašná₂ *vt1* s/he misses smth (target, date) ▸ **Ába wąží žé wagášna.** I missed the date. *1s:* **wagášna** *2s:* **yagášna** *1p:* **ųgášnabi** *Vpos:* **knašná** *Vrecip:* **gicíjašnabi** *Vredup:* **gašnášna**

gašnášna *vt1-redup* s/he misses smth over and over ▸ **Ecágen gašnášna.** He always misses it over and over.

gašpá *vt1* s/he opens smth with an axe, tool; it opens by itself ▸ **Ganúza cén tiyóba gašpáyeya.** The door blew open. (Cumberland 2005:425) *1s:* **wagášpa** *2s:* **yagášpa** *1p:* **ųgášpabi** *Vbenef:* **gíjašpa**

gašpábi *n* 25 cents, quarter

gašpábi okíse *cp* dime, 10 cents *Lit:* half a quarter

gaštágA *vt1* 1) s/he knocks, hits, beats sb (with a tool, stick) ▸ **Gitézi wįcáwagaštagakta!** I will beat the brats! ▸ **Hį́į eyáš "Ektá nįjáštagabi cá mitágoža. Yéšį."** Oh, but [she said] "No, grandson, they will probably knock you out. Do not go." (Weasel 146:522–523) 2) s/he clubs sb, smth to death *1s:* **wagáštaga** *2s:* **yagáštaga** *1p:* **ųgáštagabi**

gaštą́ *vt1* s/he pours smth out

gat'Á *vt1* s/he kills, knocks sb by striking with a club ▸ **Koška né nigát'a he?** Did this young man knock you unconscious? (Parks et al. 1999:149) ▸ **Gat'á kó įȟpéya cén.** He even knocked him dead. (Cumberland 2005:376) *1s:* **wagát'a** *2s:* **yagát'a** *1p:* **ųgát'abi** *Vdat:* **gigát'A**

ga'ú *vt1-dat* s/he comes here bringing smth to sb ▸ **Mína magá'u.** Bring me a knife. *1s:* **wagá'u** *2s:* **yagá'u** *1p:* **ųgá'ubi** *Vbenef:* **gíja'u**

ga'ųspe *vt1* s/he trains, breaks an animal with a tool, stick ▸ **Šų́gatąga wagá'ųspe.** I train the horse. *1s:* **wagá'ųspe** *2s:* **yagá'ųspe** *1p:* **ųgá'ųspebi**

gawéwe *vt1-redup* s/he hits and makes sb, smth bleed *1s:* **wagáwewe** *2s:* **yagáwewe**

gawį́ga *vi* it glides in circles *Vcont:* **gawį́ȟwįȟ**

gawį́ȟwįȟ *vcont-redup* gliding in circles ▸ **Gawį́ȟwįȟ ų́.** It kept gliding in circles.

gawį́š *vcont* bent over by itself ▸ **Cą́ žé gawį́š yįgá.** The tree is bent over.

gawį́žA *vt1* 1) s/he/it bends smth by pushing, pressing with a tool *1s:* **gawáwįža** *2s:* **gayáwįža** *1p:* **ųgáwįžabi** *vi* 2) it bends over by itself or by the action of the wind *Vcont:* **gawį́š**

gawós *pro, dem* those two yonder ▸ **Gawós núba a'ú.** Bring these two yonder. ▸ **Gawós žéci éknąga!** Put those two yonder over there! ▸ **Gawós yábįkta.** Those two yonder are gone.

gáyA *Variant:* **gáyabi** ; **jáyA** *vi-irr* 1) s/he says, said; they say, it is said ▸ **Mnį́kta gápa.** I said I would go. ▸ **"Néci úbi"** gáya. "They are here," he said. ▸ **Wamnúhe gápešį.** I did not say I had it all. ▸ **Ába nén maštáȟtiyąkta,** gáyabi. Today will be the warmest day, it is said. ▸ **"Makóce né, né'įš nitáwabįkta,"** jáya. "This land, this too will be yours," he said. *1s:* **gápa** *2s:* **gáha** 2) third-hand source when used after eyá 's/he says' ▸ **"Žé waná hįknáwaya"** eyá' gáya. "'Now I am married with that one' she said," they say. ▸ **"Gicí wakníc'eȟą"** eyá' gáya. "'So I went back home with him' she said," they say.

gazába *vt1* s/he opens smth ▸ **Gá tiyóba gazába.** So then he lifted the door. ▸ **Ektášįšį tiyóba né kó gazába [. . .]** She mistakenly opened the door [. . .] (NS 2002:20) *Vcont:* **gazám**

gazám *vcont* opening smth

gazám įȟpéyA *ph* s/he yanks smth ▸ **Ti'óba né gazám įȟpéya.** He yanked the door open.

gazó *vt1* s/he draws a line

gazógic'ų *vi-irr* s/he skates; plays hockey ▸ **Éstena gazógic'ų mnį́kte no.** I will go play hockey soon. ▸ **Hokšíbina né iyúha gazógic'ųbi.** All of the boys play hockey. *1s:* **gazówec'ų** *2s:* **gazóyec'ų** *1p:* **gazó'ųgic'ųbi**

gazógic'ų skádA *vi1* s/he plays hockey *See:* **gazógic'ų**

gazú ecų́bina *Variant:* **ga'écųbina** *n* dice

gažáža *vt1* s/he rinses sb, smth ‣ **Miní ụs dạyạ́ gažáža.** Rinse it well with water.

gažạ́k *vcont* in poor health, in agony ‣ **Gažạ́k ya'ụ́ no.** You are in poor health.

gažíbA *vt1* s/he planes smth *1s:* **wagážiba** *2s:* **yagážiba**

gažǒ *vii* s/he has diarrhea *1s:* **wagážo** *2s:* **yagážo** *1p:* **ụgážobi**

gažǒ *vt1* 1) s/he makes it whistle by spinning *vi* 2) it whistles because of the wind *vii* 3) s/he has diarrhea *1s:* **wagážo** *2s:* **yagážo** *1p:* **ụgážobi** *Adv:* **gažóya**

gažóya *adv* with a whistling sound

gažúžu *vt1* s/he pays smth off (debt); pays for smth ‣ **Iyé gažúžubi.** They are paying for it themselves. ‣ **Ecágen ụgážužubi.** We always pay for it. ‣ **Niyé yagážužu.** You are paying for it yourself. ‣ **Dágu nówa wagážužu.** I paid for all things. *1s:* **wagážužu** *2s:* **yagážužu** *1p:* **ụgážužubi** *Vabs:* **wagážužu** *Vbenef:* **gíjažužu** *Vpos:* **knažúžu** *Vrecip:* **gicíjažužubi**

gábina *n-pl* elders, old people ‣ **Gábina hụgágạbis'a.** 1) Old people used to tell fairy tales. ‣ **Gábina óhạ ecágen yịgá.** He always sits among the elders. *vs* 2) they are old, elderly, aged

gábina maswícak'ubi *cp* old age pension

gábina tíbi *cp* retirement home

gánA ; gánA *vs* s/he/it is old, elderly, aged ‣ **Nahạ́ḥ magánešị.** I am not old yet. ‣ **Gạ́na:ga hịnị́ga.** The older she got, the meaner she became. ‣ **Hạ́, gána áya duká nahạ́ḥ mawášte.** Yes, he is getting old but he is still good-looking. ‣ **Waná nína gána hịkna maníšị no.** He is very old and he cannot walk. *1s:* **magána** *2s:* **nigána** *1p:* **ụgánabi** *3p:* **gábina**

gecị́ *vt1* s/he thought smth *Usage:* used to report thoughts, ideas, or opinions but not quotes. ‣ **Wíyạ tokạ́ gecị́bi.** They thought she was a different woman. ‣ **Né mak'íkta otạ́ ịgac ecị́.** "It seems he wants to carry me," he thought. (Drummond 1976, A bear story)

-geȟ *suff* 1) specifically *Usage:* added to pronouns to indicate a specific referent. ‣ **iyé > iyégeȟ** s/he/itself, themselves > s/he/itself, themselves specifically 2) derives adverbs from stative verbs ‣ **skúya > skúyageȟ** s/he/it is sweet > sweetly

-gen₁ *encl* not *Usage:* expresses the negation of verbs but adds strong disagreement or contradiction often accompanied by a touch of sarcasm or carelessness; it is often translated as "did not . . . anyways" or "did not . . . for what I care." ‣ **Ecúktegen!** He will not do it (and do not expect him to)! ‣ **Tą́ḥca wạží ktégen.** He did not kill a deer (anyways). ‣ **Dágu wóda ogínibigen.** They can go without eating anything. (NS 2002:34) *Syn:-šị*

-gen₂ *suff* rather, sort of, fairly, somehow *Usage:* derives adverbs from verbs and adds an attenuative meaning. ‣ **owáštenagen** rather slowly ‣ **dạyágen** fairly well ‣ **awáciyạgen** s/he wonders somehow about smth

-gen₃ *Variant:* **-yagen** *suff* in the manner of *Usage:* derives adverbs of manner from verbs and adverbs. ‣ **ganúsnuza > ganúsnuzagen** it is breezy > with a breeze ‣ **ịšnána > ịšnánagen** s/he is alone > lonesomely ‣ **šikná > šiknáyagen** s/he is angry > angrily ‣ **ịkcé > ịkcéyagen** common > in an ordinary way

gepcá *vii* I thought that, it seems like *Usage:* used with 1st person only. ‣ **Nịšnána gepcámị no.** I think you are alone. ‣ **Gahómni wacíbi yuhábi gepcámị.** I thought that they were having a round dance. *1s:* **gepcámị**

-gi- *prefix-infix* to, for, of (marker of dative verbs) *Usage:* used when the action is directed to or intended for somebody else. ‣ **bazó > gibázo** s/he shows smth > s/he shows smth to sb ‣ **yawá > giyáwa** s/he counts, reads > s/he reads smth to sb *1s:-***wagí-***2s:-***yagí-**

gi- ; **k-** *pref* back to an original state or place ▸ **ní > giní** s/he/it lives > s/he comes back to life, wakes up (from hibernation) ▸ **í > kní** s/he arrives there > s/he arrives back here ▸ **yá > kná** s/he goes there > s/he goes back here

-gi- ; **-ki-** ; **-k-** *prefix-infix* on one's own (marker of possessive verbs) *Usage:* agent is acting on his/her own thing, body part, or relative; possessive verbs are of Class 1. ▸ **cįgá > gicíga** s/he wants him/her/it > s/he wants his/her own ▸ **cosyá > coskíya** s/he warms up smth > s/he warms up his/her own ▸ **yuhá > knuhá** s/he has it > s/he has, keeps his/her own *1s:* -wagi- ; -wak- ; *2s:* -yagi- ; -yak- *1p:* -ųgi- . . . -bi ; -ųk- . . . -bi

gibázo *vt1-dat* s/he shows, points, reveals smth to him/her ▸ **Ektá gibázo.** He is pointing at it to her. ▸ **Iyúhaĥ wįcágibazo.** She showed him every single one of them. ▸ **Nitúgaši gibázo.** Show it to your grandfather. ▸ **Wa'ókmabi cijíbazokta.** I will show you some drawings. *1s:* **wagíbazo** *2s:* **yagíbazo** *1p:* **ųgíbazobi** *Vcoll:* **wįcágibazo**

gibá *vt1-dat* s/he yells, shouts at sb; calls sb's attention ▸ **Magíbąšį!** Do not yell at me! ▸ **Hą'éyasą šúga mitáwa žé wagíbą.** I shouted at my dog all night long. ▸ **Magíbąc'ehą amnúpta.** When she called me I answered. *1s:* **wagíbą** *2s:* **yagíbą** *1p:* **ųgíbąbi**

gicí *post* with sb, smth (single person or object) ▸ **Duwé gicí yahí?** Who did you come with? ▸ **Mitáwįju gicí wahįkta.** I will come with my wife. ▸ **Žehą́dahą gicí wa'ų́.** Since then I live with him. ▸ **Mitášųga gicí iwá'a jé.** I always talk to my horse.

-gici- . . . **-bi** ; **-ci-** . . . **-bi** *circumfix* one another (marker of the reciprocal) *Usage:* used when two persons are acting on one another; reciprocal verbs are of Class 1. ▸ **yuhábi > gicíyuhabi** they have sb, smth > they keep smth for one another ▸ **dagúya > dagúgiciyabi** s/he is related to sb > they are related to one another ▸ **ógiya > ógiciyabi** s/he helps sb > they help one another

gicí ecúna *ph* bet ▸ **Šųk'áktagabi gicí ecúna ecámų.** I placed a bet on the horse race.

gicí kpábi *cp* twins

gicíbažibabi *vi1-recip* they poke one another *1p:* **ųgícibažibabi**

gicícobi *vi1-recip* 1) they invite one another 2) gathering (where everyone is welcome) ▸ **Gicícobi én wakpámni.** She serves at the gathering.

gicíc'u *adv* from one to another; giving smth to one another ▸ **Gá žé'ec dáguškina né kpamní hiyáyabi dúkš anéžabišį žécen né gicíc'u yegíyabi.** So they passed that child around but he did not pee on anyone as they handed him along from one to the other. (Weasel 30:85)

gicíc'ubi *vi1-recip* they give smth to one another *1p:* **ųgícic'ubi**

gicíja *vt1* s/he is with sb (as a friend or spouse); accompanies sb ▸ **Wíyą žé wécija.** I am with that woman. ▸ **Nén misúgac wécija.** I am here with my younger brother. *1s:* **wécija** *2s:* **yécija** *1p:* **ųgícijabi**

gicíjašnabi *vi1-recip* they miss one another (as with a phone call)

gicíjažužubi *vi1-recip* they pay for one another

gicíkmąbi *vi1-recip* they resemble one another

gicíkna'įškadabi *vi1-recip* they tease one another verbally

gicíknuzabi *n* 1) wedding *vi1-recip* 2) they marry within their own (people, kind) ▸ **Įjínųba niyé né nícabi cá yéciknuzabikta uká.** Next time you will marry your own kind though. (Weasel 109:341) *1p:* **ųgíciknuzabi**

gicíksuyabi *vi1-recip* they remember one another

gicíktebi *vi1-recip* they kill one another *1p:* **ųgíciktebi**

gicíktebina *vi1-recip* they cheat, defeat one another *1p:* **ųgíciktebina**

gicís *vcont* fighting ‣ **Gicís įknúta.** He is practicing boxing.

gicíʼų *n* spouse

gicíyabi *vi1-recip* they call one another ‣ **Anų́k sųgágu gicíyabi.** They both called each other "younger brother." (Cumberland 2005:353) *1p:* **ųgíciyabi**

gicíyaʼįškadabi *vi1-recip* they tease one another verbally *1p:* **ųgíciyaʼįškadabi**

gicíyudabi *vi1-recip* they eat one another (as cannibals, monsters do)

gicíyuhabi *vi1-recip* they keep smth for one another

gicízA *vt1-dat* s/he fights with sb ‣ **Ecágen gicíza.** He always fights with him. *1s:* **wéciza** *2s:* **yéciza** *1p:* **ųgícizabi** *Vcont:* **gicís**

gicízabi *vi1-recip* 1) they fight one another *1p:* **ųgícizabi** *n* 2) fight, fighting ‣ **Gicízabi wamnúpi.** I am skilled at fighting. ‣ **Wá ųs gicízabi škádabi cén.** They are doing a snowball fight.

gicízabišį *n* peace, ceasefire

gicížobi *vi1-recip* they whistle at one another

gicʼį́ *vt1-pos* s/he carries his/her own *1s:* **wécʼį** *2s:* **yécʼį** *1p:* **ųgícʼįbi**

gicį́gA *vt1-pos* s/he wants his/her own thing ‣ **Miyé wécįga.** I want it for myself. ‣ **Įjážužu waná gicįga.** She wants her paycheck now. *1s:* **wécįga** *2s:* **yécįga**

gicó *vt1-dat* 1) s/he invites sb ‣ **Miyéco žé pinámayaya.** Thank you for inviting me. ‣ **Íciyuhana cicóbi.** I invite you all. ‣ **Miyéco he?** Did you invite me? ‣ **Macóbi cén imnámna.** They invited me so I came. ‣ **Wįcá né wéco.** I invited that man. ‣ **Ųmábi žé wįcáweco.** I invited the others. 2) s/he calls sb ‣ **Agícida nįco.** The police called you. ‣ **Waží wąyáge žé gicóbi.** One one was called as witness *1s:*

wéco *2s:* **yéco** *1p:* **ųgícobi** *Vcoll:* **wįcágico** *Vrecip:* **gicícobi**

gicʼú *vt1-dat* s/he gives smth back to sb ‣ **Zizíbena né éyagu, bakšíja hį́k mícʼu.** Take this towel, fold it, and give it back to me. *1s:* **wécʼu** *2s:* **yécʼu**

gicúni *vt1-irr* s/he quits an activity; it is finished ‣ **Įbási žé gicúni.** He quit driving. ‣ **Wací yécunįšį.** You did not finish the dance. ‣ **Wayáwa gicúni híbi štén.** They will come when school finishes. ‣ **Ogíciza gicúnįkta wacégiyabi.** They pray for the war to stop. *1s:* **wécuni** *2s:* **yécuni**

gicúwa *vt1-pos* s/he treats, acts toward, cares for his/her own ‣ **Dónacʼehą tahášitku gicúwa.** For a certain time he looked after his cousin. (Drummond 1976, The boy who made peace.)

gicʼú *vt1-pos* s/he wears his/her own (clothes, jewelry) ‣ **Owá gicʼú.** Wear all your clothes on. ‣ **Oyákʼu gicʼúšį.** He is not wearing his socks. ‣ **Wówaši hayábi wécʼu.** I put on my working clothes. *1s:* **wécʼu** *2s:* **yécʼu** *1p:* **ųgícʼųbi** *Vcaus:* **gicʼúkiyA**

gicʼúkiyA *vt1-caus-pos* s/he gets his/her own to wear smth, to dress ‣ **Micį́kši owá gicʼúwakiya.** I got my son all dressed. *1s:* **gicʼúwakiya** *2s:* **gicʼúyakiya** *1p:* **gicʼúʼųkiyabi**

gídana ; gídanaȟ *adv* barely ‣ **Gídana osní no.** It is barely cold. ‣ **Tiʼóba žé gídanaȟ yušpá yįgá.** The door is barely opened.

gidą́ *vt1* s/he insists on smth *Vabs:* **wagídą**

gídąȟ *adv* finally, at last ‣ **Dágeyešį! Dáguškina žé gídąȟ įštíma'.** Shh! The baby is finally sleeping. ‣ **Gídąȟ žehągeja waʼí.** At last I reached the destination.

gigátʼA *vt1-dat* s/he kills, knocks by striking with a club sb in relation to him/her ‣ **Hį́į, miyégakta, hokšína žé.** Oh, you killed that boy of mine. (Weasel 31:98) *1s:* **wégatʼa** *2s:* **yégatʼa**

gigídA *vs* it is sticky ▸ **Kiškána né gigída.** This spoon is sticky.

gihí *vi1-pos* s/he/it leaves the nest, is fledged

gíjağA *vt1-benef* s/he makes smth for him/her ▸ **Mį́š ecéduȟ míjaǧa.** Make me one exactly like this. ▸ **Huȟnáȟyabi wįcáwejağįkta.** I will make coffee for them. ▸ **Huȟnáȟyabi cijíjaǧa.** I made coffee for you. ▸ **Nakón wóyuda wicáwejaǧa.** I made some Indian food for him. (Cumberland 2005:212) *1s:* **wéjaǧa** *2s:* **yéjaǧa** *1p:* **ųgíjaǧabi** *Vcont:* **gíjaȟ**

gijahi *vt1-benef* s/he arrives with smth for sb ▸ **Wa'ówabi wąžíȟ cíjahi.** I brought you a book. *1s:* **wéjahi** *2s:* **yéjahi**

gíjaȟ *vcont* making smth for sb ▸ **Huȟnáȟyabi míjaȟwįcaši.** Tell them to make coffee for me.

gíjaȟ iyéyA *vt1-benef* s/he makes it quickly for sb *1s:* **gíjaȟ iyéwaya** *2s:* **gíjaȟ iyéyaya**

gíjaȟnada *vs3-pos* s/he has a stain on his/her own (clothes) ▸ **Cuwíknąga mijáȟnada.** I got a stain on my coat. *1s:* **mijáȟnada** *2s:* **nijáȟnada**

gíjakni *vt1-benef* s/he brings smth back for sb ▸ **Cą́ įš doháyą gíjaknibi cén wíyeya gíjiknągabi.** They brought him a stick of a certain length and placed it ready for him. (Drummond 1976, A bear story) *1s:* **wéjakni** *2s:* **yéjakni** *1p:* **ųgíjaknibi**

gíjaksA *vt1-benef* s/he cut, chops smth for him/her ▸ **Žécen tacúba néca įš wįcágijaksa.** Then he cut the bone to get marrow for them. (Shields 63:248) *1s:* **wéjaksa** *2s:* **wéjaksa** *1p:* **ųgíjaksabi**

gíjašna *vt1-dat* s/he cuts sb else's thing with a tool (hair, grass); gives sb a haircut; mows the lawn ▸ **Pahá míjašnakta.** Cut my hair. ▸ **Pahá wéjašnakta.** I will cut his hair. *1s:* **wéjašna** *2s:* **yéjašna**

gíja'u *vt1-benef* s/he brings, comes here with smth for sb ▸ **Á! mitágoža į́kšuna žé míja'u'.** Ah! my grandson brings the beans. *1s:* **wéja'u** *2s:* **yéja'u**

gíjayA *vt1-benef* s/he takes sb, smth there for him/her ▸ **Mitą́kš, iwádope miní ektá mį́jaya wó.** Younger sister, take the boat to the water for me. (Weasel 37:55)

gíjažužu *vt1-benef* s/he pays for smth for sb ▸ **Wįkóškebi wįcáwejažužu.** I paid for the young ladies. *1s:* **wéjažužu** *2s:* **yéjažužu**

-giji- *prefix-infix* for sb's benefit, on behalf of sb, instead of sb (marker of benefactive verbs) *Usage:* the agent is acting on behalf or for the benefit of someone else; benefactive verbs are of Class 1. ▸ **nową́ > gíjinową** s/he sings > s/he sings for sb, in his/her honor ▸ **iyéska > iyégijiska** s/he converses, translates > s/he translates for sb ▸ **hí > gíjihi** s/he arrives here > s/he arrives here instead of sb *1s:* **-weji-** *2s:* **-yeji-** *1p:* **-ųgiji-** . . . **-bi**

gíjibabehą *vt1-benef* s/he rolls smth up for him/her *1s:* **wéjibabehą** *2s:* **yéjibabehą** *1p:* **ųgíjibabehąbi**

gíjibahi *vt1-benef* s/he gathers, picks up smth for him/her ▸ **Cąsága wéjibahįkta.** I will gather twigs for her. *1s:* **wéjibahi** *2s:* **yéjibahi** *1p:* **ųgíjibahibi**

gíjibakįdA *vt1-benef* s/he wipes, cleans sb else's (body part) ▸ **Dáguškina paȟní wéjibakįda.** I wiped the baby's snot. *1s:* **wéjibakįda** *2s:* **yéjibakįda** *1p:* **ųgíjibakįdabi**

gíjibaksA *vt1-benef* s/he breaks smth for him/her manually or by pressure *1s:* **wéjibaksa** *2s:* **yéjibaksa** *1p:* **ųgíjibaksabi**

gíjibasi *vt1-benef* s/he drives for him/her, drives sb around ▸ **Waná wéjibasi.** I am driving for her now. *1s:* **wéjibasi** *2s:* **yéjibasi** *1p:* **ųgíjibasibi**

gíjibasijA *vt1-benef* s/he ruins sb's thing by sitting on it ▸ **Šiná wéjibasija.** I ruined her quilt by sitting on it. *1s:* **wéjibasija** *2s:* **yéjibasija** *1p:* **ųgíjibasijabi**

gíjibasisA *vt1-benef* s/he sews smth for sb *1s:* **wéjibasisa** *2s:* **yéjibasisa** *1p:* **ųgíjibasisabi**

gíjibawįda *vt1-benef* s/he rubs smth for him/her (like a body part) ▸ **Įstó mabádį míjibawįda.** My arm is stiff, rub it for me. *1s:* **wéjibawįda** *2s:* **yéjibawįda** *1p:* **ųgíjibawįdabi**

gíjibą *vt1-benef* s/he shouts for, on behalf of him/her *1s:* **wéjibą** *2s:* **yéjibą** *1p:* **ųgíjibąbi**

gíjibąhą *vt1-benef* s/he cheers for sb ▸ **Micį́kši wéjibąhą.** I cheer for my son. *1s:* **wéjibąhą** *2s:* **yéjibąhą** *1p:* **ųgíjibąhąbi**

gíjiceyA *vt1-benef* s/he cries for sb ▸ **Dóna dagúwįcayabi žanáwa wįcágiksuyabi cén wįcágijiceyabi.** When they remembered all their many relatives, they cried for them. (Shields 59:205)

gíjihi *vt1-benef* s/he arrives, comes here instead of sb *1s:* **wéjihi** *2s:* **yéjihi** *1p:* **ųgíjihibi**

gíji'įȟpayA *vi1-benef* she/it has a miscarriage ▸ **Núbaȟ hokší gíji'įȟpaya.** She had two miscarriages. *1s:* **míji'įȟpaya** *2s:* **níji'įȟpaya** *Syn:* **hokší gíji'įȟpayA**

gíjikmųgA *vt1-benef* s/he snares smth for him/her ▸ **Iná maštín wéjikmųga.** I snared a rabbit for mom. *1s:* **wéjikmųga** *2s:* **yéjikmųga** *1p:* **ųgíjikmųgabi**

gíjiknągA *vt1-benef* s/he gets smth ready for sb; stores smth (food, wood) for sb to have on hand ▸ **Dágu niyúhana wįcágijiknąga.** She stored all kinds of things for them. ▸ **Cą́ įš doháyą gíjaknibi cén wíyeya gíjiknągabi.** They brought him a stick of a certain length and placed it ready for him. (Drummond 1976, A bear story) *1s:* **wéjiknąga** *2s:* **yéjiknąga** *1p:* **ųgíjiknągabi**

gíjiknuštą *vt1-benef* 1) s/he finishes smth for sb (work, meal) 2) s/he decides smth for sb *1s:* **wéjiknuštą** *2s:* **yéjiknuštą** *1p:* **ųgíjiknuštąbi**

gíjik'A *vt1-benef* s/he digs smth for him/her (like potatoes, roots) *1s:* **wéjik'a** *2s:* **yéjik'a** *1p:* **ųgíjik'abi**

gíjinową *vt1-benef* s/he sings for sb; sings in his/her honor ▸ **Adé wéjinowąkte no.** I will sing in honor of my father. *1s:* **wéjinową** *2s:* **yéjinową** *1p:* **ųgíjinowąbi**

gíji'o *vt1-benef* s/he shoots and hits sb, smth for him/her; kills sb, smth for him/her

gíjiteȟigA *vs1-benef* it is hard on him/her; difficult for him/her ▸ **Iná gíjiteȟiga.** It is very hard on mom. ▸ **Dágu né gíjiteȟibigeší stéya.** This thing was not hard on them, it seems. *1s:* **wéjiteȟiga** *2s:* **yéjiteȟiga** *1p:* **ųgíjiteȟigabi**

gíji'u *vt1-benef* s/he comes here instead of sb *1s:* **wéji'u** *2s:* **yéji'u** *1p:* **ųgíji'ubi**

gíji'ų *vt1-benef* 1) s/he wears sb else's own 2) s/he uses sb else's own *1s:* **wéji'ų** *2s:* **yéji'ų** *1p:* **ųgíji'ųbi**

gíjiyaǧu *vt1/2-benef* s/he finishes up a pipe for sb *1s:* **wéjimnaǧu** *2s:* **yéjinaǧu** *1p:* **ųgíjiyaǧubi**

gíjiyudA *vt1/2-benef* s/he eats sb's food ▸ **Tanó táwa žé gíjiyuda.** He ate her meat. ▸ **Žécen šųkšíjana žé wók'u hą́da gíjiyuda:ga.** So then whenever the little dog fed her, she was eating its food. (Weasel 194:128) *1s:* **wéjimnuda** *2s:* **yéjinuda** *1p:* **ųgíjiyudabi**

gíjiyudodo *vt1/2-benef* s/he cleans smth for sb *1s:* **wéjimnudodo** *2s:* **yéjinudodo**

gíjiyugadį *vt1/2-benef* s/he stretches out smth for sb *1s:* **wéjimnugadį** *2s:* **yéjimnugadį** *1p:* **ųgíjiyugadįbi**

gíjiyuǧabA *vt1-benef* s/he pulls the skin or bark off smth for him/her; skins an animal for him/her ▸ **Mikúš, nén iyúžųtų míjiyuǧaba wó.** Grandma, skin and dry this for me and stretch it into a bag. (Weasel 27:30) *1s:* **wéjiyuǧaba** *2s:* **yéjiyuǧaba** *1p:* **ųgíjiyuǧababi**

gíjiyuhA *vt1/2-benef* s/he has, keeps, carries smth for sb ▸ **Gíjiyuha maní.** He walks carrying it for her. *1s:* **wéjimnuha** *2s:* **yéjinuha** *1p:* **ųgíjiyuhabi**

gíjiyuksA *vt1/2-benef* s/he cuts smth with scissors for him/her ▸ **Sąksája wąží wéjimnuksa.** I cut a dress for her. *1s:* **wéjimnuksa** *2s:* **yéjinuksa** *1p:* **ųgíjiyuksabi**

gíjiyuška *vt1-benef* s/he unties, detaches sb, smth for him/her ‣ **Žécen wįcá né wįcágijiyuška.** So then he untied the men.

gíjiyušpa *vt1/2-benef* s/he opens smth for him/her ‣ **Míjiyušpa!** Open it for me! ‣ **Cągú wįcágijiyušpa.** He opened the path for them. *1s:* **wéjimnušpa** *2s:* **yéjimnušpa** *1p:* **ųgíjiyušpabi**

gíjiyušpi *vt1/2-benef* s/he picks berries for sb manually ‣ **Né wíbazuką cíjimnušpi.** I picked saskatoons for you. *1s:* **wéjimnušpi** *2s:* **yéjinušpi** *1p:* **ųgíjiyušpibi**

gíjiyužaža *vt1-benef* s/he washes sb, smth for him/her ‣ **"Hųų, hokšíbi, né mní nén yá hík ųgíjiyužažam,"** eyábi. "So, boys, go to the water and wash these for us," they said. (Shields 62:238) *1s:* **wéjiyužaža** *2s:* **yéjiyužaža** *1p:* **ųgíjiyužažabi**

gíjižo *vt1-benef* s/he whistles for him/her *1s:* **wéjižo** *2s:* **yéjižo** *1p:* **ųgíjižobi**

gikmą́ *vt-irr* s/he/it resembles sb; looks like sb ‣ **Wįcá nų́babi né gikmą́bi.** These two men look alike. *1s:* **wékmą** *2s:* **yékmą** *1p:* **ųgíkmąbi** *Vrecip:* **gicíkmąbi**

gikną́ *vt1* s/he pampers, cuddles, caresses, sweet talks sb ‣ **Koškášká né iyáȟpaya póskin yúza hík gikną́.** He grabbed the boy in his arms, embraced him, and caressed him. (Drummond 1976, The boy who made peace.) *Vredup:* **gikną́kną́ga**

gikną́gA *vt1-pos* s/he stores, saves, caches smth for himself/herself *Vabs:* **wagíkną̨gA**

giknúgA *vi1* s/he/it dives into water *Vcont:* **giknúk**

giknúk *vcont* diving into water ‣ **Įtó togáheya cába žé giknúkši.** Well first he [Įktomi] ordered the beaver to dive. (Drummond 1976, The flood)

giksúyA *vt1-irr* s/he remembers sb, smth ‣ **Wanúȟ ųgibišį cá.** Maybe we will not remember about it. ‣ **Niyé mayéksuya he?** As for you, do you remember me? ‣ **Mihúgagebi wįcágiksuyabi.** My parents remember them. *1s:* **wéksuya** *2s:* **yéksuya** *1p:* **ųgíksuyabi** *Vrecip:* **gicíksuyabi**

giktá *vi1* s/he gets up (from bed) ‣ **Waná hąyákena, giktá!** It is now early in the morning, get up! ‣ **Céya:ga ųká wéktašį.** Despite her constant crying I did not get up. ‣ **Giktá gicí yįgá žé yazą́.** Get up and sit with the sickly one. *1s:* **wagíkta** ; **wékta** *2s:* **yagíkta** ; **yékta** *1p:* **ųgíktąbi** *See:* **yugíkta**

giktá iyéyA *vi1* s/he/it gets up quickly ‣ **Mitúgaši nawáȟ'ųc'ehą giktá iyéwaya.** When I heard my grandfather I got up quickly. *1s:* **giktá iyéwaya** *2s:* **giktá iyéyaya**

gikté *vt1-dat* 1) s/he kills sb, smth for him/her *vt1-pos* 2) s/he kills his/her own ‣ **[. . .] waná sųgágu giktékta cén otápa.** [. . .] now she was going to kill her younger brother so she followed him. (NS 2002:24)

gimą́mąna ; **gimą́miną** *n-redup* butterfly

giná *vt1-dat* s/he asks smth of sb ‣ **Mikúši giná.** Ask my grandmother for it. ‣ **Ağúyabi magínabi.** They asked me for bread. *1s:* **wagína** *2s:* **yagína** *1p:* **ųgínabi**

giní *vi1* s/he comes back to life, wakes up (from hibernation)

giníhą *vi1* s/he is afraid ‣ **Hiyá wagínihąšį no.** No I am not afraid. ‣ **Giníhąšį, napécijiya.** Do not be afraid, I chase it away for you. *1s:* **wagínihą** *2s:* **yagínihą** *1p:* **ųgínihąbi**

ginį́ja *part* almost ‣ **Mahį́ȟpaya ginį́ja.** I almost fell. ‣ **Šų́gatąga t'á ginį́ja.** The horse almost died. ‣ **Awápa ginį́ja.** I almost hit it. ‣ **Košká žé mni'óta ginį́ja.** That boy almost drowned. *See:* **tanį́ješ**

ginówą *vi1-refl* s/he sings to himself/herself ‣ **"Duká bahá ektá yągá hík gínowąsa" gáya.** "He used to sit on a hill and sing to himself," he said. (NS 2002:4)

gipí *vs-dat* s/he/it fits into smth; s/he is large enough to fit into smth

gisába *n* spot of bare ground where the snow has melted

gísabana *n* chickadee

gisápsabA *vimp-redup* 1) there are spots of bare ground where the snow has melted ▸ **Gisápsaba hǫ́da bis'ų́kuwabi.** When there are bare spots of ground in the snow, we chase gophers. *n-redup* 2) spots of bare ground where the snow has melted

Gisníwįcayabi ecúbi *cp* Healing ceremony

gisníyA *vt1* s/he save, heals sb from an illness *1s:* **gisníwaya** *2s:* **gisníyaya** *Vcoll:* **gisníwįcaya**

gisú *vt1-pos* s/he braids his/her own hair ▸ **Mikúši dąyá gisús'a.** My grandmother always braided her hair nicely. *1s:* **wésų** *2s:* **yésų** *1p:* **ųgísųbi** *See:* **pahá gisú, págisų**

Gisúna *n* person of Asian descent *Lit:* s/he braids himself/herself

gisúna šúga *cp* chow dog *Lit:* Asian dog

gitézi *n* boy, lad, kid, brat (pejorative connotation) ▸ **Gitézi óda wįcáyuha.** She has a bunch of brats. ▸ **Gitézi wįcáwagaštagakta!** I will beat the brats.

gitú *vt1-pos* s/he wears his/her clothes or smth over the upper body part (shawl, glasses, mask) *1s:* **wétų** *2s:* **yétų** *1p:* **ųgítųbi**

-giya *suff* 1) toward ▸ **ektá > ektágiya** in, at > toward this direction 2) X by X, in a number of ways, directions, locations *Usage:* occurs mostly with numerals. ▸ **dóba > dóbagiya** four > four by four; in four different locations ▸ **nų́ba > nų́bagiya** two > two by two; in two different locations *Syn:* **-takiya**

-giyA ;-kiyA *suff* s/he causes one's own to do smth (possessive form of the causative-yA) *Usage:* creates transitive verbs from stative ones; -kiyA is used after a consonant. ▸ **šįtú > šįtúgiya** s/he/it is fat > s/he fattens his/her own ▸ **šnušnúda > šnušnúnkiya** it is dirty >

s/he dirties his/her own *1s:*-**wagiya** *2s:*-**yagiya** *1p:*-**ųgiyabi**

giyáwa *vt1-dat* s/he reads smth to sb *1s:* **wagíyawa** *2s:* **yagíyawa**

giyą́yąno *n* mourning dove

giyékiyabi (OM) *n* airplane, car *Syn:* **amų́giya, giyą́yąbi**

giyúką *vt1-dat* s/he makes room for sb ▸ **Catkú ektá giyúkąbi.** They made room for him in the honor's place. (Shields 17:206) *1s:* **wagíyuką** *2s:* **yagíyuką** *1p:* **ųgíyukąbi**

gižó *vt1-dat* s/he whistles at sb ▸ **Dóhąni macą́deskuya wagížoši.** I never whistled at my sweetheart. *1s:* **wagížo** *2s:* **yagížo** *1p:* **ųgížobi**

giyĄ́ *vi1* s/he/it flies ▸ **Wamní žé wągą́duwah giyą́'.** The eagle flies the highest. ▸ **Giyą́ úbic'ehą mowįcawamneja.** I shot and scattered them as they flew. *1s:* **wagíyą** *2s:* **yagíyą** *1p:* **ųgíyąbi** *Adv:* **giyą́yą** *See:* **ogíyĄ**

giyą́ ús'a *cp* airborne pilot

giyą́yą *adv* flying ▸ **Wamní giyą́yą én ahí.** The eagles came flying in.

giyą́yąbi *n* airplane (archaic)

gíza *vi* it creaks, squeaks

goskós *vcont* waving, swinging, flapping smth

goskóza *vt1-redup* s/he/it waves, swings, flaps smth (as bird) ▸ **"Hubá goskóza," eyá.** "Flap your wings" he said. (Weasel 3:51) *1s:* **wagóskoza** *2s:* **yagóskoza** *Vcont:* **goskós**

góza *vt1* s/he waves, swings sb, smth *Vredup:* **goskóza**

-gu- *Variant:* -ju *suff-infix* his, her, their (3rd person singular possessor) *Usage:* used with kinship and a few common nouns. ▸ **-sųga-> sųgágu** younger brother > his/her younger brother ▸ **-cųna-> cų́guna** older sister > her older sister ▸ **koná > takónagu** friend > his/her/their friend ▸ **-nekši- > nekšíju** uncle (mother's brother; father's sister's husband) > his/her uncle

gú *vi1* s/he comes back here ‣ **Wazíȟe ecíyadahą gúbi.** They left Cypress Hills to come back here. ‣ **"Tída gú!" ecíjiya.** "Come back here!" I told you. ‣ **Ȋwáštena wagú.** I came back home slowly. *1s:* **wagú** *2s:* **yagú** *1p:* **ųgúbi**

gugúša *cp* pig ‣ **Gugúša šįtų gá wįcá žé táwa.** The man owns that fat pig over there. *From:* French cocoche.

gugúša cįjána *cp* piglet *Syn:* **gugúšana**

gugúša šį *n* bacon *Lit:* pork fat

gugúša tí *cp* pigsty

gugúša yúde *cp* barley *Lit:* pig food

gugúšamnoga *n* hog

gugúšana *n* piglet, or little pig *Syn:* **gugúša cįjána**

gugúšawįyena *n* swine

gúwa *vimper* come here *Usage:* used as an imperative form only. ‣ **Gúwa! Waná ųyįkta!** Come here! We will go now! ‣ **Įhiyų pağųda! Gúwam dágu wąží ocíjimnagabįkta.** Hey ducks! Come here, I want to tell you one thing. (Drummond 1976, Įktomi and the ducks)

gú *vt1* s/he desires sb; wishes for sb ‣ **Wįkóške wąží wagú cén.** I desire a young woman. *1s:* **wagú** *2s:* **yagú**

gųgúbi *n* cucumber, pickle

gųgúma *n* wild cucumber, cucumber; pickle *Syn:* **gųgúbi**

gúza *vi1-aux* s/he pretends *Usage:* attaches to a verb and triggers e-ablaut. ‣ **t'á > t'égųza** s/he/it is dead > s/he/it pretends to be dead ‣ **huštá > huštégųza** s/he/it is lame > s/he/it pretends to be lame *1s:* -**wagųza** *2s:* -**yagųza**

Ǧ

ǧaǧána *n* cheesecloth, gauze

ǧa'įt'A *vs* s/he is exhausted, tired, out of breath *Vcaus:* **ǧa'įt'eyA**

ǧa'įt'eyA *vt1-caus* s/he exhausts, tires sb out, make sb to be out of breath ‣ **Mitášųga ǧa'įt'ewaya.**

I exhausted my horse. *1s:* **ǧa'įt'ewaya** *2s:* **ǧa'įt'eyaya**

ǧí *vs* it is light yellow; brown ‣ **Škoškóbena né ǧí.** This banana is yellow. ‣ **Búza žé ǧí hįk zí nína wógųga.** That cat is brown and yellow and very pretty. ‣ **waȟpé ǧí wí** September ‣ **waȟcáǧi** dandelion *Vcaus:* **ǧiyÁ** *Vredup:* **ǧiǧí**

ǧigíjiyA *vt1-benef* s/he paints, colors sb, smth in brown for sb

ǧigíyA *vt1-pos* s/he paints, colors, dyes his/her own brown

ǧiǧí *vs-redup* s/he/it is yellow, light brown ‣ **Zitkána táwabi abá ǧiǧíbi.** Some of his birds are yellow. (Parks et al. 1999:112)

ǧíȟtįyą *vs* it is deep yellow

ǧi'įc'iyA *vi3-refl* s/he paints himself/herself in brown

ǧijáhą *vs* s/he/it falls ‣ **Eȟá'i žécen tiyóba táwa én yuhá ǧijáhe gúza.** He reached there and at the door, carrying it, he pretended to fall. (Weasel 68:131)

ǧiyÁ *vt1-caus* s/he paints, colors, dyes smth in brown *Adv:* **ǧiyéna** *Vbenef:* **ǧigíjiyA** *Vpos:* **ǧigíyA** *Vrefl:* **ǧi'įc'iyA**

ǧiyéna *adv* brown condition ‣ **Ǧiyéna co'úba wo.** Cook it brown.

ǧóbA *vi1* s/he snores ‣ **Hą'éyasą ǧóba.** He snores all night. *1s:* **waǧóba** *2s:* **yaǧóba** *1p:* **ųǧóbabi**

ǧóbes'a *n* snorer

ǧuǧúyA *vt1-redup* s/he chars, singes smth *1s:* **ǧuǧúwaya** *2s:* **ǧuǧúyaya** *1p:* **ǧuǧú'ųyąbi**

ǧúmna *vs* it has a smell of burnt (hair), scolding

ǧuyÁ *vt1* s/he scorches, burns smth *1s:* **ǧuwáya** *2s:* **ǧuyáya**

H

há *n* skin, hide, bag, pouch, any type of container ‣ **Tągán úbi, né'ųs há zí.** They are continously outside, and because of this his skin is tanned. ‣ **Waná há ȟniȟníbi jé.** Then they always had sores on the skin. ‣ **Haskána** White man ‣ **ptehá** buffalo hide ‣ **tahá** deer, moose, elk hide ‣ **ak'įha** saddle bag

há okmábi *cp* birthmark, tattoo

háá *interj* expression indicating doubt (female speaker)

ha'ágam *adv* on the skin

hábasisA *vi1* s/he sews skins together *1s:* **wahábasisa** *2s:* **yahábasisa** *Vbenef:* **gíjibasisA**

hádi ; hądi *interj* get out; get away; get out of the way ‣ **Hádi, sam yá!** Get out, go away! ‣ **Hą:di bo misųga Įktómi iyúhana ųgásodabįkta.** My brothers get out of here! Įktomi is going to wipe us all out. (Drummond 1976, Įktomi and the ducks)

hagíkta *vt1-pos* s/he looks back ‣ **Įnážį híkna hagíkta.** He stopped and looked back. *1s:* **hawékta** *2s:* **hayékta**

hahá'aha *interj* Greetings! (as one opens the door)

hahána *vs* s/he is lively, frisky, excited ‣ **Gitézina hahábina.** Kids are lively. ‣ **šųkháhana** spirited horse *1s:* **maháhana** *2s:* **niháhana** *Adv:* **haháyena**

haháyena *adv* lively ‣ **Haháyena wa'ų́.** I am lively.

hah̃níša *n* crybaby

hámna *vs* s/he/it smells; has a body odor ‣ **Micíkši nihámna, nįknúžaža céyaga!** My son you smell, you should wash yourself! (BigEagle 2019:8) *1s:* **mahámna** *2s:* **nihámna** *1p:* **ųhámnabi**

Hásaba *nprop* person of African or African-American descent

Hásaba makóce *ngeo* Africa

Hásaba wíyą *cp* woman of African or African-American descent

Haskána *Variant:* **Haská** *nprop* person of European or Euro-Canadian descent; White man

hásuda *vs* s/he/it has a hard skin ‣ **Anáciǧoptašį cén mat'éja, mahásuda áya ko!** I did not listen to you and now I am slow with a hard skin. (BigEagle 2019:14) *1s:* **mahásuda** *2s:* **nihásuda**

hatéja *n* new clothes

hatókągic'ų *vt1-pos* s/he changes his/her own clothes *1s:* **hatókąwec'ų** *2s:* **hątókąyec'ų**

háu *interj* Hello! (male speaker to another male) ‣ **Háu koná!** Hello friend!

hayábi *n* clothes, costume, suit ‣ **Wówaši hayábi wéc'ų.** I put on my working clothes. *Syn:* **gağábi**

hayábi oktéyabi *cp* clothes hanger

hayábi opíye *cp* suitcase

hayábi owópetų *cp* clothing store

hą- *cont* night ‣ **máni > hąmáni** s/he/it walks > s/he/it walks at night

-hĄ *encl* continuative or progressive aspect marker (indicates continuous events or actions that have no time boundaries; some speakers do not ablaut the final vowel) ‣ **Mitáwįju įštímešįhą.** My wife is continuously sleepless. ‣ **Waná wįkóškehąkta.** Now she is becoming a young lady. ‣ **Mįšnána mągáhą né tamų́kašį.** I dread being alone. ‣ **Wanágaš t'áhą cén dágu né h̃ųwįmna.** This thing died long ago because it smells putrid.

-hą *suff* at a particular time; last ‣ **žé > žehą́** that > at that time, at a certain point in time ‣ **wani->waníhą** winter > last winter

hą₁ *adv* 1) yes ‣ **Huh̃náh̃yabi yacíga? Hą́, edáhą wacíga.** Do you want coffee? —Yes, I want some. ‣ **Hą́, wanúh̃.** Yes, maybe. *interj* 2) Hello! (female speaker) *See:* **háu**

hą₂ *vs* it stands, is; it is placed *Usage:* used with inanimate referents that are taller than they are large. ‣ **Mosnán hą́.** It stands upright. ‣ **Ti'óba né kudína hą́.** This door is hanging low. ‣ **Bapsúbi nécen hą́.** It is a heavy rainfall. ‣ **Miní žé mnesyá hą́.** The water is clear.

hąba *n* moccasins, shoes ‣ **Hąba žé mak'ú!** Give me those shoes! ‣ **Hąba né įmnúta!** Try these shoes on. *Cont:* **hąm- ; hąp-** *See:* **cáhąba**

hąba ecúbina *cp* moccasin game

hąba kšúbi *cp* decorated moccasins

hába oskábi *Variant:* habóska *n* quilted moccasins

hábasicu *n* moccasin soles

habí *n* juice, sap *See:* cahábi

hácogadu *adv* midnight, middle of the night
‣ **Hácogadu žehá wacíbi žedáha wakní.** I came home from the dance at midnight. ‣ **Iknúhahana hácogadu wékta.** Occasionally I wake up in the middle of the night.

háda *adv* whenever, when, when it is the case ‣ **Gisápsaba háda bis'úkuwabi.** When there are bare patches of ground, we chase gophers. ‣ **Dágu ecú háde ecéduň ecú'!** Whenever he does something he does it in the same way! ‣ **Wédu háda paǧúda žená nén iyáhabi.** In the spring those ducks land here.

ha'éyasa *adv* throughout the night, all night ‣ **Ha'éyasa wáhiha.** It snowed all night. ‣ **Ha'éyasa bá.** He shouted all night long.

-haga- *root* sister-in-law (male speaker) *1s:* **mihága** *2s:* **nihága** *3s:* **hagágu** *Vcaus:* **hagáguyA**

hagáguyA *vt1-caus* he has her as a sister-in-law

-hagaši- *root* female cross-cousin (male speaker) *1s:* **mihágaši** *2s:* **nihágaši** *3s:* **hagášico**

hagé *n* half ‣ **Dóba sám hagé ehá'i.** It is 4:30. ‣ **mázaska hagé** fifty cents

hagéya *adv* finally, at last ‣ **Hagéya yahí!** You finally arrived! ‣ **Hagéya temyá.** At last he ate it up. ‣ **Hagéya yazá.** She became sick finally.

hagéyadaha *adv* and then finally, at last ‣ **Hagéyadaha iyáyabi.** And they finally left. ‣ **Hagéyadaha dágejiyabiši.** After a while they did not say anything. (NS 2002:73)

hagíkta *vi1* s/he gets up early

hahá *interj* expression of surprise for unexpected news (male speaker)

hahébi *n* 1) night ‣ **Hahébi né šukmánukte no!** He will steal a horse tonight! ‣ **Hahébi dónaca žé ništíma?** How many nights did you sleep there? *vimp* 2) it is nighttime ‣ **Hahébi háda cuwíktu tagán ománi.** Her daughter walks outside at nighttime. *Cont:* ha-

Hahébi wanáǧi wówicak'ubi *ph* Feed the night spirits ceremony

hahébi wódabi *cp* supper

hahébic'eha *adv* last night ‣ **Hokšína žé hahébic'eha hí.** That boy arrived last night.

hakpázA *vimp* it is evening twilight

ham-; hap- *cont* shoe, pertaining to shoes ‣ **hamcóna** without moccasins, shoeless ‣ **hapkáǧA** s/he makes moccasins

hamáni *vi1* s/he walks at night ‣ **Wícá matéjana háda, ha'úmanibic'eha.** When I was a young man, we were walking at night.

ham'áyazabi *n* beaded moccasins

hamcóna *adv* without moccasins, shoeless

hanówabi *n* night song

hanúni *vi1* s/he gets lost at night *1s:* **hawánuni** *2s:* **hayánuni** *1p:* **uhánunibi**

ha'ómani *vi1* s/he/it walks at night

hapkáǧA *vi1* s/he makes moccasins

háskA *vs* s/he/it is tall, long ‣ **Nína niháske no.** You are very tall. ‣ **Dóna háska eháya'i?** How tall are you? ‣ **Wícá háske žé mani.** That tall man is walking. *1s:* **maháska** *2s:* **niháska** *1p:* **uháskabi** *Adv:* **háskeya** *Vredup:* **háskaskA**

háskaskA *vs-redup* s/he/it is very tall, long ‣ **Wikóške žé háskaskabi.** The young women are very tall.

háskeya *adv* in a long manner ‣ **Háskeya cetíbi.** They made a fire that burned in a long line. (Drummond 1976, How the woman made pemmican)

haté *n* juniper

hatéha *adv* late at night ‣ **Hatéha áya'.** It is getting late at night. (Cumberland 2005:402) ‣ **Waná hatéha no.** It is late already. *Syn:* ahátehaga

hatéša *n* cedar, red cedar

há'uka *conj* and then, when *Usage:* this conjunction has no direct equivalent in English and is loosely translated by "and (then)" or "when"; in narratives it often occurs in sentence-final position followed by a pause and functions as a clause coordinator expressing temporal cohesion between simultaneous or sequential events. ‣ **Wíyąbi né wóšpi íbis'a hą́'ųka. Wįcą́bi žé'įš dóki iyáme yábis'a hą́'ųka.** The women usually went to pick berries. And as for the men they usually went hunting. ‣ **Gicí iwá'i hą́'ųka iná hí.** I was talking with her when mom arrived.

hąwácibi *n* women's dance, night dance, moon dance

hąwí ; wí *n* 1) moon ‣ **"Hąwí océti stéya," eyábis'a.** "The moon is like a stove," they say usually. 2) sun ‣ **Hąwí tą'íšį a'óhązi no!** The sun is not visible, it is overcast! 3) month ‣ **įdú wigǎ hąwí** May

hąwí akída *cp* clock

hąwí bapsų́ *cp* wet moon, Cheshire moon (refers to the moon's winter cycle when its horns point up; when summer comes the moon "pours" out the water it had kept and which causes the summer rains) *Lit:* pouring out moon

hąwí cogą́du *cp* half moon *Syn:* **hąwí okíse**

hąwí hinąpA *vimp* it is sunrise; it dawns ‣ **Nahą́ȟ hąwí hinąpešį, gá wihíyayešį ecíyadahą éduwą.** Before sunrise he looked toward the north. (Shields 77:423)

hąwí hįnąpa *cp* sunrise

hąwí okíse *cp* half moon

hąwí ožúna *cp* full moon

hąwí togáhe oyášpe *ph* quarter moon *Lit:* first piece bitten off of the moon

hąwí ų́šį *vimp* it is a period with no moon; it is a night without a moon

hąwí waȟcá *cp* sunflower (calque from English)

hąwígagǎbi *n* clock, timer

hąwísaba *n* lunar eclipse *Lit:* black moon

hąwíyawa *n* calendar

hąwíyąba *n* moonlight

hąyáke *adv* late morning (8–9 am)

hąyákeji *adv* tomorrow ‣ **Hąyákeji nowąkta.** He will sing tomorrow. ‣ **Hąyákeji dágu dókanų?** What are you doing tomorrow? ‣ **Hąyákeji mitúgaši įmúgǎkta.** I will ask my grandfather tomorrow. ‣ **Hąyákeji né wįkóškebi híkna koškábina Nakón-wįcóȟ'age škádabįkta.** Tomorrow girls and boys will play traditional games.

hąyákena 1) *adv* early morning ‣ **Hąyákena né mázaska edą́ha mak'úbi no!** This morning they gave me some money! ‣ **Hąyákena úkta.** He will come this morning. ‣ **Hąyákena waštéc!** Good morning! ‣ **hąyákena wódabi** breakfast 2) *vimp* it is early morning ‣ **Waná hąyákena, gíkta!** It is now early morning, get up!

hąyákena cogą́du *adv* midmorning

hąyákena wódabi *cp* breakfast *Lit:* morning food

hąyákenaȟ *adv* very early in the morning

hąyákesą *adv* throughout the morning, all morning

he *part* question marker (male and female speakers) ‣ **Dágu núda he?** What are you eating? ‣ **Dágu né he?** What is this? ‣ **Waná he?** Are you ready? ‣ **Cąpásu yuką́ he?** Is there pepper? ‣ **Úkta he?** Will he come?

hé *n* horn 1s: **mitáhe** 2s: **nitáhe** 3s: **tahé**

hé'a *n* louse, lice ‣ **Hé'a wįcáyuhabi.** They have lice ‣ **Hé'a wįcáyusnuda.** She pulls lice off him.

hebíya *adv* halfway up a hill ‣ **Hebíya įnážį.** He stopped halfway up the hill.

hehébiya *adv* 1) midway, halfway ‣ **Hehébiya hí.** He came halfway. 2) before

heȟága ; heȟáge *n* elk

Heȟága hóta'į wíyą *nprop* Echo of the elk woman (Wilma Kennedy's traditional name)

hejá *n* buzzard, turkey vulture ‣ **Hejá agáwįȟ ų́.** A turkey vulture is circling.

hékiška ; kíška *n* bighorn sheep, mountain goat *Syn:* **héškoba**

hékta *adv* back then, in the past ▸ **Hékta naháȟ pté óda žehą.** There was still a lot of buffalo back then. ▸ **Hékta žé wįyą snohmáyašį no.** Back then the woman did not know who I was. ▸ **Né hékta nén aškán ḷhąktuwąbi nená ahí no!** Back in the recent past these Yankton Dakota came here.

hékta odágugiciyabi *cp* ancestors

hékta odáguye *cp* ancestor

héktac'ehą *adv* long time ago

héktam *adv* behind, in the rear ▸ **Šúga héktam máni.** The dog is walking behind. ▸ **Héktam nážį nén.** He is standing here behind.

héktapadahą *adv* from behind ▸ **Héktapadahą hí.** He arrived from behind.

héškoba *n* bighorn sheep *Lit:* bent horns *Syn:* **hékiška ; kíška**

Héwahį *nprop* surname in Carry The Kettle (spelled Haywahe) *Lit:* horn flint

heyúką *vs* s/he/it has horns *1s:* **hémayuką** *2s:* **héniyuką**

hi- *pref* doing smth while arriving here; doing smth after arriving here *Usage:* this prefix attaches to active verbs. ▸ **iyódąga > hiyódąga** s/he sits down > s/he arrives here and sits down

hí₁ *n* tooth ▸ **Mįštímikta cén hí wakpážaža.** I will brush my teeth because I am going to sleep. *1s:* **mahí** *2s:* **nihí** *1p:* **ųgíhibi**

hí₂ *vi1* s/he arrives here from there *Usage:* this verb is often translated as "to come here." ▸ **Dóhąc'ehą yahí?** When did you arrive here? ▸ **Duwé hí?** Who is arriving? ▸ **Ába né wąží ehą'i wahí.** I arrived at one o'clock today. *1s:* **wahí** *2s:* **yahí** *1p:* **ųhíbi** *Vbenef:* **gíjihi** *Vcaus:* **hikíyA** *See:* **ahí, gihí**

hí įcáǧA *vs* s/he (baby) is teething

hí oȟnóga *n* cavity

hí wįcáyušnoges'a *cp* dentist

hí wįcáyušnoges'a tíbi *cp* dental clinic

hícona *vs* s/he/it is toothless *1s:* **hímacona** *2s:* **hínicona**

higítų *vt1-pos* s/he wears false teeth *1s:* **híwetų** *2s:* **híyetų**

higítųbi *n* false teeth

hį́į *interj* expression of surprise (female speaker) ▸ **Hį́į! Tągán nína osní.** Oh my! It is cold outside.

hikíyA *vt1-caus* s/he makes sb arrive, come here *1s:* **hiwákiya** *2s:* **hiyákiya**

hímaza *n* gold tooth *Lit:* metal tooth

hinážį *vi1* s/he arrives here and stands

hináǧa *vimper* Wait! Hold on!

hinápA *vi1* s/he/it arrives here and appears; comes into sight ▸ **Téhạn šnayą hinápa.** He appeared in a distance. ▸ **Šųktógeja iyúhana hinápabi.** All the wolves appeared. ▸ **Įknúhana šúga nówa hinápabi.** Suddenly all the dogs appeared. ▸ **Waná waȟpé hinápa.** Now the leaves are coming out. *1s:* **hináwapa** *2s:* **hináyapa**

hipépena *n* ant *Lit:* sharp teeth

hiské *n* tusk

hítąga *n* molar

hiyá *adv* no ▸ **Hiyá, dáguni wacígešį.** No, I do not want anything. ▸ **Šúga žé wapášį? — Hiyá šúga žé wapášį.** Isn't the dog barking? — No the dog is not barking.

hiyábata *n* gum (body-part)

hiyákneya *adv* suddenly ▸ **Á! s'ás'a híkna hiyákneya gáyabi.** Ah! there was a sound of wings and then suddenly it came down. (NS 2002:14)

hiyáyA *vi2* 1) s/he goes, passes by *Lit:* s/he arrives and departs ▸ **Žéca šúgašana hąyákena hiyáya hųštá.** Early in the morning a red fox passed by that way, it is said. (Parks et al. 1994) *aux* 2) it happens quickly, or suddenly *Usage:* preceded by verbs. ▸ **wé hiyáya** s/he/it is bleeding

hiyéde *n* top of the shoulder

hiyó- *pref* gets, takes sb, smth *Usage:* prefixed to verbs of movement. ▸ **yá > hiyóya** s/he goes there > s/he goes there to take sb, smth *Vpos:* **kniyó-**

hiyódą̆gA *vi1/2* s/he arrives here and sits down; s/he arrives here and settles down ‣ **Écen nén hiyódą̆ga.** So they settled here.

hiyóhi *vt1* s/he arrives here to take sb, smth ‣ **"Hı̨́ı̨́, nahą̆ Pahášašana kiyómahi ųkš," eyá.** "Oh, I wish Red Hair would reach me first," she said. (Weasel 43:200) *1s:* **kiyówahi** *2s:* **kiyóyahi**

hiyó'i *vt1* s/he went, arrives there to take sb, smth *1s:* **hiyówa'i** *2s:* **hiyóya'i** *Vpos:* **kniyó'i**

hiyóyA *vt2* s/he goes there to take sb, smth ‣ **Miní hiyóya.** Go and get water. ‣ **Ųspé wą̆ží hiyóya wo.** Go and get an axe. *1s:* **hiyómna** *2s:* **hiyóna**

hiyú *vi1* 1) s/he departs, is setting to come here from there ‣ **Hiyú bo!** Come here you all! ‣ **Midáguyabi néci hiyú bo!** My relatives come over here! *1s:* **wahíyu** *2s:* **yahíyu** *1p:* **ųhíyubi** *Vcaus:* **hiyúkiyA** *vs* 2) it begins, appears, arises, turns into smth ‣ **šayá hiyúbi** measles

hiyú'įc'iyA *vi3-refl* s/he throws himself/herself down ‣ **Kogám hiyúmįc'iya.** I threw myself down in front of him. *1s:* **hiyúmįc'iya** *2s:* **hiyúnįc'iya**

hiyúkiyA *vt1-caus* s/he tosses, sends sb, smth here to him/her; sends sb here ‣ **Dágu nówa hiyúkiyabi.** They send everything here to him. ‣ **Iná wa'óyabi hiyúwakiya.** I send a letter to mom. *1s:* **hiyúwakiya** *2s:* **hiyúyakiya** *1p:* **hiyú'ųkiyabi**

hiyúweǧa *vi1/2* s/he crosses a body of water while arriving here *1s:* **wahímnuweǧa** *2s:* **wahínuweǧa**

hiyúgA *Variant:* **hiwų́gA** *vi1/3* s/he arrives here and lies down *1s:* **wahímuga** *2s:* **wahínuga**

hı̨́ *n* hair, fur, pelt ‣ **šahı̨́** woman's pubic hair ‣ **tahı̨́** ruminant's hair ‣ **[…] hı̨́ žé iyúha bóhiya yą̆gá.** […] all that remained was hair scattered around. (NS 2002:35)

hįcą́ *n* cattail

hįcą́hu *n* cattail stalk

hı̨hą́ 1 *n* 1) owl 2) dove

hı̨hą́ 2 *vimp* it falls, comes down

hı̨hą́ oȟnóga otís'a *ph* burrowing owl *Lit:* hole dweller owl

hı̨hą́ tą́ga *cp* great gray owl

hı̨hą́hana *n-redup* pigmy owl

hı̨hą́są *n* snowy owl *Lit:* off-white owl

hı̨hą́ska (OM) *n* snowy owl *Lit:* white owl

hı̨hą́wapapana *n* short-eared owl *Lit:* barking owl

hı̨ȟcá *vs* s/he/it is shaggy ‣ **Šų́ga žé nína hı̨ȟcá.** That dog is very shaggy *1s:* **hı̨mą́ȟca** *2s:* **hı̨níȟca**

hı̨ȟpáyA *vs* s/he/it collapses, falls down, falls apart, falls from smth (figuratively "s/he becomes sick") ‣ **Ową́ga hı̨ȟpáya.** The bed collapsed. ‣ **Mahı̨́ȟpaya ginı́ja.** I almost fell. *1s:* **mahı̨́ȟpaya** *2s:* **nihı̨́ȟpaya** *1p:* **ųhı̨́ȟpayabi**

hı̨knA *aux* suddenly happens, begins; sudden and sharp ‣ **ot'į́hı̨kna** it is a clap of thunder ‣ **kpáhı̨kna** it is a bullet shot

hı̨́kna ; hı̨́k *conj* and, and then *Usage:* links two verbs or two nouns together. ‣ **Tín ú hı̨́kna wóda wo!** Come in and eat! ‣ **Amápa hı̨́kna mayúȟija.** He hit me, and he woke me up. ‣ **Éyagu hı̨́kna žén ékną̆ga.** He took it and put it down there. ‣ **Ųšigiya nawáží hı̨́kna wacéwagiya.** I stand humbly and I pray. ‣ **Gamnáya:ga hı̨́k žécen aké makóce gáǧa.** He [Įktómi] spreaded out far and wide and made the earth again (Drummond 1976, The flood)

-hı̨kna- ; -hı̨kną̆- *root* husband ‣ **Hı̨knágu tayúza.** She controls her husband. ‣ **Nihı̨́kna dóki iyáya?** Where did your husband go? *1s:* **mihı̨́kna** *2s:* **nihı̨́kna** *3s:* **hı̨knágu** *1p:* **ųgíhı̨knabi**

hı̨knátų *vt1* she has a husband; is married *1s:* **hı̨knáwatų** *2s:* **hı̨knáyatų** *1p:* **hı̨kná'ųtųbi** *Vcaus:* **hı̨knátųkiya**

hı̨knátųbi *n* marriage

hı̨knátųkiyA *vt1-caus* s/he makes her marry, take a husband *1s:* **hı̨knátųwakiya** *2s:* **hı̨knátųyakiya** *1p:* **hı̨kná'ųtųkiyabi**

hı̨knáyA *vt1-caus* she marries sb; has sb for husband ‣ **Wíyą né hı̨knáyįȟtįyą.** This woman really married him. ‣ **Wíyą né hįknáyąbi wacíga.** I want to marry this woman. ‣ **Wíyą žé teyáȟina štén, hįknáya wo.** If you love this woman, then marry her. *1s:* **hįknáwaya** *2s:* **hįknáyaya** *1p:* **hįkná'ųyabi**

hįknų *vt1* s/he singes off an animal

hįktą *n* cattail fuzz

hįn *part* isn't it so?; right? ‣ **Žecéya hįn?** It is like that, isn't it? (Cumberland 2005:334)

hįnígA *vs* s/he/it is mean ‣ **Gą́na:ga hįníga.** The older she got, the meaner she became. ‣ **Wįcásta žé nína hįníga.** That man is very mean. *1s:* **mahį́nįga** *2s:* **nihį́nįga** *1p:* **ųgíhįnįgabi**

hįptéjena *vs* s/he/it has short hair

hįšmą́ *vs* s/he/it has thick hair, fur ‣ **wamnúška hįšmą́šmą** caterpillar *Vredup:* **hįšmą́šmą**

hįšmą́šmą *vs-redup* it (animal) is thick haired

hįtų́ *n* fur

ho-₁ *pref* camp circle, round enclosure

ho-₂ *cont* fish ‣ **mnaská > homnáska** it is flat, plain, smooth > goldeye ‣ **kuwá > hokúwa** s/he/it chases, hunts, goes after sb, smth > s/he fishes

hó 1) *n* voice ‣ **Hó namáȟ'ų wo!** Hear my voice! 2) *vi1* it (canine) howls ‣ **Šųkcúk'ana hó.** The coyote is howling.

hócącą *vs* s/he has a trembling voice ‣ **Mikúši hócącą i'á.** My grandmother speaks with a trembling voice.

hocógam *adv* inside a camp circle

hódodo *n* baby swing

hó'ewįcayagubi *n* tape recorder

hogákna *adv* along, around the camp circle

hogiyA *vt1* s/he cries smth out, announces smth *1s:* **howágiya** *2s:* **hoyágiya** *1p:* **ho'ų́giyabi**

hogíyes'a *n* camp crier ‣ **Wįcá žé hogíyes'a žéca.** That man is the camp crier.

hoǧą́ *n* fish ‣ **Hoǧą́ nína tą́ga.** This fish is very large. ‣ **Hoǧą́ žé huhú ožúna.** That fish is bony.

hoǧą́ǧana *n-redup* minnow

hoǧą́mna *vs* s/he/it smells like fish

hóȟna *vs* s/he has a coarse, rattling voice *1s:* **homáȟna** *2s:* **honíȟna**

hoȟpÁ *vi1* s/he coughs ‣ **Hoȟpácuna.** He is coughing all the time. ‣ **Hą'éyasą įš ho'ų́ȟpabi.** We also coughed all night. *1s:* **howáȟpa** *2s:* **hoyáȟpa** *1p:* **ho'ų́ȟpabi** *See:* **gahóȟpA**

hoȟpá pežúda *cp* cough medicine

hoȟpábi *n* cough, cold

hoȟpábi hą́ska *cp* whooping cough *Lit:* long cough

hoȟpábi téhą *cp* whooping cough *Lit:* prolongated cough

hoȟpí *n* nest *Syn:* **wahóȟpi**

ho'íyegiyA *vt1-pos* s/he recognizes sb's voice

ho'ícuwa *n* fishhook; fishing pole and line

hoká *n* heron

hóka he *adv, interj* yes, exclamation when one is eager to do smth (male speaker)

hokmúǧe *n* fishnet

hokší *cont* 1) child, baby ‣ **Hokší įyúškį.** He adores the baby. 2) boy *Usage:* occurs in personal names. ‣ **Máza hokší** Iron boy

hokší awą́yages'a *cp* babysitter

hokší gíji'įȟpayA *vi1-benef* she/it has a miscarriage ‣ **Nų́baȟ hokší gíji'įȟpaya.** She had two miscarriages. *1s:* **hokší míji'įȟpaya** *2s:* **hokší níji'įȟpaya**

hokší ogíne *vt1-pos* s/he looks for his/her own child *1s:* **hokší owéne** *2s:* **hokší oyéne**

hokší oné *vi1* s/he looks for a child *Vpos:* **hokší ogíne**

hokšícįjage *n* favored child

hokšígiksuyA *vi1* s/he remembers, thinks of his/her child *1s:* **hokšíweksuya** *2s:* **hokšíyeksuya**

hokší'įȟpayA *vi1* she/it has a miscarriage *Vbenef:* **hokší gíji'įȟpayA**

hokšíknuhA *adv* holding one's baby ‣ **Hokšíknuha yąǵá.** She sits holding her baby.

hokšína *n* boy (7–13 years old) ‣ **Hokšína né tacą́kiyutabi záptą hą́ska.** This boy is five feet tall. ‣ **Hokšína gá tába né táwa.** That boy over there owns this ball. ‣ **Hokšína žé nežémna.** That boy smells like urine. *1s:* **mitáhokšina** *2s:* **nitáhokšina** *3s:* **tahókšina** *Cont:* **hokší**

hokšína ohídiga *cp* superhero *Lit:* brave boy

hokšína wąyágabi *n* childcare

hokšína wąyágabi tíbi *np* daycare center

hokšínana *n-redup* small boy

Hokšítogapa *nprop* Jesus Christ *Syn:* **Waką́tąga cįhį́ktu** (Carry The Kettle); **Waką́tąga cįhį́tku** (OM, PR); **Waką́tąga hokšítogapa**

hokšítogapa *n* first born child in a family ‣ **Hokšítogapa wiyódahąm žecí iyódąga.** The first born son sits over to the south.

hokšíyuhA *vi2* she gives birth, is in labor *1s:* **hokšímnuha** *2s:* **hokšínuha** *Syn:* **cįjátų**

hokšíyuza *n* midwife *Lit:* she holds the child

hokšúwa *vi1* it collapses, crumbles

hokún *adv* down, below; downstairs ‣ **Hokún yubáǧe.** He pulled it down. ‣ **Opáya hokún ma'ų́nibi.** We walked down the valley. ‣ **Hokún yá!** Go downstairs!

hokún įjámna *vimp* there is a ground blizzard, drifting snow on the ground

hokúwa *vi1* s/he fishes ‣ **Hokúwa wa'óyabi opétųbikta.** They must buy a fishing permit. ‣ **Ą́ba né nína wašté cén hokúwa ųyábi.** It is a very nice day today, thus we will go fishing. *1s:* **howákuwa** *2s:* **hoyákuwa**

Hókuwa O'į́nažį *ngeo* Fort Qu'Appelle (Saskatchewan) *Lit:* place where one stops to catch fish ‣ **Hókuwa O'į́nažį gakí téhąn** Fort Qu'Appelle is far over there.

hokúwas'a *n* any kind of prey bird that catches fish

homnáska *n* goldeye *Lit:* flat fish

hón *adv, interj* yes, all right ‣ **"Wihínąpa nedám watí. Ú cá," ecíya. — "Hón."** "I live over toward sunrise. You must come," he told him. "All right." (Weasel 63:25–27)

honáǧina ; honáǧi *n* fly, house fly

honáǧina cįjábi *cp-pl* maggots

honáǧinatotobi *n* bluebottle fly

honín-giciyabi *vi1-recip* they comfort one another *1p:* **honín'ųgiciyabi**

honínyA *vt1* s/he comforts sb (like sb who is mourning) *1s:* **honínwaya** *2s:* **honíyaya** *Vrecip:* **honín-giciyabi**

hónisko *vs* s/he has a loud voice; has a voice as loud as this *1s:* **hománisko** *2s:* **honínisko**

hopépe *n* perch, pike, pickerel

hopútįhį yuką́ *cp* catfish *Lit:* the fish that has whiskers

hóta'į *vi1* 1) s/he cries for help in a ritual way (like in a vision quest) *1s:* **hówata'į** *2s:* **hóyata'į** *n* 2) camp crier

hótąga *vs* s/he has a loud voice *1s:* **hómatąga** *2s:* **hónitąga**

hotų́ *vi1* it produces a sound (refers to cries of animals) *Vredup:* **hotų́tų**

hotų́bi *n* cattle call

Hotų́mani *nprop* Hotomani (surname in Carry The Kettle) *Lit:* s/he/it walks bellowing

hotų́tų *vi1-redup* it (horse) neighs, cackles; it (cattle) whines ‣ **Šų́gatąga hotų́tų?** Is the horse neighing? *See:* **šųkhótųtų**

howáyayA *vi1-redup* it (dog) yelps ‣ **Šų́ga žé awápa cén howáyaya.** I hit the dog and it yelped. ‣ **Howáyaya ų́.** He is going around screaming.

howókšą *adv* around the camp circle ‣ **Wacónįca iyéyabi hą́da, yúdagagabina žé howókšą žécen hiyáyabi.** Whenever they found dried meat they would eat it, going around camp like that. (Weasel 81:13)

hoyáȟnana *vi2* s/he has a raspy voice *1s:* **homnáȟnana** *2s:* **honáȟnana**

hóyapsąpsą *vi1* s/he talks with a trembling voice ‣ **Hóyapsąpsą céya:ga.** She kept crying with a trembling voice.

hóyekiyA *vt1-dat* s/he sends a message to sb *Lit:* s/he sends his/her voice to sb ‣ **Žéci hóyewįcawakiyįkta!** I will send a message over

there to them. *1s*: **hóyewakiya** *2s*: **hóyeyakiya**
1p: **hóye'ųkiyabi**

hoyúdA *vi2* s/he/it eats fish *1s*: **homnúda** *2s*: **honúda**

hoyúpsicA *vi2* s/he jerks fish out of water with a line *1s*: **homnúpsija** *2s*: **honúpsija**

hú₁ *n* leg, stem, stalk, wheel ‣ **Hú ótąna yįgá.** Sit with your legs straight in front. ‣ **cą'ágąn hú** leg of a chair ‣ **hú basíbi** steering wheel ‣ **hú mįmámina** wheel *1s*: **mahú** *2s*: **nihú**

hú₂ *vt1* he has sex with her *1s*: **wahú** *2s*: **yahú** *1p*: **ųhúbi**

hú mįmámina *n* wheel *Lit*: round leg ‣ **iyécįgayena hú mįmámina** car wheel

hubákšijA *vi1* s/he pulls his/her legs to the side *1s*: **huwábakšija** *2s*: **huyábakšija**

hubákšin *adv* 1) with the legs pulled to the side ‣ **Mikúši hubákšin yįgá.** My grandmother is sitting with her legs pulled to the side. ‣ **Hubákšin mągá hą́da ksúmaya.** It hurts when I sit with my legs pulled to the side. 2) cross-legged

hucą́ *n* 1) pipe stem 2) stem, leg of an object (like a chair, table) *See*: **cąnúba įhúcą**

hucą́saba *n* black root

hucéšpu *n* 1) wart, growth *vs* 2) s/he/it has a wart ‣ **Nén hucémašpu.** I have a wart here. *1s*: **hucémašpu** *2s*: **hucénišpu**

hucíyadahą *adv* from the leg on the other side, **hucíyadahą** *adv* from the leg on the other side ‣ [. . .] **hucíyadahą yuȟnéȟneja** [. . .] [. . .] he tore up the one from the other side [. . .] (NS 2002:16)

húcoğa *n* hamstring

húda *n* root ‣ **Žé húda, žé ocíjimnaga.** That is the root I was telling you about. *Syn*: **hutką́**

húde *n* 1) base of an object, bottom ‣ **Húde žé iyútabi yámni.** The base is three feet. ‣ **cąhúde** tree stump 2) rectum, bum

Húdeša ; **Húdešana** ; **Húdešabina** *nprop* Red bottom people (band of Nakoda living in Fort Peck, Montana) ‣ **Atkúgu Húdešabi žedáhą hą́da, cįjábi į́š Húdešabi.** When the father is Red Bottom, the children also are Red Bottom. (Ryan 1998:26)

hugáše *vs* s/he stumbles, trips over *1s*: **humágaše** *2s*: **hunígaše** *Vcaus*: **hugášeyA**

hugášeyA *vt1-caus* s/he trips sb

hugáškA *vt1* s/he ties its leg; hobbles a horse ‣ **Šų́gatąga žé hugáška.** He hobbled the horse.

huhú *n* bone, bones ‣ **Hoğá žé huhú ožúna.** That fish is full of bones.

huhú mnumnúğe *cp* cartilage

huhú yazą́ *vs* s/he has, suffers from arthritis

huhú yazą́bi *n* arthritis

Huhúmasmibi *nprop* They clean bones people

huhúwanap'į *n* breastplate, necklace

Huhúžubina *ngeo* Regina (Saskatchewan) *Lit*: pile of bones ‣ **Huhúžubina žecíyadahą wahí no!** I come from around Regina! ‣ **Huhúžubina aškán nén wahí.** I arrived here in Regina recently.

huȟcá *n* hair on the hoof or paw

huȟnáğa *vs* s/he/it is burnt, scorched ‣ **Tíbi žé huȟnáğa.** That house is burnt. ‣ **Wa'ówabi nówa huȟnağa.** All the papers are burnt. *Vabs*: **wahúȟnayA** *Vcaus*: **huȟnáȟyA** *Vrefl*: **huȟnáȟ'įc'iyA**

huȟnáȟyA *vt1* s/he burns, scorches smth ‣ **Owá huȟnáȟwayįkte no.** I will put everything on fire. ‣ **Wa'ówabi nówa huȟnáȟwaya.** I burned all of the papers. *1s*: **huȟnáȟwaya** *2s*: **huȟnáȟyaya** *Vabs*: **wahúȟnayA** *Vrefl*: **huȟnáȟ'įc'iyA**

huȟnáȟyabi *n* coffee, coffee beans *Lit*: that which is scorched ‣ **Huȟnáȟyabi gáğa wo!** Make coffee! ‣ **Huȟnáȟyabi yacíga? —Hą́ edáhą wacíga.** Do you want coffee? —Yes I want some. ‣ **Huȟnáȟyabi cąšmúyabi cóna mak'ú.** Give me coffee without sugar. ‣ **Duwé huȟnáȟyabi gáğa?** Who made coffee?

huȟnáȟyabi céğa *cp* coffee pot

huȟnáȟ'įc'iyA *vi3-refl* s/he scorches smth (toasts) for himself/herself *1s:* **huȟnáȟ-mįc'iya** *2s:* **huȟnáȟ-nįc'iya** *1p:* **huȟnáȟ'ųgįc'iyabi**

húȟni *vi1* s/he rushes in *Adv:* **húȟniya**

húȟniya *vt1-caus* s/he hurries sb ▸ **Iná ecágen húȟnimaya.** Mom always hurries me.

húȟniya ; húȟniyena *adv* hurriedly, in a hurry, in a rush ▸ **Húȟniya wa'ú.** I came in a hurry. *Syn:* **įnáȟniyena**

húȟniyena *adv* hurriedly, in a rush ▸ **Húȟniyena wowádįkta.** I will eat in a hurry. ▸ **Húȟniyena wowádįkta.** I will take a quick bite. ▸ **Húȟniyena wahí.** I came in a rush.

hukwáá ; húk *interj* expression of surprise or disinterest, discontent (male speaker) ▸ **Hukwáá waná he?** What is happening now? ▸ **Hukwáá! Nežénimna.** Oh my! You smell like urine.

humnó *n* shin bone *Syn:* **cąkpé**

húsaba *n* blackleg disease *See:* **sikásaba**

hústagA *vs* s/he/it is skinny ▸ **Nína mahústaga amáya.** I am getting really skinny. ▸ **Niyé nihústaga óda wóda duká wo!** As for you, you are skinny, you should eat more! *1s:* **mahústaga** *2s:* **nihústaga** *1p:* **ųhústagabi**

husté *vs* s/he/it is lame *1s:* **mahúšte** *2s:* **nihúšte** *1p:* **ųhúštebi** *Adv:* **huštéyagen**

huštéguza *vi1* s/he pretends to be lame ▸ **Kní cén huštéguza kó cén.** As he came back, he craftily pretended to be lame. (Cumberland 2005:433) *1s:* **huštéwaguza** *2s:* **huštéyaguza**

huštéyagen *adv* with a limp ▸ **Huštéyagen maní.** He is walking with a limp.

hutką *n* root

-hų- *root* mother *Usage:* used for reference, although some speakers use the vocative form iná for both address and reference. ▸ **Mihų́ žeyá, "Nén iyódągam!"** My mother said, "Sit down here!" ▸ **Mihų́ waȟpé gáǧa.** My mother is making tea. ▸ **Nihų́ dokí iyáya he?** Where did your mother go? ▸ **Atkúgu, húgu įš nahą́ȟ níbi.** His father and his mother too are still alive. *1s:* **mihų́** *2s:* **nihų́** *3s:* **húgu** *1p:* **iná'ųyąbi** *See:* **iná**

hųcíhįtku *n* chief's son

hųgá *n* 1) chief, king ▸ **Hųgá gaȟníȟabi.** They chose a chief. ▸ **Hųgá žé mnacókta.** I will sue the chief. *1s:* **mitáhųga** *2s:* **nitáhųga** *3s:* **tahúga** *Cont:* **hųk-; hų-**-*vi1* 2) he is a chief *1s:* **wahúga** *2s:* **yahúga**

hųgágA *vi1* s/he tells a fairy tale ▸ **Gábina hųgágabis'a.** Old people used to tell fairy tales. *1s:* **wahúgagą** *2s:* **yahúgagą** *Vbenef:* **hųgágijigą**

hųgágąbi *n* fairy tale

hųgágebi *n-pl* parents ▸ **Mihúgagebi wįcágiksuyabi.** My parents remember them. *1s:* **mihúgagebi** *2s:* **nihúgagebi**

hųgágijigą *vt1-benef* s/he tells sb a fairy tale *1s:* **hųgáwejigą** *2s:* **hųgáyejigą** *1p:* **hųgá'ųgijigąbi**

Hųgájuk'a *nprop* Little chief (1839–1873); Nakoda chief killed during the Cypress Hills massacre of 1873

hų́gešį *vs* s/he/it is slow ▸ **Nína nihúgešį no.** You are very slow. *1s:* **mahúgešį** *2s:* **nihúgešį**

hųgíya *n* camp crier

hųgóȟ'abi *n* giveaway *See:* **wakpámni ecúbi**

hųgóȟ'ą *vi1* s/he does a giveaway, birthday party *1s:* **hųgówaȟ'ą** *2s:* **hųgóyaȟ'ą**

hųgóȟ'ą onówą *cp* giveaway song

húguyA *vt1-caus* s/he has her as a mother ▸ **Garcia húguwaya.** I have Garcia as a mother. ▸ **Martha húgumaya.** Martha has me as a mother. ▸ **Húguciyaȟtįyą!** I am your real mother!

hųk- ; hų- *cont* chief ▸ **wíyą > hųkwíyą** woman > queen ▸ **cįhįtku > hųcíhįtku** chief > chief's son

hųkwíyą *n* queen; queen in playing cards

Hųkwíyą ta'ába *cp* Victoria Day *Lit:* queen's day

hų́n *encl* I wonder (marker of modality) *Usage:* used when the speaker does not know the likeliness of an event. ▸ **Gakí dágu ecúbi hų́n.** I wonder what is going on over there. ▸ **Dágucen ecú hų́n.** I wonder why he did it. ▸ **Dágu dók'ų**

hų́n. I wonder what he is doing. ‣ **Dóki yúzabi hų́n.** I wonder where they caught him.

-hųna- *root* aunt (mother's sister, father's brother's wife) *Usage:* only used with 2nd and 3rd persons. *1s:* **inána** *2s:* **nihų́na** *3s:* **hų́guna** *1p:* **iná'ųyąbina** *See:* **inána**

hų́pe *n* picket, tipi peg *Redup:* **hų́pepena**

hų́pepena *n-redup* pickets, tipi pegs

hųská *n* pants, leggings ‣ **Hųská né duwé opétų he?** Who bought these pants? ‣ **Hųská žé pšopšó.** Those pants are baggy.

hųskána *n* stockings

hųskáto *n* jeans, denims ‣ **Hųskáto babóda.** He wears out his jeans.

hųskíjažе *n* garter *1s:* **mitáhųskįjažе** *2s:* **nitáhųskįjažе** *3s:* **tahų́skįjažе**

hųskógit'ų *vii* s/he wears pants ‣ **Duwé hųskógit'ųgen.** No one wore pants. (Weasel 6:123)

hųštÁ *part* people say, they say, it is said (marker of reported speech) *Usage:* some speakers ablaut this particle. ‣ **Úkta hųštá** It is said he would come. ‣ **Tawíju apá hųštá no!** People said that he beats his wife. ‣ **Dóki nį́kta hųštá žé nawáh̆'ų.** I heard you are leaving.

H̆

-h̆ *suff* 1) absolutely, the very X, exactly, specifically, at all (marks focus on demonstratives, nouns, pronouns, and negative interrogative pronouns) ‣ **nówa > nówah̆** all of these > absolutely all of these ‣ **ocágu > ocáguh̆** road > (the) specific road ‣ **miyé > miyéh̆** myself > myself specifically ‣ **duwéni > duwénih̆** nobody > nobody at all 2) some-(marks nonspecificity on indefinite interrogative pronouns and articles) ‣ **duwé > duwéh̆** who > someone ‣ **wąží > wąžíh̆** a > any 3) very, really (intensifier of gradable expressions such as manner and time adverbs; occurs obligatory with the

degree adverb **nína** 'very' in negative clauses) ‣ **éstena > éstenah̆** soon > very soon ‣ **nína ktá > nínah̆ ktáší** it is very heavy > it is not very heavy 4) derives numerals or verbs into adverbs of time or manner (indicates multiplication when used with numerals) ‣ **dóba > dóbah̆** four > four times ‣ **dágeyeší > dágeyešíh̆** s/ he does not say a thing > silently

h̆ah̆á *vimp* it is a liquid that flows ‣ **Wakpá žé dókiyo h̆ah̆á.** The river is flowing its course.

H̆ah̆átųwą *nprop* Gros Ventres, Atsina people, person of Gros Ventres, Atsina descent

h̆ah̆ų́da *n* thread, rope ‣ **H̆ah̆ų́da žé yut'į́s mnúza.** I hold the rope tightly. ‣ **H̆ah̆ų́da žé pah̆tá.** Tie the rope.

h̆amyÁ *vt1-caus* s/he scares, chases smth (animal) away

h̆ayÁ *vt1-caus* s/he blocks smth with it

h̆ą́ *n* scab

h̆cá *vi* it blooms

h̆ciná *vs* it is ragged, tattered

h̆é *n* mountain, mountain ridge ‣ **H̆é nén matų́bi no.** I was born here in the mountains.

H̆ébina *nprop* Rock mountain people (band of Stoney living in Morley, Alberta)

h̆eh̆ágana ; h̆eh̆ágągana *n* spider

h̆eh̆ágągana wakmų́ga *cp* cobweb *Syn:* **wosų́sųbina**

H̆énatųwąbina *nprop* Mountain village people (band of Nakoda living in the Little Rocky Mountains and Fort Belknap)

H̆épa *ngeo* Moose Mountain (Saskatchewan) *Syn:* **Tah̆é**

H̆ewáktųkta *nprop* Hidatsa people, person of Hidatsa descent

h̆eyám *adv* in the back, behind ‣ **H̆eyám mawánįkta.** I will walk behind. ‣ **H̆eyám ú!** Stay behind! ‣ **Žécen h̆eyám iyáya hį́k įc'ícuwa.** And then he went off and fixed himself. (Drummond 1976, Įktomi and the ducks)

h̆eyátakiya *adv* toward the hill

ȟijáȟą *vs* s/he trips, stumbles on smth and falls ‣ Įknúhanaȟ ȟijáhą. He suddenly tripped and fell. ‣ Maȟíjahą įstó wakpáksa. I tripped and broke my arm. *1s:* maȟíjahą *2s:* niȟíjahą *Vcaus:* ȟijáheyA

ȟijáheyA *vt1-caus* s/he makes sb trip, stumble

ȟmá *vs* s/he is sleepy ‣ Ȟmá kó. He was sleepy too. ‣ Hąyákena nén maȟmá. I am sleepy this morning. ‣ Macúwida ga'éca maȟmá. I am sleepy from being cold. ‣ Osnídahą ȟmá. He is sleepy because of the cold. *1s:* maȟmá *2s:* niȟmá *1p:* ųȟmábi

ȟmúyahą *vi1* 1) s/he/it buzzes, rumbles, emits a buzzing sound (motor, airplane, bee) *1s:* ȟmųyámahą *2s:* ȟmųyánihą *n* 2) rattle, maraca, band instrument

ȟná *vi* it is a rattling sound; it rattles *Vredup:* ȟnáȟna

ȟnáȟna *vi-redup* it rattles

ȟneȟnéjA *vs-redup* it is ragged ‣ Cuwíknąga mitáwa žé ȟneȟnéja. My coat is ragged.

ȟnejá *vs* it is torn ‣ Wí žé agá'oȟya ȟnejáhą. That tent is torn at an angle. (Fourstar p. 3)

ȟní *vs* 1) s/he/it has a sore *n* 2) sore, disease *Syn:* ȟníbi

ȟníbi *n* sore

ȟníbi tága *cp* cancer *Lit:* great sore

ȟniȟní *vs-redup* s/he/it has rashes, scabies ‣ Ųzé ȟniȟní. He has rashes on the buttocks.

ȟníyą *vs* s/he has the chills *1s:* maȟníyą *2s:* niȟníyą *1p:* ųȟníyąbi

ȟníyąyą *vs-redup* s/he shivers (from cold or fever) *1s:* maȟníyąyą *2s:* niȟníyąyą

ȟnó *vi1* it (animal) growls *See:* aȟnó

ȟnogéja *vs* it is hollow

ȟnokíyA *vt1* s/he makes sb, smth (a dog) growl ‣ Šúga žé ȟnowákiya. I made the dog growl. *1s:* ȟnowákiya *2s:* ȟnoyákiya

ȟó *interj* expression indicating doubt, oh! (female speaker) ‣ Ȟó! Duwé snokyéšį. Oh! People do not know that. ‣ Ȟó! Duwé žé'įš. Oh! I doubt

he is the one. ‣ Ȟó! Nįšnánašį. Oh! You are not alone.

ȟóda *vs* s/he/it is gray ‣ Šųktógeja nųba wawícąmnaga, ȟódabi no! I saw two wolves, they were gray. *1s:* maȟóda *2s:* niȟóda *Vcaus:* ȟonyÁ *Vcont:* ȟon *Vredup:* ȟonȟóda

ȟogá *n* badger ‣ Ȟogá žé mąká k'á. The badger is digging dirt. *Syn:* o'íknuhena

ȟon *vcont* gray condition ‣ Ȟon áya. It is getting gray.

ȟonȟóda *Variant:* ȟotȟóda *vs-redup-pl* they are gray

ȟon'íc'iyA *vi3-refl* s/he paints himself/herself in gray

ȟonkíjiyA *vt1-benef* s/he paints, colors sb, smth in gray for sb

ȟonkíyA *vt1-pos* s/he paints, colors, dyes his/her own gray *1s:* ȟonwágiya *2s:* ȟonyágiya

ȟonyÁ *vt1-caus* s/he paints, colors, dyes sb, smth in gray *Vbenef:* ȟonkíjiyA *Vpos:* ȟonkíyA *Vrefl:* ȟon'íc'iyA

ȟoškíškina *n* sandy, hilly terrain

ȟpąyÁ *vt1-caus* s/he soaks smth in water ‣ Į'íjuna okná ȟpąyą́ eknąga. He put it in a cup to soak. *1s:* ȟpąwáya *2s:* ȟpąyáya *1p:* ȟpą'ų́yąbi

ȟpuȟpú *vs* s/he/it is chapped, scaly, rough ‣ Nąbé niȟpúȟpu. Your hands are chapped. ‣ Įští maȟpúȟpu. I have chapped lips. ‣ Nąbé ȟpuȟpú stéȟ ųgúbi. Our hands were always chapped like that. (Cumberland 2005:328) *1s:* maȟpúȟpu *2s:* niȟpúȟpu *1p:* ųȟpúȟpubi

ȟta- *cont* in the evening

ȟtánihą *adv* yesterday ‣ Ȟtánihą t'į́kta. She would have died yesterday. ‣ Ȟtánihąc'ehą wakní. I came back home yesterday. ‣ Ȟtánihą šúga tągán gicízabi. Yesterday the dogs were fighting outside.

ȟtawódA *vi1* s/he/it eats in the evening

ȟtayédu 1) *n* evening ‣ Ȟtayédu né amnágena. The evening is still. 2) *vimp* it is evening ‣

Ȟtayédu cén tída waknį́kta. Because it is evening I will go home. *Cont:* ȟta-

-ȟtįyĄ *suff* 1) very, really, real, genuine, -est *Usage:* intensifier and superlative of stative verbs of quality and colors and some kinship verbs; as a suffix-**ȟtįyĄ** occurs before the negative, aspect, and modality enclitics. ‣ **ǧí > ǧíȟtįyą** it is yellow > it is deep yellow ‣ **dąyą́ > dąyą́ȟtįya** it is good > it is very good/best ‣ **tą́ga > tągáȟtįyą** it is big > it is very big/biggest ‣ **adéšį > adéȟtįyešį** he is not my father > he is not my real father *encl* 2) exactly, really anxious to, absolutely, at all (marks focus on active verbs and some nongradable stative verbs) *Usage:* as an enclitic-**ȟtįyĄ** occurs after the negative, aspect, and modality enclitics and does not ablaut; when used alone-**ȟtįyĄ** is a focus restrictor that translates as 'exactly'; the combination-**kteȟtįyĄ** expresses an intense desire to do something and translates as 'anxious to,' or 'really wants to'; the combination-**šįȟtįyĄ** conveys the idea that there are no other options available and translates as 'absolutely,' 'completely,' or 'at all.' ‣ **duktédu > duktéduȟtįya** it happened somewhere as such > where did it happen exactly? ‣ **yį́kta > yį́kteȟtįya** s/he will go > s/he is anxious to go, really wants to go ‣ **ogíhišį > ogíhišįȟtįya** s/he cannot do it > s/he absolutely cannot do it ‣ **dágunišį > dágunišįȟtįya** it is nothing > it is nothing at all

ȟubá wagíknągagana *cp* bat (animal) *Lit:* it saves its own wings

ȟubáhu *n* wing ‣ **wagíyą ȟubáhu máza** iron-winged thunderbird

ȟuȟúna *n* ghost, monster (invoked to scare off children)

ȟuyá *n* eagle

Ȟuyátąga *nprop* BigEagle (surname in Pheasant Rump, White Bear, and Ocean Man, Saskatchewan)

ȟųwį́ *vs* it has a rotten smell ‣ **Wį́tka ȟųwį́, tanó žé'įš ȟųwį́.** The eggs have a rotten smell, and the meat too has a rotten smell.

ȟųwį́mna *vs* s/he/it smells rank, putrid ‣ **Wanągaš t'áhą cén dágu né ȟųwį́mna.** This thing died long ago because it smells putrid.

Ȟ'

ȟ'ą́ *vi1* s/he behaves; s/he does smth (in interrogative sentences) ‣ **"Dóken ųȟ'ą́bikta he?" eyágabi.** "How will we do it?" they said. (NS 2002:42) ‣ **Įdúȟ dóken yaȟ'ą́kteší.** Certainly you cannot do anything. (NS 2002:73) *1s:* **waȟ'ą́** *2s:* **yaȟ'ą́** *1p:* **ųȟ'ą́bi**

ȟ'eyáyana *n* grapes

ȟ'oká 1) *vi1* s/he sings with a drum group; beats the drum in a powwow or dance 2) *n* singer

ȟ'oká yįgábi *cp* drum singer, member of a drum group

I

i- *pref* doing smth while arriving there from here; doing smth after arriving there from here ‣ **yeyÁ > iyéyA** s/he sends sb, smth away > s/he sends smth, sb there from here (away from speaker)

í₁ *n* mouth ‣ **Í nagítaga.** Close your mouth. *1s:* **ma'í** *2s:* **ni'í**

í₂ *vi1* s/he arrives there from here *Usage:* this verb is often translated with 'went'; triggers e-ablaut in the preceding word. ‣ **Šiyónide aškán nén í.** She arrived there in Pheasant Rump recently. ‣ **Duktéȟ í cá'.** He went somewhere else I guess. ‣ **Ą́ba waką́ žehą́ owácegiya žéci wa'í.** I went to church on Sunday. *1s:* **wa'í** *2s:* **ya'í** *1p:* **ųgíbi**

i'Á ; iyÁ *vt1* 1) s/he speaks, talks to sb, with sb ‣ **Dóhani én imá'ešį.** He never speaks to me. ‣ **Wašín'icí'a.** I am talking English to you. ‣ **Wįyą́ žé gicí i'ą́bikta.** He will speak with that woman. *vi1* 2) s/he speaks; speaks a language ▸ **Nakón'i'á wo.** Speak Nakoda. ▸ **Owáštena i'á.** Speak slowly. ▸ **I'écuna.** She is continuously yapping. ▸ **Gakí iyódąga wo, i'éšį wo.** Sit over there and do not speak. ▸ **I'á:ga gicí teȟíga.** He has a speech disability. *1s:* iwá'a *2s:* iyá'a *1p:* ųgí'abi *Vbenef:* igíji'A *Vcaus:* i'ékiyA

i'ábi *n* language ▸ **Nakón'i'ábi gídana owágaȟniǧa duká iwá'ešį.** I understand a little bit of Nakoda but I don't speak it. *Syn:* **wįcó'i'e**

I'ášijana; I'ášija; I'ásija; Iyášija; Iyásija *nprop* person of Dakota, Chippewa, Saulteaux, French, German, Ukrainian or Russian descent *Lit:* bad talker

I'áš'abi *nprop* Eashappie (surname in Carry The Kettle) *Lit:* they cheer for him/her

i'átoką *vi1* s/he talks differently

íbutagA *vt1* s/he kisses sb, smth ▸ **Micúkši íwabutaga.** I kissed my daughter. ▸ **Iná ímabutaga.** Mom kissed me. *1s:* íwabutaga *2s:* íyabutaga *Vbenef:* ígijibutagA *Vrecip:* ígicibutagabi

íbutakuwa *vt1* s/he is always seeking a kiss from sb *Lit:* chasing a kiss

íci- *pref* together ▸ **iyúhana > íciyuhana** all > everybody

ícigaška *vt1* s/he ties sb, smth together ▸ **Pagúda žé íciwįcawagaška.** I tied the ducks together. (Cumberland 2005:235) *1s:* íciwagaška *2s:* íciyagaška

ícitoką *adv* different when compared to, different altogether ▸ **Nakón-nowąbi umá wašín-nowąbi žé ícitoką.** Nakoda songs are different from English songs. (Cumberland 2005:235)

íciyuhana *adv* everybody, all the people together ▸ **Íciyuhana cicóbi.** I invite you all.

i'égabį *vi1* s/he is reluctant to talk

i'égicuni *vi1-irr* s/he is done talking *1s:* **i'éwecuni** *2s:* **i'éyecuni**

i'ékiyA *vt1-caus* s/he makes sb speak *1s:* **i'éwakiya** *2s:* **i'éyakiya**

i'éknašna *vi1* s/he had a slip of the tongue, misspoke *1s:* **i'éwaknašna** *2s:* **i'éyaknašna**

i'épina *n* chatterbox

i'éšį *vi1* 1) s/he is mute *n* 2) mute person *Lit:* s/he does not speak

ígicibutagabi *vi1-recip* they kissed one another ▸ **Ígicibutaga yągábi** They are kissing.

igíji'A *vt1-benef* s/he speaks for, on behalf of sb *1s:* **iwéji'a** *2s:* **iyéji'a**

ígijibutagA *vt-benef* s/he kisses sb for him/her *1s:* **íwejibutaga** *2s:* **íyejibutaga**

ihá (WB) *n* lips, both lips *See:* **įští**

iháȟni *n* cold sore

íkmus *vcont* with the mouth closed ▸ **Íkmus yągá.** She sits with the mouth closed.

íkmuza *vi1* s/he/it has his/her/its mouth closed *Vcont:* **íkmus**

imáǧaǧa *vs* s/he is amused, entertained by sb, smth; socializes *Vcaus:* **imáǧaǧakiyA**

imáǧaǧakiyA *vt1-caus* s/he amuses sb; makes sb glad

imnézA *vs* s/he sobers up; lifts his/her spirit up *1s:* **imámneza** *2s:* **inímneza**

iná *voc* 1) Mother! (address form) ▸ **Iná amáǧaȟpa!** Mom cover me up! **Iná! Imnámnįkteší no!** Mother! I will not go! *n* 2) my mother *Usage:* reference form. ▸ **Žé iná!** That is my mother! ▸ **Iná awámnaga.** I care for my mother. ▸ **Iná įš adé Nakón'i'ábi jé.** Mother and father always spoke Nakoda. *1s:* **mi'ína** *1p:* **iná'ųyąbi**

Iná ába *cp* Mother's Day

Iná maká *nprop* Mother Earth ▸ **Iná maká pinámayaye no, Nakón-wįcóȟ'ąge waką no!** Thank you Mother Earth, for the holy Nakoda way of life! *See:* **Mikúši Makóce, Ųjímąka**

Iná waką *cp* Holy Mary *Lit:* holy mother

inána *n* 1) my aunt (mother's sister) 2) my aunt (father's brother's wife) *Usage:* this noun occurs with 1st person singular and plural. *1s:* **inána** *2s:* **nihų́na** *3s:* **húguna** *1p:* **iná'ųyąbina**

Inína ų́bi *nprop* Quiet people (band of Nakoda that lived near Cypress Hills, Saskatchewan)

inína ų́bi *ph* silent child

inį́da *vs* s/he is anxious to start smth

i'óžuna *vs* s/he/it has a mouthful *1s:* **i'ómažuna** *2s:* **i'ónižuna**

i'óžunyapa ; i'óžuyapa *vi2* s/he gets a mouthful ▸ **Žécen iyáya cén eyáš i'óžuyapa [. . .]** Then he went, so he got a mouthful [. . .] (NS 2002:29) *1s:* **i'óžunamnapa** *2s:* **i'óžunanapa**

ísnagiya *n* lip balm

íšagiya *n* lipstick *Lit:* it makes one's mouth red

išícona *adv* 1) free 2) available ▸ **Išícona nén wa'ų́.** I am available now.

išíjA *vs* s/he feels bad because of it ▸ **Dágu imášija.** There is something wrong with me. *1s:* **imą́šija** *2s:* **inį́šija**

ítutu *vs* s/he/it drools, slobbers ▸ **Žé ítutu.** That one is slobbering. *1s:* **ímatutu** *2s:* **ínitutu** *Adv:* **ítutuya** *Vcaus:* **ítutuyA**

ítutuyA *vt1-caus* s/he makes sb drool, slobber ▸ **Ómna né ítutumaya.** This smell makes me drool.

ítutuya *adv* in a drooling, slobbering manner

íwašiju *vs* s/he is mouthy *Lit:* white man's mouth *1s:* **ímawašiju** *2s:* **íniwašiju**

íwe hiyáyA *vs-redup* s/he bleeds from the mouth *1s:* **íwe himáyaya** *2s:* **íwe hiníyaya**

íyabizA *vt2* s/he smooches sb; kisses by producing a loud sucking sound *1s:* **ímnabiza** *2s:* **ínabiza** *1p:* **ųgíyabizabi**

iyágicipebi *vi1-recip* they wait for one another

iyágiȟpayA *vt1-dat* 1) s/he grabs smth from him/her with force *vt1-pos* 2) s/he grabs his/her own ▸ **Tábana né íyagiȟpaya hį́k žécen naȟmá tągán yá.** He grabbed up his ball and then secretly went outside. (NS 2002:22)

iyágipe *vt1-dat* 1) s/he waits for sb, smth ▸ **Iyámągipešį kó kosán yá.** He did not wait

for me and passed by. *vt1-pos* 2) s/he waits for his/her own ▸ **Micį́kši iyáwagipe.** I wait for my son. *1s:* **iyáwagipe** *2s:* **iyáyagipe**

iyáhĄ *vi1* s/he/it lands ▸ **Žécen én iyáhą.** And so it landed there. ▸ **Owédu hą́da pağų́da žená nén iyáhąbi.** In the spring those ducks land here.

iyáȟpayA *vt1* s/he attacks, rapes sb; grabs sb, smth with force ▸ **Šų́ga žé búza iyáȟpaya.** The dog attacked the cat. ▸ **Cųwį́ktu iyáȟpayabi.** Her daughter got raped. ▸ **Košká né iyáȟpaya póskin yúza hį́k gikną́.** He grabbed the boy in his arms, embraced him, and caressed him. (Drummond 1976, The boy who made peace.) *1s:* **iwáyaȟpaya** *2s:* **iyáyaȟpaya** *Vdat:* **iyágiȟpayA** *Vpos:* **iyágiȟpayA**

iyákna *post* together with smth, sb ▸ **Dágu táwa teȟína žé nówa, iyákna piyábi mąká én ahíbi.** All of his treasured things are buried with him in the ground. (Shields 34:173) ▸ **Huhú žé níyuhana eyáš yamnúȟ yúdabi, tašúbana né iyákna.** They ate all of the bones, crunching them up together with the guts. (Weasel 52:377)

iyákne *post* together with ▸ **Táno né iyákna wahą́bi gáğabi.** They make a broth together with meat.

iyáksamkiyA *vt1-caus* s/he trains an animal (horse, dog) ▸ **Mitášųga iyáksamwakiyįkte no.** I will train my horse. *1s:* **iyáksamwakiyabi** *2s:* **iyáksamyakiyabi** *1p:* **iyáksamųkiyabi**

iyám *adv* along, against ▸ **Micį́kši iyám ų́ąga.** My son ran against it. ▸ **Cą'ágą yįgábi awódabi iyám éknąga.** Put the chairs along the table.

iyáme í *vi1* s/he went hunting *1s:* **iyáme wa'í** *2s:* **iyáme ya'í** *1p:* **iyáme ųgíbi** *See:* **í**

iyáme yÁ *vi2* s/he goes hunting *1s:* **iyáme mná** *2s:* **iyáme ná**

iyáni ; i'áni *vt1* s/he/it climbs on sb, smth ▸ **Cą́ iyáni.** Climb up the tree. ▸ **Néci iyáni.** Climb up here. ▸ **Hokšína žé abáhan iyáni.** That boy climbed up on that knoll. (Fourstar, p.1) *1s:* **iyáwani** *2s:* **iyáyani**

iyápa *vs* 1) s/he touches, bumps into smth 2) his/her/its heart is beating (used with c̨ądé 'heart') ‣ **c̨ądé iyápa** s/he is excited, agitated; his/her heart beats fast

iyápabi *n* pulse, heartbeat

iyápe *vt1* s/he lies waiting for sb; ambushes sb ‣ **Oc̨águ gakná iyápebi.** They are ambushed beside the road. *Vdat:* **iyágipe** *Vrecip:* **iyágicipebi**

iyápebi *n* ambush

iyápeh̨ą *vt1-dit* s/he binds, wraps smth around it

Iyásija makóce *ngeo* France, Germany, Ukraine

iyásije *n* foreign language

iyáyA₁ *vi2* s/he sets to go from here, departs from here (before or shortly after departure) ‣ **Mit̨ágena dóki inána he?** My older sister, where are you setting to go? ‣ **Wayáwa tíbi dóh̨ą inánįkta?** When will you be setting to go to school? ‣ **Owópetų imnámna.** I am setting to go to the store. *1s:* **imnámna** *2s:* **inána** *1p:* **ųgíyayabi**

iyáyA₂ *vs-aux* s/he/it gradually becomes; turns into ‣ **I̧štíma iyáya.** She fell asleep. ‣ **I̧dómni imáyaya jé.** I always become dizzy. ‣ **Miní né sábasteh̨ iyáya.** This water is turning blackish. *1s:* **imáyaya** *2s:* **iníyaya**

iyáyena *vi2* s/he (child, little animal) sets to go from here, departs from here

iyáza *adv* in succession, one after the other

iyázagen *adv* in succession, one after the other; wandering ‣ **Iyúha iyázagen híbi.** They all arrived one after the other. ‣ **Žécen iyázagen ú:ga.** So then he wandered aroung. (Shields 77:416)

iyážo *n* whistle, eagle bone whistle

iyážo k'i̧bi *n* whistle carrier

iyé *pro* 1) himself, herself, themselves, itself (emphasizes the subject or object) ‣ **Tíbi né iyé gáği̧kte no.** He will build this house himself. ‣ **Iyé onébi.** They seek it for themselves. ‣ **Ecágen miyé ecúmakiya.** She always makes me do it. ‣ **Niyé mitáwa.** You are mine. ‣ **Niyé omágipi.** I am happy for you ‣ **U̧gíye miní a'úbapsųbi.** As for us, we were baptized. *vs* 2) s/he/it/they is/are the one(s) ‣ **Iyébi he úbi žé! —H̨ą iyébi!** Is it them coming? — Yes it is them. *1s:* **miyé** *2s:* **niyé** *1p:* **u̧gíye** *3p:* **iyébi**

iyéci̧ga *adv* on his/her/its own; by himself/herself/itself ‣ **Iyéci̧ga abápsu̧.** He poured it on by himself. *1s:* **miyéci̧ga** *2s:* **niyéci̧ga** *1p:* **u̧gíyeci̧ga**

iyéci̧gamani *n* car

iyéci̧gayena ; iyéci̧gana ; iyéci̧ga ; iyéci̧gena *n* car, automobile *Syn:* **amógiyą ; amúgiyą ; i̧múgiya ; iyéci̧gamani**

iyéga kóšta *ph* even him/her/it/them ‣ **Miyéga kóšta ecámu̧ši̧ ca!** Even I would not do that. *1s:* **miyéga kóšta** *2s:* **niyéga kóšta** *1p:* **u̧gíyega kóšta**

iyégeȟ *pro* himself/herself/itself/themselves specifically ‣ **Miyégeȟ i̧ȟpémayabi.** They left me behind. *1s:* **miyégeȟ** *2s:* **niyégeȟ** *1p:* **u̧gíyegeȟ** *Syn:* **iyéȟ**

iyégeȟti̧yA ; iyéȟti̧yA *vs3* it is himself/herself/itself/themselves specifically *1s:* **miyégeȟti̧yą ; miyéȟti̧yą** *2s:* **niyégeȟti̧yą ; niyéȟti̧yą** *1p:* **u̧gíyeȟti̧yabi** *3p:* **iyéȟti̧yabi**

iyégijiska *vt1-benef* s/he interprets, translates for sb ‣ **Mikúši iyéwejiska.** I translate for my grandmother. ‣ **Mit̨ágoza iyémijiska.** My grandson translates for me. ‣ **Wašíjubi iyéwi̧cagijiska.** He translates for the White people. *1s:* **iyéwejiska** *2s:* **iyéyejiska** *1p:* **iyé'u̧gijiskabi** *See:* **iyéska**

iyégiyA *vt1-pos* s/he recognizes, finds his/her own ‣ **Iná iyéwagiya.** I found my mom. ‣ **Šúga žé iyéyagiya?** Did you find that dog of yours? ‣ **Atkúgu tíbi žé iyégiya.** She recognized her father's lodge. ‣ **"Iyégiya wo," ejíyabi.** "Find

him," they told him. (NS 2002:14) 1s: **iyéwagiya**
2s: **iyéyagiya** 1p: **iyé'ụgiyabi**

iyéhạdu *vs* it is now the time ‣ **Né waná giktá
iyéhạdu.** Now it is time to get up.

iyéȟ *pro* specifically, really him, himself, she,
her, herself, they, them, themselves, it, itself ‣
Miyéȟ watápe žemạca. I am a real hunter. *1s:*
miyéȟ *2s:* **niyéȟ** *1p:* **ụgíyeȟ** *Syn:* **iyégeȟ**

iyékapeya *adv* above, exceedingly ‣ **Iyékapeya
wasnókya.** He is exceedingly smart.

iyékiyA *vt1-caus* s/he passes smth to sb

iyéska *vi1* s/he interprets, translates, converses
‣ **Wa'ówabi ụs iyéskabi.** They translate using
a book. *Vbenef:* **iyégijiska**

iyéska ; iyéskabi *n* 1) interpreter, translator ‣
Wịcá gá iyéskabi žéca. That man over there
is an interpreter. 2) announcer

iyéš *pro* him, himself, her, herself, they, themselves as opposed to someone else; him/her on
the other hand (-š means 'adversative, uncer-
tain, contrastive') ‣ **Tim ú štén miyéš mnịkta**
If Tim comes I will go. ‣ **Miyéš dágu kábi žé
owápešị.** As for myself I did not take part
in the discussion. ‣ **Nahą́ȟ koníška, miyéš
waná magána.** You are still a young man, as
for myself I am old now. ‣ **Iyéš nínaȟ ecágen
wayáwašị.** Him, he hardly ever went to school.
1s: **miyéš** *2s:* **niyéš** *1p:* **ụgíyeš**

iyéšị *vs* it is not herself/himself/itself/them-
selves; s/he/it/they are not the one(s) *1s:* **miyéšị**
2s: **niyéšị** *1p:* **ụgíyešị**

iyéšnạna *adv* by herself/himself/itself/them-
selves; her/him/it/them alone ‣ **Miyéšnạna
mawáni.** I walk alone. *1s:* **miyéšnạna** *2s:*
niyéšnạna *1p:* **ụgíyešnạna**

iyéyA₁ *aux* s/he does smth quickly or suddenly
‣ **Gíjaȟ iyéya.** She made it quickly for him. ‣
I'écuna cén badịn iyéwaya. She talks all the
time so I suddenly nudged her. *1s:* **iyéwaya** *2s:*
iyéyaya *1p:* **ụgíyeyabi**

iyéyA₂ *vt1* s/he finds sb, smth ‣ **Šų́gatạga
iyéwayešị no.** I cannot find the horse. ‣ **Wạží
iyéyayịkta.** You will find one. *1s:* **iyéwaya** *2s:*
iyéyaya *1p:* **iyé'ụyabi** *Vpos:* **iyégiyA**

iyéyA₃ *vt1* s/he sends smth, sb there from here
(away from speaker) ‣ **Wa'óyabi iyéwaya.**
I sent the mail. *1s:* **iyéwaya** *2s:* **iyéyaya** *1p:*
iyé'ụyabi

iyóbatA *vt1* s/he patches smth ‣ **Hụská
iyówabata.** I patched the pants. *1s:* **iyówabata**
2s: **iyóyabata** *See:* **buspÁ**

iyódạgA *vi2* s/he sits down ‣ **Iyódạga ịš nạgáhạ
wóda wo!** Sit down now and eat! ‣ **Wagíyạ
sába wazíyam žéci iyódạgabi.** The black
thunderbirds sit down there to the north. ‣
Gakí ịmnódạgịkta. I will sit over there. *1s:*
imnódạga *2s:* **inódạga** *1p:* **ụgíyodạgabi** *Vcaus:*
iyódạkkiyA *Vcont:* **iyódạk**

iyódạ *n* honor

iyódạgina *vt1-pos* s/he honors his/her own *1s:*
iyódạwagina *2s:* **iyódạyagina**

iyódạk *vcont* sitting down ‣ **Ịyódạk ú wo!** Sit
down still! ‣ **Iyódạk yịgá ịštíma.** He is sleeping
in a sitting position. ‣ **Ụgịštíma hịkna iyódạk
kó ụyą́gịkta.** We will remain sleeping and sitting too. (NS 2002:33)

iyódạkiyA *vt1-caus* s/he honors sb, smth ‣ **Hụgá
žé iyódạwịcawakiya.** I honor the chiefs. *1s:*
iyódạwakiya *2s:* **iyódạyakiya**

iyódạkkiyA *vt1-caus* s/he makes sb sit down ‣
Ecén nén iyódạkwakiya. I made him sit here
like this. *1s:* **iyódạkwakiya** *2s:* **iyódạkyakiya**
1p: **iyódạk'ụkiyabi**

iyódiyegiyA *vi1* s/he/it is miserable; is having
a difficult time ‣ **Iyódiyegiya wa'ụ́.** I live in
misery.

iyógapte *Variant:* **ogápte** *n* plate, dish, shell, dipper ‣ **Iyógapte ecṹmakiya.** She makes me do
the dishes.

iyógapte sába *cp* frying pan

iyógapte škokpá *Variant:* **iyógapte oškókpa** *cp* bowl

iyógaptopi *n* cupboard

iyógipi *Variant:* **ogípi** *vs-dat* s/he is happy about sb, smth ▸ **Iyónigipi he?** Are you happy about it? ▸ **Niyé omágipi no!** I am happy for you! ▸ **Ába iyógipi!** Happy birthday! ▸ **Dąyą́ opí'įc'iya štén iyómagipi.** If he behaves, I will be happy about it. ▸ **Micį́kši ús iyómagipi.** I'm happy because of my son. ▸ **Wįcáwatųga, iyómagipi.** When I gave birth to them I was happy. ▸ **Wagágana bibína yuhá ús iyó'ųgipibi.** We are happy because my wife had a baby. *1s:* **iyómagipi** *2s:* **iyónigipi** *1p:* **iyó'ųgipibi** *Vrefl:* **iyógipi įc'íyA**

iyógipi įc'íyA *vi3-refl* s/he enjoys himself/herself *1s:* **iyógipi mįc'íya** *2s:* **iyógipi nįc'íya** *1p:* **iyógipi ųgíc'iya**

iyógipisijA *vs* s/he is sick, sad, grieving *1s:* **iyómągipisija** *2s:* **iyónįgipisija** *Vcaus:* **iyógipisinyA**

iyógipisinyA *vt1-caus* s/he saddens sb; makes sb feel bad, sorry *1s:* **iyógipisinwaya** *2s:* **iyógipisinyaya**

iyógipiši *vs-dat* s/he is displeased about sb, smth *Adv:* **iyógipišįya**

iyógipišįyA *vt1-caus* s/he offends sb ▸ **Iyógipišįciya he?** Did I offend you? *1s:* **iyógipišįwaya** *2s:* **iyógipišįyaya**

iyógipišįyą *adv* feeling sad, displeased about smth ▸ **Iyógipišįyą wa'ų́.** I am feeling depressed.

iyógipiyA *vt1-caus* s/he/it makes sb happy, satisfied ▸ **Wíyą žé iyógipiwaya.** I made that woman happy. ▸ **Híc'ehą iyógipimaya.** When she came she made me happy. *1s:* **iyógipiwaya** *2s:* **iyógipiyaya** *Vdat:* **iyógipi** *See:* **iyópiya**

iyógiši *vt1* s/he sends sb away; orders sb to stop doing smth ▸ **Dágu iyóciciši hą́da dóhąni namáyah'ųšį no.** You do not listen to anything I tell you. (Weasel 178:310)

iyóhi *vt1* 1) s/he reaches smth ▸ **Ḷ'áni žé ús iyówahi.** I reach it with a ladder. 2) s/he counts a coup (touches the enemy in battle) ▸ **Žé'ecųhą waná, owá pahá éwįcayagubi cén, iyówįcahibi kó.** By that time, since all of them had taken some hair, they had each "captured" him. (Shields 90:560) *1s:* **iyówahi** *2s:* **iyóyahi** *Vcaus:* **iyóhiya** *Vpos:* **iyógihi** *vs* 2) it extends, is long enough ▸ **Ḷ'áni žé iyóhi.** The ladder is long enough.

iyóhiyA *vt1-caus* s/he causes sb to reach it; extends, reaches toward ▸ **"Makóce iyóhiyaya štén edáhą opšíja edáhą a'ú cá" ejíya.** He said to him, "If you reach the earth, bring up some mud from there." (Drummond 1976, The flood) *1s:* **iyóhiwaya** *2s:* **iyóhiyaya** *1p:* **iyóhi'ųyabi**

iyóȟpeyA *vt1* s/he throws, drops smth into it *1s:* **iyóȟpewaya** *2s:* **iyóȟpeyaya** *1p:* **iyóȟpe'ųyabi**

iyóknągA *vt1-pos* s/he puts smth in his/her own mouth

iyók'įba *n* cradleboard

iyópegiciyabi *vi1-recip* they quarrel, scold, attack one another ▸ **Ecágen misúga iyópegiciyabi.** My younger brothers are always quarreling with one another. *1p:* **iyópe'ųgiciyabi**

iyópeyA *vt1* s/he scolds, reproves sb ▸ **Micį́kši iyówapeya no.** I scolded my son. *1s:* **iyówapeya** *2s:* **iyóyapeya** *1p:* **iyó'ųpeyabi** *Vabs:* **wawíyopegiyA** *Vrecip:* **iyópegiciyabi**

iyópiyA *vs* s/he is happy, pleased, merry

iyópsijA *vi1* s/he/it jumps ▸ **Šúgatąga gá nína iyópsijabi wayúpi.** That horse over there is good at jumping. *Vcaus:* **iyópsikiyA**

iyópsije *n* hop, jump

iyópsįpsįjamna *n-redup* chipmunk

iyóptayą *adv* 1) toward ▸ **Wakpá iyóptayą maní žehą́.** He walked toward the river. ▸ **Eyáš šųkšóšona úna néci eyáš iyóptaya agíktaga cén.** Then the little donkey came over here, and he ran toward it. (Weasel 15:141) 2) in the right way, properly ▸ **Iyóptayą iyáya.** He is going in the right way.

iyúha *quant* 1) all, every, one after the other (distributive meaning) ▸ **Amógįyą iyúha mnušnóga.** I dismantled all the cars. ▸ **Ą́ba nén iyúha ecámų.** I do it everyday. 2) none *Usage:* followed by a negated verb. ▸ **Iyúha iyútąbišį.** None of them tried to do it.

iyúhabi *vs* it is all of them ▸ **Abá žé ejé'ena cégiyabi iyúhabišį duká.** Some pray only to him; not all though. (NS 2002:5)

iyúhagen *Variant:* **iyúhage** *quant* at all, altogether *Usage:* followed by a negated verb. ▸ **Iyúhagen ú wąmnágešį.** I did not see it coming at all. ▸ **Cóȟ iyúhagen įwáknįgešį.** I will honestly avoid it altogether.

iyúhaȟ *quant* every single one of them ▸ **Iyúhaȟ wįcágibazo.** She showed every single one of them.

iyúhana *quant* all, all of them, all of it, every individual in a group, all at the same time (collective meaning) ▸ **Iyúhana dąyą́ wódabi** They all ate well. ▸ **"Mázaska iyúhana mak'ú" žeyá!** "Give me all of your money!" he said. ▸ **Šųktógeja iyúhana hįnápabi.** All of the wolves appeared. ▸ **Iyúhana wacégiyabi.** They pray in a mass.

iyúhana ówąja *cp* universe

iyúšna (CTK) *num* seven

iyúweǧa *vi2* s/he crosses a body of water while arriving, going there 1s: **imnúweǧa** 2s: **inúweǧa** 1p: **ųǧíyuweǧabi**

íyužŋna *vt2* s/he cleans a newborn's mouth 1s: **ímnužŋna** 2s: **ínužŋna**

izį́mna *vs* it is the smell of smth burning (like incense, sweetgrass) ▸ **Zizíbena izį́mna.** The cloth has a burnt smell.

izį́tkiyA ; azį́tkiyA *vt1-pos* s/he burns incense for a ritual, a smudge

ižága *n* chatterbox *Usage:* archaic. *Syn:* **i'épina**

Į
ţ

į- *pref* 1) because of, with a tool ▸ **temnít'a** > **įtémnit'a** s/he/it sweating profusely > s/he/it is sweating profusely because of smth ▸ **cesní** > **įcésni** s/he/it defecates > s/he defecates because of smth ▸ **basmíyą** > **įbásmiyą** s/he cleans the surface of smth > s/he clears, cleans the surface with smth 2) particularizes spatial adverbs ▸ **hokún** > **įhokun** down, below; downstairs > under, underneath smth ▸ **wągám** > **įwągam** up high, above, upright > above smth 3) turns some active verbs into the noun indicating a tool or instrument ▸ **aní** > **į'áni** s/he climbs > ladder ▸ **wabábnaya** > **įwábabnaya** s/he irons clothes > iron ▸ **capá** > **įcápe** s/he stabs sb, smth > fork ▸ **yušpá** > **įyúšpe** s/he opens it > key ▸ **wųgá** > **įwúga** s/he lies down > s/he lies down in bed 4) cardinal numbers in -th ▸ **yámni** > **įyámni** three > third ▸ **dóba** > **įdóba** four > fourth *Syn:* **įji-**

į *vt1* s/he wears smth on the shoulder ▸ **Wįcápaha šiná wąží į́nážį** [. . .] She stood wearing a scalp robe [. . .] (NS 2002:23) 1s: **wa'į́** 2s: **ya'į́**

į'ágam *adv* 1) over it *conj* 2) than *Usage:* indicates a comparison between two things or persons. ▸ **Įkcéya né ȟaȟ́úda ų́ wagáǧeǧe né į'ágam sudá.** It was stronger than this ordinary thread they used for sewing. (Drummond 1976, Tanning hides)

į'ágezaptą *num* fifteenth

į'ákide *n* field glasses, binoculars, telescope

į'áni *n* ladder ▸ **Į'áni žé ų́s iyówahi.** I reach it with a ladder.

į'ápA *vt1* s/he hits sb, smth with it 1s: **į'áwapa** 2s: **į'áyapa**

į'ápe *n* drumstick

įbágįza ; įbázįje *n* violin, fiddle *Syn:* **įwábagįza ; cąwábazįje**

įbáǧe'įc'iyA *vi3-refl* s/he frees himself/herself *1s:* **įbáǧemįc'iya** *2s:* **įbáǧenįc'iya** *1p:* **įbáǧe'ųgįc'iyabi**

įbáhį *n* pillow

įbáhųhųza *n* rocking chair

įbáȟage *n* pipe tamper

įbáȟnoga *n* pin

įbáȟnoge *n* punch (for making holes)

įbákca *n* comb

įbákmįkma *n* 1) wheel, tire ‣ **Įbákmįkma tí gakná yįgá.** The wheels are located beside the house. 2) wheelbarrow

įbámnaye *n* iron

įbámną *n* file

įbási *n* driver's license ‣ **Įbási žé waknúha.** I have my driver's license.

įbásise ; įbásisa *n* needle, security pin

įbáskije *n* washboard

įbásmiyą *vt1* s/he clears, cleans the surface with smth *1s:* **įwábasmiyą** *2s:* **iyábasmiyą**

įbásmiyąyą *n* anything used to clean, polish smth (polishing cloth, steal wool)

įbáspe *n* peg, stake

įbáweȟ ocągu *cp* crossroad

įbážužu *n* eraser

įbíǧA *vi* it boils, is boiling ‣ **Miní įbíǧa.** The water is boiling. ‣ **Miní įbíǧabi én éknąga.** Put it in boiling water. *Vcaus:* **įbíȟyA**

įbíȟyA *vt1-caus* s/he boils smth ‣ **Pąǧí įbíȟyabi.** They boiled potatoes. *1s:* **įbíȟwaya** *2s:* **įbíȟyaya** *1p:* **įbiȟ'ųyabi**

įbóȟkiya *n* pump

įbúskeba *n* strainer

įcáǧA *vs* s/he/it grows up ‣ **Waȟpé įcáǧa.** The flowers are growing. ‣ **Micíjabi iyúhana įcáǧabi žehą, mįš įȟpéwaya híkna dóki wówaši ecámų.** Then my kids grew up and, myself too, I divorced him and I worked somewhere. *Vabs:* **wa'įcaǧA** *Vbenef:* **įgíjicaǧA**

įcáǧabi *n* generation ‣ **Nągáhą įcáǧabi né wanáȟ'ųbišį.** Nowadays this generation does not obey.

įcáȟyA *vt1-caus* s/he grows, breeds smth; raises sb ‣ **Adé wayáȟoda óda įcáȟya.** Dad grows a lot of oats. ‣ **Aǧúyabi wayáȟoda kóya įcáȟyabi.** They grew both wheat and oats. (Schudel 1997) *1s:* **įcáȟwaya** *2s:* **įcáȟyaya**

įcápena *Variant:* **įcápe** *n* fork ‣ **Įcápena mak'ú!** Give me a fork!

įcąbahotų ; įcąmahotų *n* organ, piano

įcądešijA *vs* s/he regrets smth ‣ **Nína įcądemašija.** I regret it a lot. ‣ **Hįhą wąyága įcądešija.** She regretted seeing an owl. *1s:* **įcądemašija** *2s:* **įcądenišija** *1p:* **įcąde'ųšijabi**

įcądewašte *vs* s/he is pleased with smth; happy about smth ‣ **Hí ga'éca įcądemawašte.** When he came it made me happy.

įcągažibe *n* wood plane *Syn:* **cągážiba**

įcąwabamna *n* rasp, file

įcąyukse *n* saw

įcégiyA *vt1-dit* s/he prays to sb for smth ‣ **Žécen, įcécigiya mįš.** Now I pray to you. (Shields 23:26) *1s:* **įcéwagiya** *2s:* **įcéyagiya** *1p:* **įcé'ųgiyabi**

įcésni *vs* s/he defecates because of smth

įcésnibi *n* laxative

įcéte *n* rim

įcéti *vt1* s/he builds a fire ‣ **Žécų hík agámpadahą įcéti.** He did that and build a fire on top of it.

-įc'i- ; -įk- *prefix-infix* oneself; -self (reflexive marker) *Usage:* occurs when the subject is both agent and patient; reflexive verbs are of Class 3. ‣ **kté > įc'íkte** s/he/it kills sb, smth > s/he commits suicide; kills himself/herself ‣ **škádA > įc'íškadA** s/he plays > s/he plays with himself/herself; masturbates ‣ **yužáža > įknúžaža** s/he washes sb, smth by scrubbing > s/he washes himself/herself ‣ **wąyága > wą'įknaga** s/he sees sb > s/he sees himself/herself *1s:* **-mį̇c'i-; mį̇k-** *2s:* **-nį̇c'i-; nį̇k-** *1p:* **-ų̇gį̇c'i-; ų̇gį̇k-**

įc'íc'u *vi3-refl* s/he gives smth to himself/herself *1s:* **mį̇c'íc'u** *2s:* **nį̇c'íc'u**

įc'ícuwa *vi3-refl* s/he gets dressed *Lit:* s/he cares for himself/herself ‣ **Waná, waníyedu osnókyabi hą́da Nakóda né, įc'ícuwabi.** Now, the Nakoda people knew about winter and how to care for themselves. ‣ **Įc'ícuwa hį́k ša'įc'íya kó.** He both dressed up and painted himself in red. (Drummond 1976, Įktomi and the ducks) *1s:* **mį̇c'ícuwa** *2s:* **nį̇c'ícuwa** *1p:* **ų̇gį̇c'icuwabi**

įc'íjağA *vi3-refl* 1) s/he makes smth for himself/herself ‣ **Dágu iyúhana įc'íjağabi ų́s.** They made all of their things with it. (Drummond 1976, Tanning hides) 2) s/he turns himself/herself into sb, smth ‣ **Búza įc'íjağa.** He turned himself into a cat. *1s:* **mį̇c'íjağa** *2s:* **nį̇c'íjağa**

įc'íknąyA *vi3-refl* s/he fools himself/herself *1s:* **mį̇c'íknąyą** *2s:* **nį̇c'íknąyą** *1p:* **ų̇gį̇c'iknąyąbi**

įciknuni *vs* s/he is confused ‣ **Į́š wamą́kašką oyáde įciknuni áya.** The animal nation is getting confused. (BigEagle 2017:9) *1s:* **įcimaknuni** *2s:* **įciniknuni**

įc'íkte *vi3-refl* s/he commits suicide; kills himself/herself *1s:* **mį̇c'íkte** *2s:* **nį̇c'íkte**

įc'íkte tawácį *vi* s/he has suicidal tendencies *1s:* **įc'íkte mitáwacį** *2s:* **įc'íkte nitáwacį**

įc'ínahomni *n* bicycle

įcinową *n* brave song

įc'íškadA *vi3-refl* s/he plays with himself/herself; masturbates *1s:* **mį̇c'íškada** *2s:* **nį̇c'íškada**

įciyopegiciyabi *vi1-recip* they barter, trade with one another

įciyopekiyA *vt1-caus* s/he trades smth for it ‣ **Dágu kóšta įciyopekiya.** He traded it for anything. *1s:* **įciyopewakiya** *2s:* **įciyopeyakiya**

įciyopeyA *vt1* s/he trades, exchanges smth ‣ **Cuwį́knaga né įciyopewaya'.** I traded this shirt. *1s:* **įciyopewakiya**

įciyopeyabi *n* exchange, trade

įc'íyušnogA *vi3-refl* s/he has smth pulled out ‣ **Hí mį̇c'íyušnoga.** I had a tooth pulled out. *1s:* **mį̇c'íyušnoga** *2s:* **nį̇c'íyušnoga**

įc'íyųǧA *vi3-refl* s/he asks himself/herself about it ‣ **Įc'ímųǧįkta.** I will ask for myself. *1s:* **įc'ímųǧa** *2s:* **įc'íŋųǧa**

įcómni *vs* s/he feels lonely, sad, homesick ‣ **Ecágen įnį́comni'!** You are always sad! ‣ **Kiknábi cén įmą́comni.** They went back home so I am lonely. *1s:* **įmą́comni** *2s:* **įnį́comni**

įdáhomni *vs* s/he feels dizzy *1s:* **įmádahomni** *2s:* **įnídahomni** *Syn:* **įdómni**

įdásakyabina *n* freezer

įdáziba *n* bow

įdą́ *vs* s/he is proud *1s:* **įmádą** *2s:* **įnídą** *1p:* **ų̇gį́dąbi**

įdé *n* face ‣ **Įdé kpakį́da!** Wipe your face! ‣ **Įdé né sapsába.** He has black spots on the face. *1s:* **mi'į̇de** *2s:* **ni'į̇de**

įdé okmÁ *vt1* s/he photographs, takes a picture of sb, smth *1s:* **įdé owákma** *2s:* **įdé oyákma**

įdégatita *n* halter

įdéha *n* mask ‣ **įdéha gitú** s/he wears his/her mask

įdéȟnoga (OM) *n* pumpkin *Lit:* holes in the face *Syn:* **wįcánų̇ȟnų̇ǧena**

įdé'įbakį̇da *Variant:* **įdébakį̇de** *n* towel

įdé'ogiǧe *n* bandit *Lit:* one with a masked face

įdéša iyáyA *Variant:* **įdé šayá iyáyA** *vs* s/he blushes; is embarrassed ‣ **Mayá'įškada įdéša imáyaya.** He teased me until I was embarrassed. *1s:* **įdéša imáyaya** *2s:* **įdéša iníyaya**

Įdeša ti'óda *ngeo* Harlem (Montana) *Syn:* **Agásąm ti'óda**

įdéšitkiyA *vt1-pos* s/he furrows his/her eyebrows; looks discontent *1s:* **įdéšinwagiya** *2s:* **įdéšinyagiya**

įdóba ; įįídoba *num* fourth ‣ **ą̇ba įdóba** Thursday

įdókpazA *vs* s/he faints *1s:* **įdómakpaza** *2s:* **įdónikpaza**

įdókpaza stéya *vs* s/he feels like fainting *1s:* **įdómakpaza stéya** *2s:* **įdónikpaza stéya**

įdókšą *adv* around the face

įdómni *vs* s/he/it is dizzy ▸ **Įknúhanaȟ įdómamni!** Suddenly I felt dizzy! ▸ **Pežúda né ús įdómni.** The pills made him dizzy. *1s:* **įdómamni** *2s:* **įdónimni** *Syn:* **įdáhomni**

įdú *adv* just, simply, only ▸ **Įdú ecámų.** I just did it. ▸ **Įdú wacégiya wo!** Simply pray! ▸ **Įdú nén yįgá.** He is sitting idly here.

įdú wįǧá hąwí *Variant:* įdú wįgá hąwí *cp* May *Lit:* idle moon *Syn:* **wįbazuką hąwí**

Įdúgaȟ wįcášta *nprop* White Bear people *Lit:* common made man

įdúgam *adv* backwards, leaning back ▸ **Įdúgam yįgá.** He is sitting leaning back (as in Lazy Boy).

įdúȟ *adv* anyway, no doubt, contrary to what is expected ▸ **Įdúȟ wącímnagįkta.** I will see you anyway. ▸ **Įdúȟ níktešį.** Contrary to hope he did not survive.

įdúȟtayena ; įdútahena *adv* for nothing ▸ **Įdúȟtayena žécamų.** It did that for nothing. ▸ [. . .] **yé'įc'iya žéca įdútahena** [. . .] she threw herself at nothing (NS 2002:83)

įdúka *vs* s/he is hungry ▸ **Nína įmáduka.** I am really hungry. ▸ **Įmáduka jé.** I am always hungry. ▸ **Íš įdúkabi.** They are hungry too. ▸ **Ába wąží giktá, įdúka.** One day he got up and he was hungry. *1s:* **įmáduka** *2s:* **įníduka** *Syn:* **nodį́ t'a**

įdúya *adv* for no reason, for nothing ▸ **Įdúya hí.** They came for nothing.

įgáǧi *vs* s/he is anxious, worried about smth *1s:* **įmágaǧi** *2s:* **įnígaǧi** *1p:* **ųgígáǧibi**

įgáǧo *vt1* s/he scratches, makes a notch on smth, marks a line on smth *1s:* **įwágaǧo** *2s:* **įyágaǧo**

įgákna *adv* against, besides sb, smth *Usage:* this adverb can take person markers. ▸ **Mígakna yįgá!** Sit beside me! ▸ **Nígakna mągíkta.** I will sit beside you. *1s:* **mígakna** *2s:* **nígakna** *1p:* **ųgígakna**

įgámu *n* drumstick

įgáškena *n* tie

įgáški *n* pounder

įgázogic'ų ; įgázo *n* skates

įgážąga *vs* s/he is anxious, worried, bothered because of the lack of smth ▸ **Wóyude įmágaząga.** I am worried because I am short on food. ▸ **Iná dáguniȟ įgážągešį.** Mom is not lacking anything. *1s:* **įmágažąga** *2s:* **įnígažąga**

įgíjicaǧA *vs-benef* it (plant, cereal, fruit) grows for him/her *1s:* **įmíjicaǧa** *2s:* **įníjicaǧa**

įgíjitų *vt1-benef* s/he paints, smth for sb else *1s:* **įwéjitų** *2s:* **įyéjitų**

įgíjitųšį *vt1-benef* s/he lies for sb *1s:* **įwéjitųšį** *2s:* **įyéjitųšį**

įgíji'ų *vt1-benef* s/he paints, rubs, applies smth on him/her for sb *1s:* **įwéji'ų** *2s:* **įyéji'ų**

įgíjiyuškį *vt1/2-benef* s/he admires sb, smth for sb else *1s:* **įwéjimnuškį** *2s:* **įyéjinuškį**

įgíjiyutA *vt1-benef* s/he tries, measures, tastes sb else's ▸ **Wožábi įmíjiyuta!** Try my gravy! ▸ **"Įhyu, skúye įgíjiyutam," eyá.** "Come on, taste it to see if it is sweet," he said. (Weasel 130:249) *1s:* **įwéjiyuta** *2s:* **įyéjiyuta**

įgíjiyuǧA *vt1/3-benef* s/he asks sb for him/her ▸ **Wįkóške žé įcíjimuǧa.** I asked that girl for you. *1s:* **įwéjimuǧa** *2s:* **įyéjinuǧa**

įgíju₁ *vt1-dat* s/he smokes for sb; įgíju₂ *vt1-pos* s/he smokes his/her own thing ▸ **Hiyá, cąníska įwékcukta.** No, I will smoke my own cigarette. *1s:* **įwékcu** *2s:* **įyékcu**

įgíknucą *vt1* s/he considers smth *1s:* **įwéknucą** *2s:* **įyéknucą**

įgí'ų *vt1-pos* s/he paints, rubs, applies smth on his/her own ▸ **Įkcé mąkáge néca ús owá tacą́ įgí'ųbi.** They painted their bodies with ordinary dirt. (Shields 9:114)

iǧúǧa *n* granite

Iǧúǧa wídana *ngeo* Snake Butte (Montana) *Lit:* small island of granite

iǧúȟkiyaga *adv* barely opened ▸ [. . .] **žé wąžíȟ įštá iǧúȟkiyaga wąyága ga'éca.** [. . .] one of them barely opened his eyes and then he saw. (NS 2002:44)

įhágam *adv* after ▸ **Micúkši įhágam hí.** My daughter arrived after.

įhágapa *vs* s/he/it is younger than sb ▸ **Hokšína žé įhágapa.** That boy is younger than her. *Adv:* **įhágam**

įhákta *vt1* s/he is concerned for sb out of love ▸ **Kúgišiktu įhákta cén kníšį.** He was concerned for his grandmother so he did not come back home. *1s:* **įháwakta** *2s:* **įháyakta**

įhámnA *vt1* s/he dreams of sb, smth ▸ **Žécen įwáhamna.** I dreamed it in that way. *1s:* **įwáhamna** *2s:* **įyáhamna** *Vabs:* **wįhamnA**

įhámnabi *n* dream, vision *Syn:* **wįhámne**

įhą *n* 1) step *vi1* 2) s/he steps, takes a step ▸ **Gakí įhą.** Step over there.

įháge *vs* 1) it is the end, the last one ▸ **Žéci įháge ektá wągágana wąží tagóžakpagu hokšína gicí tí.** There at the end (of the village) an old lady lived with her grandson. (Parks & DeMallie 1994) *n* 2) the end of smth ▸ **makóce įháge** doomsday *Adv:* **įhágeda** *Vcaus:* **įhákya**

įhágeda *adv* at the end of it

įhágedaȟ *adv* at the very end of it

Įháktųwą *nprop* Yankton Dakota people, person of Yankton Dakota descent

Įháktųwąna *nprop* Yanktonai Dakota people, person of Yanktonai Dakota descent

įhákyA *vt1-caus* s/he ends, prevents smth; puts an end to smth *1s:* **įhákwaya** *2s:* **įhákyaya**

įhiyų *interj* well, all right (uttered at the beginning of a sentence) ▸ **Įhiyų aké yá, aké agú.** All right, try again, bring back more. (Drummond 1976, The flood)

įhódodogic'ų *n* swing

įhokun *adv* under, underneath smth ▸ **Įhokun maníbi.** They walked underneath it. ▸ **íyą įhokun** under a rock ▸ **iyécįgayena įhokun** under the car *See:* **hokún, kún**

įhókuwa *n* fishing pole

įhúpaȟtA *vt1* s/he ties its leg; hobbles a horse *1s:* **įhúwapaȟta** *2s:* **įhúyapaȟta** *See:* **hugáška**

įhúpaȟte *n* hobble

įhú *interj* exclamation of surprise ▸ **Įhú! Žé ktá.** Hey! That is heavy.

įȟÁ *vi1* 1) s/he laughs ▸ **Įȟá ya'ú.** You are constantly laughing. ▸ **Duwéni įȟ'éšį.** None of them laughed. ▸ **Wóganabi įȟácubina.** The old ladies kept laughing along. ▸ **Dágucen iyáȟa?** Why are you laughing? *vt1* 2) s/he laughs at sb, smth ▸ **Ųgíȟabi no.** We laugh at it. *1s:* **įwáȟa** *2s:* **iyáȟa** *1p:* **ųgíȟabi** *Vrefl:* **įȟé'įc'iyA, įknú'įȟA**

įȟá'įc'iyA *vi3-refl* s/he smiles *1s:* **įȟámįc'iya** *2s:* **įȟánįc'iya** *1p:* **įȟá'ųgįc'iyabi**

įȟát'A *vs* s/he laughs hard *Lit:* s/he laughs to death *Vcaus:* **įȟát'eyA** *Vredup:* **įȟát'at'A**

įȟát'at'A *vs-redup* s/he laughs loudly *1s:* **įȟámat'at'a** *2s:* **įȟánit'at'a**

įȟát'at'ana *n-redup* 1) laughter 2) magpie (Denig 2000[1930]:189)

įȟát'eyA *vt1-caus* s/he/it makes sb laugh to death ▸ **Mitákona įȟát'emaya.** My friend made me laugh to death. ▸ **Įȟát'emaya giníja.** I almost died laughing. (Ryan 1998:61) *1s:* **įȟát'ewaya** *2s:* **įȟát'eyaya**

įȟé *n* mountain, gravel

įȟé'įc'iyA *vi3-refl* s/he has a grimace, laughs at himself/herself unpleasantly ▸ **Įȟé'įc'iya yįgá.** She is sitting with a grimace. *1s:* **įȟémįc'iya** *2s:* **įȟénįc'iya**

įȟéyam *adv* away from; apart from ▸ **Įȟéyam nážįbi cá záptą gacéȟ.** They stood about five feet apart. (NS 2002:64)

įȟpégiciyabi 1) *vi1-recip* they divorce from one another ▸ **Waná įȟpé'ųgiciya.** We are divorced now. ▸ **Iná, adé įȟpégiciyabi.** Mom and dad are divorced. 2) *n* divorce

įȟpé'įc'iyA *vi3-refl* s/he throws himself/herself on the ground ▸ **Gamnáš įȟpé'įc'iya.**

She threw herself on the ground with her legs spread apart. *1s:* įȟpémįc'iya *2s:* įȟpénįc'iya

įȟpékiyA *vt1-dat* 1) s/he throws smth at sb 2) s/he deals the cards 3) s/he leaves smth for sb ‣ **Cą̧ žé įȟpémakiya.** He left the stick for me. *1s:* įȟpéwakiya *2s:* įȟpéyakiya *1p:* įȟpé'ųkiya

įȟpéyA *vt1-caus* 1) s/he discards, throws sb, smth away ‣ **Dágu nowá yamnáya įȟpéya.** She gossips about things. 2) s/he leaves sb, smth behind, alone; s/he/it is left behind; s/he divorces him/her ‣ **Wanúȟ įšną́ną̧ įȟpé'ųya.** Maybe we should leave her alone. ‣ **Hékta įȟpéya.** He is left behind in the race. ‣ **Įȟpéwayįkte no!** I will get divorced from her! ‣ **Waná įȟpéniyąbi?** Are you divorced now? 3) s/he banishes sb ‣ **Hųgá žé įȟpéwįcaya oyáde nedáȟą.** The chief chased them out of the reserve. *1s:* įȟpéwaya *2s:* įȟpéyaya *1p:* įȟpé'ųyabi *Vabs:* wa'įȟpeyA *Vdat:* įȟpékiyA *Vrecip:* įȟpégiciyabi *Vrefl:* įȟpé'įc'iyA

į'íjuna ; **íjuna** *n* cup, glass ‣ **Į'íjuna wąží yaknúha he?** Does she have a cup with her? ‣ **Į'íjuna né wagáptuǧa.** I cracked this cup. ‣ **Íjuna óda.** There are a lot of cups.

į'íbaȟpa *n* scraper

į'íc'i'ų *vi3-refl* s/he paints, rubs, applies smth on himself/herself *1s:* įmíc'i'ų *2s:* įníc'i'ų

į'íjaška *n* pin

į'íjuna o'égikną̧ga *cp* cupboard *Lit:* a place to put one's cup

į'íyute *n* ruler

ịjábA *vi1* s/he opens his/her mouth ‣ **Nína įjába.** Open wide. *1s:* įwájaba *2s:* įyájaba *Vcont:* įjáp- ; įjám

įjáhi *vs* it is mixed, blended with smth else ‣ **Škoškóbena gicí įjáhi.** It is mixed with bananas. *Vcaus:* įjáhiyA

įjáhiyA *vt1-caus* s/he blends, mixes smth together with it ‣ **Wíkni įjáhiwayįkta.** I will mix it with oil.

įjáhomni *n* 1) crank, lift *vt1* 2) s/he cranks up a vehicle *1s:* įwágahomni *2s:* įyágahomni

įjáȟabe wįcá *cp* whipman

įjáȟni *vt1* s/he smears smth with it ‣ **Amúǧiya žé maká įjáwaȟni.** I smeared the car with mud. *1s:* įwágaȟni *2s:* įyágaȟni

įjámna *vimp* there is a blizzard, drifting snow ‣ **Mąká agą́n įjámna.** It drifts on the ground.

įjánu *n* fan

įjánuza *vimp* there is a gust of wind (as when a car passes by)

įjánuzakiya *n* electric fan

įjáp- ; **įjám** *vcont* opening one's mouth

įjápaži *n* cushion *Lit:* something soft

įjápsįdena ; **įjápsįde** *n* whip ‣ **Ptewána įjápsįdena ús awícawagu.** I brought the cows home with a whip.

įjápsįpsįdana *n* swallow (bird)

įjáptągA *vi1* s/he opens his/her mouth wide *1s:* įwájaptąga *2s:* įyájaptąga

įjáską *vt1* s/he melts smth by heating ‣ **Wá įwájaską miní wacíga cén.** I melt snow because I want water. *1s:* įwágaską *2s:* įyágaską

įjásna *n* cymbal

įjáše *n* button, safety pin

įjáškA *vt1* 1) s/he ties sb, smth to it; ties a knot ‣ **Ȟaȟúda žé įjáška.** He tied the rope to it. ‣ **Šúga žé įwágaškakta.** I will tie up the dog to it. *1s:* įwágaška *2s:* įyágaška *1p:* ųgíjaškąbi *n* 2) lace, laces ‣ **hába įjáška** moccasin laces

įjášna *n* scissors

įjášoša *vt1-dit* s/he mixes smth into it to thicken it *1s:* įwágašoša *2s:* įyágašoša

įjášpe *n* phlegm

įjázo *n* 1) line ‣ **Wa'óyabi žén įjázo okmá.** He drew a line in the book 2) yardstick, ruler *vt1* 3) s/he draws a line on smth

ijážobi *n* line

ijážužu *n* fare, paycheck ▸ **Įjážužu waná gicíga.** Her paycheck, she wants it now.

ijáȟabe *n* whip

ijáȟtage *n* tattooing or vaccination needle

iji- *pref*-th (turns an ordinal into a cardinal number) ▸ **šákpe > ijíšákpe** six > sixth ▸ **agézaptą > iji'agezaptą** fifteen > fifteenth *Syn:* **į-**; **iji'agezaptą ; į'ágezaptą** *num* fifteenth

ijída *adv* high above ▸ **wįcá ijída hą́ska** the tallest man

ijíma *adv* next time, next ▸ **Įjíma štén mnį́kta.** Next time I will go. ▸ **Įjíma štén wamą́kaškąbi owá cašwį́catų.** Next give a name to all of the animals.

ijínapcuwąga *num* ninth

ijínažį *vi1* s/he/it stands above

ijínųba; įnúba *num* second

ijíšagowį *num* seventh

ijíšaknoǧą ; išáknoǧą *num* eighth

ijíšakpe *num* sixth

ijíwikcemna *num* tenth ▸ **ijíwikcemna šákpe** sixtieth

ijíyuha *adv* entire, whole thing (archaic)

ijóǧą *vi1* s/he/it drifts

ijú₁ *vi1* s/he smokes ▸ **Įwájuši no.** I do not smoke. ▸ **Cąnúba ųgíjukta.** Let us two smoke the pipe. ▸ **Peží wįtkó ijúbi ogíhibi.** They can smoke weed. ▸ **Cąnúba įwáju no.** I smoke the pipe. *1s:* **įwáju** *2s:* **iyáju** *1p:* **ųgíjubi** *Vdat:* **igíju** *Vpos:* **igíju**

ijú₂ *vt1* s/he chooses sb, smth ▸ **Įmáyaju.** You chose me. *1s:* **įwáju** *2s:* **iyáju**

ijú₃ *voc* Grandmother! (address form).

įká (PR) *n* reins *Syn:* **iyúdįda**

įkcé *adv* common

įkcé aǧúyabi *cp* bannock

įkcé wistó *cp* tent (with walls), prospector tent *Syn:* **wistó**

Įkcé wįcášta *cp* Indigenous person

Įkcé wįcášta owáyawa tíbi tága *ph* First Nations University of Canada (Saskatchewan)

įkcé zizíbena *cp* cotton *Lit:* common fabric

įkcéya *adv* in a common, ordinary, usual way; original ▸ **Dágu įkcéya ecų́.** What she does is common. ▸ **cąm'úzitka įkcéya** wild onion

įkcéyagen *adv* in an ordinary way ▸ **Dágu nówa įkcéyagen ecų́.** She does everything in an ordinary way.

įkíyA *vt1-caus* s/he makes him/her wear it on the shoulders *1s:* **įwákiya** *2s:* **iyákiya**

įkmúna *n* bobcat *Syn:* **bustą́ga**

įkmų́ *n* wildcat (generic); lynx

įkmų́ge *n* snare *Syn:* **wakmúga**

įkmų́tąga *n* cougar *Syn:* **búzatąga**

įknádana *vi3-refl* s/he dusts himself/herself off

įknádą *vi3-refl* s/he brags about himself/herself *1s:* **įwáknadą** *2s:* **iyáknadą**

įknádodo *vi3-refl* s/he shakes, brushes, dusts himself/herself off ▸ **Tągán įknádodo wo.** Brush yourself off outside. *1s:* **mįknádodo** *2s:* **nįknádodo** *1p:* **ųgíknadodobi**

įknáǧoǧo *vi3-refl* s/he slashes himself/herself *1s:* **mįknáǧoǧo** *2s:* **nįknáǧoǧo**

įknáhokudu *vi3-refl* s/he denigrates himself/herself *1s:* **mįknáhokudu** *2s:* **nįknáhokudu**

įknáhomni *vi3-refl* s/he turns himself/herself around

įkná'iškadA *vi3-refl* s/he teases himself/herself *1s:* **mįkná'iškada** *2s:* **nįkná'iškada** *1p:* **ųgíkna'iškadabi**

įknásto *vi3-refl* s/he smooths himself/herself by licking (as fur)

įknášikna *vi3-refl* s/he speaks angrily about himself/herself *1s:* **mįknášikna** *2s:* **nįknášikna** *1p:* **ųgíknášiknabi**

įkná'ųšįga *vi3-refl* s/he speaks pitifully of himself/herself *1s:* **mįkná'ųšįga** *2s:* **nįkná'ųšįga**

įknáwa *vi3-refl* s/he counts himself/herself in ▸ **Hokšíbina nówa įknáwabi.** All of the young men counted themselves in. *1s:* **mįknáwa** *2s:* **nįknáwa** *1p:* **ųgíknawabi**

įknázijA *vi3-refl* s/he stretches himself/herself 1*s:* **mįknázija** 2*s:* **nįknázija**

įkní *n* grease obtained from marrow, or from thin and soft layers of fat inside the stomach

įknį *vt1* s/he investigates sb, smth *Vabs:* **wa'įknį**

įknígA *vt1* s/he minds, wonders, has regards for, pays attention to sb, smth; obeys sb ▸ **Įknígešį!** Do not mind it! ▸ **Duwé įknígešįhą.** People did not mind about her. ▸ **Híbi ųká įwícawaknįgešį.** They arrived but I did not mind them. ▸ **Iyúhagen įwáknįgešį.** I will avoid it altogether. ▸ **Ecágen mikúši įwáknįga.** I always obey my grandmother. 1*s:* **įwáknįga** 2*s:* **įyáknįga** *Vcont:* **įknįk**

įknįk *vcont* mind, observe, pay attention to sb, smth ▸ **Įknįk yá.** He goes to observe. ▸ **Dágu I'ábi žé įknįk mągá.** I am sitting paying attention to what is said.

įknúdąšį *vi3-refl* s/he disrespects, brags about himself/herself; is stupid ▸ **Wašíju né įknúdąšį, nodéhą.** This White man is disrespectful and greedy. 1*s:* **mįknúdąšį** 2*s:* **nįknúdąšį**

įknúhA *vi3-refl* s/he keeps himself/herself in a certain state; cares for himself/herself ▸ **Micíkši nidáguškinešį dąyá įknúha céyaga.** My son you are not a baby, you should take good care of yourself. (BigEagle 2019:8) 1*s:* **mįknúha** 2*s:* **nįknúha** 1*p:* **ųgíknuhabi**

įknúhahana; įknúhąhąna *adv-redup* now and then, occasionally ▸ **Įknúhahana ecúbi.** They do it occasionally. ▸ **Įknúhahana hácogądu wékta.** Occasionally I wake up in the middle of the night.

įknúhana ; įknúhąnaȟ *adv* suddenly, instantly, all at once ▸ **Įknúhana šúga nówa hįnápabi.** Suddenly all the dogs appeared. ▸ **Įknúhanaȟ įdómamni!** Suddenly I felt dizzy! ▸ **Įknúhana wapšá.** All of a sudden I sneezed.

įknúhi *vt1-pos* s/he mixes his/her own 1*s:* **įwéknuhi** 2*s:* **įyéknuhi**

įknúhokunyena *adv* humbly

įknúhomni *vi3-refl* s/he turns himself/herself around ▸ **Įknúhomni škáda.** She turns herself around to play. 1*s:* **mįknúhomni** 2*s:* **nįknúhomni**

įknúȟija *vi3-refl* s/he awakens himself/herself 1*s:* **mįknúȟija** 2*s:* **nįknúȟija**

įknú'įȟA *vi3-refl* s/he laughs at himself/herself, about one's own behavior 1*s:* **mįknú'įȟa** 2*s:* **nįknú'įȟa**

įknúkca *vt3-pos* s/he thinks about his/her own

įknúknebA *vi1-refl* s/he makes himself/herself vomit ▸ **Įknúknebįkta šká:hąga.** He kept trying to make himself throw up. (Weasel 7:144) 1*s:* **mįknúkneba** 2*s:* **nįknúkneba**

įknúk'eǧA *vi3-refl* s/he scratches himself/herself 1*s:* **mįknúk'eǧa** 2*s:* **nįknúk'eǧa** *Vcont:* **įknúk'eȟ**

įknúk'eȟ *vcont* scratching oneself ▸ **Įknúk'eȟ ecámų.** I keep on scratching myself.

įknúk'ek'eǧA *vi3-refl-redup* s/he scratches himself/herself continuously ▸ **Įknúk'ek'eǧešį!** Do not scratch yourself! 1*s:* **mįknúk'ek'eǧa** 2*s:* **nįknúk'ek'eǧa** 1*p:* **ųgíknuk'ek'eǧabi** *See:* **yuk'éǧA**

įknú'otą *vi3-refl* s/he straightens himself/herself (figuratively "puts one's life back on tracks") 1*s:* **mįknú'otą** 2*s:* **nįknú'otą**

įknúptąyą *vi1-refl* s/he rolls, turns himself/herself over 1*s:* **mįknúptąyą** 2*s:* **nįknúptąyą**

įknúškąšką *vi3-refl* s/he/it moves himself/herself/itself around ▸ **Mįknúškąšką wagábį.** I hate to move around. (Cumberland 2005:395) 1*s:* **mįknúškąšką** 2*s:* **nįknúškąšką**

įknúšnogA *vi3-refl* s/he undresses himself/herself; takes off his/her clothes 1*s:* **mįknúšnoga** 2*s:* **nįknúšnoga**

įknúšnušnuda *vi3-refl* s/he dirties himself/herself 1*s:* **mįknúšnušnuda** 2*s:* **nįknúšnušnuda**

įknúš'agA *vs* she is pregnant ▸ **Wíyą žé įknúš'aga.** That woman is pregnant. 1*s:* **įmąknuš'aga**

2s: **įníknuš'aga** *Vcaus:* **įknúš'akyA** *See:*
wį'įknuš'age

įknúš'akyA *vt1-caus* he makes her pregnant 1s:
įknúš'akwaya 2s: **įknúš'akyaya**

įknúš'įš'į *vi3-refl* s/he tickles himself/herself 1s:
mįknúš'įš'į 2s: **nįknúš'įš'į**

įknútA *vi3-pos* s/he tries for, practices at smth
(activity, sport); rehearses smth (speech, play)
‣ **Gicís įknúta.** He is practicing boxing.

įknúwašte *vi3-refl* s/he makes himself/herself
look good 1s: **mįknúwašte** 2s: **nįknúwašte**

įknúwewe *vi3-refl* s/he makes himself/herself
bleed 1s: **mįknúwewe** 2s: **nįknúwewe**

įknúwįyeyA *vi3-refl* s/he gets himself/herself
ready

įknúzijA *vi3-refl* s/he stretches himself/herself
1s: **mįknúzija** 2s: **nįknúzija**

įknúžaža *vi3-refl* s/he washes, bathes him-
self/herself 1s: **mįknúžaža** 2s: **nįknúžaža** 1p:
ųgíknuzažabi

įknúžužu *vi3-refl* s/he undresses himself/
herself 1s: **mįknúžužu** 2s: **nįknúžužu** 1p:
ųgíknužužubi

įknúzA *vi3-refl* s/he dresses himself/herself in a
certain way ‣ **Cosyá mįknúzįkta!** I will dress
warm! ‣ **Wací įknúza.** She is dressed in regalia.
‣ **Wíyą įknúza.** He dressed up as a woman. ‣
Owá dąyą įknúzabi. They are all well dressed.
1s: **mįknúza** 2s: **nįknúza** 1p: **ųgíknųzabi**

įkóyakya *vt1* s/he ties, harnesses smth, connects them together (to a horse or wagon) 1s:
įkóyawakya 2s: **įkóyayakya**

įkpá *n* tip, point ‣ **Mína įkpa péna.** The knife
has a sharp tip. ‣ **peží'įkpa** hayfork ‣ **azépįkpa**
nipple, teat

įkpáȟnogA *vi3-refl* s/he pierces himself/her-
self 1s: **mįkpáȟnoga** 2s: **nįkpáȟnoga** 1p:
ųgíkpaȟnogabi

įkpák'eǧA *vi3-refl* s/he scratches himself/herself
by pushing, rubbing against smth

įkpázo *vi3-refl* s/he shows, reveals himself/her-
self ‣ **Nidúwe gaš įkpázo!** Whoever you are,
show yourself!

įkpážaža *vi3-refl* s/he washes himself/herself
by rubbing 1s: **mįkpážaža** 2s: **nįkpážaža** 1p:
ųgíkpažažabi

įkpážibA *vi3-refl* s/he makes the sign of the cross

įkpí *n* lap

įksamyA ; **įksapyA** *vt1* s/he bothers, annoys sb
‣ **Įksapciya he?** Am I annoying you? ‣ **Šúga**
žé įksammaya. The dog is bothering me. ‣
Há, nína įksapmayaye no! Yes, you annoy me
very much! 1s: **įksamwaya** 2s: **įksamyaya** *Vabs:*
wa'įksamkiyA

įkšukšuna *Variant:* **úkšukšuna** (WB) *n* bean

įkšuna *n* bag

Įktómi *nprop* 1) Įktomi (name of a trickster) ‣
"Įktómi né iyúhana nįjásodabikte no," eyá.
"Įktómi will do away with all of you," he said.
(NS 2002:44) ‣ **Né Įktómi įwóknagabi háda**
mnogédu háda aknéškana timáhen híbis'a
gáyabis'a. They used to say that lizards would
come to your tent if you told Įktomi stories in
the summertime. (Drummond 1976, Įktomi)
vs 2) s/he is a liar 1s: **įmáktomi** 2s: **įníktomi**
Syn: **įtúšįs'a**

įktú *Variant:* **įtkú** *vs* s/he/it is lit, in flames ‣
"Įnítkųktac," eyá:ga. "You will catch [on]
fire," she kept saying. (Weasel 176:266) ‣ **Gáken**
owáštena įtkúkta. That way it will burn slowly.
1s: **įmáktų** ; **įmátkų** 2s: **įníktų** ; **įnítkų** *Vcaus:*
įktúyA

įktúskiyA *Variant:* **įtkúskiyA** *vt1-pos* s/he finishes, completes his/her own task ‣ **Waná**
įktúswagiya. Now I am done with it. ‣ **Dóȟą**
įktúskiyešį. It goes on forever. 1s: **įktúswagiya**
; **įtkúswagiya** 2s: **įktúsyagiya** ; **įtkúsyagiya**

įktúsyA *Variant:* **įtkúsyA** *vt1-caus* s/he finishes,
completes smth ‣ **Waníyedu dóba né įtkųs'ųya**
štén žé wįjá'ųkįkta. After four years when we

finish it, we will tell the truth. (NS 2002:33) *1s:* į́ktų́swaya ; į́tkų́swaya *2s:* į́ktų́syaya ; į́tkų́syaya *1p:* į́ktų́s'ų̨yabi ; į́tkų́s'ų̨yabi

į́ktų́yĄ *vt1-caus* s/he makes smth burn; lights smth on fire *Vabs:* wa'į́ktų̨yĄ

į́ktų́y̨ yįgÁ *vi3* it is in flames

į́ktų́y̨abi *n* light, lamp ▸ Į́ktų́y̨abi žé sní. The lamp went out.

į́ktų́žA *vs* s/he is drunk on smth *1s:* į́mą́ktų̨ža *2s:* į́nį́ktų̨ža

į́kú *n* chin

į́kú hą́ska *cp* mountain goat *Lit:* long chin

į́kúde *n* weapon, something one shoots with (bow, crossbow, gun)

į́kúhį̨ *n* hair under the chin of a buffalo

į́kusana *n* mink *Lit:* pale chin

į́kuwa *vt1* s/he tempts, teases sb

į́mą́ka gaksá *n* farming disk

į́mą́kayupte *n* plow

į́mǫ́htagA *vt1* s/he bumps against smth, runs, crashes into smth ▸ Cą̨báza į́mǫ́htaga. He crashed into the fence.

į́mǫ́htage ; į́mǫ́htaga *n* bumper ▸ togáda į́mǫ́htage front bumper ▸ héktam į́mǫ́htage rear bumper

į́mótą̨ *vs* 1) s/he is cheeky, bold about smth ▸ Dágu nówa én į́mótą̨. He is cheeky about everything. 2) s/he is greedy *1s:* į́mą́motą̨ *2s:* į́nímotą̨

į́ną́hmA *vi1* s/he hides

į́ną́hme iyáyabi *vi2-pl* they are eloping *1p:* į́ną́hme ų̨gíyayabi

į́ną́hmegiciyabi *vi1-recip* they hide from one another *See:* wį́'į́nahma

į́ną́hmekiyA *vt1-caus* s/he hides from sb, smth ▸ Iná į́ną́hmewakiya. I hid from my mother. ▸ Agícida į́ną́hmewį̨cawakiya. I hid from the police officers. ▸ Wį̨cá žé į́ną́hmemą̨kiya. That man is hiding from me. *1s:* į́ną́hmewakiya *2s:*

į́ną́hmeyakiya *1p:* į́ną́hme'ų̨kiyabi *Vrecip:* į́ną́hmegiciyabi

į́ną́hmeya *vii* s/he is sly *1s:* į́ną́hmewaya *2s:* į́ną́hmeyaya *1p:* į́ną́hme'ų̨yabi

į́ną́hni *vii* s/he hurries; is in a rush ▸ Hą́, į́náwahnį̨kta! Yes, I will hurry! *Adv:* į́ną́hniyą̨ *Vcaus:* į́ną́hniyA

į́ną́hnigen *adv* kind of in a rush; sort of hastily

į́ną́hniyA *vt1-caus* s/he rushes sb ▸ Misų́ga į́ną́hnimayešį́. Younger brother, do not rush me.

į́ną́hniyą̨ *adv* hurriedly

į́ną́hniyena *adv* hurriedly, in a hurry *Usage:* more intense than į́ną́hniyą̨. ▸ Į́ną́hniyena wa'í. I got there in a hurry. ▸ Į́ną́hniyena tín hí He arrived in the house in a hurry.

į́nám *adv* hiding behind smth ▸ Į́nám iyódą̨gabi. They sat down hiding behind it.

į́nápcuwą̨ga ; ijínapcuwą̨ga *num* ninth

į́názam *adv* in the back of smth

į́názapadahą̨ *adv* from the back of smth, from behind smth

į́náží *vii* 1) s/he/it stops, halts ▸ Búza né dóhą̨i į́nážišį́. This cat never stops. ▸ Mawáni híkna į́wánaží. I walked and I stopped. ▸ cą̨dé į́náží s/he has a heart attack 2) s/he stands up ▸ Nazám į́náží. He stood up at the back. *1s:* į́wánaží *2s:* į́yánaží

į́nádaboǧa ; į́nádaboȟya *n* baking powder, yeast

į́ní *vii* s/he does a sweat lodge ceremony, goes into a sweat lodge *1s:* į́wánį *2s:* į́yánį

į́níbi *n* sweatlodge (structure or ceremony) ▸ Į́níbi én iyódą̨gabi. They are sitting here in the sweat lodge. ▸ Į́níbi wagáǧa štén, mini óda wacíǧa. When I make a sweat lodge, I want a lot of water. *See:* į́níbi ecúbi

į́níbi ecúbi *cp* sweatlodge ceremony

į́níbi gáǧabi *n* sweatlodge

į́nígaǧA *vii* s/he builds a sweatlodge

į́nį́tibi *cp* sweatlodge

į̧nį́hą *vs* s/he fears; is worried ‣ **Į̧nį́hą yį̧gá.** He sits in fear. *Vcaus:* į̧nį́hąyĄ

į̧nį́hąyĄ *vt1-caus* s/he/it makes sb worry ‣ **Dókiya yá hą́da į̧mą́nį̧hąyą.** When he goes away it makes me worry.

į̧nówą *vt1* s/he sings about smth *1s:* į̧wánową *2s:* į̧yánową

į̧nų́ba *num* 1) second *n* 2) double-barreled shotgun

į̧nų́ba wiyópeyabi tíbi *np* thrift store, second hand store

į̧nų́m-nažį̧ *n* second base player

į̧'ógana *n* pile, place where substances (such as ashes) are poured ‣ **cahóda į̧'ógana** pile of ashes

į̧'ówąja *adv* all over *Usage:* more intense than ówąja.

į̧'óyA ; į̧'óyayA *vi1-redup, vs* s/he yawns ‣ **Ecágen į̧'ówaya.** I am always yawning. ‣ **I'ómayecuna.** I keep on yawning. ‣ **Į̧'óyabi né'ųs.** This one is always yawning. *1s:* į̧'ówaya ; į̧'ómaya *2s:* į̧'óyaya ; į̧'óniya *1p:* į̧'ó'ųyabi

į̧pá *n* head of smth (mountain, hill)

į̧pą́hte *n* 1) hair or braid tie 2) bridle *Lit:* mouth tying tool ‣ **nį̧gé į̧pą́hta** belly-band

į̧pi *vs* s/he/it is full, sated ‣ **Nína į̧mápi, pinamayaye no.** I am very full, thank you. ‣ **Ą́ą, píyahąšį̧ ko eyáš, į̧pi cén eyáš.** Ah, then in no time at all he was full. (Weasel 87:150) *1s:* į̧mapi *2s:* į̧nipibi *1p:* ų̧gį́pibi *Vcaus:* į̧piyA *Vrefl:* į̧pi'į̧c'iyA

į̧pi'į̧c'iyA *vi3-refl* s/he sates, fills himself/herself up ‣ **Iyuhána dayą́h wódabi, nína į̧pi'į̧c'iyabi.** They all ate well and they really filled themselves. *1s:* į̧pimį̧c'iya *2s:* į̧pinį̧c'iya

į̧piyA *vt1-caus* s/he fills sb up (with food) ‣ **Dąyą́h į̧píciya!** I filled you really well! ‣ **Midáguyabi į̧piyabi.** My relatives sated him. *1s:* į̧piwaya *2s:* į̧piyaya

į̧píyaga *n* belt ‣ **wámni į̧píyaga wacíbi** eagle belt dance

į̧píyaga į̧já̧šeye *cp* belt buckle

į̧są́'į̧ *adv* out of sight ‣ **Žehą́ žéci bą́bą, gaksį́ksį, aktága hį́kna į̧są́'į̧ iyáya.** He was yelling and running back and forth and went out of sight. (Weasel 12:152)

į̧snáye *n* cream, ointment ‣ **hní į̧snáye** skin cream, rash treatment

į̧spá *n* lower part of the elbow

į̧spáse *n* point of the elbow

į̧stó *n* arm ‣ **Į̧stó mabádį̧ míjibawį̧da.** My arm is stiff, rub it for me. *1s:* ma'į̧sto *2s:* ni'į̧sto

į̧stó knağé *vt1-pos* s/he gashes his/her arm *1s:* į̧stó waknáğe *2s:* į̧stó yaknáğe

į̧stókmus *vcont* with the eyes closed ‣ **Į̧stókmus mągá.** I am sitting with my eyes closed. ‣ **Į̧stókmus wací.** She dances with her eyes closed. ‣ **Į̧stókmus wayácibį̧kta c!** You will dance with your eyes closed!

į̧stókmuza *vi1* s/he closes the eyes ‣ **Į̧stókmuza wo!** Close your eyes. *Vcont:* į̧stókmus

į̧stústA *vs* s/he is bored, fed up ‣ **Šką́šį̧ mągá cén į̧mástusta.** I am bored by sitting still. ‣ **Né miní ejéna wąyák wa'ų́ né į̧mástusta.** I am tired of only seeing this water. (NS 2002:28) *1s:* į̧mástusta *2s:* į̧nístusta

į̧š *pro* s/he, it, they too, as well ‣ **Į̧š ektá í.** He went there too. ‣ **Nína į̧š mağážu.** It rains a lot too. ‣ **Į̧š į̧dúkabi.** They are hungry too. ‣ **Mį̧š emácedu.** Me too, I am like this. *1s:* mį̧š *2s:* nį̧š *1p:* ų̧gį́š

į̧šákpe *num* 1) sixth *n* 2) pistol, handgun *Syn:* į̧yókšu

į̧škádA *vt1* s/he plays with smth *1s:* į̧wáškada *2s:* į̧yáškada

į̧škádabi *n* woman that is teased sexually

į̧šką́ *vs* s/he/it is horny *1s:* į̧mášką *2s:* į̧níšką

Į̧šką́ wacíbi *cp* lustful dance

į̧šną́na 1) *pro, adv* by himself/herself/itself, alone ‣ **Į̧šną́na o'énažį̧ ektá í.** She went to town alone. ‣ **Į̧šną́na ecú.** She did it on her own. ‣ **Mį̧šną́na mągáhą né tamúkašį.** I dread being alone. ‣ **Adé Waką́tąga nįšną́na waníką no!** Father the Creator you are the only one that is holy! 2) *vs3* s/he is alone, by himself/herself ‣ **Hǒ! Nįšną́našį.** Oh! You are not alone. *1s:* **mįšną́na** *2s:* **nįšną́na** *1p:* **ųgíšnąnabi**

išną́na ú *vi1* s/he is, stays alone; is a bachelor *Usage:* some speakers also inflect **išną́na.** ‣ **Išną́na úkta.** He will be alone. ‣ **Mįšną́na wa'ú.** I am alone. ‣ **Misų́ga išną́na ú.** My younger brother is a bachelor. *1s:* **išną́na wa'ú** *2s:* **išną́na ya'ú** *1p:* **išną́na ųk'úbi**

išną́nagen *adv* alone, in a lonesome manner ‣ **Išną́nagen ománi.** He walks around alone.

išną́naȟtįyA *vs* s/he/it is the only one *1s:* **mįšną́naȟtįyA** *2s:* **nįšną́naȟtįyA**

išną́ti ; išną́na tí *vi1* she has her menses *Lit:* she lives alone *1s:* **išną́wati ; išną́na watí** *2s:* **išną́yati ; išną́na yatí**

ištá *n* eye ‣ **Ištá sąní wąyága.** He sees with one eye.

ištá gaȟ'ó *vs* s/he is cross-eyed *1s:* **ištá magáȟ'o** *2s:* **ištá nigáȟ'o**

ištá gaškábi *n* blindfold

ištá ȟniȟní *vs* s/he/it has gummy eyes

ištá kmukmúza *vi1-redup* s/he twinkles, blinks repetitively

ištá kmúza *vi1* s/he blinks ‣ **Ištá yakmúza he?** Did you blink? *1s:* **ištá wakmúza** *2s:* **ištá yakmúza** *Vredup:* **ištá kmukmúza**

ištá kpá *vs* s/he is blind from one eye ‣ **Žé ištá kpá.** That one is blind in one eye. *1s:* **ištá wakpá** *2s:* **ištá yakpá** *See:* **ištáǧųǧA**

ištá ogástą *vt1* s/he gives sb a black eye

ištá ogáškA *vt1* s/he blindfolds sb ‣ **Ištá omágaškabi.** They blindfolded me. *1s:* **ištá owágaška** *2s:* **ištá oyágaška**

ištá ogíkma *n* mascara

ištá ostą́ *vs* s/he has a black eye *1s:* **ištá omástą** *2s:* **ištá onístą** *Syn:* **ištásabA**

ištá ošáša *vs* s/he has red eyes, bloodshot eyes ‣ **Šóda žé ús ištá omášaša.** I have red eyes

because of the smoke. *1s:* **ištá omášaša** *2s:* **ištá oníšaša**

ištá sapkíyA *vt1-pos* s/he puts eye shadow; darkens his/her eyes *1s:* **ištá sapwákiya** *2s:* **ištá sapyákiya**

Ištágitų tí *ngeo* Indian Head (Saskatchewan) *Lit:* the house of the one wearing glasses ‣ **Ištágitų tí ektá mnį́kta.** I am going to Indian Head.

ištáǧųǧA *vs* s/he is blind ‣ **Mitúgašina ištáǧųǧa.** My grandfather is blind. *Vcaus:* **ištáǧųȟyA ; ištáǧųȟkiyA**

ištáǧųȟkiyA *vt1-caus* s/he/it blinds sb ‣ **Hąwí akída cén ištáǧųȟkiya.** Looking at the sun made her blind.

ištáǧųȟyA *vt1-caus* s/he causes sb to be blind (by flashing a light) *1s:* **ištáǧųȟwaya** *2s:* **ištáǧųȟyaya**

ištáha *n* eyelid

ištáhį *n* eyelashes

ištáȟe *n* ridge of the eyebrow

ištáȟe'ųba *n* eyebrow

Ištámaškida *nprop* Japanese *See:* **Gisų́na**

ištámaza *n* glasses

ištámnįǧe *n* tear

ištásabA *vs* 1) s/he has a black eye ‣ **Awápa cén ištásaba.** I hit hit him, so he has a black eye. *1s:* **ištámasaba** *2s:* **ištánisaba** *Syn:* **ištá ostą́** *n* 2) raccoon *Syn:* **wįcá**

ištásu *n* iris, eyeball *Lit:* eye seed

ištáštana *n-redup* glasses

ištáštana sába *n-redup* sunglasses

ištátoto *vs-redup* s/he/it has blue eyes *1s:* **ištámatoto** *2s:* **ištánitoto**

ištáyabi *n* glasses

ištáyabi sába *cp* sunglasses *Lit:* black glasses

ištéjA *vs* s/he is bashful, shy, easily embarrassed, ashamed *1s:* **imášteja** *2s:* **iníšteja** *Adv:* **ištéješį** *Vabs:* **wįštéjA** *Vcont:* **ištén**

ištéješį *adv* shamelessly ‣ **Ištéješį i'á.** She spoke shamelessly.

ištén *vcont* embarrassing

įštén įc'íyA *vi3-refl* s/he makes a fool of, embarrasses himself/herself *1s:* **įštén mįc'íya** *2s:* **įštén nįc'íya**

įštényA *vt1-caus* s/he embarrasses, shames sb ‣ **Misúgabi įšténwįcawaye no!** I shamed my younger brothers! ‣ **Koná įšténmayaya.** Friend, you shamed me. *1s:* **įšténwaya** *2s:* **įštényaya**

įští *n* lower lip, lips ‣ **Įští mahpúhpu.** I have chapped lips.

įštímA *vi3* s/he sleeps, is asleep ‣ **Įštíma wo!** Sleep! ‣ **Šúga žé tągán įštíma.** The dog is sleeping outside. ‣ **Téhą mįštíma.** I slept for a long time. ‣ **Ecágen nįštíma.** You are always sleeping. ‣ **Įštímabišį otí'įga.** They do not seem to be asleep. ‣ **Waná ųgíštimabis.** Let us sleep now. *1s:* **mįštíma** *2s:* **nįštíma** *1p:* **ųgíštimabi** *Vcaus:* **įštímekiyA**

įštímat'a *n* sleepy head; someone that is hard to wake up

įštímekiyA *vt1-caus* s/he puts him/her to sleep

įštíšage *n* lipstick

įštípahte *n* Indian bridle

įštóhni *vs* s/he/it has gummy eyes *1s:* **įštómahni** *2s:* **įštónihni**

įtágapsija *n* baseball bat

įtącą *n* 1) leader, boss ‣ **agícida įtącą** policeman *vs* 2) s/he is the boss *1s:* **įmą́tącą** *2s:* **įnítącą**

įté *n* forehead

ítehą *adv* long time ‣ **Ítehą wa'ų́.** I stayed for a long time.

ítehąn *adv* from far away, far over there ‣ **Ítehąn ų́bi.** They are from far over there.

įtémnit'A *vs* s/he/it is sweating profusely because of smth *Lit:* s/he is sweating to death because of it.

įtímahen *adv-post* inside of, within an area, enclosure, pasture, field

įtkóm ; įtkúm *adv* back, back again ‣ **Dóhani įtkóm waknáší.** I will not go back. ‣ **Aké įktúm kní.** She came back again. (NS 2002:51)

įtó *adv* 1) now, well ‣ **Įtó ecúší!** Do not do it now! ‣ **Įtó gán tiwįcoda tíbi.** Well many families lived over there. ‣ **Žé omnágįkta duká įtó togáheya né žepá.** I will tell that one but first I will tell this. (NS 2002:41) *interj* 2) maybe, I guess ‣ **Įtó wanúwąkta.** I guess I will shower. ‣ **Įtó imnódągas.** I guess I will sit down.

įtógam *adv* in front of sb, smth; before time *Usage:* this adverb can be inflected with person markers. ‣ **Hųgá įtógam nawáži.** I stood in front of the chief. ‣ **Tíbi įtógam ną́ži.** He is standing in front of the house. ‣ **Šúga mítogam máni.** The dog is walking in front of me. *1s:* **mítogam** *2s:* **nítogam** *1p:* **ųgítogam** *See:* **togá**

įtúgasą *n* weasel

įtúgasąskana *n* white weasel (winter time)

įtúgasązina *n* brown weasel (summer time)

įtúpa *vt1* s/he avoids sb out of embarrassment; s/he is shy

įtúpsipsijana *n* kangaroo mouse

įtúšį *vii* 1) s/he lies, does not tell the truth ‣ **Dóhani įwátųšįšį.** I never lie. *1s:* **įwátųšį** *2s:* **įyátųšį** *n* 2) lie ‣ **Įtúšį wómagiknagešį!** Do not tell me lies! *Vbenef:* **įgíjitųšį** *Vcaus:* **įtúšįkiyA**

įtúšįkiyA *vt1-caus* s/he makes, convinces sb to lie *1s:* **įtúšįwakiya** *2s:* **įtúšįyakiya**

įtúšįs'a *n* 1) liar *vii* 2) s/he is a liar ‣ **Įwátųšįšįs'a'!** I am not a liar! *1s:* **įwátųšįs'a** *2s:* **įyátųšįs'a** *See:* **įktómi, įtúšį**

į'ų́ *vt1-dit* s/he paints, rubs, applies smth on it *Vbenef:* **įgíji'ų** *Vpos:* **įgí'ų** *Vrefl:* **į'íc'i'ų**

į'ų́tų *vt1* s/he paints smth ‣ **Miyé į'ų́watų.** I painted it myself. ‣ **Tíbi žé į'ų́watų.** I painted the house. *1s:* **į'ų́watų** *2s:* **į'úyatų** *Vbenef:* **įgíjitų**

į'ų́tų įwókma *cp* crayon, paintbrush

įwábadįja *n* shovel

įwábagįza *n* violin ‣ **Įwábagįza wamnúpišį.** I am not skilled at playing violin. *Syn:* **įbágįza**

įwábamnaya *n* iron (for clothes)

įwábasisa *n* sewing machine

įwábažáža *n* washboard

įwáci *n* dance outfit

įwáco'ųba : įwáco'ųbe *n* frying pan

įwádopa *n* canoe

įwágaška *n* bundle

įwágaškeca *n* love medicine

įwágici *vt1-dat* s/he dances over or on account of smth 1s: įwáwagici 2s: įwáyagici

įwáką *vi1* 1) s/he is an expert ‣ **Gamúbi įwáką.** He is a drum expert. 1s: įwámąką 2s: įwániką *n* 2) expert, person with a holy gift *See:* **wayápi**

įwánakąyą *n* thresher

įwá'okma ; įwó'okma ; įwókma *n* pen, pencil, chalk, any writing instrument *Syn:* **owá'okma ; owó'okma**

įwášteȟ *adv* very slowly ‣ **Įwášteȟ yá.** He went very slowly.

įwáštena *adv* slowly, carefully, softly ‣ **Įwáštena wagú.** I came back home slowly. ‣ **Įwáštenaȟ i'á.** He speaks really softly.

įwátape *n* horse used in buffalo hunting

įwátokšu *Variant:* **otókšu, tokšú** *n* truck, pickup truck, large vehicle *Lit:* that which one hauls things with 1s: **mitátokšu** 2s: **nitátokšu** 3s: **tatókšu ; tokšú**

įwátokšu tága *cp* large truck (like a trailer van) **Adé įwátokšu tága basíšį.** Dad does not drive large trucks.

įwátokšu wa'íbadįda *cp* snowplow

įwągam *adv, post* above smth ‣ **Taȟáge įwągam ta'óbi.** He was wounded above the knee. (Drummond 1976, A bear story)

įwąknage *n* 1) mirror 2) window, glass ‣ **Įwáknage né šmiyáyą.** The window is shining.

įwáyage *n* gunsight

Įwążikte *n* First kill ceremony

įwóbaska *n* bread pan

įwócape *n* long fork or stick used to fork up some puppy meat in the kettle dance or clowns' dance

įwóhe *n* cooking pot

įwóknagA *vt1* 1) s/he tells a story about smth ‣

Nağí įwóknaga. He is telling a vision. ‣ **Dágu įwóknagabi?** What are they talking about? ‣ **Né Įktómi įwóknagabi hą́da mnogédu hą́da aknéškana timáhen híbis'a gáyabis'a.** They used to say that lizards would come to your tent if you told Įktomi stories in the summertime. (Drummond 1976, Įktomi) *n* 2) legend

įyágaȟpa ; įyágaȟpe ; įyágaȟpena *n* lid, cover ‣ **Įyágaȟpa žé yušnóga.** Take the cover off. *Syn:* **agáȟpe**

įyágasam *adv* further, beyond

įyágaškabi *n* pipe pouch, bag

įyáge *n* feather on an arrow

įyágų *vi2* s/he gags because of an awful taste in the mouth

Íyaȟe wídana *ngeo* Little Rockies (Montana) *Lit:* small island of rocks

Íyaȟe wįcášta *nprop* Stoney Nakoda people, person of Stoney Nakoda descent

įyáȟtage ; įyáȟtakiya *n* trap

įyámni *num* third

įyámnigiya *adv* in all directions, scattered ‣ **Įyámnigiya iyáyabi.** They went in all directions.

įyámni-nažį *n* third base player

įyáskamyA *vt1-caus* s/he glues, seals, stamps smth on it

įyáskamye *n* stamp, tape, something that is glued on

įyáskapA *vs* s/he/it is glued, sealed, stamped *Vcaus:* **įyáskamyA**

įyá'ųba *vt1-dit* s/he blames, accuses sb for smth ‣ **Ecágen įyáma'ųba.** She blames me for it all the time. 1s: **iyáwa'ųba** 2s: **įyáya'ųba**

įyáweȟtįyą *n* computer *Syn:* **owókma wąyágabi**

įyáyuza *n* holder, anything that holds

íyą *n* stone ‣ **Íyą žé mnaská.** That stone is flat. ‣ **Íyą wąmnága žehą́ hį́k nawápsija.** I saw a stone and I kicked it.

Íyą oyáde *cp* Stone nation

íyą wašíjuti *cp* brick house

íyągA *vi3* s/he runs, speeds up, races ‣ **Nína íyąga.** He really sped up ‣ **Hokšína gicí ínągįkte no.** You will race with the boy. *1s:* **įmąga** *2s:* **įnąga** *1p:* **ųgíyągabi** *Vcont:* **íyąk** *See:* **kíyągena** *Syn:* **aktágA**

íyąges'a *n* runner ‣ **Wįcá íyąges'a žé, cagú wašté yuhá.** That man is a runner, he has good lungs. (Fourstar p. 10)

íyąȟe ; íyaȟe *n* mountain, stony hill ‣ **Íyąȟe óhą iyáme í.** He went hunting up there in the mountain. ‣ **Íyąȟe wągámneȟ íbi.** They went to the highest mountain.

Íyąȟe tága *ngeo* Rocky Mountains *Lit:* big mountains

íyąk *vcont* running ‣ **Íyąk ú.** He comes running. *Vredup:* **íyąkyąk**

íyąkyąk *vcont-redup* running around

iyéciga giyéna (WB) *cp* airplane *Lit:* flies by itself

iyéǧA *vs* it glows because of it (fire, spark, light, stove) ‣ **Océti žé iyéǧa.** The stove is glowing from the heat. *Vcaus:* **iyéȟyA**

iyéȟyA *vt1-caus* s/he/it makes smth glow

iyókšu *n* 1) cartridge 2) shotgun

iyúcą *n* handle

iyúdįda *n* reins *Syn:* **įká**

iyúhibi *n* tobacco mixed with red willow (used in ceremonies)

iyúhomni *n* steering wheel

iyúkcą *vt2* s/he thinks, has an opinion about sb, smth ‣ **Wáhįhąkta inúkcą he?** Do you think it will snow? ‣ **Dóken įnúkcą?** What do you think about it? ‣ **Žécen iyúkcąbi.** That is the way they think about it. *1s:* **įmnúkcą** *2s:* **įnúkcą** *1p:* **ųgíyukcąbi** *Vabs:* **wíyukcą** *Vpos:* **įknúkcą** *Vredup:* **iyúkcąkcą**

iyúkcąkcą *vt2-redup* s/he thinks long and hard about sb, smth

iyúksA *vt1* s/he shortens smth, to make designs on smth; measures and cuts smth ‣ **Sąksája žé iyúksa éknąga.** She shortened the dress and put it down. *1s:* **įmnúksa** *2s:* **įnúksa**

iyúkša *n* curve

iyúmą *n* sharpener, file ‣ **mína iyúmą** knife sharpener

iyúnena *n* monkey

iyúsnohą *n* sleigh

iyústo *n* pet

iyúškį *vt2* s/he admires sb, smth ‣ **Hokší iyúškį.** He adores the baby. *1s:* **įmnúškį** *2s:* **įnúškį** *Vabs:* **wa'íyuškį** *Vbenef:* **įgíjiyuškį**

iyúšnoge *n* wrench, pliers

iyúšpe *n* key

iyútA ; iyútA *vt2* s/he tests, tries, measures smth (food, drink, clothes, task) ‣ **Waȟpé né iyúta.** Try this tea. ‣ **Hába né įmnúta.** I tried these shoes. ‣ **Iyúha iyútąbišį.** None of them tried to do it. ‣ **Įyútąbi cįgíšį.** She does not want to try it on. ‣ **Dąyágen iyútešį.** He did not measure it properly. *1s:* **įmnúta** *2s:* **įnúta** *Vbenef:* **įgíjiyutA** *Vrefl:* **įknútA**

iyútabi *n* unit of measurement (centimeter, inch, foot, yard) ‣ **Įyútabi yámni nážį.** It stands three feet tall. ‣ **awódabi iyútabi** measurement of the table

iyúweǧa *n* crossing place on a river, creek

iyúžaža *n* soap, laundry soap

iyúžažamno *n* laundry soap

iyúgA *Variant:* **įwúgA** *vi3* s/he goes to bed, sleep; sleeps on smth ‣ **Ųgíyųgas!** Let us go to bed! ‣ **Žéci iyúgabi.** They slept over there. *1s:* **įmúga** *2s:* **įnúga** *1p:* **ųgíyųgabi ; ųgíwųgabi** *Vcaus:* **iyúk-kiyA ; įwúk-kiyA** *See:* **kiyúgA**

iyúgaši *vt1* s/he orders sb to go to bed *1s:* **iyúgawaši** *2s:* **iyúgayaši**

iyúǧA *Variant:* **įwúǧA** *vt3* s/he asks sb about smth ‣ **Hąyákena mitúgaši įmúǧa.** I will ask my grandfather about it tomorrow. ‣ **Niyé įnúǧa he?** Did you ask for it yourself? ‣ **Hą nitága ųgíwųǧįkta no!** Ok, we will ask your sister! ‣ **Įcímųǧįkta.** I will ask you. *1s:* **įmúǧa** *2s:* **įnúǧa** *1p:* **ųgíyųǧabi ; ųgíwųǧabi** *Vabs:* **wawíyųǧA**

Vbenef: **įgíjiyųǧA** *Vcoll:* **įwį́cayųǧA** *Vrefl:* **įc'íyųǧA**

įyų́kkiyA *Variant:* **įwų́kkiyA** *vt1-caus* s/he puts sb to bed; s/he makes sb lie down *1s:* **įyų́kwakiya** ; **įwų́kwakiya** *2s:* **įyų́kyakiya** ; **įwų́kyakiya** *1p:* **įyúk'ųkiyabi** ; **įwúk'ųkiyabi**

įzáptą *num* fifth

įzíngijiyA *vt1-benef* s/he burns incenses ritually for sb *1s:* **įzínwejiya** *2s:* **įzínyejiya**

įzínyA *vt1-caus* s/he burns incense ritually *1s:* **įzínwaya** *2s:* **įzínyaya** *1p:* **įzín'ųyabi** *Vbenef:* **įzíngijiyA** *See:* **azínyA**

įzínyabi *n* incense

įzítkiyA *vt1-caus* s/he makes smth burn ritually ▸ **Pežískuya įzítkiyabi.** They burn sweetgrass ritually.

įžáža *vi* it is washed away ▸ **Nówa įžáža.** It is all washed away.

J

jé ; jé'e *part* always, often ▸ **Híbi jé.** They come often. ▸ **Įmáduka jé.** I am always hungry. ▸ **Gicí iwá'a jé.** I always talk with him. ▸ **Waná há ȟniȟníbi jé.** Then they always had sores on the skin. ▸ **Okówąži hą́da tída wówįcagijikma jé'e.** She always writes to her folks back home once a week.

jísą *n* birthmark

jiškína ; júskina *vs* s/he/it is small ▸ **Šų́ga né jiškína.** That is a small dog. ▸ **Gáki zitką́na wąží júskina né ókta wašką́.** I am trying to shoot a very small little bird over there. (Weasel 82:29)

jónana *quant* few, little, small amount ▸ **Cąšmúyabi pšųkáką jónana mak'ú.** Give me a few candies. ▸ **Mázaska óda mnuhá iyéš jónana yuhá.** I have a lot of money, and as for him he has a little. ▸ **Eyáš jónana mak'ú.** Give me a small amount.

-ju *suff See:* **-gu**

juk'ána *vs* it is small, narrow ▸ **Wakpá juk'ána iyáyabi.** They went through the narrow river. ▸ **tahį́špa juk'ána** sewing needle ▸ **šųkcúk'ana** coyote

júsina *vs* s/he/it is small (size or age) ▸ **Júsina žé micį́kši.** The small one is my son. ▸ **Mitáwa žé júsina.** Mine is small. ▸ **Né Įktómi owóknage né wanáǧaš žé ųgégiyabis'a ųjúsibina žehą́.** They used to tell us this Įktomi story when were small. (Drummond 1976, Įktomi) *1s:* **majúsina** *2s:* **nijúsina** *1p:* **ųjúsibina** *Vredup:* **júsinana**

júsinaȟtįyĄ *vs* s/he/it is the smallest (of a group) ▸ **Búza žé júsinaȟtįyą.** That cat is the smallest.

júsinana *vs-redup* s/he/it is very small ▸ **Edáhą né hokšínana né júsinana né hokšína né.** One of them was this little boy, this very small boy. (NS 2002:20)

júsisina *n-pl-redup* children, little children

juwį́jijina *n* killdeer *Syn:* **sihújijina**

juwį́na *n* sandpiper

K

kÁ *vt1* 1) s/he/it means smth, indicates sb, smth ▸ **Né dágu kábi?** What does this mean? ▸ **Žécen waká.** That is what I mean. ▸ **Dágu yaká he?** What is wrong with you? 2) s/he chooses smth, sb ▸ **Niyé cicá.** I chose you. ▸ **Miyé mayáka he?** Did you choose me? ▸ **Žé kábi.** He has been chosen. *1s:* **waká** *2s:* **yaká** *1p:* **ųkábi**

kádA *vimp* 1) it is hot (weather, food, objects), spicy ▸ **Ą́ba káda.** It is a hot day. ▸ **Wahą́bi né káda.** This soup is hot. ▸ **Waȟpé káda edáhą wacíga.** I want some hot tea. ▸ **Káda he?** Is it spicy? ▸ **mázakada** hot metal ▸ **mníkada** hot water *vs* 2) s/he is feverish ▸ **Micų́kši nína káda no!** My daughter is really feverish! *1s:* **makáda** *2s:* **nikáda** *1p:* **ųkádabi** *Vcaus:* **kanyÁ** *Vredup:* **katkádA** *See:* **kanyágen ų́**

kádagen *adv* kind of warm

kangíyA *vt1-pos* s/he heats up his/her own thing 1s: **kanwágiya** 2s: **kanyágiya** 1p: **kan'úgiyabi**

kanyÁ *vt1-caus* s/he heats smth up ‣ **Waȟpé žé kanyá!** Heat up the tea! 1s: **kanwáya** 2s: **kanyáya** 1p: **kan'úyabi** *Adv:* **kanyágen** *Vpos:* **kangíyA**

kanyágen *adv* rather hot; feverish

kanyágen ú *vi1* s/he is feverish

kapéya *vt1-caus* s/he/it is more than, goes beyond sb, smth ‣ **Cogán kapéya.** He passed the middle point. ‣ **Mázaska obáwįǧe kapéya.** It is more than $100. *Adv:* **kapéyena** *See:* **iyékapeya**

kapéyaktagA *vi1* s/he runs faster ‣ **Eyá žeȟá kapéyaktaga.** Right away he ran all the faster. (Weasel 46:260)

kapéyena *adv* more ‣ **Kapéyena wók'u wo.** Feed him more.

katkádA *vs-redup* they are hot

ką *n* 1) muscle 2) gristle ‣ **Ką yatábi wašté.** It is nice to chew on gristle. 3) tendon, vein, artery

káda *n* plum

kágakpa *vi1* s/he taps on a vein

kągí ; kagí *n* raven

Kągí okónagiciye *cp* Crow society

Kągí Tóga *cp* Crow tribe; person of Crow descent *Lit:* raven enemy

kájusina *n* small vein

kąsú *n* plum seed

kątága *n* large artery

kąyútibA *vs* s/he has cramps; epilepsy, epileptic seizure 1s: **kąmáyutiba** 2s: **kąníyutiba**

kąyútibes'a *n* person suffering from epilepsy

kéš *conj* but, but invariably, but instead ‣ **Kuwábi kéš duwéni yúzešį.** They chased it but nobody caught it. (Parks et al. 1994) ‣ **Waȟpé wacíga duká huȟnáȟyabi kéš mak'ú.** I wanted tea but she gave me coffee instead.

keyá *n* snapping turtle

ki-₁ *pref* two, in two; separated in the middle ‣ **yuksá > okíyukse** s/he breaks, cuts smth off with scissors > canyon

ki-₂ *pref* doing smth while arriving back there (after leaving); doing smth while returning back to where s/he is from ‣ **iyódągA > kiyódągA** s/he sits down > s/he arrives back there and sits down ‣ **yųgÁ > kiyúgA** s/he lays down, goes to bed > s/he arrives back there and lays down, goes to bed

kí₁ *vi1* s/he arrives back there (after leaving); returns back to where s/he is from ‣ **Aké tiyáb kíbi cén.** Again they came back home. ‣ **Ecén wíyą žé tída kí** And so the woman returned back home. 1s: **wakí** 2s: **yakí** 1p: **ųkíbi** *See:* **knokí**

kí₂ *vt1-dit* s/he grabs, takes away smth from sb ‣ **Né hoǧá makíbi.** The fish grabbed it away from me. (Cumberland 2005:433) 1s: **wakí** 2s: **yakí** 1p: **ųkíbi**

-ki ; -ci *suff* over, around (indicates a general or approximative location) *Usage:* changes to -ci after e. ‣ **žé > žéci** that > over there ‣ **né > néci** this > over here ‣ **gá > gakí** that yonder > over there yonder

kibážį *vt1* s/he is against, jealous of sb ‣ **Sųgágu kibážį.** He is against his younger brother. *Vabs:* **wakíbažį**

kíǧe *interj* word used to ridicule sb

kiȟpá *vi1-dat* s/he dismounts, gets off from sb, smth ‣ **Waȟ'áksija žeįyúga žécen kiȟpá.** The bear laid down, and he got off of it. (Drummond 1976, A bear story) 1s: **wéȟpa** 2s: **yéȟpa**

kiȟpé ecúbi *vt3-pl* they wrestle

kiȟpé ecúbina *cp* wrestling match

ki'íyągA *vi1* s/he races *Vcont:* **ki'íyąk**

ki'íyągena ; kíyągena *n* 1) race *vi1* 2) s/he races ‣ **Ųkíyągenas!** Let us race! ‣ **Hokšíbina gáki ki'íyągenabi no.** The boys are racing over there. ‣ **Né šųkjúk'ana wąží gicí ki'íyągena.** He raced with a coyote. (NS 2002:41)

ki'íyąk *vcont* racing ‣ **Ki'íyąk ecúbinakta.** They will do a racing contest.

kijáksA *vt1* s/he cuts, chops smth in two with a tool; s/he disobeys, breaks a rule, law ‣

Wósuye žená koškábi, kijáksabi štén, wanúȟ wócaȟiya síja ehą́ųgibi ca. If those young men were to break them [laws], very bad luck could come our way. (Shields 41–42:20)

kiknÁ *vi1* s/he leaves home ‣ **Waná kikná koná!** Now it (the spirit) is leaving friend! ‣ **Kiknábi cén įmą́comni.** They left home, so I am lonely. ‣ **Kiknábi ųká nahą́ȟ bąyáhąbi stéya.** They left home but still they can be heard yelling. *1s:* **wakíkna** *2s:* **yakíkna** *1p:* **ųkíknabi**

kiškána *n* spoon ‣ **Kiškána niyúha wabáwiyakpa.** I polished all of the spoons.

kiškána tága *cp* ladle

kišné *n* lover, boyfriend *Syn:* **akíšne**

kišnégiciyabi *vi1-recip* they love one another ‣ **Kišnéyeciyabi hųštá.** You loved each other, it is said. *1p:* **kišné'ųgiciyabi**

kišnéyA *vt1* s/he loves sb romantically, steadily; s/he has a lover ‣ **Duwéȟ kišnéyaya?** Do you love someone? ‣ **Waną́gaš hą́dahą kišnéya.** Long ago he loved her steadily. *1s:* **kišnéwaya** *2s:* **kišnéyaya** *1p:* **kišné'ųyabi**

ki'úm *adv* beside, alongside ‣ **Šų́ga žé amų́giya ki'úm aktága.** The dog ran alongside the car.

-kiyA₁ *suff* s/he makes, allows, lets sb do smth, *Usage:* triggers e-ablaut and attaches to contracted verbs. ‣ **gic'ų́ > gic'ų́kiyA** s/he wears his/her own > s/he gets his/her own to wear smth, to dress ‣ **yužáža > yužážakiyA** s/he washes sb, smth by rubbing > s/he makes sb wash smth ‣ **snokyÁ > snokyékiyA** s/he knows sb, smth > s/he lets sb know smth; lets smth be known *1s:* **-wakiya** *2s:* **-yakiya** *1p:* **-ųkiyabi** *See:* **-yA**

-kiyA₂ *suff* s/he considers, regards sb, smth as *Usage:* attaches to stative verbs, and truncates a preceding word. ‣ **owáštena > owášten-kiya** slowly, carefully > s/he is happy, enjoys smth ‣ **dágu > dágukiya** it is something > s/he thinks it is something ‣ **waką́ > waką́kiya** s/he/it is holy, spiritually powerful > s/he consid-

ers, holds sb, smth as holy ‣ **ecá > ecákiya** s/he/it is thus, is of that kind > s/he considers, thinks sb is as such *1s:* **-wakiya** *2s:* **-yakiya** *1p:* **-ųkiyabi**

-kiyA₃ *suff* to, for *Usage:* triggers e-ablaut; this suffix combines the dative -gi- and the causative-yA. ‣ **hiyú > hiyúkiya** s/he departs, is setting to come here from there > s/he tosses, sends smth over to sb; sends sb over ‣ **yá > yekíya** s/he goes away from here, he departed from here > s/he sends sb, smth away to sb ‣ **įȟpéya > įȟpékiya** s/he discards, throws sb, smth away > s/he throws smth at sb; s/he leaves smth for sb *1s:* **-wakiya** *2s:* **-yakiya** *1p:* **-ųkiyabi**

-kiyA₄ *suff* *See:* **-takiya**

kiyáni *vi1* s/he arrives back there climbing up

kiyą́na *adv* close, nearby ‣ **Kiyą́na ú.** He is coming close. ‣ **Kiyą́na híbi.** They are approaching.

kiyą́naȟ *adv* very close, pretty close

kiyéna *adv* close to ‣ **Huhúžubina kiyéna tí.** She lives close to Regina.

kiyódągA *vi1/3* s/he arrives back there and sits down ‣ **Žécen wíyą žé tín kiyódąga.** So then the woman went in and sat down. *1s:* **wakímnodąga** *2s:* **yakínodąga**

kiyúȟa *vi1* it (animal) breeds, copulates ‣ **Šųkwíyena žé kiyúȟa.** That mare is breeding.

kiyúweǧa *vi1/2* s/he crosses a body of water while arriving back there *1s:* **wakímnuweǧa** *2s:* **yakínuweǧa**

kiyúgA *vi1/3* s/he arrives back there and lays down, goes to bed ‣ **Yakínųga céyaga.** You should go back to bed. ‣ **Waná yakínųgábi céyage'.** Now it is time you go back to bed. *1s:* **wakímųga** *2s:* **yakínųga**

kízA *vt1* s/he fights sb, smth ‣ **Makíziktą šką́.** He tried to fight me. ‣ **Wįcákiziktą ųšką́bi.** We tried to fight them. *1s:* **wakíza** *2s:* **yakíza** *1p:* **ųkízabi** *Vdat:* **gicízA**

kį'į *vt1* s/he throws smth at sb; stones sb *1s:* **wakį́'į** *2s:* **yakį́'į** *1p:* **ųkį́'įbi**

Kį'íbi *ngeo* Sintaluta (Saskatchewan) *Lit:* they throw stones

kį'íyegiciyA *vi1-recip* they throw smth to one another

kį'íyeyA *vt1* s/he throws, casts, propels smth ▸ **Tába žé kį'íyeya.** Throw the ball. ▸ **[. . .] eyáš tahú yubémni gá kį'íyewįcaya gáyabi.** [. . .] so he wrung their necks and threw them over there. (NS 2002:42) *1s:* **kį'íyewaya** *2s:* **kį'íyeyaya** *Vrecip:* **kį'íyegiciyA**

kmúgA *vt1* s/he snares smth ▸ **Maštín wakmúga.** I snared a rabbit. *1s:* **wakmúga** *2s:* **yakmúga** *1p:* **ųkmúgabi** *Vabs:* **wakmúgA** *Vbenef:* **gíjikmųgA**

-kna *aux* s/he feels, senses *Usage:* used with verbs or adverbs of negative feelings; triggers e-ablaut. ▸ **Nągáhą né osní ųknábi.** These days we find it cold. (Cumberland 2005:398) ▸ **osągaga > osąkkna** s/he is lonesome > s/he feels lonely ▸ **sijáya > sijáyekna** badly, poorly > s/he feels sad, badly *1s:* **-wakna** *2s:* **-yakna** *1p:* **-ųknabi**

kná *vi1* s/he goes, returns back to where s/he is from ▸ **Cída yakná he?** Are you going back home? ▸ **Yakná štén anúk éduwą.** When you go back home look both ways. *1s:* **wakná** *2s:* **yakná** *1p:* **ųknábi**

knabó *vs-pos* his/her foot (lower body part) is swollen

knagíyą *vs* s/he/it is located across

knağú *vt1-pos* s/he finishes up his/her own pipe *1s:* **waknáğu** *2s:* **yaknáğu** *1p:* **ųknáğubi**

knaháskA *vt1-pos* s/he lengthens his/her own story ▸ **Knaháska jé.** He always lenghtens his story.

knahómni *vt1-pos* s/he spins his/her own

knaȟéba *vt1-pos* s/he drinks up his/her own

knaȟpÁ *vt1-pos* s/he takes down his/her own (as a tent) *1s:* **waknáȟpa** *2s:* **yaknáȟpa** *1p:* **ųknáȟpabi**

knaȟtágA *vt1-pos* s/he bites his/her own ▸ **Ceží waknáȟtaga.** I bit my tongue. *1s:* **waknáȟtaga** *2s:* **yaknáȟtaga**

knaksÁ *vt1-pos* 1) s/he cuts his/her own with a sharp tool ▸ **Pahá knaksá.** He cut his own hair. ▸ **Wógitahą ağúyabi knaksábi.** And in spite of everything, they managed to cut their own wheat. (Drummond 1976, Early days on Carry The Kettle reserve) 2) s/he bites his/her own off *1s:* **waknáksa** *2s:* **yaknáksa** *1p:* **ųknáksabi**

knapÁ *vt1-pos* s/he carries, puts it in his/her mouth

knapšú *vi1-pos* s/he dislocates his/her thing *1s:* **waknápšų** *2s:* **yaknápšų**

knaptá *vimp* it (weather) cleared up ▸ **Mağážu né knaptá.** The rain cleared up. ▸ **Makóce iyúhana agáȟpac'ehą žehą knaptá.** When all the earth was covered [with water], the weather cleared up. (Drummond 1976, The flood)

knasní *vt1-pos* s/he smothers, puts out his/her own fire, light ▸ **Žécen, nągáȟ éyaš knasníkta škąškąnahą duká dáguge žécaš.** So now he really tried to put it [his house] out, but there was no hope of that. (Weasel 91:228) *1s:* **waknásni**; *2s:* **yaknásni** *1pl:* **ųknasnibiųknasnibi**

knasníbA *vt1-pos* s/he/it licks his/her own ▸ **Búza nąbé knasníba.** The cat is licking his paws.

knaškíškįyą *vi1-redup* s/he is very crazy, out of control

knaškíyą *vi1* s/he is crazy, out of control, insane ▸ **Knaškíyą úšį wo.** Do not be crazy. ▸ **Né knaškíyą.** This one is out of control. ▸ **Owá knaškįyąbįkte no!** They all went crazy! ▸ **Ȟtánihą, iyúha waknáškįyą** Yesterday, I was completely out of control. ▸ **Šųkknáškįyąbi** Crazy dog society *1s:* **waknáškįyą** *2s:* **yaknáškįyą** *1p:* **ųknáškįyąbi** *Vredup:* **knaškíškįyą**

knašná *vt1-pos* s/he omits smth while speaking *1s:* **waknášna** *2s:* **yaknášna** *1p:* **ųknášnabi**

knaštą *vt1-pos* s/he finishes his/her own speech ▸ **Onówą né knaštą.** He finished singing his song. *1s:* **waknáštą** *2s:* **yaknáštą** *1p:* **ųknáštąbi**

knažúžu *vt1-pos* s/he pays for his/her own *1s:* **waknážužu** *2s:* **yaknážužu** *1p:* **ųknážužubi**

knágA *vt1* s/he puts smth ready; stores smth (food, wood); has smth on hand *1s:* **waknága** *2s:* **yaknága** *1p:* **ųknágabi** *Vbenef:* **gíjiknagA** *Vpos:* **giknágA** *See:* **oknágA**

knągíyą *adv* sideways ‣ **Knągíyą yubáǧe.** He pulled it sideways.

knąyÁ *vt1* s/he fools sb ‣ **Dóhani mąknáyešį.** He never fooled me. ‣ **Wįcáwaknąyįkte no.** I will trick them. *1s:* **waknáyą** *2s:* **yaknáyą** *1p:* **ųknáyąbi** *Vabs:* **waknáyÁ** *Vcaus:* **knąyákiyA** *Vrefl:* **įc'íknąyÁ**

knąyákiyA *vt1-caus* s/he fools, tricks sb *Usage:* some speakers do not ablaut this verb. ‣ **Misúga knąyámakiya.** My younger brother tricked me. *1s:* **knąyáwakiya** *2s:* **knąyáyakiya** *1p:* **knąyá'ųkiyabi**

kné *vt1* s/he sets, puts smth in place; makes smth ‣ **Wíyeya kné.** He puts it aside, ready. *1s:* **wakné** *2s:* **yakné** *1p:* **ųknébi**

knébA *vii* s/he vomits ‣ **Mayázą híkna waknébe no.** I am sick and vomiting. *1s:* **waknéba** *2s:* **yaknéba** *1p:* **ųknébabi** *Vcaus:* **knemkíyA** *Vcont:* **knem-** *Vrefl:* **knem'íc'iyA, įknúknebA**

knegíyA *vt1* s/he makes an offering (food, cloth); blesses smth ‣ **Duwé knegíyįkta?** Who will do the blessings? *1s:* **knewágiya** *2s:* **kneyágiya** *1p:* **ųknégiyabi**

knegíyabi ; kneyábi *n* offering ‣ **tóyude kneyábi** food offering

kneknéǧa *vs-redup* s/he/it is spotted ‣ **Šúga žé kneknéǧa.** That dog is spotted. ‣ **Kneknéǧa žé núzahą.** The spotted one is fast.

knem- *vcont* vomiting

knem'íc'iyA *vi3-refl* s/he made himself/herself vomit *1s:* **knemmíc'iyA** *2s:* **knemníc'iyA**

knemkíyA *vt1-caus* s/he/it makes sb vomit ‣ **Tanó žé knemmákiya.** This meat made me vomit. *1s:* **knemwákiya** *2s:* **knemyákiya**

kneška *vs* s/he/it is spotted

kni- *pref* doing smth while arriving back here, to where s/he is from; doing smth while returning, coming home ‣ **iyódąga > kniyódąga** s/he/it sits down > s/he arrives back here and sits

kní *vii* s/he arrives back here; returns, comes home ‣ **Tída kní.** He comes home. ‣ **Ába įyámni ųkníbįkte no.** We will come home on Wednesday. ‣ **Owópetų žedáhą ųkníbi.** We came back home from the store. ‣ **Neháduhtįyą kníbi.** They came back around this time. *1s:* **wakní** *2s:* **yakní** *1p:* **ųkníbi** *Vabs:* **wakní**

knihéya *adv* steep ‣ **Né įyaȟe knihéya žén, aktága, giksúyešį.** He ran toward the steep cliff, forgetting it was there. (Weasel 12:147)

knijú *vii* s/he departs, leaves to come back here

kninážį₁ *vii* s/he arrives back here and stands ‣ **Nén ųknínažįkta mitátiyoba nén.** We will stop here at my gate. (Weasel 17:183) *1s:* **waknínawažį** *2s:* **yaknínayažį** *1p:* **kniná'ųžįbi** ; **ųknínažįbi**

kninážį₂ *vii* s/he stands his/her own ground *1s:* **knináwažį** *2s:* **knináyažį**

kninápA *vii* s/he comes out, emerges; arrives back here and reappears ‣ **Bízena nówa kninápabi.** All the gophers appeared. *1s:* **waknínąpa** *2s:* **yaknínąpa**

kniyó- *pref* gets, takes his/her own *Usage:* prefixed to verbs of movement. ‣ **hiyó'i > kniyó'i** s/he went, arrives there to take sb, smth > s/he went, arrives there to take his/her own

kniyódągA *vii/2* s/he arrives back here and sits down *1s:* **waknímnodąga** *2s:* **yaknínodąga**

kniyó'i *vt1-pos* s/he went, arrives there to take his/her own; gets his/her own back *1s:* **kniyówa'i** *2s:* **kniyóya'i**

kniyóyA *vt2-pos* s/he goes there to get his/her own ‣ **Hába nitáwa žé kniyóya.** Go and get your shoes. ‣ **"Kniyó'ųyąbiktac," eyá.** "We will go get her," they said. (NS 2002:54) *1s:* **kniyómna** *2s:* **kniyóna** *1p:* **kniyó'ųyąbi**

kniyúweǧa *vi1/2* s/he crosses a body of water while arriving, returning back here *1s:* **waknímnuweǧa** *2s:* **yaknínuweǧa**

kniyúgA *vi1/3* s/he arrives back here and lies down *1s:* **waknímųga** *2s:* **yaknínųga**

kno- *pref* bring his/her own *Usage:* used with verbs of coming and going. ‣ **kí > knokí** s/he arrives back there (after leaving); returns back to where s/he is from > s/he arrives back there (after leaving) with his/her thing; returns back home with his/her own

knokí *vt1-pos* s/he arrives back there (after leaving) with his/her thing; returns back home with his/her own ‣ **Žécen tída knokíbi hį́k iyúha yužážabi.** And then they returned back home and washed everything. *1s:* **waknóki** *2s:* **yaknóki** *1p:* **ųknókibi**

knoknók *adv* loose, loosely

Knoknók wací *cp* Loose dance (when one's limbs go in all directions, as a clown)

knubó *vt1-pos, vi1-pos* s/he/it makes his/her own swell by the action of the hands; his/her becomes swollen ‣ **Áá, hú knubó áyabi.** Ah, their legs became swollen. (Weasel 42:166) *1s:* **waknúbo** *2s:* **yaknúbo** *1p:* **ųknúbobi**

knúdA *vt1-pos* s/he eats his/her own food *1s:* **waknúda** *2s:* **yaknúda** *1p:* **ųknúdabi** *Vcont:* **knún**

knudódo *vt1-pos* s/he cleans his/her own *1s:* **waknúdodo** *2s:* **yaknúdodo** *1p:* **ųknúdodobi**

knudóȟpeya *vt1-pos* s/he has his/her thing (blanket) slung over the shoulder ‣ **Šiná žé knudóȟpeya yuhá.** He has his blanket slung over.

knudúgA *vt1-pos* s/he plucks, pulls his/her own out (eyebrow, hair) ‣ **Įštáȟe'ųba iyúha knudúga** She plucked all of her eyebrows.

knugádį *vt1-pos* s/he stretches his/her own out ‣ **Mína knugádį.** He opened out his pocket knife.

knuhÁ *vt1-pos* s/he has his/her own, carries, keeps smth with him/her ‣ **Wįcíjana gá búza wąží knuhá.** That girl over there has one cat with her. ‣ **Cuwíknąga cóza žéca yaknúhabi he?** Do you all have a warm coat with you? ‣ **Šųkcíjana né ųknúhabi.** We kept this puppy of ours. ‣ **Gugúša šį́tų́ né knuhíkteši̧.** She will not keep this fat pig of hers. ‣ **Nakón'i'abi knuhá ma'ųnibika.** We will walk carrying our Nakoda language. *1s:* **waknúha** *2s:* **yaknúha** *1p:* **ųknúhabi**

knuhá máni *vi1* s/he walks carrying his/her own ‣ **Nakón'i'abi knuhá ma'ųnibika.** We will walk carrying our Nakoda language. *1s:* **knuhá mawáni** *2s:* **knuhá mayáni** *1p:* **knuhá ma'ųnibi**

knuháši *vt1-pos* s/he orders his/her own to carry smth *1s:* **knuháwaši** *2s:* **knuháyaši**

knuȟpÁ *vt1-pos* s/he unloads his/her own; throws his/her own down *1s:* **waknúȟpa** *2s:* **yaknúȟpa** *1p:* **ųknúȟpabi**

knukcá *vt1-pos* s/he undoes his/her own braids *1s:* **waknúca** *2s:* **yaknúca**

knúknun *vcont-redup* eating his/her own ‣ **Žécen ųzé žé knúknun yáwųga.** So then he was walking along eating his own rump. (Weasel 7:135)

knuksÁ *vi1-pos* s/he cuts his/her own with scissors *1s:* **waknúksa** *2s:* **yaknúksa** *1p:* **ųknúksabi**

knuk'éǧA *vt1-pos* s/he scratches his/her own ‣ **Hą́, waná hú knuk'éǧabi.** Ah, now they scratched their legs. (Weasel 42:163) ‣ **Dágu ų́ hú waknúk'eǧa.** I scratched my leg on something. *1s:* **waknúk'eǧa** *2s:* **yaknúk'eǧa** *Vredup:* **knuk'ék'eǧA**

knuk'ék'eǧA *vt1-pos-redup* s/he scratches his/her own repeatedly ‣ **Pá knuk'ék'eǧeši!** Do not scratch your head repeatedly!

knumą́ *vt1-pos* s/he sharpens, files his/her own ‣ **Mína žé knumą́.** Sharpen your knife. ‣ **Ųspé**

waknúmąšį. I did not sharpen my axe. 1s: **waknúmą** 2s: **yaknúmą** 1p: **ųknúmąbi**

knumnézA *vt1-pos* s/he wakes up his/her own out of a drowsing, nap ‣ **Adé waknúmneza.** I woke my dad from his nap. 1s: **waknúmneza** 2s: **yaknúmneza**

knún *vcont* eating his/her own thing ‣ **Knún yįgá.** He is sitting eating his own. *Vredup:* **knúknun**

knusákiba *vt1-pos* s/he puts his/her own together manually (shoes, books) *Vcont:* **knusákim**

knusákim *vcont* putting one's own together ‣ **Knusákim éknąga.** Put your own things together.

knusnóhą *vt1-pos* s/he drags, pulls his/her own 1s: **waknúsnohą** 2s: **yaknúsnohą** 1p: **ųknúsnohąbi**

knustó ; aknústo *vt1-pos* s/he brushes his/her own hair

knušnógA *vt1-pos* s/he takes his/her own thing off (hat, coat) ‣ **Wapáha waknúšnoga.** I took off my hat. ‣ **Cuwíknąga knušnóga!** Take off your coat! 1s: **waknúšnoga** 2s: **yaknúšnoga** 1p: **ųknúšnogabi** *Vcont:* **knušnok**

knušnók *vcont* taking his/her own thing off (hat, coat)

knušpá *vt1-pos* s/he opens his/her own 1s: **waknúšpa** 2s: **yaknúšpa**

knušpú *vt1-pos* s/he picks, plucks a piece off from his/her own; s/he picks, plucks his/her own off from smth ‣ **Nécen ecú hįk éknagu ažųtka žé'ec knušpúyeyahą cén, wók'u.** And as he did that, he plucked out his own kidney and fed him. (Weasel 112:30) 1s: **waknúšpu** 2s: **yaknúšpu** 1p: **ųknúšpubi**

knuštą *vt1-pos* 1) s/he finishes his/her own thing (meal, work) ‣ **Wówaši waknúštą cén wakni.** I came home because I finished working. ‣ **Knuštąbi štén mikúši wožábi gáǧįkta.** When they are finished my grandmother will

make gravy. 2) s/he decides regarding his/her own thing ‣ **Akínijabi žé dąyą knuštąbi.** The argument was settled peacefully. 1s: **waknúštą** 2s: **yaknúštą** 1p: **ųknúštąbi** *Vcaus:* **knuštąkiyA**

knuštąkiyA *vt1-pos-caus* s/he makes sb finish his/her own 1s: **knuštąwakiya** 2s: **knuštąyakiya**

knutągA *vt1-pos* s/he makes his/her own bigger

knuwášte *vt1-pos* s/he improves, makes his/her own in a better, good way 1s: **waknúwašte** 2s: **yaknúwašte** 1p: **ųknúwaštebi**

knuwįžA *vt1-pos* s/he bends his/her own manually

knuzÁ *vt1-pos* s/he holds his/her own thing 1s: **waknúza** 2s: **yaknúza** 1p: **ųknúzabi** *Vrecip:* **gicíknuzabi**

knužáža *vt1-pos* s/he washes his/her own thing ‣ **Tacą waknúžaža.** I washed my body. ‣ **Cuwíknąga knužáža wo!** Wash your shirt! 1s: **waknúžaža** 2s: **yaknúžaža** 1p: **ųknúžažabi**

knužągA *vt1-pos* s/he mistreats, bullies his/her own; picks on his/her own (as a child, sibling) 1s: **waknúžąga** 2s: **yaknúžąga** 1p: **ųknúžągabi**

kó₁ *conj* also, too, even ‣ **Nįš kó!** You too! ‣ **Vincent kó hí.** Vincent also arrived. ‣ **Žécen kó eyá.** She even said that. *Redup:* **kóko**

kó₂ *part* marks strong emotions, irony, amazement, surprise, ridicule ‣ **Hįįį! A'ámna kó!** Oh! They are all moldy too! ‣ **Žé'įš kó!** That one too! ‣ **Kó he?** What then? ‣ **Wįcá aǧúyabi baská kó.** The man is even kneading dough. (Fourstar p. 3)

kó eštáš *ph* even if ‣ **Dágu teȟpí yužážabi kó eštáš búza hąda ságešį.** Even if leather things were washed, when it dried it did not dry hard. (Drummond 1976, Smoking hides)

kogám *adv* 1) in front, ahead, forward ‣ **Kogám aktága.** He ran ahead. ‣ **Kogám ye'įc'iya.** He threw himself forward. 2) across ‣ **Wakpá kogám wanúwą.** I swam across the river.

kogípA *vt1-dat* s/he fears sb, smth ‣ **A'ókpazą hą́da tągán yábi kowágipa.** I am afraid to go out in the darkness. *1s:* **kowágipa** *2s:* **koyágipa** *1p:* **ko'ų́gipabi** *Vabs:* **wakógipA** *Vrecip:* **ogícikopabi** *Syn:* **giníhą**

kohą́ *adv* meanwhile, while

kohą́na *adv* quickly ‣ **Kohą́na owá knuštą!** Finish them all quickly!

kókhįknA *vs* s/he/it is a sudden clicking sound ‣ **Mahí kókhįkna.** My teeth are clicking.

kokní *vimp* it is shiny, glassy, bright, translucent *Adv:* **kokníyą**

kokníyą *adv* shinily, brightly

kóko *conj-redup* even them; they too *Usage:* used with plural referent. ‣ **[. . .] héya kóko wįcábahpa.** [. . .] she even combed out all the lice. (Shields 66:286, our translation)

kokóna *adv* quickly, fast ‣ **Miyéš cądé kokóna iyámąpešį.** As for myself my heart does not beat that fast.

koktóbawįǧe *n* thousand

kokyÁ *vt1-caus* s/he/it produces a clattering, clicking sound ‣ **Hí kokyá.** He is clicking his teeth together. *Adv:* **kokyéna**

kokyéna *adv* in a clattering manner

koná *n* friend; male friend (male speaker) ‣ **Háu koná!** Hello friend! ‣ **Waná ženą́ga koná.** Now it is enough friend. ‣ **Mitákona ecúnašį!** My friend do not gamble! *1s:* **mitákona** *2s:* **nitákona** *3s:* **takónagu** *1p:* **ųgítakonabi** *Vcaus:* **konáyA**

konáyA *vt1* s/he has sb as a friend ‣ **Nínah̆ konáwayešį.** I am not really friends with him. *1s:* **konáwaya** *2s:* **konáyaya** *Vabs:* **wakónayA**

kosán *adv* beyond, onward ‣ **Waná kosán yá.** Now he passed away. ‣ **Dágu epé né kosán oyága.** He will pass on what I say. ‣ **Iyámągipešį kó, kosán yá.** He did not wait for me and passed by.

kosán yegíyA *vt1-pos* s/he passes, gives away his/her own position to sb *1s:* **kosán yewágiya** *2s:* **kosán yeyágiya**

kosą́c ną'į́ *vii* it is transparent, sheer ‣ **Sąksáją ų́ žé kosą́c ną'į́.** The dress that she is wearing is sheer.

koškáškana *n-redup* 1) teenage boy *vs* 2) he is a teenage boy ‣ **Komáškaškanahą žéhą wéksuya.** I remember when I was a teenage boy. *1s:* **komáškaškana** *2s:* **koníškaškana**

kóš *part* anyways, despite ‣ **Nistústa kóš ištímešį!** Despite being tired, do not sleep! ‣ **Mağážu kóš wi'ógizibabi.** Even though it rained they pitched up their tent. (Schudel 1997:180)

koškÁ *n* 1) young man ‣ **KoškÁ né ptéjena.** This young man is short. ‣ **KoškÁ oh̆'ą́ko.** It is a fast young man. *1s:* **mitákoška** *2s:* **nitákoška** *3s:* **takóška** *vs* 2) he is a young man ‣ **Nahą́h̆ koníška, miyéš waná magána.** You are still a young man, as for myself I am old now. *1s:* **komáška** *2s:* **koníška** *Redup:* **koškáškana, koškánana** *Vrefl:* **koškÁ'įc'ina**

koškÁ'įc'ina *vi3-refl* he thinks of himself as a young man *1s:* **koškámįc'ina** *2s:* **koškánįc'ina**

koškánana (CTK) *n-redup* teenage boy

kóšta *part* any, whichever, whoever, no matter what, even if *Usage:* marks the lack of interest on behalf of the speaker. ‣ **Duwéh̆ hí kóšta.** I do not care who arrived. ‣ **Dukté yaká kóšta.** It does not matter which one you chose. ‣ **Maktébi kóšta dókejašį.** Even if they kill me, it is nothing. ‣ **Dókeja kóšta.** I do not care. *See:* **ga kóšta**

kówa *adv* all of those (people, animals, things, ideas) ‣ **Misų́gabi mitágožabina kówa wacíwįcawakiyįktac.** I am going to make all of my little brothers and my grandchildren dance. (NS 2002:42)

kóya *Variant:* **kówa** *adv* along, with, accompanying, and ‣ **Įš kóya úkta.** He is coming along too. ‣ **Ağúyabi wayáhoda kóya įcáȟyabi.** They grew both wheat and oats. (Schudel 1997) ‣ **Wašín'i'ábi kówa wamnápiši.** I did not speak English either. (Shields 130:943)

koyágA *vt2* s/he puts on clothes, fine garment, outfit *Vcaus:* **koyákyA**

koyákyA *vt1-caus* 1) s/he connects, fastens smth to it; hangs smth ‣ **Cąbákmįkma koyákwaya.** I connected the wagon. ‣ **Cuwíknąga koyákya!** Hang your coat! 2) s/he makes sb put on clothes, fine garment, outfit ‣ **Nená koyákwayeši.** I will not put these on. *1s:* **koyákwaya** *2s:* **koyákyaya** *Vcaus:* **koyákya**

kpá *vs* it is a loud, resonant metallic sound ‣ **Kpá wága.** It is a loud clanging sound. ‣ **Kpáhįkna.** It is the sound of a bullet shot.

kpabéhą *vt1-pos* s/he rolls up his/her own thing ‣ [. . .] **kpabéhą cén aké ecú.** [. . .] she rolled it up and then she did it again. (NS 2002:22)

kpahį́ *vt1* s/he harvests smth *Vabs:* **wakpáhį**

kpaȟnéjA *vt1-pos* s/he tears, punctures his/her own by pushing ‣ **Cuwíknąga tą́ga wakpáȟneja.** I tore my coat. (Fourstar p. 7) *1s:* **wakpáȟneja** *2s:* **yakpáȟneja**

kpakcá *vt1-pos* s/he combs his/her own ‣ **Pahá kpakcá.** Comb your hair. *See:* **pahá įbákca**

kpakį́dA *vt1-pos* s/he wipes his/her own ‣ **Įdé kpakį́da.** Wipe your face. ‣ **Paȟní wakpákįda.** I wiped my snot. *1s:* **wakpákįda** *2s:* **yakpákįda**

kpakpí *vi1* it (egg) hatches

kpaksÁ *vt1-pos* s/he breaks, fractures his/her own manually or by pressure ‣ **Tahú wakpáksa.** I broke my leg. ‣ **Maȟíjahą įstó wakpáksa.** I tripped and broke my arm. *1s:* **wakpáksa** *2s:* **yakpáksa**

kpamní *vt1* s/he serves sb; passes smth around (as food in a ceremony) ‣ **Wįkóške žé wóyude kpamníkta.** That young lady will pass the food around. ‣ **Gá žé'ec dáguškina né kpamní hiyáyabi dúkš anéžabiši žécen né gicíc'u**

yegíyabi. So they passed that child around but he did not pee on anyone as they handed him along from one to the other. (Weasel 30:85) *Vabs:* **wakpámni**

kpási *vt1-pos* s/he drives his/her own vehicle *1s:* **wakpási** *2s:* **yakpási** *See:* **yekíyA**

kpasnádA *vt1-pos* s/he pushes, plants his/her own straight into the ground

kpawéğa *vt1-pos* s/he breaks his/her own by pressure ‣ **Táȟca žé hé kpawéğa.** That deer broke his horn by pressure. (Fourstar p. 18)

kpazó *vt1-pos* s/he shows his/her own *1s:* **wakpázo** *2s:* **yakpázo** *1p:* **ųkpázobi**

kpąyą́ *vt1* s/he tans a hide *Vabs:* **wakpą́yą**

kpúspA *vt1-pos* s/he daubs, patches his/her own *1s:* **wakpúspa** *2s:* **yakpúspa** *1p:* **ųkpúspabi**

ksábA *vs* s/he is wise, intelligent, prudent ‣ **Hųgá žé ní:::na ksabé cá.** The chief was a reaaaaally wise man. (BigEagle 2017:9) *1s:* **maksába** *2s:* **niksába** *Adv:* **ksamyágen**

ksahą́ *vs* it is broken ‣ **Sąní ksahą́.** It is broken on one side.

ksamyágen *adv* rather wisely, prudently ‣ **Ksamyágen i'á.** He talks rather wisely.

ksugíyA *vt1-pos* s/he/it hurts his/her own (mental or physical pain) ‣ **Cądé ksuwágiya.** I hurt my heart. *1s:* **ksuwágiya** *2s:* **ksuyágiya**

ksu'įc'iyA *vi3-refl* s/he hurts, injures himself/ herself ‣ **Dóhani ksu'įc'iyeši.** She never hurt herself. ‣ **Šųkcúk'ana né táȟca ksu'įc'iye žé kní:gabi.** The coyotes kept coming back at the injured deer. *1s:* **ksumį́c'iya** *2s:* **ksunį́c'iya**

ksuyÁ *vt1* s/he/it hurts sb ‣ **Amáyapa cén ksúmaya.** He hit me and hurt me. *1s:* **ksuwáya** *2s:* **ksuyáya** *1p:* **ksu'ų́yabi** *Vpos:* **ksugíyA** *Vrefl:* **ksu'įc'iyA**

-ktA *encl* 1) will, 'll, would (marks a potential event that is not yet realized) *Usage:* when used in the past it indicates a counterfactual event; triggers į-ablaut. ‣ **Huȟnáȟyabi edáhą**

wak'úkte no. I will give him some coffee. ‣ **Mağáźu štén kníkta.** If it rains he will leave. ‣ **Aké wącímnagįkte no.** I will see you again. ‣ **Mağáźu štén íš kiknákta.** If it had rained he would have left home. 2) expresses a suggestion, let us *Usage:* when occurring with verbs in the 1st person plural ų(g)- . . .-bi or dual ų(g)-. ‣ **Ųgíyįkte no.** Let us go.

ktá *Variant:* **tká** *vs* s/he/it is heavy ‣ **Nínaȟ ktáší.** It is not very heavy. ‣ **Cá né nína ktá.** This tree is very heavy. ‣ **Awódabi žé ktáší.** That table is not heavy. *Adv:* **ktáyagen**

ktába *vi* it is thick, doughy, adhesive *Vcaus:* **ktamyÁ**

ktamyÁ *vt1-caus* s/he thickens smth (soup, broth) ‣ **Ktamyá ecúší.** Do not thicken it too much. *1s:* **ktamwáya** *2s:* **ktamyáya** *1p:* **ktam'úyabi**

ktáyagen *adv* heavily ‣ **Ktáyagen maní.** He walks heavily.

kté *vt1* s/he/it kills sb, smth ‣ **Táȟca awánųka wakté.** I accidentally killed a deer. ‣ **Tá wąží ktébi.** They killed a moose. ‣ **Né miyé wakté né.** I am the one who killed it. *1s:* **wakté** *2s:* **yakté** *1p:* **ųktébi** *Vdat:* **gikté** *Vpos:* **gikté** *Vrecip:* **gicíktebi** *Vrefl:* **įc'íkte**

kténa *vt1* s/he cheats, beats sb (in a game) *Usage:*-ktena 'game' in compounds. *1s:* **wakténa** *2s:* **yakténa** *3p:* **ktébina** *Vrecip:* **gicíktebina**

kténas'a *n* cheater

-ktu *Variant:* **-tku** *suff* his, her (3rd person singular possessor) *Usage:* used only with kinship nouns. ‣ **-tugaši-** > **tugágišiktu** ; **tugágišitku** grandfather > his/her grandfather ‣ **-cįhį-** > **cįhíktu** ; **cįhítku** son > his/her son

Ktųsyá *ngeo* Wolseley (Saskatchewan)

ktųšíȟpayA *vs* s/he passes out ‣ **Tągán ktųšíniȟpaya.** You passed out outside. *1s:* **ktųšímaȟpaya.** *2s:* **ktųšíniȟpaya.**

ktúšya ų *vi1* s/he is mentally ill

ktúžA *vs* s/he is drunk ‣ **Waná aké nįktúža.** Now you are drunk again. *1s:* **mąktúža** *2s:* **nįktúža** *1p:* **ųktúžabi** *See:* **įktúža**

ktúžes'a *n* drunkard

kúda *adv* down *Cont:* **kún**

kudé *vt1* s/he shoots at sb, smth ‣ **Žé wakúde.** I shot that. ‣ **Pağúdatąga kudé yá.** He goes shooting at geese. *1s:* **wakúde** *2s:* **yakúde** *1p:* **ųkúdebi** *Vabs:* **wakúde**

kúdi'įc'iyA *vi3-refl* s/he ducks down

kúdina *Variant:* **kúdiyena** *adv* low, down, near the ground ‣ **Ti'óba né kudína hą.** This door is hanging low. ‣ **Waná kúdiyena gaȟmóga.** Now it is blowing close to the ground.

kukÁ *vs* 1) it is worn out, tattered ‣ **Cuwíknąga žé kuká.** The coat is tattered. ‣ **Sąksája nitáwa žé kuká.** Your dress is tattered. 2) it is rotten ‣ **Peží žé wašíjuti gakná éknąga žé iyúhana kuká.** That hay which lays beside the house is all rotten.

kún *adv* down, downward, below ‣ **Kún ú.** Come down. ‣ **Sihá kún égiknąga.** Put your feet down. *See:* **hokún**

kúna *interj* hurry up ‣ **Kúna misúga!** Hurry up young brother!

-kuši-;-kųgiši- *root* grandmother: term of reference. ‣ **Mikúši én ú.** My grandmother is there. ‣ **Nikúši iyéwejiska.** I translate for your grandmother. ‣ **Nikúši Nakón'i'a jé no!** Your grandmother always speaks Nakoda! *1s:* **mikúši** *2s:* **nikúši** *3s:* **kúgišiktu** ; **kušícu** *1p:* **ųgíkųšitku**

-kuši- tága *root + vs* great-grandmother *1s:* **mikúši tága** *2s:* **nikúši tága** *3s:* **kúgišiktu tága**

kúši wanáǧi oyáde *cp* grandmother spirit nation

kušyá *adv* sickly

kušyá ų *vi1* s/he is sickly *1s:* **kušyá wa'ų** *2s:* **kušyá ya'ų**

kutkún *adv-redup* low, very low ‣ **Kutkún iyáya.** He is descending.

kuwá *vt1* 1) s/he/it chases, hunts, goes after sb, smth *Usage:* some speakers e-ablaut this verb.

‣ **Wanúȟ! Nikúwa cá.** Beware! He might go after you. ‣ **Tašúǧa táwabi wįcákuwa jé.** He always chased their horses. 2) s/he treats, acts toward, cares for sb, smth ‣ **Wįcíjana né wakúwa.** I care for this girl. ‣ **Akí'ecen wįcákuwa.** Treat them equally. *vt1-aux* 3) s/he keeps on doing smth ‣ **Ya'íškan wakúwa** I kept on teasing him verbally. ‣ **Pá gaksá makúwabi cén úspemąkiyabi.** They kept hitting me on the head to make me learn. (Cumberland 2005:401) *1s:* **wakúwa** *2s:* **yakúwa** *1p:* **ųkúwabi** *Vcoll:* **wįcákuwa** *Vpos:* **gikúwa ; gicúwa** *Vrefl:* **įc'ícuwa**

kuwága *vt1* s/he courts sb *1s:* **wakúwaga** *2s:* **yakúwaga**

kúža *vs* s/he is weak, sick *1s:* **makúža** *2s:* **nikúža** *Adv:* **kušyá**

-kų- *root* mother-in-law ‣ **Mikų́ ába nų́bacą hí.** My mother-in-law arrived two days ago. *1s:* **mikų́** *2s:* **nikų́** *3s:* **kų́gu** *1p:* **ųgíkųbi**

K'

k'Á *vt1* s/he/it digs ‣ **Ȟogá žé mąká k'á.** The badger is digging dirt. ‣ **Típsina ųk'ábįkta.** We will dig out turnips. ‣ **Wanágaš típsina k'ábis'a** Long ago they use to dig up turnips. ‣ **Ókšą maká né k'ábi.** The ground is dug up in a circle. (Drummond 1976, Įktomi) *1s:* **wak'á** *2s:* **yak'á** *1p:* **ųk'ábi** *Vbenef:* **gíjik'A**

k'į́ *vt1* 1) s/he carries sb, smth on the back ‣ **Wanágaš šúga cuwíc'iba k'įbis'a.** Long ago dogs carried travois on their back. ‣ **"Né mak'įkta otá'įgac" ecí.** "It seems he wants to carry me," he thought. (Drummond 1976, A bear story) *1s:* **wak'į** *2s:* **yak'į** *1p:* **ųk'įbi** *Adv:* **k'íya** *Vcaus:* **k'įkíyA** *Vpos:* **gic'į** *n* 2) carrier ‣ **iyážo k'į** whistle carrier ‣ **wakák'į** battery

k'įkíyA *vt1-caus* s/he causes sb to carry smth; s/he hitches, loads smth on sb ‣ **Žén né šųkkána né cuwíc'ipa néca k'įkíya híkna.** Then she hitched the old dog to the travois. (Weasel 111:10) *1s:* **k'įwákiya** *2s:* **k'įyákiya** *1p:* **k'į'ų́kiyabi**

k'íya *adv* carrying sb, smth on the back ‣ **K'íya aktága.** He ran with him on his back.

k'ú *vt1* s/he gives smth to sb ‣ **Dágu wak'ú cén?** What can I give him then? ‣ **Mázaska wikcémna yámni mak'úbi.** They gave me 30$. ‣ **Dágu nik'ú he?** What did he give you? ‣ **Koná šųkcíjana né mak'úbi.** This puppy was given to me by my friend. ‣ **Miní waká, niyá wašté ųk'úbįkte no!** Holy water, give us good health! ‣ **Duwé iyúhana tanó cic'úbįkte no!** I will give meat to all of you! ‣ **Mázaska mayák'ųkta he?** Will you give me money? ‣ **teȟíya k'ú** s/he gives sb a hard time ‣ **wópina k'ú** s/he shows gratefulness toward sb *1s:* **wak'ú** *2s:* **yak'ú** *1p:* **ųk'úbi** *Vcoll:* **wįcák'u** *Vrecip:* **gicíc'ubi** *Vrefl:* **įc'íc'u**

k'úbi *n* power given to sb (as in a vision)

L

Lakóta *nprop* Lakota people, person of Lakota descent

M

-m- *prefix-infix* I (1st person singular) *Usage:* agent/subject of active verbs of Class 3. ‣ **įštíma > mįštíma** s/he sleeps > I sleep ‣ **ecú > ecámų** s/he does smth > I do smth

-m *suff* particular point or location, at, in, to a location or destination > there, in a place ‣ **ektá > ektám**

m *part* indicates a command made to one or many persons (male and female imperative) *Usage:* this particle is usually written attached to the verb or preceding enclitic. ‣ **Mihų́ žeyá,**

"Nén iyódągam!" My mother said, "Sit down here!" ▸ **"Né yušnábišįm!"** eyá. "Do not drop this!" he said. (NS 2002:23) ▸ **Į́hiyų pağųda! Gúwam dágu wąží ocíjimnagabįkta.** Hey ducks! Come here I want to tell you one thing. (Drummond 1976, Įktomi and the ducks)

ma- *pref* by cutting smth with a sharp tool (knife, saw) ▸ **-ksA- > maksÁ** cut > s/he cuts smth with a sharp blade

-ma- *prefix-infix* 1) I (1st person singular) *Usage:* subject of stative verbs. ▸ **stustá > mastústa** s/he is tired > I am tired ▸ **įpi > įmapi** s/he is full > I am full 2) me (1st person singular) *Usage:* patient of transitive verbs. ▸ **yucéya > mayúceya** s/he makes sb cry > s/he makes me cry ▸ **wąyága > wąmáyaga** s/he sees sb, smth > s/he sees me *pref* 3) my (1st person singular possessor) *Usage:* used with nouns for body parts. ▸ **í > ma'í** mouth > my mouth ▸ **hí > mahí** tooth > my tooth *Syn:* **mi-**

má *interj* used to call attention, or to guide the addressee's attention toward a specific sound ▸ **Má, anáğopta!** Here, listen!

magé *n* hoop

magícinųbi *vi1-recip* they steal from one another

magíjiksA *vt1-benef* s/he cuts smth for him/her with a sharp blade 1s: **mawéjiksa** 2s: **mayéjiksa**

magíjinų *vt1-benef* s/he steals smth for sb

magíksA *vt1-pos* s/he cuts his/her own with a sharp blade 1s: **mawágiksa** 2s: **mayágiksa**

magínų *vt1-dat* s/he steals smth from sb ▸ **Dóhani macíjinųkteší!** I will never steal something from you! 1s: **mawáginų** 2s: **mayáginų**

magísnejA *vt1-pos* s/he cuts, slits him/her own ▸ **Bó né magísneja.** He cut his blister.

mağá *n* 1) goose 2) generic for duck, goose, and swan

mağážu *n* 1) rain ▸ **Mağážu né knaptá.** The rain cleared up. *vimp* 2) it rains ▸ **Mağážukteší no.** It is not going to rain. ▸ **Aké mağážukte no.** It will rain again.

mağážu įkmúga ; mağážu kmúga *cp* rainbow *Lit:* rain snare

Mağážu wacíbi *cp* Rain dance

mağážu waką́ *vimp* it is a hot summer drizzle *Lit:* holy rain

mağó *vt1* s/he marks, carves smth with a sharp tool

mahé- ; mahét- *cont* under, down

mahédu *vimp* it is deep inside ▸ **Mnikábi žé mahédu.** The well is deep. *Adv:* **mahén, mahét**

mahéduȟ *adv* deeper, deep down inside ▸ **Dágu nówa mahéduȟ naȟmá.** She hides everything way down.

mahén *adv-cont* 1) inside, in, within ▸ **Nén mahén cąbų́bų.** The wood is rotten here inside. *post* 2) under, underneath ▸ **Cąšížé awódabi mahén ayáskama.** The chewing gum is stuck under the table. ▸ **Owį́ža mahén yįgá!** Stay under the blanket! *Cont:* **mahé**

mahén hayábi *cp* underwear

mahén hųská *cp* long johns, thermal underwear

mahén ų́bi *cp* underwear

mahétkiya *adv* downward ▸ **Mahétkiya ecų́ší.** Do not push it downward. ▸ **Mahétkiya badídaší.** Do not push it too deep.

mahéyįgA *vi3* s/he/it hides under 1s: **mahémąga** 2s: **mahénąga**

maȟ'ú *vt1* s/he peels smth with a sharp tool (fruit, vegetable) ▸ **Waná pąğí maȟ'ú.** Now she is peeling potatoes.

maȟnógA *vt1* s/he pierces a hole in smth with a knife, saw, or punch

maȟpíya *n* 1) sky, heaven ▸ **Adé wakátąga maȟpíyam agán yągá.** Father Great Spirit who sits in the sky. ▸ **Adé'ųyabi maȟpíya ektá nągá.** Our Father who art in heaven. 2) cloud

maȟpíya agícida *cp* airforce soldier

maȟpíyakta *adv* to the clouds

maȟpíyam *adv* in the sky

Maȟpíyato *nprop* Arapaho people, person of Arapaho descent mahpíyato *n* blue sky

ma'íc'iksA *vi3-refl* s/he cuts himself/herself with a sharp blade *1s:* **mamíc'iksa** *2s:* **maníc'iksa**

ma'íc'iškida *vi3-refl* s/he cuts, gashes himself/herself *1s:* **mamíc'iškida** *2s:* **maníc'iškida**

maká *n See:* **mąká**

maká įjápte *n* hoe

maká ogápte *n* shovel

makáda *vimp* it is hot weather (contraction of maštá káda)

makágan *adv* on the ground, on earth ‣ **Makágan iyódąga.** He sits on the ground.

makáhasaba *n* coal

makámahen ; makámahen *n* den, basement

makáto *n* clay *Lit:* blue soil

makáyutą *n* land surveyor

makóce *n* land, territory, earth, ground; homeland ‣ **Makóce né ahópa wo!** Respect the land! ‣ **Makóce wógųga.** That is a beautiful landscape. ‣ **Makócedahą bahí.** He picked it up from the ground. ‣ **Makóce téhądahą híbi.** They come from a far away land. ‣ **Céǧa K'įna oyáde tamákoce dókiya he?** Where is Carry The Kettle reserve? *3s:* **tamákoce**

makóce agícida *cp* foot soldier

makóce įdóba *cp* fourth dimension; fourth spiritual realm

makóce įháge *cp* doomsday

makóce įkúwa *cp* tractor

makóce mnaská *cp* prairie, flat land

makóce owáštejaga *cp* heaven

makóce wídaya *ph* strait *Lit:* island-like land

makóhnoga *n* cave

makómnaya *n* prairie, flat land *Syn:* **makóce mnaská**

makóšija *n* badlands

makóškiška *n* 1) rough, bumpy road 2) it is a rough, bumpy road ‣ **Ocágu okná yéšį, žé makóškiška.** Do not go through that road, it is rough.

makóti *n* earth lodge

makówąja *adv* all over the world

makpá *vt1* s/he minces smth fine

maksÁ *vt1* s/he cuts smth with a sharp blade *1s:* **mawáksa** *2s:* **mayáksa** *Vabs:* **wamáksA** *Vbenef:* **magíjiksA** *Vpos:* **magíksA** *Vredup:* **maksáksA** *Vrefl:* **ma'íc'iksA**

maksáksA *vt1-redup* s/he cuts them with a sharp blade

makú *n* chest

makú įyúskice *Variant:* **makúskice** *cp* brassiere

makúhuhu *n* sternum

makúša (CTK) *Variant:* **cątkúša** *n* American robin *Lit:* red chest

maní ; máni *vi1* 1) s/he walks ‣ **Inína mawánįkte no.** I will walk quietly. ‣ **Nųpín gakná maníbi.** They both are walking along. ‣ **Mítogam mayáni oyágihi he?** Can you walk in front of me? 2) s/he progresses, behaves as such in life *Usage:* used after an adverb. ‣ **Ótąnah máni wo.** Walk in a straight way. ‣ **Cóhtįyą mawáni.** I walk honestly. 3) s/he accompanies, walks with sb *Usage:* used with gicí and óm. ‣ **Óm mawáni.** I walk with them. *1s:* **mawáni** *2s:* **mayáni** *1p:* **ma'únibi** *Vredup:* **mánini** *See:* amáni, ománi

manín *adv* far away, in a distance ‣ **Manín wa'ú.** I have been far away. ‣ **Táhca manín owáne.** I looked for a deer far away. ‣ **Dágu manín wįcóh'ąge dágunih snokwáyešį.** I know nothing of the customs and things away from camp. (NS 2002:65) ‣ **"Écen ųgétisiye manín," eyá.** "Let us live that way, off somewhere away from camp," he said. (Weasel 163:5)

mánini *vi1-redup* s/he takes small steps (like a baby or an elder)

manú *vt1* s/he steals smth ‣ **Tanó edáhą manú.** He stole some meat. *1s:* **mawánų** *2s:* **mayánų** *1p:* **ma'únųbi** *Vbenef:* **magíjinų** *Vdat:* **magínų** *Vrecip:* **magícinųbi**

mapóbA *vt1* s/he bursts, punctures smth with a sharp tool ‣ **Niǧé mayápoba štén, nįš nén ecíknąga hík niǧé macípobįkta.** If you burst its stomach, I will put you down here and burst your stomach. (Weasel 14:134) *1s:* **mawápoba** *2s:* **mayápoba** *1p:* **ma'ųpobabi**

mas- *cont* 1) iron, metal 2) money

maskádo *vt1* 1) s/he pounds metal ▸ **Maskádo jé.** He always pounds metal. *1s:* **maswágado** *2s:* **masyágado** *n* 2) blacksmith

maskáǧA *vi1* s/he earns, makes money *1s:* **maswágaǧa** *2s:* **masyágaǧa** *1p:* **mas'ųgaǧabi** *Syn:* **maskámna**

maskáȟa *n* chain

maskámna *vi1* s/he earns money *1s:* **maswágamna** *2s:* **masyágamna** *1p:* **mas'ųgamnabi** *Syn:* **maskáǧA**

maskásodA *vi1* s/he wastes money *1s:* **maswágasoda** *2s:* **masyágasoda**

masknúsodA *vt1-pos* s/he spends his/her own money *1s:* **maswáknusoda** *2s:* **masyáknusoda**

maskúwa wíyą *cp* female prostitute

mask'ú *vt1-dat* s/he gives money to sb ▸ **Wócįs'a žé mask'ú.** Give money to the beggar. *1s:* **maswák'u** *2s:* **masyák'u**

masnéjA *vt1* s/he splits, slits smth in the middle ▸ **Cąmnáska žé masnéja.** Split the plank in the middle. *1s:* **mawásneja** *2s:* **mayásneja** *1p:* **ma'ųsnejabi** *Vpos:* **magísnejA**

masó *vt1* s/he cuts a strip *Vredup:* **masóso**

masóso *vt1-redup* s/he cuts smth in strips *1s:* **mawásoso** *2s:* **mayásoso**

maspépe *n* barbed wire

mastų́biga *n-pl* wealthy, rich people

mastų́ga *vs* s/he is rich, wealthy *1s:* **maswátųga** *2s:* **masyátųga** *Syn:* **masyúheja**

Maswícak'ubi ába *cp* Treaty Day *Lit:* give people money day

masyúhA *vi2* s/he has money ▸ **Wanáǧaš masyúhabįšį.** Long ago they did not have money. *1s:* **masmnúha** *2s:* **masnúha**

masyúheja *vs* s/he has money; is wealthy *Syn:* **mastų́ga**

masyúhešį *vi2* s/he does not have money; is poor *1s:* **masmnúhešį** *2s:* **masnúhešį**

masyúsodA *vi2* s/he spends money *1s:* **masmnúsoda** *2s:* **masnúsoda**

masyúwibi *n* metal wire

mas'ágicipabi *vi1-recip* they telephone one another

mas'ágijipA *vt1-benef* s/he telephones sb on behalf of him/her

mas'ágipA *vt1-dat* s/he telephones sb ▸ **Mas'ámayagipa he?** Did you phone me? ▸ **Duwé mas'ámagipa?** Who is calling me? *1s:* **mas'áwagipa** *2s:* **mas'áyagipa**

mas'ápA *vi1* 1) s/he makes a telephone call *Lit:* s/he hits on metal ▸ **Waná hináǧa! Togáhe mas'áwapįkta.** Wait now! First I will make a telephone call. *1s:* **mas'áwapa** *1p:* **mas'á'ųpabi** *Vbenef:* **mas'ágijipA** *Vdat:* **mas'ágipA** *Vrecip:* **mas'ágicipabi** *n* 2) telephone, telephone call

mas'ápabi *n* telegraph, telephone *Syn:* **mas'ápa**

mas'ápe *n* blacksmith *Syn:* **maskádo**

mas'íyapa *n* hammer

mas'íyapa tága *n* sledgehammer

mas'íbadįda *Variant:* **maswíbadįde** *n* shovel

mas'ínaȟtage *n* spur

mas'ípaȟte ; mąs'ípaȟte *n* bridle and bit *See:* **ipáȟte**

mas'íškadA *vt1* s/he gambles money *1s:* **mas'íwaškada** *2s:* **mas'íyaškada** *1p:* **mas'í'ųškadabi**

mas'ó'i'abi *n* telephone

mas'ók'e *n* mine for digging metal

mas'ónodA *vi1* s/he borrows money *1s:* **mas'ówanoda** *2s:* **mas'óyanoda**

mas'ówąyaga (WB) *n* bank

mas'óyuȟpe *n* bank

maškída *vt1* s/he cuts sb, smth *Vrefl:* **ma'įc'iškida**

mašpé *n* piece cut off

mašpúšpu *vt1-redup* s/he cuts smth into small pieces ▸ **Tanó mašpúšpu.** Cut the meat in small pieces. ‣ **Ecéduň mamášpušpukta.** He will cut me up the same way. (Weasel 15:144)

maštá *vimp* it is hot weather ‣ **Ába né nína maštá.** It is very hot today. ‣ **Ába né maštáňtiyįkta gáyabi.** They say today will be the warmest day. *Vredup:* **maštášta**

maštá ganúza *vimp* it is a hot wind, like a Chinook wind

maštámakoce *n* land to the south

maštášta *vimp-redup* it is very hot ‣ **Waskúyeja šašá áya žéhą nagú maštášta.** Berries start ripening and it is also very hot. (Haywahe 1992:38)

maštíja *n* rabbit *Cont:* **maštín**

Maštíja oyáde *cp* Northern Cree tribe *Lit:* rabbit people

maštíjatąga *n* jackrabbit

maštín ; maští *cont* rabbit

maštín įkmúge *cp* rabbit snare

maštín mnóga *cp* male rabbit

Maštín wacíbi *cp* Rabbit dance

maštín wakmúga *cp* rabbit snare

maštín wįyéna *cp* female rabbit

maštíjabina *n-pl* rabbit herd

maštíšpą *vs* s/he is sunburned *1s:* **maštímąšpą** *2s:* **maštínįšpą**

maštítapA *vi1* s/he follows, pursues, tracks rabbits

matánijoň *n* moss

mató *n* black bear

Mató įdénųba *nprop* Two face grizzly bear (name of Wilma Kennedy's father)

matómna *vs* s/he/it smells like bear

matónuda *n* cinnamon bear

matósaba *n* black bear

Matóska *nprop* 1) White Bear (Nakoda chief and signatory of Treaty 4, 1875) *ngeo* 2) White Bear reservation (Saskatchewan)

Matówįtko *nprop* Crazy Bear (1785–1856); Nakoda chief and negotiator of the Fort Laramie Treaty Council of 1851

mayá *n* cliff, bluff

mayá'oňnoǧa *n* hole in a rock

mayátąga *n* mountain

mayáwašiju ; mayášiju *n* little people, cave dwellers (mythic being)

Mayáwašiju wowįcak'ųbi *ph* Feed the little people ceremony

mayáyukseya *n* cut bank

máza *n* iron, metal ‣ **wagíyą ňubáhu máza** Iron wing thunderbird *Cont:* **mas-**

máza įyúkse *cp* wire cutter

máza ocágu *cp* train track

Máza Ok'á *ngeo* Zortman, Montana

máza o'ópetų *cp* hardware store

mázagiyą *n* airplane *Syn:* **giyáyabi, wádagiyą, giyékiyabi**

máza'i *n* gun muzzle

máza'ijuna *n* tin cup

mázakada *n* hot metal

mázaska *n* 1) money *Lit:* white metal ‣ **Mázaska nuhá? — Hiyá, mnuhéšį.** Do you have money? — No, I do not have any. ‣ **Mázaska óda mak'úbi.** They gave me a lot of money. ‣ **Mázaska ųkáš!** If only money was! ‣ **Mázaska éknąga.** She put money on it. 2) dollar *Usage:* usually followed by a number. ‣ **Mázaska dóba owágini.** I earned four dollars

mázaska éknągA *vt1-dat* s/he bets on sb, smth; puts money on sb, smth *1s:* **mázaska éwaknąga** *2s:* **mázaska éyaknąga**

mázaska hągé *cp* fifty cents

mázaska tíbi *cp* bank, financial institution *Syn:* **mas'ówąyaga**

mázaska wąží *cp* one dollar; loony

mázaskana *n* silver

mázaskazi *n* gold

mázasni *n* cold metal

mázaša *n* 1) penny, cent 2) copper *Lit:* red metal

mázašnoyabi *n* solder

mázawada *n* train *Lit:* iron canoe *See:* **wáda**

mázawapaha *n* helmet

mazóti *n* iron lodge

mągá *n* skunk ‣ **Mągá žé s'ámna.** The skunk stinks. *Cont:* **mąk-**

mąká ; maká *n* earth, soil, ground, dust, dirt, mud ‣ **Mąká agán bapsý.** He spilled it on the ground. ‣ **Ȟogá žé mąká k'á.** The badger is digging dirt. ‣ **Mąká né sábeȟtiyą.** The mud is pitch black.

mąkámahen *adv* underground; under the ground; below the surface of the earth

mąkámnuna *n* dust

mąkán *adv* on the ground, earth ‣ **Mąkán yųgá.** He lies down on the ground.

mąkáyuǧe *n* harrow

mąkáyuptA *vi2* s/he plows a field ‣ **Mąkáyupte yá.** He is going to plow the field. *1s:* **mąkámnupta** *2s:* **mąkánupta**

mąkáyutąbi wąží *cp* one mile

mąkázi *n* sand *Syn:* **wiyáska**

mąkíyutabi ; makíyutabi *n* mile, kilometer, unit of measurement

mąkóškąšką ; makóce škąšką *n-redup* earthquake

mąkótahena *adv* lonely place ‣ **Mąkótahena néci yągé no.** She lies over here in a lonely place. (NS 2002:73)

mąkwíkni *n* skunk oil

mąza sú *cp* lead (metal)

mi- *pref* my (1st person singular possessor) ‣ **dagúye > midáguye** relative > my relative ‣ **-kuši-> mikúši** grandmother > my grandmother ‣ **tawáci > mitáwaci** mind > my mind *Syn:* **ma-**

Mikúši makóce *nprop* Grandmother Earth

mína *n* knife ‣ **Mína žé nína péna.** This knife is very sharp. ‣ **Mína mnumą.** I sharpen the knife. *1s:* **mitámina** *2s:* **nitámina** *3s:* **tamína**

mínaha *n* sheath

Mínahąska *nprop* person of American descent

mínahąska *n* sword, sabre

mínaškoba *n* short scythe

miní *n* water ‣ **Miní mnéza.** It is pure water. ‣ **Šúga žená miní cįgábi cén kníbi.** Those dogs came home because they wanted water. ‣ **Miní waką nína niyá wašté ųk'úbįkte no!** Very sacred water, give us good health! *Cont:* **mni-**

miní abápsųbi *vs-pass* 1) s/he is baptized ‣ **Miní amábapsųbįšį.** I was not baptized. *n* 2) baptism *1s:* **miní amábapsųbi** *2s:* **miní aníbapsųbi** *1p:* **miní a'ųbápsųbi**

miní agícida *cp* navy soldier

miní iyáya *cp* flood

miní natága *cp* dam

miní ožúna *vs* it is a water blister *Usage:* usually preceded by a body part. ‣ **Ną̇bé miní omážuna.** The hand is full of water blisters.

miní sudá *cp* alcohol

miní tutá *cp* vinegar

miníȟaȟa *n* waterfall

miní'įbiǧa ; miníbiǧa *n* beer *Lit:* boiled water

miníkada *n* hot water

miníkta *adv* in, to the water ‣ **Miníkta égijikne.** He put it in the water for him. (Weasel 38:58)

miník'u *vt1* s/he waters an animal

Minínuzahą *ngeo* 1) Swift Current river 2) Swift Current (Saskatchewan)

miní skuya *n* soda pop *Lit:* sweet water ‣ **Miní skuya edáhą yacíga he?** Do you want some pop (soda)?

minísnohena *n* watersnake

Miníša *ngeo* Red River (Manitoba, North Dakota, Minnesota)

miníšaša *n-redup* wine *Lit:* red water

Minísatųwąbi *nprop* Red River people (band of Nakoda)

miníšį *vs* it is dry, arid, waterless

Miníšoše šųkcébi wįcášta *nprop* Missouri dog penis people

Miníšoše wakpá *ngeo* Missouri River

minítąga *n* lake *Redup:* **minítąktąga** *Syn:* **mné**

minítąktąga *n-redup* lakes

Miníwaką *ngeo* Manitou Beach (Saskatchewan)

miníwaką *n* 1) Holy water 2) whisky *Lit:* mysterious water ‣ **Miníwaką yaǧóba.** He is sipping a whiskey.

miníyatką *vi2* s/he drinks alcohol *1s:* **minímnatką** *2s:* **minínatką**

miníyatkes'a ; **minátkes'a** *Variant:* **yatkés'a** *n* drunkard, alcoholic

minkáš'į *n* boning knife

míšaba *n* knife used for bloodletting

mįknáge *n* crow belt *Syn:* **amįknągabi**

mįmĄ́ *vs* it is round ‣ **Tába žé mįmą́mąšį.** That ball is not round. ‣ **aǧúyabi mįmá** round bannock *Adv:* **mįméya**

mįméya *adv* roundly, circularly, in circles

mįméya wacíbi *cp* round dance

mįpšúbina *n* pocket knife

-mn- *prefix-infix* I (1st person singular) *Usage:* agent/subject of active verbs of Class 2. ‣ **yá > mná** s/he goes there > I go there ‣ **éyagu > émnagu** s/he takes sb, smth > I take sb, smth

-mna *suff* s/he/it smells *Usage:* used in compounds; triggers e-ablaut. ‣ **a'á > a'ámna** it is moldy > s/he/it has a moldy smell ‣ **skúyA > skúyemna** it is sweet > it has a sweet smell

mná *vs* s/he/it smells like

mnagíciyąbi *vi1-recip* they are grouped ‣ **Owá mnagíciyąbi.** People are all grouped. *See:* **mnayą́**

mnakápkąpa *adv* unsteadily, staggering

mnamnáska *vs-redup* it is flat

mnaská *vs* it is flat, plain, smooth ‣ **Į́yą žé mnaská.** That stone is flat. ‣ **Įwą́knage žé mnaská.** That window is smooth. ‣ **Pámnaska** Flathead person ‣ **cąmnáska** wooden board *Vredup:* **mnamnáska, mnaskáska**

mnaskáska *vs-redup* they are flat

mnayĄ́ *vt1-caus* s/he collects smth; gathers smth, sb ‣ **O'ímnayą́!** Collect the beads ‣ **Šúgatąga wikcémna záptą mnawícayąbi.** They gathered fifty horses. (Drummond 1976, The boy

who made peace) *Vabs:* **wamnáyĄ́** *Vrecip:* **mnagíciyąbi**

mną́za *n* wolverine *Syn:* **wį́kcena**

mné *n* lake *Usage:* archaic. *Syn:* **minítąga**

mnesyá *adv* clearly, in a clear manner ‣ **Miní žé mnesyá hą́.** The water is clear. *Adv:* **mnesyágen**

mnesyágen *adv* clearly ‣ **Mnesyágen įmnúkcą.** I think clearly about it.

mnézA *vs* it is clear, pure, transparent ‣ **Miní mnéza.** It is pure water. *Adv:* **mnesyá**

mni- *cont* water, liquid, alcohol ‣ **mnicógan** in the water ‣ **įštámniǧe** tear *See:* **miní**

mnicáǧa *n* frozen water

mnicógan *adv* in the water ‣ **Mnicógan škádabi.** They play in the water. ‣ **Mnicógan wa'í.** I went in the water.

mnigákna *Variant:* **mnįjákna** *adv* beside the water, at the shore

mnihĄ́ *vs* s/he/it is strong, powerful ‣ **Nína mamníhą.** I am very strong. ‣ **Mitímnobi mnihą́bi** My older brothers are strong. ‣ **Pežúda né mnihą́.** This medicine is powerful. ‣ **Žé mnihį́šįh̃tįyą.** That one is not that strong. *1s:* **mamníhą** *2s:* **nimníhą** *1p:* **ųmníhąbi** *Vcont:* **mnihé**

mnihą́šį *vs* s/he/it is weak ‣ **Wįcá žé mnihą́šį.** This man is weak.

mnihé *vcont* strong ‣ **Mnihé aníya.** You are getting strong.

mnihé'įc'iyA *vi3-refl* s/he strengthens himself/herself; has courage in himself/herself *1s:* **mnihémįc'iya** *2s:* **mnihénįc'iya**

mnihéja *vs* s/he/it is strong *1s:* **mamníheja** *2s:* **nimníheja** *1p:* **ųmníhejabi**

mnihíyeyA *vimp* there is a flood *Lit:* the water arrives suddenly

mnihúde *n* shore

mni'į́t'a áyA *vs* s/he/it is thirsty *1s:* **mni'į́mat'a áya** *2s:* **mni'į́nit'a áya**

mnijáhomni *n* windmill

mnik'ábi *n* water well

mnimáhen wáda *cp* submarine

mnimóząą *vimp* it is drizzling ‣ **Ąm'éyasąą mnimóząą.** It drizzled all day.

mni'ót'A ; miní'ot'A *vs* s/he/it drowns ‣ **Koškáą žé mni'óta giníja.** That boy almost drowned. ‣ **Téhąduwa cén miní'ot'a.** It was a long way so he drowned. (NS 2002:29) *1s:* **mni'ómat'a** *2s:* **mni'ónit'a** *Vcaus:* **mni'ót'eyAmni'ót'ekiyA** *Vrefl:* **mni'ót'e'įc'iyA**

mni'ót'e'įc'iyA *vi3-refl* s/he drowns himself/herself *1s:* **mni'ót'emįc'iyA** *2s:* **mni'ót'enįc'iyA**

mni'ót'ekiyA *vt1-caus* s/he drowns, lets sb drown

mni'ót'eyA *vt1-caus* s/he drowns sb *1s:* **mni'ót'ewaya** *2s:* **mni'ót'eyaya**

mnip'ú; mnip'úhu *n* bittern

mnísni *n* cold water

mniwáda *n* boat, ship

mniwáwąąga *n* sea creature

mniwája *n* sea, ocean

Mniwążži *ngeo* Lake Superior

mniwóhą *adv* in the water ‣ **Pağúda okíknąąge iyúha mniwóhą nųwąąbi cá wąwíįcayaga.** He saw all kinds of ducks swimming in the water. (Drummond 1976, Įktomi and the ducks)

mnóga *n* male animal *Usage:* occurs mostly in compounds.

mnogáskA *vi1* s/he has hiccups *1s:* **mnowágaska** *2s:* **mnoyágaska**

mnogédu *n* 1) summer *vimp* 2) it is summer ‣ **Mnogédu hąąda wí'otibi.** In the summer they live in a tent. *Vcont:* **mnogén** *See:* **omnédu**

mnogéhą *adv* last summer

mnogén *cont* summer

mnogén cogąądu wí *np* July *Lit:* mid-summer moon

mnogésąą ; mnogéyasąą *adv* throughout the summer, all summer ‣ **Mnogéyasąą ganúzakte né dąąyąąšį.** Unfortunately, it is going to be windy all summer. (Cumberland 2005:415)

mnowąąga *n* water monster

mnóza *n* pelican

mnuná *vs* it is fine (powder, flour, sand) ‣ **Mąąká žé mnuná.** The dust is fine.

mnuyéna *vs* it is in powder

mo- *pref* 1) by an impact from a distance (by shooting, hitting with a projectile, poking with a stick) ‣ **hušté > mohúšte** s/he/it is lame > s/he makes smth (animal) lame by shooting 2) by colliding into smth with a vehicle ‣ **mnaská > momnáska** it is flat, plain, smooth > s/he flattens smth by shooting, colliding or running over it 3) by blowing on smth; by the action of the wind, rain ‣ **sní > mosní** it burns out; burns itself out > s/he blows it out (light); the wind, rain blows smth out

mocéğ'a *vs* s/he is greedy, cheeky, disrespectful ‣ **Wįįcá žé nína mocéğ'a.** That man is very greedy.

modáą *vt1* s/he slices smth (bread, bannock) ‣ **Ağúyabi modáąbi oyágihi?** Can you slice a loaf of bread? *1s:* **mowáda** *2s:* **moyáda** *See:* **wagámna**

modápta *n* slice *Syn:* **omáksabi**

modąą *vt1* s/he bumps against sb

modįį *vs* it is stiff, inflexible; stands straight

modíįyąą *adv* stiffly

mogíciȟtagabi *vi1-recip* they bump, ram into one another from a distance

mohókšu *vt1* s/he takes smth apart by shooting

mohóyA *vt1-caus* s/he makes smth howl, cry (dog) by shooting *1s:* **mohówaya** *2s:* **mohóyaya**

mohúšte *vt1* s/he makes smth (animal) lame by shooting *1s:* **mowáhušte** *2s:* **moyáhušte**

mohúšhųza *vt1* s/he makes smth swing (branch) by shooting

moȟcáą *vs* s/he/it is tangled; sticks up ‣ **Pahá momáȟca.** I have tangled hair. *1s:* **momáȟca** *2s:* **moníȟca**

moȟcína *vt1* s/he frays smth (cloth, blanket) by shooting

moȟnógA *vt1* s/he makes a hole in smth by shooting; punches a hole with a projectile

moȟpÁ *vt1* s/he knocks sb, smth down by shooting

moȟtágA *vt1* s/he bumps, rams into sb, smth from a distance *Vrecip:* **mogíciȟtagabi**

moȟúȟuga *vt1* s/he wrecks smth by hitting, bumping, colliding into it *1s:* **mowáȟuȟuga** *2s:* **moyáȟuȟuga**

mokógA *vt1* 1) s/he makes a tapping sound by hitting with a projectile, or a stick on smth 2) s/he plays pool *Vcont:* **mokók**

mokógabi *n* pool game *See:* **omókoge**

mokók *vcont* making a tapping sound; playing pool ‣ **Mokók waškáda.** I play pool.

mokpá *vt1* s/he shatters smth into pieces by shooting *1s:* **mowákpą** *2s:* **moyákpą**

mokpékna *adv* direct, directly

moksÁ *vt1* s/he breaks smth by shooting or colliding into it *1s:* **mowáksa** *2s:* **moyáksa**

mokúkA *vt1* 1) s/he shoots and makes holes in smth ‣ **Duwé šųktí mokúka.** Someone shot and made holes in the barn. 2) s/he wears smth out *1s:* **mowákuka** *2s:* **moyákuka**

momnáska *vt1* s/he flattens smth by shooting, colliding, or running over it *1s:* **mowámnaska** *2s:* **moyámnaska**

momnéja *vt1* s/he shoots smth (birds, pot) into pieces ‣ **Iyógapte mowámneja.** I shot the plate into pieces. ‣ **Gįyą́ ųbic'ehą mowį́cawamneja.** I shot and scattered them as they flew. *1s:* **mowámneja** *2s:* **moyámneja**

mopóbA *vt1* s/he explodes, bursts smth by shooting ‣ **Tába wąží mowápoba.** I shot a ball and exploded it. *1s:* **mowápoba** *2s:* **moyápoba**

mopsą́ga *vt1* s/he shoots smth hanging from a branch and it falls *1s:* **mowápsąga** *2s:* **moyápsąga**

mopsípsįna *vi1-redup* s/he/it bounces

moptÁ *vt1* s/he digs smth with a digging stick ‣ **Žé'eca dúkš piyéniš né típsįna mopté í:ga.** Still she kept on going digging up prairie turnips. (Weasel 120:59) *Vabs:* **wamóptA**

moptą́yĄ *vt1* s/he knocks smth over by shooting

mosíjA *vt1* s/he ruins smth by shooting

moská *vt1* s/he churns smth (butter)

moskébA *vi1* it drains by leaking, dripping out ‣ **Wį́kni žé moskéba.** The oil is dripping out.

mosnádA *vs* s/he/it is upright *1s:* **momásnada** *2s:* **monísnada** *Adv:* **mosnán**

mosnán *adv* upright, straight ‣ **Mosnán éknąga.** He puts it upright. ‣ **Mosnán yįgá!** Sit up straight! ‣ **Mosnán hą́.** It stands upright.

mosnéjA *vt1* s/he splits smth open by shooting or colliding into it

mosní *vt1* 1) s/he blows it out (light) 2) the wind, rain blows smth out

mosódA *vt1* s/he shoots smth, sb down; s/he uses all of the bullets on sb, smth ‣ **Bízena nówa mowį́cawasoda.** I shot all of the gophers. *1s:* **mowásoda** *2s:* **moyásoda** *Vabs:* **wamósodA** *Vcaus:* **mosónyA** *Vcont:* **mosón**

mosón *vcont* shooting smth, sb down

mosónyA *vt1-caus* s/he has smth, sb killed by shooting ‣ **"Ee'ee-hé, né Ptéskawį mosónniyąbikte no."** "Oh, woe! This White Buffalo Woman will get all of you killed." (Weasel 108:310) *1s:* **mosónwaya** *2s:* **mosónyaya** *1p:* **mosón'ųyabi**

mošná *vt1* s/he makes smth ring by shooting

mošną́ *vt1* s/he shoots and misses smth

mošpúšpu *vt1* s/he breaks smth into pieces by shooting

mot'Á *vt1* s/he kills, stuns smth by shooting

motą́ *vs* 1) s/he is socially aggressive ‣ **Nína motą́ áya.** He is becoming very aggressive socially. 2) s/he is greedy *1s:* **momátą** *2s:* **monítą**

múhįknA *vi1* it is a heavy and sudden boom

muyá *vs* it is a drumbeat *Adv:* **muyéna**

muyákne *vt1* s/he makes a drumming sound,

a drumbeat ‣ **Owédu tįknámųmųna né muyákne.** In the springtime the partridge make a drumming sound.

muyáknebi *n* drumbeat, drumming sound ‣ **Muyáknebi žé nayáh'ų?** Do you hear the drumbeat?

muyéna *adv* like drumbeats

N

-n- *prefix-infix* 1) you (2nd person singular) *Usage:* agent/subject of active verbs of Class 2. ‣ **yá > ná** s/he goes away from here > you go away from here ‣ **éyagu > énagu** s/he takes sb, smth > you take sb, smth 2) you (2nd person singular) *Usage:* agent/subject of active verbs of Class 3. ‣ **yįgá > nągá** s/he sits on smth > you sit on smth ‣ **ecų́ > ecánų** s/he does smth > you do smth

-n-...-bi *circumfix* 1) you all (2nd person plural) *Usage:* agent/subject of active verbs of Class 2. ‣ **yá > nábi** s/he goes away from here > you all go away from here ‣ **iyáya > inánabi** s/he departs from here > you all depart from here 2) you all (2nd person plural) *Usage:* agent/subject of active verbs of Class 3. ‣ **įštíma > nįštímabi** s/he sleeps > you all sleep ‣ **iyų́ga > inų́gabi** s/he asks him > you all ask him

-n *suff* at a particular point in time or space *Usage:* contracted and adverbial form of -du. ‣ **mahédu > mahén** it is deep inside > in, within, inside ‣ **ecédu > ecén** s/he/it is like this, it happens as such, it is the right way > in the right, original way; accordingly; thus

na- ; ną- *pref* 1) by kicking, stepping, walking *Usage:* forms active verbs. ‣ **súda > nasúda** s/he/it is hard > s/he hardens smth by stepping on it 2) by internal force, heat; by itself *Usage:* forms impersonal or stative verbs. ‣ **júsina > nąjúsina** s/he/it is small > s/he/it sits in the sun and shrinks

-na₁ *suff* only (derives numbers into adverbs) ‣ **omá > omána** one of two; the other > just, only one ‣ **nų́ba > nų́mnana** two > only two ‣ **wikcémna > wikcémnana** ten > only ten

-na₂ *suff* nominalizer *Usage:* derives a verb into a noun; triggers e-ablaut. ‣ **snohá > snohéna** s/he crawls > snake ‣ **wadópa > wadópena** s/he paddles > paddler ‣ **gisų́ > Gisų́na** s/he braids his/her own hair > Asian

-na₃ *encl* small, little, cute, dear *Usage:* with nouns and verbs it indicates the small size of an entity, or the endearment/sympathy of the speaker for the person or object; it often occurs on verbs used to describe the actions of a baby or small child. ‣ **hįhá > hįháhąna** owl > pigmy owl ‣ **mihų́ > mihų́na** my mother > my dear mother ‣ **škáda > škádana** s/he plays > s/he (baby or small child) plays

-na₄ *suff* parallel kinship relation (like maternal aunt, paternal uncle) ‣ **adé > adéna** my father > my uncle (father's brother) ‣ **iná > inána** my mother > my aunt (mother's sister)

-na₅ *suff* plural of demonstratives ‣ **né > nená** this > these ‣ **žé > žená** that > those

-na₆ *suff* s/he considers, rates, has regard for sb, smth (attaches to stative verbs and triggers e-ablaut) ‣ **wašté > wašténa** it is good, nice > s/he likes sb, smth ‣ **wįjáka > wįjákena** it is true; s/he tells the truth > s/he considers sb to tell the truth; considers smth to be true *1s:* **-wana** *2s:* **-yana** *1p:* **-ųnabi**

ná *vt1* s/he asks for smth ‣ **Dágu yaná?** What did you ask for? *1s:* **waná** *2s:* **yaná** *1p:* **ųnábi** *Vabs:* **waná** *Vdat:* **giná**

nacą́gu *vt1* s/he opens a trail, path by walking in it *1s:* **nawácągu** *2s:* **nayácągu**

nadą́ í *vi1* s/he went on a raid, to war *1s:* **nadą́ wa'í** *2s:* **nadą́ ya'í** *1p:* **nadą́ ųgíbi**

nadą́dą *vt1* s/he nudges sb with the foot

nagícih'ųbi *vi1-recip* they hear, understand one another

nagíciẑįbi *vi1-recip* they defend, stand for one another

nagíȟmA *vt1-pos* s/he hides his/her own thing ▸ **Wóyude nawéȟma.** I hide my food. *1s:* **nawéȟma** *2s:* **nayéȟma**

nagíjiȟmA *vt1-benef* s/he hides sb, smth from him/her ▸ **Né hokšína hoǧá né nągíjiȟmąga.** She was hiding his fish from him. (Weasel 26:5) *1s:* **nawéjiȟma** *2s:* **nayéjiȟma**

nagíjipA *vt1-dat* s/he flees from him/her

nagíjiẑį *vt1-benef* s/he defends, stands for sb ▸ **Ecágen nacíjiẑįkta.** I will always stand for you.

nagíkįdA *vt1-pos* s/he scrapes, cleans, wipes his/her own feet ▸ **Tín ú hįkna sihá nagíkįdįkta.** Come in and wipe your feet.

nagíkukA *vt1-pos* s/he wears out his/her thing by walking (like shoes)

nagípA *vt1-pos* s/he flees to his/her own (people, place)

nagípšų *vi1-pos* s/he dislocates, sprains his/her own (knee, foot, ankle) ▸ **Sihá nayépšų.** You sprained your foot. *1s:* **nawépšų** *2s:* **nayépšų** *1p:* **na'úgipšųbi** *Syn:* **anákok-kiya**

nagítagA *vt1-pos* s/he closes, shuts his/her own ▸ **Í nagítaga.** Shut your mouth. ▸ **Maȟpíya ektá tiyóba né nągítagabi no.** The door in the sky is closed to us now. (Shields 46:27)

naǧé *vt1* s/he pushes smth into a pile (sand, snow) with the foot ▸ **Wá naǧé įȟpéwaya.** I push snow into a pile.

naǧí *n* spirit of a person or thing (stone, tree) ▸ **Naǧí wąyága.** He saw a spirit. *See:* **wanáǧi**

naǧí makóce *cp* heaven

naǧí ógiya *cp* spirit guide

Naǧítąga *n* Great Spirit

naǧóǧo *vt1* s/he slashes sb, smth (as with a knife) *Vrefl:* **įknáǧoǧo**

naǧóȟązi *n* spirit bundle

naháȟ *adv* still, yet ▸ **Naháȟ wagáǧįkte no!** I am still going to make it! ▸ **Naháȟ wówaši ecúbi.** They are still working. ▸ **Naháȟ waná he?** Are you ready yet? ▸ **Naháȟ niȟmáši?** You are not sleepy yet?

naháȟtįšį *vs* 1) it is not time yet ▸ **Cáǧa žé skákta naháȟtįšį.** The ice will melt, but not yet. *adv* 2) before time ▸ **Naháȟtįšį kó azígicuniwakiya.** I weaned him before time.

nahán ; **nahá** *adv* now, about now ▸ "**Dóken waȟ'á štén nahán wįcámnuda úkaš,**" **ecí.** "What can I do so I can eat them?" he thought. (NS 2002:42)

nahánįštaš *part* I wonder, I wish ▸ **Nahánįštaš híbi.** I wish they could have come.

nahókšu *vt1* s/he breaks, kicks smth apart

nahómni *vt1* s/he spins smth with the feet; pedals *Vpos:* **knahómni**

nahówayayA *vt1-redup* s/he makes sb squeal, cry in pain by stepping (on one's foot or tail)

naȟmÁ *vt1* s/he hides sb, smth ▸ **Dágu nówa mahéduȟ naȟmá'.** She hides everything way down. *1s:* **nawáȟma** *2s:* **nayáȟma** *1p:* **na'úȟmabi** *Vbenef:* **nagíjiȟmA** *Vpos:* **nagíȟmA** *See:* **anáȟmA**

naȟmáȟman *adv-redup* secretly, privately ▸ **Naȟmáȟman wógiciknak yįgábi.** They were talking together privately. (Cumberland 2005:405)

naȟmána ; **naȟmá** *adv* secretly, inwardly *Adv:* **naȟmáȟman**

naȟmána i'Á ; **naȟmá i'Á** *vi1* s/he whispers

naȟmáyena *adv* secretly, furtively, quietly ▸ **Naȟmáyena máni.** He walks furtively.

naȟmá kuwága *vt1* s/he has a love affair with sb *1s:* **naȟmá wakúwaga** *2s:* **naȟmá yakúwaga**

naȟmúyĄ *vt1* s/he starts an engine *1s:* **nawáȟmųyą** *2s:* **nayáȟmųyą**

naȟnéjA *vi* it tears, bursts open by inner force

naȟnógA *vt1* s/he makes a hole by stepping on, kicking smth with one's body weight ▸ **Cáǧa né nawáȟnoga.** I made a hole in the ice by stepping on it. *1s:* **nawáȟnoga** *2s:* **nayáȟnoga** *1p:* **na'úȟnogabi**

naȟtágA *vt1* s/he kicks sb, smth ‣ **Anípa he eštáš naníȟtaga?** Did he hit you or kick you? *1s:* **nawáȟtaga** *2s:* **nayáȟtaga**

naȟúga *vt1* 1) s/he cracks, crushes smth with the foot, by trampling *vs* 2) it cracks by itself ‣ **Káda cén cáǧa né naȟúga.** It is hot so it cracked the ice.

naȟ'ámya *adv* on the hillside ‣ **Naȟ'ámya mągés'a.** I habitually sit on the hillside.

naȟ'ú *vt1* s/he scrapes smth with the foot

naȟ'ų *vt1* 1) s/he hears, listens to sb, smth ‣ **Nacíȟ'ų no.** I hear you. ‣ **Hó namáȟ'ų wo.** Hear my voice. ‣ **Iná nawáȟ'ų ecámųkta duká!** I should have listened to mom! ‣ **Ųnáȟ'ųs.** Let us listen to it. ‣ **Dąyą́ nawáȟ'ų.** I hear good. 2) s/he obeys sb ‣ **Iná nawáȟ'ų ecámųkta duká!** I should have listened to mom! *1s:* **nawáȟ'ų** *2s:* **nayáȟ'ų** *1p:* **na'ų́ȟ'ųbi** *Vabs:* **wanáȟ'ų** *Vrecip:* **nagíciȟ'ųbi** *See:* **onáȟ'ų**

naȟ'ų́šį *vs* s/he is deaf *Syn:* **nuǧé kpá**

na'įc'ikmįkmąbi ; nakmį́kmąbi *n* bicycle

na'įc'iži *vi3-refl* s/he defends, stands for himself/herself *1s:* **namį́c'iži** *2s:* **nanį́c'iži**

nakį́dA *vt1* s/he scrapes smth clean with the foot *Vpos:* **nagíkįdA**

Nakóda *n* 1) Nakoda person ‣ **Nakóda hįknábi cíga.** She wanted to marry a Nakoda *vs* 2) s/he is Nakoda ‣ **Wįcá né Nakódaȟtįyą.** This man is a real Nakoda. ‣ **Namákoda no.** I am Nakoda. ‣ **Nakóda wíyąšį.** She is not a Nakoda woman. *1s:* **Namákoda** *2s:* **Naníkoda** *1p:* **Na'ų́kodabi** *Cont:* **Nakón-**

Nakóda tíbi *ngeo* Fort Belknap agency (Montana)

Nakón- *cont* related to the Nakoda, or Nakoda way of life

Nakón-caže *n* traditional Nakoda name

Nakón'i'A *Variant:* **Nakón'iyA** *vi1* 1) s/he speaks Nakoda ‣ **Nakón'ųgi'įkteȟtįyą.** We want to speak Nakoda so badly! ‣ **Né duwé Nakón'i'a he?** Who speaks Nakoda? ‣ **Nakón'iwa'ageja.** I sort of speak Nakoda. ‣

Gitézi né Nakón'i'abišį. These kids do not speak Nakoda. *vt1* 2) s/he speaks Nakoda to sb *1s:* **Nakón'iwa'a** *2s:* **Nakón'iya'a** *1p:* **Nakón'ųgi'abi**

Nakón'iyabi *Variant:* **Nakón'i'e** *n* Nakoda language ‣ **Nakón'i'abi dóken eyábi he?** How is it said in Nakoda? ‣ **Nakón'i'abi ecúgųbįkte no!** We will use the Nakoda language! ‣ **Nakón'i'abi né ųknúštąbi.** We are finished with our Nakoda language.

Nakón'įc'ina *vi3-refl* s/he behaves like a Nakoda *1s:* **Nakón-mįc'ina** *2s:* **Nakón'nįc'ina** *1p:* **Nakón'ųgįc'ina**

Nakón-makoce *n* Nakoda reservation

Nakón-nowąbi *n* Nakoda song

Nakón-wįcóȟ'age *n* Nakoda custom, tradition, way of life ‣ **Nakón-wįcóȟ'age waką no.** The Nakoda way of life is holy.

Nakón-wįcó'i'e *n* Nakoda language, word

nakpákpa *vimp-redup* there is a repetitive crackling, popping sound

naksÁ *vt1* s/he breaks smth off (with the foot or by pressure)

nakúkA *vt1* s/he crushes smth with the feet, by stepping on it ‣ **Wamnúška žé nawákuka.** I crushed that insect by stepping on it. *Vpos:* **nagíkukA**

namnáska *vt1* s/he flattens smth by stepping on it *1s:* **nawámnaska** *2s:* **nayámnaska**

namnáyA *vs* it opens up flat by itself (as flowers)

namnázA *vi1* it bursts, splits open (by internal force) ‣ **Aǧúyabi žé namnáza.** The bread burst open.

namnéja *vt1* s/he scatters smth with the foot ‣ **Waȟpéȟpe né nawámneja.** I scattered the leaves with the foot.

namóo *interj* female expression of surprise for unexpected news

namú *vt1* s/he/it makes a loud sound with the foot ‣ **Namú wą́ga.** He keeps making a thumping sound.

napÁ *vi1* s/he flees, runs away, retreats ▸ **Maštíja žé napá.** The rabbit ran away. ▸ **Nawápa duká mayúzabi.** I fled but they arrested me. ▸ **Šúga síja žé wąyága cén napá.** He ran away because he saw that bad dog. ▸ **Ecén napábic'ehą gakíñ Cągúsam, éciyadahą í.** And so they fled, over there in the United States, they went from there. *1s:* **nawápa** *2s:* **nayápa** *1p:* **na'úpabi** *Vcaus:* **napéyA** *Vdat:* **nagíjipA** *Vpos:* **nagípA** See: **onápA**

napcá *vt1* s/he swallows smth ▸ **Pežúda né napcá wo.** Swallow this medicine. *1s:* **nawápca** *2s:* **nayápca**

napcúwąga *num* nine

napcúwągana *quant* only nine

napégijiyA *vt1-benef* s/he drives, chases sb, smth away for him/her ▸ **Giníħąšį, napécijiya.** Do not be afraid, I chased it away for you. *1s:* **napéwejiya** *2s:* **napéyejiya**

Napéšį *nprop* No retreat society

Napéšį wacíbi *cp* No retreat dance

napéyA *vt1-caus* s/he drives, chases sb, smth away; makes sb flee ▸ **Šúga žé napéwaya.** I chased the dog away. *1s:* **napéwaya** *2s:* **napéyaya** *1p:* **napé'ųyabi** *Vbenef:* **napégijiyA**

nap'į *vt1* s/he wears smth on the neck ▸ **Nawáp'įc.** I wore it specifically on the neck. *1s:* **nawáp'į** *2s:* **nayáp'į** *1p:* **na'úp'įbi** *Vcaus:* **nap'įkiyA**

nap'įkiyA *vt1-caus* s/he makes sb wear it around the neck; puts smth around sb's neck ▸ **Žé yuħnéħneja hįk nap'įwįcakiya [. . .].** He tore it up in strips and tied it around their necks [. . .] (NS 2002:17) *1s:* **nap'įwakiya** *2s:* **nap'įyakiya**

napsíjA *vt1* s/he/it kicks, propels sb, smth ▸ **Íyą aké nawápsiješį no.** I did not kick a stone again. *1s:* **nawápsija** *2s:* **nayápsija** *1p:* **ųnápsijabi** *Vcont:* **napsín**

napsín *vcont* kicking, propelling

napsín ye'įc'iyA *vi3-refl* s/he propels himself/herself (as in a race)

napsínyeyA *vt1* s/he kicks sb, smth *Vrefl:* **napsín ye'įc'iyA**

napsínyeyabi *n* football

napsú *vt1* s/he spills smth by kicking it, by pushing it with the foot

napsú įħnáye *cp* ring

napšú *vt1* s/he dislocates, sprains smth with the foot or by kicking *1s:* **wanápšų** *2s:* **yanápšų** *1p:* **ųnápšųbi** *Vrefl:* **nagípšų**

naptąyA *vt1* s/he turns smth over with the foot

nasnádA *vt1* s/he sneaks, crawls up to sb *Vcont:* **nasnán**

nasnán *vcont* sneaking, crawling up to sb

nasnéjA *vt1* s/he stands on smth and breaks; breaks smth with his body weight

nasníza *vt1* 1) s/he puts a fire out by stepping on it 2) s/he/it forces out air by stepping on it

nastó *vt1* s/he straightens, smoothens smth with the foot

nasú *n* brain

nasúda *vt1* s/he hardens smth by stepping on it

nasú *vi1* s/he/it stretches out the feet and legs ▸ **Nasú yągá hįk hú knuk'éğabi.** They sat with their legs stretched out and scratched their legs. (Weasel 42:165) *1s:* **nawásų** *2s:* **nayásų**

naškóbA *vt1* s/he bends smth by body, foot pressure ▸ **Ahą hįkna naškóba.** He stepped on it and bent it.

našnógA *vi* it pops out *Vcaus:* **našnókyA**

našnókyA *vt1-caus* s/he makes smth pop out *1s:* **našnókwaya** *2s:* **našnókyaya** *1p:* **našnók'ųyabi**

našnúda *vi1* s/he slips while walking on it ▸ **Waktá nayášnuda cén.** Beware! You will slip on it.

nat'Á *vt1* s/he kicks, tramples sb to death

natágA *vt1* s/he closes, locks, shuts smth; it (wind) closes it; turns it off ▸ **A'óžąžą né natága.** Shut off the lights. ▸ **Wíyą žé ti'óba natága.** The woman shut the door. ▸ **Océti natága.** Turn the stove off. ▸ **Omníyakte žé**

núba eháʼi hą́da natágabi. The bar closes at two o'clock. *Vpos:* **nagítagA**

natáȟtų *vi* foam appears by itself

naʼų́kce *n* cowboy

nawáde *n* temple, side of the head

nawą́ga *vt1* s/he pushes sb, smth with the foot *Vcaus:* **nawą́kkiyA** *Vcont:* **nawą́k**

nawą́k *vcont* at a slow, easy gait (on a horse) ▸ **Nawą́k ų́.** The horse is at a slow gait.

nawą́kkiyA *vt1-caus* s/he/it makes it trot, run off *1s:* **nawą́kwakiya** *2s:* **nawą́kyakiya**

nawą́kwąga *vi1-redup* it (horse) trots

nawís *vcont* jealous ▸ **Nawís waʼų́.** I feel jealous.

nawízi *vi1* s/he is jealous ▸ **Waná aké nawízi cén.** As so now he is jealous again. ▸ **Wíyą žé šikná cén nawízi.** The woman was angry because she was jealous. *1s:* **nawáwizi** *2s:* **nayáwizi** *1p:* **naʼų́wizibi** *Vcont:* **nawís**

nazám *adv* aside, at the back ▸ **Nazám ecų́.** He pulls it aside. ▸ **Nazám įnáži!** Stand at the back!

nazámpadahą *adv* from behind, from the back ▸ **Tógabi owá nazámpadahą híbi.** All of the enemies arrived from behind.

nazámpagena *adv* somewhere at the back; a little further back ▸ **Nazámpagena nawáži.** I stood somewhere at the back.

nazámpagiya *adv* toward the back ▸ **Tí nazámpagiya aktága.** He ran toward the back of the house.

nazápa *post* in the back of smth, behind smth ▸ **Nazápaš wónešį.** Do not go looking around back here. (Weasel 126:172)

nazúda *vt1* s/he wears smth down

náži *vi1* 1) s/he/it stands ▸ **Tá baháġan náži.** The moose is standing on top of a hill. ▸ **Duwé nén náži?** Who is standing here? 2) s/he is, exists in a certain condition *Usage:* used after an adverb or a postposition. ▸ **Agám náži.** He is the best. ▸ **Midáguyabi nína ųšigiya náži bo!** My relatives stand in a very humble way! ▸ **Agísas náži.** He stands proudly. 3) it is, it is located *Usage:* used for objects. ▸ **Cą́ įjída náži.** It is the tallest tree. *1s:* **nawáži** *2s:* **nayáži** *1p:* **naʼų́žibi** *Vbenef:* **nagíjiži** *Vrecip:* **nagícižibi** *Vrefl:* **naʼíc'iži**

nažúde *n* nape of the neck, occiput (hollow part)

nąbáda *adv* by the hand

nąbáda yúzA *vt2* s/he holds sb's hand *Usage:* not used for greetings.

nąbáwąge *n* finger *Usage:* used in compounds only.

nąbáwąge įjíyamni *cp* ring finger *Lit:* third finger

nąbáwąge įjínuba *cp* middle finger *Lit:* second finger

nąbáwąge įjíwaži *cp* index finger *Lit:* first finger *Syn:* **waʼébazo**

nąbáwąhuge tága *cp* thumb *Lit:* big finger

nąbé *n* hand ▸ **Nąbé táwa žé pążéna.** Her hands are soft. ▸ **Nąbé miní ožúna.** The hand is full of water blisters. ▸ **Nąbé awáhą wagáhowaya.** I step on her hand and make her scream. *Cont:* **nąp-**

nąbé caktána *Variant:* **nąbé catkána** *cp* left hand

nąbé gamúbi *cp* hand drum

nąbé į́ʼáyustage *cp* handcuff

nąbé okíhąge *cp* finger joint

nąbé psųkáya *cp* fist

nąbé škádabi *cp* handgame

nąbé t'at'Á *vs* s/he has a numb hand *1s:* **nąbé mat'át'a** *2s:* **nąbé nit'át'a** *1p:* **nąbé ųt'át'abi**

nąbéyus *vcont* shaking hands ▸ **Nąbéyus waʼų́.** I am shaking his hand.

nąbéyuzA *vi2* s/he shakes hands with sb ▸ **Níš nąbénuzįkta.** You too will shake his hand. *1s:* **nąbémnuza** *2s:* **nąbénuza** *1p:* **nąbéʼųyuzabi** *Vcont:* **nąbéyus**

nąbíjaške ; nąbé įjáške *n* bracelet

nąbíkpa *n* glove, mitten ▸ **Nąbíkpa aknúštą.** He lost his gloves. ▸ **Nąbíkpa yaknúha he?** Do you have your mittens with you? ▸ **tamkápsija nąbíkpa** baseball glove

nąbímna *vs* it is delicious, sweet ▸ **Aǧúyabi né nąbímna.** The bread is delicious.

nąbó *vs* it (hand) is swollen; it swells by itself

nąbóda *vt1* s/he wears smth out with the feet ‣ **Hába ų̄ žé'įš wanągaš nąbóta.** He had worn out his moccasins long ago. (Shields 13:161)

nąbó'ųšna *n* thimble

nądáboǧA *vs* s/he/it bloats; is swollen, puffed up *1s:* **nąmádaboǧa** *2s:* **nąnídaboǧa** *Adv:* **nądáboȟyena** *Vrefl:* **nądáboǧ'įc'iyA**

nądáboȟyabi *n* yeast

nądáboȟyena *adv* bloated ‣ **Žéceya hoǧą́ né nadáboȟyena hiyéya.** In the meantime all these fish had become bloated. (Weasel 32:124)

nądáboȟ'įc'iyA *vi3-refl* s/he/it bloats, swells himself/herself/itself up (frog) ‣ **Tabéȟ'a nądáboȟ'įc'iya.** The frog is bloating itself up. *See:* **nądáboǧA**

nągáhą *adv* now ‣ **Nągáhą wawápadįkta.** Now I will do some butchering. ‣ **Nągáhą nína wówaši ecú.** Now she is in labor. *Syn:* **nahą́**

nągáhąȟ ; nągáȟ *adv* just now, right away, immediately ‣ **Nągáhąȟ hí.** She came just now.

nągáhąš ; nągáš *adv* now as compared to before; but now ‣ **Nągáš toká.** Now it is different.

nągénuna *adv* right away, immediately; temporarily ‣ **Nągénuna ecú.** Do it right away.

nągís *vcont* squeak ‣ **Cą'ówįža nągís mawáni.** I walked on this and made it squeak.

nągíza *vt1* s/he/it makes sb, smth squeak by stepping on him/her/it *Cont:* **nągís**

nągú ; nakų́ ; nągú *conj* 1) and, and also, in addition ‣ **Wahpé nągú asą́bi mnuhá.** I want tea and milk. ‣ **Mihų́ nakų́ mikúši cąpá yušpí yábi.** My mother and my grandmother are going to pick chokecherries. ‣ **Wahpé, huȟnáȟyabi nągú asą́bi mnuhá.** I have tea, coffee, and also milk. *adv* 2) more, anymore *Usage:* has the latter meaning when followed by a negated verb in -šį. ‣ **Nągú wacíga.** I want more. ‣ **Nągú eyéšį.** Do not say it anymore.

ną'įtkųyA *vt1* it lights it up

nąjúsina *vi* it sits in the sun and shrinks ‣ **Tanó žé nąjúsina iyáya.** The meat is starting to shrink.

nąkádA *vi* it becomes hot by itself, internal force

nąkéya *adv* on one's side ‣ **Nąkéya mągá.** I am leaning on the side. ‣ **Pá nąkéya yįgá.** His head is leaning on the side.

nąknábo *vi* it swells, puffs up on its own (beans, injury)

nąkpá *n* wrist

nąkpáhuhu *n* wrist bone

nąm'écųbina ; nąbé ecųbina *n* hand game

nąmgícigawįwįbi *vi1-recip* they wave the hand at one another

nąmgíjawįwį *vt1-dat* s/he waves the hand at sb *1s:* **nąmwéjawįwį** *2s:* **nąmyéjawįwį**

nąmką *n* vein of the wrist

nąmknáskaba *vi1-pos* s/he claps his/her hands; applauds

nąpcó *n* outer area of the upper arm

nąpcóga *n* palm of the hand

nąpkáwį *vi1* s/he waves *1s:* **nąmwágawį** *2s:* **nąmyágawį**

nąpkáwįwį *vi1-redup* s/he waves at sb *1s:* **nąmwágawįwį** *2s:* **nąmyágawįwį** *Vcoll:* **nąmwícagawįwį** *Vdat:* **nąmgíjawįwį** *Vrecip:* **nąmgícigawįwįbi**

nąpóbA *vi* it explodes, bursts by itself *Vcaus:* **nąpópkiyAnąpómyA**

nąpómyA *vt1-caus* s/he causes smth to explode, burst; bombs smth ‣ **Ecánaȟ nąpómyabi.** Right at that time they bombed it. *See:* **anąpomyA**

nąpómyabi *n* dynamite, fireworks

nąpópkiyA *vt1-caus* s/he makes it explode

nąpópomyabi *n-redup* popcorn

nąp'óyA *vi1* it produces steam

nąpsápsą *vi1-redup* s/he/it waggles smth ‣ **Sįdé nąpsápsą.** It waggles its tail.

nąpsíhu *n* finger *Syn:* **nąbáwąge**

nąpsíhu hąwí akída *ph* minute hand on a clock

nąpsíhušage *n* fingernail

nąpsú *n* finger *1s:* **minápsu** *2s:* **ninápsu**

nąšpá *vt1* s/he opens smth with the foot

né 1) *dem* this, these (near the speaker) ‣ **Wapáha né nų́kta he?** Are you going to wear this hat? ‣ **A'óžą̄žą né natága!** Shut off the lights! ‣ **Hųská né duktén opéyatų he?** Where did you buy these pants? 2) *pro* this, he, she, it ‣ **Duwé né he?** Who is this?

néca *vs* s/he/it is this kind ‣ **Šų̄któgeja nécabic.** They were wolves.

nécedu *adv* 1) in this way *vs* 2) s/he/it is like this ‣ **Nécedu otí'įga.** This must be the way. ‣ **Né nécedukta oyága.** He told him this would happen. *Adv:* **nécen**

nécekcen *adv-redup* in these ways, in this way for each of them

nécen *adv* in this way, like this, as such ‣ **Nécen ecú.** Do it like this. ‣ **Nécen kábi.** They mean it as such. ‣ **Nécen epá jé.** I always say it like this. ‣ **Dayą́h̄ nécen ų́bi jé no.** They always behave in a very good way. *Redup:* **nécekcen**

néci *adv* over here, here ‣ **Néci ú wo.** Come over here. ‣ **Néci ganį́yą híbi.** They came directly here.

nécidahą *adv* from over here

néciyadahą *adv* from this direction

nécų *vt1* s/he does this ‣ **Įjínųba, wįcášta ayáhibi necánųbiktešį'.** You will not bring these people here ever again. (Weasel 89:193) *1s:* **nécamų** *2s:* **nécanų**

nedábaš *adv* in this direction ‣ **Nedábaš yábišįm.** Do not go in this direction.

nedáhą *adv* from here, from a group ‣ **Nédahą ų̄gíyayį̄kte no.** We will start from here. ‣ **Hųgá žé į̄hpéwįcaya oyáde nedáhą.** The chief chased them out of the reserve.

nedáhągeja *vs* it is from around here

nedám *adv* this way (toward the speaker) ‣ **Nedám yá.** He went this way.

nedápa *adv* on this side ‣ **Nedápa yuptéjena.** Cut it shorter on this side.

nedápadahą *adv* 1) moving from here, behind, from this side 2) from the beginning, start

nédu *vimp* it is here, this is the place ‣ **"Néduc,"** **eyá.** "Here it is," he said.

néduȟ *vimp* it is right here, this is exactly the place

néduna *adv* near, close to here

nédunaȟ *adv* very near, close to here ‣ **Nedám nédunaȟ wa'ų́.** I live close to here, over this way.

né'e *vs* it is this; this is him/her/it/them *Usage:* only used in the 3rd person. ‣ **Né'e no!** This is the one!

néhą *adv* at this time, now

nehą́du *vs* it is now; it took place at this time ‣ **Įdé žé wą̄'ų́yagabišį nehą́du.** We could not see his face at this time. ‣ **Nehą́du hą́da wó'ųdabi.** We ate at this time. *Adv:* **nehą́n**

nehą́duȟ *adv* now, about this time ‣ **Nehą́duȟ owá híbi.** They all come now.

nehą́duȟtįyA *vimp* it is now specifically; it is at this time ‣ **Nehą́duȟtįyą kníbi.** They came back around this time.

nehą́geȟ *adv* this long; this far off ‣ **Nehą́geȟ maksá.** Cut it that length. ‣ **Nehą́geȟ aktága.** He ran this far off.

nehą́gejA *vs* s/he/it is about this high, tall, or far *Vredup:* **nehą́hągeja**

nehą́hągejA *vs-redup* they are about this high, tall, or far ‣ **Áá, nehą́hągeja wakmų́haza né eyáš.** Ah, so those corn stalks were about this high. (Weasel 83:45)

nehą́ktA *vimp* it is happening

nehą́n *adv-cont* at this time; now, today

né'įš *dem* this, these too; this one, these ones too ‣ **Hųgágebi né'įš snokkíciyabįkta.** The parents too would know each other. ‣ **"Makóce né, né'įš nitáwabįkta,"** **jáya.** "This land, this too will be yours," he said.

-nekši- *root* 1) uncle (mother's brother) 2) uncle

(father's sister's husband) ▸ **Wąží híšį žé minékši.** The one who did not show up is my uncle. *1s:* **minékši** *2s:* **ninékši** *3s:* **nekšíco** ; **nekšíju** *1p:* **nekšíju'ųyąbi**

nén *adv* here (precise location near the speaker), in a place ▸ **Nén úbįkta he?** Will they be coming here? ▸ **Nén mayázą'.** I ache here.

nená *dem* these here (close to the speaker) ▸ **Dágu nená he?** What are these? ▸ **Buscíjabina nená duwé táwabi he?** Whose kittens are these? ▸ **Wįcíjana nená wayáwa tíbi aktágabi.** These girls are running to school. ▸ **mitúgašibina waná iyáyabi nená** my dear late grandfathers

nenągeja *vs* it is this many; it is such amount *Usage:* when showing an amount close to the speaker.

nenąknana *adv* only these, this is all, just a bit left; less than expected (as something that is left over)

néš *pro* this one indeed, this one unlike the other ▸ **Néš omągipi.** This one, on the other hand, fit me.

nešwúges'a *n* bedwetter

né'ųs ; né'ų *conj* because of this, on account of this, therefore ▸ **Téhą yįgábi né'ųs cuwí mabádį.** I sat for too long and because of this my body is stiff. ▸ **Tągán úbi né'ųs há zí.** They are continously outside and because of this his skin is tanned.

newós *pro, dem* these two ▸ **newós įwó'okma žéca** these two pencils

neyá *vt-irr* s/he says this *Usage:* precedes or follows a quote. ▸ **"Iyé ecúšį," nepá.** I said, "He did not do it." *1s:* **nepá** *2s:* **nehá**

néžA *vi1* 1) s/he/it urinates ▸ **Yanéžįkta he?** Are you going to urinate? ▸ **Wanúň hokšína né néžąbi cíga.** Perhaps the boy wants to urinate. *1s:* **wanéža** *2s:* **yanéža** *1p:* **ųnéžąbi** 2) *n* urine *Usage:* occurs mostly in compounds. ▸ **nežémna** s/he smells urine

néžeha *n* bladder

nežémna *vs* s/he/it smells urine ▸ **Hukwá, nežénimna.** Oh my, you smell urine. *1s:* **nežémamna** *2s:* **nežénimna**

-ni- *prefix-infix* 1) you (2nd person singular) *Usage:* subject of stative verbs. ▸ **stustá > nistústa** s/he is tired > you are tired ▸ **ípi > ínipi** s/he is full > you are full 2) you (2nd person singular) *Usage:* patient of transitive verbs. ▸ **yucéya > niyúceya** s/he makes sb cry > s/he makes you cry ▸ **wąyága > wąníyaga** s/he sees sb, smth > s/he sees you 3) your (2nd person singular possessor) *Usage:* body parts and kinship nouns. ▸ **hú > nihú** leg > your leg ▸ **dagúye > nidáguye** relative > your relative

-ni *Variant:-***na** *suff* not, no *Usage:* negator used with indefinite pronouns. ▸ **dágu > dáguni, dáguna** something > none, nothing ▸ **duwé > duwéni, duwéna** someone > nobody, no one

ní *vi1* s/he/it is alive, lives ▸ **Ní'!** He is alive! ▸ **Atkúgu, húgu íš nahą́ň níbi.** His father and mother too are still alive. ▸ **Duwéni níšį.** No one survived. ▸ **Įdúň níktešį.** Contrary to hope he did not survive. *Vcaus:* **niyÁ, nikíyA** *Vpos:* **nigíyA**

-ni- . . .-bi *circumfix* 1) you (2nd person plural) *Usage:* subject of stative verbs. ▸ **stustá > nistústa** s/he is tired > you all are tired 2) you (2nd person plural) *Usage:* patient of transitive verbs. ▸ **wąyága > wąníyagabi** s/he sees sb, smth > s/he sees you all 3) your (2nd person plural possessor) *Usage:* body parts and kinship nouns. ▸ **hú > nihúbi** leg > your leg ▸ **dagúye > nidáguyabi** relative > your relative

nigíyA *vt1-pos* s/he heals, saves, rescues his/her own ▸ **Húgu gicí niyą́'ųgiya.** His mother and I healed him. ▸ **Micíkši niwágiya.** I healed my son. *1s:* **niwágiya** *2s:* **niyágiya**

niğé *Variant:* **niğá** *n* stomach, tripe, abdomen ▸ **Niğé yazą́.** He has a stomachache.

niğé húde *cp* lower part of the stomach below the navel (less common)

niğé įhókun *cp* lower part of the stomach below the navel

niğé įpáĥta *cp* cinch (strap that attaches under a horse's belly)

niğé tahésaga *cp* little children

niğé yazą *vs* s/he has a stomachache *1s:* **niğé mayázą** *2s:* **niğé niyázą** *1p:* **niğé ųyáząbi**

niğúde *n* flank, part below the ribs

nikíyA *vt1-caus* s/he saves, rescues, causes sb to live ‣ **Ni'ųkiya bo.** Save us. *1s:* **niwákiya** *2s:* **niyákiya** *1p:* **ni'ųkiyabi**

nína *adv* 1) very ‣ **Nína cądéniwašte no.** You are very kind. ‣ **Nína wasnókye no.** She is very clever. 2) really, a lot, intense, intensively; always ‣ **Nína cóza.** It is too warm. ‣ **Nína mapáyažą.** I have an intense headache. ‣ **Nína cíga.** He wants it badly. ‣ **Nína wa'écų!** He is always cursing! 3) not at all, not really *Usage:* followed by a negative verb. ‣ **Wįcá žé nínaĥ wógipiši!** This man is quite fearless!

niní *vs* it thickens, coagulates; it is sticky ‣ **Nínaĥ nįníši.** It's not too sticky.

niséhu *n* thigh (also the name of Chief Carry The Kettle's wife; Linda Cumberland field-notes 1999)

nísko *vs* it is this size, much; it is as big as this ‣ **Miní niskó no.** It is this much water. ‣ **Eknága nísko kún!** Put this much down here!

nískoga *vs* it is about this size, much ‣ **Cą wąží nískoga mak'ú.** Give me a stick about this size. *Vredup:* **nískogaga** *See:* **žískoga**

nískogaga *vs-redup* it is about this small size

niyá 1) *vs* s/he/it breathes, is alive ‣ **Niyáši iyáya.** He is starting to choke. *1s:* **waníya** *2s:* **yaníya** 2) *n* breath of life ‣ **Adé wakątąga niyá waką mak'ú no!** Father the Creator, give me the holy breath of life!

niyÁ *vt1-caus* s/he/it makes sb live; spares, allows sb to live ‣ **Misųga, miyéš nicíya.** Younger brother, I save your life myself. ‣ **Žécena niwícaya.** It allowed them to survive. (Weasel 25:47) *1s:* **niwáya** *2s:* **niyáya**

niyáhą ų *vii* s/he/it is living ‣ **Né téhą niyáhą ya'ųkta!** You will be living for a long time! ‣ **Duwéni niyáhą ųbiši.** No one is alive. *1s:* **niyáhą wa'ų** *2s:* **niyáhą ya'ų** *1p:* **niyáhą ųgúbi**

niyáwašte *vs* s/he/it is in good health

-niyą *suff* loudly, with a loud voice, audibly (often used with verbs for singing, crying, speaking, etc.) ‣ **nową > nowąniyą** s/he sings > s/he sings loudly ‣ **Aké žecíyac nowąniyą.** Just as before she sang with a loud voice from afar. (Weasel 26:14, my translation)

niyáyA *vt1-caus* s/he heals, brings sb back to life ‣ **Pežúda ųs niyąya.** He cured him using medicine.

niyúha *quant* all of these, all kinds ‣ **Kiškána niyúha wabáwíyakpa.** I polish all of the spoons. ‣ **Cą niyúha wabánaži.** I put all of the sticks up.

nįdé *n* lower part of the back, above the rump; hip ‣ **Nįdémayázą.** My rump hurts.

nįjA *vs* s/he lacks smth (needed); it is lacking ‣ **Wóyude manįja.** I lack food. *1s:* **manįja** *2s:* **ninįja**

nįktegiciyakiyabi *vii-recip* they doctor, heal one another

nįktegijikiyA *vt1-benef* s/he doctors, heals sb for him/her *1s:* **nįktewejikiya** *2s:* **nįkteyejikiya**

nįktekiyA *vt1-caus* s/he doctors, heals sb ‣ **Nįktekiyabi duká dáguniĥ kó ųs asníši.** They doctored her, but even with that she did not recover at all. (NS 2002:69) *1s:* **nįktewakiya** *2s:* **nįkteyakiya** *1p:* **nįkte'ųkiyabi** *Vabs:* **wanįktekiyA** *Vbenef:* **nįktegijikiyA** *Vrecip:* **nįktegicikiyabi**

nįséhu *n* hip bone

no *part* indicates an assertion (declarative male particle) *Usage:* triggers e-ablaut on the preceding word. ‣ **Pinámayaye no!** I thank you!

‣ **Dąyą́ wącímnage no.** It is good to see you. ‣
Aké wącímnagįkte no. I will see you again. ‣
Wadópena žemáca no. I am of the Wadopena
Tribe.

nó *vi* it is moist, fresh (as meat)

nodé *n* throat, neck ‣ **Nodé mabádįda.** My neck
is stiff.

nodé pšųpšų́ *cp* Adam's apple

nodéhą *vs* s/he is voracious; greedy for smth
(food, money) ‣ **Hokšína žé nodéhą.** That
boy is greedy. ‣ **Wašíju nína nodéhąbi.** The
White people are very greedy. *1s:* **nomádehą**
2s: **nonídehą** *1p:* **ųnódehąbi**

nodį́n t'A *vs* s/he/it is hungry, starving ‣ **Nodį́n
t'a ayéšį.** He is not that hungry. ‣ **Owá nodį́n
t'a áya.** All were starving. ‣ **Nína nodį́n t'a áya.**
He is getting really hungry. *1s:* **nodį́n mat'a** *2s:*
nodį́n nit'a *1p:* **nodį́n ųt'abi** *See:* **įdúka**

nókna *post* through this ‣ **Pestóna né, o'óna
nokná kniȟpáyįkta.** The sharp end will go
through the opening. (Weasel 49:326)

nową́ *vi1* s/he/it sings ‣ **Nową́ wo!** Sing! ‣
Dóhąda yanówąbįkta? At what time will you
sing? ‣ **Waną́gaš mitúgaši onówą nená.** Long
ago my grandfather used to sing these songs.
1s: **wanówą** *2s:* **yanówą** *Vbenef:* **gíjinową** *Vrefl:*
ginówą *See:* **įnówą**

nówa *pro* all of these (people, animals, things,
ideas) ‣ **Dáguškibina nówa nųwą́ iyáyabi.** All
the children are going swimming. ‣ **Įknúhana
šų́ga nówa hįnápabi.** Suddenly all the dogs
appeared. ‣ **Cą́ nówa škąšką́.** All of the trees
are shaking. ‣ **Mína nówa mnumą́.** I sharpen
all the knives. ‣ **Dágu snokyá nówa ogíjiyaga.**
He told him exactly all that he knew.

nową́s'a *n* singer

núda *vs* it is red, scarlet *Usage:* mostly used in
compounds. ‣ **matónuda** cinnamon bear ‣
paȟnúda turkey

núǧe *n* ear ‣ **Núǧe én owážiži.** I whispered in her
ear. *1s:* **manúǧe** *2s:* **ninúǧe** *Cont:* **nuȟ**

núǧe hąskáska *cp-redup* mule

núǧe kpá *vs* s/he/it is deaf *Lit:* pierced ears *1s:*
núǧe makpá *2s:* **núǧe nikpá** *1p:* **núǧe ųkpábi**
Syn: **naȟ'ų́šį**

núǧe oȟnóga *cp* ear holes

núǧe ų́s wa'ánaǧoptąbina *ph* hearing aid

nuȟ *cont* ear

nuȟcá *n* deaf person

nuȟ'ó'į *n* earrings *Vcaus:* **nuȟ'ó'įkiyA**

nuȟ'ó'įkiyA *vt1-caus* s/he puts earrings on sb's
ears

núni *vi1* s/he/it is lost ‣ **Šų́ga núni ca.** The dog
must be lost. ‣ **Dóhąni wanúnįkteši.** I never
get lost. *1s:* **wanúni** *2s:* **yanúni** *1p:* **ųnúnibi**

nús *vcont* fast, quickly ‣ **Nína nús iyáya.** It went
very fast. ‣ **Šų́gataǧa žé nús aktága ogíhi.** That
horse can run fast.

núskiyA *vt1-pos* s/he makes his/her own faster

núzahą *vi1* s/he/it is fast, quick ‣ **Wáda žé
núzahą.** The train is fast. ‣ **Kneknéǧa žé
núzahą.** The spotted one is fast. *Vcont:* **nús**
See: **oȟ'ą́ko, kokóna**

nų́ba *num* 1) two ‣ **Mína nų́ba éyagu.** Take these
two knives. ‣ **Mitágožabina nų́ba timáni híbi.**
Two of my grandchildren came to visit. ‣ **Nų́ba
wįcáyuhešį, dóba wįcáyuha.** She does not
have two kids, she has four. ‣ **Dobáȟ nų́ba štén
šaknóǧą.** Four times two equals eight. *vs* 2)
s/he/it is two; there are two ‣ **Ą́ba nų́ba štén
hį́kta.** He will arrive in two days. *Cont:* **nų́m-**

nų́babina *Variant:* **nų́babi** *n* twins *Lit:* they are
two ‣ **Nų́babina žé akíyecedu.** The twins look
alike. ‣ **Nų́babina wįcáyuha.** She has twins.
See: **gicí kpábi**

nų́bacą *vimp* it is a period of two days ‣ **Mikų́
ą́ba nų́bacą hí.** My mother-in-law arrived two
days ago.

nų́bagiya *adv* two by two, in two ways, in two
different directions, locations ‣ **Nų́bagiya
iyáyabi.** They went separate ways. ‣ **Nų́bagiya
egíknągabi.** They put theirs in two differ-

ent places. ▸ **Taȟpá agą́n aní žécen hú né
anų́k nų́bagiya cén hú né yuškom iyáya.** He
[Įktomni] stepped on his [diver] back, spreading his legs out and bending them crooked.
(Drummond 1976, Įktomi and the ducks)

nụbáȟ basísA *vt1* s/he double stitches smth *1s:*
nụbáȟ wabásisa *2s:* **nụbáȟ yabásisa**

nų́m- *cont* two

nų́mnana *num* only two

nų́mnanaȟ *adv* only two ▸ **Nų́mnanaȟ híbi.** Only
two came.

nų́mnụbanaȟ *adv-redup* only twice

nųpí ; nųpín *pro* both ▸ **Nųpí gakná maníbi.**
They both are walking along. ▸ **Hą́ba žé nųpín
mak'ú.** Give me both of the shoes.

nų́ške *n* 1) thing, thingy ▸ **Nų́ske wąží, uh
éyag . . . cąwák'įna wąží, uh, éyagu.** One of
those things, uh, take one of those little barrels.
(Weasel 19:34) vs) 2) it is so, as such *Usage:* used
to recall a thing that is not properly identified.
▸ **Nų́skektac.** It will be that thing.

nụwǍ *vi1* s/he/it swims, bathes, showers ▸
Wakpá kogám wanų́wą. I swam across the
river. ▸ **Dóhąni wakpá én wanų́wešį.** I never
swam in this river. ▸ **Dáguškibina nówa nụwą́
iyáyabi.** All the children went swimming. ▸ **Įtó
wanų́wąkta.** I guess I will shower. *1s:* **wanų́wą**
2s: **yanų́wą** *1p:* **ụnų́wąbi** *Vcaus:* **nụwékiyA** *See:*
anų́wǍ

nụwékiyA *vt1-caus* s/he lets sb swim ▸ **Iná
misų́ga nụwékiya.** Mom let my younger
brother swim. *1s:* **nụwą́wakiya** *2s:* **nụwą́yakiya**
1p: **nụwą́'ụkiyabi**

O

o- *pref* inside, in, into *Usage:* derives a verb into
a noun or a simple verb into a more specified
verb. ▸ **wokšú > owókšubi** s/he plants things >
garden ▸ **wóda > owóde tíbi** s/he eats > restaurant ▸ **įknúžaža > o'į́knužaža** s/he washes him-

self/herself > bathroom ▸ **maní > ománi** s/he
walks > s/he travels

ó *vt1* s/he shoots and wounds sb, smth; kills sb,
smth ▸ **Pté žé ó hį́k páda.** He shot a buffalo
and butchered it. (Cumberland 2005:432) *1s:*
wa'ó *2s:* **ya'ó** *Vbenef:* **gíji'o** *See:* **ta'ó**

o'ápe *n* hour ▸ **O'ápe šákpe ohą́.** Boil for six
hours.

obáǧe *vt1* 1) s/he pushes smth into it; fills smth
with it *Vbenef:* **ogíjibaǧe** *Vdat:* **ogíbaǧe** *n* 2)
filled pipe

óbaksA *vt1* s/he breaks smth by pressing it into
a hole

obápsụ *vt1* s/he pours smth (a liquid) into a container ▸ **Žécen mini obápsụ.** Then she poured
water in it. *Vpos:* **okpápsụ**

obásisA *vt1* s/he sews smth on it *1s:* **owábasisa**
2s: **oyábasisa** *See:* **basísA**

obáwįǧe *num* hundred ▸ **Obáwįǧe nų́ba,
žehą́geȟ mak'ú.** $200, that is how much he
gave me. ▸ **Mázaska obáwįǧe kapéya.** It is
more than a $100.

obázą *vt1* s/he sticks, inserts smth in it *Vbenef:*
ogíjibazą

obémni *vt1* s/he wraps sb, smth in it ▸ **Šiná
obémni.** She wrapped it in a blanket. ▸
Dáguškina žé obémni. Wrap the baby. *1s:*
owábemni *2s:* **oyábemni** *Vbenef:* **ogíjibemni**
Vpos: **ogíbemni** *Vrefl:* **o'į́kpemni, o'į́c'ibemni**

obóǧA *vt1* s/he blows into smth; inflates smth

obúȟni *vt1* s/he stuffs smth into it ▸ **Žén pté
hį́ụzé obúȟnibi cén ų́kce ogíhišį.** They had
stuffed his rump with buffalo fur so that he
could not fart. (Cumberland 2005:434–435)

obúktą *vt1-dit* s/he dips smth in it (as bannock in
soup) ▸ **Wasé né obútką cén cąkáhu né agán
okmá.** [He] stuck his fingers in the paint and
made a mark on her back between the shoulder blades. (Weasel 36:31) *1s:* **owábuktą** *2s:*
oyábuktą *Vpos:* **okpúktą**

obúspA *vt1* s/he plasters over smth 1s: **owábuspa** 2s: **oyábuspa**

ocápe *n* pitchfork

ocáže *n* kind, sort, species ‣ **Ocáže owácegiye ocáže nówa įš én nągáhą ópabi cén.** Today they join all different kinds of churches. (NS 2002:5)

ocábaza *n* pasture

ocágaksaksa *n-redup* pile of wood

ocágaške *n* enclosure

ocágu *n* road, street

ocágu ceskámaza *cp* highway patrol

ocágu gaȟ'ú *cp* grader

ocágu įštámniğe *cp* trail of tears (refers to the hardships that occurred during the relocation of the Western Nakoda in eastern Saskatchewan after the Cypress Hills massacre of 1873)

ocágu waká *cp* Canada/USA border; medicine line *Lit:* mysterious road

ocágugağa *n* road builder

ocáguȟe *n* gravel road

ocáguna *n* path, trail

ocágusaba *n* 1) paved road 2) drunkenness *Lit:* black road

ocáguša *n* sobriety *Lit:* red road

ocágutąga *n* highway

ocá'įyukse *n* sawmill *Syn:* **ocánakseyabi**

ocánakseyabi *n* sawmill *Syn:* **ocá'įyukse**

océsni *vi1* s/he defecates in smth 1s: **owácesni** ; **océwasni** 2s: **oyácesni** ; **océyasni** *Vredup:* **océsnisni**

océsni tíbi *cp* outhouse

océsnisni *vi1-redyp* s/he/it (child, small animal) defecates in smth

océti *n* 1) fireplace, hearth 2) stove, oven ‣ **Océti gakná nawáži.** I am standing beside the stove. ‣ **Océti natága!** Turn the stove off! 3) heater *vi1* 4) s/he lights up a stove; cooks on top of a stove 1s: **owáceti** ; **océwati** 2s: **oyáceti** ; **océwati**

océti awáyaga *cp* firekeeper

océti waká *cp* microwave *Lit:* mysterious oven

océyA *vt1* s/he cries for smth sb has 1s: **owáceya** 2s: **oyáceya**

ocógą *adv* in the center, middle ‣ **Ocógą nážibi.** They stand in the middle.

ódA *quant* 1) a lot, many, much ‣ **Hékta wanágaš mázaska óda yuhábiši.** Long ago they did not have a lot of money. ‣ **Micíkši óda ųspékta.** My son will learn a lot. *vs* 2) it is a lot; there are many *Usage:* used with 3rd person subjects only. ‣ **Šųkcúk'ana nén ódabi.** There are many coyotes here. ‣ **Wįcóyazą óda.** There are a lot of ailments. ‣ **Hékta naháȟ pté óda žehą.** There was still a lot of buffalo in the past. *Vcoll:* **wįcódabi**

odásagA *vs* it is frozen inside, on smth

o'écų *n* manner, style of doing smth

o'écųna *Variant:* **o'écųna tíbi** *n* gaming house, casino ‣ **Dóhąni o'écųna tíbi ektám né wa'íši.** I never went to the casino.

o'ékne *n* countertop

o'énaži *n* town, station *Lit:* where people stop ‣ **O'énaži ektá mníkta.** I will go to town. ‣ **Įšnána o'énaži ektá í.** She went to town alone. *Syn:* **ti'óda**

o'éti *n* campground, camp site

o'étibi *n* powwow *Syn:* **ogáğe wacíbi**

ogábodA *vi* s/he/it floats on water 1s: **omágaboda** 2s: **onígaboda** *Vcont:* **ogábon** *See:* **agábodA**

ogábon *vcont* floating on water ‣ **Ogábon iyáya.** It was floating by. ‣ **'Ogábon ų.** It is floating around.

ogádą *vt1* s/he nails smth; pounds a nail in 1s: **owágadą** 2s: **oyágadą**

ogáğe₁ *vt1* s/he gathers smth in it (as when one picks up dust after sweeping)

ogáğe₂ *n* make of smth, manner, style *Cont:* **ogáȟ**

ogáğe wacíbi *cp* powwow *Syn:* **o'étibi**

ogáȟ *vcont* making ‣ **Gamúbina ogáȟ iyéya.** He quickly made a little drum. (Weasel 2:39)

ogáȟ síjA *vs* it is hard to make ‣ **Cuwíknąga ogáȟ síja.** A shirt is hard to make.

ogáȟ wašté *vs* it is easy to make

ogáȟci *n* fringes ‣ **Ogáȟci óda.** There are a lot of fringes. *See:* **gaȟcíȟci**

ogáȟniǧA *vt1* s/he understands sb, smth ‣ **Oyágaȟniǧa he?—Hą́, owágaȟniǧe no.** Do you understand?—Yes, I understand. ‣ **Owágaȟniǧa duká iwá'ešį.** I understand it, but I do not speak it. *1s:* **owágaȟniǧa** *2s:* **oyágaȟniǧa** *1p:* **ųgógaȟniǧabi**

ogáȟnoga *vs* s/he/it is soaked in water; is wet ‣ **Tągán ogáȟnoga.** It is wet outside. ‣ **Tągán wa'ų́ cén maǧážu cén omą́gaȟnoga.** I was outside and it rained so I am wet. ‣ **Žécųbi žé ogáȟnoga amą́ǧažu eštá yužážabi dóhąni sagéšį sudášį.** By doing this it never dries out and gets hard in rain or washing. (Drummond 1976, Smoking hides) *1s:* **omą́gaȟnoga** *2s:* **oníǧaȟnoga** *Vcaus:* **ogáȟnokyA** *Vcont:* **ogáȟnok**

ogáȟnok *vcont* soaked in water

ogáȟnokkiyA *vt1-pos* s/he wets his/her own (boots, shoes, coat) ‣ **Dágucen hą́ba ogáȟnokyagiya?** Why did you wet your shoes? *1s:* **ogáȟnokwagiya** *2s:* **ogáȟnokyagiya**

ogáȟnokyA *vt1-caus* s/he gets smth wet (as shoes in a puddle) ‣ **Hą́ba né ogáȟnokwagiya.** I got my shoes wet. *Vpos:* **ogáȟnokkiyA** *Vrefl:* **ogáȟnok'ic'iyA**

ogáȟnok'ic'iyA *vi3-refl* s/he gets himself/herself wet *1s:* **ogáȟnok-mic'iya** *2s:* **ogáȟnok-nic'iya**

ogáȟtąyą *vs* it is easy to make

ogánA *vt1* s/he empties, pours smth (like ashes) down there ‣ **Aǧúyabi mnúna žé wahíyoknąga žén ogánabi.** The flour is in (poured into) the jar. (Cumberland 2005:256)

ogápsija *n* piece struck off

ogáptA *vt1* s/he ladles, dips smth out of it

ogáska *vs* s/he/it is curdled, matted ‣ [...] **iyúha baǧé kó ogáskac.** [...] it was all bunched up and matted. (Shields 65:277)

ogásni *vs* 1) it is a draft of air *n* 2) draft of air

ogáštą *vt1* s/he pours smth in it ‣ **Waskúya én ogáštą.** She poured juice in it. ‣ **Céǧa žén miní ogáštą.** Add water into the pot.

ogáwįȟ *adv* traveling around

ogáwįȟ ų́ *vii* s/he travels all over

ogíbaǧe *vt1-dat* s/he fills a pipe for sb; gives sb a smoke ‣ **Omágibaǧe wo.** Give me a smoke.

ogíbemni *vt1-pos* s/he wraps his/her own with it *1s:* **owébemni** *2s:* **oyébemni**

ogícic'ubi *vt1-recip* they pass, lend sb, smth to one another ‣ **Wašpáyąbi šką́wųga ogícic'ubi.** They busily cooked him up and passed him around. (Weasel 219:162)

ogícikopabi *vii-recip* they fear one another

ógiciyabi *vii-recip* they help each other ‣ **Owá ógiciyabi.** They all cooperate. ‣ **Wįcášta ógicizabįšį žená ógiciyabi.** These peaceful people help one another. *1p:* **ųgógiciyabi**

ogíciyagabi *vii-recip* they tell smth about one another

ogíciza *Variant:* **ogícizabi, ogícize** *n* war, battle ‣ **Ogíciza gicúnįkta wacégiyabi.** They pray for the war to stop. ‣ **Ogícize nén wįcášta wąží ta'óbi.** A man was wounded in this war. *See:* **zuyÁ**

ogíciza mniwáda *cp* battleship

Ogíciza wakpá *ngeo* Battleford River (Saskatchewan)

ogícize maká agą́ wáda *ph* tank

ogícuni *n* end of smth, closing

ogícuni onówą *cp* closing song

ógiǧe *vt1-pos* s/he covers his/her own with it ‣ **Cąwába néca, cąhá néca sihá ogíǧe.** He wrapped pine bark around his feet. (Shields 13:161) *1s:* **ówagiǧe** *2s:* **óyagiǧe**

ogíhą *vt1-pos* s/he wears his/her own footwear ‣ **Hą́ba ogíhą.** Get your shoes on. *1s:* **owéhą** *2s:* **oyéhą**

ogíhi *vt1-aux* s/he can, is able to do smth ‣ **Wacó'ųbabi ogíhišį.** She cannot cook. ‣ **Waną́ǧaš ecámų owágihi.** Long ago I was able to do it. ‣ **Waná maní ogíhibišį.** Now they are not able to walk. *1s:* **owágihi** *2s:* **oyágihi**

ógi'įc'iyA *vi3-refl* s/he helps himself/herself *1s:* **ógimįc'iya** *2s:* **óginįc'iya**

ogíjibağe *vt1-benef* s/he fills a pipe for sb *1s:* **owéjibağe** *2s:* **oyéjibağe**

ogíjibazą *vt1-benef* s/he sticks, inserts smth in it for him/her *1s:* **owéjibazą** *2s:* **oyéjibazą**

ogíjibemni *vt1-benef* s/he wraps sb, smth for sb in it ‣ **Dáguškina žé owéjibemnįkta.** I will wrap up the baby for her. *1s:* **owéjibemni** *2s:* **oyéjibemni**

ogíjigini *vt1-benef* s/he earns, gets smth for sb *1s:* **owéjigini** *2s:* **oyéjigini**

ogíjiȟįyą *vt1-benef* s/he regrets smth; is sorry about smth ‣ **Né mnéšį cén omíjiȟįyą.** I am sorry I did not go.

ogíjikmA *vt1-benef* s/he writes smth for sb ‣ **Wįcášta owįcawejikma.** I write it for the people. ‣ **Wa'óyabi né Nakón wįcášta ųgógijikmabi.** We wrote this book for the Nakoda people. *1s:* **owéjikma** *2s:* **oyéjikma** *1p:* **ųgógijikmabi**

ogíjiknągA *vt1-benef* s/he puts, stores smth away in it for sb

ogíjikšu *vt1-benef* s/he plants smth (plants, garden) for sb ‣ **Iná owéjikšu.** I plant it for my mother. ‣ **Amánibi né anúk įš dokédu omíyejikšu.** Plant both sides of this path over here for me in the same way. (Weasel 12:87) *1s:* **owéjikšu** *2s:* **oyéjikšu**

ogíjine *vt1-benef* s/he hunts for sb ‣ **Mikúši owéjine.** I hunt for my grandmother. *1s:* **owéjine** *2s:* **oyéjine** *See:* **oné**

ogíjinoda *vt1-benef* s/he borrows, rents smth for sb else ‣ **Mázaska omíjinoda.** He borrowed money for me. ‣ **Ųjí tacéğa táwa žé omíjinoda.** Borrow my grandmother's kettle. (NS 2002:44–45) *1s:* **owéjinoda** *2s:* **oyéjinoda** *See:* **onóda**

ogíjiyagA *vt1-benef* s/he tells smth to sb; tells smth for sb else ‣ **Omíjiyagawo!** Tell me! ‣ **Misúgabi owįcawejimnaga.** I told it to him on my younger brothers' behalf. ‣ **Dágu nówa owįcawejimnagįkta.** I will tell them everything. ‣ **Dágu omíjiyage anáwaȟma.** He told me something I kept as a secret. ‣ **Į́hiyų pağųda! Gúwam dágu wąží ocíjimnagabįkta.** Hey ducks! Come here, I want to tell you one thing. (Drummond 1976, Įktomi and the ducks) *1s:* **owéjimnaga** *2s:* **oyéjinaga**

ogíjiziba *vt1-benef* s/he puts up a tent for sb

ogíkmA *vt1-pos* 1) s/he writes, signs his/her own (book, name) ‣ **Micáže žé owágikmakta.** I will sign my own name. *vt1-dat* 2) s/he writes smth to, for sb ‣ **Wa'óyabi miyé owékma.** I wrote my own book. *1s:* **owágikma ; owékma** *2s:* **oyágikma ; oyékma**

ogíknągA *vt1-pos* 1) s/he puts, stores his/her own thing away in it ‣ **Iyúhana ogíknąga.** She put it all together in hers. *n* 2) bag

ogíkšu *vt1-pos* s/he plants his/her own (garden) *1s:* **owékšu** *2s:* **oyékšu**

ogíne *vt1-pos* s/he looks for his/her own ‣ **Nécen nitákona ogíne yá wo.** So go look for your friend. (NS 2002:14)

ogíni *vt1* s/he earns money, gets smth ‣ **Wóyude ogínibišį.** He did not get much food. ‣ **Mázaska dóba owágini.** I earned four dollars. ‣ **Wóyude edáhą mnuhá owágini?** Can I get some food? ‣ **Dágu wóda ogínibigen.** They can go without eating anything. (NS 2002:34) *1s:* **owágini** *2s:* **oyágini** *Vbenef:* **ogíjigini**

ogínoda *vt1-dat* s/he borrows, rents smth from sb ‣ **Adé owáginoda.** I borrowed it from my father. ‣ **Šúgatąga owįcawejinoda.** I borrowed their horses. *1s:* **owáginoda** *2s:* **oyáginoda** *See:* **onóda**

ogípi *vs-dat* s/he fits in there; is large enough (shoes, pants) ‣ **Néš ogípi.** This one, on the other hand, fits him ‣ **Hą́ba žená omágipi.** These shoes fit me. *1s:* **omágipi** *2s:* **onįgipi.**

ógiyA *vt1-dat* s/he helps sb ‣ **Dóken ócijiyįkta?** How can I help you? ‣ **Tugášina ómagiya wo.** Grandfather, help me. ‣ **Ówįcagiyabi cíga.** She wants to help people. ‣ **Mihų́ nakų mitų́wi įš wašpą́yąbi ógiyabi.** My mother and my aunt helped her cook. ‣ **Wagíyą ȟubáhu máza ówagiya.** I helped the iron-winged thunderbird. *1s:* **ówagiya** *2s:* **óyagiya** *1p:* **ųgógiyabi** *Vcoll:* **ówįcagiyA** *Vrecip:* **ógiciyA** *Vrefl:* **ógi'įc'iyA**

ógiyabi *n* helper

ogíyagA *vt1-dat* s/he tells smth to sb *1s:* **owágiya** *2s:* **oyágiya** *1p:* **ųgógiyabi** *Vcont:* **ogíyak**

ogíyak *vcont-dat* telling smth to sb

ógiyes'a *n* servant, assistant ‣ **adé Wakątąga ógiyes'a** the Lord's servant ‣ **wįcá ógiyes'a** mentor

ogíziba *vt1-pos* s/he puts up his/her own tent

ogíyĄ *vi1* s/he/it soars, flies about *Adv:* **ogíyągen**

ogíyągen *adv* flying about, flying around ‣ **Ogíyągen ų́.** He is flying around.

óǧe *vt1* s/he wraps, covers smth up with it ‣ **Ómaǧe!** Cover me up! *1s:* **ówaǧe** *2s:* **óyaǧe** *Vpos:* **ógiǧe**

oǧų́ǧA *vs* 1) s/he/it is awake ‣ **Duwé oǧų́ǧešį.** People are not awake. 2) s/he wakes up ‣ **Dágúškina oǧų́ǧįkta wací.** The baby is about to wake up. ‣ **Éstena oǧų́ǧa.** She wakes up early. ‣ **Įknúhana oǧų́ǧac.** All of a sudden he woke up. *1s:* **omáǧųǧa** *2s:* **oníǧųǧa** *1p:* **ųgóǧųǧabi**

ohá *interj* expression of surprise used in storytelling (female speaker)

ohágapa *n* 1) youngest-born child in a family *vs* 2) s/he is the youngest-born child in a family ‣ **Hokšína ohágapa.** He is the youngest boy.

óhą *post* among, in the middle, in it ‣ **Óhą hí.** He arrives in the middle. ‣ **Gábina óhą ecágen yįgá.** He always sits among the elders. ‣ **Šóda óhą yįgá.** He is sitting in the smoke.

ohÁ *vt1* s/he cooks smth by boiling ‣ **O'ápe šákpe ohá.** Boil it for six hours. ‣ **Iná pasú agástaga ohá žé nína tągáȟtiyą.** The turkey my mother boiled is very big. *Vabs:* **wóhĄ**

ohÁ *vt1* s/he wears a shoe *1s:* **owáhą** *2s:* **oyáhą** *1p:* **ųgóhąbi** *Vpos:* **ogíhĄ**

ohídigA *vi1* 1) s/he is brave, fearless ‣ **Agícida žé nína ohídiga.** That soldier is very brave. *1s:* **owáhidiga** *2s:* **oyáhidiga** *vs* 2) s/he is a wealthy, prosperous person *Vrefl:* **ohídiga įc'ína**

ohídiga ecų́ *cp* war deed

ohídiga įc'ína *vi3-refl* s/he thinks of herself/himself as brave, fearless *1s:* **ohídiga mįc'ína** *2s:* **ohídiga nįc'ína** *1p:* **ohídiga ųgíc'ína**

ohíyA *vt1* s/he wins smth (game, contest, battle) ‣ **Owáhiya!** Bingo! ‣ **Ogícizabi žé ohíyešį.** He did not win the battle. ‣ **Ohíya štén nína waštékta.** If he wins something it will be very good. *1s:* **owáhiya** *2s:* **oyáhiya** *1p:* **ųgóhiyabi**

ohíyabi *n* prize ‣ **togáhe ohíyabi** first prize *Syn:* **wo'óhiya**

ohíyes'a *n* winner

ohį́ȟpayA *vs* s/he/it falls off smth *1s:* **omáhįȟpaya** *2s:* **onį́hįȟpaya**

ohógicinabi *vi1-recip* they respect one another ‣ **Wanągaš dąyą́ iyúha ohógicinabįkta.** Long ago they would all respect one another.

ohóna *vt1* s/he respects, honors sb *Vrecip:* **ohógicinabi**

ohų́ȟnaǧa *vs* it burns inside (like a barrel of rubbish) *Vcaus:* **ohų́ȟnaȟYA**

ohų́ȟnaȟYA *vt1-caus* s/he burns smth inside (as in a barrel) *1s:* **ohų́ȟnaȟwaya** *2s:* **ohų́ȟnaȟyaya** *1p:* **ohų́ȟnaȟ'ųyabi**

ohúgaǧą *n* legend, fable

oȟnáte *adv* between ‣ **Cą́ žé oȟnáte éknąga.** Put that stick in between. ‣ **Aǧúyabi oȟnáte yįgá.** It is between slices of bread.

oȟnáte co'úbabi *cp* pie *Lit:* baked in between ‣ **taspą́ oȟnáte co'úbabi** apple pie ‣ **tanó oȟnáte**

co'**ųbabi** meat pie ‣ c**įkta oh̃náte co'ųbabi** raisin pie

o**h̃ní** vs it is dirty inside ‣ **Iyógapte oh̃ní žená bah̃pú.** Scrape those dirty plates. (Fourstar p. 8)

o**h̃nóga** n 1) hole ‣ **Oh̃nóga žé mahédu'.** The hole is deep. vs 2) it is a hole in smth ‣ **ųzóh̃noga** anus, rectum

o**h̃nóh̃nogA** vimp-redup it is full of holes

o**h̃ónageje** interj holy smokes Usage: expression of surprise for someone who has accomplished a great deed. ‣ **Oh̃ónageje! Né akída!** Holy smokes! Check this out!

o**h̃páyA** vs s/he is sad, lonely ‣ **Dóhąnih̃ omáh̃payešį.** I am never sad. 1s: **omáh̃paya** 2s: **oníh̃paya** 1p: **ųgóh̃payabi**

o**h̃péyA** vt1 s/he throws smth in it

oh̃'**ą** n action, behavior, habit, manner ‣ **Oh̃'ą wašté.** Be nice.

oh̃'**ąge** vs 1) s/he behaves, acts as such (as when joining a group) ‣ **Sijáya omáh̃'ąge.** I have bad habits. ‣ **Žécen dóken oh̃'ągekta žé, owá ogíjiyagabi.** So then told him all about what to do. (Shields 75:387) 1s: **omáh̃'ąge** 2s: **oníh̃'ąge** n 2) character, behavior See: **h̃'ą, oh̃'ą**

oh̃'**ągesijA** vs s/he behaves badly 1s: **oh̃'ągemasija** 2s: **oh̃'ągenisija**

oh̃'**ągewašte** vs s/he behaves well 1s: **oh̃'ągewawašte** 2s: **oh̃'ągeyawašte**

oh̃'**ąko** vs s/he is swift, fast ‣ **Paul né oh̃'ąko.** That Paul is very fast. ‣ **Nína oníh̃'ąko.** You are very fast. 1s: **omáh̃'ąko** 2s: **oníh̃'ąko** 1p: **ųgóh̃'ąkobi** Vredup: **oh̃'ąkoko**

oh̃'**ąkoko** vs-redup s/he/it is very fast, swift ‣ **Šųgattąga núm oh̃'ąkokobic wįcáyuha huštá.** The young man had two fast horses, it is said. (Shields 4:48)

oh̃'**ąpi** vs s/he is generous 1s: **omáh̃'ąpi** 2s: **oníh̃'ąpi**

oh̃'**ąsijA** vs s/he is stingy 1s: **oh̃'ąmasija** 2s: **oh̃'ąnisija**

o'**į** n beads ‣ **O'į mnayą.** Collect the beads.

o'**íyoh̃peyA** vt1-caus s/he throws smth in it 1s: **o'íyoh̃pewaya** 2s: **o'íyoh̃peyaya**

o'**įc'ibemni** ; o'**įkpemni** vi3-refl s/he wraps himself/herself in smth ‣ **Šiná omįc'ibemni.** I wrap myself in a blanket. 1s: **omįc'ibemni** ; **omįkpemni** 2s: **onįc'ibemni** ; **onįkpemni**

o'**įc'icuwa** vi3-refl s/he gets himself/herself ready ‣ **Hí híkna o'įc'icuwa.** He arrived and got himself ready. 1s: **omįc'icuwa** 2s: **onįc'icuwa**

o'**įc'ine** vi3-refl s/he looks for, seeks smth for himself/herself ‣ **Wacónįca ogápsija oné, o'įc'ine ųbihą.** They were looking for some dried meat for themselves. (Weasel 81:12)

o'**įhage** n end, conclusion (of a story)

o'**įh̃peya** n dump, nuisance ground ‣ **O'įh̃peya ektá mnįkta.** I am going to the dump.

o'**įjusina** n pony bead, small bead

o'**íknagA** vi3-refl s/he tells of himself/herself; makes himself/herself known 1s: **omíknaga** 2s: **onįknaga**

o'**įknuhena** n badger Lit: covers himself as he is digging along Syn: **h̃ogá**

o'**įknužaža** n 1) bathroom Lit: a place to wash oneself 2) washbasin, sink

o'**ípa** n tip, point of a shape

o'**ípa dóba** cp square Syn: **omnétų**

o'**ípa mįmą** cp circle

o'**ípa šaknóg̃ą** cp octagon

o'**ípa šákpe** cp hexagon

o'**ípa yámni** cp triangle

o'**įštima** vi3 1) s/he sleeps inside smth 1s: **omįštima** 2s: **onįštima** n 2) bed, bedroom

o'**įštima tíbi** cp hotel, motel

o'**įštimabi** n bed, room

o'**įštime síjA** vs it (bed, camp) is bad to sleep in

o'**įštime wašté** vs it (bed, camp) is good to sleep in ‣ **O'įštime wašté žé įyúta.** Try the comfortable bed.

ó'**įyahe** n ladder, stirrup

o'íyoȟpeya *vt1* s/he throws sb, smth in it ›
Miní nén o'íyoȟpeya. He threw it here in the
water. *1s:* **o'íyoȟpewaya** *2s:* **o'íyoȟpeyaya** *1p:*
o'íyoȟpe'ųya

okáda *vimp* it is hot inside *Adv:* **okánya** *See:*
ti'ókada

Ókalala *nprop* Oglala Lakota people

okánya *adv* being hot inside

oką́ *n* aisle, narrow path; vacant place › **Oká okná**
žé mawáni. I walk through the aisle.

okíknąge *adv* of all kinds, different kinds ›
Pağúda okíknąge iyúhą mniwóhą nųwą́bi cá
wąwį́cayaga. He saw all kinds of ducks swimming in the water. (Drummond 1976, Įktomi
and the ducks)

okínaží *vt1* s/he defies sb

okíse *n* half › **gašpábi okíse** dime › **hąwí okíse**
half moon

okíyA *vt1* s/he asks sb to do smth › **Dágu teȟíga**
onį́kiyįkta. He will ask you to do difficult
things. *1s:* **owákiya** *2s:* **oyákiya** *1p:* **ųgókiyabi**

okíyukse *n* canyon *Lit:* broken in two

okmÁ *vt1* s/he writes, draws smth; paints,
sketches sb, smth › **Né šá okmá.** Color it in
red. › **Wanágaš i'ábi né okmábišį.** Long ago
they did not write the language. › **Wa'óyabi**
wąží wašíju i'ábi oyákma oyágihi? Are you
able to write a letter in English? *1s:* **owákma**
2s: **oyákma** *1p:* **ųgókmabi** *Vabs:* **wa'ókmA ;**
wókmA *Vbenef:* **ogíjikmA** *Vpos:* **ogíkmA**

okmábi *n* color, mark, written production, writing process › **Dukté okmábi waštéyana?** What
color do you like? › **Okmábi žé John ecų́.** John
did the writing. › **há okmábi** birthmark, tattoo

okmátoto *n-pl* crayons

okná *post* in, through › **Cą'í̧tkų okná éknąga.**
He put it in the fire. › **Oką́ okná žé mawáni.** I
walk through the aisle. › **Ti'óba žé okná tągán**
yá. He goes out through the door. › **Į'ákide**
okná wąmnága. I saw it through a telescope.

oknágA *vt1-pos* 1) s/he tells his/her own

(story, news) 2) s/he confesses his/her own
› **Wówaȟtani oknágabi.** They confess their
sins. *Vrefl:* **o'í̧knagA**

oknápšį yįgÁ *vi3* s/he lays on the stomach

oknápšįyą *adv* 1) upside down 2) on the stomach
› **Oknápšįyą ú.** He is upside down.

oknágA *vt1* s/he puts, stores smth away in it
Vbenef: **ogíjiknąga** *Vpos:* **ogíknąga**

ókne *n* 1) coat › **ókneša** Royal Canadian Mounted
Police 2) sleeve › **Ókne mitáwa žé kuká.** My
sleeve is raggy.

oknécona *n* sleeveless vest

ókneša *n* Royal Canadian Mounted Police,
mounties *Lit:* red coat *Syn:* **cuwíknąga šašábi**

oknútątą *vt1-pos-redup* s/he feels inside of his/
her own

okókona *adv* one after the other › **Okókona**
aktágabi. They ran one after the other.

okóna *adv* friendly

okónagiciyabi *vi1-recip* 1) they are friendly, associate with one another *n* 2) society, union,
association › **Okónagiciyabi opá.** He joins
the union. › **Wíyąbi heȟága okónagiciyabi**
Elk woman society

okónagiciye *n* society

okónayA *vt1-caus* s/he is friendly with sb *1s:*
okónawaya *2s:* **okónayaya** *Vabs:* **wakónayA**

okópa *vi1* s/he is fearful, uneasy *Usage:* archaic
word. *1s:* **owákopa** *2s:* **oyákopa** *Vrecip:*
ogícikopabi

okpápsų *vt1-pos* s/he spills his/her liquid on
himself/herself

okpúktą *vt1-pos* s/he dips smth in his/her own
1s: **owákpuktą** *2s:* **oyákpuktą**

ókšą *adv* around › **Ókšą ų́bi.** They are all around.
› **Ókšą nén waká cá no!** Everything around
here is sacred! › **Ókšą akídabi ųká duwénišį.**
They looked around but there was no one. ›
Duwé iyúhana nén ókšą iyódąga bo. Every-
body sit around here. *Redup:* **ókšąkšą**

ókšądahą *adv* from all around › **Omnábi cen**

ókšadahą a'ógas'į:gabi. They had smelled him and were peeking in from all around. (Weasel 5:90)

ókšąkšą *adv-redup* all around ▸ **Ókšąkšą éduwą:ga.** He is looking all around.

okšú *vt1* s/he plants smth (seed, plant, crop) ▸ **Miyéȟ owákšu.** I planted it by myself specifically. *1s:* **owákšu** *2s:* **oyákšu** *Vabs:* **wókšu** *Vbenef:* **ogíjikšu** *Vpos:* **ogíkšu**

oktégiyA *Variant:* **otkégiyA** *vt1-pos* s/he hangs, suspends her/his own (clothes, meat) ▸ **Cąknągiyą žén tanó oktégiya.** She dried her meat there on the drying rack. *1s:* **oktéwagiya** *2s:* **oktéyagiya** *1p:* **okté'ųgiyabi**

okté'įc'iyA *Variant:* **otké'įc'iyA** *vi1-refl* s/he hangs, suspends himself/herself ▸ **ȟubá wagíknągagana cą́ én otké'įc'iyabi.** Bats hang themselves on a branch. *1s:* **otkémįc'iya** *2s:* **otkénįc'iya** *1p:* **okté'ųgįc'iyabi**

oktéyA *Variant:* **otkéyA** *vt1-caus* s/he hangs up, suspends smth ▸ **Oktéya hį́kna gabúsya.** Hang it and let it dry. *1s:* **oktéwaya ; otkéwaya** *2s:* **oktéyaya ; otkéyaya** *1p:* **okté'ųyabi ; otké'ųyabi** *Vpos:* **oktégiyA ; otkégiyA** *Vrefl:* **otké'įc'iyA ; okté'įc'iyA**

okúwašte ; okúwawašte *vs* it (animal) is tamed ▸ **Šų́ga žé okúwašte.** That dog is tamed.

ok'į́ *n* ton, a full load ▸ **ok'į́wąží** one ton

ok'į́wąži *n* bundle packed on the back

ok'ú *vt1* 1) s/he lends smth to sb ▸ **Iná amógiyą omák'u.** Mom, lend me the car. 2) s/he shares smth with sb ▸ **Piyéšį ok'úšį kó.** He was not good, he did not even share. (Cumberland 2005:433) *1s:* **owák'u** *2s:* **oyák'u** *Vrecip:* **ogícic'ubi**

óm *post* with them ▸ **Óm mawáni.** I walk with them. ▸ **Aké wíyąbi žé óm ú.** She hangs out with those women again. ▸ **Ȟaȟátųwą óm ųk'ų́bis'a.** We used to live with the Gros Ventres. *See:* **gicí**

omá *Variant:* **ųmá ; umá** *pro* 1) one of two ▸ **Omá**

žé'e. It is the other one. ▸ **Omá žé énagu?** Did you pick the other one? ▸ **Omá Nakóda wíyą žé.** The other woman is Nakoda. ▸ **Omá wąyáge žé gicóbi.** The other witness was called. 2) the others ▸ **Ųmá žé mak'ú.** He gave me the others. ▸ **Ųmábi žé wįcágico!** Invite the others! *3p:* **omábi ; ųmábi**

omáğo *n* minute

omáğe *vt1* 1) s/he marks smth into it (with a sharp instrument, knife, or pencil) ▸ **Mitágoža wa'óyabi omáğe.** My grandson made a mark in the book. *1s:* **owámaǧe** *2s:* **oyámaǧe** *n* 2) mark (made with a knife or pencil)

Omáha wacíbi *cp* Omaha dance

omáȟkaǧe *n* field

ómaka ; omáka *n* year

omáka'esą *adv* throughout the year, all year

ómakateja ; omákateja *n* New Year's Day

omákawąži *adv* annually ▸ **Omákawąži amámneza.** I have my annual checkup. ▸ **omákawąži mas'úk'ubi** annual treaty day

omáksabi *n* slice *Syn:* **modápta**

omána *pro* just, only one

ománi *vi1* s/he goes for a walk, travels, wanders ▸ **Ocą́gu škašká omáwani.** I traveled on a crooked road. *1s:* **omáwani** *2s:* **omáyani** *Vredup:* **ománini**

ománini *vi1-redup* s/he walks around

omás'ape ; omás'apa *n* telegraph, telephone office

omágakiyadahą *adv* from the other side

omáȟ *pro* either one ▸ **Omáȟ mak'ú!** Give me either one! ▸ **Mitágoža wómįjic'um omáȟ.** One of you feed my son for me. (Weasel 113:55)

omáȟtįyą *pro* this one specifically ▸ **Omáȟtįyą žé cígabi.** They want this one specifically.

omáktam *adv* other side ▸ **Omáktam ecú.** Do it on the other side.

omémega *n-redup* different things; a variety of things *Morph:* omA.

omį́tokto *adv* back and forth; taking turns ‣ **"Miyé mayúd, miyé mayúd, miyé mayúda,"** eyá omį́tkokto eyás. "Eat me, eat me, eat me!" they were saying in turn, back and forth. (Weasel 47:281)

ómna *vt1* 1) s/he/it smells, sniffs sb, smth ‣ **Wahčá né ómna!** Smell this flower! ‣ **Dágu owámna.** I smell something. *1s:* **owámna** *2s:* **oyámna** *1p:* **ųgómnabi** *n* 2) smell ‣ **Ómna mak'ú wo.** Give me a smell (tobacco).

omnáwitąga *n* large flat area, large prairie

omnáyA *vimp* it is flat

omnáyena *n* small flat area

omnédu *adv* in the summer time

omnétų *n* 1) square *vs* 2) it is square *Syn:* **o'į́pa dóba**

omnézena *vimp* it is clear (liquid) ‣ **Wóguyą há cen eyáš omnézenah.** It was tempting and just wonderfully clear. (Weasel 134:313)

omní owópetų *cp* liquor store

omníhiyohi *n* watering place

omníjiye *n* meeting, gathering ‣ **Omníjiye žén cažé wak'ú.** I voted there in the meeting.

omníjiye tą́gą *cp* conference ‣ **Nągáhą omníjiye tą́gą yuhábi.** A conference is being held now.

omníyakte *n* bar, tavern ‣ **Omníyakte žé núba ehą́'i hą́da natágabi.** The bar closes at two o'clock.

omníyupsųna *n* bar, saloon

omókoge *n* pool room ‣ **Omókoge ektá yá.** He has gone to the pool room.

omówahįtų *n* co-parent-in-law *1s:* **omówahįtų** *2s:* **nitómowahįtų** *3s:* **tómowahįtų**

oná *n* prairie fire *Vcaus:* **onáyA**

onágasni *n* firefighter

onáhma *n* secret

onáhpa *vt1* s/he caves smth in, made a hole with the foot

onáh'ų *vt1* s/he hears about smth

onákoda *n* peace ‣ **Onákoda gága.** He made peace with her. ‣ **Onákoda gahwį́cakiya.** He made them make peace.

onákodagiciyabi *vi1-recip* they are in peace with one another

onákuwes'a *n* prairie or forest firefighter

onápA *vi1* s/he flees into smth *1s:* **onáwapa** *2s:* **onáyapa** *1p:* **oná'ųpabi**

onáyA *vt1-caus* s/he sets the prairie on fire *1s:* **onáwaya** *2s:* **onáyaya**

oné *vt1* s/he looks for smth; hunts ‣ **Owánįkta né.** I will look for it. ‣ **Wį́bazuką ųgónes.** Let us go search for Saskatoon berries. ‣ **Gakí tehą́da owáne no.** I looked for it way over there. ‣ **Minékši wa'óyabi okmé žé owáne.** I am looking for a book my uncle wrote. ‣ **Oyánįkta he?** Will you go hunting? *1s:* **owáne** *2s:* **oyáne** *1pl:* **ųgonebi** *Vabs:* **wóne** ; **wa'óne** *Vbenef:* **ogíjine** *Vpos:* **ogíne** *Vrefl:* **o'į́c'ine**

onéžA *vt1* s/he urinates on/in smth; pees in bed ‣ **Ową́ga onéžįkteš ̨ųspéwakiya.** I taught him not to urinate in bed. *1s:* **owáneža** *2s:* **oyáneža**

oní *n* life ‣ **wįcóni** human life, human ways, spirit, ghost

onį́kte wací *vi1* 1) s/he is meek, submissive ‣ **Tawį́ju onį́kte wací.** His wife is submissive. 2) s/he is a coward ‣ **Ehás onį́kte wací.** He is quite a coward.

onóda *vt1* s/he borrows, rents smth *1s:* **owánoda** *2s:* **oyánoda** *Vbenef:* **ogíjinoda** *Vdat:* **ogínoda**

onówą *n* song ‣ **Duwé onówą snokyá?** Who knows these songs? ‣ **Waną́gaš mitúgaši onówą nená ahíyayas'a.** Long ago my grandfather used to sing these songs.

onúde *n* thigh

onų́wą *n* pool, swimming pool

o'óknage *n* fable, tale

o'ókšąh *adv* all around the place ‣ **Há žécen o'ókšąh éduwą.** Ah, so then he looked all around the tent. (Weasel 166:83)

o'óna *n* opening ‣ **Pestóna né, o'óna nokná**

kniȟpáyįkta. The sharp end will go through the opening. (Weasel 49:326)

o'ópiyeda *n* pocket ‣ **O'ópiyeda yubáǧe.** He pulls it out of the pocket.

o'ósnohągic'ų *n* slide

o'óye *n* scar

ópA *vt1* s/he is part of smth; joins, qualifies for smth (games, contest) ‣ **Micį́kši ópa ogíhišį.** My son cannot qualify. ‣ **Agícida owápįkte no!** I will join the army! ‣ **Ocáže owácegiye ocáže nówa įš én nągáhą ópabi cén.** Today they join all different kinds of churches. (NS 2002:5) *1s:* **owápa** *2s:* **oyápa** *1p:* **o'ų́pabi** *Adv:* **opáya**

opágiȟtA *vt1-pos* s/he ties, packs his/her own thing into a bundle ‣ **Dágu nówa opágiȟta cén.** So she tied all of her things into a bundle.

opáȟtA *vt1* s/he ties, packs smth into a bundle; ties smth in it *Vpos:* **opágiȟtA**

opáya *adv* 1) through, along, following the course of smth ‣ **Ocágu žé opáya yá.** Follow the road. 2) in, through a valley, coulee ‣ **Opáya hokún ma'ų́nibi.** We walked down the valley.

opégijitų *vt1-benef* s/he buys smth for sb ‣ **Wa'óyabi opémijitų.** Buy me a book. ‣ **Šųkcíjana wąží opégijitų.** She bought a puppy for her. ‣ **Amógįyą opécijitų.** I will buy you a car. ‣ **Dágu nowá opéwįcawejitų.** I bought stuff for them. *1s:* **opéwejitų** *2s:* **opéyejitų**

opégitų *vt1-dat* s/he buys smth from sb *1s:* **opéwagitų** *2s:* **opéyagitų**

opégitų tíbi *cp* trading post *Syn:* **Wašíju opégitųbi**

opéšį *vi1* s/he is disqualified *Vcaus:* **opéšį kiyÁ** *See:* **ópA**

opéšį kiyÁ *vt1-caus* s/he disqualifies sb *1s:* **opéšį wakíya** *2s:* **opéšį yakíya** *1p:* **opéšį ųkíyabi**

opétų *vt1* s/he buys, purchases smth ‣ **Hųská né duktén opéyatų he?** Where did you buy these pants? ‣ **Hokúwa wa'óyabi opétųbikta.** They must buy a fishing permit. *1s:* **opéwatų**

2s: **opéyatų** *1p:* **opé'ųtųbi** *Vbenef:* **opégijitų** *Vdat:* **opégitų**

opí'įc'iyA *vi3-refl* s/he behaves, occupies himself/herself ‣ **Dąyą́ opí'įc'iya štén iyómagipi.** If he behaves well I will be happy about it. *1s:* **opím'įc'iya** *2s:* **opín'įc'iya** *1p:* **opí'ųgįc'iyabi**

opšíja *n* mud ‣ **Opšíja awágana.** I am spreading mud on it. ‣ **Amúgiya mitáwa žé opšíja ožúna.** My car is full of mud inside.

opšíja gamóta *vimp* there is a dust storm

opšíje tíbi *cp* mud house

ópta *adv* across ‣ **Ptéǧa ópta mná.** I went across the lake.

optéya *n* herd ‣ **Optéya awícakin yįgá.** He is watching the herd.

osą́gaga ; o'ósągaga *vs-redup* s/he is lonesome after sb leaves *Adv:* **osą́kya ; o'ósąkya**

osą́kkna *vi1* s/he feels lonely *1s:* **osą́kwakna** *2s:* **osą́kyakna**

osą́kya ; o'ósąkya *adv* lonely, in a lonesome way ‣ **O'ósąkya mawáni.** I am walking on my own.

óska *vt1* s/he decorates smth (outfit, rawhide) with porcupine quills *Vabs:* **wóska**

óskabi *vs-pass* it is quilted

osmága *n* 1) coulee 2) crease *Cont:* **osmą́k** *Vcaus:* **osmą́kkiyA**

osmą́k *cont* crease

osmą́kkiyA *vt1-caus* s/he makes a crease on smth (pants, skirt) ‣ **Sąksą́ja osmą́kwakiya.** I made a crease on the skirt. *1s:* **osmą́kwakiya** *2s:* **osmą́kyakiya** *1p:* **osmą́kųkiyabi**

osní *vimp* it is cold weather ‣ **Osní áya.** It is getting cold. ‣ **Tągán osní he?** Is it cold outside? ‣ **Osnį́kta ca.** I guess it will be cold. *Vredup:* **osnísni**

osní núba *cp* person or animal that is two years old

osní wąžína *cp* yearling (calf)

Osníbi wįcášta *nprop* People of the cold (Stoney band)

osnídahą *adv* from, because of the cold ‣ **Osnídahą maȟmá.** I am sleepy because of the cold.

osníhąba *n* overshoes

osníkna *vi1* s/he/it feels cold *1s:* **osníwakna** *2s:* **osníyakna** *1p:* **osní'ųknabi**

osnísni *vimp-redup* it is very cold weather ‣ **Waní ų́ gáki hą́da osnísnis'a.** He wintered over there, and it was usually very cold.

osnóhą *vs* s/he/it slides

osnókyA *Variant:* **osnóhyA** *vt1* s/he understands smth; is knowledgeable about smth ‣ **Osnóhya wacíga.** I want to understand it. ‣ **Waná, waníyedu osnókyabi hą́da Nakóda né įc'ícuwabi.** Now, the Nakoda people knew about winter and how to care for themselves. *1s:* **osnókwaya** ; **osnóhwaya** *2s:* **osnókyaya** ; **osnóhyaya** *1p:* **osnók'ųyabi**

osódA *vi-coll* they are all gone *See:* **ti'ósoda**

ošá *vs* s/he/it is red inside *Vredup:* **ošáša**

ošágiyA *vt1-pos* s/he paints his/her own red inside ‣ **Žécen í né'įš ošágiyabi.** Then they also painted their lips [mouth] red. (Shields 9:115)

ošáša *vs-redup-pl* they are red inside ‣ **Įštá oníšaša no.** You have red eyes.

ošíjejA *vimp* there is a storm; it is stormy weather ‣ **Ošíjejįšį no.** It is not stormy. ‣ **Ošíjeja tagą́n hą́da, timáhen wa'ų́ jé.** Whenever there is a storm outside I always stay inside.

oškádA *vi1* 1) s/he plays inside of smth *n* 2) playground

oškáde *n* 1) picnic 2) festival 3) arena

oškáde tíbi *cp* gymnasium

ošką́šijA *vs* s/he feels uneasy, uncomfortable *1s:* **omą́škašija** *2s:* **oníškašija** *Vcaus:* **ošką́šinyA**

ošką́šinyA *vt1-caus* s/he makes sb feel uneasy, uncomfortable *1s:* **ošką́šinwaya** *2s:* **ošką́šinyaya**

oškíška *vs* it is rough, bumpy

ošódA *vs* 1) it is smoky (room, atmosphere) *n* 2) smoke from a chimney

ošódemna *vs* s/he/it smells like smoke ‣ **Dágu né ošódemna.** This thing smells like smoke.

ošpáye *n* divisions, parts of smth ‣ **ą́ba ošpáye** divisions of the day

oštéga *vs* s/he/it is peculiar, odd, weird ‣ **Wįcá žé oštéga.** That man is odd. *1s:* **omą́štega** *2s:* **oníštega**

oštéȟ'ąge *vs* s/he/it is acting strange ‣ **"Há né dágu cén né oštéȟ'ąge no,"** eyá. "Ah! This thing is acting strange," he said. (NS 2002:56)

oštéšte *adv* strangely ‣ **Gá tą́kuna né oštéšte oȟ'ą́ge:ga.** The older sister was behaving strangely. (NS 2002:20)

ošų́kminik'u *n* watering hole for horses, cattle

ošų́kyuze *n* corral

ot'Á *vs* s/he dies in, inside of (house, water)

otágipA *vt1-pos* s/he follows, pursues his/her own

otámškadabi *n* baseball diamond

otápA *vt1* s/he follows, pursues sb, smth ‣ **Táȟca otáwapa.** I followed the deer. ‣ **Honágina dókiya cén otápabi.** Flies follow him wherever he goes. (BigEagle 2019:8) ‣ **[. . .] waná sųgágu giktékta cén otápa.** [. . .] now she was going to kill her younger brother so she followed him. (NS 2002:24) *1s:* **otáwapa**; **otá'ųpabi** *2s:* **otáyapa** *Vpos:* **otágipA**

otážošA *vt1* 1) s/he spits into smth *1s:* **owátožaša** *2s:* **oyatažoša** *n* 2) spittoon

otągA *vs* it is broad, large

ótąna *adv* straight, in a straight manner, in a respectable way ‣ **Ótąna máni.** He is walking straight. ‣ **Ótąnaȟ máni wo!** Walk in the straightest way possible! (Be a good, respectable person!) ‣ **Hú ótąna yįgá.** Sit with your legs straight in front.

otéhągeȟ *adv* a while longer ‣ **Otéhągeȟ kní, dóbaȟ kní [. . .]** He returned after a while, he returned four times [. . .] (NS 2002:30)

otéȟigA *vs* 1) it is difficult, hard, problematic, sad ‣ **Dágu nówa otéȟiga ecų́kta šką́šį.** He did not try to solve all of the problems. ‣ **Né wįcóyazą né otéȟiga.** This pandemic is difficult. *n* 2) problem, trouble

otémni *vt1* s/he sweats on sb, smth

otémni'įc'iyA *vi3-refl* s/he makes himself/herself sweat in smth (as in a heavy coat) *1s:* **otémnimįc'iya** *2s:* **otémninįc'iya**

otí *n* 1) dwelling *vi1* 2) s/he lives in a dwelling ‣ **Né tíbi né owáti.** I live in this house. ‣ **Tiwįcoda duká wąžína hųgá cá, witága otí, hųštá.** There were many families but only one was chief, so he lived in a large tipi, it is said. (Parks et al. 1994) *1s:* **owáti** *2s:* **oyáti** *1p:* **ųgótibi**

otígadodo *n* broom *Lit:* house brush

otí'įgA *Variant:* **otįgA ; otá'įgA** *part* it seems, I think, apparently *Usage:* this particle can occur with the negative enclitic -šį. ‣ **Adé ú otí'įga.** It seems like my father is coming. ‣ **Úbįkteší otí'įga.** It seems they will not come. ‣ **Šikná otí'įga.** He seems angry. ‣ **Dóken šikná otí'įga.** How angry he must be. ‣ **Úšigabi otí'įgeší.** I do not think they are poor.

otíyužaže *Variant:* **otíyužaža ą́ba** *n* Saturday *See:* **ą́ba yužáža ; ą́ba tiyúžaža ; wowį́cak'u ą́ba**

ot'į́ *vimp* 1) it is thundering ‣ **Ową́hįkna hį́kta né, ot'į́cuna cén.** Lightning came about and it kept on thundering. ‣ **ot'į́hįkna** there is a sudden thunderclap *n* 2) thunder

ot'į́ apÁ *vimp* it is a thunderclap *Lit:* thunder strikes *Syn:* **hoknį́kne**

otį́da *n* clearing, opening without trees, prairies

otóką *adv* differently, unusual ‣ **Otóką i'á.** He speaks differently.

otų́weda *n* abandoned campsite

otų́yą *vs* it (sore) has pus inside

otų́ye *Variant:* **otų́we** *n* city

o'ų́knaga *vi1-coll* they (family, group) move camp *Vcont:* **o'ų́knak**

o'ų́knak *vcont-coll* moving camp ‣ **Mnogédu cén o'ų́knak ú tuktápagiya yábi.** Since it was sum-mer, they packed up and moved somewhere. (Shields 58:199)

owá *quant* all (people, things); everybody ‣ **Owá ų́bi.** They are all wearing it. ‣ **Owá įštá kmúzabi.** They all blink. ‣ **Owá mnagíciyąbi.** People are grouped. ‣ **Owá dókaš dąyą́ ų́bįkta.** Everybody will prosper.

owábazo *n* circus

owábazoti *n* theater

owácegiya tíbi *cp* church

owácegiye ; owácegiya *n* church ‣ **Owácegiya íbi.** They went to church. ‣ **Ą́bawaką žehą́ owácegiya žéci wa'í.** I went to church on Sunday. ‣ **Owácegiye én ağúyabiwaką yúdabi.** They take communion bread in church. *Syn:* **owácegiya tíbi**

owáci *vi1* 1) s/he dances inside (building, hoop) *n* 2) dance ‣ **cą'ómima owáci** hoop dance

owácibi *n* dance hall, dance arbor

owádA *vs* 1) it is lit *n* 2) lights ‣ **Owáda žé yusní.** Turn off the lights. *Vcont:* **owán**

owádasakyabi *n* fridge

owáȟna'į *vs* it is loose, not steady

owákma *n* photograph

owákpamni ti'ų́ma *cp* servery

owán *vcont* lightning, lit up

owánaȟ'ųbi *n* radio

owán-hįknA ; ową́hįknA *vimp* 1) there is lightning *n* 2) lightning, electricity, flashlight ‣ **Ową́hįkna hį́kta né, ot'į́cuna cén.** Lightning came about, and it kept on thundering.

owániyedu *adv* in the winter time

owá'okma ; owó'okma *n* pencil, pen, chalk *Syn:* **įwá'okma ; įwó'okma ; įwókma**

owápiye *n* grave, cemetery

owášpąyąbi *n* kitchen

owášpąye *n* kitchen

owášte *adv* easy, easily

owášte yuhÁ *vi2* it is easy to have

owáštege *vs* s/he/it is the best ‣ **Tanó owáštege éca maksá.** He cut the best meat.

owáštegina *vt1* s/he is excited about smth ‣ **Úbįkta cén owáštegina.** They are coming so she is excited.

owášteȟ *adv* slowly, gently

owáštejaga *vimp* it is beautiful (day) *See:* **ąm'ówaštejaga**

owáštena *adv* slowly, carefully ‣ **Owáštena i'á.** Speak slowly. ‣ **Owáštenaȟ maní.** He is walking really carefully.

owáštenagen *adv* rather slowly

owáštenkina *adv* happily

owášten-kiyA *vt1* s/he enjoys, is happy about sb, smth

owáyaco *n* courthouse ‣ **Owáyaco ektá mnįkta.** I will go to court. *See:* **yacó**

owáyacotąga *n* supreme court

owáyawa ; wayáwa tíbi *n* school (the building) ‣ **Ábawaką gicúni štén, owáyawa mnįkta.** On Monday, I will go to school. ‣ **Wayáwa tíbi dóhąn inánįkta he?** When will you go to school? ‣ **Wįkóške nená wayáwa tíbi aktágabi.** These girls are running to school.

owáyawa otókšu *cp* school bus

owáyawatąga *n* high school

owáyušnoge *n* thresher

owáyužažabi *n* laundry

owážaža *n* washtub

ową *n* spot, place *Usage:* used in compounds. ‣ **cą'ówą** floor

ową́ga agáȟpabi *cp* bedcover

ową́ga (CTK) *Variant:* **owų́ga** *n* bed ‣ **Ową́ga hįȟpáya.** The bed collapsed. ‣ **Ową́ga gakná įštíma.** He is sleeping beside the bed. *From:* Dakota owáŋka.

ówąja *adv* everywhere, all over ‣ **makówąja** all over the world ‣ **cówąja** forest ‣ **mniwą́ja** ocean

ową́yage síjA *vs* s/he/it is bad-looking; looks bad

ową́yak *vcont* looking a certain way ‣ **Nína wíyą ową́yak wašté.** That is a very nice woman to look at.

ową́yak wašté *vs* s/he/it is beautiful to look at; is good-looking

ówecoga *vs* s/he is talented

owédu *adv* in the spring time

owéšijA *vs* s/he/it is mean, vicious ‣ **Šų́ga mitáwabi iyuhana owéšijabi.** All of my dogs are mean. (Parks et al. 1999:103)

owícanebi *n* hunter

owícagaške *n* jail, prison

owícagaške awáyage *cp* prison guard

owíduka *Variant:* **owíduka tíbi** *n* toilet, bathroom, outhouse *Syn:* **o'íknužaža**

owį́ža *n* quilt, bedding sheet, blanket ‣ **Owį́ža mahén yįgá.** Stay under the blanket. ‣ **Owį́ža žé yumnáya.** Spread the blanket.

owį́ža basísA *vi1* s/he quilts *1s:* **owį́ža wabásisa** *2s:* **owį́ža yabásisa** *1p:* **owį́ža ųbásisąbi**

owį́ža wįcáȟpi *cp* starblanket

owóda *n* 1) feast *vi1* 2) s/he sits down to eat

owóde tíbi ; owóde *cp* restaurant ‣ **Owodé tíbi ektá ųgíyįkte no.** Let us go to the restaurant. ‣ **Owóde žéci ecágen íbi.** They always go to a restaurant over there.

owógana *n* trash pile

owókcą *n* thought ‣ **Mitówokcą wašté no.** My thoughts are good. *1s:* **mitówokcą** *2s:* **nitówokcą** *3s:* **towókcą**

owókma wąyágabi *cp* computer *Syn:* **iyáweȟtįyą**

owóknage *n* story, legend, fable

owókpamni ; owákpamni *n* tribal agency, rations house

owókšubi *n* garden, planted area ‣ **Owókšubi žén ų́.** She is over there in the garden.

owókteyA *Variant:* **owótkeyA** *vt1-caus* s/he hangs smth on or inside it

owónažį *n* fort

owópetų tíbi ; owópetų ; o'ópetų *n* store, shop ‣ **Owópetų tíbi imnámna.** I am setting to go to the store. ‣ **Owópetų žedáhą ųkníbi.** We came back home from the store. ‣ **hayábi owópetų**

tíbi clothing store ▸ **cáhąba owópetų tíbi** shoe store

owópina *vs* s/he is thankful, grateful ▸ **Nína owópina.** He is very thankful.

owópiye *n* pocket

owópiyena *n* woman's sewing bag

owóteȟiga *adv* difficult, hard (as in grieving)

owótkeya ába *cp* Christmas *Lit:* hanging on it [tree] day

oyábodA *vt2* s/he tears smth with the teeth *1s:* **omnáboda** *2s:* **onáboda**

oyáde *n* tribe, people, nation ▸ **Íyą oyáde** Stone nation ▸ **Maštíja oyáde** Northern Cree tribe ▸ **Kúši wanáği oyáde** Grandmother spirit nation ▸ **Oyáde toká én hí.** She arrived in a different tribe. *1s:* **mitá'oyade** *2s:* **nitá'oyade** *3s:* **ta'óyade**

oyáde omníciye *cp* band office

oyáde tí *cp* band office

oyágA *vt2* s/he announces, tells, talks about smth ▸ **Agícida owápįkte no.** I will join the army. ▸ **Ecéduȟ omnága.** I tell it exactly the way it is. ▸ **Misųga oyágįkta tayúkašį.** My younger brother is reluctant to talk about it. ▸ **Žé omnágįkta duká įtó togáheya né žepá.** I will tell that one, but first I will tell this. (NS 2002:41) *1s:* **omnága** *2s:* **onága** *Vbenef:* **ogíjiyagA** *Vdat:* **ogíyagA** *Vpos:* **oknágA** *Vrefl:* **o'íknagA**

oyákų *n* socks, stockings ▸ **Oyákų gic'úšį.** He is not wearing socks.

oyáptA *vt2* s/he has leftovers after eating ▸ **Dágu oyáptešį.** Do not leave anything over. *1s:* **omnápta** *2s:* **onápta**

oyáptabi *n* leftovers

oyátagA *vs* s/he/it is stuck after being inserted; gets stuck while going out *1s:* **omáyataga** *2s:* **oníyataga**

oyáząa *n* pain

oyáge *n* reservation

oyé *n* track, animal tracks ▸ **Táȟtįna oyé óda.**

There a lot of deer tracks. ▸ **táȟca oyé** deer tracks ▸ **maštín oyé** hare tracks ▸ **ziktán oyé** bird tracks *3p:* **oyébi**

oyé otápA *vt1* s/he follows sb's tracks *1s:* **oyé otáwapa** *2s:* **oyé otáyapa**

oyébi *n-pl* tracks

oyé'opA *vi1* s/he tracking sb, smth; follows the tracks of sb, smth

oyúğe *vt2* s/he rakes smth into a pile manually *1s:* **omnúğe** *2s:* **onúğe**

oyúha síjA *vs* it is difficult to have

oyún síjA *vs* it is not good to eat

oyún wašté *vs* it is good to eat; tastes good ▸ **Dágu co'úba né oyún wašté.** What she cooks taste good. *See:* **yunwášteya**

oyúskeba *n* drain

oyútą *vt2* s/he feels inside of smth *Vpos:* **oknútątą**

oyútątą *vt2-redup* s/he feels inside smth

Oyúweğa *ngeo* Malta (Montana)

oyúzA *vt2* s/he digs smth out *1s:* **omnúza** *2s:* **onúza**

oyúze síjA *vs* it is difficult to hold ▸ **Tašų́ge né oyúze síja.** His horse is hard to hold.

oźázą iyáyA *vi2* s/he staggers *1s:* **oźázą imnámna** *2s:* **oźázą inána**

ozíba *vt1* s/he puts up a tent ▸ **Wí nitáwa žé owáziba.** I put up your tent. ▸ **Ozíba waknúštą.** I finished putting mine up. *1s:* **owáziba** *2s:* **oyáziba** *1p:* **ųgózibabi** *Vbenef:* **ogíjiziba** *Vpos:* **ogíziba**

ozį́kta *Variant:* **ozį́tka** *n* 1) rosehip 2) tomato

ozį́kta hábi *Variant:* **ozį́tka hábi** *cp* ketchup

ozį́kta tága *Variant:* **ozį́tka tága** *cp* tomato

ožíži *vi1* s/he whispers ▸ **Núğe én owážiži.** I whispered in her ear. *1s:* **owážiži** *2s:* **oyážiži**

ožúna *vs* it (container) is full; it is full of it ▸ **Ųkce ožúna.** It is full of poop. ▸ **Hoğá žé huhú ožúna.** That fish is full of bones. ▸ **Nąbé yazą žé tų ožúna.** That sore hand is full of pus. ▸ **Amúgiya mitáwa žé opšíja ožúna.** My car is full of mud. ‣ **Nąbé miní omážuna.** My hand is full of water blisters. *1s:* **omážuna** *2s:* **onížuna** *Vcaus:* **ožúya**

ožútų *vt1* s/he fills smth ‣ **Wį́kni owážutų.** I filled it with gasoline. *1s:* **owážutų** *2s:* **oyážutų** *Vabs:* **wóžutų**

ožútųbi *n* bag *Syn:* **wóžutų**

ožúyA *vt1-caus* s/he fills smth ‣ **Eyáš ožúya.** Fill it up sufficiently. ‣ **Céǧa žé miní ožúya.** Fill the bucket with water.

P

pá *n* 1) head ‣ **Ąbáhotųna žé pá gaksá.** He beheaded the chicken. ‣ **Pá nąkéya yįgá.** His head is leaning on the side. 2) hair *Usage:* in certain constructions only. ‣ **pá šagíya** s/he dyed his/her hair red ‣ **págisų** s/he braids his/her hair *1s:* **mapá** *2s:* **nipá** *1p:* **ųgípabi** *See:* **hį́**

pádA *vt1* s/he butchers an animal ‣ **Pté páda.** He is butchering a buffalo. *See:* **wapádA**

-padahą *suff* moving from a location ‣ **nedám > nedápadahą** this way > from here, from the start ‣ **nazám > nazámpadahą** behind > from behind ‣ **caktá > caktápadahą** left > from the left side

pąǧí *n* potato ‣ **Pąǧí šašá žená éyagu.** Take those red potatoes. ‣ **Pąǧí įbíhyabi.** They boiled potatoes.

págisų *vt1-pos* s/he braids his/her hair

pagǧúda *n* duck *Cont:* **pagǧún**

Pagǧúda wacíbi *cp* Duck dance

pagǧúdasaba *n* American black duck

pagǧúdatąga *n* goose *Lit:* big duck

pagǧúdatąga skána *cp* snow goose

pagǧún *cont* duck ‣ **Pagǧún kuwé iyáya.** He went duck hunting.

pagǧúncija *n* duckling

pahá *n* hair, head hair ‣ **Pahá yúzešį!** Do not pull her hair! ‣ **Pahá cįcá.** His hair is curly. ‣ **Pahá kpakcá!** Comb your hair! ‣ **Pahá gašnábi**

wacíga. I want a haircut. *1s:* **mapáha** *2s:* **nipáha** *1p:* **ųgípahabi** *Cont:* **pa-**

pahá éyagu *Variant:* **wįcápaha éyagu** *vt2* s/he scalps sb, an enemy ‣ **Žécen eyáš wįcápaha éyagu žená kówa aknéwįcakiya hį́kna.** So then he took those scalps, and he made them take all of them back. (NS 2002:73–74) *1s:* **pahá émnagu** *2s:* **pahá énagu**

pahá gašnábi *cp* haircut ‣ **Pahá gašnábi wacíga.** I want a haircut.

pahá gíjisų *vt1-benef* s/he braids his/her hair for him/her *1s:* **pahá wéjisų** *2s:* **pahá yéjisų** *1p:* **pahá ųgíjisųbi**

pahá gisų́ *vt1-pos* 1) s/he braids his/her own hair *1s:* **pahá wésų** *2s:* **pahá yésų** *n* 2) braid

pahá įbákca *cp* hair brush, comb

pahá wanį́jA *vs* s/he/it is bald-headed

pahásapsabA *vs-redup* s/he has black hair *1s:* **pahámasapsaba** *2s:* **pahánisapsaba** *1p:* **pahá'ųsapsababi**

pahásąsą *vs-redup* s/he has light grey hair ‣ **Wįcá žé pahásąsą áya'.** That man is getting gray-haired. (Cumberland 2005:402)

paháska *vs* s/he has gray hair

paháskaskana *vs-redup* s/he has pure white hair

pahášaša *vs-redup* s/he has red hair

Paházizi *nprop* George A. Custer, colonel of the American Army, defeated at the battle of Little Big Horn (1839–1876)

paházizi *vs-redup* s/he has blond hair

pahį́ *n* 1) porcupine ‣ **Pahį́ ǧuyábi.** They singe a porcupine. 2) porcupine quill ‣ **pahį́ pahá** porcupine quill hat

pahį́ pahá *cp* porcupine quill hat

pahú *n* nape of the neck

pahňáda *n* bridge of the nose

pahňí *n* snot, mucus ‣ **Waktá! Pahňí anį́gastagakta.** Beware! He will throw snot on you.

pahňí agástaga *cp* turkey *Lit:* the gooey snot *Syn:* **pasú agástaga**

pahní įbákįda *cp* handkerchief

pahnúda *n* turkey *Lit:* red snot

pahpúhpu *vs* s/he has dandruff

pahtÁ *vt1* s/he ties smth up *See:* apáhtA

paknážųtka *n* hog-nosed snake

pakóya *Variant:* pakówa *adv* all over the head
  ‣ **Éc pakówa aknáštą cén eyáš įknúžaža kó
  eyáš.** So he splashed water over his head and
  even bathed. (Weasel 97:94)

pakóyakyA *vt1* s/he ropes an animal by the head
  (steer, horse)

pamáknena *adv* with the head bowed ‣
  Pamáknena nážį. He stood with his head
  bowed.

Pámnaska *nprop* Flathead tribe, person of Flathead descent *Lit:* flat head

Panána ; Panáne *nprop* Arikara, Pawnee tribe;
  person of Arikara, Pawnee descent

Pásaba *nprop* Pasap (surname in White Bear,
  Saskatchewan) *Lit:* black head

pasú *n* beak; tip of the nose

pasú agástaga *n* turkey *Syn:* **pahní agástaga,
  póǧe agástaga**

Pasú ohnóga *cp-prop* Nez Perce tribe, person of
  Nez Perce descent *Lit:* pierced nose *Syn:* **Póǧe
  ohnóga ; Póhnoga**

pasúhąska *n* elephant *Lit:* long nose

pašéja *n* dried-up skull

pat'á *n* dumb, stupid person *Lit:* dead head *See:*
  tawácį ecédušį, įknúdašį, wasnókyešį

patkášana ; patkášina *n* slough turtle

páwe *vs* s/he has a nosebleed *1s:* **pámawe** *2s:*
  pániwe

pawíwina *n-redup* fontanelle

payážą *vs* s/he has a headache ‣ **Ecágen
  pamáyazą.** I always have a headache. ‣ **Nína
  mapáyažą.** I have a big headache. *1s:* **pamáyazą
  ; mapáyažą** *2s:* **paníyazą ; nipáyazą**

pąǧí gakúkabi *cp* mashed potatoes

pąǧí háska *n* parsnip

pąǧíska *n* white Irish potato

pąǧískuya *n* sweet potato

pąpá *vs* it is soft (like suede)

pąšpáža *vs-redup* it is soft ‣ **Pąšpáža híkna
  šnušnúda.** It is soft and slimy.

pąšpážena *vs-redup* it is soft and small (like down
  feathers)

pążéna *vs* it is soft ‣ **Wá pážena.** The snow is
  soft. ‣ **Nąbé táwa žé pążéna.** Her hands are
  soft. *Vredup:* **pąšpážena**

péda *n* fire, matches *Cont:* **pen-**

pedáha *n* ember, charcoal, spark

pédamna *vs* s/he/it smells like fire, smoke

pedížaža *n* oil lantern

pedíhpaya *n* ashes

pehágina *n* sandhill crane

Pehágina wací *cp* Sandhill crane dance

pen- *cont* fire

péna *vs* it is sharp ‣ **Mína žé nína péna.** This
  knife is very sharp. ‣ **Mína įkpa péna.** The
  knife has a sharp tip. *Vredup:* **pepéna**

penákpakpa *n-redup* 1) fire crackles *vimp* 2) the
  fire crackles

pencóna *adv* without a fire

pen'íškadA *vi1* s/he plays with fire; pokes a fire

penkákna *adv* near the fire ‣ **Penkákna náži
  žé.** She is the one standing near the fire. *Syn:*
  penkáyena

penkáyena *adv* near the fire *Syn:* **penkákna**

pen'ókša *adv* around a fire

pensníya *adv* without a fire

penyúza *n* parhelion, sun dog *Lit:* it holds fire

pe'óhnoga *n* idiot, person that is not smart *Lit:*
  holes in the head

pepéna *vs-redup* it is prickly, sharp

pepéšį *vs-redup-pl* they are dull *Usage:* used
  with inanimates. ‣ **Mína ženáwa pepéšį.** All
  of those knives are dull.

pesnéda *n* crown of the head *Syn:* **peyéde**

pésto *vs* it is a sharp point

péstona *vs* it is pointed

péšį *vs* it is dull (as a knife, axe blade) *Vredup:* **pepéšį**

péšna *vs* s/he/it is bald-headed ‣ **Wašíju žé péšna.** The White man is bald-headed. *1s:* **pemášna** *2s:* **peníšna**

peyéde *n* crown of the head *Syn:* **pesnéda**

peží *n* grass, hay

peží amíknąk wacíbi *cp* Grass dance

peží įcápe *cp* hayfork

peží įyúǧe *cp* rake

peží ogáǧe *cp* rake

peží paȟtábi *cp* hay bale

peží wįtkó *cp* marijuana, cannabis *Lit:* crazy grass ‣ **Peží wįtkó įjúbi ogíhibi.** They are permitted to smoke weed. ‣ **Waná peží wįtkó įjúbi ecánų?** Do you smoke weed now?

pežígabuza *n* dried hay

pežíȟoda *n* sagebrush *Lit:* gray grass

peží'ijašta *n* lawnmower

peží'įkpa *n* hayfork

pežískuya *n* sweetgrass

Pežískuya bahá *ngeo* Sweet Grass Hills (Montana) *Syn:* **A'įkpoǧą oyúze**

pežíšeja *n* straw

pežíto *n* 1) bluejoint grass *vs* 2) s/he/it is blue-green, green

pežúda *n* medicinal plant, medicine in general ‣ **Pežúda né mnihą.** This medicine is powerful. ‣ **Pežúda né ús įdómni.** The pills made him dizzy. ‣ **Pežúda né ús mayášpuya.** This medicinal plant makes me itchy.

Pežúda éyagu ecúbi *ph* Medicine Ceremony *Lit:* medicine-taking ceremony

pežúda tíbi *cp* pharmacy

pežúda wašíjuti *cp* clinic, medical office

pežúda wįcášta *cp* 1) medicine man 2) doctor

pežúda wíyą *cp* nurse

pežúdasaba *n* blackroot, Culver's root *Lit:* black medicine

pežúdasije *n* bad medicine; drug (cannabis, cocaine) ‣ **Pežúdasije yuhá c!** He has bad medicine. *See:* **peží wįtkó**

pí *n* liver *1s:* **mapí** ; **matápi** *2s:* **nipí** ; **nitápi** *3s:* **pí** ; **tapí** *See:* **tapí**

pi'écų *vt3* s/he repairs, fixes smth ‣ **Piyáhą iyúha pi'écų.** He fixed it all in a minute. *1s:* **pi'écamų** *2s:* **pi'écanų**

pigíjiyA *vt1-benef* s/he makes a bed for sb ‣ **Micúkši owága piwéjiyes'a.** I usually make my daughter's bed. *1s:* **piwéjiya** *2s:* **piyéjiya**

pigíyA₁ *vt1-pos* s/he buries his/her own relative

pigíyA₂ *vt1-pos* s/he makes his/her own bed ‣ **Owága piwágiya.** I made my bed. *1s:* **piwágiya** *2s:* **piyágiya**

píȟpiǧana *n-redup* carrot

piȟyá *vimp* it is a loud sound

piȟyá kné *vt1* s/he/it makes noise

piȟyáhą *vi1* s/he is noisy

pi'íc'iyA *vi3-refl* s/he/it moves around

-pija *vs-aux* it is easy, worth it, feasible, good to do, -able *Usage:* suffixed to verbs. ‣ **yuhá > yuhápija** s/he has smth, sb > it is worth having ‣ **ecú > ecúpija** s/he does smth > it can be done, it is doable

piná *vt1* s/he is thankful for smth ‣ **Nína dąyą pi'únabic.** We are very thankful for it. *1s:* **piwána** *2s:* **piyána** *1p:* **pi'únabi**

pináyA *vt1-caus* 1) s/he pleases sb, makes sb be grateful ‣ **Micíkši pinámaya.** My son pleased me. 2) s/he thanks sb *Lit:* s/he pleases him/her ‣ **Pinámayaye no!** I thank you! (lit. you please me) ‣ **Né wowádįkte né'įš pinámayaya.** For what I am about to eat, I thank you. *1s:* **pináwaya** *2s:* **pináyaya** *1p:* **piná'ųyabi**

piyá *adv* anew, again, in a different location ‣ **Piyá ųgétibi.** We camped in a different place.

piyÁ₁ *vt1* s/he buries sb, smth *Vpos:* **pigíyA**

piyÁ₂ *vt1* s/he makes a bed *1s:* **piwáya** *2s:* **piyáya** *Vbenef:* **pigíjiyA** *Vpos:* **pigíyA**

piyá ecú *vt3* s/he does smth again; renews,

remodels, renovate smth ‣ **Timáhen piyá
ecúbi.** They are remodeling the inside. ‣ **Aké
piyá ecánųkta he?** You will renew it again? *1s:*
piyá ecámų *2s:* **piyá ecánų** *1p:* **piyá ecúgųbi**

piyábi *n* scaffold

piyáhą *adv* in a minute ‣ **Piyáhą iyúha piyécų.**
He fixed it all in a minute.

piyáhąšį *adv* in no time ‣ **Ą́ą́, píyahąšį ko eyáš,
įpi cén eyáš.** Ah, then in no time at all he was
full. (Weasel 87:150)

piyéniš *adv* instead, still, notwithstanding ‣
Žé'eca dúkš piyéniš né tį́psįna mopté í:ga.
Still she kept on going digging up prairie tur-
nips. (Weasel 120:59)

pizí *n* gall

p'ó *vimp* 1) it is steam; it steams *n* 2) mist, vapor,
steam

póǧe *n* nose *Cont:* **poȟ-**

póǧe agáštaga *cp* turkey *Syn:* **pasú agástaga**

Póǧe oȟnóga ; Póȟnoga *nprop* Nez Perce people,
person of Nez Perce descent

poȟ- *cont* nose

poȟkáwe *vt1* s/he hits and makes his/her nose
bleed

poȟžó *vi1* s/he/it snorts *Lit:* s/he/it whistles
through the nose

poȟ'óȟnoga *n* nostril

póskin *adv* hugging, embracing; around the
neck ‣ **Póskin mayúza wo.** Hold me around
the neck.

póskin knúzA *vt1-pos* s/he hugs, embraces
his/her own ‣ **Micį́kši póskin waknúza.** I
hugged my son. *1s:* **póskin waknúza** *2s:* **póskin
yaknúza**

póskin yúzA *vt1* s/he hugs, embraces sb ‣ **Koškά
né iyáȟpaya póskin yúza hį́k giknᾳ.** He
grabbed the boy in his arms, embraced him,
and caressed him. (Drummond 1976, The boy
who made peace.) *1s:* **póskin mnúza** *2s:* **póskin
núza** *Vpos:* **póskin knúzA**

p'oyáhą *vimp* it is misty, foggy

psá *n* cattail root

psį́ *n* wild rice, rice

pšÁ *vi1* s/he sneezes ‣ **Nína wapšá'!** I sneeze a lot!
‣ **Įknúhana wapšá.** All of a sudden I sneezed.
1s: **wapšá** *2s:* **yapšá** *1p:* **ųpšábi** *Vcaus:* **pšakíyA,
pšayÁ** *See:* **apšÁ**

pšakíyA *vt1-caus* s/he makes sb sneeze *1s:*
pšawákiya *2s:* **pšayákiya**

pšayÁ *vt1-caus* s/he/it causes sb to sneeze *1s:*
pšawáya *2s:* **pšayáya**

pšopšó *vs* it is baggy, loose ‣ **Hųská žé pšopšó.**
These are baggy pants.

pšųká *vs* s/he is round, spherical ‣ **Sįdé žé pšųká,
tᾴga.** Its tail was big and round. (Cumberland
2005:387) *Adv:* **pšųkáyenaȟ ; pšųkáya** *Vredup:*
pšųkáka

pšųkáka *vs-redup* it is round, spherical

pšųkáya *adv* hunched, crouched down, lying in
a spherical shape

pšųkáyenaȟ *adv* hunched, crouched down, lying
in a spherical shape ‣ **Pšųkáyenaȟ wųgáwųga.**
She stayed crouched down. (Weasel 125:147)

ptᾴ *n* otter

ptᾳptᾴyA *vi1-redup* s/he/it rolls over and over

ptᾳyÁ *vi1* s/he turns over

ptᾳyédu *n* fall

ptᾳyésᾳ *adv* throughout the fall, all fall

pté *n* 1) buffalo (generic term) ‣ **Pté žé nína
tᾴga.** A buffalo is very big. ‣ **Hékta naháȟ
pté óda žehᾳ.** There were still a lot of
buffalo in the past. 2) female buffalo 3) domestic cow ‣ **Pté páda.** He is butchering a cow.

pté oyádena *cp* buffalo people

pte'ágan yįgábi *ph* bull riding

pte'áwᾳyage *n* cowboy

ptecį́jana *n* calf *Lit:* young bovid

ptecónica *n* dried buffalo meat

ptéǧa *n* slough, lake ‣ **Ptéǧa žé búza.** The slough
is dry. ‣ **Ptéǧa ópta mná.** I went across the lake.

Pteǧábina *nprop* Swamp people (band of Stoney)

ptehá *n* buffalo hide

pte'ícaȟyA *vi1-caus* s/he raises cattle

ptéjena *vs* s/he/it is short ▸ **Koška né ptéjena.** This boy is short. *1s:* **maptéjena** *2s:* **niptéjena** *1p:* **ųptéjenąbi**

ptemnóga *n* bull ▸ **Ptemnóga žé takpéya.** The bull charged him.

pte'ógijine *vt1-benef* s/he looks for a cow or cattle for sb else *1s:* **pte'ówegine** *2s:* **pte'óyegine**

pte'ógine *vt1-pos* s/he looks for his/her cow, or herd *1s:* **pte'ówene** *2s:* **pte'óyene**

pte'ónaži *n* corral

pte'óne *vi1* s/he looks for a cow, or herd *1s:* **pte'ówane** *2s:* **pte'óyane** *Vbenef:* **pte'ógijine** *Vpos:* **pte'ógine**

pte'óye *n* buffalo tracks

ptepá *n* buffalo skull

pteptéǧana *n-pl-redup* little sloughs

pteská *n* white, albino buffalo

ptešíȟ'ą *n* buffalo monster

ptešína *n* buffalo robe

ptéšį *n* buffalo tallow

ptewánųwą *n* cattle, domestic cow

ptewíyena *n* female buffalo, domestic cow

ptewówaši *n* ox

pteyúhA *vi2* 1) s/he is a rancher *1s:* **ptemnúha** *2s:* **ptenúha** *n* 2) rancher

ptíhą *adv* last fall ▸ **Ptíhą žéci wa'í.** I went there last fall.

pudé *n* upper lip, area under the nose ▸ **Pudé knašná!** Shave!

pudéhįšmą *n* mustache *Lit:* hairy upper lip

putíhį *n* whiskers, beard

putíhįšmą *vs* s/he has a beard

S

-s *suff* let us do smth *Usage:* exhortative suffix placed on the dual form; the meaning 'we' includes the speaker plus at least another person. ▸ **ųyá > ųyás** we go > let us go ▸ **na'ȟ'ų > na'ȟ'ųs** we listen > let us listen ▸ **wó'ųda > wó'ųdas** we eat > let us eat

sábA *vs* s/he/it is black ▸ **Cuwíknąga sába né duwé táwa?** Whose black coat is this? ▸ **Šúga sába mitáwabi.** My dogs are black. *1s:* **masába** *2s:* **nisába** *1p:* **ųsábabi** *Adv:* **sapyá** *Vcaus:* **samyÁ** *Vcont:* **sap-; sam-** *Vpos:* **sapkíyA** *Vredup:* **sapsábA** *Vrefl:* **sap'íc'iyA**

sábeȟtiyĄ *vs* it is pitch black ▸ **Mąká né sábeȟtiyą.** The mud is pitch black.

ságA *vs* it is dried hard (like smth wet that dried up) ▸ **Cuwíknąga mitáwa sága.** My coat is dry. ▸ **Žécųbi žé ogáȟnoga amáǧažu eštá yužážabi dóhani sagéšį sudášį.** By doing this it never dries out and gets hard in rain or washing. (Drummond 1976, Smoking hides) *Vcaus:* **sakyÁ**

sakím *adv* together, joined ▸ **Sakím híbi.** They came here together. ▸ **Hába žé sakím éknąga.** Put the shoes together. ▸ **Wanąǧaš koškábi núm ecágen sakím ųbis'a gáyabi.** Long ago there were two young men who were always together. (NS 2002:13)

sakípa *adv* two of something

sakkíjiyA *vt1-benef* s/he dries smth for him/her

Sakná *nprop* person of Metis descent, mixed blood *From:* French (le)s anglais.

sakné *Variant:* **sakyé** (OM) *n* cane, crutch ▸ **Sakyé ųs mawáni.** I walk using a cane.

saknégitų *vt1-pos* s/he uses his/her cane ▸ **Saknégitų hinápa.** She appeared using a cane. (Weasel 172:200) *1s:* **saknéwet'ų** *2s:* **saknéyet'ų**

sakyÁ *vt1-caus* s/he dries smth that is wet *1s:* **sakwáya** *2s:* **sakyáya** *1p:* **sak'ųyabi** *Vbenef:* **sakkíjiyA**

sám ; sám *post* 1) beyond, over, across *Usage:* short form of sápa. ▸ **Bahá sám žéci wa'í.** I went over the hill. ▸ **Sám yá!** Go away! ▸ **Tíbi táwa žé ocągu sám há.** His house is across the street.

(Cumberland 2005:408) 2) and, in addition to *Usage*: when used in counting it is placed between decades and cardinal numbers, and between hundreds and decades. ‣ **Dóba sám hągé ehą'i.** It is 4:30. ‣ **wikcémna núm sám dóba** twenty-four ‣ **wikcémna napcúwąga sám šagówį** ninety-seven ‣ **obáwįğe sám wąží sám agénųba** one hundred and twelve ‣ **obáwįğe sám napcúwąga wikcémna yámni sám šaknoğa** nine hundred and fifty-eight

samyÁ *vt1-caus* s/he blackens sb, smth; paints, colors, dyes smth in black *Vrefl*: **sap'įc'iyA**

sap- ; sam- *cont* black

sap'įc'iyA *vi3-refl* s/he blackens, paints himself/ herself in black

sapkíyA *vt1-pos* s/he blackens his/her own *1s*: **sapwágiya** *2s*: **sapyágiya**

sapsábA *vs-redup* it is black spotted, black here and there ‣ **Įdé né sapsába.** He has black spots on the face. *n* 2) pitch, tar

sapyá *adv* blackly, darkly ‣ **Miní žé sapyá iyáya.** That liquid will turn pitch black.

są *vs* it is beige, faded, off-white

sąksája *n* dress ‣ **Sąksája awábasisa.** I sew it on the dress. *1s*: **mitásąksaja** *2s*: **nitásąksaja** *3s*: **tasąksaja**

sąní *adv* single, one side ‣ **Sąní ksahá.** It is broken on one side. ‣ **Įštá sąní wąyága.** He sees with one eye.

sąnína *adv* on one side only ‣ **Sąnína t'at'á.** He is paralyzed on one side only.

sąpana *adv* further on, over ‣ **Sąpana yįgá!** Move over!

sewí *vs* it is sour ‣ **Asábi žé sewí.** That milk is sour. ‣ **Naháȟ sewíšį.** It is not sour yet.

sewímna *vs* it has a rancid, sour smell ‣ **Asábi né sewímna.** This milk has a rancid smell.

si- *cont* foot

sicą *n* shin *Syn*: **cąkpé**

sicógądu *n* arch of the foot

sicóna ; sicóco ; sicócona *adv* barefoot ‣ **Sicóna**

yįgá. He is barefoot. ‣ **Sicóco ú.** He is going about barefoot. ‣ **Sicócona mawánįkta.** I will walk barefoot.

sicúha *n* foot sole ‣ **Sicúha mašóga.** My foot soles are callous.

sihá *n* foot ‣ **Sihá nibó.** You have swollen feet. ‣ **Sihá kún égiknąga!** Put your feet down! ‣ **Sihá s'ámna.** He has stinky feet. *1s*: **masíha** *2s*: **nisíha**

Sihábi *nprop* Foot people (band of Nakoda)

Sihásaba *nprop* Blackfoot people, person of Blackfoot descent

sihásaba *n* Canada goose *Lit*: black feet

siháškoba *n* clubfoot

sihú *n* bone of the lower leg

sihújijina *n* killdeer *Syn*: **juwíjijina**

sihúšaša *n* mallard duck *Lit*: red lower leg bones

síjA *vs* 1) s/he/it is bad, hard, difficult, harmful, unpleasant ‣ **Yawábi síja.** It is hard to read. ‣ **Dágu síja awáci.** He is tormented. ‣ **Šúga síja žé wąyága cén napá.** He ran away because he saw that bad dog. ‣ **wagágana tawácį síja** old wicked lady ‣ **cądésija** s/he is sad, brokenhearted 2) s/he/it is ugly *1s*: **masíja** *2s*: **nisíja** *1p*: **ųsíjabi** *Adv*: **sijáya** *Vcont*: **sin- ; šin- ; sij-**

sijá akípa *vi1* s/he encounters, is afflicted with bad luck; it is bad luck

sijáyA *vi* it is wrong ‣ **Sijáyįkta otí'įga.** I think there is something wrong.

sijáya *adv* badly, poorly ‣ **Sijáya eyá.** He curses. ‣ **Sijáya oȟ'áge no.** He has bad habits. ‣ **Dágu sijáya ayákipakte no.** You will encounter something bad.

sijáyekna *vs* s/he feels sad, badly ‣ **Įšnána yįgá cén sijáyekna.** She feels sad because she is alone. *1s*: **sijáwayekna** *2s*: **sijáyayekna**

síjecų *vt3* s/he does smth bad

síjeȟtįyA *vs* s/he/it is the worst, wildest, meanest, ugliest *Usage*: used to describe behavior and appearance. ‣ **Búza ódabi wąží síjeȟtįya.** There are a lot of cats, but one is the wildest.

síjena *n* 1) ugly person *vs* 2) s/he is ugly *1s:*
masíjena *2s:* **nisíjena**

sijúpsąpsą *vi1-redup* it (dog) waggles its tail

siką́ *n* ankle, calf ‣ **Siką́ mabádįda.** My leg is stiff.

siką́saba *n* blackleg disease, infectious bacterial
disease (livestock)

siką́zina *n* snipe

siksíja *vs-redup* they are bad

sin- ; **šin-** *vcont* bad ‣ **wókcą > šinwókcą** s/he
thinks > s/he thinks it is bad

sináₚsą *vcont* shaking his/her foot ‣ **Sináₚsą
yįgá.** She is sitting shaking her foot.

sináₚsąpsą *vi1-redup* s/he/it shakes his/her foot
Vcont: **sináₚsą**

sinúₚin *n* both feet

sipá *n* toe, toes

sipášage *n* toenail *Syn:* **sišáge**

sipátąga *n* big toe, big toes ‣ **Sipátąga ksumáya**
I hurt my big toe.

sišáge *n* toenail *Syn:* **sipášage**

sit'át'A *vs* s/he has a numb foot *1s:* **simát'at'a**
2s: **sinít'at'a**

-siye *suff* let us do smth *Usage:* archaic form of the
exhortative *-s.* ‣ **éti > ųgéti** s/he camps there >
we (two) camp there ‣ **"Écen ųgétisiye manín,"**
eyá. "Écen ųgétisiye manín," eyá. "Let us live
that way, off somewhere away from camp," he
said. (Weasel 163:5)

siyéda *n* heel; Achilles tendon

siyéda wagádu *cp* high heels

síyutabi *n* so many feet (length) *Usage:* followed
by a number. ‣ **Įš síyutabi dóba gašná.** It cut a
four-foot swath [of wheat]. (Drummond 1976,
Early days on Carry The Kettle reserve)

sįdé *n* tail ‣ **Sįdé hąskáskabi.** They have long
tails.

sįdédena *n-redup* tailbone, coccyx *Syn:* **sįdéhuhu**

sįdégoskoza *n* mule deer

sįdéhuhu *n-redup* tailbone, coccyx *Syn:* **sįdédena**

sįdéȟna *n* rattlesnake *Syn:* **wó'ošija**

sįdésaba *n* black-tailed deer

sįdéšana *n* red fox *Lit:* red tail *Syn:* **šų́gašana** ;
šųkšána

sįdéžada *n* sparrow

skagíjiyA *vt1-benef* s/he paints, colors sb, smth
in white for sb

skagíyA *vt1-pos* s/he whiten, paints, colors, dyes
his/her own in white

ska'íc'iyA *vi3-refl* s/he whitens, paints himself/
herself in white *1s:* **skamíc'iya** *2s:* **skaníc'iya**

skána *Variant:* **ská** *vs* s/he/it is white *Usage:* the
short variant occurs mostly in compounds. ‣
Skána žé waná iyáya. The white one is now
gone. ‣ **Búza skána gá asą́bi yatką́.** That white
cat over there is drinking milk. ‣ **mázaska**
money ‣ **šųkská** white horse ‣ **cąníska** cigarette *Vcaus:* **skayÁ** *Vredup:* **skaskána, skaská**

skaská *vs-redup-pl* they are white (inanimate
plural)

skaskána *vs-redup* s/he/it is pure white

skayÁ *vt1-caus* s/he whitens, paints sb, smth in
white *1s:* **skawáya** *2s:* **skayáya** *Adv:* **skayéna**
Vbenef: **skagíjiyA** *Vpos:* **skagíyA** *Vrefl:*
ska'íc'iyA

skayéna *adv* white condition

ską́ *vimp* it thaws, melts ‣ **Wá né ską́ giníja.**
The snow is almost all melted. *Vcaus:*
ską́yA

ską́yA *vt1-caus* s/he/it melts smth ‣ **Cáǧa
ską́wáya, miní mnatką́kta.** I will melt the
ice and drink the water. ‣ **Wá žé ską́wáya'.**
I melted the snow. *1s:* **ską́wáya** *2s:* **ską́yáya**
1p: **ską́'úyabi**

skébA *vs* it is empty, drained *Vbenef:* **skemkíjiyA**
Vcaus: **skemyÁ** *Vcont:* **skem-** *Vpos:* **skemkíyA**

skem- *vcont* empty, drained

skemkíjiyA *vt1-benef* s/he drains, bails smth out
for sb else *1s:* **skemwéjiya** *2s:* **skemyéjiya**

skemkíyA *vt1-pos* s/he drains, bails out his/her
own

skemyÁ *vt1-caus* s/he drains, bails out smth

skuskú *vs* s/he/it (dog, wolf, coyote, horse) is mangy; is missing spots of fur

skúyA *vs* it is sweet ‣ **Skúya he?** Is it sweet? ‣ **Cǎšmúyabi pšųkáka nína skúya.** This candy is very sweet. ‣ **cǎdéskuya** sweetheart, girlfriend

skúyageȟ *adv* in a soft, sweet manner ‣ **Skúyageȟ i'á.** He is sweet-talking.

skúyemna *vs* it has a sweet smell ‣ **A'įkpapsų né skúyemna.** This perfume has a sweet smell.

skuyéyA *vt1-caus* s/he sweetens smth ‣ **Huȟnáȟyabi né skuyéwaya.** I sweeten the coffee. *1s:* **skuyéwaya** *2s:* **skuyéyaya**

smagá *vs* s/he/it has thin hair

smismí *vs* s/he/it is bare, thinned out ‣ **Cą né smismí, waȟpé dágunišį.** This tree is bare, it has no leaves.

smiyáyą *vs* it shines

smuyá *vs* it is smooth

sná *n* lotion, oil *Vcaus:* **snayÁ**

snagíyA *vt1-pos* s/he rubs, oints his/her own with grease, oil, lotion ‣ **Mató wįkni snagíya.** He rubs his with bear grease. *1s:* **snawágiya** *2s:* **snayágiya**

sna'įc'iyA *vi3-refl* s/he rubs himself/herself with grease, oil, lotion ‣ **Iyúha ús sna'įc'iya bo.** Rub yourselves with all of it. *1s:* **snamįc'iya** *2s:* **snanįc'iya**

Sna'ót'e *nprop* half-breed, Whiteman *Usage:* archaic. *Lit:* drown in grease *Syn:* **Wašíju**

snayÁ *vt1-caus* s/he rubs sb, smth with grease, oil, lotion *Vpos:* **snagíyA** *Vrefl:* **sna'įc'iyA**

sní₁ *vs* s/he/it is cold ‣ **Sní he?** Is it cold? *Adv:* **sniyą́** *See:* **bosní**; **mosní**

sní₂ *vs* it burns out; burns itself out ‣ **Įktúyąbi žé sní.** The lamp went out. *Vcaus:* **sniyÁ**

sníbA *vt1* s/he/it licks sb, smth ‣ **Šų́gaƭąga žé štušténa sníba.** The horse is licking the salt. *1s:* **wasníba** *2s:* **yasníba** *Vredup:* **snísniba**

snigíjiyA *vt1-benef* s/he cools smth off for him/her ‣ **Mikúši sniwéjiya.** I cooled it off for my grandma. *1s:* **sniwéjiya** *2s:* **sniyéjiya**

snigíyA *vt1-pos* s/he cools off his/her own *1s:* **sniwágiya** *2s:* **sniyágiya**

snigíyabi *n* ice cooler

snísniba *vt1-redup* s/he/it licks sb, smth

sniyÁ *vt1* s/he cools smth off *Vbenef:* **snigíjiyA** *Vpos:* **snigíyA**

sniyą́ *adv* cold, cool condition ‣ **Sniyą́ egíknąga.** I put mine down to cool off.

sníza *vs* it is flat, has no air in it

snohą́ *vi1* s/he/it crawls, creeps ‣ **Snohą́ yá:ga.** He was going creeping. *Adv:* **snohą́dugen**

snohą́dugen *adv* sliding ‣ **Snohą́dugen hiyáya.** He went sliding.

snohéna *n* 1) snake (generic) *Lit:* crawler ‣ **Snohéna wąmnága.** I see a snake. ‣ **Snohéna waníjabi.** There are no snakes. 2) garter snake

snohéna pežúda *cp* snake medicine

Snohéna wįcášta *nprop* Shoshone people, person of Shoshone descent *Lit:* snake people

snokkíciyabi *vi1-recip* they know one another ‣ **Eyáš snokkíciyabi.** They know one another quite well. ‣ **Hųgágebi né'įš snokkíciyabįkta.** The parents too would know each other. *1p:* **snok'ų́giciyabi**

snokyÁ *Variant:* **snohyÁ** (PR, OM) ; **snonyÁ** (WB) *vt1* 1) s/he knows sb, smth ‣ **Dóken ecų́bi snokwáyešį.** I do not know how to do it. ‣ **Timáni wahí duká dóki inánabi žé snohwáyešį.** I came to visit, but I do not know where you all went. ‣ **Hékta žé wíyą snohmáyašį no!** Back then the woman did not know who I was. ‣ **Né'įš snokyábi cįgá.** This one wants to know. *vi1* 2) s/he understands ‣ **Snohyáyešį no.** You do not understand. *1s:* **snokwáya ; snohwáya** *2s:* **snokyáya ; snohyáya** *1p:* **snok'ų́yabi ; snoh'ų́yabi** *Vcaus:* **snokyékiyA** *Vrecip:* **snokkíciyabi**

snokyékiyA *vt1-caus* s/he lets sb know smth; lets smth be known ‣ **Iná snokyékiyešį!** Do not let mom know!

snúga *n* 1) foreskin 2) idiot, a person who is pretending not to know anything

sódA *vs* s/he is extinct, gone; perishes *Vcont:* **són** *See:* **osódA**

són *vcont* being extinct, gone, perishing

són áyA *vs* it is becoming extinct *Usage:* not used with humans. ‣ **Dágu nówa són áya.** All kinds (of species) are disappearing.

spą́ *vs* it is damp

steȟ *part* like, in the manner of, somewhat, -ish, as if *Usage:* triggers e-ablaut. ‣ **Šų́ga steȟ awáȟnoga.** I growl at him like a dog. ‣ **Snokyé steȟ škáda.** He plays somewhat skillfully. ‣ **Miní né sába steȟ iyáya.** This water is turning blackish. ‣ **Snokyé steȟ ecų́.** He did it as if he knew it.

sten *part* declarative female particle ‣ **Naȟ'ų́ oką́ eyį́kte žé wayápišį jé'e sten.** He understands all right, but when he tries to speak he cannot do it. (Cumberland 2005:338)

stéyA *part* it seems like; like ‣ **Aké wáȟiȟakta stéya no.** It seems like it will snow again. ‣ **Ecágen žéci ų́bi stéya.** It seems they are always over there. ‣ **Šų́ga stéya awáȟnoga.** I growl at him like a dog. ‣ **Miyé stéya.** He is just like me. ‣ **Aktúgu stéya.** He is just like his father. ‣ **"Hąwí océti stéya," eyábis'a.** "The moon is like a stove," they say usually.

stó *vs* it is rectangular, oblong

stohą́skA *vs* it has a long oblong shape

stustÁ *vs* s/he/it is tired ‣ **Mastústa áyaȟ!** I am getting tired! ‣ **Nistústa? —Hiyá mastústešį.** Are you tired? —No I am not tired. ‣ **Wa'úkta ų́ká mastústa.** I was to come but I am tired. *1s:* **mastústa** *2s:* **nistústa** *1p:* **ų̱stústabi** *Adv:* **stustáyagen** *Vcaus:* **stustéyA**

stustáyagen *adv* boringly ‣ **Nén stustáyagen mą̱gá.** I am sitting here bored.

stustéyA *vt1-caus* s/he tires sb ‣ **Stustémayaye no!** You are tiring me! ‣ **Stustéciya he?** Am I tiring you? *1s:* **stustéwaya** *2s:* **stustéyaya** *1p:* **stusté'ų̱yąbi**

sú *n* 1) seed, pellet ‣ **ağúyabisu** wheat kernel 2) bullet *Redup:* **susú ; susúna**

sudá *vs* 1) it is hard, solid ‣ **Žécų̱bi žé ogáȟnoga amáğažu eštá yužážabi dóhąni sagéšį sudášį.** By doing this it never dries out and gets hard in rain or washing. (Drummond 1976, Smoking hides) ‣ **asą́bi sudá** cheese ‣ **cąní sudá** twisted tobacco ‣ **cąsúda** ash 2) s/he/it is strong, tough ‣ **Tanó né sudá.** This meat is tough. *1s:* **masúda** *2s:* **nisúda** *1p:* **ų̱súdabi** *Adv:* **sudáya ; sudáyagen** *Vredup:* **suksúda** *Vrefl:* **sudá'įc'iyA**

sudá'įc'iyA *vi3-refl* s/he makes himself/herself hard *1s:* **sudámįc'iya** *2s:* **sudánįc'iya**

sudáya *adv* firmly, hard, strongly, solidly ‣ **Sudáya mnúza.** I held it firmly. ‣ **Sudáya cáğa.** It is frozen solid.

sudáyagen *adv* kind of hard, solid ‣ **Maką́ né sudáyagen áya.** The soil is getting kind of hard.

suksúda *vs-redup* they are hard

susméja *n* dragonfly

susú ; susúna *n-redup* testicles

susú éyagu *vt2* s/he castrates a male *1s:* **susú émnagu** *2s:* **susú énagu**

susú éyagubi *cp* castrated male

susú maksÁ *vt1* s/he gelds, castrates an animal *1s:* **susú wamáksa** *2s:* **susú yamáksa**

-sų̱ga- *root* 1) younger brother (male or female speaker). 2) younger male parallel cousin (male or female speaker). *1s:* **misų̱́ga ; misų́** (vocative) *2s:* **nisų̱́ga** *3s:* **sų̱gágu** *1p:* **ų̱gísų̱ga** *Vcaus:* **sų̱gáguyA** *Vrecip:* **sų̱gágugiciyabi**

sų̱gágugiciyabi *vi1-recip* they have one another as younger brother

sųgáguyA *vt1-caus* s/he has him as a younger brother ‣ **"Sųgáguciyįktac" eyá.** "I will have you as my younger brother," he said.

sųkpé *n* muskrat ‣ **Sųkpé kuwá.** He hunts muskrat.

sųkpétawode *n* bitterroot *Lit:* muskrat food

S'

-s'a *encl* 1) often, usually, habitually *Usage:* used on verbs; triggers e-ablaut. ‣ **Nína waštés'a.** It is usually very good. ‣ **Mikúši žeyés'a.** My grandmother often says that. ‣ **Wanágaš mitúgaši onówą nená nowás'a.** Long ago my grandfather used to sing these songs. 2) agent, one who does smth *Usage:* derives agentive nouns with or without pejorative connotations. ‣ **yatkés'a** drunkard ‣ **ištímes'a** sleeper ‣ **ağóbas'a** snorer ‣ **adé wakátąga ógiyes'a** the Lord's servant

s'ámna *vs* s/he/it stinks ‣ **Mągá žé s'ámna.** That skunk stinks. ‣ **Sihá mas'ámna.** I have stinky feet. *1s:* **mas'ámna** *2s:* **nis'ámna** *1p:* **ųs'ámnabi**

s'ás'a *vi* it is a swooping sound (as of wings) ‣ **Á! s'ás'a hįkna hiyákneya gáyabi.** Ah! there was a sound of wings and then suddenly it came down. (NS 2002:14)

Š

-š *suff* 1) as opposed to, on the other hand (adversative suffix) *Usage:* with pronouns it indicates a contrast between two referents. ‣ **niyé > niyéš** yourself > yourself on the other hand 2) serves to put emphasis on nouns, adverbs, and verbs and is translated as 'indeed' ‣ **waná > wanáš** now > now indeed ‣ **aké > akéš** again > again indeed

šá *vs* s/he/it is red ‣ **Wagíyą šá wiyóȟpeyam žéci iyódągabi.** The Red Thunderbirds sit there to the west. *1s:* **mašá** *2s:* **nišá** *1p:* **ųšábi** *Adv:* **šayá** ; **šayéna** *Vredup:* **šašá**

šába *vs* it is dirty *Vcaus:* **šamyÁ** *Vcont:* **šam**

šagé *n* nail, hoof, claw ‣ **įkmú šagé** lynx claw ‣ **sipášage** toenail

šágeja *vs* s/he/it is kind of red

šagíjiyA *vt1-benef* s/he paints, colors sb, smth in red for sb *1s:* **šawéjiya** *2s:* **šayéjiya**

šagíyA *vt1-pos* s/he reddens, paints his/her own in red ‣ **Pahá šagíya** She dyed her hair red.

Šagówį océti *nprop* Seven council fires

šagówį (PR, OM, WB, FP) *num* 1) seven *vs* 2) s/he/it is seven; there are seven *Syn:* **iyúšna**

Šahíya *nprop* Cree people (generic term), person of Cree descent

Šahíya wašíju *nprop* Gros Ventres, Atsina people, person of Gros Ventres, Atsina descent *Lit:* White Cree

Šahíyena *nprop* Cheyenne people, person of Cheyenne descent *Lit:* Little Cree

Šahíyeskąbi *nprop* Piapot Cree people, person of Piapot Cree descent *Lit:* Cree translator

ša'ímna *vs* s/he/it is pink

ša'íc'iyA *vi3-refl* s/he reddens, paints himself/herself in red ‣ **Wasé ús ša'íc'iya.** He painted his face with red ocher. ‣ **Įc'ícuwa hįk ša'íc'iya kó.** He both dressed up and painted himself in red. (Drummond 1976, Įktomi and the ducks) *1s:* **šamíc'iya** *2s:* **šaníc'iya**

ša'í'ų *vt1-dit* s/he paints, applies red paint on sb, smth ‣ **Žécen né'jš ša'í'ų wahíkpe né.** So then this other one painted an arrow red. (Weasel 39:97) *1s:* **ša'íwa'ų** *2s:* **ša'íya'ų**

šaknóğą *num* 1) eight *vs* 2) s/he/it is eight; there are eight

šaknóğana *quant* only eight

šákpe *num* 1) six ‣ **Įyútabi šákpe nawáží.** I am six feet tall. ‣ **O'ápe šákpe oȟá.** Boil it for six hours. *vs* 2) s/he/it is six; there are six

šakpéȟ *adv* six times

šákpena *quant* only six

šam- *vcont* dirty

šam'íc'iyA *vi3-refl* s/he/it dirties himself/herself/itself ▸ **Škáda háda ní:::naȟ šam'íc'iya húšta.** When he played he always got very dirty. (BigEagle 2019:4) *1s:* **šammíc'iya** *2s:* **šamníc'iya**

šamyÁ *vt1-caus* s/he darkens, dirties sb, smth *1s:* **šamwáya** *2s:* **šamyáya** *Vrefl:* **šam'íc'iyA**

šašá *vs-redup-pl* they are red ▸ **Waskúyeja šašá áya žéȟą nagú maštášta.** Berries start ripening, and it is also very hot. (Haywahe 1992:38) ▸ **"Wąžíȟ yadúwąbi štén įštá né nišášabiktac"** eyága. "If one of you opens your eyes, your eyes will be red," he said. (NS 2002:43) *1s:* **mašáša** *2s:* **nišáša** *1p:* **ųšášabi**

šašána *vs-redup* 1) it is orange *n* 2) candies (idiolectal)

šašté *n* pinkie, little finger

šató (WB) *vs* s/he/it is purple

šayÁ *vt1-caus* s/he reddens, paints sb, smth in red *Adv:* **šayéna** *Vbenef:* **šagíjiyA** *Vpos:* **šagíyA** *Vrefl:* **ša'íc'iyA**

šayá *adv* red condition ▸ **Tacá šayá áya.** His body is turning red.

šayá hiyúbi *cp* measles *Lit:* it turns red

šą *n* vagina

šąhí *n* woman's pubic hair

šąmná *vs* her vagina smells

šéba *n* black person *Usage:* obsolete.

šéjA *vs* it is dry, dead ▸ **pašéja** dried-up skull ▸ **cášeja** dead tree

-ši *vt1-dit-aux* s/he tells, asks, orders, commands sb *Usage:* attaches to or follows a preceding verb. ▸ **Íš uwáši.** I told her to come too. ▸ **Umáyaši he?** Are you telling me to come here? ▸ **Iyéska mašíbi.** They asked me to translate. ▸ **Huȟnáȟayabi gaȟší.** Tell him to make coffee. *1s:* **-waši** *2s:* **-yaši**

-šic'e- *root* brother-in-law (female speaker) *1s:* **mišíc'e** *2s:* **nišíc'e** *3s:* **šic'étku** *1p:* **šic'étku'ųyąbi**

-šic'eši- *root* male cross-cousin (female speaker) *1s:* **mišíc'eši** ; **mišík'eši** *2s:* **nišíc'eši** ; **nišík'eši** *3s:* **šic'éšicu** *1p:* **šic'éšitku'ųyąbi**

šigíjikna *vt1-benef* s/he takes up for sb in anger *1s:* **šiwéjikna** *2s:* **šiyéjikna**

šiȟ'ą *n* beast, monster ▸ **Šiȟ'ą éniyagukta.** The beast will take you.

šijéją (PR) *n* otter *Syn:* **ptą**

-šijepą- *root* sister-in-law (female speaker) *1s:* **mišíjepą** *2s:* **nišíjepą** *3s:* **šijépągu** *1p:* **šíjepągu'ųyąbi**

-šijepąši- *root* female cross-cousin (female speaker) ▸ **Mišíjepąši wanįje!** My cross-cousin is gone! *1s:* **mišíjepąši** *2s:* **nišíjepąši** *3s:* **šijépąšicu** *1p:* **šijépąšitku'ųyąbi**

šikná *vi1* s/he/it is mad, angry ▸ **Waktá šiwákna!** Beware! I am angry! ▸ **Šikná stéya no.** He is angry it seems. *1s:* **šiwákna** *2s:* **šiyákna** *1p:* **ši'úknabi** *Adv:* **šiknáya** ; **šiknáyagen** *Vbenef:* **šigíjikna** *Vcaus:* **šiknáyA**

šiknákiyA *vt1-caus* s/he is mad at sb *1s:* **šiknáwakiya** *2s:* **šiknáyakiya** *1p:* **šikná'ųkiyabi**

šiknáyA *vt1-caus* s/he makes sb mad

šiknáya *adv* angrily ▸ **Šiknáya i'ábi.** They talk angrily.

šiknáyagen *adv* kind of angry ▸ **Šiknáyagen ú.** She is feeling kind of angry.

šiná *n* blanket, robe ▸ **Mikúši šiná basísa.** My grandmother sews the blanket. ▸ **Mary šiná gáǧa žé opéwatų no.** I bought the blanket Mary made.

šinágaȟci *n* fringed shawl

šinágaȟciȟcibi *n-redup* fringed shawl

šin'ákipa *vt1, vi1* s/he encounters smth bad; is afflicted with bad luck ▸ **Wįcášta wąží, šin'ákipa dagúwįcaya žé t'á háda wašíknabi, žén okónagiciya né, wįcágico hík.** If a man experiences something bad, [as] when one of his relatives dies and they are mourning him, he invites the dance society. (Shields 42:34)

šináknekneǧa *n-redup* Hudson Bay blanket

šinásaba *n* Catholic

šinásaba wašíjuwaką *cp* Catholic priest

šinásaba wįcáwaką *cp* Catholic priest *Lit:* black robe priest

šinášoga *n* Pendleton blanket

šinwókcą *vi1* s/he thinks it is bad

šiptó *n* abalone shell

šiyága *n* large, black diving bird *Cont:* **šiyák**

šiyágo *n* American coot, mud hen

šiyák'o ; šiyágo *n* boil *Lit:* to be hit by a šiyága

Šiyó *ngeo* Sheho (Saskatchewan)

šiyó *n* prairie chicken, pheasant, grouse; domestic chicken

šiyójusina *n* quail

Šiyónide *nprop* 1) Pheasant's Rump (Nakoda chief and signatory of Treaty 4 in 1876) *ngeo* 2) Pheasant Rump reservation (Saskatchewan)

Šiyóša *ngeo* Red Pheasant reservation (Saskatchewan)

šiyótąga *n* greater sage-grouse, sage hen *Lit:* big grouse

-šį- *root* female friend (woman speaking) *1s:* **mišį́** *2s:* **nišį́** *3s:* **šį́tku**

-šį *encl* not, in- *Usage:* expresses the negation of verbs, adverbs, particles, and pronouns; triggers e-ablaut. ‣ **wacímnaga > wacímnagešį** I see you > I did not see you ‣ **įwátųšį > įwátųšįšį.** I lie > I did not lie ‣ **miyé > miyéšį** it is me > it is not me *Syn:* **-gen**

šį *n* fat *Usage:* used only in compounds. ‣ **pté > ptéšį** buffalo > buffalo tallow ‣ **ųzé > ųzéšį** rump > rump fat

šįtú *vs* s/he/it is fat ‣ **Gugúša šįtú né knuhábįkteši.** They will not keep this fat pig. ‣ **Nína nišį́tų no!** You're very fat! *1s:* **mašį́tų** *2s:* **nišį́tų** *1p:* **ųšį́tųbi** *Vcaus:* **šįtúyA**

šįtúgijiyA *vt1-benef* s/he fattens an animal for sb ‣ **Mikúši gugúša šįtúwejiya.** I fatten my grandma's pig for her. *1s:* **šįtúwejiya** *2s:* **šįtúyejiya**

šįtúgiyA *vt1-pos* s/he fattens his/her own animal

šįtúyA *vt1-caus* s/he fattens an animal ‣ **Búza šįtúwaya.** I fatten the cat. *Vbenef:* **šįtúgijiyA** *Vpos:* **šįtúgiyA**

škádA *vi1* 1) s/he plays ‣ **Tągán škáda wo!** Play outside! ‣ **Nisúga timáhen šųktí gakná škáda.** Your younger brother is playing beside the barn. ‣ **Mitákona gicí waškáda.** I play with my friend. ‣ **Dáguškina né škádana.** The baby is playing. *vt1* 2) s/he plays a musical instrument ‣ **Įbázije škáda.** He plays the fiddle. *1s:* **waškáda** *2s:* **yaškáda** *1p:* **ųškádabi** *Vcaus:* **škatkíyA** *Vcont:* **škat- ; škan-**

škanwáyupiya *vt2* s/he is skilled at playing games *1s:* **škanwámnupiya** *2s:* **škanwánupiya**

škat- ; škan- *vcont* playing ‣ **Škan yá.** Go and play.

škatkíyA *vt1-caus* s/he lets sb play ‣ **Mihú tągán škatmákiya.** Mom lets me play outside. *1s:* **škatwákiya** *2s:* **škatyákiya** *1p:* **škat' úkiyabi**

šką *vt1* 1) s/he tries to do smth ‣ **Giksúyešįkta šką!** Try not to forget about it! ‣ **Waštékta šką.** He is trying to be good. ‣ **Nakón'i'abi šką.** Try to talk Nakoda. *vi1* 2) s/he is busy ‣ **Nína šką.** She is very busy. 3) s/he moves, behaves ‣ **Wéskuya táwa šką he?** How is her diabetes level? 4) s/he feels thus ‣ **Mikúši dóken yašką he?** My grandmother, how are you feeling? ‣ **Dąyá wašką.** I am doing fine. *1s:* **wašką** *2s:* **yašką** *1p:* **ųškábi** *Vredup:* **škąšką**

šką́hįknA *vi* it moves suddenly; it is a sudden movement

šką́šį *adv* calm, still, quiet ‣ **Šką́šį ųyį́gabis.** Let us stay still. ‣ **Šką́šį wa'ánaǧoptą yįgábi.** They were sitting still and listening.

šką́šį yįgÁ *vi3* s/he is sitting still ‣ **Šką́šį yįgá bo.** You all sit still. *1s:* **šką́šį mągá** *2s:* **šką́šį nągá** *1p:* **šką́šį ųyį́gabi**

škąšką *vs-redup* s/he/it moves, shakes; it shakes, moves by inner force ‣ **Ganúza cén cą́ nówa škąšką.** It is windy, thus all the trees are shaking. ‣ **Waȟpé nówa škąšká.** All the leaves are shaking. ‣ **Nąbé nišką́šką.** Your hand is shaking. *Adv:* **škąškáyą**

škąškáyą *adv* with a moving motion

škejá *n* fisher

škiška *Variant:* **kšikšá** (PR) *vs* it is crooked, curly, wavy ‣ **Ocą́gu škiška omáwani.** I traveled on a crooked road.

škóbA *vs* it is bent, crooked, curved ‣ **Cą́ né škóba.** This stick is bent. *Adv:* **škomyá**

škóbena *vs* it is slightly crooked

škokpá *vs* *vs* it is hollow, caved in

škomyá *adv* in a bent, crooked, curved shape ‣ **Škomyá hą́.** It is crooked.

škoškóbena *n-redup* banana *Lit:* it is slightly curved ‣ **Duwé škoškóbena né nik'ú he?** Who gave you this banana? ‣ **Škoškóbena gicí ijáhi.** It is mixed with bananas.

šmá *vs* it is deep ‣ **Mnik'ábi žé šmá.** The well is deep! ‣ **Wá né nína šmá'!** That snow is very deep.

šmú *vs* it leaks, drips ‣ **Wį́kni šmú.** Grease is dripping.

šmúwąga *vs* it is dripping (as a faucet)

šná *vs* it rings, jingles

šnašnána *n* dancing bell

šnašnáyena *adv* jingling

šnayá *vi* it shows; is visible, uncovered, bare ‣ **Pá žé žé'įš šnayášį.** His head was not visible. (Cumberland 2005:321) ‣ **Dókedukte žéš, šnayáktac.** Whatever might have happened will show. (Shields 27:88)

šnayą́ *Variant:* **šna'įyą** *adv* clearly, in plain sight ‣ **Téȟą šnayą́ hįnápa.** He appeared clearly at a distance. ‣ **Šnayą́ nážį.** He is standing in plain sight.

šnišníyena *adv* naked, with no clothes on ‣

Šnišníyena mįštímįkte no! I will not sleep naked!

šnó *vi* s/he/it melts *Vcaus:* **šnoyá**

šnošnóna *vs* it is soft

šnoyÁ *vt1* s/he melts, renders fat; fries smth ‣ **Wį́kni šnowáya.** I melt the lard. ‣ **Wá šnowáya.** I melted snow. ‣ **Pąǧí šnoyá.** She fried potatoes. *1s:* **šnowáya** *2s:* **šnoyáya** *1p:* **šno'ų́yabi**

šnušnúda₁ *vs-redup* it is slippery, slimy ‣ **Cáǧa žé šnušnúda.** The ice is slippery. ‣ **Pąšpą́ža hį́kna šnušnúda.** It is soft and slimy.

šnušnúda₂ *vs-redup* s/he/it is dirty *1s:* **mašnúšnuda** *2s:* **nišnúšnuda** *Vcaus:* **šnušnúnkiyA** *Vcont:* **šnušnún** *Vrefl:* **šnušnún įc'íyA**

šnušnún *vcont* dirty

šnušnún įc'íyA *vi3-refl* s/he dirties himself/herself

šnušnúnkiyA *vt1-pos* s/he dirties his/her own ‣ **Hųská šnušnúnkiya.** He dirtied his pants. *1s:* **šnušnúnwagiya** *2s:* **šnušnúnyagiya**

šóda *n* smoke ‣ **Šóda óhą yįǧá.** He is sitting in the smoke. *Cont:* **šon-** *Vcaus:* **šonyÁ** *See:* **ošóda**

šóga *vs* it is thick ‣ **Teȟpí né šóga.** This buckskin is thick. ‣ **Cup'ó šóga.** The fog is thick. ‣ **Sicúha mašóga.** My foot soles are callous. *1s:* **mašóga** *2s:* **nišóga** *Adv:* **šokyá**

šokyá *adv* thickly, extensively

šon- *cont* smoke

šonyÁ *vt1-caus* s/he smokes smth (such as meat) ‣ **Tanó šonwáya.** I smoke meat. *1s:* **šonwáya** *2s:* **šonyáya** *1p:* **šon'ų́yabi**

šošéna *n* waterfall

šóšobina *n-pl* puppies

špą́ *vs* 1) s/he/it is cooked 2) s/he/it is burned ‣ **Waȟą́bi káda yatką́ gá cagá špą́.** He drank hot soup and burned his palate. (Fourstar p. 9)

špągíyA *vt1-pos* s/he cooks, bakes his/her own ‣ **Ųzé né špągíya.** He burned his own rump. (Weasel 6:125)

špą́'įc'iyA *vi3-refl* s/he burns himself/herself *1s:* **špámįc'iya** *2s:* **špánįc'iya** *1p:* **špą́'ųgíc'iyabi**

špášį *vs* it is raw, not cooked

špášį yúdabi *cp* watermelon *Lit:* it is eaten raw

špąyÁ *vt1-caus* 1) s/he cooks, bakes smth ▸ **Pąǧí, típsina, wakmúhaza įš špąyą́.** She cooked potatoes, turnips, and corn too. ▸ **Duktám ináne žehą́ pağúda žená špąwícawaya.** While you were gone I cooked these geese. (Cumberland 2005:416) 2) s/he brands an animal (sheep, steer) *1s:* **špąwáya** *2s:* **špąyáya** *1p:* **špą'ų́yąbi** *Vabs:* **wašpáyÁ** *Vpos:* **špągíyA** *Vrefl:* **špá'įc'iyA**

Špe'óna ; Špe'úna *nprop* person of Mexican or Spanish descent *From:* French espagnol.

špušpúna *n* particles

štén *conj* 1) if when, if then ▸ **Įníduka štén, wóda wó.** If you are hungry, then eat. 2) when, whenever, in, at, on, next ▸ **Hąyákena štén ağúyabisaga edáhą wacíga.** In the morning I want some toast. ▸ **Hąhébi štén mikúši nągú mitúgaši timánibįkta.** At night my grandmother and my grandfather will come visit. ▸ **Įníbi ųgáğabi štén, miní odá ųcígabi no!** When we make a sweatlodge, we want a lot of water. ▸ **Ábawaką štén wa'úkta.** I will come next Sunday. 3) equals (in arithmetic) ▸ **Dóba aké nų́ba štén šákpe.** Four plus two equals six.

štúda *vs* it is thawed, defrosted, soft *Vcaus:* **štunyÁ**

štunyÁ *vt1-caus* s/he thaws, defrosts smth ▸ **Tanó štunyá!** Thaw the meat! *1s:* **štunwáya** *2s:* **štunyáya**

štuštÁ *vs* it is salty *Vcaus:* **štuštéya**

štušténa *n* 1) salt ▸ **Eháš štušténa óda ecų́.** She used too much salt. ▸ **Štušténa agána.** He pours salt on it. *vs* 2) it is salty ▸ **Nína štušténa.** It is very salty. *Vbenef:* **štušténagijiya** *Vpos:* **štušténagiya**

štušténa sába *cp* pepper

štušténagijiyA *vt1-benef* s/he salts sb's food *1s:* **štušténawejiya** *2s:* **štušténayejiya**

štušténagiyA *vt1-pos* s/he salts his/her own food *1s:* **štušténayagiya** *2s:* **štušténawagiya** *1p:* **štušténa'ųgiyabi**

štušténasapsaba *n-redup* pepper *Lit:* black salt

štuštéyA *vt1-caus* s/he salts smth

šubé *n* guts, intestines ▸ **mató šubé** bear guts *1s:* **mašúbe** *2s:* **nišúbe**

šúža *vimp* it clatters

šų́ ; wíyaga šų́ *n, cp* longest feathers on the wing

šúǵa *n* 1) dog ▸ **Duktén šúǵa žé wąnága he?** Where did you see that dog? ▸ **Įknúhąna šúǵa nówa hįnápabi.** Suddenly all the dogs appeared. ▸ **Wanáǵaš šúǵa cuwíc'iba k'įbis'a.** Long ago dogs were harnessed to a travois. 2) horse *Usage:* in possessed forms only. ▸ **Mitášųǵa iyáksamwakíya.** I train my horse. ▸ **Tašų́ǵe né oyúze síja.** His horse is hard to hold. *1s:* **mitášųǵa** *2s:* **nitášųǵa** *3s:* **tašúǵa** *Cont:* **šųk-** *Redup:* **šúǵagana**

šúǵa įdé pšųká *ph* bulldog *Syn:* **šųkpátąga**

šúǵa káda *cp* hot dog

Šúǵa núda *nprop* Red dog (1855–1925); Nakoda chief

šúǵa tína *cp* doghouse

šúǵagana *n-redup* lapdog

šųǵámna *vs* s/he/it smells like a dog

šųǵána *n* old horse

šúǵašana *Variant:* **šųkšána** (PR) *n* red fox *Lit:* red canine *Syn:* **sįdéšana**

šúǵatąga *Variant:* **šųktáǵa** (PR) *n* horse *Lit:* big dog ▸ **Mitúǵaši šúǵatąga wagíbazo.** I showed the horse to my grandfather. ▸ **Šúǵatąga t'á giníja.** The horse almost died. ▸ **Mitášųktąga né.** That is my horse. *1s:* **mitášųǵa** *2s:* **nitášųǵa** *3s:* **tašúǵa**

šúǵatągana *n* little horse *1s:* **mitášųgena** *2s:* **nitášųgena** *3s:* **tašúǵena**

šúǵawį *n* female dog, bitch

šųǵícoco *vt1-redup* s/he calls his/her own dogs ▸ **Žécen tągápadahą wíyą wąží šųǵícoco, ú níyąc. nah̃ų́.** Then from outside he heard a woman calling her dogs. (Shields 50:81)

šų̃hpéna *n* colt

šųk- *cont* dog, horse, sheep ‣ **šųkcíjana** puppy ‣ **šųksába** black horse ‣ **šųgána** old horse

šųkcé *n* dog penis

Šųkcébina wįcášta *nprop* Dog penis people (band of Nakoda)

Šųkcíjana wóhąbi ecúbi *ph* Puppy soup ceremony

šųkcíjana *n* puppy

šųkcúk'ana *n* coyote *Lit:* small canine ‣ **Šųkcúk'ana nén ódabi.** There are many coyotes here. ‣ **Šųkcúk'ana kuwá awícaya.** The coyote kept coming back at them.

šųkháhana *n* spirited, lively horse

šųkháskusku *n* mangy dog, coyote, wolf; unkept dog

šųkhéwąga *n* sheep

šųkhéyuke ; šųkhéyuką *n* sheep *Lit:* horned canine

šųkhéyuke cįjá *cp* lamb

šųkhíša *n* bay horse, reddish horse *Lit:* red hair horse

šųkhíto *n* bluish, gray horse *Lit:* blue hair horse

šųkhítokneška *n* straight-eyed horse, blue roan horse

šųkhí *n* wool

šųkhíȟca *n* shaggy dog

šųkhíȟpayA *vs* s/he falls, dismounts from a horse 1s: **šųkmáhįȟpaya** 2s: **šųkníhįȟpaya**

šųkhótųtų *vi1-redup* 1) it (wolf, coyote, dog) howls 2) it (horse) neighs

Šųkknáškįyąbi *nprop* Crazy dog society

šųkknékneǧa *n* pinto horse *Lit:* spotted horse

šųkkúwa *vi1* s/he chases, handles, pursues horses 1s: **šųkwákuwa** 2s: **šųkyákuwa**

šųkmánų *vi1* s/he steals a horse, horses ‣ **Hąhébi né šųkmánųkte no.** He will steal horse tonight. 1s: **šųkmáwanų** 2s: **šųkmáyanų** 1p: **šųkmá'unųbi**

šųkmínik'u *vi1* s/he waters horses

šųkmnóga *n* stallion

šųknábe *n* paw with claws, hoof

šųknídeska *n* Appaloosa

šųkpámnikiyabi *n* rodeo

šųkpámnina *n* bucking horse

šųkpásikiyA *vt1-caus* s/he drives a horse (toward a place) *Vcoll:* **šųkpásiwįcakiya**

šųkpásiwįcakiyA *vt1-coll* s/he drives horses (toward a place) 1s: **šųkpásiwįcawakiyA** 2s: **šųkpásiwįcayakiyA**

šųkpáša *n* strawberry roan horse *Lit:* red head horse

šųkpátąga *n* bulldog *Syn:* **šúga įdé pšųká**

šųkpúdehąska *n* hound

šųksába ; šúgasaba *n* black horse

šųksídeksa *n* bobtail horse *Lit:* horse with a cut-off tail

šųksíhamaza *n* horseshoe

šųksíde *n* horse tail

šųkská *n* white horse ‣ **Šųkská agán-yągá.** She is riding the white horse.

šųkskúsku *n* mangy horse

šųkšáge *n* hoof of a horse

šųkšágemaza *n* horseshoe

šųkšóšona *Variant:* **šųkšóšo ; šúšubina ; šųkšúšu** *n* donkey, mule

šųkšpáya ; šųkšpáye *n* horse brand

šųktáwap'i *n* horse collar

šųktí *n* stable, barn *Lit:* horse house ‣ **Šųktí héktam nážį.** He is standing behind the barn.

šųktógeja *n* wolf *Lit:* bluish canine ‣ **Šųktógeja nén ódabišį.** There are not many wolves here. ‣ **Šųktógeja iyúhana hįnápabi.** All of the wolves appeared. ‣ **Šųktógeja a'ókšą'ųyąbi.** The wolves encircled us. *Syn:* **šųktógena ; šųktóga**

Šųktógeja Ébazo *ngeo* Wolf Point (Montana)

šųktógena ; šųktóga *n* wolf *Syn:* **šųktógeja**

šųktúske *n* stunted horse

Šųkwácibi *n* Horse dance

šųkwágįc'į *n* pack animal (horse or dog)

šųkwícaȟtįyaną *n* old stallion

šųkwíyena *n* mare ‣ **Šųkwíyena žé kiyúȟa.** That mare is breeding.

šųkwówaši *n* work horse

šųkyúhųhųza *n* pacer (horse that lifts the front and back leg on the same side, and rocks or "shakes" side to side as it moves forward) *Lit:* shaking horse

šųkzí *n* buckskin horse; sorrel horse

šųk'áktagabi *n* horse race

šųk'áktakkiyA *vt1-caus* s/he rides a horse, makes a horse run *1s:* šųk'áktakwakiya *2s:* šųk'áktakyakiya *1p:* šųk'áktak'ųkiyabi

šųk'ák'įgit'ų *vi1* s/he saddles a horse

šųk'ápeskana *n* palomino horse *Lit:* white mane

šųk'ášpąyĄ *vi1* s/he brands horses *1s:* šųk'ášpąwayą *2s:* šųk'ášpąyayą

šųk'áyumnaya *n* horse blanket

šųk'íjapšįde *n* horse whip

šųk'íyopsikiyA *vt1-caus* s/he makes a horse prance, jump *1s:* šųk'íyopsiwakiya *2s:* šųk'íyopsiyakiya

šųk'íȟceya *n* Cayuse, horse or pony of little value *Lit:* common horse

šųk'įkiyA *vt1* s/he gallops a horse *1s:* šųk'įwakiya *2s:* šųk'įyakiya

šųk'įkoyakya *vi1* s/he harnesses a horse, ties a horse to a wagon *1s:* šųk'įkoyawakya *2s:* šųk'įkoyayakya

šųk'ógijine *vt1-benef* s/he looks for sb else's horse, or horses *1s:* šųk'ówejine *2s:* šųk'óyejine

šųk'ógine *vt1-pos* s/he looks for his/her own horse, horses *1s:* šųk'ówene *2s:* šųk'óyene

šųk'óhabi *n* boiled dog, puppy soup

šųk'ókuwasije *n* bronc

šųk'óne *vi1* s/he looks for a horse or horses *1s:* šųk'ówane *2s:* šųk'óyane *Vpos:* šųk'ógine

šųk'ówode *n* place where horses feed

šųk'óye *n* horse, dog tracks

šųk'ųze *n* dog rump

Š'

š'á *vi* it is a roaring sound ▸ [...] š'áwąga dóken oȟ'ągebi [...] making the noises they used to with their activities. (Shields 47:51) *Vredup:* š'aš'á *See:* agíš'a

š'ágA *vs* s/he/it is strong *Adv:* š'akyÁ *See:* mnihĄ́

š'akyá *adv* strongly

š'aš'á *vi-redup* it is a continuous roaring sound

T

ta- *n* ruminant (generic meaning; moose, deer, elk, buffalo, antelope) *Usage:* occurs in compounds. ▸ pí > tapí liver > ruminant's liver ▸ šagé > tašáge nail, claw, hoof > ruminant's hoof

ta-...-bi *circumfix* their (3rd person plural possessor) ▸ šiná > tašínabi blanket > their blanket

-ta- *pref* marker of alienable possession (friend, object, animal) ▸ šiná > mitášina blanket > my blanket ▸ šúgatąga > nitášųga horse > your horse ▸ koná > takónagu friend > his/her friend *1s:* mitá- *2s:* nitá- *3s:* ta-...-gu

tá *n* moose ▸ Tá bahágąn nážį. The moose is standing on top of a hill.

t'Á *vs* s/he/it dies, is dead ▸ Šúgatąga t'á giníja. The horse almost died. ▸ Ȟtánihą t'įkta. She would have died yesterday. ▸ Wikcémna yámni giníja, mitúgaši t'á žé. It has been almost thirty years since my grandfather died. (Cumberland 2005:421) *1s:* mat'á *2s:* nit'á *1p:* ųt'ábi

tába *n* ball ▸ Tába žé mįmámašį. That ball is not round. *Cont:* tap-; tam-

tába yukába *cp* baseball glove

tábana *n* small ball

tábapabi *n* baseball bat

tabéda *n* ruminant's back

tabéȟ'a *Variant:* tabéȟ'ana ; tabáȟ'a *n* frog ▸ Tabéȟ'a nądáboȟ'įc'iya. The frog is bloating.

tabéȟ'a tawį́ wí *cp* April

tabéȟ'ana táwode *cp* mushroom *Lit:* frog food

t'ábi *n* deceased person

tacą ; tącą *n* body, carcass; body and soul, whole being 1s: **mitácą** 2s: **nitácą**

tacákiyutabi *n* foot (unit of measurement) ‣ **Hokšína né tacákiyutabi záptą hą́ska.** This boy is five feet tall.

tacéhuba *n* ruminant's jaw

Tácehubana *ngeo* Moose Jaw (Saskatchewan)

tacésni *n* manure

tacúba *n* animal marrow

tacúba ą́ba *cp* Friday *Lit:* animal marrow day *Syn:* **ą́ba įzáptą; tanó yúdabišį**

tadé *n* wind *See:* **tadéyąba ; tadé'ąba**

tadé omní tą́ga *ph* whirlwind

tadé'uya *n* cardinal directions, world quarters *Lit:* from where the wind blows

tadé'uya dóba *cp* four cardinal directions

tadéwam *adv* facing the wind ‣ **Owá tadéwam ma'ų́nibi.** We all walked facing the wind.

tadéyąba ; tadé'ąba *vimp* it is a windy day

tagípA *vt1-pos* s/he follows, pursues his/her own 1s: **tawágipa** 2s: **tayágipa** 1p: **ta'ų́gipabi**

-tagošku- *root* stepchild 1s: **mitágošku ; mitágoš** (vocative form) ; **mitágoškubina** (vocative form) 2s: **nitágóšku** 3s: **tagóšku**

-tagoža- ; -tagóžakpa- *root* grandchild ‣ **Tagóžakpagu aktášį.** He disowned his grandchild. ‣ **Mitágožabina nų́ba timáni híbi.** Two of my grandchildren came to visit. 1s: **mitágoža** 2s: **nitágoža** 3s: **tagóžakpagu** 1p: **ų́gítagožakpagu ; ų́gítagožabi**

tahá *n* deer, moose, elk hide

tahá ogádą *vt1* s/he pegs a hide down

tahásaga *n* rawhide bag; parfleche

tahą́guyA *vt1-caus* he is his brother-in-law ‣ **"Háu tahą́gucįyįktac," eyá.** "Hello, I am your brother-in-law," he said. (Drummond 1976, The boy who made peace.) 1s: **tahą́guwaya** 2s: **tahą́guyaya**

tahé *n* horns of a ruminant

tahékiškana *n* horn spoon

tahį́špa *n* awl

tahį́špa juk'ána *cp* sewing needle *Lit:* small awl ‣ **Tahį́špa juk'ána ų́s wagáğeğe.** I sewed it with a needle.

tahú *n* neck, nape of the neck ‣ **Tahú kpaksá.** He broke his neck.

tahúbaza *n* currant

tahúhąska *n* giraffe

tahúša *n* turkey

tahúto *n* mallard duck

tahą́ge *n* knee

tahą́ge huhú ; tahą́gena *n* kneecap

tahą́ge kné *vii* s/he kneels down

tahą́ge kné yįgÁ *vi3* s/he is sitting on his/her knees 1s: **tahą́ge kné mągá** 2s: **tahą́ge kné nągá**

tah̆ca *n* deer ‣ **Tah̆ca otáwapa.** I followed the deer. ‣ **Tah̆ca waktékta.** I will kill a deer. ‣ **Šųkcúk'ana né tah̆ca ksu'íc'iye žé kní:gabi.** The coyotes kept coming back at the injured deer.

tah̆camnoga *n* stag ‣ **Tah̆camnoga tanó žé wąkanašį.** That stag meat is not tender.

tah̆cawįyena *n* doe

tah̆cįjana ; tah̆tįjana *n* 1) deer (generic); herd of deer 2) white-tailed deer

tah̆cįtano *n* venison

Tah̆é *ngeo* Moose Mountain (Saskatchewan) *Syn:* **Ȟépa**

tah̆pá *n* back (body part) ‣ **Tah̆pá mayáza.** I have a backache. ‣ **Tah̆pá agán aní žécen hú né anúk núbagiya cén hú né yuškom iyáya.** He [Įktomni] stepped on his [diver] back, spreading his legs out and bending them crooked. (Drummond 1976, Įktomi and the ducks)

tah̆tú *vi* it has foam

taką *n* 1) sinew 2) deer, moose gristle

taką́heja *n* raspberry

-takiya *Variant:* **-kiya** *suff* toward ‣ **bahá > bahátakiya** hill > toward the hill ‣ **mah̆píya > mah̆píyatakiya** sky > toward the sky ‣ **wazíya > wazíyatakiya** North > toward the North

-takona- *root* one's friend ‣ **Mitákona pinámayaya!** Thank you my friend! ‣ **Nitákona a'ú.** Bring your friend. *1s:* **mitákona** *2s:* **nitákona** *3s:* **takónagu** *1p:* **ųgítakonabi** *Vrecip:* **takónagiciyabi** *See:* **koná**

takónagiciyabi *Variant:* **takónagugiciyabi** *vii-recip* they are friends ‣ **Takónagugiciyabi hį́kna dágu wóyuha waštéšte nówa į́š gicíc'ubi.** The friendship was reciprocated, and they exchanged gifts including fine clothes and other things. (Shields 15:181)

takónagutų *vt1* s/he makes friends

takpégiciyabi *vii-recip* they charged one another

takpéya *vt1* s/he/it charges, runs against, attacks sb ‣ **Ptemnóga žé takpéya.** The bull charged him. *Vrecip:* **takpégiciyabi**

tam'ápA *vii* s/he hits a ball *1s:* **tam'áwapa** *2s:* **tam'áyapa**

Tamínabina *nprop* They have sharp knives people (band of Nakoda)

tamkápsija nąbį́kpa *n* baseball glove

tamkápsijabi *n* baseball, softball *See:* **tapškáda**

tamní *n* placenta

tamškádA ; tapškádA *vii* s/he plays baseball, ball

tamškádabi *n* baseball

tamyúkaba įtáčą *cp* baseball coach

tanó *n* meat, flesh *Lit:* fresh ruminant ‣ **Tanó štúnya!** Thaw the meat! ‣ **Tanó edáhą manú.** He stole some meat. ‣ **Atkúgu tanó edáhą k'ú.** He gave his father some meat.

tanícona *adv* breathless

Tanį́debina *nprop* Buffalo hip people (band of Nakoda)

tanį́ǧa *n* tripe of an animal

taníješ *Variant:* **tanį́š** *adv* almost ‣ **Taníješ žécedukta ųká.** It almost happened in this way.

taníya *n* 1) his/her/its breath 2) breath, air, oxygen, atmosphere ‣ **Taníya žé dókiyo iyáya tą'į́šį.** The air dissipates in all directions. *Adv:* **taníyešį**

taníyešį *adv* breathless, out of breath ‣ **Taníyešį įt'áhą.** He is out of breath.

tanį́k'e *vs* it is an old thing

tanį́n ; tąnį́na *adv* ahead of time, ahead of others; already ‣ **Tanį́n togáda hí.** He arrived ahead of time. ‣ **Tąnį́na kpąyą́bi.** They were already tanned.

tanį́n wanį́je *cp* stillborn infant *Lit:* s/he/it is gone ahead of time

tanó maksáksabi *cp* hamburger

tanó obáząbi *cp* sausage

tanó owópetų *cp* butcher shop

tanó yažímkiya *cp* sandwich

tanó yúdabišį *n* Friday *Lit:* meat is not eaten

tanóyukpąbi *n* ground beef, hamburger

ta'ó *vt1* s/he/it wounds sb, smth ‣ **Žé watá'oga.** I sort of wounded it. ‣ **Šų́ga žé ta'ó.** He wounded that dog. *1s:* **watá'o** *2s:* **yatá'o**

ta'óbi *n* wound

tap- ; tam- *cont* ball ‣ **tamkápsijabi** baseball, softball

tapÁ *vt1* s/he follows, pursues sb, smth *1s:* **tawápa** *2s:* **tayápa** *1p:* **ta'ų́pabi** *Vabs:* **watápA** *Vpos:* **tagípA**

tapí *n* ruminant's liver *See:* **pí**

tapkápsijektena *n* ballgame

tapnápsijabi *n* football

tapškádabi ; tamškádabi *n* baseball

tapškádabi wapáha *cp* baseball cap, helmet

tapų́ ; tapó *n* cheek

tapų́šage *n* rouge for the cheeks

tasį́de *n* ruminant's tail

taskákpa *n* wood tick

taspǫ́ *n* 1) hawthorn fruit 2) apple 3) fruit *Usage:* in compounds only. ‣ **taspǫ́ ǧí** orange ‣ **taspǫ́ pestóstona** pear *Syn:* **taspǫ́spąna**

taspǫ́ cogądu co'úbabi *ph* apple pie *Lit:* it is baked with apples in the middle

taspǫ́ ǧí *cp* orange *Lit:* orange apple, orange fruit ‣ **Asą́bi yatką́ wo, hį́kna taspǫ́ ǧí yúda!** Drink your milk, and then eat your orange!

taspǫ́ ǧí hįšmą ; taspǫ́ hįšmą *cp* peach *Lit:* hairy orange *Syn:* **taspǫ́hįtųtų**

taspǫ́ ǧí tą́ga *cp* The grapefruit

taspą̆ ǧí tutá *cp* lemon *Lit:* sour orange

taspą̆ pestóstona *cp* pear *Lit:* pointed fruit

taspą́cą *n* apple tree

taspą́ǧiǧi *n-redup* orange

taspą́hạbi *n* apple juice

taspą́hịtụtụ *n-redup* peach *Syn:* **taspą̆ ǧí hịšmą ; taspą̆ hịšmą**

taspą́hu *n* hawthorn bush

taspą́spạna *n-redup* 1) hawthorn berries 2) crabapple

tašáge *n* ruminant's hoof

tašiyapopobena *n* meadowlark

tašnáheja *n* striped gopher

tašnáheja akída wí *ph* October *Lit:* gopher looks back moon

tašnáheja ȟóda *cp* grey squirrel

tašnáheja ȟóda hagíkta wí *ph* October

tašnǫ́ ų́ *vi1* s/he is single; he is a bachelor *1s:* **tašnǫ́ wa'ų́** *2s:* **tašnǫ́ ya'ų́**

tašų́kkiyA *vt1-caus* s/he makes smth his/her own dog ‣ **Ųmá né tašų́kkiya cén ųmá į́š gá tašų́kkiya.** He gave the other one a dog for his own. (Weasel 171:179)

t'at'Á *vs-redup* s/he/it is numb, paralyzed *1s:* **mat'át'a** *2s:* **nit'át'a**

tatą́ga *n* male buffalo

tatą́ga cạgáȟa *cp* buffalo corral, fence

Tatą́ga magé *nprop* Buffalo hoop (Victor Sammy's traditional name)

tatą́ga oȟpáye *cp* buffalo jump

tatą́ga wapáha *cp* buffalo headdress

tatą́gabina *n-pl* bison herd

tatą́gaha *n* buffalo hide

tatą́gašina *n* buffalo robe

tatą́k *cont* buffalo

Tatą́k wacíbi *cp* Buffalo dance

tatézi *n* ruminant's stomach

tatógana *n* antelope

tatók'ana *n* butterfly

táwa *pro* 1) his/her ‣ **Cuwíknạga nitáwa wašté no.** Your coat is nice. ‣ **Mitáwa žé júsina.** Mine is small. *vs* 2) s/he owns it, it is his/her own ‣ **Duwé né táwa?** Who owns this? ‣ **Búza né nitáwa he?** Is this cat yours? ‣ **Žé táwabi.** They own that. ‣ **Žé miyé mitáwašị.** That is not mine. ‣ **"Makóce né, né'į́š nitáwabịkta,"** **jáya.** "This land, this too will be yours," he said. *1s:* **mitáwa** *2s:* **nitáwa** *1p:* **ųgítawabi** *3p:* **tawábina**

tawácị *n* 1) mind; his/her mind, mindset, goal ‣ **tawácị wịyą́** a woman of good will ‣ **Tawácị ų́s iyéskabi.** They converse using their mind. *vs* 2) s/he thinks thus ‣ **Dóken nitáwacị?** How do you think? ‣ **Žécen tawácị.** That is the way she thinks. *1s:* **mitáwacị** *2s:* **nitáwacị** *1p:* **ųgítawacịbi**

tawácị dạyą́ *vs* s/he is considerate *1s:* **mitáwacị dạyą́** *2s:* **nitáwacị dạyą́** *1p:* **ųgítawacịbi dạyą́**

tawácị dạyą́šị *vs* s/he is moody; feels bad ‣ **Ecų́šị cén tawácị dạyą́šị.** She did not do it because she felt bad. ‣ **Wịhamni né ų́s tawácị dạyą́šị.** He is moody because of a dream. *1s:* **mitáwacị dạyą́šị** *2s:* **nitáwacị dạyą́šị** *1p:* **ųgítawacịbi dạyą́šị**

tawácị ecédušị *vs* s/he is stupid ‣ **Hokšína žé tawácị ecédušị.** That boy is stupid. *1s:* **mitáwacị ecédušị** *2s:* **nitáwacị ecédušị** *1p:* **ųgítawacịbi ecédušị**

tawácị hą́skA *vs* s/he is patient *1s:* **mitáwacị hą́ska** *2s:* **nitáwacị hą́ska** *1p:* **ųgítawacịbi hą́ska**

tawácị nų́ba *vs* s/he is undecided *1s:* **mitáwacị nų́ba** *2s:* **nitáwacị nų́ba** *1p:* **ųgítawacịbi nų́ba**

tawácị otóką *vs* s/he is strange *1s:* **mitáwacị otóką** *2s:* **nitáwacị otóką** *1p:* **ųgítawacịbi otóką**

tawácị síjA *vs* 1) s/he has a wicked mind ‣ **Wagą́gana žé tawácị síja.** That old lady has a wicked mind. *1s:* **mitáwacị síja** *2s:* **nitáwacị síja** *1p:* **ųgítawacịbi síja** *n* 2) bad habits

tawácị wašté *vs* 1) s/he has good mind *1s:* **tawácị mawášte** *2s:* **tawácị yawášte** *n* 2) good mind

Tawáhacąga wašté *nprop* Prettyshield (surname in Carry The Kettle, Saskatchewan)

-tawįju- ; **-tawį-** *root* wife ‣ **Mitáwįju céyešį wo.** My wife, do not cry. ‣ **Jim tawįju wací iyáya.** Jim's wife went dancing. ‣ **Mitáwįju tamnúza.** I control my wife. *1s:* **mitáwįju** ; **mitáwį** *2s:* **nitáwįju** ; **nitáwį** *3s:* **tawįju** *1p:* **ųgítawįjubi**

tawįjutų *vii* 1) he has sb for a wife, he is married *1s:* **tawįjuwatų** *2s:* **tawįjuyatų** *1p:* **tawįju'ųtųbi** *n* 2) married man

tawįyą *vt1* he has her as a wife ‣ **Tawįciyą.** I have you as a wife.

táwįyena *n* female moose

tayúzA *vt2* s/he controls sb, smth ‣ **Hįknágu tayúza.** She controls her husband. *1s:* **tamnúza** *2s:* **tanúza**

tayúkašį *vt3* s/he is reluctant to, dreads smth ‣ **Žéci yábi tayúkašį.** He dreads going there. ‣ **Wįyą žé gicí i'ábįkta tamúkašį.** I am reluctant to speak with that woman. ‣ **Ecúbi tayúkabįšį.** They are reluctant to do it. *1s:* **tamúkašį** *2s:* **tanúkašį** *1p:* **ta'úyųkabišį**

tažó *n* saliva, spit

tažóšA *vii* s/he spits ‣ **Micíkši nína tažóša.** My son spits a lot. *1s:* **tawážoša** *2s:* **tayážoša**

tažúška *n* deerfly

tažúškatąga *n* horsefly

tažúkta *Variant:* **tažútka** *n* ruminant's kidney

tąbá *n* white birch

t'A *vs* s/he/it dies, is dead · **Šúgatąga t'a ginįja.** The horse almost died. ‣ **Ȟtanihą t'íkta.** She would have died yesterday. ‣ **Wikcemna yamni ginįja, mitugaši t'a že.** It has been almost thirty years since my grandfather died. (Cumberland 2005:421) *1s:* **mat'a** *2s:* **nit'a** *1p:* **ųt'abi**

t'a'ihpayA *vs* s/he faints, loses consciousness

tąbáwada *n* birchbark canoe

tącócona *vs* s/he is naked *1s:* **tąmácocona** *2s:* **tąnícocona**

Tącówaci *Variant:* **Tącó wacíbi** *cp* Naked dance

tágA *vs* s/he/it is big, large ‣ **Tága žé nitáwa.** The big one is yours. ‣ **Wópina tága wak'ú no.** I give great thanks. ‣ **Waȟ'ákšija sába tága žé wąyága cén napá.** He fled because he saw that big black bear. *1s:* **matága** *2s:* **nitága** *3s:* **tágįkta** *1p:* **ųtágabi** *Redup:* **tágaga** *Vredup:* **tąktágA**

-tąga- ; **-tą-** *root* 1) younger sister (female speaker) ‣ **Há nitąga ųgíwųgįkta no.** Ok, we will ask your younger sister. 2) female parallel cousin (female speaker) *1s:* **mitąga** ; **mitą** *2s:* **nitąga** ; **nitą** *3s:* **tągágu** *1p:* **ųgítągagubi**

tągabina *n-pl* elders

tágaga *n-redup* mature person *3p:* **tágabiga**

tągán ; **tągáda** *adv* outside ‣ **Tągán osní he?** Is it cold outside? ‣ **Tągán yá škáda wo.** Go and play outside. ‣ **Tągán a'óžąžą.** It is sunny outside. ‣ **Šúga žé tągán įštíma.** The dog is sleeping outside.

tągana *vs* s/he/it is kind of big, grown up ‣ **Gá waná tągana cén hokúwa íges'a, hokšína né.** So, now that he was kind of grown up, this little boy would go fishing. (Weasel 26:2)

tągápadahą *Variant:* **tągápada** *adv* from the outside ‣ **Žécen tągápadahą wíyą wąží šųgícoco, ú níyąc. naȟ'ú.** Then from outside he heard a woman calling her dogs. (Shields 50:81) ‣ **Tągápada tiyóba žé yús ú.** He was holding the door from the outside. (Cumberland 2005:400)

-tągena- ; **-tąguna-** *root* 1) older sister (male speaker) 2) older female parallel cousin (male speaker) *1s:* **mitągena** *2s:* **nitągena** *3s:* **táguna** *1p:* **ųgítągenabi**

-tąhą- ; **-tahą-** *root* brother-in-law (male speaker) *1s:* **mitą́hą** *2s:* **nitą́hą** *3s:* **tahácu** ; **tahágu** *Vcaus:* **tahą́guya**

-tąhąši- *root* male cross-cousin (male speaker) ‣ **Tą́hą́ši, ą́ba dayą́ yuhá!** Cousin, have a good day! *1s:* **mitą́hąši** *2s:* **nitą́hąši** *3s:* **tahą́šicu** ; **tahą́šitku**

tą'į *vs* s/he/it is visible, apparent; famous ‣ **Hąwí tą'į́šį a'óhązi no.** The sun is not visible, it is overcast. *1s:* **matą́'į** *2s:* **nitą́'į** *1p:* **ųtą́'įbi**

ţạ'íšị *vs* s/he/it disappears, is out of sight, lost ▸ **Dókiya ta'íšị.** She disappeared somewhere. ▸ **Ịknúhạnaȟ ta'íšị.** It disappeared suddenly. ▸ **Mitáwacị dókedu ţạ'íšị.** I am very undecided. ▸ **Yuwágan eyáya ecédu dóki kowá eyáya ţạ'íšị.** It lifted him up, then it took him out of sight. (NS 2002:15) *1s:* **matá'ịšị** *2s:* **nitá'ịšị** *1p:* **ụtá'ịbiši** *Adv:* **ţạ'íyạ**

ţạ'íyạ *adv* in sight, visible ▸ **Ţạ'íyạ yịgá.** He is visible.

-ţạkši- *root* younger sister (male speaker) ▸ **Mitákšịȟtịyešị.** She is not my real sister. ▸ **Mitákši Nakón'i'a cíga.** My little sister wants to speak Nakoda. *1s:* **mitákši** *2s:* **nitákši** *3s:* **ţạkšítkuna** ; **ţạkšíju** *1p:* **ụgítạkšitkubina** *Vcaus:* **ţạkšíjuyA**

ţạkšíjuyA *vt1-caus* he has her as a younger sister

ţạktágA *vs-redup* they are big, large ▸ **Ịštá ţạktágabi.** They have big eyes. ▸ **Šụktógeja núba wawícạmnaga'. Ţạktágabi'!** I saw two wolves. They were big!

ţạníjana *n* gnat, sandfly

ţạsákt'A *vs* s/he is frightened, scared *1s:* **ţạsákmat'a** *2s:* **ţạsáknit'a** *1p:* **ţạsák'ụt'abi** *Vcaus:* **ţạsákt'ekiyA, ţạsákt'eyA**

ţạsákt'ekiyA *vt1-caus* s/he frightens, scares sb *1s:* **ţạsákt'awakiya** *2s:* **ţạsákt'ayakiya** *1p:* **ţạsákt'a'ụkiyabi**

ţạsákt'eyA *vt1-caus* s/he frightens, scares sb to death ▸ **A! Dohágeja ţạsákt'ewịcaya hụštá'.** He really scared them to death, it is said. (Shields 18:220) *1s:* **ţạsákt'ewaya** *2s:* **ţạsákt'eyaya** *1p:* **ţạsákt'e'ụyabi**

tegíciȟinabi *vt1-recip* they love one another *1p:* **te'ụgiciȟinabi**

t'egúza *vii* s/he plays dead *1s:* **t'ewágụza** *2s:* **t'eyágụza**

téhạ *adv* 1) late ▸ **Téhạ kníšị.** He got back late. 2) long time ▸ **Téhạ mạgá** I sat down for a long time. ▸ **Téhạ mịštíma.** I have been asleep for a

long time. ▸ **Téhạ wạcímnagešị.** I did not see you for a long time.

téhạc'ehạ *adv* long time ago

téhạduwa *adv* a long distance, far away ▸ **Téhạduwa wa'íšị.** I did not go far. ▸ **Téhạduwa cén miní'ot'a.** It was a long way, so he drowned. (NS 2002:29)

tehạduwaȟ *adv* a very long distance, really far away ▸ **Eyáš gáki téhạduwaȟ kó ká.** She meant really far away over there. (Weasel 45:238)

téhạn *adv* far away, in a distance ▸ **Téhạn tí.** He lives far away. ▸ **Téhạn šnayá hịnápa.** He appeared clearly at a distance.

Téhạn Nakóda *nprop* Stoney Nakoda people, person of Stoney Nakoda descent *Lit:* far away Nakoda

téhạpadahạ ; **téhạdahạ** *adv* far from over there ▸ **Makóce téhạdahạ híbi.** They come from a far away land.

tehígA *vs* s/he/it is hard, difficult, critical ▸ **Ecúbi tehíga.** It is difficult to do. ▸ **Snokyíkte žé tehígešị.** It is not difficult to understand. ▸ **Cạšmúyabi pšụkáka nína yatábi tehíga.** These candies are very hard to chew. *Syn:* **otéȟigA**

tehína *vt1* s/he loves, holds on to smth, cherishes sb (like a relative), prizes smth and does not want to part with it ▸ **Temáyaȟina he? — Hạ tecíȟina no!** Do you love me? — Yes, I love you! ▸ **Macádeskuya tewáȟina cá no!** I really love my sweetheart. *1s:* **tewáȟina** *2s:* **teyáȟina** *1p:* **te'úȟinabi** *Vabs:* **watéȟina** *Vrecip:* **tegíciȟinabi**

tehíšị *vii* 1) it is easy ▸ **Nakón'i'abi tehíšị.** The Nakoda language is easy. 2) it is cheap ▸ **Cuwíknạga žé tehíšị.** This coat is cheap. *Adv:* **tehíšịyạ**

tehíšịyạ *adv* easily, without difficulty ▸ **Tehíšịyạ máni.** He walks easily. ▸ **Tehíšịyạȟ ecámụkte no.** I will do it very easily.

tehíyạ *adv* with difficulty, poorly ▸ **Tehíyạ yịgá.** He is in critical shape. ▸ **Tehíyạ wa'ú.** I am having a rough time. ‣ **Teȟíyą wįcáyak'ubi no!** You are giving them a rough time!

teȟpí *n* raw hide, buckskin ‣ **Teȟpí né šóga.** This buckskin is thick.

teȟpí hųská *cp* deerhide legging

teȟpí sąksája *cp* buckskin dress

teȟpíhąba *n* hide moccasins

teȟpípąpą *n* soft hide (like deer hide)

teȟpíšina *n* deerskin robe

t'ejá *vs* s/he is slow at moving ‣ **Anáciǧoptašį cén mat'eja, mahásuda áya ko!** I did not listen to you, and now I am slow with a hard skin! (BigEagle 2019:14) *1s:* **mat'éja** *2s:* **nit'éja** *1p:* **ųt'éjabi**

téjana ; téja *vs* 1) s/he/it is young (humans, animals) 2) it is new (things) ‣ **Iyécįgayena téja táwabi.** They own that new car. *1s:* **matéjana** *2s:* **nitéjana** *1p:* **ųtéjanabi** *Vredup:* **tektéjana**

tektéjana *vs-redup* they are new)

temní *vs* 1) s/he/it sweats *n* 2) sweat *1s:* **temámni** *2s:* **tenímni** *Vcaus:* **temníyA**

temní'įc'iyA *vi3-refl* s/he causes himself/herself to sweat *1s:* **temnímįc'iya** *2s:* **temnínįc'iya**

temnímna *vs* s/he/it smells of sweat

temníšmu *n* sweat drop

temníyA *vt1-caus* s/he/it causes sb to sweat *Vrefl:* **temní'įc'iyA**

temyÁ *vt1* s/he/it eats it all, devours smth ‣ **Iyúha temwįcayabi.** All were eaten up. (NS 2002:15) *1s:* **temwáya** *2s:* **temyáya** *Vabs:* **watémyA** *Vcaus:* **temyékiyA** *Vpos:* **tepkíyA**

temyékiyA *vt1-caus* s/he makes sb eat smth; stuffs sb (as a baby) ‣ **Taspą́ nówa temyéwakiya.** I made him eat all of the apples. *1s:* **temyéwakiya** *2s:* **temyéyakiya**

tepkíyA *vt1-pos* s/he eats up, devours his/her own ‣ **Tepkíye no!** He devoured his (meal). ‣ **Owá temwágiya.** I ate all of my own. *1s:* **temwágiya** *2s:* **temyágiya**

-teya- *root* co-wife *Usage:* obsolete. *1s:* **mitéya** *2s:* **nitéya** *3s:* **téyagu**

tezíȟnina *n* baby with the umbilical cord severed

tí *vi1* 1) s/he lives somewhere (house, place, area) ‣ **Nén watí.** I live here. ‣ **Húgu Céǧa K'ína ektá tí.** His mother lives in Carry The Kettle. ‣ **Duktén yatí?** Where do you live? *n* 2) house, place *Usage:* used mostly in compounds, or with a demonstrative. ‣ **gugúša tí** pigsty ‣ **Watí žé.** That is my house. ‣ **Tí žé į'ų́watų.** I painted her house. *1s:* **watí** *2s:* **yatí** *3s:* **tí** *1p:* **ųtíbi**

ti'ágaȟpa *n* roof *Syn:* **ti'ą́gam**

ti'ágasam *n* entrance, inside of a buiding

ti'ánagidą *vt1-pos* s/he flees, runs to his/her home

ti'ą́gam *n* roof *Syn:* **ti'ágaȟpa**

tíbi *n* house, dwelling, any type of structure ‣ **Tíbi žé yuhókšubi.** They destroyed the house. ‣ **Wayáwa tíbi dóhąn inánįkta?** When will you be setting to go to school? ‣ **Tíbi né miyé wagáǧa.** I am building this house myself. ‣ **Tíbi žé huȟnáǧa.** That house is burnt.

Tíbi háska *nprop* Long lodge (Nakoda chief and signatory of Treaty 4)

tíbi owáyužažabi *cp* laundromat

tíbi tą́ga *cp* Sun dance arbor

tíbi tokšú *cp* trailer house

tibúspA *vi1* s/he daubs a house, plasters a hole in a wall *1s:* **tiwábuspa** *2s:* **tiyábuspa** *1p:* **ti'ų́buspabi**

ticáktu *n* separate part of a building; private room

ticé *n* top part of a tipi where the poles are tied up

ticéda *n* smoke hole

ticógam *adv* in the center of a camp circle, room

ticóna *vs* s/he is homeless

ticówaknąga ; ticéwaknąga *n* flag

ticówaknąga onówą *cp* flag song

tída *Variant:* **cída** *adv* home, at home, homewards *Usage:* often used with going/returning verbs. ‣ **Tída kní.** He is arriving home. ‣ **Waná tída waknįkta.** I will return home now. ‣ **Cída ųknábi.** We are returning home. ‣ **Tíde yįgábi waštéwana.** I like sitting at home. *Cont:* **tín, cín**

tigádodo *vi1* s/he sweeps the floor of the house

tigáǧes'a *n* carpenter

tihókun *n* cellar, cold storage room; downstairs ‣ **Tihókun ékne.** Put it in the cellar. ‣ **Micįkši tihókun ú.** My son is downstairs.

tihúda *n* bottom of a tipi

tiȟáha *n* omasum

tiȟéyam *adv* behind the tent, house

ti'íyaza *adv* from house to house; all throughout camp ‣ **Žé ti'íyaz[a] ųdóbabi né ti'íyaz ųgánabikta.** The four of us will go all throughout the camp and pour it around. (Weasel 59:507) ‣ **Žécen hųgíye žé ti'íyaza yá ga'éca, wąží iyéya.** Then the camp crier went all around the camp, and then he found one. (Shields 26:69)

ti'įc'ijaǧA *vi3-refl* s/he builds a house for himself/herself *1s:* **timįc'ijaǧa** *2s:* **tinįc'ijaǧa**

ti'íjaškabi *n* tipi flap

ti'įktu *n* house in flames, arson

ti'íyužaža *n* mop ‣ **Ti'íyužaža žé baskíja.** Squeeze the mop.

tijáǧA *vi1* s/he builds a house; erects a tent, lodge *Vrefl:* **ti'įc'ijaǧA**

tijáǧabi *n* Sun dance arbor

tijáȟ *cont* Sun dance ‣ **tijáȟ wacíbi** Sun dance ‣ **Tijáȟ wanówą.** I sang Sun dance songs.

tijáȟ wacíbi *np* Sun dance

tijákna *adv* beside a dwelling, house ‣ **Amúgiyą žé tijákna yįgá.** The car is beside the house.

tikíyana *adv* near a tent

timágini *vt1-pos* s/he visits his/her relative or sb else's relatives ‣ **Dóhą mitúgaši timáyaginįkta?** When will you visit my grandfather? ‣ **Wéhą timáwįcagini.** Last spring she visited her relatives. *1s:* **timáwagini** *2s:* **timáyagini** *1p:* **timá'ųginibi**

timáhen *adv* inside smth, in (building, car) ‣ **Wí timáhen yįgá.** He is sitting in the tent. ‣ **Šúga wąží iyécįgana timáhen ú.** There is a dog in the car. ‣ **Timáhen dágunišį.** There is nothing inside.

timáhen úbi *cp* slipper

timáhentahą *adv* from indoors, from the inside ‣ **Wíyą úkta timáhentahą.** The woman will come from indoors.

timáni *vi1* s/he visits ‣ **Micįkši tawíju gicí timáni úbįkta.** My son and his wife are coming to visit. ‣ **Timáni wahí duká dóki inánabi žé snohwáyešį.** I came to visit, but I do not know where you all went. *1s:* **timáwani** *2s:* **timáyani** *1p:* **timá'ųnibi** *Vpos:* **timágini**

-timno- *root* 1) older brother (female speaker) ‣ **Mitímnobi mnihábi.** My older brothers are strong. 2) older male parallel cousin (female speaker) *1s:* **mitímno** *2s:* **nitímno** *3s:* **timnógu** *1p:* **ųgítimnobi ; ųgítimno**

-timnona- *root* older male parallel cousin (female speaker) *1s:* **mitímnona** *2s:* **nitímnona** *3s:* **timnóguna** *1p:* **ųgítimnona**

tín *adv* inside a house *Usage:* often pronounced **cín.** ‣ **Tín ú!** Come in! ‣ **Tín úkta cįgá.** She wants to come in.

ti'óba ; tiyóba *n* door ‣ **Ti'óba apápa.** He is knocking lightly on the door. ‣ **Ti'óba né kudína hą.** This door is hanging low. *1s:* **mitáti'oba** *2s:* **nitáti'oba**

ti'ócogamkiya *adv* toward the center of a camp circle, room

ti'óda *n* town, village *Lit:* many houses *Syn:* **otų́we**

ti'ódatąga *n* city

ti'óganu *n* house fan

ti'ógasni *vimp* there is a draft of cold air in a house

ti'ógijine *vt1-benef* s/he looks for a house, room for sb else *1s:* **ti'ówejine** *2s:* **ti'óyejine**

ti'ógijinoda *vt1-benef* s/he rents a house for sb else ▸ **Micúkši ti'ówejinoda.** I rent a house for my daughter. *1s:* **ti'ówejinoda** *2s:* **ti'óyejinoda**

ti'ógine *vt1-pos* s/he looks for his/her own house, room

ti'óȟnoga *n* smoke hole of a tipi

ti'ókadA *vimp* it is a hot dwelling

ti'ókšą ; tiwókšą *adv* around the house, camp ▸ **Koškábi nówa šųk'áganyąk tiwókšą wįnówąbis'a.** All of the young men used to ride horseback around the camp, singing love songs. (NS 2002:5)

ti'ónapA *vi1* s/he takes refuge, shelter inside

ti'óne *vi1* s/he looks for a home to buy, room to rent *1s:* **ti'ówane** *2s:* **ti'óyane** *Vbenef:* **ti'ógijine** *Vpos:* **ti'ógine**

ti'ónoda *vi1* s/he rents a house *1s:* **ti'ówanoda** *2s:* **ti'óyanoda** *Vbenef:* **ti'ógijinoda**

ti'ósni *vimp* it is a cold dwelling, house

ti'ósnikiya *n* air conditioning

ti'ósodA *vi-coll* people are all gone, have all left the house

ti'óšpaye *n* group of relatives, extended family

ti'óšijámna *vimp* it is a smelly house, dwelling

ti'óškadabi ti'úma *cp* gymnasium

ti'óšmu *vimp* there is dripping in a dwelling

tipésto *n* pointed tipi

típsina ; típšina *n* wild turnip ▸ **Típsina ųk'ábįkta.** We will dig out turnips.

Tiská Óda *ngeo* Chinook (Montana)

Titága *ngeo* Edmonton (Alberta) *Lit:* big lodge

titóką *n* See: **atítoką**

ti'úma *n* room

tiwáhe *n* family, household

tiwįcodA *vs-coll* there are many families ▸ **Įtó**

gán tiwįcoda tíbi. Well, there are many families living over there.

tiyám *adv* toward home; at home ▸ **Tiyám maní acíknįkta.** I will walk you home. ▸ **Tiyám wa'úšį.** I am not at home.

tiyám kní *cp* homerun

tiyápkiya *adv* toward home ▸ **Tiyápkiya nagípa.** He fled toward his home.

tiyóba įyúšpena *cp* doorknob

tiyóbaska (PR) *n* police, police car *Lit:* white doors

tiyógas'į *vi11* s/he peeks inside a tent

tiyóškadA *vi1* s/he plays in a lodge, house

tiyúdada *vi2* s/he cleans, tidies up a house *1s:* **timnúdada** *2s:* **tinúdada**

tiyúwąga *vi2* s/he takes a lodge down ▸ **Koškábi nówa tiyúwągabi.** All of the young men took the lodge down. *1s:* **timnúwąga** *2s:* **tinúwąga**

tiyúžaža *vi2* s/he cleans a house; washes the floor *1s:* **timnúžaža** *2s:* **tinúžaža**

tiyúžaža wįcášta *cp* janitor

tizí *n* belly

tįknámųmųna *n* partridge, grouse *Lit:* it tickles its wings/feathers

tįpsinaǧi *n* carrot *Syn:* **píȟpiǧana**

tįpšina skúye *cp* sugar beet

tįpšinašaša *n* beet *Lit:* red turnip

t'įsyá *adv* tightly ▸ **T'įsyá núzįkta.** You will hold onto it tightly.

tįšnága *n* 22° halo, circular halo around the sun on cold winter days

tįšnága bašnóga *cp* half halo around the sun, especially in March *Lit:* it takes its halo off

tó *vs* 1) s/he/it is blue ▸ **Mihų wašíju tíbi tó wąží okná tí.** My mother lives in a blue house. ▸ **Įštá tó.** His eyes are blue. ▸ **hųskáto** blue jeans, denims 2) s/he/it is green ▸ **wa'ówabitoto** paper money *1s:* **monó** *2s:* **nitó** *Adv:* **toyéna** *Vcaus:* **toyÁ** *Vredup:* **totóna**

togá *adv* before, ahead of time ‣ **Iyé, togá hí.** He, himself, arrived before.

Tóga *nprop* Gros Ventre, Atsina tribe, person of Gros Ventre, Atsina descent

tóga *n* enemy *Cont:* **tók-** *Vcaus:* **tógayA** *Vrecip:* **tógagiciyabi**

Togá giyą *nprop* First to fly (1887–1971); Nakoda chief, also known as Joshua Wetsit

togáda *adv* 1) ahead, in front, in the lead, in the first place ‣ **Togáda yá.** He is taking the lead. ‣ **Togáda hí.** He came first. 2) in the future, later ‣ **Togáda žéci yá.** He will go over there later. ‣ **Togáda dágu ecánųħtįyįkta?** What will you do exactly in the future?

togádagiya *adv* in the future ‣ **Dókaš togádagiya amógįyą opécijitų.** Maybe one day I will buy you a car. ‣ **Togádagiya štén gitézibina nená tawácį nągú cądé waš'ága ománibįkta.** In the future the kids will walk with a strong mind and heart.

tógagiciyabi *vii-recip* they are enemies, at war against one another *1p:* **tóga'ųgiciyabi**

togágihĄ *vs* 1) s/he is in the lead; s/he is the first *n* 2) leader

togáhe *adv, num* 1) first, the first, one in the first place ‣ **Togáhe sihá ħniħníbi.** First they had scabs on their feet. ‣ **togáheħ** the very first one *vs* 2) s/he/it is the first; is in the lead

togáhe įnážįbi *cp* first base player

togáheħ *num* the very first one

togáheya *adv* first, in the first place ‣ **Įtó togáheya cába žé giknúkši.** Well first he [Įktomi] ordered the beaver to dive. (Drummond 1976, The flood) ‣ **Žé omnágįkta duká įtó togáheya né žepá.** I will tell that one, but first I will tell this. (NS 2002:41)

togáħ *adv* ahead of time; first ‣ **Miyéš togáħ wakní.** As for myself, I came home ahead of time. ‣ **Micúkši togáħ yazą́.** My daughter got sick first.

togáħtani *adv* early evening

togáħtįyĄ *vs* s/he/it is the very first ‣ **Togáħtįyą žehą žeyá.** He said that in the very first place.

togám *adv* ahead, in the lead ‣ **Togám ų́.** He remains ahead. ‣ **Togám nážį.** He stood in front.

togámpadahą *adv* from somewhere else ‣ **Žécen togámpadahą híbi.** So then they arrived from somewhere else.

togápa *n* 1) first born child in a family *vs* 2) s/he is the oldest child of a family ‣ **Mąkóce né miyé wagáǧa cén matógapa.** I made this earth myself, so I am the oldest. (NS 2002:32) *1s:* **matógapa** *2s:* **nitógapa** *Adv:* **togám**

tógayA *vt1-caus* s/he has sb as an enemy

togíjikšu *vt1-benef* s/he hauls, transports smth for sb else ‣ **Adé towéjikšu.** I haul it for my father. *1s:* **towéjikšu** *2s:* **toyéjikšu**

togíjiyA *vt1-benef* s/he paints, colors sb, smth in blue for sb

togíknąga *adv* different kinds ‣ **Íyą nówa togíknąga.** All kinds of rocks.

togíyA *vt1-pos* s/he paints, colors, dyes his/her own blue

tohe; tihe. *n* his/her place, house, bed ‣ **Tíbi né miyé matóhe.** This house is my own place. *1s:* **matóhe ; mitóhe** *2s:* **nitóhe**

toħmísu *n* rope, leather rope

tóħtįyĄ *vs* it is purple *Lit:* intense blue

to'í'ebi *n* one's language; his/her/their language

to'įc'iyA *vi3-refl* s/he paints himself/herself in blue *1s:* **tomįc'iya** *2s:* **tonįc'iya**

tók- *cont* enemy

tokám *adv* away from ‣ **Waħ'áksija né yúda hįk tokám iyáya.** The bear ate it and went away.

tokámpadahą *adv* from a different place ‣ **Tokámpadahą hí.** He arrived from a different place.

tokána *n* gray fox; swift fox

Tokána wacíbi *Variant:* **Tokána owáci** *cp* Fox dance

toką́ *vs* 1) it is different ‣ **Nągáš toką́.** Now it is different. ‣ **Gídąna toką́.** It is a little bit different. ‣ **Wíyą toką́ gecíbi.** They thought she was a different woman. (Drummond 1976, A bear story) *adv* 2) different, differently ‣ **Duwéh̃ toką́ hí.** Somebody different came.

Toką́bi *nprop* Strangers people

toką́h̃ṭiyą *adv* quite differently

toką́ką *vs-redup* they are different ‣ **Duká nągú toką́ką ahíyayes'a.** He used to sing different songs. (NS 2002:4)

toką́yą *adv* differently ‣ **Toką́yą ecú!** Change your ways!

tokšú *vt1* s/he/it hauls, transports smth from one place to another ‣ **Owá to'úkšubi.** We hauled all of it. *1p:* **to'úkšubi** *Vbenef:* **togíjikšu**

tóktamakoce *n* enemy territory ‣ **Tóktamakoce ektá múgįkta no.** I will lie dead in enemy territory. (Shields 78:434, our translation)

Toktí *ngeo* Hays (Montana) *Syn:* **Agáda**

tóna *vs* s/he/it is light blue

tónah̃ṭiyĄ *vs* s/he/it is very light blue

tósabA *vs* s/he/it is dark blue, almost black *Lit:* black blue

tosą́ *vs* it is light blue *Lit:* pale blue *See:* **są́**

tošá *vs* it is purple *Syn:* **tóh̃ṭiyĄ**

-toška- *root* nephew (brother's son; female speaker) *1s:* **mitóška** *2s:* **nitóška**

tošúda *n* area near the door, or door flap inside a tipi

totóba *vs* it is damp, wet

totóna *vs-redup* s/he/it is light blue

tó'ų *n* homeland *1s:* **mitó'ų** *2s:* **nitó'ų** *3s:* **tó'ų**

toyÁ *vt1-caus* s/he colors, paints, dyes smth blue *Adv:* **toyéna** *Vbenef:* **togíjiyA** *Vpos:* **togíyA** *Vrefl:* **to'íc'iyA**

toyéna *adv* blue, green condition

tóyude kneyábi *cp* food offering

-tožą- ; **-tožąna-** *root* niece (brother's daughter; female speaker) *1s:* **mitóžąna** *2s:* **nitóžąna** *3s:* **tožą́gu**

-tugaši- tą́ga *root+vs* great-grandfather *1s:* **mitúgaši tą́ga** *2s:* **nitúgaši tą́ga**

-tugaši- ; **-tugą́ši-** ; **-tugągiši-** *root* grandfather ‣ **Jim žé mitúgašina.** Jim is my grandfather. ‣ **Nitúgaši įwúǧa.** Ask your grandfather. ‣ **Tugą́gišiktu cažé yuhá.** He has his grandfather's name. ‣ **Tugą́gišiktu anágipa.** He runs to his grandfather for protection. *1s:* **mitúgaši** *2s:* **nitúgaši** *3s:* **tugą́gišiktu** (CTK) ; **tugą́šicu, tugą́šitku** (PR, OM) *1p:* **ųgítugągišitku**

tugą́šina ; **tugą́šina** *n* 1) Grandfather! (address form). ‣ **Tugášina ceyá wa'ú no.** Grandfather, I am constantly crying. 2) creator 3) president

tugí *n* shell, seashell, pearl

tugígina *n* snail

Tugíska wakpá *ngeo* Musselshell River (Montana)

tugískana *n* white shell

túǧa *vs* s/he is hunched back *1s:* **matúǧa** *2s:* **nitúǧa**

tuh̃mą́ǧa *n* bee ‣ **Tuh̃mą́ǧa tahú yah̃tága.** The bee stung him on the neck.

tuh̃mą́ǧa cesní *cp* honey *Lit:* bee feces

tuh̃mą́h̃ṭaga *n* wasp, bumblebee

tuh̃mą́h̃ti *n* beehive, bumblebee nest ‣ **Tuh̃mą́h̃ti žé wagámneja.** I scattered the bumblebee nest by hitting on it.

tušú *n* tipi pole, lodge pole

tušúda *n* place near the entrance of a tipi ‣ **Yusnúda hį́k tušúda gán k'į́'įyeya.** He pulled him out and tossed him over there to the place by the door. (Weasel 164:38)

tutÁ *vs* it is sour, bitter, astringent ‣ **Cąšmúyabi pšųkáka tutá.** These candies are sour. ‣ **taspą́ ǧí tutá** lemon

tutú *vs* s/he/it has a messy behind

tų́₁ *n* pus ‣ **Nąbé yazą́ žé tų́ ožúna.** That sore hand is full of pus.

tų́₂ *vt1-dit* 1) s/he puts smth on sb *Usage:* occurs almost exclusively in compounds. ‣ **acáštų** s/he names sb after another person 2) *vt1* s/he bears smth; is equipped with smth; is in relation with smth *Usage:* occurs almost exclusively in compounds. ‣ **tawį́jutų** he has sb for wife, he is married ‣ **hįknátų** she has a husband; is married ‣ **sįtų́** s/he/it is fat (lit. s/he/it bears fat) *1s:* **watų́** *2s:* **yatų́** *1p:* **ųtų́bi** *Vpos:* **gitų́**

tų́₃ *vt1* 1) she bears a child, gives birth to sb; lays an egg ‣ **Ą́bahotuna wį́tka óda tų́.** The chicken laid many eggs. (Cumberland 2005:356) *1s:* **watų́** *2s:* **yatų́** *1p:* **ųtų́bi** *Vcoll:* **wįcátųga** *vs-pass* 2) s/he/it is born *Usage:* inflects like a stative verb when used in the passive voice with -bi. ‣ **Tahé nén matų́bi no.** I am born here in Moose Mountains. ‣ **Céǧa K'į́na én matų́bi.** I was born in Carry The Kettle. *1s:* **matų́bi** *2s:* **nitų́bi** *See:* **togápa**

-tųga- ; -tųgą- *root* father-in-law *1s:* **mitų́ga** *2s:* **nitų́ga** *3s:* **tųgą́gu** ; **tųgágu** *Vcaus:* **tųgáguyA**

tųgáguyA *vt1-caus* s/he has him as a father-in-law *1s:* **tųgáguwaya** *2s:* **tųgáguyaya**

Tųgášina makóce *ngeo* United States of America *Syn:* **Cągúsam**

-tųška- *root* nephew (sister's son; male speaker) *1s:* **mitų́ška** *2s:* **nitų́ška** *3s:* **tųškágu** ; **tųškácu** ; **tųšká**

-tųwį- ; -tųwįna- *root* 1) aunt (father's sister) 2) aunt (mother's brother's wife) ‣ **Iná, mitų́wį įš nén ų́bi.** My mom and my aunt too live here. *1s:* **mitų́wį** ; **mitų́wįna** *2s:* **nitų́wį** ; **nitų́wįna** *3s:* **tųwį́ju** ; **tųwį́juna**

tųyą́ *vs* it (sore) suppurates, emits pus

-tųžą- *root* niece (sister's daughter; male speaker) *1s:* **mitų́žą** *2s:* **nitų́žą** *3s:* **tųžą́co**

U

ú *vi1* s/he comes, arrives here from there ‣ **Wa'úkte no.** I will be coming. ‣ **Néci ú!** Come here! ‣ **Ú ciší.** I tell you to come. ‣ **Nahą́h́ úkta he?** Is he yet to come? *1s:* **wa'ú** *2s:* **ya'ú** *1p:* **ųk'úbi** *Vbenef:* **gíji'u** *Vcaus:* **ukíyA**

ubí *n* tail of bird

ubížade *n* barn swallow *Lit:* forked tail

ukíyA *vt1-caus* s/he makes sb come here *1s:* **uwákiya** *2s:* **uyákiya**

úna *vi1* s/he (child, little animal) comes, arrives here from there ‣ **Eyáš šųkšóšona úna néci eyáš iyóptaya agíktaga cén.** Then the little donkey came over here, and he ran toward it. (Weasel 15:141)

utÁ *vi1* s/he fires, shoots, discharges a weapon ‣ **Utábi ųspém'įc'iya.** I taught myself how to shoot. *See:* **a'útA**

utábi *n* sound of a shotgun

uyá *vimp* the wind blows this way ‣ **Tadé uyá né, cą́ né yuksá.** The wind blew this way and broke the tree.

Ų

-ų- ; -ųg- *prefix-infix* 1) we two (1st person dual) *Usage:* subject of active and stative verbs; -ųg-occurs before a vowel. ‣ **maní > ma'ųni** s/he walks > we two walk ‣ **įštíma > ųgíštima** s/he sleeps > we two sleep ‣ **ípi > ųgípi** s/he is full, sated > we two are full, sated 2) us two (1st person dual) *Usage:* patient of transitive verbs. ‣ **yucéya > ųyúceya** s/he makes sb cry > s/he makes us two cry or we two make sb cry ‣ **wąyága > wą'ų́yaga** s/he sees sb, smth > s/he sees us two or we two see sb, smth

-ų- . . .-bi ;-ųg- . . .-bi *circumfix* 1) we (1st person plural) *Usage:* subject of active and stative verbs. ‣ **wąyága > wą'ų́yagabi** s/he sees sb, smth > we see sb ‣ **ištíma > ųgį́štimabi** s/he sleeps > we sleep ‣ **į́pi > ųgį́pibi** s/he is full, sated > we are full, sated 2) us (1st person plural) *Usage:* patient of transitive verbs. ‣ **yucéya > ųyúceyabi** s/he makes sb cry > s/he makes us cry or we make sb cry ‣ **wąyága > wą́ų́yagabi** s/he sees sb, smth > s/he sees us or we see sb

ų́₁ *vi1* 1) s/he/it is, lives, exists ‣ **Né téhą niyáhą ya'ų́kta!** You will be living for a long time! ‣ **Ȟaȟátųwą óm ųk'ų́bis'a.** We used to live with the Gros Ventres. 2) s/he stays, lives somewhere ‣ **Waná nén wa'ų́.** Now I live here. 3) s/he feels; exists, is in a certain way ‣ **Dóken ya'ų́? — Dąyą́ wa'ų́.** How are you? — I am fine. ‣ **Síjaȟ ųk'ų́bi.** We are getting along bad. ‣ **Mitúgašibi dóken i'ábi žé įyúkcą wa'ų́.** I am thinking of how my grandfathers spoke. *vi1-aux* 4) s/he does continuously; goes around doing smth ‣ **Įȟá ya'ų́.** You are continuously laughing. ‣ **Tugášina ceyá wa'ų́ no!** Grandfather I am going, crying! *1s:* **wa'ų́** *2s:* **ya'ų́** *1p:* **ųk'ų́bi**

ų́₂ *vt3* 1) s/he wears smth ‣ **Wapáha né nų́kta he?** Are you going to wear this hat? ‣ **Dáguškina žé ų́.** The baby is wearing it. ‣ **Ų́ nážį.** She is standing wearing it. ‣ **Cuwíknąga žé ziyéna ų́.** He wears a yellow shirt. ‣ **Wįkóške né šiná ayázabi ų́.** This young woman was wearing a beaded shawl. 2) s/he uses smth ‣ **Mína žé ų́.** Use that knife. ‣ **Iyé táwa žé ų́.** He uses his own. ‣ **Štušténa jónana ų́bi emą́giyabi.** They told me to use a little bit of salt. *1s:* **mų́** *2s:* **nų́** *1p:* **ųk'ų́bi** *Vbenef:* **gíji'ų** *Vcaus:* **ųkíyA** *Vpos:* **gic'ų́**

ų́ca *vt1* s/he imitates sb

ųgí- *pref* our (1st person dual possessor) ‣ **dagúye > ųgídaguye** relative > our relative ‣ **šiná > ųgítašina** blanket > our blanket ‣ **táwa > ųgítawa** s/he owns it, it is his/her own; his/her > we two own it, it is our own

ųgí-...-bi *circumfix* our (1st person plural possessor) ‣ **dagúye > ųgídaguyabi** relative > our relative ‣ **šiná > ųgítašinabi** blanket > our blanket ‣ **táwa > ųgítawa** s/he owns it, it is his/her own; his/her > we two own it, it is our own

ų́'į *n* hazelnut

ųji *voc* Grandmother! (address form).

Ųjímąka *nprop* Grandmother Earth

ųká₁ *voc* Grandfather! (address form). *Syn:* **gagá**

ųká₂ *conj, encl* *See:* **duká**

ųkáš *part, conj* if, if only (marker of optative modality) ‣ **Mázaska mnuhá ųkáš no.** If only I had money. ‣ **Naȟ'ų́ ųkáš, aké epéšį ca.** If he had been listening, I would not have to say it again. ‣ **Tawáci dąyą́ ųkáš waštékta oká.** It would be nice if he had a straight mind.

ų́kca *vi1* s/he farts *1s:* **ų́wakca** *2s:* **ų́yakca** *Vredup:* **ų́kcakcaya**

ų́kca iyéyA *vi1* s/he/it farts suddenly, unexpectedly

ų́kcakcaya *vi1-redup* s/he walks along farting *1s:* **ų́kcakcawaya** *2s:* **ų́kcakcayaya**

ų́kcana *vi1* it (baby) farts

ųkcé *n* feces *Redup:* **ųkcékcena**

ųkcékcena *n-redup* 1) cactus, prickly pear cactus 2) fig

ųkcékiǧa *n* magpie

ųkcémna *vs* it smells like feces

ųkíyA *vt1* s/he makes sb wear smth ‣ **Cuwíknąga žé ųkíya.** Make him wear his coat. *1s:* **ųwákiya** *2s:* **ųyákiya**

ų́na *vt3* s/he uses smth small; s/he/it (baby, child) wears smth

ųpą́ *n* female elk

ų́s *Variant:* **ų́** *post* using it, with it, because of it *Usage:* occurs after the word for the thing or body part used. ‣ **Sakyé ų́s mawáni.** I walk with a cane. ‣ **Wa'ówabi ų́s iyéskabi.** They translate using a book. ‣ **Wįhámne né ų́s tawáci dąyą́šį.** He is moody because of this dream. ‣ **Pežúda né ų́s mayášpuya.** I am itchy because of this medicine. ▸ **Dágu ų́ hú waknúk'eǧa.** I scratched my leg on something.

ús įbásisa *ph* sewing machine

ųspé₁ *vs* s/he learns, acquires a skill ▸ **Micíkši óda ųspékta.** My son will learn a lot. ▸ **Iyábi ųspéc.** He learned to walk on his own. (Cumberland 2005:396) *1s:* **ųmáspe** *2s:* **ųníspe** *1p:* **ųgų́spebi** *Vabs:* **wa'ų́spe** *Vcaus:* **ųspékiyA** *Vcoll:* **ųspéwįcakiyA** *Vrefl:* **ųspé'įc'iyA**

ųspé₂ *n* axe ▸ **Ųspé waknúmąšį.** I did not sharpen my axe.

ųspéhudana *n* hatchet ▸ **Ųspéhudana žé giksúyešį.** Do not forget the hatchet.

ųspé'įc'iyA *vi3-refl* s/he learns smth on his/her own ▸ **Utábi ųspém'įc'iya.** I taught myself how to shoot. *1s:* **ųspémįc'iciya** *2s:* **ųspénįc'iciya**

ųspékiyA *vt1-caus* s/he teaches smth to sb ▸ **Né duwé ųspénijiya he?** Do you have someone to teach you? ▸ **Ową́ga onéžiši žécen ųspéwakiya.** I teach him not to pee in bed. ▸ **Dóken ecúbi ųspémąkiya.** Teach me how to do it. ▸ **Duktén ųspéwįcayakiya?** Where do you teach? ▸ **Wįcábi ųspéwįcakiyebįšį, ecén núš.** These men do not teach them, that is the way it is. *1s:* **ųspéwakiya** *2s:* **ųspéyakiya** *1p:* **ųspé'ųkiyabi**

ų́ši *vs* s/he/it is pitiful *1s:* **ų́maši** *2s:* **ų́niši**

ų́šiga *vs* s/he is poor, pitiful ▸ **Ų́šigabi otí'įgešį.** I do not think they are poor. ▸ **Midáguyabi nína ų́šigabi.** My relatives are very poor. *1s:* **ų́mašiga** *2s:* **ų́nišiga** *1p:* **ųgų́šigabi**

ų́šigiya *adv* pitifully, humbly ▸ **Midáguyabi nína ų́šigiya nážį bo!** My relatives stand very humbly!

ų́ši'įc'ina *vi3-refl* s/he pities, humbles himself/herself ▸ **Nína ų́ši'įc'ina i'á.** He spoke very pitifully. *1s:* **ų́šimįc'ina** *2s:* **ų́šinįc'ina**

ų́šina *vt1* s/he pities, has compassion for sb ▸ **Ų́šimana wo.** Pity me. ▸ **Wįcá žé ų́šiwana.** I pity that man. ▸ **Cądé mayúką cén ų́šiwana.** I pity him because I have a heart *1s:* **ų́šiwana**

2s: **ų́šiyana** *Vabs:* **wa'ų́šina** *Vcoll:* **wawįca'ų́šina** *Vrefl:* **ų́ši'įc'ina**

ų́šiya *adv* pitifully, humbly

Ų́šiya máni *nprop* 1) Ocean Man (Nakoda chief) *ngeo* 2) Ocean Man reservation (Saskatchewan) *Lit:* lame walker

ųwą́šį *adv* still, quiet ▸ **Ųwą́šį nągíkta.** You will stay still.

ųwą́ži *n* one place ▸ **Dóhąni ųwą́ži ų́šį.** She did not stay in one place.

ųzé *n* buttocks ▸ **Ųzé ȟniȟní.** He has rashes on the buttocks. *1s:* **ma'ų́ze** *2s:* **ni'ų́ze**

ųzéšį *n* rump fat

ųzíhektam ; ųzéktam *adv* backward ▸ **Ųzéktam nážị.** He stands backward.

ųzímani *vi1* s/he walks backward *Adv:* **ųzímaniya**

ųzímaniya *adv* backward

ųzį́kpakįdA *vi1-pos* 1) s/he wipes his/her own buttocks, behind *n* 2) toilet paper

ųzóȟnoga *n* anus, rectum

ųzóžuha *n* pants

W

wa- *pref* things, stuff (marker of an indefinite object) *Usage:* derives nouns or abstract verbs of Class 1. ▸ **hąbí > wahą́bi** juice > broth ▸ **pahá > wapáha** hair > hat ▸ **co'ų́ba > wacó'ųba** s/he roasts smth > s/he roasts things

-wa- *prefix-infix* I (1st person singular) *Usage:* agent/subject of active verbs of Class 1. ▸ **hí > wahí** s/he arrives here > I arrive here ▸ **mapí > mawáni** s/he walks > I walk

wá *n* 1) snow ▸ **Nína wá gaȟmóga.** The snow is blowing away hard. ▸ **Wá yupšų́ka.** He made it into a snowball. *vs* 2) s/he/it is snowy ▸ **Makóce én dóhąni wášį.** The land that is never snowy.

wá yupšų́kabi *cp* snowball

wa'ágąn *adv* on the snow ▸ **Wa'ágąn įȟpéya.** He dropped it on the snow.

wa'ágiciyazabi *vi1-recip* they bead for one another

wa'ágijiyaza *vt1-benef* s/he beads for sb *1s:* **wa'áwejimnaza** *2s:* **wa'áyejimnaza**

wa'águ *vi1-abs* s/he brings back things

wa'áhopA *vi1-abs* s/he shows respect for people, things

wa'áhopabi *n* respect ‣ **Wa'áhopabi dágu snokyábišį.** They do not have any respect. (Cumberland 2005:361)

wa'á'i'A *vi1-abs* s/he gossips about things ‣ **Wįcą́bi wa'á'i'abišįs'a.** Men don't usually gossip. *See:* **a'í'A**

wa'á'i'abi *n* gossip

wa'ákinija *vi1-abs* s/he debates, argues over things ‣ **Gicí wa'áwakinija** I am debating with him. *1s:* **wa'áwakinija** *2s:* **wa'áyakinija**

wa'ákipa *vi1-abs* s/he meets someone, people

wa'áknaza *vt1-pos* s/he does his/her own beadwork

wa'ákni *vi1-abs* s/he brings things back home *1s:* **wa'áwakni** *2s:* **wa'áyakni**

wa'ámnezA *vi1-abs* 1) s/he examines, scrutinizes, studies things *n* 2) examiner

wa'ámnoša *n* red-wing blackbird

wa'ánagijiǧoptą *vt1-benef* s/he listens to what sb has to say *1s:* **wa'ánawejiǧoptą** *2s:* **wa'ánayejiǧoptą**

wa'ánaǧoptą *vi1-abs* s/he listens to things ‣ **Wa'ánaǧoptą nážį.** He stands to listen. ‣ **Wa'ánaǧoptą wa'í.** I went there to listen. ‣ **Šką́šį wa'ánaǧoptą yįgábi.** They were sitting still and listening. *Vbenef:* **wa'ánagijiǧoptą**

wa'ánąptA *vi1-abs* s/he stops, blocks, forbids things *1s:* **wa'ánąwapta** *2s:* **wa'ánąyapta**

wa'ániya hiyáya *cp* ski-doo (snowmobile)

wa'ánowes'a *n* chanting doctor

wa'ápe *vi1-abs* s/he waits for things, people ‣ **Néci wa'ápe.** Wait over here.

wa'ápes'a *n* beater

wa'áskamyA *vi1-abs* s/he sticks things

wa'ás'į *vi1-abs* s/he wishes *1s:* **wawá'as'į** *2s:* **wayá'as'į**

wa'ášnoya *vi1-abs* s/he solders things

wa'áwąyagA *vi1-abs* s/he looks, watches things

wa'áwąyage ; wa'áwąyaga *n* guard, patrol

wa'áyaza *vi1-abs* s/he beads *1s:* **wa'ámnaza** *2s:* **wa'ánaza** *Vbenef:* **wa'ágijiyaza** *Vpos:* **wa'áknaza** *Vrecip:* **wa'ágiciyazabi**

wa'áyazabi ; wa'áyaza *n* beadwork

wa'áyuptA *vi1-abs* s/he answers ‣ **Duwé wa'áyuptįkta?** Who will answer? *1s:* **wa'ámnupta** *2s:* **wa'ánupta**

wa'ázinyA *vi1-abs* s/he smudges things ritually

wa'ážutųbi *n* regalia, decorated outfit

wábaha *n* eagle staff, banner

wábah̃ta ; wóbah̃te *n* sacred bundle ‣ **Wabáh̃ta awą́yagįkta.** He will look after the sacred bundles.

wabáksA *vi1-abs* s/he breaks things manually or by pressure

wabámnayA *vi1-abs* s/he irons clothes

wabásisA *vi1-abs* s/he sews, mends things

wacápA *vi1-abs* s/he stabs people

Wacápe óda *nprop* Stabbed many times (woman from Carry The Kettle who had been stabbed many times by Blackfeet warriors)

wacą́ǧa *n* sweetgrass

wacą́h̃iyA *vs* s/he is lucky ‣ **Maskámna cén wacą́h̃iya.** He was lucky to win this money. ‣ **Žécen wacą́h̃iya į́kusąna kóko wįcáyuza.** When they were lucky, they also caught mink. (Shields 68:305) *1s:* **wacą́h̃imaya** *2s:* **wacą́h̃iniya** *Vrefl:* **wacą́h̃'įc'iyA**

wacą́h̃iyeja *vs* s/he is lucky, fortunate *1s:* **wacą́h̃imayeja** *2s:* **wacą́h̃iniyeja** *Vrefl:* **wacą́h̃'įc'iyA**

wacą́h̃'įc'iyA *vi3-refl* s/he is lucky *1s:* **wacą́h̃-mįc'iya** *2s:* **wacą́h̃-nįc'iya**

wacégiyA *vi1-abs* s/he prays ‣ **Iyúhana wacégiyabi.** They pray in a mass. ‣ **Nągáhą wacé'ųgiyabi.** Now we pray together. ‣ **Ų́šigiya nawážį**

híkna wacéwagiye no. I stand humbly and I pray. ▸ **Ecén íš wacéwagiye no.** That is the way I pray. *1s:* **wacéwagiya** *2s:* **wacéyagiya** *1p:* **wacé'ųgiyabi**

wacégiyabi *n* prayer, ceremony

wacéğuğu *n-redup* pieces of tallow

wacį 1) *vi3* s/he feels like doing smth ▸ **Nowábi ecú wacámį.** I feel like singing. (Cumberland 2005:395) *1s:* **wacámį** *2s:* **wacánį** 2) *n* mind, plan, goodwill ▸ **Tawácį dąyáší.** He is moody. ▸ **Tawácį ecéduší.** He is stupid. ▸ **Tawácį wašté no!** She has a good mind! *1s:* **mitáwacį** *2s:* **nitawacį** *3s:* **tawácį** 3) *part* it is about to happen; intentive, prospective, or imminent event *Usage:* triggers e-ablaut. ▸ **Mağážu wacį no.** It is about to rain. ▸ **Dágúškina oğúğįkta wacį** The baby is about to wake up. ▸ **Wáhįhe wáci.** Looks like it is about to snow. (Cumberland 2005:43)

wací *vi1* 1) s/he dances ▸ **Dóhąn wa'úcibįkta?** When will we dance? ▸ **Dąyá wayáci no.** You dance well. ▸ **Wawácįkteší no.** I will not dance. ▸ **Wa'úci céyaga.** Let us dance. ▸ **Wanágaš wacíbi né ecén.** Long ago they danced like this. *1s:* **wawáci** *2s:* **wayáci** *1p:* **wa'úcibi** *Vcaus:* **wacíkiyA** *n* 2) dance ▸ **Šųkwáci** Horse dance

wací įknúza *vi1* s/he is dressed in regalia

wací okónagiciye *cp* dance committee

wacíbi *n* dance ▸ **Hácogądu žehá wacíbi žedáhą wakní.** I came home from the dance at midnight.

wacíbi ecúbinas'a *np* dance contestant

wacíbi įknúza *cp* costume

wacígiyA *vt1-pos* s/he depends on his/her own will

wacį'įc'iyA *vi3-refl* s/he depends on himself/ herself

wacíkiyA *vt1-caus* s/he makes sb dance ▸ **Né míš imáduka cen wacíciciyabic.** It was just me—I was hungry so I made you dance. (Weasel 4:69) ▸ **Misúgabi mitágožabina kówa**

waciwįcawakiyįktac. I am going to make all of my little brothers and my grandchildren dance. (NS 2002:42) *1s:* **wacíwakiya** *2s:* **wacíyakiya** *1p:* **wací'ųkiyabi**

wacís'a *n* dancer ▸ **Micúkši wacís'a yuká.** My daughter is a dancer.

wacíyA *vt1* s/he depends on sb, smth ▸ **Midáguyabi wacíwįcawaya.** I depend on my relatives. *1s:* **wacíwaya** *2s:* **wacíyaya** *1p:* **wací'ųyabi** *Vpos:* **wacígiyA** *Vrefl:* **wací'įc'iyA**

wacíhe *n* feather, plume tied up in the hair

wací'iyogipi *vs* s/he feels happy ▸ **Ąbédu nén wací'iyomagipi.** I feel happy today. *1s:* **wací'iyomagipi** *2s:* **wací'iyonigipi**

wacíko *vs* s/he is quick to anger ▸ **Adé tawácį wacíko ús tehíya mawáni.** Because dad angered quickly I behave problematically. *1s:* **wamácįko** *2s:* **wanícįko**

wacímnezA *vs* s/he thinks clearly *1s:* **wacímamneza** *2s:* **wacínimneza**

wacíšijA *vs* s/he is cranky ▸ **Hąyákena štén ecágen wacímašija.** When it is early morning I am always cranky. *1s:* **wacímašija** *2s:* **wacínišija**

wacítųší *vi1* s/he/it is thoughtless ▸ **Dąyá wóknagabi žená wacítųší no.** Those nice stories are thoughtless. *1s:* **wacíwatųší** *2s:* **wacíyatųší**

wacógądu *vs* it is in the middle of the snow *Adv:* **wacógąn**

wacógąn *adv* in the middle of the snow ▸ **Wacógąn yįgá.** He is sitting in the middle of the snow.

wacógu *vi1-abs* s/he threatens people

wacóğuğu *n* Indian popcorn

wacó'įc'iba *vi3-abs-refl* s/he cooks smth for himself/herself *1s:* **wacómįc'iba** *2s:* **wacónįc'iba**

wacónice *n* dried meat *Syn:* **coníca**

wacó'ųba *vi1-abs* s/he roasts, fries, cooks things *Vrefl:* **wacó'įc'iba** *See:* **co'úba**

wacúwiska *n* grizzly *Syn:* **wağí**

wáda *n* 1) canoe, boat, ship ‣ **Wáda ųgítawabi.** We own canoes. ‣ **Wáda awáyaga.** He is looking after the canoe. 2) train, engine ‣ **Wáda žé yá.** The train is going. ‣ **Wáda žé núzahą.** The train is fast.

wáda įtókšu *cp* freight car

wáda o'įnažį *cp* train depot

wádagiyą *n* airplane; aircraft carrier *Lit*: flying canoe

wádagiyą o'įnažį *cp* airport

wadágu'įc'ina *vi3-refl* s/he feels, thinks greatly of himself/herself 1s: **wadágumįc'ina** 2s: **wadágunįc'ina**

wadáguyA *vi1-abs* s/he has relatives

wadáguye *n* friendship

wádapa *n* tractor

wadásakyA *vi1-abs* s/he freezes things

wadó *n* canoe

wadó k'į *vt1* s/he does a portage 1s: **wadó wak'į** 2s: **wadó yak'į** 1p: **wadó ųk'įbi**

wadó'įnažį *n* train station

wadópa *vi1* s/he paddles 1s: **wadówapa** 2s: **wadóyapa** 1p: **wadó'ųpabi** *Vcont*: **wan-watóm**

Wadópena ; Wadópana *nprop* Paddler people (band of Nakoda living in Fort Peck, Montana and Pheasant Rump, Saskatchewan) *Lit*: paddler

wadóptom *vcont-redup* paddling

wa'ébazo *n* index finger *Syn*: **wa'ébazo; nąbáwąge įíiwažį**

wa'écagici'ųbi *vi1-recip* they do things for one another

wa'écagiįų *vt1/3-benef-abs* s/he does things, works for sb 1s: **wa'écawejimų** 2s: **wa'écayejinų**

wa'écų *vi3-abs* 1) s/he does things 2) s/he curses, does bad things ‣ **Nína wa'écų.** He curses a lot. *Vbenef*: **wa'écagiįų** *Vrecip*: **wa'écagici'ųbi**

wagágA *vi1-abs* s/he makes things; produces ‣ **Wagágas'a žé John ecú.** John conducted the production. *Vbenef*: **wagíjijağA**

wagágas'a *n* producer

wagágeğe *vi1-abs* s/he sews things

wagágeğe wíyena *cp* seamstress

wagáhi *vi1-abs* s/he rummages around, ransacks ‣ **wagáhi wíyopeyabi** garage sale *Vpos*: **wagíjahi**

wagáȟci *vi1-abs* s/he slits things; cuts fringes

wagámna *vi1-abs* s/he slices, makes slices (of meat)

wagápabi *n* pemmican

wagágana ; wagága *n-redup* 1) elderly woman ‣ **Wagágana žé tawácį síja.** That old lady has a wicked mind. 3p: **wagágabina** 2) my wife (form of address) *Usage*: archaic. ‣ **Wagágana bibína yuhá ús iyómagipi.** I am happy because my wife had a baby.

wagán *adv* up ‣ **Wagán ámnakta.** I will lift it up.

wagíc'į *vi1-abs* s/he packs things, packs a horse

wagídą *vi1-abs* s/he is determined, insistant ‣ **Miyé wawágidą hík né zuyéyabi mįš ówapa.** I insisted, and I myself joined the war party. (NS 2002:73) 1s: **wawágidą** 2s: **wayágidą**

wagíjahi *vt1-pos* s/he rummages through his/her own

wagíjijağA *vt1-abs-benef* s/he makes things for sb 1s: **wawéjijağa** 2s: **wayéjijağa**

wagíknągA *vt1-abs-pos* s/he saves, caches his/her own things (food, provisions)

wagíyą *n* thunderbird ‣ **Wagíyą šá wiyóȟpeyam žéci iyódągabi.** The Red Thunderbirds sit there to the west.

wagíyą ȟubáhu máza *np* iron-winged thunderbird

wağéyaga *n* prayer cloth ‣ **Wağéyaga wąží awáhi.** I brought a prayer cloth. *Syn*: **wó'įye**

wağí *n* grizzly *Syn*: **wacúwiska**

wağínųba *Variant*: **wanáği núba** *n* homosexual person *Lit*: two spirited

wahąbi *n* soup, broth ‣ **Tanó įš wahąbi cįgá he?** Does he want meat and soup? ‣ **Wahąbi edáhą gáğa.** Make some soup. ‣ **Wahąbi žé káda.** The soup is hot.

wahácąga *n* shield

wahą́ba *n* snowshoe(s) ‣ **Wahą́ba gic'ų́.** Put your snowshoes on.

wahą́bi éyagu *cp* ladle

wahéc'ų *vi1-abs* s/he packs things in bundles, breaks camp for traveling *Vpos:* **wahégic'ų**

wahégic'ų *vi1-abs-pos* s/he packs his/her things in bundles, breaks his/her camp for traveling

Wahíkiyabi *n* 1) Yuwipi, Tie up, Calling of the spirits ceremony; shaking tent 2) radio (object); radio broadcast

Wahíkiyabi ecúbi *cp* Yuwipi, Tie up, Calling of the spirits ceremony; shaking tent

wahíyoknąga *Variant:* **wahí'oknąga** *n* bottle, glass; jar, cooking pot

wahį́ *n* flint

wahį́bahpa *vi1-abs* s/he scrapes the hair off a hide *1s:* **wahį́wabahpa** *2s:* **wahį́yabahpa**

wáhįhĄ *vimp* it snows ‣ **Wáhįhįkte no.** It will snow. ‣ **Tągán éduwą wáhįhą.** Look outside, it is snowing. ‣ **Wáhįhącuna.** It keeps snowing. ‣ **Hą'éyasą wáhįhą.** It snowed all night. ‣ **Wáhįhe wácį.** Looks like it is about to snow. (Cumberland 2005:43)

wahį́heya *n* mole *Syn:* **wahé'ağa**

wáhįhpa *vimp* it is a snowfall ‣ **Nína wáhįhpa.** It is a very heavy snowfall.

wahį́kpe; wahį́kpa. *n* flint, flint arrowhead; arrow *1s:* **mitáwahįkpe** *2s:* **nitáwahįkpe** *Redup:* **wahį́kpekpena**

wahį́kpekpena *n-redup* little bow and arrows used by children

wahį́tka *n* hide scraper *Redup:* **wahį́tkatkana**

wahį́tkatkana *n-redup* hide scrapers

wahį́tušina *n* robe with hair

wahógu *vi1* s/he gives advice, dares ‣ **Wahógušį ecúšį!** You do not dare do that! *Vcaus:* **wahógukiyA**

wahógukiyA *vt1-caus* s/he lectures, advises sb ‣ **Mikúši wahógumakiya.** My grandmother lectured me. ‣ **Žéci yéšį wahógukiya.** He advises him not to go over there. ‣ **Ecágen**

įš wahógu'ukiyabi. They always lectured us. *1s:* **wahóguwakiya** *2s:* **wahóguyakiya** *1p:* **wahógu'ukiyabi**

wahóhpi *n* nest ‣ **Ziktábina né cąwą́gąduh wahóhpi gáğabi.** Those birds made a nest way up there in the tree. *Syn:* **hohpí**

wahóhpiya *n* rookery

wahóyA *Variant:* **įwáhoyA** *vt1-dit* s/he promises sb to do smth ‣ **Ecámukte wahówaya.** I promised to do it. ‣ **Mike wahómaya timánįkta.** Mike promised me he will visit. *1s:* **wahówaya** *2s:* **wahóyaya** *1p:* **wahó'uyabi**

wahú núba *cp* two-legged creature

wahúhna *vi1-abs* s/he burns things; sets junk on fire

wahúkeza ; wahúkeza *n* spear

wahcá *n* flower, blossom ‣ **Wahcá né ómna.** Smell this flower.

wahcáği *n* dandelion

wahcánebi *n* decoration

wahé'ağa *n* mole *Syn:* **wahį́heya**

wahéyaga *n* cloth offering

wahníca *n* white poplar

Wahníca wakpá *ngeo* Poplar (Montana)

wahpáya o'ópetu *cp* thrift store

wahpé *n* 1) leaf ‣ **wahpé tą́ga** cabbage ‣ **wahpé ği wí** September ‣ **wahpé wóšma wí** June 2) tea ‣ **Duwé wahpé cįgá?** Who wants tea? ‣ **Wahpé né iyúta.** Taste this tea.

wahpé cąní *cp* kinnikinnick *Lit:* leaf tobacco

wahpé ce'ága *cp* peppermint

wahpé céğa *cp* teapot

wahpé ği wí *ph* September *Lit:* yellow leaves moon

wahpé ijáhibi *cp* salad

wahpé tą́ga *cp* cabbage; lettuce *Lit:* big leaves

wahpé wóšma wí *ph* June *Lit:* thick leaves moon

wahpécağa ; wahpé acáğa *n* iced tea

wahpéhpena *n-redup* flower (with leaves)

wahpésaba *n* black tea

wahpétaheya *n* caterpillar *Lit:* leaf's louse

waȟpéto *n* green tea

waȟpétoto hạwí *cp* May

waȟpétoya hą *adv* in the spring time *Lit:* when the green leaves come out

waȟpézizi hạwí *cp* September

waȟtáni *vi1-abs* s/he sins *1s:* **wawáȟtani** *2s:* **wayáȟtani** *See:* **wówaȟtani**

waȟtánis'a *n* sinner

waȟtége *vs* it is not good ‣ **Dágu waȟtége.** It is good for nothing.

waȟténašị *vt1* s/he hates, dislikes sb, smth (taste, task, person) ‣ **Wayáwabi waȟtéwanašị.** I do not like to study. ‣ **Ecágen ecúbi waȟtéwanašị.** I hate doing it all the time. ‣ **Wíyą žé waȟténašị.** She dislikes that woman. ‣ **Dágu epé žé waȟténašị.** He disliked what I said. *1s:* **waȟtéwanašị** *2s:* **waȟtéyanašị** *1p:* **waȟté'ụnabišị**

waȟtéšị *vs* 1) s/he/it is worthless *1s:* **wamáȟtešị** *2s:* **waníȟtešị** *interj* 2) Oh the wretch! *Usage:* uttered when one is ready to spank a kid.

waȟtéšịȟtiyą *interj* for God's sake, scrap, I will fix you, you miserable thing *Usage:* expression of disgust, exasperation.

waȟúbagoza *n* thunderbird

waȟ'ạkšija *n* bear (generic; refers possibly to the extinct prairie grizzly) *Lit:* s/he is fierce

waȟ'ạkšija tawóde *cp* bearberry

wa'ịcaȟye *n* farmer, agricultor *Syn:* **wókšus'a**

wa'ịbadịda *n* snowplow ‣ **Waktá! Wa'ịbadịda žé ú.** Watch out! The snowplow is coming. *Syn:* **ịwátokšu wa'ịbadịda**

wa'ịbaspa *n* tent peg

wa'ịcaǧA *vi1-abs* it (crops, plants) grows *Vcaus:* **wa'ịcaȟyA** *Vrefl:* **wa'ịc'icaǧa**

wa'ịcaȟyA *vi1-abs* s/he grows things, breeds animals

wa'ịc'icaǧa *vi3-refl* it is his/her fault ‣ **Žé níš wanịc'icaǧabišị iyé wa'íc'icaǧabi.** It was not your fault, it was their fault. (Cumberland 2005:132) *1s:* **wamịc'icaǧa** *2s:* **wanịc'icaǧa**

wa'íȟpeyA *vi1-abs* s/he throws things away

wa'íknị *vi1-abs* s/he investigates

wa'íksamkiyA *vi1-abs* s/he pesters, causes trouble; is bothersome ‣ **Híbi hịk wa'íksamkiyabi.** They arrived and caused trouble. *1s:* **wa'íksamwakiya** *2s:* **wa'íksamyakiya**

wa'íktụyą *vi1-abs* s/he sets things on fire (house, building, junk)

wa'íyuškị *vi1-abs* s/he is friendly *1s:* **wawá'iyuškị** *2s:* **wayá'iyuškị**

wakákana *vi1-redup* they (meat) are tender, soft ‣ **Huhú wakákana yúdabikta.** They ate soft bones.

wakána *vi1* it (meat) is tender, soft *Vredup:* **wakákana**

wakányA *vi1-abs* s/he warms things ‣ **Nínaȟ wakányešị.** Do not warm it up too much. *1s:* **wakánwaya** *2s:* **wakányaya**

waką *vs* 1) s/he/it is holy, spiritually powerful ‣ **Miní waką niyá wašté ụk'úbịkte no!** Sacred water, give us good health! ‣ **Mikúši, Albert wịcášta waką he? Hiyá, waką ụkáš, mịš mawáką cá!** Grandma, is Albert a holy man?—No, if he is holy, I am holy too! 2) s/he/it is mysterious, magical *Usage:* occurs with words for European objects. ‣ **océti waką** microwave oven ‣ **ocágu waką** Canada/USA border; medicine line *1s:* **mawáką** *2s:* **niwáką** *1p:* **ụwákąbi** *adv* 3) in holy manner ‣ **Waką iyódągabi.** They are fasting. *Adv:* **wakáya** *Vcaus:* **wakákiyA** *Vredup:* **wakáką**

waką awókcą *cp* spirituality

waką í *vi1* s/he went for a vision quest *1s:* **waką wa'í** *2s:* **waką ya'í**

waką iyódągA *vi1* s/he fasts *1s:* **waką imnódąga** *2s:* **waką inódąga** *1p:* **waką ụgíyodągabi**

waką iyódągabi *n* fast *Lit:* sit sacredly

Waką tíbi *ngeo* St Paul's Mission (Montana)

Wakáȟežabina *nprop* Little girls people (band of Nakoda living in Fort Peck, Montana)

wakáȟ'ą *vi1* s/he conjures

wakáką *vs-redup* s/he/it is kind of holy, very holy

wakąkiyA *vt1-caus* s/he considers sb, smth as holy ‣ **Ȟaȟátųwą cąnúpa né waką́kiyabi.** The Gros Ventres considered the pipe as holy. (Drummond 1976, The pipe of peace)

wakákni *n* electricity *Usage:* obsolete. *Lit:* it brings power

wakák'į *n* battery

wakásija ; wakášija *n* 1) evil-spirited being (like Įktomi or the Christian devil) *vs* 2) s/he/it is evil-spirited

Wakátąga *n* Great Spirit, Mystery (traditional); God, Lord, Holy Father (Christian)

Wakátąga cįhį́ktu *Variant:* **Wakátąga cįhį́tku** *nprop* Jesus Christ *Lit:* the Great Spirit's son

Wakátąga cįhį́tku ųktébi *ph* Good Friday *Lit:* we killed God's son

Wakátąga cįhį́tku yuhábi ába *ph* Christmas

Wakátąga gicúni ába *np* Boxing day

Wakátąga hokšítogapa *nprop* Jesus Christ

wakáya *adv* in a holy way, spiritually correct way ‣ **Wakáyą wąyága.** It [spirit] watches over him. ‣ **Dágu wakáyą ecúšį.** He did not do it in a holy way. ‣ **Wakáyą iyódąga.** She is fasting.

wakíbaži *vi1-abs* 1) s/he is against, opposes people or things *n* 2) grudge

wakmúhaza ; wakmúhąza *n* corn ‣ **Pągí, típsina, wakmúhaza íš špąyá.** She cooked potatoes, turnips, and corn too.

wakmúhazaskuya *n* sweet corn

wakmúhaząkneğe *n* Indian corn

wakmúgA *vi1-abs* 1) s/he snares animals *n* 2) snare ‣ **heȟágągana wakmúga** cobweb ‣ **maštín wakmúga** rabbit snare *Syn:* **įkmúge**

wakmúges'a *n* trapper

wakmúha ; wakmúha *n* gourd rattle ‣ **Adé, wakátąga wakmúha waką́ mak'ú no.** Father, Creator, give me the holy rattle. ‣ **Wakmúha né minékši gága.** My maternal uncle made this rattle.

waknáyA *vi1* s/he fools people

wakní *vi1-abs* s/he returns, arrives home bringing meat

wáknibi *n* game, meat brought back from a hunt

waknúžąga *n* cruelty, bullying

wakógipA *vi1-abs* s/he is afraid of things (spiritually); is a coward *1s:* **wakówagipa** *2s:* **wakóyagipa**

wakónayA *vi1-abs* s/he is friendly

wakpá *n* river ‣ **Wakpá juk'ána iyáyabi.** They went through the narrow river.

wakpá gáğabi *cp* irrigation ditch

Wakpá juk'ána *ngeo* Milk River (Montana) *Lit:* small river *Syn:* **Asábi wakpá**

wakpádahą *adv* from the river ‣ **Wįbazuką wakpádahą hí.** He arrived from Saskatoon.

wakpáhį *vi1-abs* s/he harvests grain, cereals *1s:* **wawákpahį** *2s:* **wayákpahį** *1p:* **wa'úkpahįbi**

wakpámni *vi1-abs* s/he serves ‣ **Gicícobi én wakpámni.** She serves at the gathering.

wakpámni ecúbi *cp* giveaway ceremony

wakpána *n* creek

wakpáyA *vi1-abs* s/he tans

Wakpé núzahą *ngeo* Swift Current River (Saskatchewan)

wakpógiya *n* kingfisher *Lit:* it flies over the river *Syn:* **žós'a**

waktá *vi1* 1) s/he is expectant for sb or smth to happen ‣ **Waktá mągá.** I am sitting expecting it. 2) s/he/it is alert, careful, aware of smth ‣ **Mitášųga nína waktá.** My dog is very alert. ‣ **Waktá šiwákna!** Beware! I am angry! ‣ **Nínaȟ waktášį.** He is very careless. ‣ **Waktá duktén mayáni.** Watch where you walk! *1s:* **wawákta** *2s:* **yawákta** *1p:* **ųwáktabi** *Adv:* **waktáȟ**

waktá ų́ *vi1* s/he is expectant, anticipating smth, anxious, alert *1s:* **waktá wa'ų́** *2s:* **waktá ya'ų́**

waktáȟ *adv* on the lookout, expectantly ‣ **Waktáȟ mągá.** I am on my guard.

waktáȟtįyA *vs* s/he is alert; is on his/her guard *1s:* **wamáktaȟtįyą** *2s:* **waníktaȟtįyą**

waktášį *adv* carelessly ▸ **Waktášį ecámų.** I did it carelessly.

waktáya *adv* in anticipation, expectantly ▸ **Waktáya mągá.** I am sitting alert.

Wakté wacíbi *cp* Scalp, victory dance

wakúde *vi1-abs* s/he shoots things; hunts

wakúdebi *n* shooting, hunting

wak'į *n* backpack

wak'įtáwa *vi3* it (horse) is saddled *Lit:* it has a saddle ▸ **Šų́gatąga wak'įtáwa.** The horse is saddled.

wak'įgitų *vi1-abs* s/he carries things on the back

wak'ú *n* gift, present

wamáhen *adv* under the snow ▸ **Wamáhen ųškádabi.** They played under the snow. ▸ **Wamáhen yįgá iyéwaya.** I found it sitting under the snow.

wamáksA *vi1-abs* s/he cuts things with a sharp blade

wamánų *vi1-abs* s/he steals things ▸ **Dóhąni wamáwanųšį.** I never stole. ▸ **Ecágen wamáyanų.** You steal stuff all the time. ▸ **Gitézi wamánųbis'a.** The brats usually steal stuff. *1s:* **wamáwanų** *2s:* **wamáyanų** *1p:* **wamá'ųnųbi**

wamánųs'a *vi1* 1) s/he is a thief ▸ **Wamáyanųs'a no!** You are a thief! *n* 2) thief

wamą́kamani *n* bear

wamą́kašką *n* 1) creature, animal 2) bear *Lit:* that which moves on earth

wámini *n* snow water ▸ **Wámini né yaktą́.** Drink that snow water.

wamnáyas'a *n* collector

wamnáyĄ *vi1-abs* s/he gathers, collects things

wamní *n* golden eagle *Usage:* also used as a generic term. ▸ **Wamní žé wągáduwah̃ giyą́'.** The eagle flies the highest.

Wamní įpíyaga wacíbi *cp* Eagle belt dance

wamní šagé *cp* eagle claw

Wamní wacíbi *cp* Eagle dance

wamníkneška *n* spotted eagle

Wamníwaš'aga *nprop* Strongeagle (surname)

wamnónįja *n* orphan ▸ **Wamnónįja žemáca.** I am an orphan.

wamnónįja hąwí *cp* March *Lit:* orphan moon (because orphans would die toward the end of winter)

wamnúmnu *vi* there are fine snow particles blowing

wamnúška *n* insect (generic), ant, bug, worm

wamnúška hįšmášmą *cp* caterpillar *Lit:* furry insect

wamnúška mnaská *cp* bedbug *Lit:* flat insect

wamnúška pašáša *cp* red ant *Lit:* red-headed ant

wamnúška sapsábina *cp* cricket

wamnúškaša *n* flea *Lit:* red insect

wamópąbi *n* cornball (pemmican made of ground corn)

wamóptA *vi1-abs* s/he digs with a digging stick ▸ **Éé né duktén wamópte niyúhana wąyága.** Aha! He saw where she had been digging all these. (Weasel 122:93)

wamósodA *vi1-abs* s/he shoots down, kills all the game ▸ **Dąyą́h̃ né nén wamó'ųsodabikta.** We will easily shoot many of them here. (Weasel 144:486) *1s:* **wamówasoda** *2s:* **wamóyasoda** *1p:* **wamó'ųsodabi**

wan- *cont* canoe

waná₁ *adv* now, already ▸ **Waná wóyadabįkte no.** You will eat now. ▸ **Waná tída waknį́kta.** I am coming home now. ▸ **Nahą́h̃ waná he?** Are you ready yet? ▸ **Waná wóda he?** Is he already eating?

waná₂ *vi1-abs* s/he asks for things *1s:* **wayána** *2s:* **wawána**

wanągaš *adv* long ago ▸ **Wanągaš wanįja.** He passed away long ago. ▸ **Wanągaš ecámų céyaga.** I should have done that a long time ago. ▸ **Wanągaš Šiyóša ektá wa'í.** I went to Red Pheasant long ago.

wanáǧi *n* spirit, soul, ghost (of an unknown referent)

Wanáǧi ába *cp* Halloween

wanáǧi ocágu *cp* Milky Way

Wanáǧi wacíbi *cp* 1) Northern Lights; aurora borealis 2) Ghost dance

wanáȟ'ų *vi1-abs* s/he obeys ‣ **Wanáȟ'ųbišį.** They are disobeying. ‣ **Iná, adé dágeyabi háda, wanáȟ'ųbišį.** Whenever mom and dad are saying something, they disobey. *1s:* **wanáwaȟ'ų** *2s:* **wanáyaȟ'ų** *1p:* **waná'ųȟ'ųbi**

wanáp'į *n* necklace

wanáse *vi1-abs* s/he goes on a buffalo hunt *Usage:* this verb is usually followed by a coming/going verb. ‣ **Aké waná, "Wanáse ųyábikte nó:," eyá.** Once again he said, "We are going on a buffalo hunt." (Weasel 146:518)

wanágaš wįcášta *cp* people from long ago

wanágažašį *vs* it is not too long ago, recently ‣ **Wanágažašį hí žehá.** Not too long ago he came.

wanéhadu *vimp* 1) at this time, in time ‣ **Wanéhadu hįšį.** He did not arrive in time. *vs* 2) s/he/it is of this age ‣ **Micúkši wanéhadu néca, tapkápsijekten[a], tabákapsijabikta gáye nówa.** He said for all those who are the same age as my daughter to play a ballgame. (Weasel 37:42)

wanéyasą *adv* throughout the winter

wani- *cont* winter

wani ú *vi1* s/he spends the winter somewhere ‣ **Waní ú gakí háda osnísnis'a.** He wintered over there, and it was usually very cold. *1s:* **waní wa'ú** *2s:* **waní ya'ú** *1p:* **waní ųk'úbi**

waníha *adv* last winter ‣ **Waníha cą'íyutabi yámni wagáksa.** Last winter I chopped three cords of wood.

waníjA *vs* 1) s/he/it lacks; there is none ‣ **Snohéna waníjabi.** There are no snakes. ‣ **I'ábi háda í waníjabi.** When they speak they have no mouth. ‣ **Pahá waníjabi.** They are bald. 2)

s/he passed away; is dead ‣ **Wanágaš wanįja.** He passed away long ago.

wanítA *vs* s/he is vigourous, industrious, ambitious ‣ **Naháȟ wanínita.** You are still vigorous. *1s:* **wamánita** *2s:* **wanínita**

waníyedu *n* 1) winter ‣ **Waníyedu štén wó'ųknagabįkte no.** Next winter we will tell stories. ‣ **Waníyedu dóna eháki he?** How old is he? ‣ **Mató waníyedu ábé'ištima.** The bear sleeps during the winter days. 2) year *Usage:* used only in counting the age of someone. ‣ **Waníyedu dóna eháyaki?** How old are you? *vimp* 3) it is winter ‣ **Waná waníyedu.** Now it is winter. *Cont:* **wani**

waníyedu cogána *adv* midwinter

waníyedu úbis'a *ph* chickadee *Lit:* they stay in the winter

wan'ídopa *n* paddle, oar

waníktekiyA *vi1-abs* s/he doctors, heals

waníktekiyA ; níktekiyA *vt1-caus* s/he heals, doctors sb *Vbenef:* **níktegijikiyA** *Vrecip:* **níktegiciyakiyabi**

waníktekiyes'a *n* doctor

wanúȟ *adv* maybe, might ‣ **Wanúȟ hokšína né néžąbi cíga.** Maybe the boy wants to urinate. ‣ **Wanúȟ ųgíksuyabišį ca'.** We might not forget about it.

wanúyabi *n-pl* small animals

wa'óȟnoga *n* hole, cave

wa'ókmA ; wókmA *vi1-abs* 1) s/he writes things 2) s/he has debts, has credit in a store ‣ **Nína wa'ówakma.** I have a lot of debts. *1s:* **wa'ówakma** *2s:* **wa'óyakma** *Vbenef:* **wógijikmA** *n* 3) credit

wa'ókmabi *n* letter, written word, drawing ‣ **Wa'ókmabi wabážužu.** I erased the words.

wa'ókmabi waká *cp* email *Lit:* mysterious letter

wa'ókmabi wa'ówabi *cp* bill, amount owed

wa'ókmas'a *n* writer, author, painter, scribe

wa'óne *vi1-abs* s/he looks for things *1s:* **wa'ówane** *2s:* **wa'óyane**

wa'óštena *vs* s/he/it (small thing, baby, child) is cute

wa'óštenąga *Variant:* **wawóštenąga** *vs* s/he/it is cute ▸ **Koná, šųkšįjana né wawóštenąga. Né wacíga.** Friend, this puppy is cute. I want this one. (Parks et al. 1999:102)

wa'ówabitoto *n* paper money *Lit:* green paper

wa'óyabi *n* card game

wa'óyabi ; wa'ówabi ; wóyabi *n* paper, letter, book ▸ **Wa'óyabi bakšíja.** Fold the paper. ▸ **Wa'óyabi knuhéšį hí.** She arrived without her book. ▸ **Wa'óyabi žená wabážužu.** I erased it off the papers.

wa'óyabi ecúbina *cp* deck of cards

wa'óyabi iyáskamye *cp* stamp

wa'óyabi oyúħpe *cp* post office

wa'óyabi šóga *ph* cardboard

wa'óyabi tága *cp* book

wa'óyabi waką *cp* 1) Bible, legal document 2) email

wapá *vi1* it (dog) barks ▸ **Šúga wapábi.** The dogs are barking. ▸ **Šúga žé wapášį? —Hiyá, wapášį.** Isn't the dog barking? —No, he is not barking. *Vredup:* **wapápa**

wapádA *vi1-abs* s/he butchers meat ▸ **Nągáhą wawápadįkta.** Now I will do some butchering.

wapáği *n* yellow-hooded blackbird *Lit:* yellow hat

wapáha *n* cap, hat, bonnet ▸ **Wapáha tó žé waknúha.** I have my blue hat with me. ▸ **Wapáha waknúšnoga.** I took off my hat. *1s:* **mitáwapaha** *2s:* **nitáwapaha** *Cont:* **wapa-**

wapápa *vi1-redup* it (dog) barks repeatedly ▸ **Eyáš šúgana né eyáš, ząkzága wapápa ų.** Well, the little dog was whining and barking. (Weasel 197:174)

wapépe *n* thistle

wapéša *n* roach headgear

wapíwacį *vs* s/he/it is clean ▸ **Amógiyą žé wapíwacįšį.** The car is not clean.

wasáza *vs* s/he/it is ill-tempered, touchy ▸ **Nína wanísaza!** You are very touchy! *1s:* **wamásaza** *2s:* **wanísaza**

wasé *n* clay, ochre, paint of any color ▸ **Wasé ús ša'íc'iya.** He painted his face with red ochre.

wasé gitú *vt1-pos* s/he wears paint, war paint *1s:* **wasé wétų** *2s:* **wasé yétų** *1p:* **wasé ųgítųbi**

Wasé oyúze *ngeo* red ochre collecting place

Wasé wakpá *ngeo* Lodge Pole (Montana)

waséğina *n* yellow paint

waską *n* melting snow

Wasképana *nprop* person of European, Euro-Canadian descent, White man *Usage:* idiolectal.

waskúya ; wóskuya *n* 1) berries, fruit *Lit:* something sweet 2) juice ▸ **Waskúya én ogášta.** She poured juice in the glass.

waskúyeja *n* berries

wásmuna *n* buckshot

wasná *n* suet; tallow, grease

wasnásnaheja *n-redup* 1) kingbird 2) catbird

wasnókkiyA *vt1-caus* s/he teaches smth to sb *1s:* **wasnókwakiya** *2s:* **wasnókyakiya**

wasnókyA *Variant:* **wasnóhyA** *vi1-abs* 1) s/he is clever, knowledgeable ▸ **Mary nína wasnókya.** Mary is very clever. ▸ **Hugá žé wasnókya wicá žecá.** The chief was a clever man. *n* 2) wisdom *See:* **wasnókyeja**

wasnókyabi *n* knowledge

wasnókya-įc'ina *Variant:* **wasnóhya-įc'ina** *vi3-refl* s/he thinks himself/herself as clever, knowledgeable *1s:* **wasnóhya-mįc'ina ; wasnókya-mįc'ina** *2s:* **wasnóhya-nįc'ina ; wasnókya-nįc'ina**

wasnókye įc'ína *cp* know-it-all

wasnókye wacį *cp* nosy person

wasnókyeja *vi1-abs* s/he is intelligent, knowledgeable; knows a lot of things ▸ **Wįcášta nína**

wasnókyeja. This man is very knowledgeable. *1s:* **wasnókwayeja** *2s:* **wasnókyayeja**

wasóbi *n* rope from raw hide

waspą́ *n* Chinook wind

wasú *n* hail *Lit:* snow pellets

wasú hįhą́ *vimp* it is hailing

wasúsmuna *n* small hail stone, sleet, gresil

wašáša *n* berry, berries (generic) ‣ **wašáša hą́wi** July

wašáša wí *cp* July *Lit:* berries ripening month

wašíjahpą *n* junk, trash

Wašíju *n* 1) minor spirit, deity ‣ **mayáwašiju** dwarf, caveman ‣ **Wašíju wążí** One spirit (personal name) 2) European people, person of European descent, Caucasian, White man ‣ **Wašíju né įknúdąšį nodéhą.** This White man is disprespectful and greedy. ‣ **Hą́, Wašíju žemáca.** Yes, I am of European descent. *vs* 3) s/he is of European descent ‣ **Waníšiju he?** Are you Caucasian? *1s:* **Wamášiju** *2s:* **Waníšiju** *Cont:* **Wašín** *Syn:* **Haskána, Haská, Sna'ót'e, Wasképana**

Wašíju opégitųbi *cp* trading post *Syn:* **opégitų tíbi**

wašíju tíbi ; wašíjuti *cp* house, framed house *Lit:* White man's house ‣ **Wašíju tí mitáwa wíyopewayešį no.** I did not sell my house.

Wašíju wążí *nprop* One Spirit (personal name)

Wašíjusaba *cp* person of African or African-American descent *See:* **Hásaba**

Wašíjusaba makóce *ngeo* Africa *Lit:* land of the black White man

Wašíjusaba wíyą *cp* woman of African or African-American descent

wašíkna *vi1-abs* 1) s/he mourns; is bereaved by the death of a relative ‣ **Žé iyúha wašíknabi.** They are all mourning. ‣ **Iná wanį́jac'ehą, nína wašíwakna.** When my mother passed away I was really bereaved. *1s:* **wašíwakna** *2s:* **wašíyakna** *n* 2) sacrifice

wašíkna įc'íyA *vi3-refl* s/he sacrifices himself/herself *1s:* **wašíkna mįc'íya** *2s:* **wašíkna nįc'íya**

wašíknabi *n* mourner

Wašín *cont* in a White man, European manner; pertaining to White people

Wašín'i'A *vi1* 1) s/he speaks English ‣ **Ecágen Wašín'i'abi.** They always speak English. ‣ **Iná Wašín'i'ešį cén awéjimnupta.** Mom does not speak English, so I answered for her. *vt1* 2) s/he speaks, talks to sb in English ‣ **Wašín'ici'a.** I am talking English to you. ‣ **Dóhąni Wašín'ici'įktešį no!** I will never talk to you in English! *1s:* **Wašín'iwa'a** *2s:* **Wašín'iya'a** *1p:* **Wašín'ųgi'abi**

Wašín'i'abi *n* English language

Wašín'įc'ina *vi3-refl* s/he behaves like a White person ‣ **Misúga wašín'įc'ina.** My younger brother behaves like a White man. *1s:* **Wašín-mįc'iya** *2s:* **Wašín-nįc'iya** *1p:* **Wašín'ųgįc'iya**

wašį́ *n* suet, fat

Wašį́ azínyabina *nprop* Fat-smoker people (band of Nakoda, Saskatchewan)

wašką́škąyabi *n* movie, movies, cinema ‣ **Wašką́škąyabi ektá iyáyabi.** They went to the movies.

wašmá *vimp* it is deep snow ‣ **Dókiya nówa wašmá.** The snow is deep everywhere.

wašmú *n* melted snow

wašną́ *n* 1) pemmican, dried goods 2) fat, grease, lard

wašpá'įc'iyA *vi3-refl* s/he cooks for himself/herself ‣ **Wašpą́mįc'iya ko owágihišįc.** I cannot even cook for myself. (Shields 83:492) *1s:* **wašpą́mįc'iya** *2s:* **wašpą́nįc'iya** *1p:* **wašpá'ųgįc'iya**

wašpáyA *vi1-abs* s/he cooks things ‣ **Mikúši nína wašpáyąbi wayúpi.** My grandmother is very skilled at cooking. ‣ **Mihų́ nakú mitúwi įš wašpáyąbi ógiyabi.** My mother and my aunt also helped her cook. *Vrefl:* **wašpá'įc'iyA**

wašpáyes'a *n* cook, chef ‣ **Wašpáyes'a žécabi wacíga.** I want to be a chef.

wašté *vs* 1) it is good, nice (event, temperature, object) ‣ **Ába wašté.** It is a nice day. ‣ **Cuwíknaga nitáwa wašté no.** Your coat is nice. ‣ **Huhúžubina ocágu wašté ųkáš.** If only the streets of Regina were good. 2) s/he is pretty, handsome, nice ‣ **Šúga né wašté.** This dog is nice. ‣ **Waštékta šká.** He is trying to be nice. *1s:* **mawášte** *2s:* **niwášte** *1p:* **ųwáštebi** *Adv:* **waštéya** *Vredup:* **waštéšte**

waštégicinabi *vi1-recip* they like, love one another ‣ **Wanágaš koškáwašté'ųgicinabi.** Long ago a boy and I were in love. *1p:* **wašté'ųgicinabi**

waštégina *vt1-dat* s/he enjoys, loves, is pleased with smth ‣ **I'ábi waštégina.** She enjoys talking. ‣ **Nína wacíbi waštéwagina.** I really like dancing. ‣ **Žécen nína wašté a'íc'icida gá, nína waštégina hųštá, hokšína né.** So then when this boy looked at himself, he looked good and so he was very happy, it is said. (Shields 67:291) *1s:* **waštéwagina** *2s:* **waštéyagina** *1p:* **wašté'ųginabi**

waštéȟtiyA *vs* it is very good, the best, nicest ‣ **Ecú žé waštéȟtiya.** She did the very best. ‣ **Huȟnáȟyabi né waštéȟtiyeší.** This coffee is not the best.

wašté'įc'ina *vi3-refl* s/he boasts about himself/herself *1s:* **waštémįc'ina** *2s:* **wašténíc'ina**

waštéjaga *vs* s/he is kind, good natured, pleasant to live with *1s:* **mawáštejaga** *2s:* **niwáštejaga** *1p:* **ųwáštejagabi**

waštémna *vs* s/he/it smells good ‣ **Hukwá, wašténimna no!** Oh girl, you smell good! *1s:* **waštémamna** *2s:* **wašténimna**

wašténa *vt1* s/he likes, loves sb, smth ‣ **Šá žé miyé waštéwana.** I, myself, like the color red. ‣ **Huȟnáȟyabi, asábi cóna waštéwana.** I like coffee without milk. *1s:* **waštéwana** *2s:* **waštéyana** *1p:* **wašté'ųnabi** *Vdat:* **waštégina** *Vrecip:* **waštégicinabi** *Vrefl:* **wašté'įc'ina**

waštéšte *vs-redup* they (objects) are good, nice

waštéya *adv* nicely, in a good manner, well ‣ **Mitáwacį waštéya eháwa'i.** I reach my mindset, goal with a good heart.

waš'ágA *vs* s/he/it is strong ‣ **Togádagiya štén gitézibina nená tawácį nagú cádé waš'ága ománibįkta.** In the future the kids will walk with a strong mind and heart. *Vcaus:* **waš'akyA** *See:* **š'ágA**

waš'áke *adv* unbearably ‣ **Waná waš'áke yįgá.** Now he is unbearably sick.

waš'akyA *vt1-caus* s/he makes smth strong

watánįjoǧa *n* moss growing in sloughs

watápA *vi1-abs* s/he follows, pursues; hunts buffalo ‣ **Watápe yá.** He has gone hunting.

watápe *n* buffalo hunter, hunter; elderly man, ancestor ‣ **Watápe žemáca no.** I am a hunter. ‣ **Watápe hékta wóknagabis'a.** Long ago the ancestors used to tell stories.

watápe wíya *cp* elderly woman *Lit:* buffalo chaser woman

watá *n* bait

watéȟina *vi1-abs* s/he is stingy ‣ **Wašíju né nína watéȟina.** This White man is very stingy. *1s:* **watéwaȟina** *2s:* **watéyaȟina** *1p:* **waté'ųȟinabi**

watéjaga *vs* s/he is young and strong ‣ **Wamátejaga žehá wéksuya.** I remember when I was young. *1s:* **wamátejaga** *2s:* **wanítejaga**

watéjana *vs* s/he/it is new ‣ **Watéjana ųká.** I guess he is new.

watémyA *vi1-abs* s/he/it eats everything, the whole thing (as an animal) *Vbenef:* **watépkijiyA**

watépkijiyA *vt1-benef* s/he eats, devours sb else's food *1s:* **watémyejiya** *2s:* **watémwejiya**

watókąkna *vi1-abs* s/he feels uneasy around strangers

watókna *vs* it (animal) is wild, untamed ‣ **Šúga žé naháȟ watókna.** That dog is still wild.

watóm *vcont* paddling ‣ **Watóm hí.** He came paddling.

watpá *n* train engine

wa'úcana *n* monkey

wa'úspe *vi1-abs* s/he is learned, knowledgeable

wa'úspekiyA, wó'uspekiyA *vt1-abs-caus* 1) s/he teaches sb things ▸ **Wó'uspenikiya okná ecú.** Do it following what he told you. (Shields 24:53) *n* 2) teacher

wa'úspekiyes'a *n* teacher

wa'úspewicakiya *n* male teacher

wa'úspewiyakiya *n* female teacher

wa'úšina *vi1-abs* s/he pities people, is kind to people *Vcoll:* **wawíca'ušina**

wawá'ušigina *vi1* s/he is kind, good-natured, likes people ▸ **Micúkši wawá'ušigina.** My daughter is good-natured.

wawáyupi *vi1-abs* s/he is skillful

wawága *n* huge animal, creature (like a dinosaur)

wawíyopekiyA *vi1-abs* s/he scolds people *1s:* **wawíyopewakiya** *2s:* **wawíyopeyakiya** *1p:* **wawíyope'ukiyabi**

wawíyugA *vi3-abs* s/he asks questions; investigates ▸ **Ecágen wawímuga.** I ask questions all the time. ▸ **Né'is i'ábi né'us, ecágen wawíyuga.** This one is talking and always asking questions. ▸ **Wawíyugabi žé wacígeši.** I do not want them to investigate. ▸ **Duwé wawíyugeši.** No one was asking questions. *1s:* **wawímuga** *2s:* **wawínuga**

wayáco *n* court judge ▸ **wayáco wicá** judge (male) ▸ **wayáco wíya** judge (female)

wayáhoda *n* oats *Lit:* the thing one chokes on

wayáȟtagA *vi1-abs* s/he/it bites ▸ **Šúga žé ȟnó hádaha, wayáȟtages'a.** When that dog growls, it usually bites. (Parks et al. 1999:139)

wayá'iškadA *vi2-abs* s/he teases, plays jokes on people *1s:* **wamná'iškada** *2s:* **waná'iškada**

wayá'iškada síje *cp* dirty joke

wayá'iškades'a *n* joker, teaser

wayápi *vi2-abs* s/he is skilled at speaking ▸ **Naȟ'ú oká eyíkte žé wayápiši jé'e sten.** He understands all right, but when he tries to speak

he cannot do it. (Cumberland 2005:338) *1s:* **wamnápi** *2s:* **wanápi**

wayásijA *vi2-abs* s/he bad-mouths, speaks ill of things, people

wayáwa *vi2-abs* 1) s/he counts things 2) s/he reads things, has the ability to read 3) s/he studies, goes to school, is a student ▸ **Wayáwabi waȟtéwanaši.** I do not like studying. ▸ **Wayáwa gicúni híbi štén.** They will come when school finishes. *1s:* **wamnáwa** *2s:* **wanáwa** *1p:* **wa'úyawabi**

wayáwa tágaȟtiya *cp* university

wayáwa wicášta *cp* student

wayáwa wókmA *vi1-abs* s/he writes, does his/her homework ▸ **Hayákeji wayáwa wókma žé waná ecúbis'a.** They should write that homework for tomorrow.

wayáwabi *n* schooling, studying, school (as a learning process)

wayáwawicakiye *Variant:* **wayáwawicakiya** *n* school teacher *Lit:* s/he teaches people to read

wayúhA *vi2-abs* s/he has things ▸ **Wamnúhe gápeši.** I did not say I had it all. *1s:* **wamnúha** *2s:* **wanúha**

wayúheja *vi2-abs* s/he is wealthy

wayú'iȟes'a *n* joker, buffoon

wayúksA *vi1-abs* s/he cuts things; alters clothing

wayúpi *vi2* s/he is skilled, good at smth ▸ **Šúgataga gá nína iyópsijabi wayúpi.** That horse over there is a very good jumper. ▸ **Gicízabi wamnúpi.** I am skilled at fighting. *1s:* **wamnúpi** *2s:* **wanúpi** *1p:* **wa'úyupibi** *Adv:* **wayúpiyagen** *Vabs:* **wawáyupi**

wayúpiyagen *adv* in a skillful manner ▸ **Wayúpiyagen ecú.** Do it in a skillful manner.

wayúžaža *vi2-abs* s/he washes things by scrubbing; does laundry ▸ **Ába yužáža hádaha wamnúžaža.** On Saturdays I do laundry. *1s:* **wamnúžaža** *2s:* **wanúžaža** *1p:* **wa'úyužažabi**

wazíca *n* pine tree

Wazíȟe *ngeo* Cypress Hills (Saskatchewan) ‣ **Wanáğaš, Wazíȟe ektá étibi žén.** Long ago, people were camped there at Cypress Hills.

Wazíȟe wįcášta *nprop* Carry The Kettle people (band of Nakoda living in Carry The Kettle, Saskatchewan) *Lit:* Cypress Hills people

Wazíya *nprop* Santa Claus

wazíyada *adv* north; in, to the north

wazíyada wí hinápagiya *ph* northeast

wazíyam *adv* in, to the north ‣ **Wagíyą sába wazíyam žéci iyódągabi.** The Black Thunder-birds sit over in the north.

Wazíyam wįcášta *cp* Inuit tribe, person of Inuit descent *Lit:* northern people

wazíyatakiya ; wazíyakiya *adv* northward, toward the north

wazíziyA *vt1-caus* s/he smokes a hide *1s:* **wazíziwaya** *2s:* **wazíziyaya** *1p:* **wazízi'ųyabi**

wažúšteja *n* strawberry

wą₁ *n* arrow *Usage:* archaic.

wą₂ *n* bullsnake

wą'éya *n* provisions

wága *vi-aux* again and again, one after the other, repetitively *Usage:* marks a repetitive action that occurs in a short time frame. ‣ **Namú wága.** He keeps making a thumping sound. ‣ **Šną wága.** There is a repetitive jingling sound.

wągám ; wągán *adv* up high, above, upright ‣ **Wągám éknąga.** Put it upright.

wągámkiya *adv* uphill, upward ‣ **Wągámkiya yábi teȟíga.** It is hard to go uphill.

wągámneȟ *adv* highest point, top, highest part of smth ‣ **Įyáȟe wągámneȟ íbi.** They went to the highest mountain.

wągádahą *adv* from above

wągáduwa *vs* 1) it is high, highly placed, of value *adv* 2) way above, way up there, high up ‣ **Wągáduwa ecú.** He stacked it high up. *Adv:* **wągán**

wągáduwa éknągA *vt1* s/he promotes sb to a higher position *1s:* **wągáduwa éwaknąga** *2s:* **wągáduwa éyaknąga**

wągáduwaȟ *adv* way up there, at the highest point ‣ **Wamní žé wągáduwaȟ giyą́!** The eagle flies the highest!

wągáduwaȟtįyĄ *vs* s/he/it is the highest, at the highest point

wągíciknagabi *vi1-recip* they see one another *1p:* **wą'ų́giciknagabi**

wągíknagA *vt1-pos* s/he sees his/her own (relative)

wąhį́ *n* arrowhead

wą'íc'iknagA *vi3-refl* s/he sees himself/herself *1s:* **wąmíc'iknaga** *2s:* **wąníc'iknaga**

wája *adv* single (archaic); one *Usage:* the meaning "one" is found only in White Bear and Fort Peck. ‣ **mniwája** ocean

wájaȟ *adv* one time, one time specifically; once *Usage:* used in introducing a tale, or story. ‣ **Įtó wájaȟ iyópsija.** For once, jump. (Fourstar p. 25)

wájanaȟ *adv* only once; one more time ‣ **Žeȟájaȟ wájanaȟtįyą wájanaȟ wa'úcibikta.** One more time, we will dance just one more time. (Weasel 100:148; our translation)

wájanaȟtįyĄ *vs* it is only once; it is one more time *Adv:* **wájanaȟ**

wąyágA *vt2* 1) s/he/it sees sb, smth ‣ **Aké wacímnagabįkte no.** I will see you all again. ‣ **Duktén šúga žé wąnága he?** Where did you see the dog? ‣ **Duwé wąnága?** Who did you see? ‣ **Dáguni wąmnágeší no.** I did not see anything. *vi2* 2) s/he/it sees; s/he has sight ‣ **Įštá saní wąyága.** He sees with one eye. ‣ **Wąmnága owágihi.** I can see. *1s:* **wąmnága** *2s:* **wąnága** *1p:* **wą'úyagabi** *Vcont:* **wąyák** *Vpos:* **wągíknagA** *Vrecip:* **wągíciknagabi** *Vrefl:* **wą'íc'iknagA**

wąyáge *n* witness ‣ **Wąží wąyáge žé gicóbi.** One was called as witness.

wąyágešį *n* blindness

wąyák *vcont* seeing ‣ **Wąníyąk wahí.** I came to see you. (Cumberland 2005:406)

wąyák í *vt1* s/he went to check on sb, smth *1s:* **wąyák wa'í** *2s:* **wąyák ya'í** *1p:* **wąyák ųgíbi**

wąyák'eyagubi *n* prisoner

wąží *num* 1) one ‣ **Ába né wąží ehá'i wahí.** I arrived at one o'clock today. ‣ **Wąží ehá'i.** It is one o'clock. ‣ **Lumsden mąkíyutabi wikcémna núm sám wąží.** Lumsden is 21 miles distant. ‣ **aké wąží** one more *art* 2) a, an ‣ **Šųkwówaši wąží opéwatų.** I bought a work horse. ‣ **Tá wąží ktébi.** They killed a moose. ‣ **Makóce wąží iyéyabi.** They found a land. ‣ **Wąží wąmnága hąda, waktékta no!** When I see a deer, I will kill it! ‣ **Owóde wąží ecágen én íbi.** They always go to a restaurant.

wąží ehá'i *cp* hour

wąžíĥ *num* 1) one in particular, a certain one (marker of focus) ‣ **Wąžíĥ ecú!** Do only one! *det* 2) any, a single one *Usage:* used with nonspecific, hypothetical referent. ‣ **Wįcášta háska wąžíĥ wąwícanaga he?** Did you see any tall men? (Cumberland 2005:363)

wąžíĥtįyą *adv* once again ‣ **Wąžíĥtįyą ecú.** Do it once again.

wąžíkšina *adv-redup* one by one, one after the other ‣ **Wąžíkšina i'ábi.** They spoke one after the other.

wąžína *num* only one ‣ **Tiwícoda duká wąžína hųgá cá witąga otí, hųštá.** There were many families but only one was chief, so he lived in a large tipi, it is said. (Parks et al. 1994)

wąžínaĥ *adv* only one, just one of a group ‣ **Wąžínaĥ hí.** Just one of them arrived.

wąžínaĥtįyĄ *vs* s/he/it is the only one of a group *Syn:* **įšnánaĥtįyĄ**

wąžíniĥ *det* not one, not a single one of a group ‣ **Wįcábi né wąžíniĥ snokyábišį.** None of the men knew it.

wążu *n* quiver; bag for powder and balls

wé *n* 1) blood *vs* 2) s/he/it bleeds ‣ **Nína wé.** It bleeds a lot. ‣ **Dágucen niwé he?** Why are you bleeding? *1s:* **mawé** *2s:* **niwé** *Vcaus:* **weyÁ**

wé hiyáyA *vs-redup* s/he/it is bleeding *1s:* **wé himáyaya** *2s:* **wé hiníyaya**

wé hiyú *vs* s/he/it starts bleeding *1s:* **wé mahíyu** *2s:* **wé nihíyu**

Wé wįcášta *nprop* tribe of Blood (Kainai), person of Blood descent

wé yazóges'a *cp* leech *Lit:* blood sucker

wédu *n* 1) spring ‣ **Wédu ába édu én wóknąkmąkiyabi.** On this spring day they want me to tell a story. (Shields 44:3) *vimp* 2) it is spring

wéhą *adv* last spring ‣ **Wéhą timáni.** She visited last spring

weĥáĥa *vs* s/he has a hemorrhage, bleeds constantly ‣ **Ecágen wemáĥaĥa.** I am always bleeding. *1s:* **wemáĥaĥa** *2s:* **weníĥaĥa**

wemná *vs* s/he/it smells like blood *Adv:* **wemnáya**

wemnáya *adv* smelling of blood

wé'opta *n* vein, artery

wésije *vs* s/he has blood poisoning *1s:* **wémasije** *2s:* **wénisije**

wéskuya *n* diabetes ‣ **Wéskuya yuhá.** She has diabetes. ‣ **Wéskuya nitáwa yašká he?** How is your diabetes level?

weyÁ *vt1-caus* s/he causes sb to bleed

wéyuskeba t'Á *vs* s/he/it dies from bleeding *1s:* **wéyuskeba mat'á** *2s:* **wéyuskeba nit'á**

wí₁ *n* 1) sun ‣ **Wí awágaĥpa ca.** I must cover the sun. (BigEagle 2017:) 2) moon 3) month ‣ **wįcógądu wí** December *Syn:* **hąwí**

wí₂ *n* lodge, tent, tipi ‣ **Wí žé ųgáǧabi.** We set up the tent. ‣ **Wí timáhen yįgá.** He is sitting in the tent. *Redup:* **wíwina**

wí yašpábi *ph* last quarter of the moon

wída *n* island

wídana *n* small island

wídaya *adv* like an island ‣ **makóce wídaya** strait

wígiyuta *vt1-dat* s/he talks in sign language to sb, makes signs to sb *1s:* **wíwagiyuta** *2s:* **wíyagiyuta**

wíhinąpa *n* east

wíhinąpatakiya *adv* eastward, toward the east

wihínįknaga *vs* s/he/it is ugly

wihíyaye *n* time

wihíyayešį *n* north ‣ **Wihíyayešį ecíyadahą éduwą.** He looked toward the north. (Shields 77:423)

wí'įšį'įyaya *vimp* the sun sets; it is sunset

wikcémna *num* 1) ten ‣ **Micíkši mázaska wikcémna yuhá.** My son has $10. *vs* 2) it is ten, there are ten ‣ **Mázaska wikcémnašį.**

wikcémna dóba *num* forty

wikcémna iyúšna (CTK) *num* seventy

wikcémna napcúwąga *num* ninety

wikcémna nųba *num* twenty

wikcémna šagówį (PR, OM) *num* seventy

wikcémna šaknóǧą *num* eighty

wikcémna šákpe *num* sixty

wikcémna yámni *num* thirty

wikcémna záptą *num* fifty

wikcémnana *num* only ten

wináhomni *n* clock

wi'ógiziba *vi1-pos* s/he erects, puts up his/her own tent ‣ **Maǧážu kóš wi'ógizibabi.** Even though it rained, they pitched up their tent. (Schudel 1997:180)

wi'ómni *n* twister wind, whirlwind, dust devil

wí'oti *vi1* 1) s/he lives in a tent ‣ **Mnogédu hąda wí'otibi.** They live in a tent in the summer. *1s:* **wí'owati** *2s:* **wí'oyati**

wi'óti ; wiyóti *n* tipi, dwelling, lodge

wi'ówa *n* painted tipi

wi'óząbi *n* tipi lining

wi'óziba *vi1* s/he erects, puts up a tent *Vpos:* **wí'ogiziba**

wistó *n* tent (with walls), prospector tent *Syn:* **įkcé wistó**

wišíjena *n* pitiful tent

wíšoga *n* canvas

witąga *n* large tipi

witéȟi sųgágu hawí *cp* December *Lit:* hard moon's little brother

witéȟi wí ; witéȟi hawí *cp* January *Lit:* difficult moon

wiwí *n* swamp, marsh; quicksand

wiwína *vi* it is swampy ‣ **Makóce né wíwina.** This land is swampy.

wíwina *n-redup* small tent

wíyaga *n* feather

wíyaga wapáha *cp* feather hat, warbonnet

wíyaga wapáha sįdé yuké *ph* war bonnet with trailer

wiyákpa *vs* it is shiny, bright, polished *Adv:* **wiyákpaya** *Vredup:* **wiyákpakpa**

wiyákpakpa *vs-redup* it is shiny; it shines brightly

wiyákpaya *adv* shining, sparkling, reflective ‣ **Napsú įȟnáye wiyákpaya yįgá.** The ring is shining

wiyáska *n* sand

wíyašpuna *n* shrew

wiyéknašį *adv* very, a lot ‣ **John wiyéknašį tąga.** John is very big. ‣ **Wiyéknašį ganúza.** It is very windy. ‣ **Wiyéknašį ecú.** He did a lot. ‣ **Wiyéknašį įštímabi.** They are sleeping soundly.

wiyódahą *n* 1) south ‣ **wiyódahą ektá** to the south 2) noon, midday ‣ **wiyódahą wódabi** dinner

wiyódahą sám *adv* afternoon

wiyódahąm *adv* in, to the south ‣ **Hokšítogapa wiyódahąm žéci iyódąga.** The first-born son sits over to the south.

wiyódahątakiya *adv* southward, toward the south

wiyó'es'a *adv* throughout the afternoon, all afternoon

wiyóhạbam *adv* in, to the east ‣ **Kúši wanáǧi oyáde wiyóhạbam žéci iyódạga.** The Grandmother spirit nation sits over in the east.

wiyóħpeya *Variant:* **wiyóħpaye** *n* 1) west ‣ **wiyóħpeya ektá** toward/to the west 2) sunset

wiyóħpeyada *adv* at, in the west

wiyóħpeyam *adv* in, to the west ‣ **Wagíyạ šá wiyóħpeyam žéci iyódạgabi.** The Red Thunderbirds sit over there in the west.

wiyóħpeyatakiya *adv* westward, toward the west

wíyopegiyA *vt1-pos* s/he sells his/her own thing ‣ **Šúgatạga žé obáwiǧe wíyopewagiya.** I sold my horse for $100. *1s:* **wíyopewagiya** *2s:* **wíyopeyagiya** *1p:* **wíyope'ųgiyabi**

wíyopeyA *vt1-caus* s/he sells smth ‣ **Búza né wíyopeyiktešị.** She will not sell this cat. ‣ **Amóǧiyạ wíyopewaya.** I sold the car. ‣ **Wašíju tí mitáwa wíyopewayešị no.** I did not sell my house. *1s:* **wíyopewaya** *2s:* **wíyopeyaya** *1p:* **wíyope'ųyabi** *Vpos:* **wíyopegiyA**

wíyopeyabi *n* sale ‣ **wagáhi wíyopeyabi** garage sale

wíyukcạšị *vi2* s/he bold, brave *1s:* **wímnukcạšị** *2s:* **wínukcạšị**

wíyuta *vi2* s/he talks in sign language, makes signs *1s:* **wímnuta** *2s:* **wínuta** *1p:* **wí'ųyutabi** *Vdat:* **wígiyuta**

wị- *cont* woman ‣ **wịkúwa** he chases, bothers women ‣ **wịtáge** old woman

-wị *suff* woman (in personal names); female (animals)

wíbaħte *n* string

wíbazukạ *n* Saskatoon berries ‣ **Wíbazukạ ųkónes.** Let us go search for Saskatoon berries.

wíbazukạ hạwí *cp* June *Syn:* **ịdú wiǧá hạwí**

wíbazukạ sába *cp* blackberry

wíbazukạ stestéyena *ph-redup* wild currant *Lit:* like a small Saskatoon berry

wíbazukạ stéya *ph* blueberry *Lit:* like a Saskatoon berry *Syn:* **a'úyabi**

Wíbazukạ wakpá *ngeo* Saskatoon (Saskatchewan) *Lit:* Saskatoon berry river ‣ **Wíbazukạ wakpá ektá yáħtịyạ.** He really intends to go to Saskatoon.

wíbuspa *n* glue

-wịca- *pref* them (3rd person plural) *Usage:* animate patient of transitive verbs. ‣ **wạyága > wạwícayaga** s/he sees him/her > s/he sees them ‣ **k'ú > wịcák'u** s/he gives smth to him/her > s/he gives smth to them

wịcá *n* 1) man ‣ **Wịcá gá ịš aǧúyabi yúda.** That man over there too is eating bread. ‣ **Wịcá žé nína mocéǧ'a.** That man is very greedy. *vs* 2) he is a man *1s:* **wịmáca** *2s:* **wịníca** *1p:* **wị'úcabi**

wịca- ; wịc- *cont* human *Usage:* in compounds only. ‣ **wịcáħniħni** smallpox ‣ **wịcíšta** human eye ‣ **wịcó'i'e** language, word

wịcá ógiyes'a *cp* mentor

wịcá pagášna *cp* barber

wịcábaǧe *n* announcer

wịcábo *n* human swelling

wịcácaže *n* name, personal name ‣ **Dágu wịcácaže wašté yak'ú.** You gave it a real name. (Weasel 136:359)

wịcágasodabi *n* massacre

wịcáħca *n* my husband (address form). *Usage:* archaic. *See:* **-hịkna-**

wịcáħniħni *n* smallpox ‣ **Wịcáštabi wịcáħniħni yuhábi hạda nína yazábi jé.** When people had smallpox they were always very sick.

wịcáħpi *n* star ‣ **Wịcáħpi óda.** There are a lot of stars. ‣ **ạba ú wịcáħpi** Venus

wịcáħpi éstenaħ *ph* Venus *Lit:* early morning star *Syn:* **ạba ú wịcáħpi**

wịcáħpi iyúšna *cp* Big Dipper constellation *Lit:* seven stars

Wịcáħpimaza *nprop* Ironstar (surname in Carry The Kettle)

wįcáȟtįyana ; wįcáȟtįyą *n* 1) elderly man, senior 2) he is an elderly man, senior *1s:* **wįmácaȟtįyąna** *2s:* **wįnícaȟtįyąna** *1p:* **wį'úcaȟtįyąbina**

wįcá'įc'ina *vs3-refl* 1) she thinks she is a man *1s:* **wįcámįc'ina** *2s:* **wįcánįc'ina** *n* 2) tomboy

wįcákneška *n* gooseberry

wįcáktA *vi1* she becomes manly

wįcákte *n* killer, assassin

wįcák'ubi ecúbi *n* Give Away ceremony *Syn:* **wakpámni ecúbi**

wįcánaǧi *n* human spirit ‣ **wįcánaǧi úbi žén** where the human spirits are

wįcánodį *n* famine

wįcánuȟnuǧe *n* squash *Lit:* human ears

wįcánųȟnųǧena *n* pumpkin

wįcápa *n* human skull

wįcápaha *n* human scalp

wįcápahagaǧabi *n* wig

Wįcápaȟe *ngeo* Skeleton Hill or Skull Mountain (burial site near Sintaluta [Saskatchewan] and one of the former names for Carry The Kettle reservation)

wįcášta *n* 1) man, adult male ‣ **cą'ágan yįgábi wįcášta** chairman 2) person (of both sexes), people *Usage:* both in the singular and plural. ‣ **wįcášta owáyawa** student ‣ **Ába wąką štén wįcášta onowabįkta no!** On Sunday the people are going to sing. 3) tribe (collective plural) ‣ **Osní wįcášta** Northern Nakoda ‣ **Snohéna wįcášta** Shoshone people, person of Shoshone descent

Wįcášta háska *nprop* Tall man (Armand McArthur's traditional name)

wįcášta tága *cp* giant

wįcášta toką *cp* alien *Lit:* different people ‣ **Wįcášta toką né coyáya he?** Do you believe in aliens?

Wįcášta wįcáȟpi *cp* Star people

wįcášta wįcáyawabi *cp* census

wįcát'a *n* human corpse, dead person

wįcátaca *n* body part

wįcátašną ú *vi1* he is a bachelor *1s:* **wįcátašną wa'ú** *2s:* **wįcátašną ya'ú**

wįcátągaga *n* middle-aged man

wįcátągana *n* gull

wįcáteja *n* new, young man

wįcátųga *vt1-coll* she bears twins, triplets ‣ **Wįcáwatųga, iyómagipi.** When I gave birth to them I was happy. *1s:* **wįcáwatųga** *2s:* **wįcáyatųga**

wįcáwaką *n* Holy man ‣ **Wįcáwaką žéca.** He is a Holy man.

wįcáwiza ; wįcáwizija *n* widower

wįcáwodes'a *n* cannibal, maneater

wįcáwoȟa *n* son-in-law

wįcáyuza tíbi *cp* hospital *Lit:* house where they bring people

wįcá *n* raccoon

wįcógądu sųgágu wí *ph* November *Lit:* midwinter's little brother moon ‣ **Ába įjíšakpe wįcógądu sųgágu hąwí'ehą.** It was on the sixth of November.

wįcógądu wí *cp* December *Lit:* midwinter moon

wįcíjana *n* 1) girl ‣ **Wįcíjana né asábi k'ú.** Give this girl milk. ‣ **Wįcíjana gá búza wąží k'úbi.** They gave that girl a cat. ‣ **Wįcíjana žé wó'įškade baháya yuhá.** That girl has a lot of toys. *vs* 2) she is a girl ‣ **Wįnícįjana he?** Are you a girl? *1s:* **wįmácįjana** *2s:* **wįnícįjana** *1p:* **wį'úcįjabina** *Redup:* **wįcíjanana**

wíc'į *n* leather

wíc'į hųská *cp* chaps

wįcíde éyagu *vt2* 1) s/he photographs, takes a picture of sb; makes footage of sb *1s:* **wįcíde émnagu** *2s:* **wįcíde énagu** *n* 2) camera *Lit:* it takes human faces

wįcíde oyábi *ph* picture, painting, photograph ‣ **Wįcíde oyábi óda yuhá.** She has a lot of pictures.

wįcíjanana *n-redup* little girl

wįcíspa *n* human elbow

Wįcíspayazą *ngeo* Calgary (Alberta) *Lit:* human elbow aching

wįcíšnąna *adv* alone *Usage:* used for humans.

wįcíšta *n* human eye

wįcíšta yazá hąwí *np* March *Lit:* sore eyes moon *Syn:* **wamnónija hąwí**

wįcódabi *vs-coll* there a lot of people, it is crowded

wįcógądu *n* midwinter

wįcóhą *n* crowd

wįcóho *n* human voice

wįcóho éyagu *ph* recorder, recording device *Lit:* it takes human voice

wįcóȟ'ą *n* deed, act of bravery

wįcóȟ'age *n* way of life, culture, tradition ‣ **Nakón wįcóȟ'age tewáȟina cá no!** I really cherish my Nakoda traditions!

wįcó'i'abi *n* 1) language, word 2) letter

wįcó'i'e *n* language, word

wįc'óne *vi1-coll* s/he looks for people *1s:* **wįc'ówane** *2s:* **wįc'óyane**

wįcóni *n* human life, health, ways, spirit; ghost ‣ **Wįcóni ųk'ú bo!** Give us life! (when addressing the spirits) ‣ **Wįcóni ųgáknibi.** We brought the way of life back to him. ‣ **Nakón-wįcóni** Nakoda ways

wįcóni wašté *vs* s/he is in good health *1s:* **wįcóni mawášte** *2s:* **wįcóni niwášte** *1p:* **wįcóni ųwaštebí**

wįcóti *n* village

wįcó'ųcağa *n* generation

wįcóyazą *vs-coll* 1) people are sick from an epidemic *n* 2) illness, epidemic disease ‣ **Wįcóyazą óda.** There are a lot of ailments. ‣ **Né wįcóyazą né otéȟiga.** This pandemic is difficult. ‣ **Wįcóyazą síja cá Įkcé wįcášta oyáde iyúha ecéyabi.** All of the Indigenous people suffered from a severe epidemic.

wįcóyazą tíbi *cp* hospital

wįcóye *n* human footprint

wįcúzi oyúgode *cp* Bigfoot, Sasquatch

wída *vi1* s/he/it crawls ‣ **Dáguškina žé waná wída.** The baby is now crawling. ‣ **Bibína wída cén taȟáge ektá babóda.** The baby crawls so he wears out his knees (on his pants). *Vcont:* **wįwín**

wídáyąga *vs* she is a fine woman, lady

wídukA *vs* s/he relieves himself/herself (urinate, defecate); uses the bathroom ‣ **Wíduke í.** He went to the bathroom *1s:* **wímaduka** *2s:* **wíniduka** *1p:* **wį'údukabi** *See:* **owíduka**

wįgúnową *n* love song

wíhamnA *vi1-abs* s/he dreams about things; has a vision ‣ **Wíwahamna žén i'á'.** She spoke in my dream. ‣ **Wíhamna cá.** He has a vision at the moment. *1s:* **wíwahamna** *2s:* **wíyahamna**

wįhámne *n* dream, vision ‣ **Wįhámne né ųs tawáci dąyáši.** He is moody because of this dream. *Syn:* **įhámnabi**

wįhámnes'a *n* someone who has visions; dreamer

wįhíknątų *n* married woman

wíȟ'aȟ'ą *vi1-redup* it (cattle, horse) is grazing ‣ **Šúgatąga né wįȟ'aȟ'ą yá:gabi.** The horses were grazing along.

wį'íde éyagu wįcášta *ph* cameraman

wį'íȟpeyA *vi1* he divorces his wife *1s:* **wį'íȟpewaya** *2s:* **wį'íȟpeyaya**

wį'íknuš'age *n* pregnant woman

wį'ínaȟmA *vi1* he elopes, runs away with a married woman *Usage:* can also be used when a woman elopes with a man. *1s:* **wį'ínawaȟma** *2s:* **wį'ínayaȟma**

wį'ínową *n* love song *Usage:* usually a song about a woman or about what the couple could do if they got together.

wį'íyape *vi1* he is waiting for her, stalking her

wįjágicinabi *vi1-recip* 1) they agree with one another 2) they believe in one another

wįjákA *vi1* 1) s/he tells the truth ▸ **Wįjákešį
otí'įga.** I guess he is not telling the truth. ▸
Cóȟ wįjáyaka? Are you telling the truth?
▸ **Waníyedu dóba né įtkųs'ųya štén žé
wįjá'ųkįkta.** After four years when we finish
it, we will tell the truth. (NS 2002:33) *vs* 2) it is
true ▸ **Žé wįjáka.** That is true. ▸ **Žé wįjákešį.**
That is not true. *1s*: **wįjáwaka** *2s*: **wįjáyaka** *1p*:
wįjá'ųkabi *Adv*: **wįjákeya** *See*: **cóȟ, cóȟtįyĄ**

wįjákabi *n* truth

wįjákena *vt1* s/he considers sb to tell the truth;
considers smth to be true

wįjákeya *adv* truthfully, honestly ▸ **Nína
wįjákeya i'á.** He spoke very truthfully. ▸
Wįjákeya ecú. He did it honestly. ▸ **Wįjákeya
eyá.** He confirms it in speech.

wįjána *vt1* 1) s/he agrees with sb, smth 2) s/he
believes (in) sb, smth; is confident in sb, smth
1s: **wįjáwana** *2s*: **wįjáyana** *1p*: **wįjá'ųnabi** *Vrecip*: **wįjágicinabi**

wíjaska *n* pemmican

wíjaskabi *n* pemmican, dried meat with crushed
chokecherries

wįkcena *n* wolverine *Syn*: **mnáza**

wįkni *n* 1) fat, grease ▸ **Mató wįkni snagíya.** He
rubs his with bear grease. ▸ **mąkwįkni** skunk
oil 2) oil, gasoline ▸ **Wįkni bapsų́.** He spilled
oil. ▸ **Wįkni owážutų.** I filled it with gasoline.

wįkni įbápsų *cp* gas station

wįkni owáco'ųba *cp* frying pan

wįkni pedížąžą *n* oil lantern

wįkniskana ; wįkniska *n* lard, shortening

wįkóške *n* 1) young woman ▸ **Waná wįkóške
hąkta.** Now she is becoming a young woman.
vs 2) she is a young woman ▸ **Cųwįtku núm
wįkóškebi.** His two daughters were young girls.
(Parks et al. 1994) ▸ **Waná wįkóškehąkta.** Now
she is becoming a young lady. *1s*: **wįmákoske**
2s: **wįníkoške** *Redup*: **wįkóškenana** (CTK) ;
wįkóškeškena

wįkóškenana (CTK) *n-redup* teenage girl

wįkóškeškena *n-redup* teenage girl

wįkta *Variant*: **wįtka** *n* egg

wįkta šagíyabi *cp* Easter *Lit*: eggs are painted red

wįktaǧi *n* yolk

wįktés'a *n* wifebeater

wįktó *Variant*: **wįtkó** *vs* s/he is crazy

wįktógaǧA *Variant*: **wįtkótkogaǧA** *vi1* 1) s/he
makes a fool out of himself/herself ▸ **Owá
wįktó'ųgaǧabi.** We all made a fool of ourselves. *1s*: **wįktówagaǧa** *2s*: **wįktóyagaǧa**
1p: **wįktó'ųgaǧabi** *n* 2) fool dancer, clown ▸
Wįktógaǧabi wówįcak'u wo! Feed the clowns!
Adv: **wįktóya**

Wįktógaǧe wacíbi *Variant*: **Wįktógaǧa wacíbi**
cp Clown dance, Fool dance

wįktókto *Variant*: **wįtkótko** *vs-redup* s/he is bad,
crazy; misbehaves ▸ **Wįktókto cén wagábe.** He
misbehaved, so I spanked him. ▸ **Wįktóktobi
cén wósijabi.** They ruined it because they
were bad. *1s*: **wįmáktokto ; wįmátkotko** *2s*:
wįníktokto ; wįnítkotko *1p*: **wį'ų́ktoktobi ;
wį'ų́tkotkobi**

wįktóktoga i'Á *vi1* s/he speaks backward as in
a Clown ceremony

wįktóktoyagen *adv* crazily, foolishly ▸
Wįtkótkoyagen ú. He behaves crazily.

wįktówį ; wįtkówį *n* foolish, loose woman

wįktóya *adv* clowning, foolishly ▸ **Wįktóya wa'ų́.**
I clown around.

wįkúwa *vi1* he chases, courts, flirts with a
woman ▸ **Wįkúwešį wo!** Do not chase girls!
1s: **wįwákuwa** *2s*: **wįyákuwa**

wįk'ú *vt1* s/he gives him a wife, daughter in marriage ▸ **Wanągaš wįmák'u.** Long ago I was
given in marriage.

wįk'úbi *n* daughter given away for marriage

wįnówą *vi1* he sings a love song ▸ **Koškábi nówa
šųk'áganyąk tiwókšą wįnówąbis'a.** All of the

young men used to ride horseback around the camp, singing love songs. (NS 2002:5)

wį́nwįda *adv-redup* here and there ‣ [. . .] **wį́nwįda cúwąja.** [. . .] it is forested here and there. (NS 2002:36)

wį'ógine *vt1-pos* he looks for his wife *1s:* **wį'ówene** *2s:* **wį'óyene**

wį'óne *vi1* he looks for a girl, woman *1s:* **wį'ówane** *2s:* **wį'óyane** *Vpos:* **wį'ógine**

wį́pena *n* weapon

wį́štejA *vs-abs* s/he is ashamed

wįšwį́žena *vs* it is flexible, pliable

wįtą́ga *vs* she is a mature woman

wįwáštega *n* beautiful woman

wįwázija *n* widow

wįwį́n *vcont-redup* crawling along ‣ **Wįwį́n ú.** He is crawling all over on all fours.

wįwóguga *n* beautiful woman

wįwóȟpa *vi1* he purchases a bride

wįwóȟpabi *n* bride price

wíyą *n* 1) woman ‣ **Wíyą žé wagáȟniȟa.** I chose that woman. ‣ **Wiyą́ žé wóguga.** That woman is beautiful. ‣ **Wíyą žená ağúyábi gáǧabi he?** Are these women making bannock? *vs* 2) s/he is a woman ‣ **Hiyá, wįmáyą.** No, I am a woman. ‣ **Nakóda wíyąšį.** She is not a Nakoda woman. *1s:* **wįmáyą** *2s:* **wįníyą** *1p:* **wį'úyąbi** *Cont:* **wį-,-wį**

wíyą omnéza *cp* nurse

wįyą́bi heȟága okónagiciyabi *ph* Elk woman society

wįyą́ša *n* penny, cent *Lit:* red woman *Syn:* **mázaša**

wįyáteja₁ *n* young (new) woman *See:* **téjana**

wįyáteja₂ *n* cranberry

wįyą́wašóga *n* nickel *Lit:* thick woman

wįyą́woȟa *n* daughter-in-law

wíyena *n* 1) female animal *Usage:* used in nominal compounds. ‣ **ptewíyena** female buffalo, domestic cow ‣ **gugúšawįyena** swine 2) doe

wíyeyA *adv* ready ‣ **Cą́ íš doháyą gíjaknibi cén wíyeya gíjiknągabi.** They brought him

a stick of a certain length and placed it ready for him. (Drummond 1976, A bear story) *Vrefl:* **įknúwįyeyA**

wíyįktA ; wį́ktA *vi* he is becoming effeminate

wíyukcą *vi2-abs* s/he thinks, ponders about things; forms his/her opinion about smth ‣ **Žécen wíyukcą.** That is the way he thinks. ‣ **Bağé nécen wíyukcą bo.** You all think about it as a group. *1s:* **wį́mnukcą** *2s:* **wį́nukcą** *1p:* **wį'ų́yukcąbi**

wíyų *vt1* s/he uses smth ‣ **Hųgóȟ'a štén wíyų wo.** Use it for a give away.

wo- *pref* food *Usage:* used in compounds. ‣ **k'ú > wók'u** s/he gives smth to sb > s/he feeds sb

wo *encl* indicates a command made to a single person by a male speaker (singular male imperative) ‣ **Tín ú wo.** Come in. ‣ **Nén iyódąga wo.** Sit down here. ‣ **Cądéwašte wo.** Be kind.

wó'ahope *n* respect, observance for customs, social rules

wó'ayupte *n* answer

wóbagą *vs-abs* s/he/it is respected *1s:* **wómabagą** *2s:* **wónibagą**

wócakne *n* scaffold *Usage:* archaic.

wócažeyada *n* words of a song ‣ **Nakón-nowąbi abá wócažeyada yuká.** Some Nakoda songs have words. (Cumberland 2005:256)

wócegiya *n* 1) Medicine ceremony 2) church service ‣ **Wócegiya íbi.** They went to the church service.

wócegiya óhą ú *vi1* s/he/it is Christian *1s:* **wócegiya óhą wa'ú** *2s:* **wócegiya óhą ya'ú** *1p:* **wócegiya óhą ųk'úbi**

wócegiya wįcášta *cp* church minister

wócegiye *n* 1) religion, spirituality ‣ **Wócegiye én ağúyabiwaką yúdabi.** They take communion bread in (Christian) religion. 2) prayer ‣ **Dágu wócegiya ecúbįkta hą́da úbi.** They used it whenever they held prayer meetings. (Drummond 1976, The pipe of peace)

wócį *vi1-abs* s/he begs ‣ **Wócį híbi.** They came begging. ‣ **Hó namáȟ'ų wo, wówacį no!** Hear my voice, I am begging! ‣ **Éstena wócįbįkta.** They will be begging soon. *1s:* **wówacį** *2s:* **wóyacį**

wócįs'a *n* beggar ‣ **Wócįs'a žé mask'ú.** Give money to the beggar.

wódA *vi1* s/he/it eats ‣ **Waná wó'ųdabįkte no.** We are going to eat now. ‣ **Mįš wówadįkteȟtįyą.** I want to eat too. ‣ **Húȟniyena wowádįkta.** I will eat in a hurry. ‣ **Waná wo'ųdas.** Let us eat now. ‣ **Né wowádįkte né'įš pinámayaya.** For what I am about to eat, I thank you. *1s:* **wówada** *2s:* **wóyada** *1p:* **wó'ųdabi** *Vcaus:* **wonkíyA** *Vcont:* **won-** ; **wo-**

wódabi *n* feast, meal ‣ **wogíksuya wódabi** Memorial feast ‣ **hąyákena wódabi** breakfast ‣ **wiyódahą wódabi** dinner

wódaguya *n* kinship, relatives

wódes'a *n* eater; one who eats all the time

wódešįyą *adv* without eating

wó'ecų *n* work, occupation, ceremony ‣ **Wó'ecų žé wįcák'ubi.** They gave them those ceremonies.

wóga ; **wóğa** *n* grasshopper

wógağe *n* product; crafted item, object

wógamna *n* flat strips of meat prepared for drying

wógiciknagA *vi1-recip* they tell stories to one another *Vcont:* **wógiciknak**

wógiciknak *vcont-recip* telling stories to one another ‣ **Naȟmáȟman wógiciknak yįgábi.** They were talking together privately. (Cumberland 2005:405)

wógidą *vi1* s/he gets, gains honors *Adv:* **wógidąya**

wógidąya *adv* gaining honor ‣ **Wógidąya ųyábi.** We are going to gain honor.

wógíjic'u *vt1-benef* s/he feeds sb for him/her ‣ **Hokšína né wómijic'u wo.** Feed this boy for me. *1s:* **wówejic'u** *2s:* **wóyejic'u**

wógijikmA *vt1-benef* s/he writes to or for him/her ‣ **Okówąži hąda tída wówįcagijikma jé'e.** She always writes to her folks back home once a week. *1s:* **wówejikma** *2s:* **wóyejikma**

wógijišpi *vt1-benef* s/he picks berries for sb *1s:* **wówejišpi** *2s:* **wóyejišpi** *1p:* **wó'ųgijišpibi**

wógiknagA *vt1-dat* s/he tells sb a story ‣ **Įtúšį wómagiknagešį.** Do not lie to me. ‣ **Žén yįgá wómagiknąga.** He sat there telling me his stories. *1s:* **wówagiknaga** *2s:* **wóyagiknaga**

wogíksuya wódabi *cp* Memorial feast

wóginihąga *vs* s/he/it is fearsome, dangerous, ferocious ‣ **Wakpá žé wóginihąga.** The river is dangerous.

wógitahą *adv* regardless, in spite of ‣ **Wógitahą ağúyabi knaksábi.** And in spite of everything, they managed to cut their own wheat. (Drummond 1976, Early days on Carry The Kettle reserve)

wógųga *vs* s/he/it is beautiful, pretty (woman only, landscape, event) ‣ **Ąbédu wógųga.** It is a beautiful day ‣ **Makóce wógųga.** It is a beautiful landscape ‣ **Wíyą žé wógųga.** That woman is beautiful, attractive. *Adv:* **wógųya**

wogúgana *n* pretty woman

wógųya *adv* attractive, in an attractive manner; tempting ‣ **Wógųya wacíbi.** They are dancing prettily. ‣ **Á! wįkóške wógųya įcága.** Ah! this young woman had grown attractive. (NS 2002:86) ‣ **Dágu wógųya wówadįkte no.** I will eat something delicious. ‣ **Wógųyą hą cen eyáš omnézenaȟ.** It was tempting and just wonderfully clear. (Weasel 134:313)

wóhą *vi1-abs* s/he cooks things by boiling ‣ **Wóyahą he?** Are you cooking? *1s:* **wówahą** *2s:* **wóyahą**

wóhena *n* cook

wóȟįyą *vi1* s/he pouts *1s:* **wówaȟįyą** *2s:* **wóyaȟįyą**

wó'imağağa *vs* s/he/it is amusing, enjoyable *Vrefl:* **wó'imağağa'įc'iyA**

wó'imağağa'įc'iyA *vi3-refl* s/he enjoys, amuses himself/herself

wó'išijA *vs* s/he/it is vicious, terrible *1s:* **wó'imašija** *2s:* **wó'inisija**

wó'įcağe *n* vegetation

wó'įškada ; **wó'įškade** *n* toy, teddy bear ‣ **Wįcíjana žé wó'įškade baháya yuhá.** That girl has a lot of toys.

wó'įšte *n* eagle feather, plume, down feathers

wo'įštéjaga *vs* s/he/it is shameful *1s:* **wó'įmaštejaga** *2s:* **wó'įništejaga**

wó'įštenyagen *adv* shamefully

wó'įye *n* cloth offering used in Sun dances ‣ **Wó'įye mitáwa žé ahómįjitą'į.** He blessed my sacred cloth.

wókcą *vi1* s/he thinks, plans on doing smth

wókcąšį wįcášta *cp* thoughtless person

wókeya *n* man-made shelter

wókmes'a *n* artist

wóknagA *vi1-abs* 1) s/he tells stories ‣ **Waníyedu štén wó'ųknagabįkte no!** Next winter we will tell stories. ‣ **Wįjáke wówaknaga.** I am telling a true story. ‣ **Anągiħmą wóknaga.** He is telling it secretly. ‣ **Watápe hékta wóknagabis'a.** Long ago the ancestors used to tell stories. *vi1-abs-pos* 2) s/he tells his/her own story *1s:* **wówaknaga** *2s:* **wóyaknaga** *1p:* **wó'ųknagabi** *Vcaus:* **wóknakkiyA** *Vcont:* **wóknak** *Vdat:* **wógiknagA** *Vrecip:* **wógiciknagA**

wóknagabi *n* storytelling ‣ **Wóknagabi wayápi.** He is an expert in storytelling.

wóknak *vcont* telling stories ‣ **Adé wóknak hįgá.** Dad sat telling stories.

wóknakkiyA *vt1-caus* s/he makes sb tell his/her story ‣ **Wédu ąba édu én wóknąkmąkiyabi.** On this spring day they want me to tell a story. (Shields 44:3)

wókoyage *n* clothes, fancy clothes, outfit

wókpą *n* bag used to store meat

woksÁ *vt1* s/he breaks his/her word; betrays sb

wókšu *vabs* s/he plants things (garden, crops) *1s:* **wówakšu** *2s:* **wóyakšu**

wókšus'a *n* farmer, gardener *Syn:* **wa'įcaħye**

wók'u *vt1* s/he feeds sb, an animal ‣ **Gugúša žé wók'u.** Feed that pig. ‣ **Šúga wówįcak'ubįšį** The dogs were not fed. *1s:* **wówak'u** *2s:* **wóyak'u** *1p:* **wó'ųk'ubi** *Vbenef:* **wógíjic'u** *Vredup:* **wók'uk'u**

wók'uk'u *vt1-redup* s/he keeps feeding sb, an animal

Wómnapta *ngeo* Montmartre (Saskatchewan)

wón *vcont* eating ‣ **Won ú.** Come eat. ‣ **Won ųyas.** Let us go eat. ‣ **Adé wón yįgá.** Dad is sitting eating. ‣ **Wíyąbi níyuhana wón a'íbi cen.** All the women would take food. (Cumberland 2005:354) *Vredup:* **wónwon**

wóne *vi1-abs* s/he hunts, looks for things

won'égijikne *vt1-benef* s/he sets the table for sb ‣ **Iná won'éwejikne.** I set the table for mom. *1s:* **won'éwejikne** *2s:* **won'éyejikne**

won'ékne *vi1* s/he sets the table *1s:* **won'éwakne** *2s:* **won'éyakne** *Vbenef:* **won'égijikne**

wónhi *vi1* s/he arrives here from there to eat *1s:* **wónwahi** *2s:* **wónyahi** *1p:* **wón'ųyabi**

wonkíyA *vt1-caus* s/he made sb eat

wónwon *vcont* eating repeatedly

wo'óhiya *n* prize *Syn:* **ohíyabi**

wó'ope *n* law

wó'ošija *n* rattlesnake ‣ **Wó'ošija wanįjabi nén.** There are no rattlesnakes here. *Syn:* **sįdéħna**

wópaħtA *vi1-abs* s/he watches people, things, a game *1s:* **wópawaħta** *2s:* **wópayaħta** *1p:* **wópa'ųħtabi**

wópaħte *n* onlooker

wópaħtes'a *n* spectator

wópetų *vi1-abs* 1) s/he buys things; shops ‣ **Dohą́n štén wópetų nįkta?** When are you going shopping? ‣ **Wįcíjana žé wópetų yéšį.** The little girl did not go shopping. *n* 2) merchant

wópina *n* thanks, gratitude ‣ **"Wópina!" epá.** I

said, "Thanks!" ▸ **"Wópina!" eyécųna.** He kept on saying, "Thanks!" *Vcaus:* **wópinaya**

wópina ába *cp* Thanksgiving day

wópina k'ú *vt1* s/he gives gratitude ▸ **Wópina tága cic'ú no.** I give great thanks. ▸ **Ába wašté né wópina wak'ú no!** For this beautiful day I give thanks. *1s:* **wópina wak'ú** *2s:* **wópina yak'ú** *1p:* **wópina ųk'úbi**

wópina onówą *cp* Thanksgiving song

wópinayA *vt1-caus* s/he makes sb thankful

wópiya *vi1-abs* s/he wraps up things; it is wrapped up ▸ **Dąyą́ wópiya.** It is well wrapped up.

wópiyabi *n* burial

wópiye *n* box, container

wópiyena *n* medicine bundle

wósijA *vi1-abs* 1) s/he causes trouble, does bad things ▸ **Wįktóktobi cén wósijabi.** They did bad things because they were misbehaving. ▸ **Dóken ecágen wósija hų́n.** I wonder why he always causes trouble. *Adv:* **wósijeya** *n* 2) something bad, evil, disastrous

wósija akípa *vi1* s/he encounters, is afflicted with bad luck; it is bad luck *1s:* **wósija awákipa** *2s:* **wósija ayákipa**

wósijeya *adv* acting problematically, troublesome ▸ **Dókedu wósijeya įȟpéya.** Somehow he got out of trouble.

wóska *vi1-abs* s/he does quillwork ▸ **Iná wóska:ga.** Mom was quilling.

wosų́sųbina *n* cobweb *Syn:* **ȟeȟágagana wakmų́ga**

wóšma *n* 1) brush, thick bush *vs* 2) it is dense, tightly packed

wóšpi *vi1-abs* s/he picks berries, things ▸ **Wįkóškebi wóšpibįkteȟtįyą.** The girls are anxious to pick berries. ▸ **Wóšpi íbi.** They went to pick berries. *1s:* **wówašpi** *2s:* **wóyašpi** *1p:* **wó'ųšpibi** *Vbenef:* **wógijišpi**

wóštejA *vs* s/he/it is strange *1s:* **wómašteja** *2s:* **wóništeja**

wóšuye *n* rule

wot'Á *vs* s/he/it dies at a distance ▸ **Gakí wot'á.** He died over there.

wótawa *n* medicine bundle; war charm

wóteȟą *vs* s/he/it is taking long

wóteȟiga *n* distress

wóteȟina *n* value, object of love or admiration

wótijaǧa ; tijáǧabi *n* medicine lodge, Sun dance arbor *Cont:* **tijáȟ**

wótijaǧa anówąbi *cp* Sun dance singing

wót'į *vi1* s/he makes noises when speaking ▸ **Wóyat'įbi no!** You guys are noisy! *1s:* **wówat'į** *2s:* **wóyat'į**

wotkícuni *vi1* s/he finishes eating ▸ **Wotkícuni áya.** He is finishing eating. *1s:* **wotwécuni** *2s:* **wotyécuni**

wótųye *n* medicine bag

wó'ųspe *n* lesson

wówacįye *vs-abs* s/he is dependable *1s:* **wómawacįye** *2s:* **wóniwacįye**

wówaȟtani *n* sin ▸ **Wówaȟtani oknágabi.** They confess their sins. ▸ **Ábédu nén wówaȟtani cóna mawánįkta.** May I walk with no sins today.

wówaši hayábi *cp* working clothes, coveralls ▸ **Wówaši hayábi wéc'ų.** I put on my working clothes.

Wówaši *nprop* O'Watch (surname in Carry The Kettle, Saskatchewan)

wówaši *n* 1) job, work, occupation; workplace ▸ **Wówaši mnįkta.** I am going to work. ▸ **Mitáwįju wówaši dahą́ awákni.** I picked up my wife at work. 2) servant, worker *1s:* **mitáwowaši** *2s:* **nitáwowaši** *3s:* **tawówaši**

Wówaši ába *cp* Labor day

wówaši ecágiji'ų *vt1-benef* s/he works for sb ▸ **Wanáǧaš wówaši ecámįji'ųbi.** They worked for me long ago. *1s:* **wówaši ecáweji'ų** *2s:* **wówaši ecáyeji'ų**

wówaši ecų́ *vi3* 1) s/he works, does his/her work ▸ **Dayágen wówaši ecámų.** I do my work with ease. ▸ **Nahą́ȟ wówaši ecų́bi.** They are still

working. 2) she is in labor ‣ **Nągáhą nína
wówaši ecú.** Now she is in labor. *1s:* **wówaši
ecámų** *2s:* **wówaši ecánų** *1p:* **wówaši ecúgųbi**
Vbenef: **wówaši ecágiji'ų** *Vcaus:* **wówaši
ecúkiyA**

wówaši ecúkiyA *vt1-caus* s/he puts sb to work;
hires sb *1s:* **wówaši ecúwakiya** *2s:* **wówaši
ecúyakiya**

wówaši įc'íkni *vi3* s/he arrives back here looking
for work ‣ **Įmáduka cén wówaši mįc'íkni.** I
am hungry, so I have come looking for work.
(Weasel 11:81) *1s:* **wówaši mįc'íkni** *2s:* **wówaši
nįc'íkni**

wówaši okíyA *vt1-caus* s/he hires sb *1s:* **wówaši
owákiya** *2s:* **wówaši oyákiya** *Vcoll:* **wówaši
owícakiyA**

wówašikiyA *vt1-caus* s/he hires sb; makes sb
work *1s:* **wówašiwakiya** *2s:* **wówašiyakiya**
1p: **wówaši'ųkiyabi**

wówaš'age *n* energy, strength, power ‣ **Mastústa
cén wówaš'age mnuhéšį.** I am tired, thus I do
not have energy.

wówayatąga *num* million

wówįcak'u *n* rations

wowįcak'u ába *cp* Saturday *Lit:* rations day

wówįhaga *vs* s/he/it is funny ‣ **Nína wówįhaga!**
It is very funny! ‣ **Wówįhaga mnawá ús įwáha.**
I am laughing because I read something funny.
1s: **wóma'įhaga** *2s:* **wóni'įhaga**

wówįjaka *n* belief

wóyapte *n* table scraps

wóyawa tága *cp* million

wóyawabi *n* number *Syn:* **yawábi**

wóyude *Variant:* **wóyuda** *n* food, groceries
Lit: the thing one eats ‣ **Wóyude awágu.**
I brought food. ‣ **Wóyude mák'u wo!** Give
me food! ‣ **Šúga né wóyuda edáhą cįgá.** The
dog wants some food. ‣ **Wóyude mitáwa
žé iyúha yúdabi.** They ate all of my food. *1s:*
mitáwoyude *2s:* **nitáwoyude** *3s:* **tawóyude;
tóyude** *Cont:* **wo-**

wóyude owópetų ; owópetų *cp* grocery store
‣ **Owópetų žén wówaši ecúšį.** She does not
work at the grocery store.

wóyuha *n* belongings, one's things ‣
**Takónagugiciyabi híkna dágu wóyuha
waštéšte nówa íš gicíc'ubi.** The friendship was reciprocated, and they exchanged
gifts, including fine clothes and other things.
(Shields 15:181)

wóža *vi1-abs* s/he cooks things (into a stew,
porridge)

wóžabi *n* Saskatoon soup, berry soup; gravy, stew
‣ **Mikúši wóžabi gágįkta.** My grandmother
will make gravy.

wóžaža *vi1-abs* s/he washes things *1s:* **wówažaža**
2s: **wóyažaža**

wóžu *n* quiver

wóžuha *n* leather bag

wóžutų *vi1-abs* 1) s/he fills bags or sacks *n* 2) full
bag, bag or sack filled with smth; medicine
bundle ‣ **Wóžutų cic'úkta.** I will give you a
full bag. *Syn:* **ožútųbi**

Y

ya- *pref* action done with the mouth, teeth (biting, chewing, speaking) *Usage:* derives a stative
verb into a transitive verb. ‣ **háska > yaháska**
s/he/it is long > s/he lengthens a story ‣ **céya >
yacéya** s/he cries > s/he makes sb cry by speech

-ya- *prefix-infix* you (2nd person singular) *Usage:*
agent/subject of active verbs of Class 1. ‣ **hí >
yahí** s/he arrives here > you arrive here ‣ **maní
> mayáni** s/he walks > you walk

-ya-...-bi *circumfix* you all (2nd person plural)
Usage: agent/subject of active verbs of Class 1.
‣ **nowá > yanówąbi** s/he sings > you all sing
‣ **nážį > nayážįbi** s/he stands > you all stand

-ya *suff* derives manner adverbs from stative
verbs *Usage:* a nasalised version -yą occurs
after a preceding syllable that has either a nasal

consonant or a nasal vowel; triggers e-blaut. ▸
ítutu > ítutuya s/he has slobbering mouth > in
a slobbering manner ▸ **wósija > wósijeya** s/he
causes trouble, does bad things > acting problematically ▸ **kokní > kokníyą** shiny, glassy,
bright, translucent > shinily, brightly ▸ **teȟį́šį
> teȟį́šiyą** it is easy > easily *Adv:*-**yagen**

-yA *suff* 1) s/he causes, makes, lets sb do it; causes,
lets sb be in a state or condition ▸ **cądéšija >
cądéšinya** s/he is sad > s/he makes sb sad ▸
búza > busyá it is dry > s/he dries smth 2) have,
adopt someone as a relative or friend ▸ **adé >
adéya** my father > s/he has him as a father ▸
húgu > húguya his/her mother > s/he adopted
her as a mother ▸ **koná > konáya** friend > s/he
has him/her as a friend *See:* -**kiyA**

yÁ *vi2* s/he goes away from here, he departed
from here *Usage:* triggers e-ablaut on a preceding word. ▸ **Sám yá!** Go away! ▸ **Yá bo!** You
all go! ▸ **Wayáwa tíbi dóken ná?** Where do
you go to school? ▸ **Ą́ba įzáptą štén wópetu
mnį́kta.** I will go shopping on Friday. *1s:* **mná**
2s: **ná** *1p:* **ųgíyabi**

yacéyA *vt2* s/he makes sb cry by speech

yacó *vt2* s/he sues, summons, takes sb to court ▸
Waktá! Niyácokta. Beware! He will sue you.
▸ **Hųgá žé mnacókta.** I will sue the chief. *1s:*
mnacó *2s:* **nacó** *1p:* **ųyácobi**

yadą́₁ *vt2* s/he praises sb, smth *Vrefl:* **įknádą**

yadą́₂ *vt2* s/he extracts smth by sucking

yadą́biga *participle* s/he is one who is highly
praised

yadį́da *vt2* s/he pulls smth with the teeth *1s:*
mnadį́da *2s:* **nadį́da** *1p:* **ųyádįdabi**

-yagen *suff* kind of, somewhat, rather *Usage:* creates manner adverbs from stative and active
verbs, but also from adverbs; in many cases
there is no attenuative meaning. ▸ **sudá >
sudáyagen** hard, firm > kind of hard ▸ **šikná
> šiknáyagen** s/he/it is mad, angry > angry ▸

stustá > stustáyagen s/he is tired > boringly,
bored

yağóba *vt2* s/he sips a beverage ▸ **Miníwaką
yağóba.** He is sipping a whisky.

yağú *vt2* s/he finishes up a pipe *Vbenef:* **knağú**
Vpos: **gíjiyağu**

yaháskA *vt2* s/he lengthens a story *1s:* **mnaháska**
2s: **naháska** *Vpos:* **knaháskA**

yahį́ȟpayA *vt2* s/he pulls smth with the teeth *1s:*
mnahį́ȟpaya *2s:* **nahį́ȟpaya**

yahóda *vi2* s/he chokes, gags on smth *1s:*
mnahóda *2s:* **nahóda** *1p:* **ųyáhodabi**

yahókšu *vt2* s/he breaks up a plan verbally ▸
Dágu eyábi ȟáda yahókšu. Whenever they
talk she breaks their plan. *1s:* **mnahókšu** *2s:*
nahókšu

yahókudu *vt2* s/he denigrates sb *1s:* **mnahókudu**
2s: **nahókudu** *Vrefl:* **įknáhokudu**

yahéba *vt1* s/he drinks smth up *1s:* **mnahéba** *2s:*
nahéba *1p:* **ųyáhebabi** *Vpos:* **knahéba**

yaȟnáda *vt2* s/he grabs smth with the teeth

yaȟnéjA *vt2* s/he tears smth with the teeth

yaȟnógA *vt2* s/he/it gnaws a hole in smth, chews
smth up (like a mouse chewing on clothes)

yaȟtágA *vt2* s/he bites sb, smth ▸ **Tuȟmáğa tahú
yaȟtága.** The bee stung him on the neck. *1s:*
mnaȟtága *2s:* **naȟtága** *1p:* **ųyáȟtagabi** *Vabs:*
wayáȟtagA *Vcaus:* **yaȟtákyA** *Vpos:* **knaȟtágA**

yaȟtákyA *vt1-caus* s/he traps

yaȟúga *vt2* s/he cracks, crunches smth with
the teeth (peanuts, candies) *1s:* **mnaȟúga** *2s:*
naȟúga

yaȟúgabi *n* peanut, any kind of nut ▸ **Yaȟúgabi
žé duȟáȟa.** The peanuts are dimpled.

yaȟúgabi tą́ga *cp* coconut ▸ **Yaȟúgabi tą́ga
gaȟúga.** He cracked the coconut.

yaȟ'ú *vt2* s/he peels smth with the teeth *1s:*
mnaȟ'ú *2s:* **naȟ'ú**

ya'íškadA *vt2* s/he teases sb verbally ▸
Mayá'įškadešį Quit teasing me! ▸ **Hokšína
žé niyá'įškada he?** Is that boy teasing you?

‣ **Mayá'íškada įdé šahímaya.** He teased me until I was embarrassed. *1s:* **mna'íškada** *2s:* **na'íškada** *Vabs:* **wayá'íškadA** *Vcoll:* **wįcáya'íškadA** *Vcont:* **ya'íškan** *Vrecip:* **gicíya'įškadabi** *Vrefl:* **įkná'įškadA**

ya'íškan *vcont* teasing verbally ‣ **Ya'íškan wakúwa mnašíkna.** I teased verbally and made him angry.

ya'íyowas *vcont* in an echo-like manner ‣ **Ya'íyowas nowąbi.** They sing by echo.

ya'íyowaza *vi2* s/he/it produces an echo (by speech or singing) *Adv:* **ya'íyowas**

ya'íȟA *vt2* s/he makes sb laugh by speech

ya'íškade *n* joke

yajúsina *vt2* s/he belittles sb ‣ **I'á hąda wįcáyajusina.** When she talks she belittles them.

yakpą́ *vt2* s/he chews smth in fine pieces

yaksÁ *vt2* s/he bites, chews smth off *1s:* **mnaksá** *2s:* **naksá** *1p:* **ųyáksabi** *Vpos:* **knaksÁ**

yaktą́ *Variant:* **yatką́** *vt2* 1) s/he drinks smth ‣ **Wámini né yaktą́.** Drink that snow water. ‣ **Dágu natką́?** What are you drinking? ‣ **Dágu yatką́bi yacígabi he?** What do you all want to drink? ‣ **Cáǧa skąwáya, miní mnaktį́kta.** I will melt the ice, and I drink the water. *vi2* 2) s/he drinks, consumes (alcohol) ‣ **John nécen emą́giya "Yatkéšį wo!"** John told me, "Do not drink!" *1s:* **mnatką́** *2s:* **natką́** *1p:* **ųyátkąbi**

yaktés'a *n* alcoholic, drunkard *See:* **minátkes'a**

yaktų́š *vcont* talking crazily ‣ **Yaktų́š i'á.** She is talking crazily about him.

yaktų́žA *vt2* s/he makes sb crazy by talking *1s:* **mnaktų́ža** *2s:* **naktų́ža** *Vcont:* **yaktų́š**

yamná *vt2* s/he acquires smth by speech; convinces sb about smth *Adv:* **yamnáya**

yamnáya *adv* acquiring smth by speech; convincing, gossiping ‣ **Wóknaga hąda dágu nówa yamnáya įȟpéya.** Whenever he tells stories he gossips about everything

yámni *num* 1) three ‣ **Cįjábi yámni mnuhá.** I have three children. ‣ **Yámni yazą́bišį.** Three were not sick ‣ **Waníhą cą'íyutabi yámni wagáksa.** Last winter I chopped three cords of wood. *vs* 2) s/he/it is three; there are three ‣ **Húde žé įyútabi yámni.** The bottom is three feet.

yámnigiya *adv* three by three, in three ways, in three different directions, locations ‣ **Yámnigiya éwaknągįkta.** I will put them in three different locations.

yámniȟ *adv* three times ‣ **Ptį́hą žéci wa'í yámniȟ.** I went there three times last fall.

yámnina *num* only three

yamnúǧa *vt2* s/he crushes smth with the teeth (candy, ice) ‣ **Šų́ga žé huhú yamnúǧa.** That dog is crushing a bone. *Vcont:* **yamnúȟ**

yamnúȟ *vcont* crushing smth with the teeth ‣ **Yamnúȟ ámna.** I crushed it with the teeth. ‣ **Huhú žé níyuhana eyáš yamnúȟ yúdabi, tašúbana né iyákna.** They ate all of the bones, crunching them up together with the guts. (Weasel 52:377)

ya'ónihą *vt2* 1) s/he congratulates, honors sb by speech ‣ **Adé ya'ówanihą.** I honor my dad. ‣ **Wįcá žé nína ya'ónihąbi.** They praise this man highly. 2) s/he brags about smth ‣ **Ecágen ya'ónihą eyá.** He is always bragging about it. *1s:* **ya'ówanihą** *2s:* **ya'óyanihą**

ya'ótą *vt2* s/he straightens smth with the teeth

ya'ótą'į *vi2* s/he announces smth, tells the news *Vcoll:* **ya'ótą'į wįcákiyA**

yapÁ *vt2* s/he carries, puts smth in the mouth ‣ **Cuwí cogán yapá hį́k ektá iyopsija.** She grabbed him in the chest with her mouth and jumped in there. (Weasel 39:105) *Vpos:* **knapÁ**

yapíyagen *adv* in a verbally skillful manner ‣ **Yapíyagen žeyá.** He said that in a skillful manner.

yapíja *vt2* s/he memorizes, mentions smth; speaks highly of smth, sb ‣ **Nína dąyá yapíja.** He praises him highly.

yapsú *vt2* s/he spills smth from his/her mouth *1s:* **mnapsú** *2s:* **napsú**

yaptúǧA *vt2* s/he breaks, cracks smth with the teeth

yasíjA *vt2* s/he bad-mouths sb, ruins smth by speech ▸ **Ecágen mayásija.** She is always bad-mouthing me ▸ **Dágu nówa yasíja.** She ruins everything by what she says. ▸ **Mnasíja cén cądéšinwaya.** I bad-mouthed her and made her feel bad. *1s:* **mnasíja** *2s:* **nasíja** *1p:* **ųyásijabi** *Vabs:* **wayásijA** *Vcoll:* **wįcáyasijA**

yaskíja *vt2* s/he sucks the juice out of smth

yasmísmį *vt2-redup* s/he cleans the meat off a bone with the teeth; s/he chews it clean ▸ **Iyé yasmísmį.** He chews it clean himself. ▸ **Nínaȟ mnasmísmįšį.** I did not clean it up much. *1s:* **mnasmísmį** *2s:* **nasmísmį**

yasníbA *vt2* s/he/it licks sb, smth *Vpos:* **knasníbA**

yasnóhą *vt2* s/he pulls sb, smth with the mouth ▸ **Hį́į, tatą́ga wążí yasnóhą akníbi.** Oh, they dragged one buffalo back using their mouths. (Weasel 86:120) *1s:* **mnasnóhą** *2s:* **nasnóhą** *1p:* **ųyásnohąbi**

yastó *vt2* s/he/it smooths smth down by licking (as a candy) *Vrefl:* **įknásto**

yašíkna *vt2* s/he angers sb verbally ▸ **Ya'įškan wakúwa mnašíkna.** I teased and angered him verbally. *1s:* **mnašíkna** *2s:* **našíkna** *Vrefl:* **įknášikna**

yašnógA *vt2* s/he/it pulls smth out of it with the teeth

yašpÁ *vt2* s/he breaks, cracks smth open with the teeth (like a peanut) *Vredup:* **yašpášpA**

yašpášpA *vt2-redup* s/he nibbles, bites a piece off sb, smth

yašpú *vt2* s/he bites smth off it *1s:* **mnašpú** *2s:* **našpú** *1p:* **ųyášpubi**

yašpúya *vs* s/he is itchy ▸ **Niyášpuya he?** Are you itchy? ▸ **Pežúda né ús mayášpuya.** I am itchy because of this medicine. *1s:* **mayášpuya** *2s:* **niyášpuya** *1p:* **ųyášpuyąbi**

yaštą́ *vt2* s/he stops talking about smth ▸ **Yaštą́ žehą́, awįcakidaga.** After he finished singing, he looked at them. (Shields 85:507) *1s:* **mnaštą́** *2s:* **naštą́** *1p:* **ųyáštąbi** *Vpos:* **knaštą́**

yatÁ *vt2* s/he chews smth ▸ **Ką́ yatábi wašté.** It is nice to chew on gristle. ▸ **Mitúgaši cąníyatabi yatá.** My grandfather chews tobacco. *1s:* **mnatá** *2s:* **natá** *1p:* **ųyátabi** *Vredup:* **yatátA** *See:* **yakpą́**, **yaȟnógA**

yat'Á *vt2* s/he/it bites sb to death; kills sb by ingesting poison

yatátA *vt2-redup* s/he/it chews smth fine ▸ **Žécen dágucen yatáta hį́kna tíbi né agá[m]padahą, bóȟ yeyá.** So then he chewed something or other up and blew it onto the lodge. (Weasel 105:265) *1s:* **mnatáta** *2s:* **natáta** *1p:* **ųyátatabi**

yawá *vt2* 1) s/he counts smth ▸ **Yawá bo.** All of you count. 2) s/he reads smth ▸ **Yawábi síja.** It is hard to read. ▸ **Wa'ówabi waką́ yawá.** He is reading the Bible. ▸ **Wówįȟága mnawá cén įwáȟa.** I am laughing because I read something funny. *1s:* **mnawá** *2s:* **nawá** *1p:* **ųgíyawabi** *Vabs:* **wayáwa** *Vdat:* **giyáwa** *Vrefl:* **įknáwa**

yawábi *n* number *Syn:* **wóyawabi**

yawášte *vt2* s/he makes smth sound good; says nice things about sb, smth ▸ **Hí hį́kna nína yawášte.** He arrived and said really nice things about him. *1s:* **mnawášte** *2s:* **nawášte** *1p:* **ųyáwaštebi**

yazá *vt2* s/he laces, beads smth

yazą́ *vs* 1) s/he is sick ▸ **Nína mayázą jé.** I am always very sick. 2) s/he is hurt; feels pain in a body part *Usage:* always preceded by a body part. ▸ **Nigé mayázą.** I have a stomachache.

yazóga *vt1* s/he/it (baby) sucks on smth *1s:* **mnazóga** *2s:* **nazóga** *Vcaus:* **yazókkiyA** *Vcont:* **yazók**

yazók *vcont* sucking ▸ **Yazók wa'ų́.** I go around sucking on it.

yazókkiyA *vt1-caus* s/he makes him/her suck on smth ▸ **Yazókwįcakiyabi né'įš dáguge.**

They could not nurse them. (Weasel 24:39) *1s:* **yazókwakiya** *2s:* **yazókyakiya**

yažó *vi1* s/he/it blows into smth (whistle, instrument) *1s:* **mnažó** *2s:* **nažó**

yągÁ *See:* **yįgÁ**

yegíciyabi *vi1-recip* they send smth to one another

yegíjiciyA *vt1-benef* s/he sends sb, smth away for sb ▸ **Ogíhišį cén yewéjiciya.** I send it away for her because she is not able. *1s:* **yewéjiciya** *2s:* **yeyéjiciya**

yéğA *vi* it glows, glitters *Adv:* **yeȟyą́**

yeȟyą́ *adv* glittering, glowing ▸ **Péda yeȟyą́ hą́.** The fire is glowing.

ye'į́c'iyA *vi3-refl* s/he propels himself/herself, gets himself/herself going ▸ **Kogám ye'į́c'iya.** He threw himself forward. ▸ **Įtógam napsín yemį́c'iya.** I propelled myself ahead (as in a race). ▸ **Gá écen eyáš húgu žé banážį ye'į́c'iya.** Then his mother got up quickly. (NS 2002:83) *1s:* **yemį́c'iya** *2s:* **yenį́c'iya** *1p:* **ye'ų́gįc'iyabi**

yekíyA *vt1-dat* 1) s/he sends sb, smth away to sb ▸ **"Né yewákiya štén į́š gá yekíyįkta, ga'į́š, ga'į́š, ga'į́š".** "When I throw it to that one over there, he will throw it to that one over there, to that one over there, to that one over there." (NS 2002:23) *vt1* 2) s/he starts, turns smth on (car, engine) ▸ **Amų́giya žé yekíya.** Start the car. *1s:* **yewákiya** *2s:* **yeyákiya** *1p:* **yé'ų́kiyabi**

yeyÁ *vt1-caus* 1) s/he sends sb, smth away ▸ **Dágu nówa yewáya.** I send everything away. *vi-aux* 2) propel ▸ **Ganúza cén tiyóba gašpáyeya.** The door blew open. (Cumberland 2005:425) *1s:* **yewáya** *2s:* **yeyáya** *Vbenef:* **yegíjiciyA** *Vdat:* **yekíyA** *Vrecip:* **yegíciyabi** *Vrefl:* **ye'į́c'iyA**

yįgÁ₁ *Variant:* **yągÁ** *vi3* 1) s/he is sitting on, in smth ▸ **Adé waką́tąga maȟpíyam agą́n yągá.** My Holy Father who sits in the sky. 2) it is, it is located (used for broad-based objects) ▸ **Napsú įȟnáye wiyákpaya yįgá.** The ring is shining. ▸ **Žéci yįgá.** It is over there. *vi3-aux* 3)

s/he remains doing, does continously; stays ▸ **Iná mitą́kši į́š gicí i'á mągá jé.** I always sit down and discuss in length with both my mom and aunt. ▸ **Žewágiya mągá.** I kept on saying that. ▸ **Įštímašį yįgá.** He is sleeplessly. ▸ **Ųwą́šį nągį́kta.** You will stay still. *1s:* **mągá** *2s:* **nągá** *1p:* **ųyą́gabi** *Vcaus:* **yįgékiyA**

yįgÁ₂ *Variant:* **yągÁ, hįgÁ, įgÁ** *vi3-aux* s/he remains doing, does continously; stays ▸ **Įštímašį yįgá.** He is sleeplessly. ▸ **Ųwą́šį nągį́kta.** You will stay still. ▸ **Žewágiya mągá.** I kept on saying that. ▸ **Iná mitą́kši į́š gicí i'á mągá jé.** I always sit down and discuss in length with both my mom and aunt. ▸ **Ųgį́štima hį́kna iyódąk kó ųyą́gįkta.** We will remain sleeping and sitting too. (NS 2002:33) *1s:* **mągá** *2s:* **nągá** *1p:* **ųyą́gabi**

yįgékiyA *Variant:* **yągékiyA** *vt1-caus* s/he makes sb sit ▸ **Yuhá yągékiya.** He put [the baby] on her lap. (Weasel 33:138)

yu- *pref* 1) manually (with the hand, fingers), by pulling *Usage:* derives transitive verbs of Class 2 from stative or intransitive verbs. ▸ **bemní > yubémni** s/he/it is twisted > s/he twists smth manually ▸ **škóba > yuškóba** it is bent > s/he bends smth manually ▸ **snoȟą́ > yusnóȟą** s/he/it crawls > s/he drags, pulls smth along 2) s/he/it causes sb, smth to be ▸ **sóda > yusóda** s/he/it is extinct, gone; perishes > s/he wastes, spends, uses smth up (money, supplies) ▸ **šá > yušá** s/he/it is red > s/he dyes smth in red ▸ **waką́ > yuwáką** s/he/it is holy, spiritually powerful > s/he consecrates sb, smth 3) derives instrumental adverbs ▸ **wągám > yuwą́gan** up high, above, upright > pulled up, upright ▸ **mahén > yumáhen** in, under > pulled in, tucked in, under

yu'ásni *vt2* s/he comforts, soothes sb *1s:* **mnu'ásni** *2s:* **nu'ásni**

yubáğe *vt2* s/he gathers scattered things into the hand ▸ **O'ópiyeda yubáğe.** He pulls it out of the pocket. *1s:* **mnubáğe** *2s:* **nubáğe** *1p:* **ųyúbağebi** *Vcont:* **yubáẖ**

yubáẖ *adv* in a united way ‣ **Gicí yubáẖ ųbi.** They live in a united way.

yubéhą *vt2* s/he twists, rolls smth (rope, tobacco) ‣ **Cąní yubéhą.** He is twisting tobacco.

yubémni *vt2* s/he twists smth manually ‣ [...] **eyáš tahú yubémni gá kį'íyewįcaya gáyabi.** [...] so he wrung their necks and threw them over there. (NS 2002:42) ‣ **Awįcayutątą duwé wąží šįtų hąda éyagu hįk tahú yubémni.** He felt them over and when there was a fat one, he took it and twisted its neck. (Drummond 1976, Įktomi and the ducks) *1s:* **mnubémni** *2s:* **nubémni** *1p:* **ųyúbemnibi**

yubízA *vt2* s/he makes smth (gopher) squeal when picking it up *1s:* **mnubíza** *2s:* **nubíza** *1p:* **ųyúbizabi**

yubó *vt2* s/he/it makes his/her own swell by action of the hands *Vpos:* **knubó**

yubųbų *vt2* s/he makes it crumble manually

yucába *vi2* it (horse) trots *Vredup:* **yucápcaba**

yucápcaba *vi2-redup* it (horse) trots along

yucącą *vt2* s/he/it shakes smth back and forth

yucéyA *vt2* s/he makes sb cry manually (pinching, cuddling too vigorously) ‣ **Dóhąni mayánuceyešį no.** You never made me cry. *1s:* **mnucéya** *2s:* **nucéya** *1p:* **ųyúceyabi**

yucíca *vt2* s/he curls smth

yúdA *vt2* s/he/it eats smth ‣ **Peží yúda.** He is eating hay. ‣ **Dóhą yúda?** When did she eat it? ‣ **Škoškóbena wąží núda he?** Are you eating a banana? *1s:* **mnúda** *2s:* **núda** *1p:* **ųyúdabi** *Vbenef:* **gíjiyudA** *Vcaus:* **yunkíyA** *Vcont:* **yún ;** **yút** *Vpos:* **knúdA** *Vrecip:* **gicíyudabi**

yudáda *vt2* s/he cleans smth (sweep, dust, wipe)

yudą́ *vt2* s/he pulls smth with a jerk

yudáyą *vt2* s/he does a good job, makes it better, repairs smth ‣ **Yudáyąkta wašką́.** I am trying to make it better.

yúdešįyą *adv* without eating smth

yudįda *vt2* s/he pulls sb, smth toward himself/herself ‣ **Iná mayúdįda.** Mother pulled me (toward her). *1s:* **wayúdįda** *2s:* **yayúdįda**

yudódo *vt2* s/he cleans smth *Vbenef:* **gíjiyudodo** *Vpos:* **knudódo**

yudúgA *vt2* s/he plucks, pulls smth out (as the feathers of a bird) *Vpos:* **knudúgA**

yu'écedu *vt2* s/he corrects, realigns smth *1s:* **mnu'écedu** *2s:* **nu'écedu**

yugádį *vt2* s/he stretches smth out *Vbenef:* **gíjiyugadį** *Vpos:* **knugádį**

yugíkta *vt2* s/he gets sb up manually; wakes sb up

yugˇábA *vt2* s/he pulls the skin or the bark off smth; skins an animal *1s:* **mnugˇába** *2s:* **nugˇába** *1p:* **ųyúgˇababi** *Vbenef:* **gíjiyugˇabA**

yugˇą́ *vt2* s/he lifts up a cover

yugˇé *vt2* s/he rakes smth manually

yuhÁ *vt2* 1) s/he has, possesses smth ‣ **Dágu nuhá?** What do you have? ‣ **Wóyude óda ųyúhabi.** We have a lot of food. 2) s/he carries sb, smth ‣ **Gakí yuhá éknąga.** Carry it and put it over there. ‣ **Yuhá ú.** He is coming carrying it. 3) she gave birth to a child ‣ **Cįjátųga ecá, núbabina wįcáyuha.** She gave birth, she has twins. 4) s/he holds smth (meeting, ceremony) ‣ **Gahómni wacíbi yuhábi gepcámį.** I thought that they were having a round dance. 5) s/he keeps, looks after, treats sb, smth ‣ **Dayą́ mayánuha.** You treated me well. *adv* 6) carry, hold, have with one *Usage:* precedes verbs of traveling. ‣ **Yuhá ú.** He comes here carrying it. ‣ **Yuhá máni** She walks carrying it. *1s:* **mnuhá** *2s:* **nuhá** *1p:* **ųyúhabi** *Vabs:* **wayúhA** *Vbenef:* **gíjiyuhA** *Vcaus:* **yuhákiyA** *Vpos:* **knuhÁ** *Vrecip:* **gicíyuhabi** *Vrefl:* **a'įknuhA ;** **įknúhA**

yuhá máni *vi1* s/he walks carrying smth *1s:* **yuhá mawáni** *2s:* **yuhá mayáni** *1p:* **yuhá ma'ųnibi**

yuhá ų́ *vt1* s/he continues having smth

yuhákiyA *vt1-caus* s/he makes sb have, carry, keep smth *1s:* **yuháwakiya** *2s:* **yuháyakiya**

yuhána *vt2* s/he (baby, small child) has sb, smth

yuhápija *vs* it is worth having

yuháši *vt1* s/he orders sb to carry smth *1s:* **yuháwaši** *2s:* **yuháyaši**

yuháskA *vt2* s/he lengthens smth

yuhíyayA *vt2* s/he sets to go from here, departs from here with sb, smth (before or shortly after departure) ‣ **Duktám yuhíyaya wa'óyabi nená.** Go away and take these cards with you. (Weasel 62:9)

yuhį́hpayA *vt2* s/he pulls smth down

yuhókšu *vt2* s/he breaks, wrecks, destroys, dismantles smth ‣ **Tíbi žé yuhókšubi.** They destroyed the house. ‣ **Žená owá yuhókšu hį́k tiyóba žé yuška.** He took all of them apart and untied the door. (NS 2002:72)

yuhókuda *vt2* s/he lowers smth by pulling *Vcont:* **yuhókun**

yuhókun *vcont* lowering smth by pulling

yuhómni *vt2* s/he rotates, turns sb, smth around ‣ **Magíbą cén mayúhomni.** She shouted at me, and it made me turn around. *1s:* **mnuhómni** *2s:* **nuhómni** *1p:* **ųyúhomnibi** *Vrefl:* **įknúhomni**

yuhótų *vt2* s/he makes smth sound manually; plays a musical instrument with the hands

yuhówayA *vt2* s/he makes sb scream in pain by pinching, pressing on a body part

yuhų́hųza *vt2* s/he jerks, shakes smth manually *1s:* **mnuhų́hųza** *2s:* **nuhų́hųza**

yuȟcína *vt2* s/he/it tears, frays smth (cloth, blanket, coat) ‣ **Šiná žé yuȟcínabi.** They tore the blanket into rags. *1s:* **mnuȟcína** *2s:* **nuȟcína** *1p:* **ųyúȟcinąbi**

yuȟíja *vt2* s/he wakes sb up by pushing or shaking ‣ **Hąyákenaȟ yuȟíja.** He woke him up early in the morning. ‣ **Amápa hį́kna mayúȟija.** He hit me and he woke me up. ‣ **Téhą mįštíma, ųká šų́ga mayúȟijabi.** I had been sleeping for a long time, but then the dogs woke me up. *1s:* **mnuȟíja** *2s:* **nuȟíja** *1p:* **ųyúȟijabi** *Vrefl:* **įknúȟija**

yuȟná *vt2* s/he makes smth rattle, ring by pulling; shakes a rattle

yuȟnáda *vt2* s/he claws, grabs sb, smth with the claws, nails

yuȟná'į *vt2* s/he peels smth off *1s:* **mnuȟná'į** *2s:* **nuȟná'į**

yuȟnéȟnejA *vt2-redup* s/he tears smth into strips manually ‣ **Hųská žé ųmá knušnóga hį́k yuȟnéȟneja.** He took off one of his leggings and tore it up. (NS 2002:16) *1s:* **mnuȟnéȟneja** *2s:* **nuȟnéȟneja**

yuȟnéjA *vt2* s/he tears smth manually (paper, cloth) ‣ **Wa'óyabi žé mnuȟnéja.** I tore the paper. *1s:* **mnuȟnéja** *2s:* **nuȟnéja** *1p:* **ųyúȟnejabi** *Vredup:* **yuȟnéȟnejA**

yuȟnógA *vt2* s/he makes a hole in smth with an instrument or manually *1s:* **mnuȟnóga** *2s:* **nuȟnóga**

yuȟpÁ *vt2* s/he unloads smth; throws smth down *1s:* **mnuȟpá** *2s:* **nuȟpá** *1p:* **ųyúȟpabi** *Vpos:* **knuȟpÁ**

yuȟ'ú *vt2* s/he scrapes, peels smth manually ‣ **Céǧa né mnuȟ'ú.** I scraped this pot. ‣ **Yuȟ'úšį yúda.** He is eating it without peeling it. *1s:* **mnuȟ'ú** *2s:* **nuȟ'ú**

yu'į́domni *vt2* s/he/it twists sb around to make him/her dizzy

yu'į́ȟA *vt2* s/he makes sb laugh (by speaking, tickling, goofing around)

yu'į́ktų *Variant:* **yu'į́tkų** *vt1* s/he/it lights, turns smth on (light, stove, fire) ‣ **Miyé mnu'į́ktų.** I turned on the lights myself. ‣ **Péda žé yu'į́ktų!** Light the fire! *1s:* **mnu'į́ktų ; mnu'į́tkų** *2s:* **nu'į́ktų ; nu'į́tkų**

yu'į́nažį *vt2* s/he stops smth, sb; cuts the motor off (car, engine) ‣ **Dóȟani mnu'į́nažįkte no.** I will never stop it. *1s:* **mnu'į́nažį** *2s:* **nu'į́nažį**

yu'į́škadA *vt2* s/he teases, plays jokes on sb; s/he plays with sb sexually *1s:* **mnu'į́škada** *2s:* **nu'į́škada**

yu'įštimA *vt2* s/he soothes sb to sleep manually

yukábA *vt2* s/he catches a rapid or flying object with the hand

yukám-nažį *n* catcher

yuką₁ *vi2* s/he makes room *1s:* **mnuką** *2s:* **nuką** *1p:* **ųyúkąbi** *Vdat:* **giyúką**

yuką₂ *vs* 1) it is, it exists, there is/are *Usage:* applies only to 3rd person animate or inanimate referents. ‣ **Tašúgasaba mitáwa yuką.** There is a black horse that is mine. ‣ **Cąpásu yuką he?** Is there pepper? ‣ **Huhúžubina wacíbi yuką.** There is a dance in Regina. ‣ **Ağúyabi wašté yuką.** There is good bannock. ‣ **Mázaska yukášį.** There is no money. ‣ **Yuką, duktékten.** There are, here and there. (Cumberland 2005:421) 2) s/he has smth; it exists for sb *Usage:* said of body parts, states, personal behavior. ‣ **Cądé mayúką cén úšiwana.** I pity him because I have a heart *1s:* **mayúką** *2s:* **niyúką**

yukcá *vt2* s/he uncoils, unravels smth manually *1s:* **mnukcá** *2s:* **nukcá** *Vredup:* **yukcákca**

yukcákca *vt2-redup* s/he keeps on uncoiling, unraveling smth manually

yukcá *vt2* s/he discusses smth ‣ **Dóken gicí yukcákta he?** How will he discuss this thing with him? *1s:* **mnukcá** *2s:* **nukcá** *1p:* **ųyúkcąbi** *See:* **įyúkcą**

yukmá *vt2* s/he sharpens smth by grinding ‣ **Mína yukmá!** Grind the knife!

yukmí *vt2* s/he pulls out plants from the ground; weeds smth ‣ **Mnukmí ámna.** I am weeding. (Cumberland 2005:403) *1s:* **mnukmí** *2s:* **nukmí** *1p:* **ųyúkmibi**

yukmíja *vt2* s/he pulls sb's hair *Vcont:* **yukmín**

yukmíkmA *vt2* s/he/it (horse) is pulling smth (wagon)

yukmín *vcont* pulling sb's hair ‣ **Yukmín yúza.** He grabbed him by the hair.

yukógA *vt2* s/he makes a rattling sound manually

yukpá *vt2* s/he crushes, grounds smth manually or with a grinder (grain, meat) *1s:* **mnukpá** *2s:* **nukpá**

yuksÁ *vt1* s/he breaks, cuts, trims smth off with scissors ‣ **Nųpín yuksá.** Cut it apart. ‣ **Tadé uyá né, cá né yuksá.** The wind blew this way and broke the tree. *1s:* **mnuksá** *2s:* **nuksá** *1p:* **ųyúksabi** *Vabs:* **wayúksA** *Vbenef:* **gíjiyuksA** *Vpos:* **knuksÁ** *Vredup:* **yuksáksA**

yuksáksA *vt2-redup* s/he breaks smth into pieces; s/he breaks them (objects)

yukúda *vt2* s/he dims the light down

yukúkA *vt2* s/he crushes smth between the fingers

yuk'éğA *vt2* s/he/it scratches sb, smth manually ‣ **Nén yuk'éğa.** Scratch here. ‣ **Yuk'éğešį.** Do not scratch it. *1s:* **mnuk'éğa** *2s:* **nuk'éğa** *1p:* **ųyúk'eğabi** *Vpos:* **knuk'éğA** *Vrefl:* **įknúk'eğA**

yumáhen *adv* pulled in, tucked in, under ‣ **Šiná yumáhen éknąga.** Tuck him under the blanket.

yumá *vt2* s/he sharpens smth (knife, axe) ‣ **Mína nówa mnumá.** I sharpen all the knives. *1s:* **mnumá** *2s:* **numá** *Vpos:* **knumá**

yumnáyA *vt2* s/he spreads smth out flat (paper, rug, sheet) ‣ **Owíža žé yumnáya!** Spread the blanket! ‣ **Yusnúda cén dágu yumnáya [...]** He pulled him out, and he spread that thing out [...] (NS 2002:29) *Vredup:* **yumnáyayA**

yumnáyayA *vt2-redup* s/he spreads them out flat (hides)

yumnázA *vt2* s/he tears, rips smth open manually

yumnéja *vt2* s/he scatters smth manually *Vcont:* **yumnén** *Vredup:* **yumnémneja**

yumnémneja *vt2-redup* s/he scatters smth manually (something small as beads)

yumnén *vcont* scattering smth manually ‣ **Yumnén éwaknąga.** I put it down and scattered it.

yumnézA *vt2* s/he rouses, wakes sb up ‣ **Mitúgaši mnumnézįkta.** I will wake grandfather. ‣

Yumnézįkta šką. He will try to wake him up. *1s:* **mnumnéza** *2s:* **numnéza** *1p:* **ųyúmnezabi** *Vpos:* **knumnézA**

yumnú *vt2* s/he crumbles, spreads smth around manually; spreads smth fine ▸ **Opšíja né iyúha yumnú.** He crumbled all of the dirt. *1s:* **mnumnú** *2s:* **numnú** *1p:* **ųyúmnubi**

yún ; yút *vcont* eating smth ▸ **Yún máni.** He walks eating it. *Vredup:* **yúnyun**

yunkíyA *vt1-caus* s/he makes, lets sb eat smth ▸ **Žén iyé togáhe žé yunwákiye no.** It is she whom I am letting eat first. (NS 2002:82) *1s:* **yunwákiya** *2s:* **yunyákiya** *1p:* **yun'ųkiyabi**

yunwášteya *adv* in a tasteful manner ▸ **Dágu nówa yunwášteya ecú.** She makes everything taste good.

yúnyun *vcont-redup* eating it repeatedly

yu'ónihą *vt2* s/he honors, respects, defers to him/her/it

yu'ótą *vt2* s/he straightens sb, smth *Vrefl:* **įknú'otą**

yu'ówadA *vt2* 1) s/he lights smth up *n* 1) flashlight, car headlights

yupéšį *vs* it is dull by wear

yupí *vt2* s/he does smth skillfully *1s:* **mnupí** *2s:* **nupí** *1p:* **ųyúpibi** *Adv:* **yupíya ; yupíyagen** *Vabs:* **wayúpi**

yupíbiga *vs-pass* s/he is honored ▸ **Agícida né akní cén yupíbiga.** The returning soldier was honored. *1s:* **mayúpibiga** *2s:* **niyúpibiga** *1p:* **ųyúpibiga**

yupíja *vi2* s/he is good at smth

yupípiya *adv-redup* very well ▸ **Nína yupípiya wómąk'u jé.** He always feeds me very well. (Weasel 193:111)

yupíya *vs* 1) it is valuable ▸ **Amųgiya né dágu yupíyašį.** This car is worthless. ▸ **Dágu yupíyašį nówa ahí.** He brought a whole bunch of junk. *adv* 2) well, in a skillful, good manner, nicely ▸ **Yupíya ecú.** It is made in a skillful manner. ▸ **Yupíya wa'ú.** I am going well. ▸ **Áa, yupíya ecá'įc'ų.** Ah, she prepared herself nicely. (Weasel 191:57) *Adv:* **yupíyagen** *Redup:* **yupípiya**

yupíyagen *adv* skillfully, handsomely ▸ **Yupíyagen įknúza.** He dressed himself in finery.

yupsų́ *vt2* s/he spills smth from a container manually *1s:* **mnupsų́** *2s:* **nupsų́**

yupšų́ka *vt2* s/he made smth into a ball *1s:* **mnupšų́ka** *2s:* **nupšų́ka**

yuptÁ *vt2* s/he breaks, turns over, plows smth ▸ **Ꞣyą žé mnuptá.** I turned the rock over. ▸ **Miyé mnuptákte no.** I will plow it myself. *1s:* **mnuptá** *2s:* **nuptá**

yuptą́yA *vt2* s/he turns smth over manually *Vrefl:* **įknúptąyA**

yuptéjena *vt2* s/he cuts smth shorter (with scissors) ▸ **Nedápa yuptéjena.** Cut it shorter on this side.

yús *vcont* holding sb, smth ▸ **Yús mągá.** I hold on to it. ▸ **Yús a'ú.** He pulls, comes with him toward here. ▸ **Tągápada tiyóba žé yús ų́.** He was holding the door from the outside. (Cumberland 2005:400)

yús náyuzA *vt2* s/he holds, grasps, clinches on smth

yusákiba *vt2* s/he puts smth together manually *Vcont:* **yusákim** *Vpos:* **knusákiba**

yusíjA *vt2* s/he ruins, destroys smth manually *1s:* **mnusíja** *2s:* **nusíja** *1p:* **ųyúsijabi**

yusíjabi *n* damage

yuská *vt2* s/he kneads smth (dough, powder) into shape ▸ **Dąyą́ꞣ yuskábi.** It is very well kneaded. *Vredup:* **yuskáska**

yuskáska *vt2-redup* s/he clenches smth in the hand ▸ **Žécen iyáya cén eyáš i'óžuyapa híkna nąbé ų́s eyáš yuskáska yuhá gú gáya.** Then he went, so he got a mouthful, and then holding it in all of his paws, he brought it back. (NS 2002:29)

yuskébA *vt2* s/he empties smth out; drains smth (oil in a car, hose, pipe) ‣ **Wį́kni žé amų́giya edáhą mnuskéba.** I drained the oil from the car. *1s:* **mnuskéba** *2s:* **nuskéba** *1p:* **ųyúskebabi**

yuskíjA *vt2* s/he squeezes smth manually ‣ **Ti'íyužaža žé baskíja.** Squeeze the mop.

yuskíyA *vt1* s/he makes sb hold sb, smth

yusní₁ *vt2* s/he squeezes the liquid out; milks a cow ‣ **Wókšu wįcášta žé asą́bi yusní.** The farmer is milking it. *1s:* **mnusní** *2s:* **nusní** *1p:* **ųyúsnibi**

yusní₂ *vt2* s/he turns, dims smth off manually (heat, gas) *1s:* **mnusní** *2s:* **nusní**

yusníza *vt2* 1) s/he squeezes the air out 2) s/he produces a small, silent fart

yusnóhĄ *vt2* s/he drags, pulls smth along *Vpos:* **knusnóhĄ**

yusnúda *vt2* s/he pulls smth out (plant) ‣ **Dágu yusnúda.** He pulls a piece out of it. ‣ **Hé'a wįcáyusnuda.** She pulls lice off him. ‣ **Hą́ba žená yusnúda.** Take those shoes out. *1s:* **mnusnúda** *2s:* **nusnúda** *1p:* **ųyúsnudabi** *Vcont:* **yusnún**

yusnún *vcont* pulling smth out

yusódA *vt2* s/he wastes, spends, uses smth up (money, supplies) *1s:* **mnusóda** *2s:* **nusóda**

yusúda *vt2* s/he hardens, toughens smth; confirms smth

yušá *vt2* s/he dyes smth red ‣ **Zizíbena žé mnušá.** I dyed the cloth red. *1s:* **mnušá** *2s:* **nušá**

yušíkna *vt2* s/he angers sb

yušká *vt2* s/he unties, detaches smth ‣ **Žená owá yuhókšu hį́k tiyóba žé yuška.** He took all of them apart and untied the door. (NS 2002:72) *1s:* **mnušká** *2s:* **nušká** *1p:* **ųyúškabi** *Vbenef:* **gíjiyuška**

yuškášką *vt2* s/he shakes smth manually back and forth ‣ **Nína yuškášką.** Shake it hard. *Vrefl:* **įknúškašką**

yuškí *vi* it shrinks *Vcaus:* **yuškíyA**

yuškíyA *vt1-caus* s/he causes smth to shrink

yuškóbA *vt2* s/he bends smth manually *1s:* **mnuškóba** *2s:* **nuškóba** *1p:* **ųyúškobabi** *Vcont:* **yuškóm**

yuškóm *vcont* in a crooked manner ‣ **Yuškóm iyáya.** It went crooked.

yušná *vt2* s/he rattles, rings a bell by pulling, by the force of the wind

yušną́ *vt2* s/he drops smth ‣ **Céǧa žé yušną́.** He dropped the pot. ‣ **"Né yušną́bišį́m!" eyá.** "Do not drop this!" he said. (NS 2002:23)

yušnógA *vt2* s/he jerks, pulls smth out from another object; takes, removes smth off (cork, tooth, root, clothes) ‣ **Ganų́za žé yušnóga.** The wind uprooted it. ‣ **Hí mayúšnoga.** He pulled my tooth out. ‣ **Įyágahpa žé yušnóga.** Take the cover off. ‣ **Hayábi žé yušnóga!** Take his clothes off. *1s:* **mnušnóga** *2s:* **nušnóga** *1p:* **ųyúšnogabi** *Vpos:* **knušnógA** *Vredup:* **yušnóšnogA** *Vrefl:* **įknúšnogA ; įc'íyušnogA**

yušnóšnogA *vt2-redup* s/he dismantles smth by pulling

yušnúšnuda *vt2* s/he dirties sb, smth manually *1s:* **mnušnúšnuda** *2s:* **nušnúšnuda** *Vrefl:* **įknúšnušnuda**

yušpá *vt2* 1) s/he opens smth by pulling, to open with an instrument *1s:* **mnušpá** *2s:* **nušpá** *1p:* **ųyúšpabi** *Vbenef:* **gíjiyušpa** *Vpos:* **knušpá** *vs* 2) it is opened ‣ **Ti'óba žé yušpábi.** Is the door opened?

yušpí *vt2* s/he picks smth (small things, beads, berries) *1s:* **mnušpí** *2s:* **nušpí** *Vabs:* **wóšpi** *Vbenef:* **gíjiyušpi**

yušpú *vt2* s/he picks, plucks a piece off smth *1s:* **mnušpú** *2s:* **nušpú** *1p:* **ųyúšpubi** *Vpos:* **knušpú**

yuštą́ *vt2* 1) s/he releases, lets sb, smth go ‣ **Éstena yuštą́bįkta.** They will release him soon. ‣ **Dóhąni wįcá žé yuštą́ktešį.** She will never let that man go. 2) s/he finishes smth *1s:* **mnuštą́**

2s: **nuštą́** 1p: **ųyúštąbi** *Vbenef:* **gíjiknuštą** *Vpos:*
knuštą́

yuš'į́š'į *vt2* s/he tickles sb 1s: **mnuš'į́š'į** 2s: **nuš'į́š'į**

yuš'į́yeya *vt2-caus* 1) s/he/it frightens, startles
sb ▸ **A! mitágožana yus'į́yewicayaye no,"** eyá.
"Ah! You frightened my grandchildren," he
said. (Cumberland 2005:140) 1s: **yų́š'į́yewaya**
2s: **yų́š'į́yeyaya** *vs* 2) s/he is frightened, scared,
afraid

yut'Á *vt2* s/he kills sb by strangulation 1s: **mnut'á**
2s: **nut'á** 1p: **ųyút'abi**

yutą́gA *vt2* s/he makes smth bigger *Vpos:*
knutą́gA

yutą́tą *vt2-redup* s/he feels sb, smth manually,
he gropes women's private parts

yutą́tą máni *vi1* s/he feels her way while walking (as in the dark)

yutéba *vt2* s/he wears smth out (as a knife blade)

yutíba *vt2* s/he scorches, burns smth

yut'į́s *adv* tightly ▸ **Ȟaȟų́da žé yut'į́s mnúza.** I
hold the rope tightly.

yut'į́zA *vt2* s/he tightens smth up by stretching
▸ **Ȟaȟų́da žé mnut'į́zįkta.** I will tighten the
rope. ▸ **Yut'į́mayaza.** You squeeze me tight. 1s:
mnut'į́za 2s: **nut'į́za** 1p: **ųyút'iząbi** *Adv:* **yut'į́s**

yútkna *vt1* s/he eats smth while going back

yutóką *vt2* s/he disguises, makes sb, smth look
different, changes smth manually

yuwáką *vt2* s/he consecrates, blesses sb, smth
with the hands ▸ **Duwé yazą́ hą́da Jesus
yuwáką** When someone was sick, Jesus blessed
him. 1s: **mnuwáką** 2s: **nuwáką**

yuwákąbi *n* blessing

yuwášte *vt2* s/he makes smth nice manually;
redoes smth in a better way 1s: **mnuwášte** 2s:
nuwášte 1p: **ųyúwaštebi** *Vpos:* **knuwášte** *Vrefl:*
įknúwašte

yuwą́ga *vt2* s/he knocks sb, smth down manually; takes smth down 1s: **mnuwą́ga** 2s: **nuwą́ga**
1p: **ųyúwągabi**

yuwą́gan ; yuwą́gam *adv* pulled up, upright ▸
Awódabi žé yuwą́gan mnúza. I held the table
upright. ▸ **Yuwą́gam aknábi.** They took it out,
pulling upwards. (Cumberland 2005:233)

yuwéǧA *vt2* s/he breaks smth manually *Vredup:*
yuwéȟweǧA

yuwéȟweǧA *vt2-redup* s/he breaks many things
manually ▸ **Žécen cą́ ówa yuwéȟweǧa cen
eyáš.** So then he broke up a lot of wood. (Weasel 4:70)

yuwéwe *vt2* s/he makes sb bleed manually 1s:
mnuwéwe 2s: **nuwéwe** *Vrefl:* **įknúwewe**

yuwí *vt2* s/he binds smth ▸ **Masyúwibi ų́s
yuwíbi.** They bind it using metal wire. 1s:
mnuwí 2s: **nuwí** 1p: **ųyúwibi**

yuwíbi *n* something woven

yuwídana *quant* small amount ▸ **Waȟpé
yuwídana mak'ú.** Give me a small amount
of tea.

yuwį́yeyA *vt2* s/he makes smth ready 1s:
mnuwį́yeya 2s: **nuwį́yeya**

yuwį́žA *vt2* s/he bends smth manually *Vpos:*
knuwį́žA

yuwógųga *vt1* s/he decorates smth manually

yúzA *vt2* 1) s/he holds, pulls, grabs, nabs,
catches sb, smth ▸ **Né yúza.** Hold this. ▸ **Pahá
yúzešį!** Do not pull her hair! ▸ **Nawápa duká
mayúzabi.** I fled, but they arrested me. ▸ **Búza
žé mnúza.** I caught the cat. 2) s/he marries sb
▸ **Wįcá né yúzabi wacíga.** I want to marry this
man. 1s: **mnúza** 2s: **núza** 1p: **ųyúzabi** *Vcaus:*
yuskíyA *Vcont:* **yús** *Vpos:* **knuzÁ** *See:* **oyúzA**

yuzámni *vt1* s/he spreads smth open; opens a
book 1s: **mnuzámni** 2s: **nuzámni**

yuzé *vt2* s/he picks smth manually (as a piece
of meat)

yuzíjA *vt2* s/he stretches smth manually 1s:
mnuzíja 2s: **nuzíja** 1p: **ųyúzijabi** *Vrefl:* **įknúzijA**

yuzíksijabina *n* elastic

yuzípaȟtA *vt1* s/he tightens smth up ‣ **Yuzípaȟta ca.** He might have tightened it up. *1s:* **yuzípawaȟta** *2s:* **yuzípayaȟta**

yužá *vt2* s/he cooks smth into a stew; puts smth in a stew *Vabs:* **wóža**

yužáža *vt2* s/he washes sb, smth by rubbing ‣ **Dáguškina yužáža.** Bathe the baby. ‣ **Žená yužážabišį.** Those are not washed. *1s:* **mnužáža** *2s:* **nužáža** *1p:* **ųyúžažąbi** *Vabs:* **wayúžaža** *Vbenef:* **gíjiyužaža** *Vcaus:* **yužážakiyA** *Vpos:* **knužáža** *Vrefl:* **įknúžaža**

yužážakiyA *vt1-caus* s/he makes sb wash smth ‣ **Iyógapte ecágen yužážamakiya.** She always makes me wash the dishes. *1s:* **yužážawakiya** *2s:* **yužážayakiya** *1p:* **yužáža'ųkiyabi**

yužą́gA *vt2* s/he mistreats, bullies sb; picks on sb ‣ **Mayúžągešį wo!** Do not bully me! ‣ **Ecágen yužą́ga.** He always picks on her. ‣ **Koškábina né niyúžągabikte no.** These boys will bully you. *1s:* **mnužą́ga** *2s:* **nužą́ga** *1p:* **ųyúžągabi** *Vcont:* **yužą́k** *Vpos:* **knužą́gA**

yužą́k *vcont* mistreating, bullying sb; picking on sb

yužíbA *vt2* s/he pinches sb, smth with the fingers ‣ **Įstó mayúžiba.** She pinched me on the arm. *Vpos:* **knužíbA** *Vrecip:* **gicíknužibabi** *Vrefl:* **įknúžibA**

yužúžu *vt2* s/he undresses sb, takes smth apart *Vrefl:* **įknúžužu**

yužúžu wacíbi *cp* stripper

yužúžu wíyą *cp* female stripper

yužų́ *vt2* s/he pulls it out manually ‣ **Yužų́kta šką́.** He is trying to pull it out. *1s:* **mnužų́** *2s:* **nužų́**

yų̨gÁ *Variant:* **wų̨gÁ** *vi3* s/he/it lies down; lays in a reclining position ‣ **Mąkán yų̨gá.** He laid down on the ground. *1s:* **mų̨gá** *2s:* **nų̨gá** *1p:* **ųyų́gabi** *Adv:* **yų̨gáya**

yų̨gáya *adv* in a lying, reclining position ‣ **Mąkán yų̨gáya ecú.** He put it flat on the ground.

Z

zakté *vs* s/he is mischievous ‣ **Wíyą gá zaktébi né'ųs.** This woman over there is one that fools around *1s:* **zamákte** *2s:* **zaníkte**

zaktébi *n* person who fools around; who is mischievous

zaktéwįyą *n* mischievous woman

záptą *num* 1) five ‣ **Ecágen záptą apá hą́da hí.** He always arrives at five. *vs* 2) s/he/it is five; there are five

zaptą́ȟ *adv* five times

záptąna *quant* only five

zągÁ *vi1* s/he /it whines *Vredup:* **zągzą́gA**

zągzą́gA *vi-redup* s/he/it whines ‣ **Eyáš šų́gana né eyáš, zągzą́ga wapápa ú.** Well, the little dog was whining and barking. (Weasel 197:174)

zązą́ *vs* it is stringy, long and thin ‣ **Zizíbena né zązą́ hą́.** This cloth is stringy.

zezéya *adv* hanging down, dangling

zí *vs* s/he/it is yellow, golden, dark yellow, tan, brown ‣ **Búza zí wąží mnuhá.** I have a brown cat. ‣ **Šų́ga zí gá nitáwabi he?** Does that brown dog belong to you all? ‣ **Búza žé ǧí hį́k zí nína wóguǧa.** That cat is brown and yellow and very pretty. *Vcaus:* **ziyÁ** *Vredup:* **zizí**

zibéna *vs* it is thin *Adv:* **zipzímyenaȟ** *Vredup:* **zipzíbena**

zigíjiyA *vt1-benef* s/he paints, colors sb, smth in yellow for sb

zigíyA *vt1-pos* s/he paints, colors, dyes his/her own yellow ‣ **Pahá ziwágiya.** I dyed my hair yellow.

zi'íc'iyA *vi3-refl* s/he paints himself/herself in yellow, golden, blond

ziktą́ǧina *Variant:* **zitką́ǧina** *n* goldfinch

ziktán *cont* bird ‣ **Ziktán wakúwa.** I am chasing birds.

ziktána *Variant:* **zitkána** *n* bird ‣ **Ziktábina né cąwą́gąduȟ wahóȟpi gáǧabi.** Those birds

made a nest way up there in the tree. *Cont:*
ziktán

ziktána wakmų́ha *Variant:* **zitkána wakmų́ha**
  cp hummingbird *Lit:* rattling bird

ziktásaba *Variant:* **zitkásaba** *n* blackbird

ziktáto *Variant:* **zitkánato ; zitkáto** *n* bluebird,
  bluejay

zinyÁ *vt1-caus* s/he smokes smth ‣ **Tanó žé**
  zinwáya. I smoked the meat. *1s:* **zinwáya** *2s:*
  zinyáya

zipzíbena *vs-redup* it is thin

zísaba *vs* it is dark brown

ziyÁ *vt1-caus* s/he paints, colors, dyes smth in yellow *Adv:* **ziyéna** *Vbenef:* **zigíjiyA** *Vpos:* **zigíyA**
  Vrefl: **zi'íc'iyA**

ziyéna *adv* yellow condition ‣ **Cuwíknąga žé**
  ziyéna ų́. He wears a yellow shirt.

zizí *vs-redup-pl* they are yellow golden, dark
  yellow, tan, brown *Usage:* used for inanimate
  plural.

zizíbena *n* cloth, fabric ‣ **Zizíbena izį́mna.** The
  cloth has a burnt smell. *Adv:* **zizímyena**

zizíbena cuwíknąga *cp* T-shirt

zizíbenaȟ *adv* thin ‣ **Žécen né bamnáskacuna**
  hį́k nén zizíbenaȟ ecú. Then this one kept
  on flattening it out, and he made it thin. (NS
  2002:30)

zizíbenaskana *n* muslin

zizímnąna *vs* it is thin ‣ **Wa'óyabi žé nína**
  zizímnąna. That paper is very thin.

zizímyena *adv* thinly

zizímyenaȟ ; zipzímyenaȟ *adv* thinly ‣
  Zipzímneyaȟ gamnábi. It was sliced up very
  very thin. (Drummond 1976, How the woman
  made pemmican)

zizína *n* 1) gold *vs* 2) s/he/it is gold

zuyÁ *vi1* 1) s/he goes on the warpath *adv* 2) going
  on the warpath *Usage:* used before verbs of
  going.

zuyé í *vi1* s/he went to war *1s:* **zuyé wa'í** *2s:* **zuyé**
  ya'í *1p:* **zuyé ųgíbi**

zuyé onówą *n* war song

zuyéska *n* soldier ‣ **zuyéska onówą** soldier song

zuyés'a *n* warrior

zuyés'a tíbi *cp* warrior lodge society

zuyéyabi *n* war party

zųzúja *n* flicker

Ž

žádA *vs* it is forked, branched

žąžą́ *vs* s/he/it is transparent ‣ **Wahíyoknąga**
  žé žąžą́. That jar is transparent.

žé *Variant:* **hé** *dem* 1) that (near the listener), general reference demonstrative *Usage:* triggers
  e-ablaut on the preceding word. ‣ **Wíyą žé**
  įknúš'aga. That woman is pregnant. ‣ **Duktén**
  šų́ga žé wąnága he? Where did you see that
  dog? ‣ **Cuwíknąga žé teȟíšį.** That coat is cheap.
  ‣ **Wóyude mitáwa žé iyúha yúdabi.** They ate
  all of my food. *art* 2) the *Usage:* definite topic
  marker. ‣ **Mína žé nína péna.** The knife is very
  sharp. ‣ **Dáguškina žé ų́.** The baby is wearing it.
  comp 3) that *Usage:* marker of complement and
  relative clauses. ‣ **Ecú žé wąmnága.** I saw that
  she did it. ‣ **Ȟtánihą wíyą nową́ žé snohwáya.**
  I know the woman who sang yesterday. ‣ **Tą́ga**
  žé nitáwa. The big one is yours. *pro* 4) he, she,
  it ‣ **Žé kábi.** He was chosen.

žéca *vs* s/he/it is of a certain kind (nationality,
  tribe, trade, behavior, condition) ‣ **Dágu žéca**
  he? Of what tribe is she? ‣ **Mi'áde wašpáyes'a**
  žéca no. My father is a chef. ‣ **Agícida žéca.**
  He is a soldier. ‣ **Comáȟtiyąȟtiyą wįcášta**
  žemáca. I am a very honest man. ‣ **Wamnónija**
  žemáca. I am an orphan. *1s:* **žemáca** *2s:* **ženíca**
  1p: **že'ų́cabi**

žécan *adv* in the meantime, during that time,
  then ‣ **Žécan nén wa'ų́.** In the meantime I
  stayed here.

žécedu *adv* 1) in the correct way, thus, like that
  ‣ **Žécedu ecú.** He is doing it right. ‣ **Žécedu**

eyábi. They say it like that. *vs* 2) it is like that, it happened like that ‣ **Žécedu!** It is so! ‣ **Wayáwawįcakiye eyé žéceduȟtįyą.** He said it exactly like the teacher. *1s:* **žemácedu** *2s:* **ženícedu** *Adv:* **žécen**

žéceduȟ *adv* exactly in that way ‣ **Žéceduȟ ecúbįkta.** They will do it exactly in that way.

žécedušį *vs* 1) it is incorrect; it is not in that way *adv* 2) incorrectly ‣ **Žécedušį ecú.** He is doing it incorrectly.

žéceȟ *adv* exactly in that way

žécen 1) *conj* so, thus, then ‣ **Wíyąbi wašpáyabi žécen iyuhána iyógipiya wó'ųdabįkta.** The women are cooking so we will all eat happily. ‣ **Žécen žedáhą iyáyabi.** So they moved from there. ‣ **Žécen waká.** That is what I mean. 2) *adv* in this way, as such, in a given style ‣ **Žécen eyá.** It is said in this way. ‣ **Šahíyabi žécen įš ecú.** She did it in the Cree style.

žecéš *adv* only that (contrary to one's expectation) ‣ **Mázaska žecéš no!** That is all the money!

žecéya *adv* really, actually ‣ **Žecéya hín?** It is like that, isn't it? (Cumberland 2005:334)

žéci *adv* around there, over there, there ‣ **Žéci wa'í žehą.** I arrived over there. ‣ **Mihú owáyawa žéci amá'įkta.** My mother will take me over there. ‣ **Wagíyą sába wazíyam žéci iyódągabi.** The Black Thunderbirds sit there to the north.

žécipadahą *adv* from over there ‣ **Žécipadahą wahí.** I arrived from over there.

žéciya *adv* over there, over that way

žecíyadahą *adv* from that direction, from over there ‣ **Huhúžubina žecíyadahą wahí no.** I come from around Regina.

žecíyo *adv* at destination, at an end point ‣ **Eháš žecíyo wa'í.** I arrived at destination.

žéciyota *adv* that way

žécu *vt3* s/he does that; acts in that way ‣ **Žécušį!** Do not do that! ‣ **Dágucen žécanų?** Why did you do that? ‣ **Įdúȟtayena žécamų.** It did that for nothing. ‣ **Ecágen žécanųs'a he?** Do you do it as such usually? ‣ **Žécųkta wahóya.** He promised to do it. (2005:396) *1s:* **žécamų** *2s:* **žécanų** *1p:* **ųžécųbi** *Vredup:* **žécųcų**

žécųcų *vt3-redup* s/he keeps doing that

žécųhą *adv* while

žedábaš *adv* in that direction

žedáhą *Variant:* **žedáhą** *adv* 1) from there, from it ‣ **Céǧa K'įna žedáhą yahí?** Are you arriving from Carry The Kettle? ‣ **Žécen žedáhą iyáyabi.** After that the people moved from there. ‣ **Žedáhą mak'ú.** Give me some from it. ‣ **Hácogądu žehą wacíbi žedáhą wakní.** I came home from the dance at midnight. *vs* 2) s/he/it is from there ‣ **Micíkši ženídahąc.** My son you are from there. ‣ **Céǧa K'įna že'ųdahąbi.** We are from Carry The Kettle. *1s:* **žemádahą** *2s:* **ženídahą** *1p:* **že'ųdahąbi**

žedáhąȟ *adv* from that time ‣ **Žén gicí'ų cén žedáhąȟ owáštengina úbi.** They stayed together there, and so from that time on they were happy. (NS 2002:87)

žedám *adv* that way (away from speaker) ‣ **Žedám édųwą!** Look that way! ‣ **Žedám iyáya.** He went in that direction.

žedápadahą *adv* moving from there, that way ‣ **Žedápadahą úbi.** They come from there.

žedápkiya *adv* toward that direction

žédu *vimp* it is there, that is the place

žéduȟ *vs* it is right there, that is exactly the place ‣ **Žéduȟ wanįca.** That is exactly where he passed away.

žédunaȟ *adv* exactly there ‣ **Žédunaȟ éknąga.** Put it exactly there.

žé'e *vs* it is that; that is him/her/it/them *Usage:* (only used in the 3rd person). ‣ **Žé'e he?** Is that the one? ‣ **Omá žé'e.** It is the other one.

žé'eȟtįyą *vs* it is really that; that is really him/her/it/them ‣ **Há žé'eȟtįyą!** Yes, it is really her!

žehą́ ; **žéhą** *adv* 1) then, at that time, at a certain point in time *Usage:* often translates the English past tense. ‣ **Komáškaškanahą žéhą wéksuya.** I remember when I was a teenage boy. ‣ **Waníyedu yámni žehą́ waníja.** He passed away three years ago. ‣ **Duktám ináne žehą́ pağúda žená špąwícawaya.** While you were gone I cooked these geese. (Cumberland 2005:416) 2) last *Usage:* with days of the week. ‣ **ába įnų́ba žehą́** last Tuesday ‣ **Ábawaką žehą́ owácegiya žéci wa'í.** I went to church last Sunday.

žéhąc'ehą *adv* at that time in the past ‣ **Žéhąc'ehą iyúha híbi.** They all arrived at that time.

žehą́dahą *adv* from then on, and so now, since then ‣ **"Žehą́dahą néci ųg'ų́bi ųká," eyá.** "From then on we lived here," she said. ‣ **Žehą́dahą nén íšį.** He did not leave this place since then.

žehą́du *vs* it was at that time, then ‣ **Žehą́du hádahą waȟpé įcáğa nagú pežíto įš ahínąpa cén.** During that time the leaves grow, and the grass sprouts as well. (Haywahe 1992:31) *Adv:* **žehą́n**

žehą́duga *vs* it took/it will take place at about that time ‣ **Yahį́kta háda žehą́tuga he?** At what time will you arrive?

žehą́duȟ *adv* at that time specifically, right at that time ‣ **Žehą́duȟ cihį́ktu gicí bašpá yá.** Right at that time he burst in with his son.

žehą́ga *n* end of a story ‣ **Dukác žehą́ga no.** Supposedly this is the end of the story.

žehą́geȟ *adv* only that far off, only that much ‣ **Obáwįǧe nų́ba, žehą́geȟ mak'ú.** $200, that is how much he gave me.

žehą́geja *vs* 1) it is that long, far, size; since then ‣ **Makóce makíyutabi dóba žehą́geja.** The land is 4 km long. ‣ **Huhúžubina mąkíyutabi wikcémna šaknóğą žehą́geja.** Regina is 80 km distant. *adv, n* 2) distance, destination ‣ **Gídąȟ**

žehą́geja wa'í. At last I reached the destination. *See:* **gahą́geja**

žehą́n *adv-cont* at that time, just when ‣ **Žehą́n timáhen ú.** At that time he came inside. ‣ **Waknúštąkta wašką́ žéhan hí.** She arrived here just when I was trying to finish it. ‣ **Įjínųba žén žehą́n mįštíma.** The second time there then I slept.

žehą́naga *conj* and so now, and after that, and at that time ‣ **Žehą́naga agícida cuwíknąga šašábi žená awícahibi.** And after that they brought in the RCMP.

žeháš *adv* but now

žé'įš *dem* that, those too; that one, those ones too ‣ **Žé'įš kó!** That one too! ‣ **Tanó žé'įš ȟųwí.** That meat too is rotten.

žejíyA *vt1-dat* s/he says that to sb *Usage:* precedes or follows a quote. ‣ **Iyé né šųkšóšone žejíya.** It was this donkey that told him to say that. (Weasel 17:198)

žektágiya *adv* toward that direction (away from speaker) ‣ **Žektágiya iyáya.** He left in that direction.

žékžena *dem-redup* each of them, those

žekžéš *pro-redup* only that one ‣ **Hokšína žekžéš wąmnága.** I only saw that one boy.

žén *adv* there ‣ **Cągúsam wanágaš žén watí, waná nén wa'ú.** Long ago I lived there in the USA, and now I live here. ‣ **Iyúha žén étibi.** People were camped there.

žená *dem* those (not far from speaker) ‣ **Wíyą žená ağúyábi gáğabi he?** Are those women making bannock? ‣ **Žená yužážabišį.** Those are dirty, not washed. ‣ **Žená mak'ú.** She gave me those. *Redup:* **žékžena**

ženáwa *dem* all of those ‣ **Mína ženáwa pepéšį.** All of those knives are dull.

ženą́ga *vs* it is enough, sufficient ‣ **Žená́ga wo!** That is enough! ‣ **Waná ženą́ga koná.** Now it is enough friend.

ženágeja *vs* it is some; it is an unspecified amount ▸ **Pągí né ženágeja ahí.** He arrives with some potatoes.

ženáknana *adv* only those

ženíyuha *adv* all of that

žepcá *vi1* I think that, I thought that *Usage:* used with 1st person only. ▸ **Mį́š žepcá.** I think alike.

žé'ų *vi1* s/he/it is like that, as such

žé'ųs *conj* that is why, because of that, on account of this, therefore ▸ **Žé'ųs owéjimnaga.** That is why I told him that. ▸ **Mį́š wąmnáges'a žená žé'ųs k'ábi.** I used to see these myself, and that is what they dug them for. (Drummond 1976, Įktomi)

žewós *pro, dem* those two ▸ **Žewós ecų́bi.** Those two did it.

žeyÁ *vt-irr* s/he says that *Usage:* precedes or follows a quote. ▸ **Mihų́ žeyá, "Nén iyódągam!"** My mother said, "Sit down here!" ▸ **"Mázaska iyúhana mak'ú," žeyá.** "Give me all your money!" he said. ▸ **Žé omnágįkta duká įtó togáheya né žepá.** I will tell that one, but first I will tell this. (NS 2002:41) *1s:* **žepá** *2s:* **žehá** *Vdat:* **žejíyA**

žíyasą *adv* all that time ▸ **Duká žíyasą nahą́ȟ badį́n iyéya:ga [. . .]** But all that time, they continued to push it out [. . .] (NS 2002:31)

žį́skoga *vs* it is about that size ▸ **"Eyáš žį́skogaš dąyą́ktac," eyá.** "Well it is just the right size, it will be well," he said. (NS 2002:31)

žó *vi1* 1) s/he whistles *1s:* **wažó** *2s:* **yažó** *1p:* **ųžóbi** *n* 2) whistle *Vredup:* **žóžo**

žós'a *n* kingfisher *Syn:* **wakpógįya**

žóžó *vi1-redup* s/he/it whistles repeatedly

žubína *n* pile

Affixes

Ø- *prefix* his, her, its (3rd person singular possessor) *Usage:* used with body parts. ▸ **mapá-nipá-pá** my head-your head-his/her/its head ▸ **-pa-** > **pá** head > his/her/its head **-i-** > **í** head > his/her/its head ▸ **ma'í-ni'í-í** my mouth-your mouth-his/her/its mouth

-Ø-₁ *prefix-infix* 1) him, her, it (3rd person singular) *Usage:* unmarked form of an active verb; this affix is placed after the object/patient marker and before the verb stem. ▸ **wąmnága** > **wąyága** I see him > s/he sees him/her 2) he, she, it (3rd person singular) *Usage:* unmarked form of an active verb; this affix is placed before the subject/agent marker. ▸ **wąmáyaga** > **wąyága** s/he sees me > s/he sees him/her

-Ø-₂ *prefix-infix* 1) he, she, it (3rd person singular) *Usage:* unmarked form of a stative verb. ▸ **nistústa** > **stustá** you are tired > s/he is tired 2) his, her, its (3rd person singular) *Usage:* unmarked form of a possessed noun. ▸ **mahí** > **hí** my tooth > his/her/its tooth

-' *part* indicates an assertion (gender neutral declarative particle) ▸ **Ní'!** He is living! ▸ **Nén mayáza'.** It aches here. ▸ **Há, maȟmá'.** Yes, I am sleepy. ▸ **Waná yakínųgábi céyaga'.** Now it is time you go back to bed. ▸ **Nén astústagen mągá'.** I am sitting here kind of tired. (Cumberland 2005:339)

-'h *encl* joke (joking enclitic) *Usage:* used to turn a statement into a counterfactual one, and is used in teasing or joking (Cumberland 2005:339). ▸ **Mawánų epcá 'h.** I am thinking of stealing it.

English/Nakoda

A

a *art prep* in Nakoda the English article *a* is often translated with a bare noun 1) **wąží** num, art one; a, an 2) **cá** det such a person, such a kind, at such a time; a, an, the

axe *n* **ųspé** n axe

abalone *n* **šiptó** n abalone shell

abdomen *n* **niǧé, niǧá** n stomach, tripe, abdomen

able *adj* **ogíhi** vt1-aux s/he can, is able to do smth (follows a verb)

-able *suff* **-pija** vs-aux it is easy, worth it, feasible, good to do, -able (suffixed to verbs)

about *adj adv prep* 1) **a-** pref about, for a reason 2) **wacį** vi3, n, part s/he feels like doing smth; mind, plan, goodwill; it is about to happen; intentive, prospective, or imminent event 3) **gacén** adv about, approximately 4) **gacéȟ** adv about

above *pp adv* 1) **įjída** adv high above 2) **įjínaži** vs s/he/it stands above 3) **wągám** adv up high, above, upright ‣ **wągádahą** adv from above ‣ **wągáduwa** adv way above, way up there 4) **iyékapeya** adv above, exceedingly

absolutely *adv* 1) **-ȟ** suff absolutely, the very X, exactly, specifically, at all (marks focus on demonstratives, nouns, pronouns, and negative interrogative pronouns) 2) **-ȟtįyą** suff, encl exactly, really anxious to, absolutely, at all (marks focus on active verbs and some non-gradable stative verbs)

accident *n* 1) **gaptáyĄ** vt1, vii s/he/it knocks, hits smth down; the wind knocks, hits smth down; s/he has a car accident 2) **mo-** pref by an impact from a distance (by shooting, hitting with a projectile, poking with a stick); by colliding into smth with a vehicle; by blowing on smth; by the action of the wind, rain

accidentally *adv* **awánųka** adv accidentally

accompany *v* 1a) **gicí yá** vi2 s/he goes there with him/her/it 1b) **óm yá** vi2 s/he goes there with them 2) **éyaya** vt1 s/he takes, sets to go with sb, smth there 3) **gicíja** vt1 s/he is with sb (as a friend or spouse); accompanies sb

accompanying *adj* **kóya, kówa** adv along, with, accompanying, and

accuse *v* **įyá'ųba** vt1-dit s/he blames, accuses sb for smth

ache *v n See:* **sick**

acquire *v* **yamná** vt2 s/he acquires smth by speech; convinces sb about smth ‣ **yamnáya** adv acquiring smth by speech; convincing, gossiping

across *prep adv adj* 1) **ópta** adv across 2) **knagíyą** vs s/he/it is located across 3) **sám ; sąm** post beyond, over (short form of sápa); across 4) **agásam** adv across smth (camp, road) ‣ **agásampadahą** adv from there across to here ‣ **cągúsampadahą** n from across the border 5) **kogám** adv in front, ahead, forward; across

act *v n* 1) **žécų** vt3 s/he does that; acts in that way 2) **kuwá** vt1 s/he treats, acts toward, cares for sb, smth ‣ **gicúwa** vt1-pos s/he treats, acts toward, cares for his/her own

action *n* **oȟ'ą́** n action, behavior, habit, manner

actually *adv* **žecéya** adv really, actually

Adam's apple *cp* **nodé pšų́pšų́** cp Adam's apple

add *v* **a'ópeyA** vt1-caus s/he adds on smth ‣ **a'ópekiyA** vt1-caus s/he adds smth onto it

addition *n* **nągų́, nakų́** conj, adv and, and also, in addition; more, anymore (when followed by a negated verb)

admiration *n* **wóteȟina** n value, object of love or admiration

admire *v* **iyúškį** vt2 s/he admires sb, smth ‣ **igíjiyuškį** vt1/2-benef s/he admires sb, smth for sb else

adopt *v* 1) **cįjáya** vt1 s/he adopts a child 2) **hokšícijage** n favored child 3) **-ya** suff consider, adopt, have someone as a relative or friend (derives verbs of kinship from the 3rd person noun or 1st person noun)

advise *v* **wahógų** vi1 s/he gives advice, dares ‣ **wahógųkiyA** vt1-caus s/he lectures, advises sb

affected *adj* **ecéya** vs s/he/it is in such disposition; is affected by smth; happens

afraid *adj* 1) **giníhą** vi1 s/he is afraid 2) **kogípa** vt1 s/he fears sb, smth ‣ **wakógipa** vi1-abs s/he is afraid of things (spiritually); is a coward

Africa *ngeo* 1) **Hásaba makóce** ngeo Africa 2) **Wašíjusaba makóce** ngeo Africa

African *nprop* 1) **Hásaba** nprop person of African or African-American descent ‣ **Hásaba wíyą** cp woman of African or African-American descent 2) **Wašíjusaba** nprop person of African or African-American descent ‣ **Wašíjusaba wíyą** cp woman of African or African-American descent

after *adv prep conj* 1) **įhágam** adv after 2) **okókona** adv one after the other 3) **iyázagen** adv in succession, one after the other; wandering 3) **hiyó-** pref after smth, to get smth (prefixed to verbs of movement) 5) **žehą́naga** conj and so now, and after that, and at that time 6) **dohą́geȟ** adv after a while 7) **iyúha** quant all, every, one after the other (has a distributive meaning); none (followed by a negated verb)

afternoon *n* 1) **wiyódahą sám** adv afternoon 2) **wiyó'esą** adv throughout the afternoon, all afternoon

again *adv* 1) **aké** adv again; another one, one more (usually followed by one); plus 2) **piyá** adv anew, again, in a different location 3) **wažíȟtiyą** adv once again 4) **wą́ga** vi-aux again and again, one after the other, repetitively (marks a repetitive action that occurs in a short time frame) 5) **įtkóm ; įtkúm** adv back, back again

against *prep* 1) **iyám** adv along, against 2) **igákna** adv against, besides sb, smth (this adverb can take person markers) 3) **kibážį** vt1 s/he is against, jealous of sb ‣ **wakíbažį** vi1-abs, n s/he is against, opposes people or things; grudge

age *n v* **ehą́ki** vi1 s/he reaches, arrives at a certain point; s/he is of a certain age (used after the numbers of winters/years)

agent *n* **adéyabi** n reservation agent, Indian agent

ago *adj adv* 1) **waną́gaš** adv long ago ‣ **waną́gažašį** vs it is not too long ago; recently 2) **téhąc'ehą** adv long time ago 3) **héktac'ehą** adv long time ago

agonize *v* **cąyák ų́** vi1 s/he/it agonizes in pain

agony *n* **gažą́k** adv in poor health, in agony

agree *v* **wįjána** vt1 s/he agrees with sb, smth; s/he believes (in) sb, smth; is confident in sb, smth ‣ **wįjágicinabi** adv they agree with one another; they believe in one another)

ah *exclamation* **á ; há** exclamation ah (expressed surprise, or when someone has noticed something)

ahead *adv* 1) **tanį́n ; tąnį́na** adv ahead of time, ahead of others; already 2) **togám** adv ahead, in the lead 3) **togáȟ** adv ahead of time; first 4) **togáda** adv ahead, in front, in the lead, in the first place; in the future, later 5) **kogám** adv in front, ahead, forward; across

air *v n* 1) **gamnúyA** vt1 s/he/it (wind) airs out smth ▸ **gamnúkiyA** vt1-caus s/he churns, airs out smth 2) **taníya** n his/her/its breath; breath, air, oxygen, atmosphere

air conditioner *cp* **ti'ósnikiya** n air conditioning

airplane *n* 1) **wádagiya** n airplane, aircraft carrier 2) **mázagiya** n airplane 3) **iyéciga giyéna** (WB) *cp* airplane 4) **giyékiyabi** (OM) n airplane, car 5) **giyáyabi** n airplane (archaic)

airport *n* **wádagiya o'ínaži** *cp* airport

aisle *n* **oká** n aisle, narrow path; vacant place

alas *interj* **é'ehe** interj alas

alcohol *n* **miní sudá** *cp* alcohol

alert *adj* **waktá** vii s/he is expectant for sb or smth to happen; s/he/it is alert, careful, aware of smth ▸ **waktáya** adv in anticipation, expectantly ▸ **waktáȟtiyA** vs s/he is alert; is on his/her guard

alien *n* **wicášta toká** *cp* alien

alike *adj adv* 1) **akí'ecedu** vs they are alike ▸ **akí'ecen** adv-cont equally, the same, alike 2) **akí-** pref same, alike, both, joined

all *n pro adv adj* 1a) **iyúha** quant all, every (has a distributive meaning, one after the other); 1b) none (followed by a negated verb) ▸ **iyúhabi** vs it is all of them ▸ **niyúha** quant all of these, all kinds ▸ **ženíyuha** adv all of that 1b) **iyúhana** quant all, all of them, all of it, every individual in a group, all at the same time (collective meaning) 2) **iyúhagen** quant at all, altogether 3) **owá** quant all (people, things); everybody ▸ **nówa** pro all of these (people, animals, things, ideas) ▸ **kówa** adv all of those (people, animals, things, ideas) 4) **-cuna** encl all the time; keep on doing (marks a frequent action or event) *See:* **at all**

alliance *n* **ceškámaza** n council, alliance (refers to council members to whom a badge was given); police officer (used in Carry The Kettle)

allow *v* 1) **ecúkiyA** vt1 s/he allows smth, sb to do smth 2) **-kiyA** suff s/he makes, allows, lets sb do smth (triggers e-ablaut and attaches to contracted verbs) *See:* **let**

all right *exclam adj adv* **hón** *interj* yes, all right

almost *part* 1) **giníja** adv almost 2) **taníješ ; taníš** adv almost

alone *adj* 1) **išnána** adv, vs3 by himself/herself/itself, alone; s/he is alone, by himself/herself ▸ **išnána ú** vii s/he is, stays alone; is a bachelor (some speakers also inflect išnána) ▸ **išnánagen** adv alone, in lonesome manner ▸ **wicíšnana** adv alone (used for humans) 2) **iyéšnana** adv by herself/himself/itself/themselves; her/him/it/them alone 3) **ejé'ena ; ejéna** adv only, simply, alone, just

along *adv prep* 1) **iyápa** adv against it, touching it ▸ **iyám** adv-cont along, against 2) **opáya** adv through, along, following the course of smth; in, through a valley, coulee 2) **kóya, kówa** adv along, with, accompanying, and 3) **ki'úm** adv beside, alongside

already *adv* 1) **waná** adv now, already 2) **tanín ; tanína** adv ahead of time, ahead of others; already

also *adv* 1) **kó** conj also, too, even ▸ **kóko** conj-redup even them; they too 2) **nagú ; nakú** conj, adv and, and also, in addition; more, anymore (when followed by a negated verb in -ši)

although *conj See:* **but**

altogether *adv n* **iyúhagen** quant at all, altogether

always *n* 1) **ecágen** adv constantly, always, all the time 2) **jé ; jé'e** part always, often (marker of the habitual modality) 3) **nína** adv very; really, a lot, always, intense, intensively; not at all, not really (followed by a negative verb in -ši)

amazement *n* **kó** part marks strong emotions, irony, amazement, surprise, ridicule

ambush *n v* 1a) **iyápe** vt1 s/he lies waiting for sb; ambushes sb 1b) **iyápebi** n ambush

American *nprop* 1) **Cągúsam wįcášta** nprop American people, person of American descent 2) **Mínahąska** nprop person of American descent

American robin *cp* 1) **makúša** (CTK) n American robin 2) **cątkúša** n American robin

among *prep* **óhą** post among, in the middle, in it

amount *n* 1) **jónana** quant few, little, small amount 2) **yuwídana** adv small amount 3) **ganágeja** vs it is that many; it is such an amount

amuse *v* **imágağa** vs s/he is amused, entertained by sb, smth; socializes ‣ **imágağakiyA** vt1-caus s/he amuses sb; makes sb glad ‣ **wó'imağağa** vs s/he/it is amusing, enjoyable ‣ **wó'imağağa'įc'iyA** vi3-refl s/he enjoys, amuses himself/herself

an *art See:* **a**

ancestor *n* 1a) **hékta odágugiciyabi** cp ancestors 1b) **hékta odáguye** cp ancestor 2) **watápe** n buffalo hunter, hunter; elderly man; ancestor

and *conj* 1) **hįkna ; hįk** conj and (links two verbs or two nouns together) 2) **gá** conj and (links two clauses) 3) **nągú ; nakú** conj, adv and, and also, in addition; more, anymore (when followed by a negated verb in -šį) 4) **žehánaga** conj and so now, and after that, and at that time 5) **sám ; sám** post beyond, over; and, in addition to (when used in counting it is placed between decades and cardinal numbers, and between hundreds and decades) 6) **kóya ; kówa** adv along, with, accompanying, and 7) **hą'ųka** conj and then, when

anger *v n* 1) **yušíkna** vt2 s/he angers sb 2) **yašíkna** vt2 s/he angers sb verbally 3) **šigíjikna** vt1-benef s/he takes up for sb in anger 4) **wacíko** vs s/he is quick to anger

angle *n* **agá'ohya** adv at an angle

angrily *adv* 1) **šiknáya** adv angrily 2) **įknášikna**

vi3-refl s/he speaks angrily about himself/herself

angry *adj* **šikná** vii s/he/it is mad, angry ‣ **šiknáyagen** adv kind of angry

animal *n* 1) **wanúyabi** n-pl small animals 2) **wamákašką** n creature, animal; bear 3) **wawága** n huge animal, creature (like a dinosaur)

anxious *adj* 1) **įgáği** vs s/he is anxious, worried about smth 2) **įgážąga** vs s/he is anxious, worried, bothered because of the lack of smth 3) **inída** vs s/he is anxious to start smth) 4) **-ȟtįyA** suff, encl exactly, really anxious to, absolutely, at all (marks focus on active verbs and some nongradable stative verbs)

announce *v* 1) **hogíyA** vii s/he cries out, announces 2) **oyágA** vt2 s/he announces, tells, talks about smth 3) **ya'ótą'į** vi2 s/he announces smth, tells the news

announcer *n* 1) **éyabaha** n hilltop announcer 2) **wįcábağe** n announcer 3) **iyéska ; iyéskabi** n interpreter, announcer

annually *adv* **omákawąži** adv annually

another *adj pro* 1) **aké** adv again; another one, one more (usually followed by one); plus 2) **-gici-...-bi ; -ci-...-bi** circumfix one another (marker of the reciprocal; used when two persons are acting on one another; reciprocal verbs are of Class 1)

answer *v* 1) **ayúptA** vt2 s/he answers sb ‣ **wa'áyuptA** vii-abs s/he answers ‣ **agíjiyuptA** vt1-benef s/he answers for him/her ‣ **agíciyuptabi** vii-recip they answer to one another ‣ **a'įc'iyuptA** vi3-refl s/he answers a question s/he had 2) **wó'ayupte** n answer

ant *n* 1) **hipépena** n ant 2) **wamnúška pašáša** cp red ant

antelope *n* **tatógana** n antelope

anus *n* **ųzóȟnoga** n anus, rectum

any *adj pro adv* 1) **dágu** pro, quant, vs thing, something; what; any, none (when followed by a negated verb); it is something 2) **wąžíȟ** num, det one in particular, a certain one (marker of focus); any, a single one (nonspecific, hypothetical referent) 3) **eyáš** adv sufficient, enough, only, well enough; any, anyways 4) **-ga kóšta** part any, no matter which/who/what (lack of interest)

anybody *pro* **duwéga kóšta** pro anyboby, just anybody, no matter who

anymore *adv* **nągú ; nakú** conj, adv and, and also, in addition; more, anymore (has the latter meaning when followed by a negated verb in -šį)

anything *pro* 1) **dáguga kóšta** pro anything, just anything, whatever, whichever one 2) **dagúȟ** pro something, anything

anyway *adv* 1) **įdúȟ** adv anyway, no doubt, contrary to what is expected 2) **eyáš** adv sufficient, enough, only, well enough; any, anyway

anywhere *adv* 1) **dókiya** adv wherever (followed by a positive verb of movement); anywhere (followed by a negated verb of movement); where to (functions like an interrogative stative verb and occurs in sentence-final position) 2) **duktédugaš** adv wherever, anywhere

apart *adv* **įȟéyam** adv away from; apart from

Appaloosa *n* **šųknídeska** n Appaloosa

appear *v* 1) **hinápA** vi1 s/he/it arrives here and appears; comes into sight 2) **kninápA** vi1 s/he comes out, emerges; arrives back here and reappears 3) **hiyú** vi1, vs s/he departs, is setting to come here from there; it begins, appears, arises, turns into smth

apple *n* **taspą́** n hawthorn fruit; apple; fruit (in compounds)

apple tree *cp* **taspą́cą** n apple tree

approximately *adv* See: **about**

April *n* **tabéȟ'a tawį wí** cp April

April fool *cp* **aknáyabi hąwí** cp April fool

Arapaho *nprop* **Maȟpíyato** nprop Arapaho people, person of Arapaho descent

arch *n v adj* **sicógądu** n arch of the foot

area *n* **omnáyena** n small flat area

arena *n* **oškáde** n picnic; festival; arena

argue *v* **akínija** vt1 s/he debates, argues over smth ‣ **wa'ákinija** vi1-abs s/he debates, argues over things

argument *n* **akínijabi** n argument, dispute, quarrel

Arikara *nprop* **Panána ; Panáne** nprop Arikara, Pawnee people, person of Arikara, Pawnee descent

arm *n* 1) **įstó** n arm 2) **nąpcó** n upper arm 3) **įstó knağé** vt1-pos s/he gashes his/her arm

armpit *n* **acóga ; acógena** n armpit

army *n* **agícida** n warrior, soldier, police; army

around *adv adj prep* 1) **ókšą** adv around ‣ **ókšąkšą** adv-redup all around ‣ **ókšądahą** adv from all around ‣ **a'ókšą** adv around smth; around camp ‣ **o'ókšąȟ** adv all around the place 2) **cą'ókšą ; cąwókšą** adv around the bush 3) **ti'ókšą ; tiwókšą** adv around the house, camp 4) **howókšą** adv around the camp circle 5) **įdókšą** adv around the face 6) **-ki; -ci** suff over, around (indicates a general or approximative location)

arrive *v* 1a) **hí** vi1 s/he arrives here from there (this verb is often translated as "to come here") ‣ **gíjihi** vt1-benef s/he arrives, comes here instead of sb ‣ **hikíyA** vt1-caus s/he makes sb arrive, come here ‣ **wónhi** vi1 s/he arrives here from there to eat 1b) **hi-** pref doing smth while arriving here; doing smth after arriving here ‣ **hiyúweğa** vi1/2 s/he crosses a body of water while arriving here ‣ **hiyúgA ; hiwúgA** vi1/3 s/he arrives here and lies down ‣ **hináži** vi1 s/he arrives here and stands 2) **hiyóhi** vt1 s/he arrives here to take sb, smth 3) **ahí** vt1, vi-coll s/he arrives here with sb, smth; they arrive here as a group ▸ **gíjahi** vt1-benef s/he arrives with smth for sb 4a) **í** vi1 s/he arrives there from here (this verb is often translated with "went") ▸ **hiyó'i** vt1 s/he went, arrives there to take sb, smth ▸ **kniyó'i** vt1-pos s/he went, arrives there to take his/her own; gets his/her own back 4b) **i-** pref doing smth while arriving there from here; doing smth after arriving there from here ▸ **iyúweǧa** vi2 s/he crosses a body of water while arriving, going there 5) **a'í** vt1 s/he takes, brings, arrives with sb, smth there 6a) **kí** vi1 s/he arrives back there (after leaving); returns back to where s/he is from ▸ **knokí** vt1-pos s/he arrives back there (after leaving) with his/her thing; returns back home with his/her own 6b) **ki-** pref doing smth while arriving back there (after leaving); doing smth while returning back to where s/he is from ▸ **kiyúweǧa** vi/2 s/he crosses a body of water while arriving back there 7a) **kní** vi1 s/he arrives back here, to where s/he is from; returns, comes home ▸ **wakní** vi1-abs s/he returns, arrives home bringing meat 7b) **kni-** pref doing smth while arriving back here, to where s/he is from; doing smth while returning, coming home ▸ **kniyúweǧa** vi1/2 s/he crosses a body of water while arriving, returning back here 8) **ehą́'i** vi1 s/he/it reaches, arrives at a certain point; it is such hour, day of the week, year 9) **ehą́ki** vi1 s/he reaches, arrives at a certain point; s/he is of a certain age (used after the numbers of winters/years)

arrow *n* **wąhį́, wahį́kpe, wahį́kpa** n flint, flint arrowhead; arrow ▸ **wahį́kpekpena** n-redup little bow and arrows used by children ▸ **wą́** n arrow (archaic)

arson *n* **ti'į́ktu** n house in flames, arson

artery *n See:* **vein**

arthritis *n* 1a) **huhú yazą́bi** n arthritis 1b) **huhú yazą́** vs s/he has, suffers from arthritis

artist *n* **wókmes'a** n artist

as if *ph* 1) **steň** part like, in the manner of, somewhat, -ish, as if 2) **gaca** encl as if; something is unlikely to happen (often conveys a sense of ridicule)

ash *n* 1) **cąsúda** n ash tree; hardwood 2) **caȟóda** n ash tree

ashamed *adj* **ištéjA** vs s/he is bashful, shy, easily embarrassed, ashamed ▸ **wį́štejA** vs-abs s/he is ashamed

ashes *n.pl* 1) **cuȟé** n ashes 2) **pedį́ȟpaya** n ashes 3) **caȟóda** n ashes; coal

Asian *nprop* **Gisų́na** nprop person of Asian descent (Chinese, Japanese) *See:* **Japanese**

aside *adv* **batógam** adv pushed aside

ask *v* 1) **ná** vt1 s/he asks for smth ▸ **waná** vi1-abs s/he asks for things ▸ **giná** vt1-dat s/he asks smth of sb 2) **iyúǧA, iwúǧA** vt3 s/he asks sb about smth ▸ **wawíyuǧA** vi3-abs s/he asks questions ▸ **igíjiyuǧA** vt1/3-benef s/he asks sb for him/her ▸ **ic'íyuǧA** vi3-refl s/he asks himself/herself about it 3) **okíyA** vt1 s/he asks sb to do smth 4) **-ši** vt1-dit-aux s/he tells, asks, orders, commands sb (attaches or follows a preceding verb)

assertion *v* 1) **no** part indicates an assertion (declarative male particle; triggers e-ablaut on the preceding word) 2) **cé** part declarative female particle 3) **-'** part indicates an assertion (gender neutral declarative particle) 4) **c** part indicates a strong assertion (gender neutral declarative particle)

association *n* **okónagiciyabi** vi1-recip they are friendly, associate to one another; society, union, association

at *prep* 1) **én** post, adv in, into, on, onto, at, to; here, there) 2) **ektá** post at, in, to a location or destination ▸ **ektáktaš** post-redup at, in, to various locations or destinations; wherever 3) **ehą́** adv then, as it happened, at a specific point in the past (often translates the English past tense) 4) **žehą́ ; žéhą** adv then, at that time, at a certain point in time (often translates the English past tense); last 5) **a-** pref on, onto, over, at 6) **é-** pref to, at, there, toward, in this direction; they (marks the collective plural form of some intransitive verbs)

at all *ph* 1) **nína** adv very; really, a lot, intense, intensively; always; not at all, not really (followed by a negative verb in -šį) 2) **iyúhagen** quant at all, altogether 3) **-ȟ** suff absolutely, the very X, exactly, specifically, at all (marks focus on demonstratives, nouns, pronouns, and negative interrogative pronouns) 4) **-ȟtįyA** suff, encl exactly, really anxious to, absolutely, at all (marks focus on active verbs and some nongradable stative verbs)

Atsina *nprop See:* **Gros Ventres**

attack *v n* 1) **iyáȟpayA** vt1 s/he attacks, rapes sb; grabs sb, smth with force ‣ **iyágiȟpayA** vt1-dat s/he grabs smth from him/her with force 2) **takpéya** vt1 s/he/it charges, runs against, attacks sb 3) **iyópegiciyabi** vi1-recip they quarrel, scold, attack one another

attention *n* **įknígešį** vt1 s/he does not care for sb, smth; s/he does not pay attention to sb, smth

attractive *adj* **wógu̧ya** adv attractive, in an attractive manner

August *n* 1) **cąpá sapsába ha̧wí ; cąpásaba wí** cp August 2) **cąpá waštéšte ha̧wí** cp August

aunt *n* 1a) **inána** n my aunt (mother's sister; father's brother's wife) 1b) **-hu̧na-** root aunt (mother's sister, father's brother's wife) 2) **-tu̧wį- ; -tu̧wįna-** root aunt (father's sister; mother's brother's wife)

author *n* **wa'ókmas'a** n writer, author, painter, scribe

available *adj See:* **free**

avoid *v* **įtú̧pa** vt1 s/he avoids sb out of embarrassment; s/he is shy

awaken *v* **įknúȟija** vi3-refl s/he awakens himself/herself

away *adv adj* 1) **téha̧n** adv far away, in a distance

‣ **įteha̧n** adv from far away, far over there 2) **duktám** adv away from a place; to somewhere 3) **gadám** adv over there, away in that direction 4) **manín** adv far away, in a distance 5) **tokám** adv away, away from 6) **įȟéyam** adv away from; apart from

awl *n* **tahį́špa** n awl

B

baby *n* 1) **dáguškina** n, vs baby, infant, child; s/he/it is a baby 2) **bibína** n baby 3) **tezíȟnina** n baby with the umbilical cord severed 4) **hokší-** cont child, baby; boy (occurs in personal names) 5) **-na** suff small, little, cute, dear (with nouns and verbs it indicates the small size of an entity, or the endearment/sympathy of the speaker for the person or object; it often occurs on verbs used to describe the actions of a baby or small child) ‣ **da̧yá̧na** vs s/he/it (small thing, baby, child) is well ‣ **ú̧na** vt3 s/he uses smth small; s/he/it (baby, child) wears smth 6) **hokšíknuha** adv holding one's baby

babysit *v* **awícawa̧yagA** vt1-coll s/he watches over people, babysits children

babysitter *n* **hokší awá̧yages'a** cp babysitter

bachelor *n* 1) **tašná̧ ú̧** vi1 s/he is single; he is a bachelor ‣ **wícatašná̧ ú̧** vi1 he is a bachelor 2) **įšná̧na ú̧** vi1 s/he is, stays alone; is a bachelor (some speakers also inflect įšná̧na)

back₁ *n adv* 1) **nazápa** post in the back of smth, behind smth ‣ **nazám** adv aside, in the back ‣ **nazámpadaha̧** adv from behind, from the back ‣ **nazámpagiya** adv toward the back 2) **įnázam** adv in the back of smth ‣ **įnázapadaha̧** adv from the back of smth, from behind smth 3) **hékta** adv back then, in the past 4) **įtkóm ; įtkúm** *adv* back, back again 5) **hagíkta** vt1-pos s/he looks back 6) **ȟeyám** adv in the back, behind 7) **giní** vi1 s/he comes back to life, wakes up (from hibernation) 8) **gi- ; k-** pref back to an original state or place

back₂ *n* 1) **taȟpá** n back (body part) 2) **tabéda** n ruminant's back 3) **nįdé** n lower part of the back above the rump; hip

back and forth *ph* **omįtokto** adv back and forth; taking turns

backpack *n* **wak'į** n backpack

backrest *n* **cą'íjaškabi** n backrest

backward *adv adj* 1) **įdúgam** adv backward, leaning back 2) **ųzíhektam ; ųzéktam** adv backward 3) **ųzímani** vi1 s/he walks backward ‣ **ųzímaniya** adv backward

bacon *n* **gugúša šį** cp bacon

bad *adj n adv* 1) **síjA** vs s/he/it is bad, hard, difficult, harmful, unpleasant; s/he/it is ugly ‣ **sin-, šin-, sij-** vcont bad ‣ **siksíja** vs-redup they are bad 2) **šinwókcą** vi1 s/he thinks it is bad 3) **wósijA** vi1-abs s/he causes trouble, does bad things 4) **wįktókto, wįtkótko** vs-redup s/he is bad, crazy; misbehaves

badger *n* 1) **ȟogá** n badger 2) **o'íknuhena** n badger

badlands *n-pl* **makóšija** n badlands

bad-mouth *v* **yasíjA** vt2 s/he bad-mouths sb, ruins smth by speech ‣ **wayásijA** vi2-abs s/he bad-mouths, speaks ill of things, people

bag *n* 1) **įkšuna** n bag 2) **wóžuha** n leather bag 3a) **wóžutų** vi1-abs, n s/he fills into bags or sacks; full bag, bag or sack filled with smth; medicine bundle 3b) **ožútųbi** n bag 4) **tahásaga** n rawhide bag; parfleche 5) **wážu** n quiver; bag for powder and balls 6) **iyágaškabi** n pipe pouch, bag 7) **owópiyena** n woman's sewing bag 8) **wókpą** n bag used to store meat 9) **ogíknągA** vt1-pos; n s/he puts, stores his/her own thing away in it; bag

baggy *adj* **pšopšó** vs it is baggy, loose

bail *v n See:* **drain**

bait *n* **watą** n bait

bake *v See:* **cook**

baking powder *cp* **inádaboǧa ; nądáboȟyabi ; inádaboȟya** n baking powder, yeast

bald *adj* 1) **péšna** vs s/he/it is bald-headed 2) **pahá wanįjA** vs s/he/it is bald-headed

ball *n* 1) **tába** n ball ‣ **tábana** n small ball ‣ **tap- ; tam-** cont ball ‣ **tapškádA** vi1 s/he plays ball, baseball 2) **tapkápsijektena** n ballgame 3) **wá yupšúkabi** cp snowball 4) **yupšúka** vt2 s/he made smth into a ball

balm *n* **ísnagiya** n lip balm

banana *n* **škoškóbena** n-redup banana

band office *cp* 1) **oyáde omníciye** cp band office 2) **oyáde tí** cp band office

bandit *n* **įdé'ogiǧe** n bandit

banish *v* **įȟpéyA** vt1-caus s/he banishes sb

bank *n v* 1) **mázaska tíbi** cp bank, financial institution 2) **mas'ówąyaga** (WB) n bank 3) **mas'óyuȟpe** n bank

bannock *n* 1) **aǧúyabi** n flour; bread, bannock ‣ **aǧúyabi mįmá** cp round bannock ‣ **aǧúyabi océti ągán** ph bannock baked on top of a stove ‣ **aǧúyabi šnoyábi** cp fried bannock 2) **įkcé aǧúyabi** cp bannock

baptism *n* **miní abápsųbi** vs-pass, n s/he is baptized; baptism

bar *n* 1) **omníyakte** n bar, tavern 2) **omníyupsųna** n bar, saloon

barbed wire *cp* **maspépe** n barbed wire

barber *n* **wįcá pagášna** cp barber

bare *adj* **smismí** vs s/he/it is bare, thinned out

barefoot *adv adj* **sicóna ; sicóco ; sicócona** adv barefoot

barely *adv* 1) **gídana ; gídanaȟ** adv barely 2) **iǧúȟkiyaga** adv barely opened

bark₁ *n* **cąhá** n bark

bark₂ *v* **wapá** vi1 it (dog) barks ‣ **wapápa** vi1-redup it (dog) barks repeatedly

barley *n* **gugúša yúde** cp barley

barrel *n* **cąwák'į** n wood barrel

base *n See:* **bottom**

baseball *n* 1) **tamkápsijabi** n baseball, softball 2) **tamškádA, tapškádA** vi1 s/he plays baseball, ball ‣ **tamškádabi** n baseball

baseball bat *cp* 1) **įtágapsija** n baseball bat 2) **tábapabi** n baseball bat 3) **cą́ ųs apábi** ph bat (baseball bat, hockey stick)

baseball cap *cp* **tapškádabi wapáha** cp baseball cap, helmet

baseball glove *cp* **tamkápsija nąbį́kpa** cp baseball glove

bashful *adj* **įštéjA** vs s/he is bashful, shy, easily embarrassed, ashamed

bat *n* **ȟubá wagíknągagana** cp bat (animal) *See:* **baseball bat**

bathe *v* 1) **įknúžaža** vi3-refl s/he bathes, washes himself/herself 2) **nųwą́** vi1 s/he/it swims, bathes, showers

bathroom *n* 1) **owį́duka ; owį́duka tíbi** n toilet, bathroom, outhouse 2) **o'į́knužaža** n bathroom; washbasin, sink

battery *n* **waką́k'į** n battery

Battleford River (Saskatchewan) *ngeo* **Ogíciza wakpá** ngeo Battleford River (Saskatchewan)

battleship *n* **ogíciza mniwáda** cp battleship

bayonet *n* **cótągawahukeza** n bayonet

be *v*

EXISTENCE

1) **ų́** vi1, vi1-aux s/he/it is, lives, exists; s/he stays, lives somewhere; s/he feels, is in a certain way; s/he does continuously; goes around doing smth ‣ **žé'ų** vi1 s/he/it is like that, as such 2) **yuką́** vs it is, it exists, there is/are (applies only to 3rd person animate or inanimate referents); s/he has smth; it exists for sb (said of body parts, states, personal behavior) 3) **waníjA** vs s/he/it lacks; there is none; s/he passed away; is dead

IDENTIFICATION

4) **é** vs used to specify, or clarify the identity of something or somebody previously mentioned ‣ **éš** vs it is it; it is indeed (expresses a contrast between an expected event and what actually occurs) 5) **é'e** vs it is him/her/it/them (only used in the 3rd person) ‣ **žé'e** vs it is that; that is him/her/it/them (only used in the 3rd person) ‣ **žé'eȟtįyA** vs it is really that; that is really him/her/it/them (only used in the 3rd person) 6) **iyé** pro, vs himself, herself, themselves, itself (emphasizes the subject or object); s/he/it/they is/are the one ‣ **iyéšį** vs it is not her/him/it/themselves; s/he/it/they are not the one(s) 7) **duwé** pro, n, vs who, anyone; person; s/he is someone

CLASSIFICATION

8) **ecá** vs s/he/it is thus, is of that kind 9) **néca** vs s/he/it is this kind 10) **žéca** vs s/he/it is of a certain kind (nationality, tribe, trade, behavior, condition) 11) **dókeja** vs it is a matter, way, kind, concern; what is it like? ‣ **dókejašį** vs there is nothing wrong with him/her/it; it is all good; it doesn't matter 12) **ecédu** vs, adv s/he/it is like this, it happens as such, it is the right way; equally, the same way, the right way ‣ **nécedu** adv, vs in this way; s/he/it is like this ‣ **žécedu** adv, vs in the correct way, thus, like that; it is like that, it happened like that

LOCATION

13) **nážį** vi1 s/he/it stands, stands up; s/he is, exists in a certain condition (used after an adverb or a postposition); it is, it is located (used for objects) 14) **yįgÁ ; yągÁ** vi3 s/he is sitting on, in smth; it is, it is located (used for broad-based objects)

ACCOMPANY

15) **gicíja** vt1 s/he is with sb (as a friend or spouse); accompanies sb

bead *n v* 1) **o'į́** n beads 2) **o'į́jusina** n pony bead, small bead 3) **yazá** vt2 s/he laces, beads smth 4) ‣ **ayáza** vt2 s/he laces beads on smth ‣ **ayázabi**

vi2-pass it is beaded ‣ **wa'áyaza** vi1-abs, n s/he beads; beadwork ‣ **wa'ágijiyaza** vt1-benef s/he beads for sb ‣ **wa'ágiciyazabi** vi1-recip they bead for one another ‣ **wa'áknaza** vt1-pos s/he does his/her own beadwork

beadwork *n* **wa'áyazabi ; wa'áyaza** n beadwork

beak *n* **pasú** n beak; tip of the nose

bean *n* **įkšukšuna** (CTK) ; **ųkšukšuna** (WB) n-redup bean

bear₁ *n* 1) **waȟ'ą́kšija** n bear (generic; refers possibly to the extinct prairie grizzly) 2) **mató** n black bear ‣ **matónuda** n cinnamon bear ‣ **matósaba** n black bear ‣ **matómna** vs s/he/it smells like bear 3) **wamą́kamani** n bear *See:* **grizzly**

bear₂ *v* 1) **tų́** vt1-dit, vt1 s/he puts smth on sb; s/he bears smth; is equipped with smth; is in relation with sb (occurs almost exclusively in compounds) *Vpos:* **gitų́** 2) **tų́** vt1, vs-pass she bears a child, gives birth to sb; s/he/it is born *Vcoll:* **wįcátųga**

bearberry *n* **waȟ'ą́kšija tawóde** cp bearberry

beard *n* 1) **putį́hį** n beard 2) **putį́hįšmą** vs s/he has a beard

beast *n* **šiȟ'ą́** n beast, monster

beater *n* 1) **wa'ápes'a** n beater 2) **wįktés'a** n wifebeater

beautiful *adj* 1) **wógųga** vs4 s/he/it is beautiful, pretty (woman only, landscape, event) 2) **owáštejaga** vimp it is beautiful (day) ‣ **ąm'ówaštejaga** vimp it is a beautiful day 3) **wįwáštega** n beautiful woman 4) **owáyak wašté** vs s/he/it is beautiful to look at; is good-looking

beaver *n* 1) **cába** n beaver ‣ **cap-; cam-** cont beaver ‣ **camką́na** n old beaver 2) ‣ **capkúwa** vi1 s/he hunts beaver

Beaver Creek (Saskatchewan) *ngeo* **Cába wakpá** ngeo Beaver Creek (Saskatchewan)

Beaver Hills (Alberta) *ngeo* **Cába ȟé** ngeo Beaver Hills (Alberta; located east of Edmonton)

because *conj* 1) **ús ; ų** post using it, with it, because of it (occurs after the word for the thing or body part used) ‣ **né'ųs ; né'ų** conj because of this, on account of this, therefore ‣ **žé'ųs** conj that is why, because of that, on account of this, therefore 2) **cén** conj then, so, thus, therefore, because, that is why 3) **į-** pref because of, with a tool; particularizes spatial adverbs

become *v* 1) **áyA** vs-aux s/he becomes, turns into, starts to (used after impersonal and stative verbs) 2) **iyáyA** vs-aux s/he/it gradually becomes; turns into

bed *n* 1) **ową́ga** (CTK) ; **owų́ga** n bed 2a) **o'į́štima** vi3, n s/he sleeps inside smth; bed, bedroom 2b) **o'į́štimabi** n bed, bedroom 3) **tóhe, tíhe** n his/her place, house, bed 4) **iyúgA, įwúgA** vi3 s/he goes to bed, sleep; sleeps on smth ‣ **įyúkkiyA, įwúkkiyA** vt1-caus s/he puts sb to bed; s/he makes sb lie down ‣ **iyúgaši** vt1 s/he orders sb to go to bed ‣ **kiyúgA** vt1 s/he arrives back there and lays down, goes to bed 5) **piyÁ** vt1 s/he makes a bed ‣ **pigíjiyA** vt1-benef s/he makes a bed for sb ‣ **pigíyA** vt1-pos s/he makes his/her own bed

bedbug *n* **wamnúška mnaská** cp bedbug

bedcover *n* **ową́ga agáȟpabi** cp bed cover

bedroom *n* 1a) **o'į́štima** vi3, n s/he sleeps inside smth; bed, bedroom 1b) **o'į́štimabi** n bed, bedroom

bee *n* **tuȟmą́ǧa** n bee

beef *n* **tanóyukpąbi** n ground beef, hamburger

beehive *n* **tuȟmą́ȟti** n beehive, bumblebee nest

beer *n* **miní'įbiǧa, miníbiǧa** n beer

beet *n* 1) **típšinašaša** n-redup beet 2) **típšina skúye** cp sugar beet

before *prep* 1) **togá** adv before, ahead of time 2) **įtógam** adv in front of sb, smth; before time 2) **hehébiya** adv midway, half-way; before

beg *v* **wócį** vi1-abs s/he begs

beggar *n* **wócįs'a** n beggar

behave *v* 1) **ȟ'ą́** vi1 s/he/it behaves; s/he does

smth (in interrogative sentences) 2) **oȟ'áge** vs s/he behaves, acts as such (as when joining a group) ‣ **oȟ'ágesijA** vs s/he behaves badly ‣ **oȟ'ágewašte** vs s/he behaves well 3) **opí'įc'iyA** vi3-refl s/he behaves, occupies himself/herself 4) **šką́** vt1, vii s/he tries to do smth; s/he is busy; s/he moves, behaves 5) **Wašín'įc'ina** vi3-refl s/he behaves like a White person 6) **Nakón'įc'ina** vi3-refl s/he behaves like a Nakoda 7) **maní ; máni** vii s/he walks; s/he progresses, behaves as such in life (used after an adverb); s/he accompanies, walks with sb (used with gicí and óm)

behavior *n* 1a) **oȟ'ą́** n action, behavior, habit, manner 1b) **oȟ'áge** n character, behavior

behind *prep adv adj* 1) **héktam** adv behind, in the rear ‣ **héktapadahą** adv from behind 2) **ȟeyám** adv in the back, behind ‣ **tiȟéyam** adv behind the tent, house 3) **nazápa** post in the back of smth, behind smth ‣ **įnázapadahą** adv from the back of smth, from behind smth 4) **įȟpéyaA** vt1-caus s/he discards, throws sb, smth away; s/he leaves sb, smth behind, alone; s/he/it is left behind; s/he divorces from him/her; s/he banishes sb 5) **aháge** adv, vs last, last one; behind; s/he/it is the last

beige *adj* **są́** vs it is beige, faded, off-white

belief *n* 1) **wówįjaka** n belief 2) **coná** vt1, n s/he believes sb, smth; belief

believe *v* 1) **coyá** vt1 s/he believes in sb, smth 2) **coná** vt1, n s/he believes sb, smth; belief 3) **wįjána** vt1-dat, vt1 s/he agrees with sb, smth; s/he believes (in) sb, smth; is confident in sb, smth ‣ **wįjágicinabi** vii-recip they agree with one another; they believe in one another)

belittle *v* **yajúsina** vt2 s/he belittles sb

bell *n* **šnašnána** n dancing bell

belly *n* **tizí** n belly

below *adv adj prep n* 1) **hokún** adv down, below; downstairs 2) **mąkámahen** adv underground; under the ground; below the surface of the earth

belt *n* **įpíyaga** n belt

bend *v n* 1) **bawį́žA** vt1 s/he bends smth by pushing on it 2) **gawį́žA** vt1, vi s/he/it bends smth by pushing, pressing with a tool; it bends over by itself or by the action of the wind ‣ **gawį́š** vcont bent over by itself 3) **agáwįžA** vt1 s/he bends over sb, smth; it bends over smth under its own weight ‣ **agáwįš** vcont bent over sb, smth; draped over smth; bent under its own weight 4) **yuwį́žA** vt2 s/he bends smth manually ‣ **knuwį́žA** vt1-pos s/he bends his/her own manually 5a) **baptúza** vii s/he bends forward, stoops over ‣ **baptús** vcont bent forward 5b) **batúža** vii s/he bends over; stoops down 6) **škóbA** vs it is bent, curved, crooked 7) **gaškóbA** vt1 s/he makes a bent in smth (permanently); bends it with a tool 8) **naškóbA** vt1 s/he bends smth by body, foot pressure 9) **yuškóbA** vt2 s/he bends smth manually

berry *n* 1a) **waskúya ; wóskuya** n berries, fruit; juice 1b) **waskúyeja** n berries 2) **wašáša** n berry, berries (generic) 3) **wóšpi** vii-abs s/he picks berries, things ‣ **wógijišpi** vt1-benef s/he picks berries for sb

beside *prep adv* 1) **gakná** adv beside, along sb, smth ‣ **mnigákna, mnįjákna** adv beside the water, at the shore ‣ **tijákna** adv beside a dwelling, house 2) **ki'úm** adv beside, alongside

best *adj adv n* 1) **waštéȟtįyĄ** vs it is very good, the best, nicest 2) **owáštege** vs s/he/it is the best

bet *n v* 1) **gicí ecúna** *ph* bet 2) **mázaska éknągA** vt1-dat s/he bets on sb, smth; puts money on sb, smth

better *adv adj v n* 1) **yudą́yą** vt2 s/he does a good job, makes it better, repairs smth 2) **yuwášte** vt2 s/he makes smth nice manually; redoes smth in a better way ‣ **knuwášte** vt1-pos s/he improves, makes his/her own in a better, good way

between *prep adv* **ohnáte** adv between

beyond *adv* 1) **sám ; sąm** post beyond, over (short form of sápa); across 2) **iyágasam** adv further, beyond 3) **kapéya** vi1-caus s/he/it is more than, goes beyond sb, smth

Bible *n* **wa'óyabi waką** *cp* Bible, legal document; email

bicycle *n* 1) **na'íc'ikmįkmąbi ; nakmíkmąbi** n bicycle 2) **įc'ínahomni** n bicycle

big *adj* **tągA** vs s/he/it is big, large ‣ **tąktágA** vs-redup they are big, large ‣ **tágana** vs s/he/it is kind of big, grown up

Big Dipper *nprop* **wįcáȟpi iyúšna** *cp* Big Dipper constellation

Big Eagle *nprop* **Ȟuyátąga** nprop BigEagle (surname in Pheasant Rump, White Bear, and Ocean Man, Saskatchewan)

Bigfoot *n* **wįcúzi oyúgode** *cp* Bigfoot, Sasquatch

bigger *adj* **yutągA** vt2 s/he makes smth bigger ‣ **knutągA** vt1-pos s/he makes his/her own bigger

bighorn sheep *cp* 1) **héškoba** n bighorn sheep 2) **hékiška ; kíška** n bighorn sheep, mountain goat

bill *n v* **wa'ókmabi wa'ówabi** *cp* bill, amount owed

bind *v n* 1) **yuwí** vt2 s/he binds smth 2) **iyápehą** vt1-dit s/he binds, wraps smth around it

binoculars *n* **į'ákide** n field glasses, binoculars, telescope

birch *n* **tąbá** n white birch

bird *n* 1) **ziktána, zitkána** n bird ‣ **ziktán** cont bird 2) **bustáges'a** n unidentified spring bird 3) **hokúwas'a** n any kind of prey bird that catches fish

birth *n* 1) **tų** vt1 s/he wears, puts smth on; s/he bears smth; she bears a child, gives birth 2) **duktén tųbi** *cp* place of birth 3a) **yuhá** vt2, adv s/he has, possesses smth; s/he carries sb, smth; s/he gave birth to a child; s/he holds smth (meeting, ceremony); s/he keeps, looks

after, treats sb, smth; carry, hold, have with one (precedes verbs of traveling) 3b) **hokšíyuha** vi2 she gives birth, is in labor 4) **cijátų** vi she gives birth (human and animal)

birthmark *n* **jísą** n birthmark, blemish

bitch *n* ‣ **šúgawį** n female dog, bitch

bite *v n* 1) **yaȟtágA** vt2 s/he bites sb, smth ‣ **wayáȟtagA** vi1-abs s/he/it bites ‣ **knaȟtágA** vt1-pos s/he bites his/her own 2) **yaksÁ** vt2 s/he bites, chews smth off ‣ **knaksÁ** vt1-pos s/he cuts his/her own with a sharp tool; s/he bites his/her own off 3) **yat'Á** vt2 s/he/it bites sb to death; kills sb by ingesting poison 4) **yašpášpA** vt2-redup s/he nibbles, bites a piece off sb, smth 5) **yašpú** vt2 s/he bites smth off it

bitterroot *n* **sųkpétawode** n bitterroot

black *adj* 1) **sábA** vs, n s/he/it is black; pitch, tar ‣ **sap- ; sam-** vcont black ‣ **samyÁ** vt1-caus s/he blackens sb, smth; paints, colors, dyes smth in black ‣ **sapsábA** vs-redup s/he/it is black-spotted, black here and there ‣ **sap'íc'iyA** vi3-refl s/he blackens, paints himself/herself in black ‣ **sapyá** adv blackly, darkly ‣ **sábeȟtiyĄ** vs s/he/it is pitch black 2) **šéba** n black person

black eye *n* 1) **įštásabA** vs s/he has a black eye 2) **įštá ostą** vs s/he has a black eye ‣ **įštá ogástą** vt1 s/he gives sb a black eye

blackberry *n* **wįbazuką sába** *cp* blackberry

blackbird *n* **ziktásaba ; zitkásaba** n blackbird *See:* **red-winged blackbird**

blacken *v See:* **black**

Blackfoot *nprop* **Sihásaba** nprop Blackfoot people, person of Blackfoot descent

blackleg *n* **sikásaba** n blackleg disease, infectious bacterial disease (livestock) (Latin gangraena emphysematosa) 2) **húsaba** n blackleg disease

blackroot *n* **pežúdasaba** n blackroot, Culver's root

blacksmith *n* 1) **maskádo** vt1 s/he pounds metal; blacksmith 2) **mas'ápe** n blacksmith

bladder *n* **nežeha** n bladder

blame *v n* **iyá'ụba** vt1-dit s/he blames, accuses sb of smth

blanket *n* 1) **šiná** n blanket, robe 2) **šináknekneǧa** n-redup Hudson Bay blanket 3) **šinášoga** n Pendleton blanket 4) **owížа** n quilt, bedding sheet, blanket 5) **šųk'áyumnaya** n horse blanket 6) **ak'ímaheda** n saddle blanket

bleed *v* 1) **wé** n, vs blood; s/he/it bleeds ‣ **weyÁ** vt1-caus s/he causes sb to bleed ‣ **wé hiyáyA** vs-redup s/he/it is bleeding ‣ **wé hiyú** vs s/he/it starts bleeding 2) **weháha** vs s/he has a hemorrhage, bleeds constantly 3) **gawéwe** vt1-redup s/he hits and makes sb, smth bleed ‣ **pohkáwe** vt1 s/he hits and makes his/her nose bleed 4) **yuwéwe** vt2 s/he makes sb bleed manually ‣ **iknúwewe** vi3-refl s/he makes himself/herself bleed 5) **íwe hiyáyA** vs-redup s/he bleeds from the mouth 6) **wéyuskeba t'Á** vs s/he/it dies from bleeding

bless *v* 1) **cégiyA** vt1 s/he blesses sb, smth; s/he supplicates, prays 2) **awácegiyA** vt1 s/he prays over, blesses sb, smth 3) **awákąyA** vt1-caus s/he blesses, consecrates sb 4) **yuwáką** vt2 s/he consecrates, blesses sb, smth with the hands 5) **ahógijitạ'į** vt1-benef s/he blesses smth for him/her 6) **knegíyA** vt1 s/he offers smth (food); blesses smth

blessing *n* **yuwákạbi** n blessing

blind *adj v* 1) **ištáǧųǧA** vs s/he is blind ‣ **ištáǧųhkiyA** vt1-caus s/he/it blinds sb ‣ **ištáǧųhyA** vt1-caus s/he causes sb to be blind (by flashing a light) 2) **ištá kpá** vs s/he is blind in one eye

blindfold *v n* **ištá ogáškA** vt1 s/he blindfolds sb ‣ **ištá gaškábi** n blindfold

blindness *n* **wạyágešį** n blindness

blink *v n* **ištá kmúza** vi1 s/he blinks ‣ **ištá kmukmúza** vi1-redup s/he twinkles, blinks repetitively

blizzard *n* **ijámna** vimp there is a blizzard, drifting snow ‣ **hokún ijámna** vimp there is a ground blizzard, drifting snow on the ground

bloat *v* **nạdáboǧA** vs s/he/it bloats; is swollen, puffed up ‣ **nạdáboh'ịc'iyA** vi3-refl s/he/it bloats, swells himself/herself/itself up (frog)

bloated *adj* **nạdábohyena** adv bloated

block *v n* 1) **agášeyA** vt1 s/he blocks smth with a tool (as a cable to hold the door); holds smth open 2) **hayÁ** vt1-caus s/he blocks smth with it

Blood *nprop* **Wé wịcášta** nprop tribe of Blood (Kainai), person of Blood descent

blood *n* 1) **wé** n, vs blood; s/he/it bleeds ‣ **wemná** vs s/he/it smells like blood ‣ **wemnáya** adv smelling of blood 2) **wésije** vs s/he has a blood poisoning

bloom *v n* **hcá** vi it blooms

blossom *n See:* **flower**

blow *v n*

WITH THE MOUTH

1) **bóǧA** vi1 s/he blows on smth (on a candle) ‣ **bóh** vcont blowing on smth ‣ **bóh'iyeyA** vt1 s/he sends smth away by blowing ‣ **bohkíyA** vt1-caus s/he blows, inflates smth ‣ **bohpóǧa** vt1-redup s/he blows on smth; cools smth by blowing on it repetitively ‣ **abóǧA** vt1 s/he blows smth (like medicine) on sb, smth ‣ **obóǧA** vt1 s/he blows into smth; inflates smth 2) **mo-** pref by blowing on smth; by the action of the wind, rain) ‣ **mosní** vt1 s/he blows it out (light); the wind, rain blows smth out

BY THE ACTION OF WIND

3) **gahmógA** vs the wind is blowing smth off 4) **uyá** vimp the wind blows this way 5) **ga-** pref by striking, hitting with an intrument; by the blowing wind; by the heat of the sun; by itself

blue *adj* 1) **tó** vs s/he/it is blue, green 2) **toyÁ** vt1-caus s/he colors, paints, dyes smth blue ‣ **togíjiyA** vt1-benef s/he paints sb, smth in blue for sb ‣ **togíyA** vt1-pos s/he colors, paints, dyes his/her own blue ‣ **to'íc'iyA** vi3-refl s/he paints himself/herself in blue ‣ **toyéna** adv blue, green condition 3) **tóna** vs s/he/it is light blue ‣ **tónaȟtįyĄ** vs s/he/it is very light blue ‣ **totóna** vs-redup s/he/it is light blue 4) **tosĄ** vs s/he/it is light blue 5) **tósabA** vs s/he/it is dark blue, almost black

blue sky cp **maȟpíyato** n blue sky

blueberry n 1) **wíbazukĄ stéya** ph blueberry 2) **a'úyabi** n blueberry

bluebird n **ziktáto, zitkánato, zitkáto** n bluebird, bluejay

blue-green adj **pežíto** n, vs bluejoint grass; it is blue/green

bluejay n See: **bluebird**

bluejoint grass cp **pežíto** n, vs bluejoint grass; it is blue/green

blush v **įdéša iyáyA ; įdé šayá iyáyA** vs s/he blushes; is embarrassed

box n **wópiye** n box, container ‣ **cą'ópiya ; cąwópiye** n trunk, storage box

box elder cp **cąšúška** n box elder

board n 1) **cą'ótąga** n board 2) **cąmnáska** n wooden board, plank

boarding school cp **ektá úbi owáyawa** ph boarding school

boast v **wašté'įc'ina** vi3-refl s/he boasts about himself/herself

boat n 1) **wáda** n canoe, boat, ship; engine, train 2) **mniwáda** n boat, ship

bobcat n 1) **bustĄga** n bobcat 2) **įkmúna** n bobcat

body n 1) **tacĄ ; tącĄ** n body, carcass; body and soul, whole being ‣ **wįcátacą** n human body 2) **cuwí** n waist, chest; body (animals and humans)

bodyguard n See: **guardian**

boil₁ adj v 1) **įbíǧA** vi1 it boils, is boiling ‣ **įbíȟyA** vt1-caus s/he boils smth 2) **amópša** vt1 s/he boils smth over, to a high temperature 3) **ohĄ** vt1 s/he cooks smth by boiling ‣ **wóhĄ** vi1-abs s/he cooks things by boiling

boil₂ n **šiyák'o ; šiyágo** n boil

Boxing day cp **WakĄtąga gicúni ába** np Boxing day

bomb n v **nąpómyA** vt1-caus s/he causes smth to explode, burst; bombs smth

bone n 1) **huhú** n bone, bones 2) **sihú** n bone of the lower leg

book n 1) **wa'óyabi ; wa'ówabi** n paper, letter, book 2) **wa'óyabi tĄga** cp book

boom n v **múhįknA** vi1 it is a heavy and sudden sound boom

boot n 1) **cąšíhąba** n rubber boots 2) **cáhąba háske** cp cowboy boots

border n 1) **ocągu wakĄ ; cągúwakĄ** cp Canada/ USA border; medicine line 2) **cągúsam** adv across the border 3) **cągúsampadahą** adv from across the border 4) **cągúwakĄ wa'áwąyaga** cp border patrol

bored adj **įstústA** vs s/he is bored, fed up

boringly adv **stustáyagen** adv boringly

born adj 1) **tú** vt1, vs-pass she bears a child, gives birth to sb; s/he/it is born (inflects like a stative verb when used in the passive voice with -bi) 2) **togápa** n, vs first born child in family; s/he is the oldest child in a family 3) **hokšítogapa** n first born child in a family 4) **ohágapa** n, vs youngest-born child in a family; s/he is the youngest-born child in a family

borrow v 1) **onóda** vt1 s/he borrows, rents smth ‣ **ogíjinoda** vt1-benef s/he borrows, rents smth for sb else ‣ **ogínoda** vt1-dat s/he borrows, rents smth from sb 2) **mas'ónoda** vi1 s/he borrows money

both pro conj adj 1) **nųpí ; nųpín** pro both ‣ **sinúpin** n both feet 2) **anúk** adv both sides, ways ‣ **anúkadahą** adv on each sides, ends, both ways

bother v 1) **įksamyA ; įksapyA** vt1 s/he bothers, annoys sb ‣ **wa'íksamkiyA** vi1-abs s/he pesters, causes trouble; is bothersome 2) **įgážąga** vs s/he is anxious, worried, bothered because of the lack of smth

bottle *n* **wahíyoknąga ; wahí'oknąga** n bottle, glass; jar, cooking pot

bottom *n* 1) **húde** n base of an object, bottom; rectum, bum) 2) **tihúda** n bottom of a tipi

bounce *v* 1) **mopsípsįna** vi1-redup s/he/it bounces 2) **gapsíja** vt1 s/he makes smth bounce, jump by striking; propels by striking

bow *n* **įdáziba** n bow

bowed *adj* **pamą́knena** adv with the head bowed

bowl *n* 1) **iyógapte škokpá, iyógapte oškókpa** cp bowl 2) **cą'ógapte** n wooden bowl

boy *n* 1) **hokšína** n boy (7–13 years old) ‣ **hokšínana** n-redup small boy ‣ **hokší** cont child, baby; boy (occurs in personal names) 2) **koškánana** (CTK) **; koškáškana** (OM) n-redup, vs teenage boy; he is a teenage boy 3) **gitézi** n boy, lad, kid, brat (pejorative connotation)

boyfriend *n* **kišné** n lover, boyfriend

bracelet *n* **nąbíjaške ; nąbé įjáške** n bracelet

brag *v* **įknádą** vi3-refl s/he brags about himself/herself

braid *n v* **gisú** vt1-pos s/he braids his/her own hair ‣ **pahá gisú** vt1-pos, n s/he braids his/her hair; braid ‣ **págisų** vt1-pos s/he braids his/her hair ‣ **pahá gíjisų** vt1-benef s/he braids his/her hair for him/her

brain *n* **nasú** n brain

branch *n v* **cąbáwįža** n low-hanging branch bent under its own weight 2) **žáda** vs it is forked, branched

brand *v n* 1) **špąyÁ** vt1-caus s/he cooks, bakes smth; s/he brands an animal (sheep, steer) 2) **ašpáyĄ** vt1 s/he brands a horse, cattle ‣ **šųk'ášpąyĄ** vi1 s/he brands horses 3) **šųkšpáya ; šųkšpáye** n horse brand

brassiere *n* **makú įyúskice ; makúskice** cp brassiere

brat *n* **gitézi** n boy, lad, kid, brat (pejorative connotation)

brave *adj* 1) **ohídigA** vi1, vs s/he is brave, fearless; s/he is a wealthy, prosperous person ‣

ohídiga įc'ína vi3-refl s/he thinks of herself/himself as brave, fearless 2) **wíyukcą́šį** vs s/he is bold, brave

bread *n* **ağúyabi** n flour, bread, bannock ‣ **ağúyabiwaką** n communion bread

break *v n* 1) **ksahą́** vs it is broken 2) **baksÁ** vt1 s/he breaks, cuts smth off with an instrument (like a chainsaw) ‣ **kpaksÁ** vt1 s/he breaks, fractures his/her own ‣ **óbaksA** vt1 s/he breaks smth by pressing it into a hole 3) **moksÁ** vt1 s/he breaks smth by shooting or colliding into it 4) **naksÁ** vt1 s/he breaks smth off (with the foot or by pressure) 5) **woksÁ** vt1 s/he breaks his/her word; betrays sb 6) **yuksÁ** vt1 s/he breaks, cuts, trims smth off with a tool (like scissors) ‣ **yuksáksA** vt2-redup s/he breaks smth into pieces; s/he breaks them (objects) 7) **yašpÁ** vt2 s/he breaks, cracks smth open with the teeth (like a peanut) 8) **bahókšu** vt1 s/he breaks, wrecks smth by sitting, putting his/her weight on it 9) **gahókšu** vt1 s/he breaks, wrecks, dismantles smth by hitting; the wind blows smth down 10) **nahókšu** vt1 s/he breaks, kicks smth apart 11) **yahókšu** vt2 s/he breaks up a plan verbally 12) **yuhókšu** vt2 s/he breaks, wrecks, destroys, dismantles smth 13) **yuwéğA** vt2 s/he breaks smth manually ‣ **yuwéȟweğA** vt2-redup s/he breaks many things manually 14) **gapsága** vt1 s/he/it breaks, cuts smth (rope) by hitting; the wind breaks smth; smth breaks, rips by itself 15) **nasnéjA** vt1 s/he stands on smth and breaks; breaks smth with his body weight 16) **bašíba** vt1 s/he breaks smth by putting pressure 17) **asnígiya** vi1-pos s/he rests, takes a break from his/her activity 18) **wahéc'ų** vi1-abs s/he packs things in bundles, breaks camp for traveling ‣ **wahégic'ų** vi1-abs-pos s/he packs his/her things in bundles, breaks his/her camp for traveling

breakfast *n* **hąyákena wódabi** cp breakfast

breast *n* 1a) **azé** n breast, udder 1b) **azépįkpa** n nipple, teat

breastfeed *v* **azé yazókkiyA** vt1-caus she breastfeeds a baby

breastplate *n* **huhúwanap'į** n breastplate, necklace

breath *n* 1) **niyá** vs, n s/he/it breathes, is alive; breath of life 2) **taníya** n his/her/its breath; breath, air, oxygen, atmosphere 3) **ǧa'ít'eyA** vt1 s/he exhausts, tires sb out, make sb be out of breath

breathe *v* **niyá** vs, n s/he/it breathes, is alive; breath of life

breathless *adj* 1) **taníyešį** adv breathless, out of breath 2) **tanícona** n breathless

breechcloth *n* 1) **coknága** n breechcloth ‣ **coknák** cont breechcloth 2) **coknákkitų** vt1-pos s/he wears a breechcloth

breed *v* 1) **įcáȟyA** vt1-caus s/he grows, breeds smth; raises sb ‣ **wa'įcaȟyA** vi1-abs s/he grows things, breeds animals 2) **kiyúȟa** vi1 it (animal) breeds, copulates

breezy *adj* **ganúsnuza** vimp it is breezy ‣ **ganúsnuzagen** adv with a breeze

bride *n* **wįwóȟpa** vi1 he purchases a bride ‣ **wįwóȟpabi** n bride price

bridge *n* 1) **cągáȟtųbi** n beaver dam, bridge 2) **paȟnáda** n bridge of the nose

bridle *n* **įpáȟte** n bridle hair or braid tie ‣ **mąs'įpaȟte** ; **mas'įpaȟte** n bridle and bit

bring *v* 1) **agú** vt1 s/he brings sb, smth back here ‣ **wa'águ** vi1-abs s/he brings back things ‣ **gagú** vt1-dat s/he brings sb, smth coming back here 2) **a'í** vt1 s/he takes, brings, arrives with sb, smth there 3) **akní** vt1 s/he comes with, brings sb, smth home, here ‣ **wa'ákni** vi1-abs s/he brings things back home, here ‣ **gíjakni** vt1-benef s/he brings smth back here for sb ‣ **gakní** vt1-dat s/he brings smth back here to sb 4) **a'ú** vt1 s/he brings, comes here bringing sb, smth ‣ **gíja'u** vt1-benef s/he brings,

comes here with smth for sb ‣ **ga'ú** vt1-dat s/he comes here bringing smth to sb 5) **ahí** vt1 s/he arrives here bringing sb, smth ‣ **gahí** vt1-dat s/he arrives here bringing sb, smth to him/her 6) **niyáyA** vt1 s/he heals sb, brings sb back to life 7) **kno-** pref bring his/her own (used with verbs of coming and going)

broad *adj* **otágA** vs it is broad, wide

bronc *n* **šųk'ókuwasije** n bronc

broom *n* **otígadodo** n broom

brother *n* 1) **-timno-** root older brother (female speaker); older male parallel cousin (female speaker) 2) **-cįna-** root older brother (male speaker); older male parallel cousin (male speaker) 3) **-sųga-** root younger brother (male or female speaker); younger male parallel cousin (male or female speaker) ‣ **sųgáguyA** vt1-caus s/he has him as a younger brother ‣ **sųgágugiciyabi** vi1-recip they have one another as younger brother

brother-in-law *n* 1) **-šic'e-** root brother-in-law (female speaker) 2) **-tąhą-** ; **-taȟą-** root brother-in-law (male speaker) ‣ **tahą́guyA** vt1-caus he is his brother-in-law

brown *adj* **zísabA** vs it is dark brown

brush *v* **knustó** ; **aknústo** vt1-pos s/he brushes his/her own hair

buck *v* *n* 1) **bamní** vi1 it (horse, bull) bucks ‣ **bamnímni** vi1-redup it (horse, bull) bucks repetitively 2) **šųkpámnina** n bucking horse

bucket *n* 1) **céǧa** n kettle, pot; bucket, pail ‣ **ceȟ-** cont kettle, pot; bucket, pail 2) **cáceǧa** n wooden pail

buckle *n* **įpíyaga įją́šeye** cp belt buckle

buckshot *n* **wásmuna** n buckshot

buffalo *n* 1) **pté** n buffalo (generic term); female buffalo; domestic cow (in compounds) 2) **pteská** n white, albino buffalo 3) **tatága** n male buffalo ‣ **taták** cont buffalo ‣ **tatágabina** n-pl buffalo herd 4) **ptepá** n buffalo skull 5)

pte'óye n buffalo tracks 6) **pté oyádena** cp buffalo people

buffalo berry *cp* **dágušašana** n-redup buffalo berry

buffalo dance *cp* **tatą́k wacíbi** cp buffalo dance

Buffalo hip people *nprop* **Tanį́debina** nprop Buffalo hip people (band of Nakoda)

Buffalo hoop *nprop* **Tatą́ga magé** nprop Victor Sammy's traditional name

buffalo jump *cp* **tatą́ga oȟpáye** cp buffalo jump

build *v* **ti'į́c'ijaǧA** vi3-refl s/he builds a house for himself/herself

bull *n* **ptemnóga** n bull

bull riding *cp* **pte'ágan yį́gábi** ph bull-riding

bulldog *n* 1) **šų̨kpátąga** n bulldog 2) **šų́ga įdé pšų̨ká** ph bulldog

bullet *n* 1) **sú** n seed, pellet; bullet 2) **cúú** interj imitation of the sound of a bullet

bullsnake *n* **wą́** n bullsnake

bully *v n* 1) **yužą́ga** vt2 s/he mistreats, bullies sb; picks on sb ‣ **yužą́k** vcont mistreating, bullying sb; picking on sb ‣ **knužą́ga** vt1-pos s/he mistreats, bullies his/her own; picks on his/her own (as sibling, child) 2) **waknúžąga** n cruelty, bullying

bum *n* **húde** n base of an object, bottom; rectum, bum

bumblebee *n* **tuȟmą́ȟtaga** n wasp, bumblebee

bump *v n* 1) **moȟtágA** vt1 s/he bumps, rams into sb, smth from a distance ‣ **mogíciȟtagabi** vi1-recip they bump, ram into one another from a distance 2) **įmóȟtagA** vt1 s/he bumps against smth, runs, crashes into smth 3) **modą́** vt1 s/he bumps against sb 4) **iyápa** vs s/he touches, bumps into smth; his/her/its heart is beating

bumper *n* 1) **įmóȟtage ; įmóȟtaga** n bumper 2) **togáda įmóȟtage;** cp front bumper 3) **héktam įmóȟtage** cp rear bumper

bumpy *adj* **makóškiška** n, vs rough, bumpy road; it is a rough, bumpy road

bundle *v n* 1) **obáȟta** vt1 s/he ties, packs smth into a bundle ‣ **obágiȟta** vt1-pos s/he ties, packs his/her thing into a bundle 2) **wábaȟta ; wóbaȟte** n sacred bundle 3) **wópiyena** n medicine bundle 4) **wótawa** n medicine bundle; war charm 5) **įwágaška** n bundle 6) **naǧóȟazi** n spirit bundle 7) **ok'į́wąži** n bundle packed on the back

burial *n* **wópiyabi** n burial

burn *v* 1) **huȟnáǧa** vs s/he/it is burnt, scorched ‣ **wahúȟnayA** vi1-abs s/he burns things; sets junk on fire ‣ **huȟnáȟyA** vt1-caus s/he burns, scorches smth 2) **ohúȟnaǧa** vs it burns inside (like a barrel of rubbish) ‣ **ohúȟnaȟyA** vt1-caus s/he burns smth inside (as in a barrel) 3) **įktúyA** vt1-caus s/he makes smth burn; lights smth on fire 4) **špą́** vs s/he/it is cooked; s/he/it is burned ‣ **špąyÁ** vt1-caus s/he cooks, bakes smth; s/he brands an animal (sheep, steer) ‣ **špą́'įc'iyA** vi3-refl s/he burns himself/herself 5) **sní** vs it burns out; burns itself out 6) **įzínyA** vt1-caus s/he burns incense ritually ‣ **įzítkiyA** vt1-caus s/he makes smth burn ritually ‣ **įzíngijiyA** vt1-benef s/he burns incense ritually for sb 7) **aǧúmna** vs it smells scorched, burnt 8) **yutíba** vt2 s/he scorches, burns smth

burp *v n* **abámnu** vii s/he/it belches, burps

burrowing owl *cp* **hįhą́ oȟnóga otís'a** ph burrowing owl

burst *v* 1) **bapóbA** vt1 s/he explodes, bursts smth by sitting or pressing on it ‣ **mapóbA** vt1 s/he bursts, punctures smth with a sharp tool ‣ **mopóbA** vt1 s/he explodes, bursts smth with a pointy object, a gun ‣ **nąpóbA** vi s/he/it explodes, bursts by itself 2) **namnázA** vii it bursts, splits open (by internal force)

bury *v* 1) **piyá** vt1 s/he buries sb, smth ‣ **pigíyA** vt1-pos s/he buries his/her own relative 2) **agáhi** vt1 s/he buries, covers smth, sb up with mud, earth

bush *n See:* **forest**

bustle *n* **amį́knągabi** n dance bustle, Crow belt

busy *adj* **šką** vt1, vi1 s/he tries to do smth; s/he is busy; s/he moves, behaves; s/he feels thus

but *conj* 1) **duká ; oká ; ųká** conj but, although, even though 2) **éyaš** conj but, and yet 3) **kéš** conj but, but invariably, but instead

butcher *v n* 1) **pádA** vt1 s/he butchers an animal ‣ **wapádA** vi1-abs s/he butchers meat 2) **tanó owópetų** cp butcher shop

butter *n* **asábi wíkni** cp butter

butterfly *n* 1) **tatók'ana** n butterfly 2) **gimámąna ; gimáminą** n-redup butterfly

buttocks *n-pl* 1) **ųzé** n buttocks 2) **ųzíkpakįdA** vi1-pos, n s/he wipes his/her own buttocks; toilet paper

button *n* **ijáše** n button, safety pin

buy *v n* **opétų** vt1 s/he buys, purchases smth ‣ **opégijitų** vt1-benef s/he buys smth for sb ‣ **opégitų** vt1-dat s/he buys smth from sb ‣ **wópetų** vi1-abs, n s/he buys things; merchant

buzz *v n* **ȟmúyahą** vi1, n s/he/it buzzes, rumbles, emits a buzzing sound (motor, airplane, bee); rattle, band instrument

buzzard *n* **hejá** n buzzard, turkey vulture

by *prep* this preposition has no single word equivalent in Nakoda; it is expressed either by the verb itself or by an instrumental prefix

C

cabbage *n* **waȟpé tága** cp cabbage; lettuce

cabin *n* **cą'óti** n log cabin

cache *v n* See: **save**

cake *n* **ağúyabiskuya** (PR) n cake, cookie

calendar *n* **hąwíyawa** n calendar

calf *n* **ptecíjana** n calf

Calgary (Alberta) *ngeo* **Wįcíspayazą** ngeo Calgary (Alberta)

call *n v* 1) **egíya ; ejíya** vt1-dat; vs-pass s/he tells sb smth; s/he/it is called (by a name) 2) **gicó** vt1-dat s/he invites sb; calls sb ‣ **gicíyabi** vi1-recip

they call one another ‣ **šųgícoco** vt1-redup s/he calls his/her own dogs 3) **cažéyadA** vt2 s/he calls sb's name

calm *adj v* 1) **amnézena** vimp it is calm, a day without a breeze 2) **škášį** adv calm, still, quiet

camera *n* **wįcíde éyagu** vt2, n s/he photographs, takes a picture of sb; makes a footage of sb; camera

cameraman *n* **wį'íde éyagu wįcášta** ph cameraman

camp *n v* 1) **éti** vi1 s/he camps there (in a remote place) ‣ **o'éti** n campground, campsite 2) **ho-** pref camp circle, round enclosure ‣ **hocógam** adv inside a camp circle ‣ **hogákna** adv along, around the camp circle ‣ **hogíyes'a** n camp crier ‣ **howókša** adv around the camp circle 3) **ti'ókša ; tiwókša** adv around the house, camp 4) **wahéc'ų** vi1-abs s/he packs things in bundles, breaks camp for traveling ‣ **wahégic'ų** vi1-abs-pos s/he packs his/her things in bundles, breaks his/her camp for traveling 5) **ti'íyaza** adv from house to house; all throughout camp

camp crier *cp* 1) **hogíyes'a** n camp crier 2) **hóta'į** vi1 s/he cries for help in a ritual way (like in a vision quest); camp crier

campsite *n* **otúweda** n abandoned campsite

can *modal* See: **able**

Canada *ngeo* 1) **Cągúsam** ngeo United States of America; Canada 2) **Cąwám** ngeo Canada

cancer *n* **ȟníbi tága** cp cancer

candidate *n* **akínįjabi** n candidate

candy *n* 1) **cąšmúyabi pšųkáka** cp candy 2) **šašána** vs-redup, n it is orange; candies (idiolectal)

cane *n* **sakné** (CTK) ; **sakyé** (OM) n cane, crutch ‣ **saknégitų** vt1-pos s/he uses his/her cane

cannabis *n* **peží wįtkó** cp marijuana, cannabis See: **drug**

cannibal *n* **wįcáwodes'a** n cannibal, maneater

cannon *n* **cótąktąga** n-redup cannon

canoe *n* 1) **wadó** n canoe 2) **įwádopa** n canoe 3) **wáda** n canoe, boat, ship; engine, train ‣ **tąbáwada** n birchbark canoe

canvas *n* **wíšoga** n canvas

canyon *n* **okíyukse** n canyon

car *n* 1) **iyécįgayena ; iyécįgana ; iyécįga ; iyécįgena** n car, automobile 2) **iyécįgamani** n car 3) **amógiyą ; amúgiyą ; įmúgiya** (archaic) n car, automobile

card *n* 1) **wa'óyabi** n card game 2) **įȟpékiyA** vt1-dat s/he throws smth at sb; s/he deals the cards; s/he leaves smth for sb

cardboard *n* **wa'óyabi šóga** cp cardboard

cardinal *adj* **tadé'uya** n cardinal directions, world quarters ‣ **tadé'uya dóba** cp four cardinal directions

cards *n* **wa'óyabi ecúbina** cp deck of cards

care *v n* 1) **awáyagA** vt2 s/he cares, watches, looks after sb, smth ‣ **awágiciyagabi** vi1-recip they watch, care for one another ‣ **awágijiknagA** vt1-benef s/he watches, cares for sb, smth for him/her ‣ **awáknagA** vt1-pos s/he cares, watches over his/her own ‣ **awá'įc'įknagA** vi3-refl s/he cares for himself/herself 2) **kuwá** vt1 s/he/it chases, hunts, goes after sb, smth; s/he treats, acts toward, cares for sb, smth ‣ **gicúwa** vt1-pos s/he treats, acts toward, cares for his/her own 3) **įknúhA** vi3-refl s/he keeps himself/herself in a certain state; cares for himself/herself 4) **įknígešį** vt1 s/he does not care for sb, smth; s/he does not pay attention to sb, smth

carefully *adv* 1) **dąyągen** adv carefully, fairly well, properly, with ease 2) **įwáštena** adv slowly, carefully, softly 3) **owáštena** adv slowly, carefully

carelessly *adv* **waktášį** adv carelessly

caress *v* **giknǫ** vt1 s/he pampers, cuddles, caresses, sweet talks to sb

carpenter *n* 1) **tigáȟes'a** n carpenter 2) **cągážibe** n carpenter

carrier *n* 1) **k'į** vt1, n s/he carries sb, smth on the back; carrier 2) **iyážo k'įbi** n whistle carrier

carrot *n* 1) **típsinaǧi** n carrot 2) **píȟpiǧana** n carrot

carry *v* 1) **k'į** vt1, n s/he carries sb, smth on the back; carrier ‣ **k'íya** adv carrying sb, smth on the back ‣ **k'įkíyA** vt1-caus s/he causes sb to carry smth; s/he hitches, loads smth on sb ‣ **cąk'į** vi1 s/he carries wood on the back 2) **wak'įgitų** vi1-abs s/he carries things on the back 3) **yuhá** vt2, adv s/he has, possesses smth; s/he carries sb, smth; s/he gave birth to a child; s/he holds smth (meeting, ceremony); s/he keeps, looks after, treats sb, smth; carry, hold, have with one (precedes verbs of traveling) ‣ **gíjiyuhA** vt1-benef s/he has, keeps, carries smth for sb ‣ **yuhákiyA** vt1-caus s/he makes sb have, carry, keep smth ‣ **knuhÁ** vt1-pos s/he has his/her own thing, carries, keeps smth with him/her ‣ **yuháši** vt1 s/he orders sb to carry smth ‣ **knuháši** vt1-pos s/he orders his/her own to carry smth ‣ **yuhá máni** vi1 s/he walks carrying smth ‣ **knuhá máni** vi1 s/he walks carrying his/her own 4) **cąknúhA** vi1-pos s/he carries his/her own wood 5) **yapÁ** vt2 s/he carries, puts smth in the mouth ‣ **knapÁ** vt1-pos s/he carries, puts smth in his/her mouth

Carry The Kettle people *nprop* 1) **Céǧa K'įna wįcášta** nprop Carry The Kettle people (band of Nakoda living in Carry The Kettle, Saskatchewan) 2) **Wazíȟe wįcášta** nprop Carry The Kettle people (band of Nakoda living in Carry The Kettle, Saskatchewan)

Carry The Kettle (Saskatchewan) *ngeo* **Céǧa K'įna** ngeo Carry The Kettle reservation (Saskatchewan)

cartilage *n* **huhú mnumnúǧe** cp cartilage

cartridge *n* **įyókšu** n cartridge; shotgun

case *n* **gamúbiha** n drum case

casino *n* **o'écuna ; o'écuna tíbi** n gaming house, casino

cast *v n See:* **throw**

castrate *v* 1) **susú éyagu** vt2 s/he castrates a male 2) **susú maksÁ** vt1 s/he gelds, castrates an animal

castrated *adj* **susú éyagubi** cp castrated male

cat *n* **búza** n cat ▸ **bus-** cont cat, feline ▸ **buskúwa** vi1 s/he chases cats ▸ **bus'óye** n cat, feline tracks

catbird *n* **wasnásnaheja** n-redup kingbird; catbird

catch *v n* 1) **yúzA** vt2 s/he holds, pulls, grabs, nabs, catches sb, smth; s/he marries sb 2) **yukábA** vt2 s/he catches a rapid or flying object with the hand

catcher *n* **yukám-nažį** n catcher

caterpillar *n* 1) **wahpétaheya** n caterpillar 2) **wamnúška hišmášmą** cp caterpillar

catfish *n* **hopútįhį yuká** cp catfish

Catholic *n adj* 1) **šinásaba** n Catholic priest 2) **šinásaba wašíjuwaką ; šinásaba wįcáwaką** cp Catholic priest

cattail *n* 1) **hįcá** n cattail ▸ **hįcáhu** n cattail stalk 2) **hįktá** n cattail fuzz 3) **gamúbi** n drum; cattail stem and fuzz 4) **psá** n cattail root

cattle *n* **ptewánuwą** n cattle, domestic cow

cattle call *cp* **hotúbi** n cattle call

cause *v n* 1) **-kiyA** suff s/he makes, allows, lets sb do smth (triggers e-ablaut and attaches to contracted verbs) 2) **-yA** suff s/he causes, makes, lets sb do it; causes, lets sb be in a state or condition 3) **-giyA ; -kiyA** suff s/he causes one's own to do smth (possessive form of the causative -yA; creates transitive verbs from stative ones; -kiyA is used after a consonant) 4) **yu-** pref s/he/it causes sb, smth to be

cave *n* **makóȟnoga** n cave

caved *adj* **škokpá** vs it is hollow, caved in

cavity *n* **hí oȟnóga** cp cavity

Cayuse *n* **šuk'įkceya** n Cayuse, horse or pony of little value

ceasefire *n* **gicízabišį** n peace, ceasefire

cedar *n* 1) **hatéša** n cedar, red cedar 2) **a'íkpoǧa** vi3-refl, n s/he blows smth (medicine, perfume) on himself/herself; cedar; Indian perfume (sweet pine, cedar)

cellar *n* **ti'ókun** n cellar, cold storage room

cemetery *n* **owápiye** n grave, cemetery

census *n* **wįcášta wįcáyawabi** cp census

cent *n* 1) **mázaša** n penny, cent; copper 2) **gašpábi** n twenty-five cents, quarter ▸ **gašpábi okíse** cp dime, ten cents 3) **mázaska hągé** cp fifty cents

center *n* 1) **ocógan** adv in the center, middle 2) **ticógam ti'ócogamkiya** adv, adv in the center of a camp circle, room, toward the center of a camp circle, room

ceremony *n* 1a) **ecúbi** n ceremony 1b) **wó'ecu** n work, occupation, ceremony 2) **wacégiyabi** n prayer, ceremony 3) **Cąnúba oȟpáǧa ecúbi** ph Pipe ceremony 4) **Gisníwįcayabi ecúbi** cp Healing ceremony 5) **Hąhébi wanáǧi wówįcak'ubi** ph Feed the night spirits ceremony 6) **inípi ecúbi** cp sweat lodge ceremony 7) **Įwážikte** n First kill ceremony 8) **Mayáwašiju wowįcak'ubi** ph Feed the little people ceremony 9) **Pežúda éyagu ecúbi** ph Medicine Ceremony 10) **Šukcíjana woȟábi ecúbi** ph Puppy soup ceremony 11) **Wahíkiyabi ecúbi** cp Yuwipi, Tie up, Calling of the spirits ceremony; shaking tent 12) **wakpámni ecúbi** cp giveaway ceremony

chain *n* **maskáȟa** n chain

chair *n* 1) **cą'ágan yįgábi** (CTK) **; cą'ágan yągábi ; cą'ágan** (PR, OM, WB) cp chair 2) **įbáhuhuza** n rocking chair

chairman *np* **cą'ágan yįgábi wįcášta** np chairman

chalk *n See:* **pen**

change *v n* **hatókągic'u** vt1-pos s/he changes his/her own clothes

chapped *adj* **ȟpuȟpú** vs s/he/it is chapped, scaly, rough

chaps *n-pl* **wíc'į huská** cp chaps

charge *v n* **takpéya** vt1 s/he/it charges, runs against, attacks sb ‣ **takpégiciyabi** vi1-recip they charged one another

charm *n v* **wótawa** n medicine bundle; war charm

chase *v n* 1) **kuwá** vt1 s/he/it chases, hunts, goes after sb, smth; s/he treats, acts toward, cares for sb, smth) ‣ **gikúwa** vt1-pos s/he treats, acts toward, cares for his/her own ‣ **biskúwa** vi1 s/he chases, looks for gophers ‣ **buskúwa** vi1 s/he chases cats ‣ **šukkúwa** vi1 s/he chases, handles, pursues horses ‣ **wikúwa** vi1 he chases, courts, flirts with a woman 2) **hamyÁ** vt1-caus s/he scares, chases smth (animal) away

Chase the pot dance *ph* **Cehkúwabi** n Chase the pot dance

chatterbox *n* 1) **i'épina** n chatterbox 2) **eyés'a** n chatterbox, blabbermouth 3) **ižága** n chatterbox (archaic)

cheap *adj adv* **tehįšį** vi1 it is easy; it is cheap

cheat *v* **kténa** vt1 s/he cheats, beats sb (in a game) ‣ **gicíktebina** vi1-recip they cheat, defeat one another

cheater *n* **kténas'a** n cheater

check *v* **wąyák í** vt1 s/he went to check on sb, smth *See:* **examine**

cheek *n* **tapú ; tapó** n cheek

cheer *v n* 1) **gíjibąhą** vt1-benef s/he cheers for sb 2) **agíš'a** vi1 s/he cheers, emits a war cry

cheese *n* **asábi sudá** cp cheese

cheesecloth *n* **ğąğána** n cheesecloth, gauze

cherish *v* **tehína** vt1 s/he loves, holds on to smth, cherishes sb (like a relative), prizes smth and does not want to part with it

chest *n* 1) **makú** n chest 2) **cuwí** n waist; chest 3) **cešká** n upper chest

chew *v n* 1) **yatÁ** vt2 s/he chews smth 2) **yahnógA** vt1 s/he/it gnaws a hole in smth, chews smth up (like a mouse chewing on clothes) 3) **yakpá** vt2 s/he chews smth in fine pieces 4) **yaksÁ** vt2

s/he bites, chews smth off 5) **yasmísmí** vt2-redup s/he cleans the meat off a bone with the teeth; s/he chews it clean

Cheyenne *nprop* **Šahíyena** nprop Cheyenne people, person of Cheyenne descent

chick *n* **ąbáhotųna cijána** cp chick

chickadee *n* 1) **waníyedu úbis'a** ph chickadee 2) **gísabana** n chickadee

chicken *n* 1) **ąbáhotųna ; ąbáhotų** n chicken 2) **šiyó** n prairie chicken, pheasant, grouse; chicken

chief *n* 1) **hųgá** n, vs, cont chief, king; he is a chief, chief *Cont:* **hųk-** ; **hų-** 2) **agícida wi'óti hųgá** np chief of the warrior lodge

child *n* 1) **cijá** n child; one's child ‣ **cij-** cont child ‣ **cijáyA** vt1 s/he adopts a child ‣ **cijódA** vs-coll s/he has many children; there are many children 2) **hokší** cont child, baby; boy (occurs in personal names) 3) **hokšícijage** n favored child 4) **hokšína wąyágabi** cp childcare 5) **inína úbi** ph silent child 6) **júsisibina** n-pl-redup children, little children 7) **gitézi** n boy, lad, kid, brat (pejorative connotation) 8) **nigé tahésaga** cp little children 9) **ohágapa** vs, n s/he is the youngest child in a family; youngest child in a family 10) **togápa** vs, n s/he is the oldest child in a family; first-born child 11) **tų́** vt1 s/he wears smth; s/he bears smth; she bears a child, gives birth 12) **yuhÁ** vt2 s/he has, possesses smth; s/he carries sb, smth; s/he gave birth to a child; s/he holds smth (meeting, ceremony); s/he keeps, looks after, treats sb, smth; carry, hold, have with one (precedes verbs of traveling) 13) **duwéni aktúguyešį** cp illegitimate child

child-in-law *n* -tagošku- root child-in-law

chill *n* **hníyą** vs s/he has the chills

chin *n* 1) **įkú** n chin 2) **cehúba** n chin and jaw area

Chinook (Montana) *ngeo* **Tiská óda** ngeo Chinook (Montana)

chipmunk *n* 1) **cąyúpipina** n-redup chipmunk 2) **iyópsipsijamna** n-redup chipmunk

3) **cąkáhukneknegˇana** n-redup striped chipmunk

Chippewa *nprop See:* **Saulteaux**

choke *v* 1) **gaktÁ** vi1 s/he chokes on smth 2) **yahóda** vi2 s/he chokes, gags on smth

chokecherry *n* 1) **cąpá** n chokecherry; pin cherry ‣ **cą-** cont chokecherry 2) **cągáški** vi1 s/he pounds chokecherries

choose *v* 1) **gaȟníğA** vt1 s/he selects, chooses sb, smth; elects, votes for sb 2) **kÁ** vt1 s/he/it means smth, indicates sb, smth; s/he chooses smth, sb 3) **įjú** vt1 s/he chooses sb, smth

chop *v* 1) **gaksÁ** vt1 s/he cuts, chops smth with a tool (axe) ‣ **gíjaksA** vt1-benef s/he cuts, chops smth for him/her ‣ **gaksáksA** vt1-redup s/he chops smth into pieces ‣ **cągáksaksA** vi1-redup s/he chops wood into kindling; chops wood ‣ **kijáksA** vt1 s/he cuts, chops smth in two with a tool; s/he disobeys, breaks a rule, law 2) **gasnéjA** vt1 s/he chops smth in two, splits smth in two by hitting

Christian *n adj* **wócegiya óhą ų́** vi1 vii s/he/it is Christian

Christmas *n* 1) **ą́bawaką tą́ga** cp Christmas 2) **owótkeya ą́ba** cp Christmas 3) **waką́tąga cįhį́tku yuhábi ą́ba** ph Christmas

chubby *adj* **ašį́tųgeja** vs s/he/it is kind of fat, chubby

church *n* 1a) **owácegiya** n church (building or institution) 1b) **owácegiya tíbi** cp church (building) 2) **wócegiya** n medicine ceremony; church service

churn *v* **moská** vt1 s/he churns smth (butter)

cigar *n* 1) **cąníska tą́ga** n cigar 2) **cąnísaba** n cigar

cigarette *n* **cąníska** cp cigarette

cinch *n* **nigˇé įpáȟta** cp cinch, bellyband

circle *n* 1) **o'ípa mįmą́** cp circle 2) **gamímą** vi1 s/he/it forms a circle ‣ **gamímeya** adv in a circle 3) **mįméya** adv roundly, circularly, in circles 4) **ho-** pref camp circle, round enclo-sure ‣ **hocógam** adv inside a camp circle *See:* **round**

circling *adj* **agáwįȟ** vcont circling

circus *n* **owábazo** n circus

city *n* 1) **ti'ódatąga** n city 2) **otų́we ; otų́ye** n city

clatter *v* 1) **šúža** vimp it clatters 2) **kokyÁ** vt1-caus s/he/it produces a clattering, clicking sound ‣ **kokyéna** adv in a clattering manner

claw *n See:* **nail**

clay *n* **makáto** n clay

clean *adj v* 1) **yudódo** vt2 s/he cleans smth ‣ **knudódo** vt1-pos s/he cleans his/her own ‣ **gíjiyudodo** vt1/2-benef s/he cleans smth for sb 2) **yudáda** vt2 s/he cleans smth (sweep, dust, wipe) ‣ **tiyúdada** vi2 s/he cleans, tidies up a house 3) **wapíwacį** vs s/he/it is clean 4) **bakį́dA** vt1 s/he wipes, brushes sb, smth off; cleans the surface of smth ‣ **gíjibakįdA** vt1-benef s/he wipes, cleans sb else's (body part) 5) **basmíyą** vt1 s/he clears, cleans the surface of smth ‣ **įbásmiyą** vt1 s/he clears, cleans the surface with smth 6) **yasmį́smį** vt2-redup s/he cleans the meat off a bone with the teeth; s/he chews it clean 7) **nakį́dA** vt1 s/he scrapes smth clean with the foot ‣ **nagíkįdA** vt1-pos s/he scrapes, cleans, wipes his/her own feet 8) **tiyúžaža** vi2 s/he cleans a house; washes the floor 9) **íyuzˇųna** vt2 s/he cleans a new-born's mouth

clear *v adj* 1) **mnézA** vs it is clear, pure, transparent ‣ **mnesyá** adv clearly, in a clear manner 2) **omnézena** vimp it is clear (liquid) 3) **knaptá** vimp it (weather) cleared up 4) **gasódA** vi, vt1 it (sky) cleared up; s/he massacres, wipes out sb 5) **basmíyą** vt1 s/he clears, cleans the surface of smth 6) **gadáda** vt1 s/he shakes off, clears smth off

clearing *n* **otį́da** n clearing, opening without trees, prairies

clearly *adv* 1) **mnesyá** adv clearly, in a clear manner ‣ **mnesyágen** adv clearly 2) **šnayą́ ; šna'íyą** adv clearly, in plain sight

clench *v* **yuskáska** vt2-redup s/he clenches smth in the hand

clever *adj* See: **knowledgeable**

cliff *n* **mayá** n cliff, bluff

climb *v n* 1) **aní** vt1 s/he steps, climbs, walks over smth ‣ **aníni** vt1-redup s/he steps, climbs, walk over smth here and there 2) **iyáni ; i'áni** vt1 s/he/it climbs on sb, smth ‣ **kiyáni** vi1 s/he arrives back there climbing up 3) **cą́'áni ; cą'íyani** vi1 s/he climbs up a tree

climber *n* **anís'a** n climber

clinic *n* **pežúda wašíjuti** cp clinic, medical office

clock *n* 1) **hąwígağabi** n clock, timer 2) **hąwí akída** cp clock 3) **wináhomni** n clock

close₁ *v* 1) **natágA** vt1 s/he closes, locks, shuts smth; it (wind) closes it; turns it off ‣ **nagítagA** vt1-pos s/he closes, shuts his/her own 2) **įstókmuza; įstókmus** vi1, vcont s/he closes the eyes, with the eyes closed 3) **íkmuza** vi1 s/he/it has his/her/its mouth closed ‣ **íkmus** vcont with the mouth closed

close₂ *adv* 1) **kiyą́na** adv close, nearby ‣ **kiyą́naȟ** adv very close, pretty close 2) **kiyéna** adv close to 3) **éduna** adv close ‣ **édunaȟ** adv close by, near ‣ **néduna** adv near, close to here ‣ **nédunaȟ** adv very near, close to here 4) **aškáyena** adv close

cloth *n* 1) **wağéyaga** n prayer cloth 2) **wó'įye** n cloth offering used in Sun dances

clothes *n* 1) **hayábi** n clothes, costume, suit ‣ **hayábi oktéyabi** cp clothes hanger ‣ **hayábi opíye** cp suitcase ‣ **hayábi owópetų** cp clothing store ‣ **wówaši hayábi** cp working clothes ‣ **hatéja** n new clothes 2) **gağábi** n clothes 3) **wokóyage** n clothes, fancy clothes, outfit 4) **babódA** vt1 s/he wears out a piece of cloth-

ing 5) **gic'ų́** vt1-pos s/he wears his/her own (clothes, jewelry) 6) **hatókągic'ų** vt1-pos s/he changes his/her own clothes

clothing store *cp* **hayábi owópetų tíbi** cp clothing store

cloud *n* **maȟpíya** n sky, heavens; cloud ‣ **maȟpíyakta** adv to the clouds

cloudburst *n* **amáȟpiya naȟnéjA** vimp there is a cloudburst, a sudden heavy rainfall

cloudy *adj* 1) **amáȟpiya** vimp, n it is cloudy; cloud 2) **a'óhązi** vimp it is cloudy, overcast

clown *v n* 1) **wįktogağA, wįtkótkogağA** vi1 s/he makes a fool out of himself/herself; fool dancer, clown 2) **wįktóya** adv clowning, foolishly

Clown dance *cp* **Wįtkógağe wacíbi, Wįtkógağa wacíbi** cp Clown or Fool dance

clubfoot *n* **siháškoba** n clubfoot

coach *n* **tamyúkaba įtącą** cp baseball coach

coal *n* 1) **makáhasaba** n coal 2) **caȟóda** n ashes; coal ‣ **caȟóda océti** cp coal stove

coat *n* 1) **cuwíknąga** n coat, shirt ‣ **cuwíknąga hąska** cp long coat, shirt 2) **ókne** n coat; sleeve ‣ **oknécona** n sleeveless vest

cobweb *n* 1) **ȟeȟágągana wakmúğa** cp cobweb 2) **wosúsubina** n cobweb

coconut *n* **yahúgabi tą́ga** cp coconut

coffee *n* **huȟnáȟyabi** n coffee, coffee beans

coil *v n* **gakšá** vt1 s/he coils, rolls smth up

cold₁ *adj n* 1) **sní** vs s/he/it is cold 2) **osní** vimp it is cold weather ‣ **osnísni** vimp-redup it is very cold weather ‣ **osnídahą** adv from, because of the cold ‣ **osníkna** vi1 s/he/it feels cold 3) **ąm'ósni** vimp it is a cold day 4) **bus'ósni** vimp it is a dry cold 5) **ti'ósni** vimp it is a cold dwelling, house 6) **cuwída** vs s/he is cold, chilly (used with animate referents only)

cold₂ *n* **hoȟpábi** n cough, cold

cold sore *cp* **iháȟni** n cold sore

collar *n v* **šųktáwap'i** n horse collar

collarbone *n* **cemnóhu** n collarbone, clavicle

collect *v* **mnayÁ** vt1-caus s/he collects smth; gathers smth, sb ‣ **wamnáyÁ** vi1-abs s/he gathers, collects things

collector *n* **wamnáyas'a** n collector

collide *v* **mo-** pref by colliding into smth with a vehicle

color *n* **okmábi** n color, mark, written production, writing process

colt *n* **šuȟpéna** n colt

comb *n v* 1) **ibákca ; pahá ibákca** n, cp comb, hairbrush 2) **bakcá** vt1 s/he combs, brushes sb, smth ‣ **kpakcá** vt1-pos s/he combs his/her own

come *v* 1) **ú** vi1 s/he comes, arrives here from there ‣ **gíji'u** vt1-benef s/he comes here instead of sb ‣ **ukíyA** vt1-caus s/he makes sb come here ‣ **úna** vi1 s/he (child, little animal) comes, arrives here from there 2) **gú** vi1 s/he comes back here 3) **gúwa** vi1 come here (imperative form only) 4) **kninápa** vi1 s/he comes out, emerges 5) **giní** vi1 s/he comes back to life, wakes up (from hibernation)

comfort *v n* 1) **yu'ásni** vt2 s/he comforts, soothes sb 2) **honínyA** vt1 s/he comforts sb (like sb who is mourning) ‣ **honín-giciyabi** vi1-recip they comfort one another

command *n* 1) **wo** encl indicates a command made to a single person by a male speaker (singular male imperative) 2) **bo** encl indicates a command made to two or more persons by a male speaker (plural male imperative) 3) **m** encl indicates a command made to one or many persons (male and female imperative) 4) **-ši** vt1-dit-aux s/he tells, asks, orders, commands sb (attaches or follows a preceding verb)

committee *n* **wací okónagiciye** cp dance committee

common *adj n* **ikcé** adv common ‣ **ikcéya** adv in a common, ordinary, usual way

common water-crowfoot *cp* **á'ana sihá** cp common water-crowfoot

compact *v adj* **gasúda** vimp the wind compacts the snow

complete *v* **iktúsyA ; itkúsyA** vt1-caus s/he finishes, completes smth ‣ **iktúskiyA ; itkúskiyA** vt1-pos s/he finishes, completes his/her own task

computer *n* 1) **iyáweȟtiya** n computer 2) **owókma wayágabi** cp computer

concerned *adj* **ihákta** vt1 s/he is concerned for sb out of love

conference *n* **omníjiye tága** cp conference

confess *v* **oknágA** vt1-pos s/he tells his/her own (story, news); s/he confesses

confirm *v* **yusúda** vt2 s/he hardens, toughens smth; confirms smth

confused *adj* **iciknuni** vs s/he is confused

congratulate *v* **ya'óniha** vt2 s/he congratulates, honors sb by speech; s/he brags about smth

conjure *v* **wakáȟ'a** vi1 s/he conjures

connect *v* 1) **koyákyA** vt1 s/he connects, fastens smth to it; hangs smth 2) **ikóyakyA** vt1 s/he ties, harnesses smth, connects them together (to a horse or wagon)

consecrate *v* 1) **awákayA** vt1-caus s/he blesses, consecrates sb 2) **yuwáka** vt2 s/he consecrates, blesses sb, smth with the hands

consider *v* 1) **-na** suff s/he considers, rates, has regard for sb, smth (attaches to stative verbs and triggers e-ablaut) 2) **-kiyA** suff s/he considers, regards sb, smth as (attaches to stative verbs)

considerate *adj* 1) **tawáci dayá** vs s/he is considerate 2) **cadé yuká** vs s/he is considerate

console *v* **catkáspeyA** vt1-caus s/he consoles, tends to sb's heart

constipate *v* **cesní oyátaga** vs s/he/it is constipated

contest *n See:* **game**

continously *adv* **yigÁ ; yagÁ** vi3-aux s/he remains doing, does continously; stays

continue *v* 1) **yuhá'u** vt1 s/he continues having

smth 2) **áyA** vi2-aux s/he does it continuously, constantly

control *v n* 1) **tayúzA** vt2 s/he controls sb, smth 2) **knaškį́yą** vi1 s/he is crazy, out of control, insane ‣ **knaškį́škįyą** vi1-redup s/he is very crazy, out of control

convince *v* **yamná** vt2 s/he acquires smth by speech; convinces sb about smth ‣ **yamnáya** adv acquiring smth by speech; convincing, gossiping

cook *v n* 1) **ohą́** vt1 s/he cooks smth by boiling ‣ **wóhą** vi1-abs s/he cooks things by boiling ‣ **wóhena** n cook 2) **špąyą́** vt1 s/he cooks, bakes smth; s/he brands an animal (sheep, steer) ‣ **wašpą́yĄ** vi1-abs s/he cooks things ‣ **špągíyA** vt1-pos s/he bakes, cooks his/her own ‣ **wašpą́įc'iyA** vi3-refl s/he cooks for himself/herself ‣ **awášpąyĄ** vi1 s/he cooks a feast ‣ **wašpáyes'a** n cook, chef 3) **co'ų́ba** vt1 s/he roasts; fries; cooks smth ‣ **wacó'ųba** vi1-abs s/he roasts, fries, cooks things ‣ **wacó'įc'iba** vi3-abs-refl s/he cooks smth for himself/herself ‣ **cogíjiba** vt1-benef s/he cooks smth for sb 4) **yužá** vt2 s/he cooks smth into a stew; puts smth in a stew ‣ **wóža** vi1-abs s/he cooks things (into a stew, porridge)

cooked *adj* **špą́** *vs* s/he/it is cooked; s/he/it is burned

cookie *n* 1) **ağúyabi skuskúyena** (CTK) cp-redup cookie 2) **ağúyabiskuya** (PR) n cake, cookie

cool *adj v* 1) **sniyÁ** vt1 s/he cools smth off ‣ **snigíyA** vt1-pos s/he cools off his/her own ‣ **snigíjiyA** vt1-benef s/he cools smth off for him/her ‣ **sniyą́** adv cold, cool condition 2) **bohpóğa** vt1-redup s/he blows on smth; cools smth by blowing on it repetitively

cooler *n* **snigíyabi** n ice cooler

coot *n* **cahpá** n American coot, mud hen

co-parent-in-law *n* **omówahįtų** n co-parent-in-law

copper *n* **mázaša** n penny, cent; copper

cord *n* **cą'į́yutabi** n cord of wood

corn *n* **wakmúhaza ; wakmúhąza** n corn

cornball *n* **wamópąbi** n cornball (pemmican made of grounded corn)

corpse *n* **wįcát'a** n human corpse, dead person

corral *n* 1) **ošų́kyuze** n corral 2) **cągáĥa** n corral ‣ **tatą́ga cągáĥa** cp buffalo corral, fence 3) **pte'ónažį** n corral

correct *adj v* **yu'écedu** vt2 s/he corrects, realigns smth

costume *n* **wacíbi įknúza** cp costume

cotton *n* **įkcé zizíbena** cp cotton

cougar *n* 1) **búzatąga** n cougar 2) **įkmútąga** n cougar

cough *v n* 1a) **hohpÁ** vi1 s/he coughs 1b) **hohpábi** n cough, cold 2) **gahóhpA** vt1 s/he causes sb to cough by hitting

could *modal See:* **able**

coulee *n* 1) **gahé** n ravine, coulee, cut bank; mountain, hill 2) **osmą́ga** n coulee; crease 3) **opáya** adv through, along, following the course of smth; in, through a valley, coulee

council *n* **ceškámaza** n council, alliance (refers to council members to whom a badge was given); police officer (used in Carry The Kettle)

count *v n* 1) **yawá** vt2 s/he counts smth; s/he reads smth ‣ **wayáwa** vi2-abs s/he counts things; s/he reads things, has the ability to read; s/he studies, goes to school, is a student ‣ **giyáwa** vt1-dat s/he reads smth to him/her ‣ **įknáwa** vi3-refl s/he counts himself/herself in 2) **sám ; sąm** post beyond, over; and, in addition to (when used in counting it is placed between decades and cardinal numbers, and between hundreds and decades)

countertop *n* **o'ékne** n countertop

coup *n* **iyóhi** vt1, vs s/he reaches smth; s/he counts a coup; it extends, is long enough

court₁ *v* 1) **kuwága** vt1 s/he courts sb 2) **wįkúwA** vi1 he chases, courts, flirts with a woman

court₂ *n* **owáyaco** n court, courthouse ▸ **owáyacotąga** n supreme court

cousin *n* 1) **-cųna-** root older sister (female speaker); older female parallel cousin (female speaker) 2) **-tąga- ; -tą-** root younger sister (female speaker); female parallel cousin (female speaker) 3a) **-timno-** root older brother (female speaker); older male parallel cousin (female speaker) 3b) **-timnona-** root older male parallel cousin (female speaker) 4) **-cįna-** root older brother (male speaker); older male parallel cousin (male speaker) 5) **-tągena ; -tąguna** root older sister (male speaker), older female parallel cousin (male speaker) 6) **-sųga-** root younger brother (male speaker); younger male parallel cousin (male speaker) 7) **-šijepąši-** root female cross-cousin (female speaker) 8) **-šic'eši-** root male cross-cousin (female speaker) 9) **-hągaši-** root female cross-cousin (male speaker) 10) **-tąhąši-** root male cross-cousin (male speaker)

cover *v n* 1) **agáȟpA** vt1 s/he covers sb, smth with it (blanket, lid, roof) ▸ **aknáȟpA** vt1-pos s/he covers his/her own ▸ **a'íknaȟpA** vi3-refl s/he covers himself/herself with smth like mud, earth, leaves 2) **agáȟpe ; iyágaȟpa ; iyágaȟpe** n cover, lid 3) **óǧe** vt1 s/he wraps, covers up smth with it ▸ **ógiǧe** vt1-pos s/he covers his/her own with it 4) **agáhi** vt1 s/he buries, covers sb, smth up with mud, earth

cow *n* 1) **pté** n buffalo (generic term); female buffalo; domestic cow (in compounds) 2) **ptewíyena** n female buffalo, domestic cow 3) **ptewánųwą** n cattle, domestic cow

coward *adj* **onįkte wacį** vi1 s/he is meek, submissive; s/he is a coward

cowboy *n* 1) **na'ųkce** n cowboy 2) **pte'áwąyage** n cowboy

co-wife *n* **-teya-** root co-wife (obsolete)

coyote *n* **šųkcúk'ana** n coyote

crabapple *n* **taspąspąna** n-redup hawthorn berries; crabapple

crack *v n* 1) **gaȟúga** vt1 s/he cracks smth; cracks smth open; crushes smth with a tool 2) **yaȟúga** vt2 s/he cracks, crunches smth with the teeth (peanuts, candies) 3) **gaptúǧA** vt1 s/he chips, cracks smth with a tool 4) **yaptúǧA** vt2 s/he breaks, cracks smth with the teeth 5) **yašpÁ** vt2 s/he breaks, cracks smth open with the teeth (like a peanut)

crackle *n v* 1) **nakpákpa** vimp-redup there is a repetitive crackling, popping sound 2) **penákpakpa** n-redup, vimp fire crackles; the fire crackles

cradleboard *n* **iyók'įba** n cradleboard

cramp *n* **kąyútiba** vs s/he has cramps; suffers from epilepsy

cranberry *n* **wįyáteja** n cranberry

crank *n v* **įjáhomni** n, vt1 crank, lift; s/he cranks up a vehicle

cranky *adj* **wacįšijA** vs s/he is cranky

crash *v n* **imóȟtagA** vt1 s/he bumps against smth, runs, crashes into smth

crawl *v* 1) **snohÁ** vi1 s/he/it crawls, creeps 2) **wįda** vi1 s/he/it crawls ▸ **wįwín** vcont-redup crawling along ▸ **wįwín ų** vi1 s/he/it crawls all over 3) **nasnádA** vt1 s/he sneaks, crawls up to sb ▸ **nasnán** vcont sneaking, crawling up to sb

crayon *n* 1) **į'útų įwókma** cp crayon, paintbrush 2) **okmátoto** n-pl crayons

crazily *adv* 1) **wįtkótkoyagen** adv crazily, foolishly 2) **yaktúš** vcont talking crazily

crazy *adj* 1) **wįktó; wįtkó** vs s/he is crazy ▸ **wįktókto, wįtkótko** vs-redup s/he is bad, crazy; misbehaves ▸ **awįktoktogA; awįtkotkogA** vs-redup s/he is somehow crazy, retarded 2) **agíktųžA** vt1 s/he goes crazy over sb, smth 3) **yaktúžA** vt2 s/he makes sb crazy by talking 4) **knaškíškiyą** vi1-redup s/he is very crazy, out of control

Crazy Bear *nprop* **Matówįtko** nprop Crazy Bear (1785–1856); Nakoda chief and negotiator of the Fort Laramie Treaty Council of 1851

Crazy dog society *cp* **Šųkknáškįyąbi** nprop Crazy dog society

creak *v* **gíza** vs it creaks, squeaks ‣ **gíza wą́ga** vs it is a creaky, squeaky sound

cream *n* **įsnáye** n cream, ointment

crease *n* **osmą́ga** n coulee; crease ‣ **osmą́k** cont crease) ‣ **osmą́kkiyA** vt1-caus s/he makes a crease on smth (pants, skirt)

creature *n* 1) **wawą́ga** n huge animal, creature (like a dinosaur) 2) **mniwáwą́ga** n sea creature

credit *n* **wa'ókmA ; wókmA** vi1-abs, n s/he writes things; s/he has debts, has credit in a store; credit

Cree *nprop* 1) **Šahíya** nprop Cree people (generic term), person of Cree descent 2) **Šahíyeskąbi** nprop Piapot Cree tribe, person of Piapot Cree descent 3) **Maštíja oyáde** nprop Northern Cree tribe

creek *n* **wakpána** n creek

cricket *n* **wamnúška sapsábina** cp-redup cricket

critical *adj See:* **difficult**

crocodile *n* **aknéška tága** cp crocodile

crooked *adj* 1) **škóbA** vs it is bent, curved, crooked ‣ **škóbena** vs it is slightly crooked ‣ **škomyá** adv in a bent, curved, crooked shape ‣ **yuškóm** vcont in a crooked manner 2) **bemní** vs s/he/it is twisted, crooked 3) **škišká** (CTK) ; **kšikšá** (PR) vs it is crooked, curly, wavy

cross *v n adj* 1) **abáweǧa** n cross ‣ **cą'ábaweǧa** n wooden cross 2) **iyúweǧa** vt2, n s/he crosses a body of water while arriving, going there; crossing place on a river, creek 3) **cąwáką** n Sun dance tree, center pole; wood cross 4) **įkpážiba** vi3 s/he does the cross sign

cross-eyed *adj* 1) **įštá gaȟ'ó** vs s/he is cross-eyed 2) **anúk éduwą** cp cross-eyed person

crossroad *n* **įbáweȟ ocą́gu** cp crossroad

crotch *n* 1) **canópa** n crotch 2) **caná ; caną́** n area inside the thigh from hip to the knee; crotch, genital area

crouch *v See:* **hunched**

Crow *nprop* **Ką́ǧí Tóga** cp Crow tribe; person of Crow descent

crow *n* **á'ana** n crow

crow belt *cp* 1a) **amíknągabi** n dance bustle, crow belt 1b) **mįknáge** n crow belt

Crow belt dance *np* **Amíknąga wacíbi** cp Crow belt dance

Crow society *cp* **Ką́ǧí okónagiciye** cp Crow society

crowd *n* **wįcóhą** n crowd

crowded *adj* **wįcódabi** vs-coll there a lot of people, it is crowded

crowhop *n* **á'ana sihá iyópsije** ph crow hop (a style of bucking where the horse's back is arched and all four legs come off the ground)

crown *n* 1) **peyéde** n crown of the head 2) **pesnéda** n crown of the head

cruelty *n* **waknúžąga** n cruelty, bullying

crumble *v* 1) **bųbų́** vs it crumbles (as rotten wood or dried bannock) ‣ **yubų́bų** vt2 s/he makes it crumble manually ‣ **cąbų́bų** vs, n it is rotten wood; rotten wood 2) **hokšúwa** vi1 it collapses, crumbles 3) **bakpą́** vt1 s/he sits on smth and makes it crumble 4) **yumnú** vt2 s/he crumbles, spreads smth around manually; spreads smth fine

crush *v* 1) **-ȟuga** root crushed, cracked (eggshell, berries, nut) ‣ **gaȟúga** vt1 s/he cracks smth; cracks smth open; crushes smth with a tool ‣ **naȟúga** vt1, vs s/he cracks, crushes smth with the foot, by trampling; it cracks by itself 2) **kuká** vs it is raggy, worn out, tattered ‣ **bakúka** vt1 s/he crushes smth by sitting on it ‣ **gakúka** vt1 s/he/it crushes, mashes smth up (with a tool, by hitting, by the action of the wind) ‣ **nakúka** vt1 s/he crushes smth with the feet, by stepping on it ‣ **yukúka** vt2 s/he crushes smth between the fingers 3) **-kpą** root crush, crumble, ground smth fine ‣ **gakpá** vt1 s/he crushes, pulverizes, grounds smth fine using a tool ‣ **yukpá** vt2 s/he crushes, grounds smth manually or with a grinder (grain, meat) 4) **yamnúǧa** vt2 s/he crushes smth with the teeth (candy, ice) ‣ **yamnúȟ** vcont crushing smth with the teeth 4) **gaškí** vt1 s/he crushes, pounds, grinds smth; pulverizes berries using a stone 5) **wįjáskabi** n pemmican, dried meat with crushed chokecherries

crust n **ayúȟuga** n crust

cry v n 1) **céyA** vii s/he cries ‣ **gíjiceyA** vt1-benef s/he cries for sb ‣ **gacéyA** vt1 s/he made sb cry by pushing, hitting ‣ **océyA** vt1 s/he cries for smth sb has ‣ **yacéyA** vt2 s/he makes sb cry by speech ‣ **yucéyA** vt2 s/he makes sb cry manually (pinching, cuddling too vigorously) 2) **nahówayayA** vt1-redup s/he makes sb squeal, cry in pain by stepping (on one's foot or tail) 3) **hóta'į** vii, n s/he cries for help in a ritual way (like in a vision quest); camp crier 4) **hogíyA** vt1 s/he cries smth out, announces smth 5) **agíš'a** vii s/he cheers, emits a war cry

crybaby n 1) **ceyés'a** n crybaby 2) **haȟníša** n crybaby

cucumber n 1) **gųgúma** n wild cucumber, cucumber; pickle 2) **gųgúbi** n cucumber, pickle

cuddle v **gikną** vt1 s/he pampers, cuddles, caresses, sweet talks sb

culture n **wįcóȟ'ąge** n way of life, culture, custom, tradition ‣ **Nakón-wįcoȟ'ąge** n Nakoda culture, custom, tradition, way of life

cup n **į'íjuna** ; **íjuna** n cup, glass ‣ **máza'įjuna** n tin cup

cupboard n **į'íjuna o'égiknąga** cp cupboard

cure v n See: **heal**

curl v n **yucíca** vt2 s/he curls smth

curlew n **cuwíjina** n curlew

curly adj 1) **cicá** vs s/he/it is curly (hair) 2) **škišká** vs it is crooked, curly, wavy

currant cp 1) **tahúbaza** n currant 2) **wį́bazuką stestéyena** ph-redup wild currant

curse v n 1) **wa'écų** vi3-abs s/he does things; s/he curses, does bad things 2) **sijáya eyÁ** vi s/he curses; speaks badly

curve n 1) **įyúkša** n curve 2) **cąškóba** n curved tree, stick

curved adj See: **crooked, bent**

cushion n **įjápąži** n cushion

cut v n 1) **yuksÁ** vt1 s/he cuts, trims smth off with scissors ‣ **gíjiyuksA** vt1/2-benef s/he cuts smth with scissors for him/her ‣ **knuksÁ** vii-pos s/he cuts his/her own with scissors ‣ **wayúksA** vii-abs s/he cuts things; alters clothing ‣ **ayúksA** vt2 s/he cuts smth off with scissors; alters a piece of clothing ‣ **įyúksA** vt1 s/he shortens smth, to make designs on smth; measures and cuts smth 2) **baksÁ** vt1 s/he breaks, cuts smth off manually or by pressure (as with a chainsaw) ‣ **gíjibaksA** vt1-benef s/he breaks smth for him/her manually or by pressure ‣ **kpaksÁ** vt1-pos s/he breaks his/her own manually or by pressure ‣ **wabáksA** vii-abs s/he breaks things manually or by pressure 3) **gaksÁ** vt1 s/he cuts, chops smth off with a tool (axe) ‣ **gíjaksA** vt1-benef s/he cut, chops smth for him/her ‣ **kijáksA** vt1 s/he s/he cuts, chops smth in two with a tool; s/he disobeys, breaks a rule, law) 4) **maksÁ** vt1 s/he cuts smth off with a sharp blade ‣ **wamáksA** vii-abs s/he cuts things with a sharp blade ‣ **magíjiksA** vt1-benef s/he cuts smth for him/her with a sharp blade ‣ **magíksA** vt1-pos s/he cuts his/her own with a sharp blade ‣ **maksáksA** vt1-redup s/he cuts them with a sharp blade ‣ **ma'íc'iksA** vi3-refl s/he cuts himself/herself a sharp blade ‣ **amáksA** vt1 s/he cuts smth off with a sharp blade 5) **maškída** vt1 s/he cuts sb, smth ‣ **ma'íc'iškida** vi3-refl s/he cuts, gashes himself/herself 6) **gapsága** vt1 s/he/it breaks, cuts smth (rope) by hitting; the wind breaks smth; it breaks, rips by itself 7) **gašná** vt1 s/he cuts smth short with a tool (hair, grass); mows the lawn ‣ **gíjašna** s/he cuts sb else's thing with a tool (hair, grass); gives sb a haircut; mows the lawn 8) **mašpúšpu** vt1-redup s/he cuts smth into small pieces 9) **yuptéjena** vt2 s/he cuts smth shorter (with scissors)

cut bank *cp* 1) **gaȟé** n ravine, coulee, cut bank; mountain, hill) 2) **mayáyukseya** n cut bank

cut off *v* **yu'ínaži** vt2 s/he stops sb, smth; cuts the motor off (car, engine)

cute *adj* 1) **wa'óštenaga ; wawóštenaga** vs s/he/it is cute 2) **wa'óštena** vs s/he/it is (small thing, baby, child) is cute 3) **-na** encl small, little, cute, dear

cutter *n* **máza iyúkse** cp wire cutter

cymbal *n* **ijásna** n cymbal

Cypress Hills (Saskatchewan) *ngeo* **Wazíȟe** ngeo Cypress Hills (Saskatchewan)

D

Dakota *nprop* 1) **Iȟáktuwa** nprop Yankton Dakota people, person of Yankton Dakota descent 2) **Iȟáktuwana** nprop Yanktonai Dakota people, person of Yanktonai Dakota descent 3) **I'ášijana ; I'ášija ; I'ásija ; Iyášija ; Iyásija** nprop person of Dakota, Chippewa, Saulteaux, French, German, Ukrainian, or Russian descent

dam *n* 1) **miní natága** cp dam 2) **cagáȟtubi** n beaver dam; bridge

damage *n v* **yusíjabi** n damage

damp *adj* 1) **spá** vs it is damp 2) **totóba** vs it is damp, wet

dance *v n* 1a) **wací** vi1, n s/he dances; dance ‣ **wacíkiyA** vt1-caus s/he makes sb dance ‣ **iwágici** vt1-dat s/he dances over or on account of smth 1b) **wacíbi** n dance 2) **owáci** vi1, n s/he dances inside (building, hoop); dance

dance hall *cp* **owácibi** n dance hall, dance arbor

dancer *n* 1) **wacís'a** n dancer 2) **wacíbi ecúbinas'a** cp dance contestant 3) **wiktogağa, witkótkogağa** n fool dancer; clown 4) **ca'ómima yuhá wací** ph hoop dancer

dandelion *n* 1) **waȟcáği** n dandelion 2) **gabúzena** n dandelion

dandruff *n* **paȟpúȟpu** vs s/he has dandruff

dangerous *adj* **wóginihaga** vs s/he/it is fearsome, dangerous, ferocious

dark *adj n* 1) **a'ókpazA** vimp it is a dark night; in the darkness 2) **aháziga** vimp it is kind of dark

darken *v* 1) **aházikiyA** vt1 s/he darkens smth 2) **šamyÁ** vt1 s/he darkens, dirties sb, smth

darkly *adv* **sapyá** adv blackly, darkly *See:* **black**

daub *v* 1) **buspÁ** vt1 s/he daubs, patches smth ‣ **kpúspA** vt1-pos s/he daubs, patches his/her own ‣ **abúspA** vt1 s/he daubs, glues, tacks smth onto it ‣ **obúspA** vt1 s/he daubs, plasters over smth ‣ **tibúspA** vi1 s/he daubs a house, plasters a hole in a wall 2) **agástagA** vt1 s/he daubs, pastes, throws, pours out a gooey substance (as to make it stick)

daughter *n* 1) **-cukši- ; -cuwi-** root daughter 2) **cuwíktuyA, cuwítkuyA** vt1-caus s/he adopts a daughter 3) **wik'úbi** n daughter given away for marriage

daughter-in-law *n* **wiyáwoȟa** n daughter-in-law

dawn *n v* 1) **ába ú** vimp it is dawn, daybreak 2) **gamnézA** vimp it is morning twilight, dawn 3) **hawí hinápA** vimp it is sunrise; it dawns

day *n* 1) **ába** n, vimp day, daylight; it is day ‣ **am- ; ap-** cont day ‣ **abéyas'a ; ábaneyas'a** adv all throughout the day, all day; everyday ‣ **am'ówaštejaga** vimp it is a beautiful day ‣ **apšíjA** vimp it is a gloomy day ‣ **apšíjeja** vimp it is a stormy day; a day with bad weather ‣ **tadéyaba ; tadé'aba** vimp it is a windy day 2)

ąbédu n day 3) **-cą** vimp it is a day, twenty-four hours ▸ **dónacą** adv several days; how many days ▸ **núbacą** vimp it is a period of two days

daycare n **hokšína wąyágabi tíbi** np daycare center

daydream n **ąmwíhamna** n daydream

dead adj n adv 1) **wanįjA** vs s/he/it lacks; there is none; s/he passed away; is dead 2) **t'Á** vs s/he/it dies, is dead 3) **t'egúza** vi1 s/he plays dead 4) **šéjA** vs it is dry, dead ▸ **cášeja** n dead tree

deadfall n **cąkníyaȟpe** n deadfall

deaf adj 1) **naȟ'úšį** vs s/he is deaf 2) **núǧe kpá** vs s/he/it is deaf 3) **nuȟcá** n deaf person

deal v n **įȟpékiyA** vt1-dat s/he throws smth at sb; s/he deals the cards; s/he leaves smth for sb

dear adj **-na** encl small, little, cute, dear (with nouns and verbs it indicates the small size of an entity, or the endearment/sympathy of the speaker for the person or object; it often occurs on verbs used to describe the actions of a baby or small child)

deathbed n 1) **dąyášį yįgá** cp deathbed 2) **dogíš yįgÁ** vi3 s/he is dying; s/he is on his/her deathbed

debate v n **akínija** vt1 s/he debates, argues over smth ▸ **wa'ákinija** vi1-abs s/he debates, argues over things

deceased adj **t'ábi** n deceased person

December n 1) **witéȟi sųgágu hąwí** cp December 2) **wįcógądu wí** cp December

decide v 1a) **gíjiknuštą** vt1-benef s/he finishes smth for sb (work, meal); s/he decides smth for sb 1b) **knuštą́** vt1-pos s/he finishes his/her own thing (meal, work); s/he decides regarding his/her own thing

decorate v 1) **yuwógųga** vt1 s/he decorates smth manually 2) **óska** vt1 s/he decorates smth (outfit, rawhide) with porcupine quills

decoration n **waȟcánebi** n decoration

deed n 1) **ohídiga ecú** cp war deed 2) **wįcóȟ'ą** n deed, act of bravery

deep adj 1) **šmá** vs it is deep ▸ **wašmá** vimp it is deep snow 2) **mahédu** vimp it is deep inside ▸ **mahéduȟ** adv deeper, deep down inside 3) **ǧíȟtįyĄ** vs it is deep yellow

deer n 1) **táȟca** n deer ▸ **ta-** n ruminant (generic meaning; moose, deer, elk, buffalo; occurs in compounds) 2) **taȟcíjana** ; **táȟtįjana** n deer (generic), herd of deer; white-tailed deer 3) **sįdégoskoza** n mule deer 4) **sįdésaba** n black-tailed deer

deerfly n **tažúška** n deerfly

defecate v 1) **cesní** vs, n s/he/it defecates, takes a shit; feces, dung, shit ▸ **cesníyA** vt1-caus it makes sb defecate 2) **acésni** vt1 s/he defecates on sb, smth ▸ **acégicisnibi** vi1-recip they defecate on one another ▸ **a'íc'icesni** vi3-refl s/he defecates on himself/herself 3) **océsni** vi1 s/he defecates in smth ▸ **océsnisni** vi1-redup s/he/it (child, small animal) defecates in smth 4) **įcésni** vs s/he defecates because of smth 5) **wíduka** vs s/he relieves himself/herself (urinate, defecate); uses the bathroom

defend v 1) **nagíjižį; nagícižįbi** vt1-benef, vi1-recip s/he defends, stands for sb, they defend, stand for one another 2) **na'íc'ižį** vi3-refl s/he defends, stands for himself/herself

deflate v **basníza** vt1 s/he deflates smth by pressing, sitting on it (cushion, ball)

defrost v See: **thaw**

defy v **okínažį** vt1 s/he defies sb

demolish v **bažúžu** vt1 s/he erases smth by pushing; s/he demolishes, make smth fall apart by putting pressure

den n **makámahen** ; **makámahen** n den, basement

denigrate v **yahókudu** vt2 s/he denigrates sb ▸ **įknáhokudu** vi3-refl s/he denigrates himself/herself

dental clinic cp **hí wįcáyušnoges'a tíbi** cp dental clinic

dentist n **hí wįcáyušnoges'a** cp dentist

depart *v* 1) **iyáyA** vi2 s/he sets to go from here, departs from here (before or shortly after departure) ▸ **iyáyena** vi2 s/he (little one, child) sets to go from here, departs from here 2) **yuhíyayA** vt2 s/he sets to go from here, departs from here with sb, smth (before or shortly after departure) 3) **knijú** vi1 s/he departs, leaves to come back here 4) **hiyú** vi1, vs s/he departs, is setting to come here from there; it begins, appears, arises, turns into smth

depend *v* **wacį́** vi3, n, part s/he feels like doing smth; mind, plan, goodwill; it is about to happen; intentive, prospective, or imminent event ▸ **wacį́giyA** vt1-pos s/he depends on his/her own will ▸ **wacį́'įc'iyA** vi3-refl s/he depends on himself/herself wacíya ▸ **wacíyA** vt1 s/he depends on sb, smth

depot *n* **wáda o'į́nažį** cp train depot

design *n v* **wóknikne** n design, pattern

desire *v n* 1) **gų́** vt1 s/he desires sb; wishes for sb 2) **cįgÁ** vt1 s/he wants, desires smth; is inclined to smth

despite *prep n v* 1) **kóš** part anyway, despite 2) **wógitahą** adv regardless, in spite of 3) **duká ; oká ; ųká** *conj* but, although, even though, despite

destroy *v* 1) **yusíjA** vt2 s/he ruins, destroys smth manually 2) **yuhókšu** vt2 s/he breaks, wrecks, destroys, dismantles smth

detach *v* **yušká** vt2 s/he unties, detaches smth ▸ **gíjiyuška** vt1-benef s/he unties, detaches sb, smth for him/her

determined *adj See:* **insistent**

devil *n* **wakášijA ; wakášijA** n, vs evil-spirited being (like Įktomi or the Christian devil); s/he/it is evil-spirited

devour *v* 1a) **temyÁ** vt1 s/he eats it all, devours smth ▸ **tepyékiyA** vt1-caus s/he makes sb eat smth; stuff sb (as a baby) ▸ **tepkíyA** vt1-pos s/he eats, devours his/her own 1b) **watémyA** vi1-abs s/he/it eats everything, the whole thing (as

an animal) ▸ **watépkijiyA** vt1-benef s/he eats, devours someone else's food

dew *n* 1) **acú** vs it is covered with dew 2) **cuȟpá** vimp, n it is a heavy dew; dew

diabetes *n* 1) **cąšmúyabi yazá** vs s/he has diabetes; is diabetic 2) **wéskuya** n diabetes

diamond *n* **otámškadabi** n baseball diamond

diamond willow *cp* **coǧážija** n diamond willow

diarrhea *n* 1) **cesní ȟaȟá** vs s/he/it has diarrhea 2) **cesní hiyáyA** vi2 s/he/it has diarrhea 3) **cešnóšno** vi1-redup s/he has soft stool, diarrhea 4) **gažó** vt1 ; vi ; vi1 s/he makes it whistle by spinning; it whistles because of the wind; s/he has diarrhea

dice *n* **gazú ecúbina ; ga'écubina** n dice

die *v See:* **dead** 1) **t'Á** vs s/he/it dies, is dead 2) **wot'Á** vi1 s/he/it dies at a distance 3) **ot'Á** vs s/he dies in, inside of (house, water) ▸ **ga'įt'eyA** vs s/he/it died of old age 4) **dogį́š yįgÁ** vi3 s/he is dying; s/he is on his/her deathbed

different *adj* 1) **toką** vs ; adv it is different; different, differently ▸ **tokáką** vs-redup they are different ▸ **ícitoką** adv different when compared to, different altogether ▸ **titóką** n different tent ▸ **yutóką** vt2 s/he disguises, makes sb, smth look different, changes smth manually 2) **núbagiya** adv two by two; in two ways, in two different directions 3) **piyá** adv anew, again, in a different location 4) **togíknąga** adv different kinds 5) **omémega** n-redup different things; a variety of things

differently *adj* 1) **toká** adv different, differently ▸ **tokáȟtįyą** adv quite differently ▸ **tokáyą** adv differently ▸ **otóką** adv differently, unusual 2) **i'átoką** vi1 s/he talks differently

difficult *adj* 1) **teȟígA** vs s/he/it is hard, difficult, critical ▸ **gíjiteȟiga** vs1-benef it is hard on him/her; difficult for him/her 2) **otéȟigA** vs, n it is difficult, hard, problematic, sad; problem, trouble ▸ **owóteȟiga** adv difficult, hard (as in grieving) 3) **verb + síjA** vs s/he/it is hard, difficult to ▸ **oyúze síjA** vs it is difficult to hold

difficulty *n* **teȟíyą** adv with difficulty, poorly ▸ **teȟíšįyą** adv easily

dig *v* 1) **k'Á** vt1 s/he/it digs ▸ **gíjik'A** vt1-benef s/he digs smth for him/her (like potatoes, roots) 2) **oyúzA** vt2 s/he digs smth out 3) **moptÁ** vt1 s/he digs smth with a digging stick ▸ **wamóptA** vii-abs s/he digs with a digging stick

dim *v* **yukúda** vt2 s/he dims the light down

dime *n* **gašpábi okíse** cp dime

dimension *n* **makóce įdóba** cp fourth dimension; fourth spiritual realm

dimpled *adj* **duȟáȟa** vs it is dimpled

dip *v n* 1) **obúktą** vt1-dit s/he dips smth in it (as bannock in soup) ▸ **okpúktą** vt1-pos s/he dips smth in his/her own 2) **ogáptA** vt1 s/he ladles, dips smth out of it

direction *n* 1) **dókiyo** adv in which direction, direction, course 2a) **dokíkiyota** adv-redup in some direction 2b) **dókikiya** adv-redup in some direction; toward some places 3) **dókiyadahą** adv from which direction, where 4) **ektágiya** adv toward this direction 5) **gákiyota** adv in that direction 6) **néciyadahą** adv from this direction 7) **núbagiya** adv two by two; in two ways, in two different directions, locations 8) **yámnigiya** adv three by three; in three ways, in three different directions, locations ▸ **iyámnigiya** adv in all directions, scattered 9) **žecíyadahą** adv from that direction, from over there 10) **žektágiya** adv toward that direction (away from speaker) 11) **nedábaš** adv in this direction 12) **žedábaš** adv in that direction ▸ **žedápkiya** adv toward that direction 13) **tadé'uya dóba** cp four cardinal directions 14) **-giya** suff toward; X by X, in a number of ways, directions, locations 15) **é-** pref to, at, there, toward, in this direction; they (marks the collective plural form of some intransitive verbs)

directly *adv* 1) **gadíyą ; ganíyą** adv directly, straight; in a beeline, straight line 2) **mokpékna** adv direct, directly

dirty *adj v* 1) **šnušnúda** vs-redup s/he/it is dirty ▸ **šnušnún** vcont dirty ▸ **šnušnúnkiyA** vt1-pos s/he dirties his/her own ▸ **šnušnún įc'íyA** vi3-refl s/he dirties himself/herself 2) **yušnúšnuda** vt2 s/he dirties sb, smth manually ▸ **įknúšnušnuda** vi3-refl s/he dirties himself/herself 3) **šábA** vs it is dirty ▸ **šam-** vcont dirty ▸ **šamyÁ** vt1-caus s/he darkens, dirties sb, smth ▸ **šam'íc'iyA** vi3-refl s/he/it dirties himself/herself/itself 4) **oȟní** vs it is dirty inside

disappear *v* **tą'íšį** vs s/he/it disappears, is out of sight, lost

disc harrow *cp* **įmáka gaksá** cp disc harrow

discard *v See:* **throw**

discontent *adj* **įdéšitkiyA** vt1-pos s/he furrows his/her eyebrows; looks discontent

discuss *v* **yukcá** vt2 s/he discusses smth

disease *n* 1) **ȟní** vs, n s/he/it has a sore; sore, disease 2) **ceȟníbi** n syphilis, sexual disease ▸ **ceȟníȟnibi** n-redup sexual diseases (in the form of viscous spots, rashes)

disguise *v* **yutóką** vt2 s/he disguises, makes sb, smth look different, changes smth manually

dish *n See:* **plate**

dismantle *v* 1) **yuhókšu** vt2 s/he breaks, wrecks, destroys, dismantles smth 2) **yušnóšnogA** vt2-redup s/he dismantles smth by pulling

dismount *v* **kiȟpá** vii-dat s/he dismounts, gets off from sb, smth

disobey *v* **kijáksA** vt1 s/he cuts, chops smth in two with a tool; s/he disobeys, breaks a rule, law)

disown *v* **aktášį** vt1 s/he rejects, does not want, disowns sb

displeased *adj* **iyógipiši** vs-dat s/he is displeased about sb, smth ▸ **iyógipišįyą** adv feeling sad, displeased about smth

disqualify *v* **opéšį** vi1 s/he is disqualified ▸ **opéšį kiyÁ** vt1-caus s/he disqualifies sb

disrespect *v n* **įknúdąšį** vi3-refl s/he disrespects, brags about himself/herself; is stupid

distance *n* 1) **žehą́geja** adv, n about that size (measurement, distance); since then; distance, destination 2) **dohą́yą** adv for a certain time, distance, length 3) **téhąduwa** adv a long distance, far away ▸ **tehą́duwaȟ** adv a very long distance, really far away

distress *n* **wóteȟiga** n distress

ditch *n* **wakpá gáǧabi** cp irrigation ditch

dive *v n* **giknúgA** vi1 s/he/it dives into water ▸ **giknúk** *vcont* diving into water

division *n* **ošpáye** n divisions, parts of smth

divorce *v n* 1) **įȟpéyA** vt1 s/he discards, throws sb, smth away; s/he leaves sb, smth behind, alone; s/he/it is left behind; s/he divorces from him/her; s/he banishes sb ▸ **wį'į́ȟpeyA** vi1 he divorces from his wife 2) **įȟpégiciyabi** vi1-recip, n they divorce from one another; divorce

dizzy *adj* 1) **įdómni** vs s/he/it is dizzy ▸ **ga'į́domni** vt1 it (wind) makes him/her dizzy ▸ **yu'į́domni** vt2 s/he/it twists sb around to make him/her dizzy 2) **įdáhomni** vs s/he feels dizzy

do *v* 1a) **ecú** vt3 s/he does smth ▸ **ecágiji'ų** vt1/3-benef s/he does smth for sb ▸ **ecúkiyA** vt1-caus s/he allows smth, sb to do smth ▸ **ecágic'ų** vt3-pos s/he does his/her own ▸ **ecágici'ųbi** vi1-recip they did smth for one another ▸ **ecá'įc'ų** vi3-refl s/he prepares, does smth to himself/herself ▸ **nécų** vt1 s/he does this ▸ **žécų** vt3 s/he does that; acts in that way ▸ **žécųcų** vt3-redup s/he keeps doing that ▸ **ecúpija** vs it can be done ▸ **síjecų** vt3 s/he does smth bad ▸ **piyá ecú** vt3 s/he does smth again; renews, remodels, renovate smth 1b) **wa'écų** vi3-aux s/he does things; s/he curses, does bad things ▸ **wa'écagijų** vt1-benef-abs s/he does things, works for sb ▸ **wa'écagici'ųbi** vi1-recip they do things for one another 2) **dágecų** vi3 s/he

does smth ▸ **dágecųšį** vs nothing is done, it is a waste of time 3) **dóku** vi3-irr s/he/it does what? 4) **ú** vi1-aux s/he does continuously, goes around 5) **áyA** vi2-aux s/he does it continuously, constantly 6) **yįgÁ** ; **yągÁ** vi3-aux s/he remains doing, does continously; stays 7) **ȟ'ą́** vi1 s/he behaves; s/he does smth (in interrogative sentences)

doable *adj* **ecúpija** vs it can be done

doctor *n v* 1) **pežúda wįcášta** cp medicine man; doctor 2) **wa'ánowes'a** n chanting doctor 3a) **nįktekiyA** vt1-caus s/he heals, doctors sb ▸ **nįktegicikiyabi** vi1-recip they doctor, heal one another ▸ **nįktegijikiyA** vt1-benef s/he doctors, heals sb for him/her 3b) **wanį́ktekiyA** vi1-abs s/he doctors, heals ▸ **wanį́ktekiyes'a** n doctor

doe *n* **wíyena** n female animal; doe ▸ **tȟą́cawįyena** n doe

dog *n* 1) **šų́ga** n dog, canine; horse (in possessed forms only) ▸ **šų́gagana** n-redup lap dog ▸ **šųk-** cont dog, horse, sheep 2) **šų́gawį** n female dog, bitch 3) **gisų́na šų́ga** cp chow dog 4) **šųkháskusku** n mangy dog, coyote, wolf; unkept dog 5) **šųgámna** vs s/he/it smells like a dog 6) **šųk'óhąbi** n boiled dog, puppy soup 7) **tašų́kkiyA** vt1-caus s/he makes smth his/her own dog 8) **šųgícoco** vt1-redup s/he calls his/her own dogs

Dog penis people *nprop* **Šųkcébina wįcášta** nprop Dog penis people (band of Nakoda)

doghouse *n* **šų́ga tína** cp doghouse

doll *n* **dáguškiškina** n-redup doll

dollar *n* **mázaska; mázaska wąží** n, cp money; dollar (usually followed by a number), one dollar; loony

donkey *n* **šųkšóšona** ; **šųkšóšo** ; **šúšubina** ; **šųkšúšu** n donkey, mule

doomsday *n* **makóce įhą́ge** cp doomsday

door *n* 1) **ti'óba** ; **tiyóba** n door 2) **tošúda** n area near the door, or door flap inside a tipi

doorknob *n* **tiyóba įyúšpena** cp doorknob

double stitch *n* **nųbáн̃ basísA** vt1 s/he double stitches smth

doubt *v n* 1) **cet'úknA** vt1 s/he doubts, disbelieves sb, smth ‣ **cet'ǘ'įc'iknA** vi3-refl s/he doubts him/herself 2) **н̃ó** interj expression indicating doubt (female speaker)

dough *n* **ağúyabi baská** cp dough

dove *n* **giyą́yąno** n mourning dove

down *adv prep v n adj* 1) **kúda** adv down ‣ **kún** adv down, downward, below 2) **hokún** adv down, below; downstairs

downstairs *n-pl adj adv* **tihókun; hokún** adv, adv downstairs, down, below; downstairs

downward *adv adj* 1) **mahétkiya** adv downward 2) **kún** adv down, downward, below 3) **gakún** adv downward

dozen *n* **agénųba** num twelve; dozen ‣ **wį́kta agénųba** cp egg dozen

draft *n* **ogásni** vs, n it is a draft of air; draft of air ‣ **ti'ógasni** vimp there is a draft of cold air in a house

drag *v n* **yusnóн̃Ą** vt2 s/he drags, pulls smth along ‣ **knusnóн̃Ą** vt1-pos s/he drags, pulls his/her own

dragonfly *n* **susméja** n dragonfly

drain *v n* 1) **skébA** vs it is empty, drained ‣ **skemkíjiyA** vt1-benef s/he drains, bails smth out for sb else ‣ **skemyÁ** vt1-caus s/he drains, bails out smth ‣ **skem-** vcont empty, drained ‣ **skemkíyA** vt1-pos s/he drains, bails out his/her own 2) **baskébA** vt1 s/he drains, empties smth out by pushing 3) **buskébA** vt1 s/he strains, drains a liquid (by pressing) 4) **moskébA** vi1 it drains by leaking, dripping out 5) **yuskébA** vt2 s/he empties smth out; drains smth (oil in a car, hose, pipe) 6) **oyúskeba** n drain

draw *v* 1) **okmÁ** vt1 s/he writes, draws smth; paints, sketches sb, smth 2) **gazó ; įjázo** vt1, n, vt1 s/he draws a line, line; yardstick, ruler; s/he draws a line on smth

drawing *n* **wa'ókmabi** n letter, written word, drawing

dream *v n* 1) **įhámnA** vt1 s/he dreams sb, smth ‣ **wį́hamnA** vi1-abs s/he dreams about things; has a vision 2) **awį́hamnA** vt1 s/he dreams about sb, smth 3) **įhámnabi ; wįhámne** n dream, vision

dress₁ *n v adj* **sąksája** n dress ‣ **abáн̃nan sąksája** cp silk dress ‣ **teн̃pí sąksája** cp buckskin dress ‣ **teн̃pí sąksája ogáн̃cibi** cp fringed buckskin dress

dress₂ *v* 1) **įc'ícuwa** vi3-refl s/he gets dressed 2) **įknúzA** vi3-refl s/he dresses himself/herself in a certain way ‣ **wací įknúza** cp s/he is dressed in regalia 3) **gic'úkiyA** vt1-caus-pos s/he gets his/her own to wear smth, to dress

drift *v* **įjóğą** vi1 s/he/it drifts

driftwood *n* **cą'íjjoğą** n driftwood

drink *v n* 1) **yaktÁ; yatkÁ** vt2 s/he drinks smth; drinks, consumes (alcohol) 2) **miníyatkÁ** vi2 s/he drinks alcohol 3) **yaн̃éba** vt1 s/he drinks smth up ‣ **knaн̃éba** vt1-pos s/he drinks up his/her own 4) **įyútA; iyútA** vt2 s/he tests, tries smth (food, drink, clothes, task)

drip *v n* 1) **šmú** vs it leaks, drips ‣ **šmúwąga** vs it is dripping (as a faucet) ‣ **ti'óšmu** vimp there is dripping in a dwelling 2) **moskébA** vi1 it drains by leaking, dripping out

drive *v* 1) **basí** vi1, vt1 s/he drives; s/he drives smth ‣ **gíjibasi** vt1-benef s/he drives for sb, drives sb around ‣ **kpási** vt1-pos s/he drives his/her own vehicle ‣ **abási** vt1 s/he drives sb, smth 2) **šųkpásikiyA** vt1-caus s/he drives a horse (toward a place) ‣ **šųkpásiwįcakiyA** vt1-coll s/he drives horses (toward a place) 3) **napéyA** vt1-caus s/he drives sb away; chases sb, smth away; makes sb flee ‣ **napégijiyA** vt1-benef s/he drives, chases sb, smth away for him/her

driver *n* **basíbi** n driver

drizzle *n* 1) **mnimózą** vimp it is drizzling 2) **mağážu waką** cp it is a hot summer drizzle

drool *v* **ítutu** vs s/he/it drools, slobbers ‣ **ítutuya** adv in a drooling, slobbering manner ‣ **ítutuyA** vt1-caus s/he/it drools, slobbers

drop *v n* 1) **yušną** vt2 s/he drops smth 2) **iyóȟpeyA** vt1 s/he throws, drops smth into it 3) **temníšmu** n sweat drop

drown *v* **mni'ót'A ; miní'ot'A** vs s/he/it drowns ‣ **mni'ót'eyA** vt1-caus s/he drowns sb ‣ **mni'ót'ekiyA** vt1-caus s/he drowns, lets sb drown ‣ **mni'ót'e'įc'iyA** vi3-refl s/he drowns himself/herself

drug *n* **pežúdasije** n bad medicine; drug (cannabis, cocaine) *See:* **cannabis**

drum *n v* 1) **gamúbi** n drum ‣ **nąbé gamúbi** cp hand drum ‣ **cągámubi** n log drum ‣ **gamúbina** n small drum 2) **gamú** vt1 s/he beats on smth; makes a drumming sound 3) **muyá** vs it is a drumbeat 4) **ȟ'oká** vi1 s/he sings with a drum group; beats the drum in a powwow or dance ‣ **ȟ'oká yįgábi** cp drum singer

drumbeat *n* 1) **muyá** vs it is a drumbeat ‣ **muyéna** adv like drumbeats 2) **muyákne** vt1 s/he makes a drumming sound, a drumbeat ‣ **muyáknebi** n drumbeat, drumming sound

drumstick *n* 1) **įgámu** n drumstick 2) **gamúyabi** n drumstick 3) **į'ápe** n drumstick

drunk *adj* **ktúžA** vs s/he is drunk ‣ **įktúžA** vs s/he is drunk on smth

drunkard *n* 1) **miníyatkes'a ; minátkes'a ; yatkés'a** n drunkard, alcoholic 2) **ktúžes'a** n drunkard

drunkenness *n* **ocągusaba** n paved road; drunkenness

dry *adj v* 1) **búza** vs it is dry ‣ **bus-** vcont dry ‣ **busyÁ** vt1-caus s/he dries smth 2) **gabúza** vt1 it is dried by the wind, sun ‣ **gapúskiyA** vt1-pos s/he dries, lets his/her own (clothes, blanket) dry in the wind, sun ‣ **gabúsyA** vt1-caus s/he

dries, lets smth dry in the wind, sun 3) **miníši** vs it is dry, arid, waterless 4) **ságA** vs it is dried hard (like smth wet that dried up) ‣ **sakkíjiyA** vt1-benef s/he dries smth for him/her ‣ **sakyÁ** vt1-caus s/he dries smth that is wet 5) **šéjA** vs it is dry, dead

duck *n v* 1) **pağúda** n duck ‣ **pağún** cont duck 2) **pağúdasaba** n American black duck 3) **sihúšaša** n mallard duck 4) **amnóto ; amnótona** n teal, blue-winged duck 5) **kúdi'įc'iyA** vi3-refl s/he ducks down

Duck dance *np* **Pağúda wacíbi** cp duck dance

duckling *n* **pağúncija** n duckling

dull *adj* 1) **péší** vs it is dull (as a knife, axe blade) ‣ **pepéší** vs-redup-pl, they are dull (used with inanimates) 2) **yupéší** vs it is dull by wear

dumb *adj See:* **stupid**

dump *n* **o'íȟpeya** n dump, nuisance ground

during *prep* 1) **žécan** adv in the meantime, during that time, then 2) **ecána** adv during that time, meanwhile

dusk *adj v n* 1) **aháži** vimp it is dusk, dark 2) **ahážiga** vimp it is kind of dark

dust *n v* 1) **mąkámnuna** n dust 2) **mąká ; maká** n earth, soil, dust, dirt 3) **cą'ókpa** n sawdust 4) **gadódo** vt1 s/he shakes, brushes, dusts smth off, s/he pecks sb, smth ‣ **įknádodo** vi3-refl s/he shakes, brushes, dusts himself/herself off 5) **įknádana** vi3-refl s/he dusts himself/herself off 6) **wi'ómni** n twister wind, whirlwind, dust devil 7) **opšíja gamóta** vimp there is a dust storm

dye *n v* **yušá** vt2 s/he dyes smth in red *See:* see the different colors for other verbs of this type

dynamite *n* **nąpómyabi** n dynamite, fireworks

E

each *pro adv* 1) **anúkadahą** adv on each side, ends 2) **-gici-...-bi ; -ci-...-bi** circumfix one another (marker of the reciprocal; occurs when two subjects are acting on one another; reciprocal verbs are of Class 1) 3) **žékžena** dem-redup each of them, those

exactly *adv* 1) **ecéduȟ** adv exactly 2) **duktéduȟ** adv exactly as such 3) **žéceȟ** adv exactly in that way 4) **-ȟ** suff absolutely, the very X, exactly, specifically, at all (marks focus on demonstratives, nouns, pronouns and negative interrogative pronouns) 5) **-ȟtįyA** suff, encl exactly, really anxious to, absolutely, at all (marks focus on active verbs and some nongradable stative verbs)

eagle *n* 1) **wamní** n golden eagle (also used as a generic term) 2) **anúkasą** n bald eagle 3) **ȟuyá** n eagle

Eagle belt dance *np* **Wamní įpíyaga wacíbi** cp Eagle belt dance

Eagle dance *np* **Wamní wacíbi** cp Eagle dance

examine *v* **amnézA** vt1 s/he examines, scrutinizes sb, smth ‣ **wa'ámnezA** vi1-abs, n s/he examines, scrutinizes, studies things; examiner ‣ **agíjimnezA** vt1-benef s/he examines sb, smth for him/her ‣ **agímnezA** vt1-pos s/he examines his/her own ‣ **agícimnezabi** vi1-recip they examine, observe, scrutinize one another ‣ **a'íc'imnezA** vi3-refl s/he examines himself/herself

examiner *n* **wa'ámnezA** vi1-abs, n s/he examines, scrutinizes, studies things; examiner

ear *n* 1) **núǧe** n ear ‣ **nuȟ** cont ear 2) **núǧe oȟnóga** cp ear holes

early *adv* 1) **éstena** adv early, soon, right away ‣ **éstestena** adv-redup very early, soon, quickly 2) **hąyákena** adv, vimp early morning; it is early morning ‣ **hąyákenaȟ** adv very early in the morning 3) **hągíkta** vi1 s/he gets up early 4) **togáȟtani** adv early evening

earn *v* 1) **ogíni** vt1 s/he earns money, gets smth 2) **gamná** vt1 s/he slices meat for drying; s/he earns money ‣ **maskámna** vi1 s/he earns

money 3) **gaktú** vt1, vi1 s/he slices meat for drying; s/he earns money 4) **maskáǧA** vi1 s/he earns, makes money

earrings *n-pl* **nuȟ'ó'į** n earrings ‣ **nuȟ'ó'įkiyA** vt1-caus s/he puts earrings on sb's ears

earth *n* 1) **mąká ; maká** n earth, soil, ground, dirt ‣ **mąkán** adv on the ground, earth 2) **makóce** n land, territory, earth, ground; homeland

earthquake *n* **mąkóškąšką ; makóce škąšką** n-redup earthquake

Eashappie *nprop* **Í'áš'abi** nprop Eashappie (surname in Carry The Kettle)

easily *adv* 1) **dąyáȟ** adv easily; very well, thoroughly 2) **teȟíšįyą** adv easily

exasperation *n* **waȟtéšįȟtįyą** interj for God sake!; scrap! (expression of disgust, exasperation)

east *n adv* 1) **wíhinąpa** n east 2) **wíhinąpatakiya** adv eastward, toward the east 2) **wiyóhąbam** adv in, to the east

Easter *n* **wįkta šagíyabi** cp Easter

eastward *adv* **wíhinąpatakiya** adv eastward, toward the east

easy *adj adv* 1) **teȟíšį** vi1 it is easy; it is cheap 2) **owášte** adv easily, easy ‣ **owášte yuhÁ** vs it is easy to have 3) **ogáȟtąyą** vs it is easy to make ‣ **ogáȟ wašté** vs it is easy to make 4) **-pija** aux it is easy, worth it, feasible, good to do, -able

eat *v* 1) **wódA** vi1 s/he/it eats ‣ **won-** vcont eating ‣ **wódešįyą** adv without eating ‣ **wonkíyA** vt1 s/he made sb eat ‣ **wotkícuni** vi1 s/he finishes eating ‣ **owóda** n; vs feast, s/he sits down to eat 2) **yúdA** vt2 s/he/it eats smth ‣ **gíjiyudA** vt1/2-benef s/he eats sb's food ‣ **yún- ; yút** vcont eating smth ‣ **yúnyun** vcont-redup eating it repeatedly ‣ **yunkíyA** vt1-caus s/he makes, lets sb eat smth ‣ **knúdA** vt1-pos s/he eats his/her own thing ‣ **knún** vcont eating his/her own ‣ **knúknun** vcont-redup eating his/her own ‣ **gicíyudabi** vi1-recip they eat one another (as cannibals, monsters do) ‣ **yúdešįyą** adv without eating smth ‣ **oyún wašté** vs it is good to eat; tastes good ‣ **oyún síjA** vs it is not good to eat 3) **ȟtawóda** vi1 s/he/it eats in the evening 4) **hoyúdA** vi2 s/he/it eats fish 5a) **temyÁ** vt1 s/he eats it all, devours smth ‣ **tepyékiyA** vt1-caus s/he makes sb eat smth; stuff sb (as a baby) ‣ **tepkíyA** vt1-pos s/he eats, devours his/her own 5b) **watémyA** vi1-abs s/he/it eats everything, the whole thing (as an animal) ‣ **watépkijiyA** vt1-benef s/he eats, devours someone else's food

eater *n* **wódes'a** n eater; one who eats all the time

eau de cologne *np* **a'íc'ibapsųpsų** n-redup eau de cologne

exceedingly *adv* **iyékapeya** adv above, exceedingly

exchange *n v See:* **trade**

echo *n v* 1) **ya'íyowaza** vi2 s/he/it produces an echo by speech or singing ‣ **ya'íyowas** vcont in an echo-like manner 2) **ga'íyowaza** vt1 s/he produces an echo by bouncing, hitting smth; it makes an echo ‣ **ga'íyowas** vcont in an echo-like manner

excited *adj* 1a) **cadé iyápa** vs s/he is excited, agitated; his/her heart beats 1b) **cadé kokóna iyápa** vs s/he is excited; his/her heart beats quickly 2) **owáštegina** vt1 s/he is excited about smth

exclusively *adv* **ejé** adv only, nothing but, exclusively

Edmonton (Alberta) *ngeo* **Titága** ngeo Edmonton (Alberta)

effeminate *adj* **wíyįktA ; wíktA** vi1 he is becoming effeminate

egg *n* **wíkta, wítka** n egg ‣ **wíkta agénųba** cp egg dozen

exhausted *adj* 1a) **bastó yįgÁ** vi3 s/he sits down tuckered out, exhausted 1b) **bastó yųgÁ** vi3 s/he lies down tuckered out, exhausted 2) **ğa'ít'A** vs s/he is exhausted, tired, out of breath ‣

ğa'ít'eyA vt1-caus s/he exhausts, tires sb out, make sb be out of breath

eight *n adj* **šaknóğa** num, vs eight; s/he/it is eight; there are eight ‣ **šaknóğana** quant only eight

eighteen *adj n* **agéšaknoğa** num eighteen

eighth *adj n* **ijíšaknoğa ; įšáknoğa** num eighth

eighty *n* **wikcémna šaknóğa** num eighty

exist *v* 1) **ų́** vi1, vi1-aux s/he/it is, lives, exists; s/he/it stays somewhere; s/he feels; exists, is in a certain way; s/he does continuously; goes around doing smth 2) **nážį** vi1 s/he/it stands, stands up; s/he is, exists in a certain condition (used after an adverb or a postposition) 3) **yuká** vs it is, it exists, there is/are (applies only to 3rd person animate or inanimate referents); s/he has smth; it exists for sb (said of body parts, states, personal behavior)

elastic *n* **yuzíksijabina** n elastic

elbow *n* 1) **įspá** n lower part of the elbow ‣ **wįcíspa** n human elbow 2) **įspáse** n point of the elbow

elder *n* 1) **gábina** n-pl elders, old people 2) **tágabina** n-pl elders 3) **watápe** n buffalo hunter, hunter; elderly man, ancestor 4) **watápe wíyą** cp elderly woman

electricity *n* 1) **owán-hįknA ; owáhįknA** vimp, n there is lightning; lightning, electricity, flashlight 2) **wakákni** n electricity (obsolete)

elephant *n* **pasúhąska** n elephant

eleven *num* **agéwąži** num eleven

elk *n* 1) **heȟága ; heȟáge** n elk 2) **ųpá** n female elk

Elk woman society *cp* **wįyábi heȟága okónagiciyabi** ph Elk Woman society

elope *v* 1) **įnáȟmA** vi1 s/he hides, elopes ‣ **wį'ínaȟmA** vi1 he elopes, runs away with a married woman (can also be used when a woman elopes with a man) 2) **įnáȟme iyáyabi** vi2-pl they are eloping

email *n* 1) **wa'ókmabi waká** cp email 2) **wa'óyabi waká** cp Bible, legal document; email

embarrass *v* 1) **įštéjA** vs s/he is bashful, shy, easily embarrassed, ashamed ‣ **įštén** vcont embarrassing ‣ **įštényA** vt1-caus s/he embarrasses, shames sb ‣ **įštén įc'íyA** vi3-refl s/he makes a fool of, embarrasses himself/herself 2) **įdéša iyáyA ; įdé šayá iyáyA** vs s/he blushes; is embarrassed 3) **įtúpa** vt1 s/he avoids sb out of embarrassment; s/he is shy

ember *n* **pedáȟa** n ember, charcoal, spark

embroider *v See:* **decorate**

emerge *v* 1) **kninápA** vi1 s/he comes out, emerges; arrives back here and reappears 2) **énapA** vi1-coll they emerge, rise

empty *v adj* 1) **bapsú** vt1 s/he pours, spills a liquid out; empties a container 2) **skébA** vs it is empty, drained ‣ **skem-** vcont empty, drained ‣ **baskébA** vt1 s/he drains, empties smth out by pushing ‣ **yuskébA** vt2 s/he empties smth out; drains smth (oil in a car, hose, pipe) 3) **ogánA** vt1 s/he empties, pours smth (like ashes) down there

encircle *v* **a'ókšąyA** vt1 s/he encircles, surrounds sb, smth

enclosure *n* **ocágaške** n enclosure

encounter *v* 1) **akípa** vt1 s/he meets sb; encounters, experiences smth 2) **sijá akípa** vi1 s/he encounters, is afflicted with bad luck; it is bad luck ‣ **wósija akípa** vi1 s/he encounters, is afflicted with bad luck; it is bad luck ‣ **šin'ákipa** vt1, vi1 s/he encounters smth bad; is afflicted with bad luck

end *n* 1) **įhágе** vs, n it is the end, the last one, the end of smth ‣ **o'íhągе** n end, conclusion (of a story) ‣ **įhákyA** vt1-caus s/he ends, prevents smth; puts an end to smth ‣ **įhágеda** adv at the end of it ‣ **įhágеdaȟ** adv at the very end of it 2) **ogícuni** n end of smth, closing 3) **žecíyo** adv at destination, at an end point 4) **anúkadahą** adv on each side, end, both ways 5) **cą'íkpa** n treetop; end, tip of a stick 6) **žehágа** n end of a story

enemy *n* 1) **tóga** n enemy ‣ **tógayA** vt1-caus s/he has sb as an enemy ‣ **tók-** cont enemy ‣ **tógagiciyabi** vi1-recip they are enemies, at war against one another 2) **tóktamakoce** n enemy territory

energy *n* 1) **wówaš'age** n energy, strength, power 2) **cíga** adv with energy, strenuously

engine *n* **watpá** n train engine

English *n adj* 1a) **Wašín'i'A** vi1, vt1 s/he speaks English; s/he speaks, talks to sb in English 1b) **Wašín'i'abi** n English language

enjoy *v* 1) **waštégina** vt1 s/he enjoys, loves, is pleased with smth 2) **iyógipi įc'íyA** vi3-refl s/he enjoys herself/himself 3) **wó'imağağa** vs s/he/it is amusing, enjoyable) ‣ **wó'imağağa'įc'iyA** vi3-refl s/he enjoys, amuses himself/herself

enough *adj* 1) **ženága** vs it is enough, sufficient 2) **eyáš** adv sufficient, enough, only, well enough; any, anyways

enroll *v* **cažé ópegiyA** vi1-pos s/he votes, puts his/her name down to become a member; enrolls in an organization

entrance *n* **ti'ágasam** n entrance, inside of a building

expectant *adj n* **waktá** vi1-abs s/he is expectant for sb or smth to happen; s/he/it is alert, careful, aware of smth ‣ **waktá ú** vi1 s/he is expectant, anticipating smth, anxious, alert ‣ **waktáȟ** adv on the lookout, expectantly ‣ **waktáya** adv in anticipation

experience *v n See:* **encounter**

expert *n* **įwáką** vi1, n s/he is an expert; expert, person with a holy gift

epidemic *n* **wįcóyazą** vs-coll, n people are sick from an epidemic disease; illness, epidemic

epilepsy *n* 1) **kąyútibA** vs s/he has cramps; suffers from epilepsy, epileptic seizure 2) **kąyútibes'a** n person suffering from epilepsy

explode *v* 1) **bapóbA** vt1 s/he explodes, bursts smth by sitting or pressing on it 2) **napóbA** vi s/he/it explodes, bursts by itself ‣ **napómyA** vt1-caus s/he causes smth to explode, burst;

bombs smth ‣ **nąpópkiyA** vt1-caus s/he makes it explode; it explodes by itself 3) **mopóbA** vt1 s/he explodes, bursts smth by shooting 4) **baptų́ǧa** vt1 s/he squishes, explodes smth by pushing, sitting on it

equal *v* **štén** conj if . . . when, if . . . then; when, whenever, in, at, on, next; equals (in arithmetic)

equally *adv* 1) **akí'ecen** adv-cont equally, the same, alike 2) **ecédu** vs, adv s/he/it is like this, it happens as such, it is the right way; equally, the same way, the right way

erase *v* **bažúžu** vt1 s/he erases smth by pushing; s/he demolishes, make smth fall apart by putting pressure

eraser *n* **įbážužu** n eraser

erect *v* 1) **wi'óziba** vi1 s/he erects, puts up a tent ‣ **wi'ógiziba** vi1-pos s/he erects, puts up his/her own tent 2) **tijáǧA** vi1 s/he builds a house; erects a tent, lodge

escape *v n See:* **flee**

extend *v* **iyóhi** vt1, vs s/he reaches smth; s/he counts a coup; it extends, is long enough ‣ **iyóhiyA** vt1-caus s/he causes sb to reach it; extends, reaches toward

-eth *suff* **ijí-** ; **į-** pref creates ordinal numbers from cardinal numbers

extinct *adj* **sódA** vs s/he is extinct, gone; perishes ‣ **són** vcont being extinct, gone, perishing ‣ **són áyA** vs it is becoming extinct (not used with humans)

even *adj adv v* 1) **kó** conj also, too, even ‣ **kóko** conj-redup even them; they too 2) **iyéga kóšta** ph even him/her/it/them

even if *ph* **kó eštáš** ph even if

evening *adv n* 1) **ȟtayédu** n, vimp evening; it is evening ‣ **ȟta-** cont in the evening ‣ **ȟtawóda** vi1 s/he/it eats in the evening 2) **a'ókpaza** vimp it is a dark evening 3) **hąkpázA** vimp it is evening twilight 4) **togáȟtani** adv early evening

evenly *adv* **ki-** pref two, in two; separated in the middle; evenly

evergreen *n* **cąwába** n evergreen tree, pine tree

every *adj* 1) **iyúhaȟ** quant every single one of them 2) **iyúhana** quant all, all of them, all of it, every individual in a group, all at the same time (collective meaning) 3) **dokíyo nówaȟ** ph in every which way

everything *pro* 1) **dágu nówa** pro everything 2) **dágugu** pro-redup everything, all things

everywhere *adv* **ówaja** adv everywhere, all over ‣ **makówaja** n all over the world

evil *adj* **wakąsijA** ; **wakąšijA** n, vs evil-spirited being (like Įktómi or the Christian devil); s/he/it is evil-spirited

eye *n* 1) **įštá** n eye ‣ **įštá ošášA** vs s/he has red eyes, bloodshot eyes ‣ **įštátoto** vs s/he/it has blue eyes ‣ **įštá ȟniȟní** vs s/he/it has gummy eyes 2) **dųwÁ** vi1 s/he opens his/her eyes 3) **įstókmuza** vi1 s/he closes the eyes ‣ **įstókmus** vcont with the eyes closed 4) **aknák** adv following, trailing, keeping an eye on, together, along

eye shadow *cp* **įštá sapkíyA** vt1-pos s/he puts on eye shadow; darkens his/her eyes

eyeball *n See:* **iris**

eyebrow *n* **įštáȟe'ųba** n eyebrow

eyelashes *n-pl* **įštáhį** n eyelashes

eyelid *n* **įštáha** n eyelid

F

fabric *n* **zizíbena** n fabric, cloth

face *n v* 1) **įdé** n face 2) **įdókšą** adv around the face 3) **édųwą** ; **édųwą** vi1 s/he looks, faces in a direction

faint *v* **įdókpazA** vs s/he faints ‣ **įdókpaza stéyA** vs s/he feels like fainting

fairly *adj* **-gen** suff rather, sort of, fairly, somehow (derives adverbs from verbs and adds an attenuative meaning)

fall₁ *n* 1) **ptąyédu** n fall, autumn 2) **ptąyésą** adv throughout the fall, all fall 3) **ptį́hą** adv last fall

fall₂ *v n* 1) **hįȟpáyA** vs s/he/it collapses, falls down, falls apart, falls from smth (figuratively "s/he becomes sick") ▸ **ohįȟpayA** vs s/he/it falls off smth ▸ **ahįȟpayA** vt1 s/he/it falls on sb, smth 2) **šųkhįȟpayA** vs s/he falls from a horse 3) **hįhą́** vimp it falls, comes down 4) **ȟijáhą** vs s/he trips on smth and falls 5) **bažúžu** vt1 s/he erases smth by pushing; s/he demolishes, make smth fall apart by putting pressure

family *n* 1) **tiwáhe** n family, household 2) **ti'óšpaye** n group of relatives, an extended family 3) **tiwį́codA** vs-coll there are many families

famine *n* **wįcánodį** n famine

famous *adj* 1) **cažé ótagaga** vs-redup s/he/it has a great, famous name 2) **cažé tą'į́** vs s/he is famous; his/her name is famous

fan *v n* n electric fan 1) **ganú** vt1 s/he fans sb, smth ▸ **ganúnu** vt1-redup s/he fans sb, smth continuously 2) **įjánu** n fan ▸ **ti'óganu** n house fan ▸ **įjánųzakiya** n electric fan

far *adv adj* 1) **téhạn** adv far away, in a distance ▸ **įtehạn** adv from far away, far over there ▸ **įtehą** adv far from, away ▸ **téhạduwa** adv a long distance, far away ▸ **teháduwaȟ** adv a very long distance, really far away ▸ **téhạpadahą, téhạdahą** adv far from over there 2) **manín** adv far away, at a distance 3) **nehágeȟ** adv this long; this far off ▸ **žehą́geȟ** adv only that far off, only that much ▸ **gahágeȟ** adv that far, not so far off 4) **nehágejA** vs s/he/it is about this high, tall, or far ▸ **nehą́hagejA** vs-redup they are about this high, tall, or far

fare *n See:* paycheck

farmer *n* 1) **wa'įcaȟye** n farmer, agricultor 2) **wókšus'a** n farmer, gardener

fart *v n* 1) **ųkca** vii s/he farts ▸ **ųkcakcaya** vii-redup s/he walks farting along ▸ **ųkcana** vii it (baby) farts ▸ **ųkca iyéyA** vii s/he/it farts suddenly, unexpectedly 2) **yusníza** vt2 s/he squeezes the air out; s/he produces a small, silent fart

fast₁ *adj* 1) **núzahą** vs s/he/it is fast, quick ▸ **nús** vcont fast, quick 2) **oȟ'ą́ko** vs s/he is swift, fast ▸ **oȟ'ą́koko** vs-redup s/he/it is very fast, swift 3) **kokóna** adv quickly, fast

fast₂ *n v* 1a) **waką́ iyódągA** vi2 s/he fasts 1b) **waką́ iyódągabi** cp fast

faster *adj* 1) **kapéyaktagA** vii s/he runs faster 2) **núskiyA** vt1-pos s/he makes his/her own faster

fat *n v* 1) **šį** n fat (used only in compounds) ▸ **wašį́** n suet, fat ▸ **ųzéšį** n rump fat 2) **šįtú** vs s/he/it is fat ▸ **ašį́tųgeja** vs s/he/it is kind of fat, chubby 3) **įkní** n grease obtained from marrow or from thin and soft layers of fat inside the stomach ▸ **wį́kni** n fat, grease; gas, oil

Fat-smoker people *np* **Wašį́ azínyabina** nprop Fat-smoker people (band of Nakoda, Saskatchewan)

father *n* 1) **adé** voc, n father (address); my father, dad (reference); Father, paternal spirit ▸ **adéyA** vt1-caus s/he has him as a father 2) **aktúgu, atkúgu** n her/his father ▸ **aktúguyA, atkúguya** vt1-caus s/he has him as a father 3) **waką́tąga** n Great Spirit, Mystery (traditional); God, Lord, Holy Father (Christian)

father-in-law *n* -tųga- ; -tuga- root father-in-law ▸ **tųgáguyA** vt1-caus s/he has him as a father-in-law

Father's Day *cp* **Adé ą́ba** cp Father's Day

fatten *v* **šįtúyA** vt1-caus s/he fattens an animal ▸ **šįtúgijiyA** vt1-benef s/he fattens an animal for sb ▸ **šįtúgiyA** vt1-caus s/he fattens his/her own animal

fault *n* **wa'įc'icaǧa** vi3-refl it is his/her fault

fear *v n* 1) **kogípa** vt1-dat s/he fears sb, smth ▸ **ogícikopabi** vii-recip they fear one another 2) **įníhą** vs s/he fears; is worried

fearful *adj* **okópa** vii s/he is fearful, uneasy (archaic word)

fearsome *adj* **wóginihąga** vs s/he/it is fearsome, dangerous, ferocious

feast *n* 1a) **wódabi** n feast, meal ‣ **wogíksuya wódabi** cp Memorial feast 1b) **owóda** n ; vi1 feast; she sits town to eat 2) **awášpąyĄ** vi1 s/he cooks a feast

feather *n* 1) **wíyaga** n feather ‣ **wíyaga wapáha** cp feather hat 2) **wó'įšte** n eagle feather, plume, down feathers 3) **wacįhe** n feather, plume tied up in the hair 4) **iyáge** n feather on an arrow 5) **šų ~ wíyaga šų** n, cp longest feathers on the wing

February *n* **ąmhąska wí** cp February

feces *n* 1) **ųkcé** n feces 2) **cesní** vs, n s/he/it defecates, takes a shit; feces, dung, shit

feed *v n* 1) **wók'u** vt1 s/he feeds sb, an animal ‣ **wógíjic'u** vt1-benef s/he feeds sb for him/her ‣ **wók'uk'u** vt1-redup s/he keeps feeding sb, an animal 2) **a'ų** vt1 s/he feeds the fire with smth ‣ **agí'ų** vt1-pos s/he feeds the fire with his/her own

Feed the little people ceremony *ph* **Mayáwašiju wowįcak'ųbi** ph Feed the Little People ceremony

feel *v n*

PHYSICAL OR EMOTIONAL EXPERIENCE

1) **wacį** vi3, n s/he feels like doing smth; mind, plan, goodwill; it is about to happen; intentive, prospective, or imminent event ‣ **awácį** vt3, vs s/he feels, thinks about smth, has smth on the mind; it is a purpose 2) **išíjA** vs s/he feels bad because of it ‣ **cądé yasíjA** vt2 s/he makes sb feel bad by speech 3) **šką** vt1, vi1 s/he tries to do smth; s/he is busy; s/he moves, behaves; s/he feels thus 4) **-kna** aux s/he feels, senses (used with verbs or adverbs of negative feelings; triggers e-ablaut) 5) **ų** vi1 s/he/it is, lives, exists; s/he/it stays somewhere; s/he feels; exists, is in a certain way 6) **tawácį dąyą́šį** vs s/he is moody; feels bad

TOUCH

7) **yutątą** vt2-redup s/he feels sb, smth manually, he gropes women's private parts ‣ **yutątą máni** vi1 s/he feels her way while walking (as in the dark) 8) **oyútą** vt2 s/he feels inside of smth ‣ **oyútątą** vt2-redup s/he feels inside smth ‣ **oknútątą** vt1-pos-redup s/he feels inside of his/her own 9) **ayútątą** vt2-redup s/he feels around with the hands ‣ **a'įknutątą** vi3-refl s/he feels himself/herself in search of smth

feline *adj See:* **cat**

female *adj n* **wíyena** n female animal (used in nominal compounds); doe

fence *v n* 1a) **cąbáza** vi1, n s/he puts up a fence; fence ‣ **cą'įkpaza** vt3-pos s/he fences his/her own field, garden 1b) **cąbázabi** n fence

festival *n* **oškáde** n picnic; festival; arena

feverish *adj* **kádA** vi, vs it is hot (weather, food, objects), spicy; s/he is feverish ‣ **kanyágen** adv rather hot; feverish ‣ **kanyágen ų** vs s/he is feverish

few *adv* 1) **dónągen** adv few 2) **ganáknana** adv just a few, less than expected, little bit less 3) **ganáknanaȟ** adv very few, way less than expected 3) **jónana** quant few, little, small amount

field *n* 1) **omáȟkağe** n field 2) **mąkáyuptA** vi2 s/he plows a field

fifteen *num* **agézaptą** num fifteen

fifteenth *adj n* **ijí'agezaptą** ; **į'ágezaptą** num fifteenth

fifth *adj n* **įzáptą** num fifth

fifty *num* **wikcémna záptą** num fifty

fig *n* **ųkcékcena** n-redup fig

fight *v n* 1) **kízA** vt1 s/he fights sb, smth ‣ **gicís** vcont fighting ‣ **gicízA** vt1-dat s/he fights with sb ‣ **gicízabi** vi1-recip they fight one another 2) **gicízabi** n fight, fighting

file *v n* 1) **bamná** vt1 s/he files, rubs smth against it (like a piece of metal) 1) **įbámną** n file, rasp ‣ **įcáwabamna** n rasp, file 2) **abámną** vt1 s/he files smth smooth with a rasp 3) **įyúmą** n sharpener, file

fill *v n* 1) **ožúyA** vt1-caus s/he fills smth 2) **ožútų** vt1 s/he fills smth ‣ **wóžutų** vi1-abs s/he fills into bags or sacks; full bag, bag or sack filled with smth; medicine bundle 3) **ogíbağe** vt1-dat s/he fills a pipe for sb; gives sb a smoke ‣ **ogíjibağe** vt1-benef s/he fills a pipe for sb

find *v n* **iyéyA** vt1 s/he finds sb, smth ‣ **iyégiyA** vt1-pos s/he recognizes, finds his/her own

fine *adj* **mnuná** vs it is fine (powder, flour, sand)

finger *n* 1) **nąpsíhu ; nąpsú** n finger 2) **nąbáwąge** n finger (used in compounds only) 3) **nąbáwąhųge tága** cp thumb 4) **nąbáwąge įjíwažį** cp index 5) **nąbáwąge įjínųba** cp middle finger 6) **nąbáwąge įjíyamni** cp ring finger 7) **šašté** n pinkie, little finger 8) **nąbé okíhąge** cp finger joint 9) **ébazo** vt1 s/he points his/her finger at sb, smth

fingernail *n* **nąpsíhušage** n fingernail

finish *v* 1) **knuštą́** vt1-pos s/he finishes his/her own thing (meal, work) ‣ **knuštą́kiyA** vt1-pos-caus s/he makes sb finish his/her own 2) **įktų́syA ; įtkų́syA** vt1-caus s/he finishes, completes smth ‣ **įktúskiyA ; įtkų́skiyA** vt1-pos s/he finishes, completes his/her own task 3) **gicúni** vt1-irr s/he quits an activity; it is finished ‣ **wotkícuni** vi1 s/he finishes eating

fire *n v* 1) **péda** n fire, match ‣ **pen-** cont fire ‣ **penkákna** adv near the fire ‣ **penkáyena** adv near the fire ‣ **pencóna** adv without a fire ‣ **pensníya** n without a fire ‣ **pen'ókša** adv around a fire 2) **pedáħa** n ember, charcoal, spark 3) **pedį́ħpaya** n ashes 4) **pedį́žaža** n oil lantern 5) **įktų́yA** vt1-caus s/he makes smth burn; sets smth on fire ‣ **wa'įktųyA** vi1-abs s/he sets things on fire (house, building, junk) 6) **cą'įtku** n fire, open fire ‣ **cą'įtkųyA** vt1-caus

s/he makes a fire 7a) **cetí** vii s/he builds a fire; starts a stove ‣ **ce'íc'iti** vi3-refl s/he builds a fire for himself/herself ‣ **cegíti** vt1-pos s/he builds his/her own fire ‣ **cegíjiti** vt1-benef s/he builds a fire for sb 7b) **acéti** vt1 s/he builds a fire on smth 7c) **įcéti** vt1 s/he builds a fire in smth 8) **a'ų́** vt1 s/he feeds the fire with smth ‣ **agí'ų** vt1-pos s/he feeds the fire with his/her own 9) **cą'ózina** n forest fire 10) **oná** n prairie fire ‣ **onáyA** vt1-caus s/he sets the prairie on fire 11) **utá** vii s/he fires, discharges a weapon

firefighter *n* 1) **onákuwes'a** n prairie or forest firefighter 2) **onágasni** n firefighter

firefly *n* **cąyéğa** n firefly

firekeeper *n* **océti awáyaga** cp firekeeper

fireplace *n* 1) **océti** n fireplace, hearth; stove, oven; heater ‣ **océti awáyaga** cp firekeeper 2) **cetíbi** n fireplace

fireworks *n* **napómyabi** n dynamite, fireworks

firmly *adv* **sudáya ; sudáyagen** adv firmly, hard, strongly, solidly

first *adj adv n* 1a) **togáhe** adv, num, vs first, the first, one in the first place; s/he/it is the first; is in the lead ‣ **togáheħ** num the very first one 1b) **togáħ** adv ahead of time; first 2) **togágihĄ** vs ; n s/he is in the lead; s/he is the first; leader

First kill ceremony *ph* **Įwą́žikte** n First kill ceremony

First Nations University of Canada *nprop* **Įkcé wįcášta owáyawa tíbi tága** nprop First Nations University of Canada (Saskatchewan)

First to fly *nprop* **Togá giyą́** nprop First to fly (1887–1971); Nakoda chief also known as Joshua Wetsit

fish *n v* 1) **hoğą́** n fish ‣ **ho-** cont fish ‣ **hoyúdA** vi2 s/he eats fish ‣ **hoğámna** vs s/he/it smells like fish 2) **hokúwa** vii s/he fishes 3) **hoyúpsicA** vi2 s/he jerks fish out of water with a line

fisher *n* **škejá** n fisher

fishhook *n* **ho'įcuwa** n fishhook; fishing pole and line

fishnet *n* **hokmúǧe** n fishnet

fist *n* **nąbé psųkáya** cp fist

fit *v n* **gipí** vs-dat s/he/it fits into smth; s/he is large enough to fit into smth ‣ **ogípi** vs-dat s/he fits in there; is large enough (shoes, pants)

five *num* **zápta** num, vs five; s/he/it is five; there are five ‣ **zaptą́h̃** adv five times ‣ **záptana** quant only five

flag *n* 1) **ticówaknąga ; ticéwaknąga** n flag 2) **gaȟmógena** n flag

flag song *cp* **ticówaknąga onówą** cp flag song

flame *n* 1) **įktų́, įtkų́; įktų́yą yįgÁ; ti'į́ktų** vs, vi3, n s/he/it is lit, in flames, it is in flames, house in flames, arson

flank *n* **niǧúde** n flank, part below the ribs

flap *n v* 1) **ti'į́jaškabi** n tipi flap 2) **goskóza** vt1-redup s/he/it waves, swings, flaps smth (as bird) ‣ **goskós** vcont waving, swinging, flapping smth

flashlight *n* **yu'ówadA** vt2, n s/he lights smth up; flashlight, car headlights

flat *adj n adv* 1) **mnaská** vs it is flat, plain, smooth ‣ **mnaskáska** vs-redup they are flat ‣ **mnamnáska** vs-redup it is flat ‣ **cągámnaska** n board, flat piece of wood 2) **omnáya** vimp it is flat ‣ **omnáyena** n small flat area ‣ **makómnaya** n prairies, flat land 3) **namnáya** vs it opens up flat by itself (as flowers) 4) **omnáwitąga** n large flat area, large prairie 5) **sníza** vs it is flat, has no air in it

Flathead *nprop* **Pámnaska** nprop Flathead tribe, person of Flathead descent

flatten *v* 1) **bamnáska** vt1 s/he flattens smth by pushing, or with his/her body weight 2) **gamnáska** vt1 s/he flattens smth down by striking, beating, hewing (as a piece of wood) 3) **momnáska** vt1 s/he flattens smth by shooting, colliding, running over it 4) **namnáska** vt1 s/he flattens smth by stepping on it

flea *n* **wamnúškaša** n flea

fledge *v* **gihí** vi1-pos s/he/it leaves the nest, is fledged

flee *v* 1) **napÁ** vii s/he flees, runs away, retreats ‣ **napéyA** vt1-caus s/he drives sb away; chases sb, smth away; makes sb flee ‣ **nagíjipA** vt1-benef s/he flees from him/her ‣ **nagípA** vt1-pos s/he flees to his/her own (people, place) ‣ **onápA** vii s/he flees into smth 2) **ti'ánagidą** vt1-pos s/he flees, runs to his/her home

flexible *adj* **wįšwį́žena** vs it is flexible, pliable ‣ **cąwįšwįžena** n piece of wood that is flexible

flicker *n* **zųzúja** n flicker

flint *n* 1) **wahį́** n flint 2) **wahį́kpekpena** n-redup little bow and arrows used by children

float *v* 1) **ogábodA** vi s/he/it floats on water ‣ **ogábon** vcont floating on water 2) **agábodA** vi s/he/it floats on smth ‣ **agábon** vcont floating on smth ‣ **agábonbon** vcont-redup floating around on smth

flood *n v* **mnihíyeyA** vimp there is a flood

floor *n* 1) **cą'ówįža ; cą'ówiža** n wooden floor, mat 2) **cą'ówą** n floor 3) **cą'ónaži̧** (WB) n floor 4) **tigádodo** vii s/he sweeps the floor of the house

flour *n* 1) **aǧúyabi** n flour; bread, bannock 2) **aǧúyabi mnúna** cp flour

flow *v* 1) **ȟaȟá** vimp it is a liquid that flows 2) **a'ú** vimp it flows, comes, oozes out

flower *n* **waȟcá** n flower, blossom

fly *n v* **honáǧina ; honáǧi** 1) n fly (generic); housefly ‣ **honáǧinatotobi** n bluebottle fly 2) **giyÁ** vii vii s/he/it flies ‣ **giyáyą** adv flying 3) **ogíyÁ** vii s/he/it soars, flies about ‣ **ogíyągen** adv flying about; flying around

fox *n* 1) **tokána** n grey fox; swift fox 2) **sįdéšana** n red fox 3) **šúgašana** n red fox

Fox dance *np* **Tokána wacíbi, Tokána owáci** cp Fox dance

foam *n v* **taȟtų́** vi it has foam ‣ **nataȟ̃tų** vi foam appears by itself

fog *n See:* **foggy**

foggy *adj* **cup'ó** vimp, n it is foggy; fog

fold *v n* **bakšíja** vt1 s/he folds smth over by pushing (blanket, clothes)

follow *v* 1) **aknáyA** vt2 s/he/it follows sb, smth along 2) **tapÁ** vt1 s/he follows, pursues sb, smth ▸ **watápA** vi1-abs s/he follows, pursues; hunts buffalo ▸ **tagípA** vt1-pos s/he follows, pursues, tracks his/her own 3) **otápA** vt1 s/he follows, pursues sb, smth ▸ **otágipA** vt1-pos s/he follows, pursues his/her own 4a) **oyé otápA** vt1 s/he follows sb's tracks 4b) **oyé'opA** vi1 s/he tracking sb, smth; follows the tracks of sb, smth 5) **tapÁ** vt1 s/he follows, pursues, tracks sb, smth ▸ **maštį́tapA** vi1 s/he follows, pursues, tracks rabbits

fontanelle *n* **pawíwina** n-redup fontanelle

food *n* 1) **wóyude ; wóyuda** n food, groceries 2) **wo-** pref food (used in compounds) 3) **tóyude kneyábi** cp food offering

fool *v n* 1) **knąyÁ** vt1 s/he fools sb ▸ **waknáyĄ** vi1-abs s/he fools people ▸ **knąyákiyA** vt1-caus s/he fools, tricks sb ▸ **įc'íknąyĄ** vi3-refl s/he fools himself/herself 2) **aknáya** n fool 3) **įštén įc'íyA** vi3-refl s/he makes a fool of, embarrasses himself/herself 4) **a'į́hąbi įc'íyA** vi3-refl s/he makes a fool, laughing stock of himself/herself 5) **zaktébi** n person who fools around; who is mischievous

foot *n* 1) **sihá** n foot ▸ **si-** cont foot ▸ **sinúpin** n both feet 2a) **tacą́kiyutabi** n foot (unit of measurement) 2b) **síyutabi** n so many feet (length; followed by a number) 3) **na- ; ną-** pref by kicking, stepping, walking (forms active verbs); by internal force, heat; by itself (forms impersonal or stative verbs)

Foot people *cp* **Sihábi** nprop Foot people (band of Nakoda)

footage *n* **wįcį́de éyagu** vt2, n s/he photographs, takes a picture of sb; makes a footage of sb; camera

football *n* 1) **tapną́psijabi** n football 2) **napsínyeyabi** n football

footprint *n* **wįcóye** n human footprint

for *prep* this word has no single word equivalent in Nakoda, but it can be translated by a dative, a causative or a benefactive verb 1a) **-gi-** prefix-infix to, for, of (marker of dative verbs; action is directed to or intended for somebody else) 1b) **-kiyA** suff to, for 2) **-giji-** prefix-infix for sb's benefit, on behalf of sb, instead of sb (marker of benefactive verbs; the agent is acting on behalf of or for the benefit of someone else; benefactive verbs are of Class 1)

force *n* **na- ; ną-** pref by kicking, stepping, walking (forms active verbs); by internal force, heat; by itself (forms impersonal or stative verbs) ▸ **nąkádA** vi it becomes hot by itself, internal force

forehead *n* **įté** n forehead

foreskin *n* **snúga** n foreskin; idiot, a person who is pretending not to know anything

forest *n* 1) **cówąja ; cą'ókšą ; cąwókšą** n, adv forest, bush, around the bush, forest 2) **cą'óhą ; cąwóhą** adv in a wooded area, in the bush, forest 3) **cąwóšma** n, vs dense bush, forest 4) **cą'óda** n bush

Forest villagers people *nprop* **Cątúwąbi** nprop Forest villagers or Wood villagers people

forget *v* **agíktųžA** vt1-pos s/he forgets about his/her own; s/he forgets

forgive *v* **agíktųžA** vt1-dat s/he forgives sb for smth

fork *n v* 1) **įcápena ; įcápe** n fork 2) **įwócape** n long fork or stick used to fork up some puppy meat in the kettle dance or clowns' dance 3) **cązáda** n fork in a sacred tree

forked *adj* **žádA** vs it is forked, branched

fort *n* **owónaží** n fort

Fort Belknap agency *cp* **Nakóda tíbi** ngeo Fort Belknap agency (Montana)

Fort Qu'Appelle *cp* **Hókuwa o'įnažį** ngeo Fort Qu'Appelle (Saskatchewan)

forty *num* **wikcémna dóba** cp forty

forward *adv adj v n* **kogám** adv in front, ahead, forward; across

four *adj n* **dóba** num, vs four ; s/he/it is four; there are four ‣ **dóm** cont four ‣ **dóbana** num only four ‣ **dóbagiya** adv four by four, in four ways, in four directions, locations ‣ **dóbaȟ** adv four times

fourteen *num* **agédoba** num fourteen

fourth *n adj* **ijídoba ; įdóba** num fourth

forty *n* **wikcémna dóba** num forty

France *ngeo* **Iyásija makóce** ngeo France, Germany, Ukraine

free *v adj* 1) **įbáǧe'įc'iyA** vi3-refl s/he frees himself/herself 2) **išícona** adv free, available

freeze *v* 1) **daságA** vs s/he/it is frozen, freezing ‣ **dasákyA** vt1-caus s/he freezes smth ‣ **wadásakyA** vi1-abs s/he freezes things 2) **odásagA** vs it is frozen inside, on smth 3) **agácaǧa** vs it is frozen, icy

freezer *n* **įdásakyabina** n freezer

freight car *cp* **wáda įtókšu** cp freight car

French *nprop* **I'ášijana ; I'ášija ; I'ásija ; Iyášija ; Iyásija** nprop person of Dakota, Chippewa, Saulteaux, French, German, Ukrainian, or Russian descent

fresh *adj* **nó** vi it is moist, fresh (as meat)

Friday *n* 1) **ába įzáptą** cp Friday 2) **tacúba ába** cp Friday 3) **tanó yúdabiši** cp Friday

fridge *n* **owádasakyabi** n fridge

friend *n* 1) **koná** n friend; male friend (male speaker) ‣ **konáyA** vt1 s/he has sb as a friend 2) **-takona-** root one's friend ‣ **takónagiciyabi ; takónagugiciyabi** vi1-recip they are friends 3) **takónagutų** vt1 s/he makes friends 4) **-šį-** root female friend (woman speaking)

friendly *adv* 1) **okóna** adv friendly ‣ **okónayA** vt1-caus s/he is friendly with sb ‣ **wakónayA**

okónagiciyabi vi1-abs, vi1-recip s/he is friendly, they are friendly, associate with one another; society, union, association 2) **wa'íyuškį** vi1-abs s/he is friendly

friendship *n* **wadáguye** n friendship

frighten *v* 1) **tąsákt'A** vs s/he is frightened, scared ‣ **tąsákt'ekiyA** vt1-caus s/he frightens, scares sb ‣ **tąsákt'eyA** vt1-caus s/he frightens, scares sb to death 2) **yuš'íyeyA** vt2-caus, vs s/he/it frightens, startles sb; s/he is frightened, scared, afraid

fringe *n* 1) **ogáȟci** n fringes 2) **gaȟcíȟci** vt1-redup s/he cuts fringes ‣ **wagáȟci** vi1-abs s/he slits things; cuts fringes

frog *n* **tabéȟ'a ; tabéȟ'ana ; tabáȟ'a** n frog

from *prep* 1) **-padahą** suff moving from a location ‣ **nedápadahą** adv moving from here, behind, from this side; from the beginning, start ‣ **žedápadahą** adv moving from there, that way ‣ **nazámpadahą** adv from behind, from the back ‣ **caktápadahą** adv from the left side ‣ **įnázapadahą** adv from the back, from behind ‣ **tokámpadahą** adv from a different place 2) **-dahą** suff from that point on ‣ **nedáhą** adv from here, from a group ‣ **edáhą** vs s/he/it is from (a place or tribe); is a member of a group ‣ **žedáhą ; žedą́hą** adv, vs from there, from it; s/he/it is from there ‣ **duktédahą** adv from where, where 3) **ecíyadahą** adv from there ‣ **nécidahą** adv from over here ‣ **žecíyadahą** adv from that direction, from over there ‣ **gákiyadahą** adv from over there, yonder ‣ **dókiyadahą** adv from which direction, where from 4) **žehą́dahą** adv from that time

front *v n adj* 1) **togáda** adv ahead, in front, in the lead, in the first place; in the future, later 2) **įtógam** adv in front of sb, smth; before time 2) **kogám** adv in front, ahead; across

frost *n adj* 1) **cuȟéwaga** vimp, n there is hoar-frost; hoarfrost 2) **acúȟewaga** vs it is frosted, covered with frost; there is hoarfrost

frozen *adj* **agácaǧa** vs it is iced, frozen over

fruit *n* **taspą́** n hawthorn fruit; apple; fruit (in compounds)

fry *v* **co'úba** vt1 s/he roasts; fries; cooks smth ‣ **wacó'uba** vi1-abs s/he roasts, fries, cooks things ‣ **cogíjiba** vt1-benef s/he cooks smth for sb

full *adj* 1) **ožúna** vs it (container) is full; it is full of it 2) **ípi** vs s/he/it is full, sated ‣ **ípiyA** vt1-caus s/he fills sb up (with food) ‣ **ipí'ic'iyA** vi3-refl s/he sates, fills himself/herself up

funny *adj* **wówįȟaga** vs s/he/it is funny, hilarious

fur *n* 1) **hį** n hair, fur, pelt 2) **hįtú** n fur

furrow *v* **įdéšitkiyA** vt1-pos s/he furrows his/her eyebrows; looks discontent

further *adv adj v* 1) **sápana** adv further on, over 2) **iyágasam** adv further, beyond

future *n* **togáda** adv ahead, in front, in the lead, in the first place; in the future, later ‣ **togádagiya** adv in the future

G

gag *v* **iyágu** vi2 s/he gags because of an awful taste in the mouth

gait *n v* **nawą́k** vcont at a slow, easy gait (on a horse)

gale *n* **ganúza tágA** vimp, n it is a gale wind (between 63–87 km/h); gale wind

gall *n* **pizí** n gall

gallop *v* 1) **gadónawaga** vi1 it (horse) gallops ‣ **gadónawąk** vcont galloping ‣ **gadónawąkkiyA** vt1-caus s/he makes a horse gallop 2) **šųk'íkiyA** vt1-caus s/he gallops a horse

gamble *v* 1) **ecúna** n, vi3 game; s/he gambles 2) **mas'íškadA** vt1 s/he gambles money

gambler *n* **ecúnas'a** n gambler, player

game *n* 1) **ecúbina ; ecúna** n game, any kind of contest 2) **nąm'écubina ; nąbé ecúbina ; nąbé škádabi** cp handgame 3) **hába ecúbina** cp moccasin game 4) **caȟ'íjahomni** n game of tops played on ice 5) **tapkápsijektena** n ballgame 6) **wa'óyabi** n card game 7) **wáknibi** n game, meat brought back from a hunt

garden *n* **owókšubi** n garden, planted area

garter *n* **huskíjaǧe** n garter

gas *n* **wíkni** n fat, grease; gas, oil

gas station *cp* **wíkni ibápsu** cp gas station

gash *v* 1) **ma'íc'iškida** vi3-refl s/he cuts, gashes himself/herself 2) **istó knaǧé** vt1-pos s/he gashes his/her arm

gasp *v n* **céya ot'át'A** vi1-redup s/he gasps after crying

gather *v* 1) **gaǧé** vt1 s/he rakes, gathers, sweeps smth together (leaves, snow) ‣ **ogáǧe** vt1 s/he gathers smth in it (as when one picks up dust after sweeping) 2) **yubáǧe** vt2 s/he gathers scattered things into the hand ‣ **yubáȟ** vcont in a united way 3) **bahí** vt1 s/he gathers, picks up smth ‣ **gíjibahi** vt1-benef s/he gathers, picks up smth for him/her 4) **mnayÁ** vt1-caus s/he collects smth; gathers smth, sb ‣ **wamnáyA** vi1-abs s/he gathers, collects things 5) **cagíjine** vt1-benef s/he gathers firewood for sb 6) **baǧé'ic'iyabi** vi1-refl they gather themselves

gathering *n* 1) **gicícobi** vi1-recip, n they invite one another; gathering (where everyone is welcome) 2) **omníjiye** n meeting, gathering

gauze *n See:* **cheesecloth**

geld *v See:* **castrate**

generation *n* 1) **icáǧabi** n generation 2) **wicó'ucaǧa** n generation

generous *adj* **oȟ'ápi** vs s/he is generous

genitalia *n* **cetápą** (OM) n male genitalia (penis and testicles)

George A. Custer *nprop* **Paházizi** nprop George A. Custer, colonel of the American Army, defeated at the battle of Little Big Horn (1839–1876)

German *nprop* **I'ášijana ; I'ášija ; I'ásija ; Iyášija ; Iyásija** nprop person of Dakota, Chippewa, Saulteaux, French, German, Ukrainian, or Russian descent

get off *v* **kihpá** vi1-dat s/he dismounts, gets off from sb, smth

get out *v* **hádi ; hạdi** interj get out; get away; get out of the way

get up *v* 1) **giktá** vi1 s/he gets up (from bed) ‣ **giktá iyéyA** vi1 s/he/it gets up quickly 2) **yugíkta** vt2 s/he gets sb up manually; wakes sb up

ghost *n* 1) **ecábišị** n invisible spirit, ghost 2) **hǔhǔna** n ghost, monster (invoked to scare off children) *See:* **spirit**

Ghost dance *n* **Wanáǧi wacíbi** n 1) Northern Lights; aurora borealis; 2) Ghost dance

giant *n* **wịcášta tága** cp giant

gift *n* **wak'ú** n gift, present

giraffe *n* **tahúhạska** n giraffe

girl *n* 1) **wịcíjana** n ; vs girl; she is a girl ‣ **wịcíjanana** n-redup little girl 2) **wịkóške** n young woman ‣ **wịkóskenana** (CTK) n-redup teenage girl ‣ **wịkóškeškena** n-redup teenage girl

girlfriend *n* **cạdéskuya** n girlfriend, sweetheart

give *v* 1) **k'ú** vt1 s/he gives smth to sb ‣ **gic'ú** vt1-dat s/he gives smth back to sb ‣ **gicíc'ubi** vi1-recip they give smth to one another ‣ **gicíc'u** adv from one to another; giving smth to one another ‣ **ịc'íc'u** vi3-refl s/he gives smth to himself/herself 2) **wịk'ú** vt1 s/he gives him a wife, daughter in marriage

giveaway *n* 1) **hụgóh'a** vi1 s/he does a giveaway, birthday party 2) **Hụgóh'abi** n giveaway 3) **Wakpámni ecúbi** cp giveaway ceremony 4) **Wịcák'ubi ecúbi** cp giveaway ceremony

glass *n* See: **bottle**

glasses *n.pl* 1) **ịštámaza** n glasses 2) **ịštáštana** n-redup glasses 3) **ịštáyabi** n glasses 4) **ị'ákide** n field glasses, binoculars, telescope

glide *v* **gawíǧa** vi it glides in circles ‣ **gawíhwịh** vcont-redup gliding in circles

glitter *v* **yéǧA** vi it glitters ‣ **yehyá** adv glittering

glove *n* 1) **nạbíkpa** n glove, mitten 2) **tamkápsija nạbíkpa** cp baseball glove 3) **tába yukába** cp baseball glove

glow *v n* 1) **yéǧA** vi it glows, glitters ‣ **yehyá** adv glittering, glowing 2) **iyéǧA** vi1 it glows because of it (fire, spark, light, stove) ‣ **iyéhyA** vt1-caus s/he/it makes smth glow

glue *v n* 1) **gastágA** vt1 s/he daubs, pastes, throws, pours out a gooey substance (as to make it stick); s/he glues smth 2) **ayáskamyA** vt1-caus s/he glues, sticks, pastes smth onto it 3) **askámyabi** n glue 4) **wíbuspa** n glue

gnat *n* **tạníjana** n gnat, sandfly

go *v* 1) **yÁ** vi2 s/he goes away from here, s/he departed from here ‣ **áyA** vt2 s/he leaves, takes, goes with sb, smth there 2) **hiyóyA** vt2 s/he goes there to take sb, smth ‣ **kniyóyA** vt2-pos s/he goes there to get his/her own 3) **iyáyA** vi2 s/he sets to go from here, departs from here (before or shortly after departure) ‣ **éyayA** vt2 s/he takes, sets to go with sb, smth there ‣ **yuhíyayA** vt2 s/he sets to go from here, departs from here with sb, smth (before or shortly after departure) 4) **kná** vi1 s/he goes, returns back to where s/he is from ‣ **yútkna** vt1 s/he eats smth while going back 5) **akné** vi1 s/he goes back to smth, somewhere 6) **kniyóyA** vt2-pos s/he goes to get his/her own ‣ **kniyó'i** vt1-pos s/he went after his/her own; gets his/her own back 7) **kuwá** vt1 s/he/it chases, hunts, goes after sb, smth 8) **zuyÁ** vi1 s/he goes on the war path ‣ **zuyé í** vi1 s/he went to war 9) **hádi, hạdi** interj get out; get away; get out of the way

God *nprop* 1) **Wakạtạga** n Great Spirit, Mystery (traditional); God, Lord, Holy Father (Chris-

tian) 2) **tugášina; tugášina** n Grandfather!;
creator; president

gold *n adj* 1) **zizína** vs gold; s/he/it is gold 2)
mázaskazi n gold

goldeye *n* **homnáska** n goldeye

goldfinch *n* **ziktážina ; zitkážina** n goldfinch

gone *adj* **osódA** vi-coll they are all gone ‣ **ti'ósodA**
vi-coll people are all gone, have all left the
house

good *adj* 1) **wašté** vs it is good, nice (event, temperature, object); s/he is pretty, handsome, nice
‣ **waštéya** adv nicely, in a good manner, well ‣
waštéšte vs-redup they (objects) are good, nice
‣ **waštéȟtiyA** vs it is very good, the best, nicest
2) **waštéjaga** vs s/he is kind, good-natured,
pleasant to live with 3) **wįcóni wašté** vs s/he is
in good health 4) **yawášte** vt2 s/he makes smth
sound good; says nice things about sb, smth
5) **yuwášte** vt2 s/he makes smth nice manually; redoes smth in a better way ‣ **įknúwašte**
vi3-refl s/he makes himself/herself look good
6) **dąyą́ ; dayą́** vs, adv s/he/it is well, good, all
right; is in good health (after an illness); well,
properly 7) **dókejašį** vs there is nothing wrong
with him/her/it; it is all good; it does not matter 8) **yupíja** vi2 s/he is good at smth

Good Friday *cp* **Waką́tąga cįhį́ktu ųktébi** ph
Good Friday

good-looking *adj* **ową́yak wašté** vs s/he/it is
beautiful to look at; is good-looking

goose *n* 1) **mağá** n goose; generic for duck,
goose, and swan 2) **sihásaba** n Canada goose
3) **pağų́datąga** n goose 4) **pağų́datąga skána**
cp snow goose

gooseberry *n* **wįcákneška** n gooseberry

gopher *n* 1) **bízena** n gopher, ground squirrel ‣
bis- cont rodent such as gopher, prairie dog,
mouse, rat; squealing 2) **bisknékneğa** n-redup
spotted gopher, thirteen-lined ground squirrel 3) **cąkáhuknekneğa** n striped gopher 4)

tašnáheja n striped gopher 5) **biskúwa** vi1 s/
he chases, looks for gophers

Gophers *nprop* **Bízebina** nprop Gopher people (Nakoda band living near Maple Creek,
Saskatchewan)

gossip *v n* 1a) **a'í'A** vt1 s/he gossips about sb,
smth ‣ **agíci'i'abi** vi1-recip they gossip about
one another ‣ **wa'á'i'A** vi1-abs s/he gossips about things 1b) **wa'á'i'abi** n gossip 2)
awógiciknagabi vi1-recip they talk, gossip
about one another 3) **yamnáyA** adv acquiring
smth by speech; convincing, gossiping

grab *v* 1) **iyáȟpayA** vt1 s/he attacks, rapes sb;
grabs sb, smth with force ‣ **iyágiȟpayA** vt1-
dat ; vt1-pos s/he grabs smth from him/her
with force; s/he grabs his/her own 2) **yuȟnádA**
vt2 s/he claws, grabs sb, smth with the claws,
nails 3) **yaȟnádA** vt2 s/he grabs smth with the
teeth 4) **kí** vt1-dit s/he grabs, takes away smth
from sb

grader *n* **ocągu gaȟ'ú** cp grader

grandchild *n* **-tagoža- ; -tagóžakpa-** root
grandchild

grandfather *n* 1) **-tugaši- ; -tugąši- ; tugągiši-**
root grandfather 2) **tugášina ; tugášina** n
Grandfather! (address form); creator; president 3) **ųká** voc Grandfather! (address form)
4) **gagá** voc Grandfather! (address form)

grandmother *n* 1) **-kuši-** root grandmother (reference) 2) **ųjí** voc Grandmother! (address form)

Grandmother Earth *nprop* 1) **Mikúši makóce**
nprop Grandmother Earth 2) **Ųjímąka** nprop
Grandmother Earth

granite *n* ** įğúğa** n granite

grapefruit *n* **taspą́ ğí tą́ga** cp grapefruit

grapes *n* **ȟ'eyáyana** n grapes

grass *n* **peží** n grass, hay

Grass dance *np* **Peží amíknąk wacíbi** cp Grass
dance

grasshopper *n* **wóga ; wóğa** n grasshopper

gratitude *n* **wópina** n gratitude, thanks

grave *n* **owápiye** n grave, cemetery

gravy *n* **wóžabi** n Saskatoon soup, berry soup; gravy, stew

gray *adj n* 1) **ȟóda** vs s/he/it is gray ‣ **ȟon** vcont gray condition ‣ **ȟonȟóda** ; **ȟotȟóda** vs-redup-pl they are gray 2) **ȟonyÁ** vt1-caus s/he paints, colors, dyes sb, smth in gray ‣ **ȟonkíjiyA** vt1-benef s/he paints, colors sb, smth in gray for sb ‣ **ȟonkíyA** vt1-pos s/he paints, colors, dyes his/her own gray ‣ **ȟon'íc'iyA** vi3-refl s/he paints himself/herself in gray

graze *v* **wíȟ'aȟ'a** vi1-redup it (cattle, horse) is grazing

grease *n v* 1) **wíkni** n fat, grease; gas, oil 2) **íkni** n grease obtained from marrow, or from thin and soft layers of fat inside the stomach 3) **wašná** n pemmican, dried goods; fat, grease, lard 4) **sná; snagíyA** n, vt1-pos lotion, oil, s/he greases, oints smth ‣ **sna'íc'iyA** vi3-refl s/he rubs himself/herself with grease, oil, lotion 5) **asnáyA** vt1-caus s/he rubs sb, smth with grease

Great spirit *cp* 1) **Wakátąga** n Great Spirit, Mystery (traditional); God, Lord, Holy Father (Christian) 2) **Naǧítąga** n Great spirit

greater sage-grouse *cp* **šiyótąga** n greater sage-grouse, sage hen

great-grandfather *cp* **-tugaši- tága** root + vs great-grandfather

great-grandmother *cp* **-kuši- + tága** root + vs great-grandmother

greedy *adj* 1) **nodéhą** vs s/he is voracious; greedy for smth (food, money) 2) **mocéǧ'a** vs s/he is greedy, cheeky, disrespectful 3) **motá** vs s/he is socially aggressive; s/he is greedy ‣ **ímótą** vs s/he cheeky, bold about smth; s/he is greedy

green *adj n* **pežíto** n, vs bluejoint grass; s/he/it is blue-green, green *See:* **blue**

grieve *v* **iyógipisijA** vs s/he is sick, bad, sad, grieving

gristle *n* 1) **ką** n muscle; gristle; tendon, vein, artery 2) **taką** n sinew; deer, moose gristle

grizzly *n* 1) **waǧí** n grizzly 2) **wacúwiska** n grizzly

groceries *n-pl* **wóyude** ; **wóyuda** n food, groceries

grocery store *cp* **wóyude owópetų** cp grocery store

groove *n* **gagúda** vt1 s/he makes a groove, notch with an axe

grope *v n* **yutátą** vt2-redup s/he feels sb, smth manually, he gropes women's private parts

Gros Ventres *nprop* 1) **Ȟaȟátųwą** nprop Gros Ventres, Atsina people, person of Gros Ventres, Atsina descent 2) **Šahíya wašíju** nprop Gros Ventres people, person of Gros Ventres, Atsina descent 3) **Tóga** nprop Gros Ventres, Atsina people, person of Gros Ventres, Atsina descent

ground *n* 1) **mąkán** adv on the ground, earth 2) **makóce** n land, territory, earth, ground; homeland 3) **kúdina ; kúdiyena** adv low, down, near the ground 4) **gisába** n spot of bare ground where the snow has melted ‣ **gisápsabA** vimp-redup there are spots of bare ground where the snow has melted; spots of bare ground where the snow has melted

groundhog *n* **bízena tága** cp groundhog

group *n v* 1) **mnagíciyąbi** vi1-recip they are grouped 2) **ahí** vi-coll they arrive here as a group 3) **baǧé** adv together, bunched up, as a group 4) **iyúha** adv as a group, together

grouse *n* **šiyó** n prairie chicken, pheasant, grouse; domestic chicken

grove *n* **cąwídaga** n grove of trees

grow *v* 1) **įcáǧA** vs s/he/it grows up ‣ **wa'ícaǧA** vi1-abs it (crops, plants) grows ‣ **įgíjicaǧA** vs-benef it (plant, cereal, fruit) grows for him/her ‣ **wa'íc'icaǧa** vi1-refl it is his/her fault 2) **įcáȟyA** vt1-caus s/he grows, breeds smth; raises sb ‣ **wa'ícaȟyA** vi1-abs s/he grows things, breeds animals

growl *v* 1) **ȟnó** vii it (animal) growls ‣ **ȟnokíyA** vt1-caus s/he makes sb, smth (a dog) growl 2) **aȟnó** vt1 s/he/it growls over at sb, smth

grown up *adj n* **tȧgana** vs s/he/it is kind of big, grown up

grudge *v n* **wakíbaži** vii-abs, n s/he is against, opposes people or things; grudge

guard *n* **wa'áwayaga ; wa'áwayage** n guard, patrol

guardian *n* 1) **awȧyages'a** n guardian, bodyguard 2) **owícagaške awȧyage** cp prison guard

guess *n v* 1) **cen** encl must be, I guess, or what (expresses uncertainty) 2) **ȧtó** adv; interj now, well; maybe, I guess

guitar *n* **cabáhotuna yucéya** cp guitar

gull *n* **wicátagana** n gull

gulp *v n* **agáskA** vt1 s/he gulps a liquid; gets drunk

gum₁ *n* **cašį** n resin, gum; chewing gum; rubber

gum₂ *n* **hiyábata** n gum

gummy *adj* **ȧštóȟni** vs s/he/it has gummy eyes

gun *n* **cótaga** n gun

gunpowder *n* **caȟnísaba** n gunpowder

gunshot *n* **utábi** n sound of a shotgun

gunsight *n* **ȧwȧyage** n gunsight

gust *n* **ȧjánuza** vimp there is gust of wind (as when a car passes by)

gut *n v* **šubé** n guts, intestines

gymnasium *n* 1) **oškáde tíbi** cp gymnasium 2) **ti'óškadabi ti'ȧma** cp gymnasium

H

habit *n* 1) **oȟ'ȧ** n action, behavior, habit, manner 2) **tawáci síja** cp bad habits

hail *n* **wasú** n hail

hailing *v* **wasú hȧȟȧ** vimp it is hailing

hailstone *n* **wasúsmuna** n small hail stone, sleet, gresil

hair *n* 1) **pahá** n hair ‣ **pa** cont hair ‣ **paháska** vs s/he has gray hair ‣ **paháskaskana** vs-redup s/

he has pure white hair ‣ **pahášaša** vs-redup s/he has red hair ‣ **pahásapsabA** vs-redup s/he has black hair ‣ **pahásąsą** vs-redup s/he has light grey hair ‣ **paházizi** vs-redup s/he has blond hair 2) **hį** n hair, fur, pelt ‣ **cehį** n man's pubic hairs ‣ **ikúhį** n hair under the chin of a buffalo ‣ **šąhį** n woman's pubic hair 3) **huȟcá** n hair on the hoof or paw 4) **hįšmá** vs s/he/it has thick hair, fur ‣ **hįšmȧšmą** vs-redup it (animal) is thick-haired 5) **smagá** vs s/he/it has thin hair

haircut *n* 1) **pahá gašnábi** cp haircut 2) **gíjašna** vt1-dat s/he cuts sb else's thing with a tool (hair, grass); gives sb a haircut; mows the lawn

half *n adj* 1) **hagé** n half 2) **hehébiya** adv midway, halfway; before 3) **okíse** n half

half moon *n* 1) **hawí cogȧdu** cp half moon 2) **hawí okíse** cp half moon

halfway *adj adv* **hebíya** adv halfway up a hill

Halloween *n* **Wanáǧi ȧba** cp Halloween

halo *n* 1) **tįšnága** n 22° halo, circular halo around the sun on cold winter days 2) **tįšnága bašnóga** cp half halo around the sun, especially in March

halter *n* **ȧdégatita** n halter

hamburger *n* 1) **tanó maksáksabi** cp hamburger 2) **tanóyukpabi** n ground beef, hamburger

hammer *n* **mas'íyapa** n hammer

hamstring *n* **húcoǧa** n hamstring

hand *n* 1) **nabé** n hand ‣ **nam** cont hand 2) **nabé catkána** cp left hand 3) **nabáda** adv by the hand 4) **napcóga** n palm of the hand 5) **yu-** pref with the hand, manually, pulling toward the actor 6) **namgíjawiwi** vt1-dat s/he waves the hand at sb ‣ **namgícigawiwibi** vii-recip they wave the hand at one another) 7) **nabé t'at'Á** vs s/he has a numb hand 8) **namknáskaba** vii-pos s/he claps his/her hands; applauds

hand drum *cp* **nabé gamúbi** cp hand drum

handcuff *n* **nabé į'áyustage** cp handcuff

handkerchief *n* **paȟní įbákįda** cp handkerchief

handle *n* **iyúcą** n handle

hang *v* 1) **oktéyA ; otkéyA** vt1-caus s/he hangs up, suspends smth ‣ **oktégiyA ; otkégiyA** vt1-pos s/he hangs, suspends her/his own (clothes, meat) ‣ **okté'įc'iyA ; otké'įc'iyA** vi1-refl s/he hangs, suspends himself/herself ‣ **owókteyA ; owótkeyA** vt1-caus s/he hangs smth on or inside it 2) **koyákya** vt1 s/he connects, fastens smth to smth, hangs smth 3) **zezéya** adv hanging down, dangling 4) **agázeze** adv hanging down, dangling

hanger *n* **hayábi oktéyabi** cp clothes hanger

hanging *adj* 1) **zezéya** adv hanging down, dangling 2) **agázeze** adv hanging down from smth, dangling

happen *v* 1) **ecédu** vs, adv s/he/it is like this, it happens as such, it is the right way; equally, the same way, the right way ‣ **žécedu** adv, vs in the correct way, thus, like that; it is like that, it happened like that 2) **dókedu** vs, adv s/he/it happened as such; for whatever reason, whatever happens; somehow 3) **duktédu** vimp it happened somewhere as such 4) **hįknA** aux suddenly happens, begins; sudden and sharp 5) **ecéya** vs s/he/it is in such disposition; is affected by smth; happens ‣ **egíjiceya** vs-benef it happens for sb, to sb 6) **nehą́ktA** vimp it is happening 7) **waktá** vi1 s/he is expectant for sb or smth to happen; s/he/it is alert, careful, aware of smth 8) **wacį́** vi3, n, part s/he feels like doing smth; mind, plan, goodwill; it is about to happen; intentive, prospective, or imminent event 9) **awánuȟ** adv unexpectedly, as it happens 10) **dókeȟ'ą** adv how it happened

happily *adv* **owáštenkina** adv happily

happy *adj* 1) **iyópiyA** vs s/he is happy, pleased, merry 2) **iyógipi ; ogípi** vs-dat s/he is happy about, because of sb, smth ‣ **iyógipiyA** vt1-caus s/he/it makes sb happy 3) **wacį́'iyogipi** vs s/he feels happy 4) **įcą́dewašte** vs s/he is pleased with smth; happy about smth 5) **imą́ǧaǧakiyA** vt1-caus s/he amuses sb; makes sb glad

hard *adj* 1) **sudá** vs it is hard, solid; it is strong, tough ‣ **sudáya** adv firmly, hard, strongly, solidly ‣ **sudáyagen** adv kind of hard, solid ‣ **suksúda** vs-redup they are hard ‣ **sudá'įc'iyA** vi3-refl s/he makes himself/herself hard 2) **hásuda** vs s/he/it has a hard skin 3) **teȟígA** vs s/he/it is hard, difficult, critical ‣ **gíjiteȟígA** vs1-benef it is hard on him/her; difficult for him/her 4) **otéȟigA** vs, n it is difficult, hard, problematic, sad; problem, trouble ‣ **owóteȟiga** adv difficult, hard (as in grieving) 5) **sága** vs it is dry, hard (like smth wet that dried up) 6) **síja** vs s/he/it is bad, hard, difficult, harmful, unpleasant 7) **ogáȟ síja** vs it is hard to make

harden *v* 1) **nasúda** vt1 s/he hardens smth by stepping on it 2) **yusúda** vt2 s/he hardens, toughens smth; confirms smth

hardware store *cp* **máza o'ópetų** cp hardware store

hardwood *n* **cąsúda** n ash tree; hardwood

Harlem (Montana) *ngeo* 1) **Agásąm ti'óda** ngeo Harlem (Montana) 2) **Įdéša ti'óda** ngeo Harlem (Montana)

harness *v n* **šųk'į́koyakyA** vi1 s/he harnesses a horse, ties a horse to a wagon

harrow *n* **mąkáyuǧe** n harrow

harvest *v n* **kpahį́** vt1 s/he harvests smth ‣ **wakpáhį** vi1-abs s/he harvests grain, cereals

hat *n* 1) **wapáha** n cap, hat, bonnet ‣ **tatą́ga wapáha** cp buffalo headdress ‣ **wíyaga wapáha** cp feather hat, war bonnet ‣ **wíyaga wapáha sįdé yuké** ph war bonnet with trailer 2) **pahį́pahá** cp porcupine quill hat 3) **wapéša** n roach headgear

hatch *v* **kpakpí** vi1 it (egg) hatches

hatchet *n* **ųspéhudana** n hatchet

hate *v n* 1) **waȟténašį** vt1 s/he hates, dislikes sb, smth (taste, task, person) 2) **gabį́** vi1-aux s/he is reluctant, hates doing smth (follows a verb)

haul *v n* **tokšú** vt1 s/he/it hauls, transports smth from one place to another ▸ **togíjikšu** vt1-benef s/he hauls, transports smth for sb else

have *v* 1) **yuhÁ** vt2, adv s/he has, possesses smth; s/he carries sb, smth; s/he gave birth to a child; s/he holds smth (meeting, ceremony); s/he keeps, looks after, treats sb, smth; carry, hold, have with one (precedes verbs of traveling) ▸ **yuhána** vt2 s/he (baby, small child) has sb, smth ▸ **wayúhA** vi1-abs s/he has things ▸ **gíjiyuhA** vt1/2-benef s/he has, carries smth for sb ▸ **yuhákiyA** vt1-caus s/he makes sb have, carry, keep smth ▸ **knuhÁ** vt1-pos s/he has his/her own thing, carries, keeps smth with him/her ▸ **a'íknuhA** vi3-refl s/he has, keeps smth for himself/herself ▸ **yuhá ú** vt1 s/he continues having smth ▸ **yuhápija** vs it is worth having ▸ **oyúha síjA** vs it is difficult to have ▸ **owášte yuhÁ** vs it is easy to have 2) **masyúheja** vs s/he has money; is wealthy 3) **wayúheja** vi2-abs s/he is wealthy 4) **yuká** vs s/he has smth; it exists for sb (said of body parts, states, personal behavior) 5) **cijódA** vs-coll s/he has many children; there are many children 6) **-yA** suff s/he has somebody as a relative; is in relation to someone (also cause, make, let)

Havre (Montana) *ngeo* **Bahásaba** ngeo Havre (Montana)

hawk *n* 1) **cedá** n hawk 2) **cášká** n hawk, chicken hawk

hawthorn *n* **taspá** n hawthorn fruit; apple; fruit (in compounds) ▸ **taspáspana** n-redup hawthorn berries; crabapple ▸ **taspáhu** n hawthorn bush

hay *n* 1) **pež* í** n grass, hay 2) **pežígabuza** n dried hay

hay bale *cp* **pež* í pahtábi** cp hay bale

hayfork *n* 1) **pež* í'íkpa** n hayfork 2) **pež* í icápe** n hayfork

Hays (Montana) *ngeo* 1) **Toktí** ngeo Hays (Montana) 2) **Agáda** ngeo Hays (Montana)

Haywahe *nprop* **Héwahi** nprop surname in Carry The Kettle

hazelnut *n* **ú'í** n hazelnut

he *pro* 1a) **-Ø-** prefix-infix he, she, it (3rd person singuler, unmarked form of an active or stative verb) 1b) **-Ø-** prefix-infix he, she, it (3rd person singular, unmarked form of a stative verb) 2) **né** dem, pro this, these (near the speaker); this, he, she, it 3) **žé** dem, art, comp, pro he, she, it

head *n v* 1) **pá** n head ▸ **pamáknena** adv with the head bowed 2) **ipá** n head of smth (mountain, hill) 3) **peyéde, pesnéda** n crown of the head 4) **nawáde** n temple, side of the head 5) **gamúbipa** n drum head 6) **pakóya, pakówa** adv all over the head 7) **awáciya** adv for the sake of it, in a contemplative manner; heading for a place

headache *n* **payáža** vs s/he has a headache

headlight *cp See:* **light**

hexagon *n* **o'ípa šákpe** cp hexagon

heal *v* 1) **asní** vs s/he is healed, has recovered from an illness; is well again ▸ **agísni** vs-dat s/he heals, recovers from smth (wound, illness) 2) **gisníyA** vt1 s/he saves, heals sb from an illness 3) **asníyA** vt1-caus s/he heals sb ▸ **asní'íc'iyA** vi3-refl s/he heals, relieves himself/herself 4) **niyáyA** vt1-caus s/he heals sb, brings sb back to life ▸ **nigíyA** vt1-pos s/he heals, saves, rescues his/her own 5) **níktekiyA** vt1-caus s/he heals, doctors sb ▸ **wan̨íktekiyA** vi1-abs s/he doctors, heals ▸ **níktegijikiyA** vt1-benef s/he doctors, heals sb for him/her ▸ **níktegicikiyabi** vi1-recip they doctor, heal one another 6) **wa'ánowa** vi1-abs s/he heals by chanting

health *n* 1) **wicóni wašté** vs s/he is in good health 2) **gažák** vcont in poor health, in agony

hear *v* **nah̨'ú ; onáh̨'ú** vt1, vt1 s/he hears, listens to sb, smth; s/he obeys sb, s/he hears about smth

hearing aid *cp* **núğe ús wa'ánağoptabina** ph hearing aid

heart *n* 1) **cądé** n heart; feelings, emotions, sentiment ‣ **cąt-** cont heart 2) **cądéwašteya** adv with a good heart)

heart attack *cp* **cądé įnážį** vs s/he has a heart attack

heartbeat *n* **iyápabi** n pulse, heartbeat

heartless *adj* **cądé wanįjA** vs s/he is heartless

heat *v n* 1) **kanyÁ** vt1-caus s/he heats smth up ‣ **kangíyA** vt1-pos s/he heats up his/her own thing 2) **ga-** pref by striking, hitting with an intrument; by the blowing wind; by the heat of the sun; by itself 3) **na-** ; **ną-** pref by kicking, stepping, walking (forms active verbs); by internal force, heat; by itself (forms impersonal or stative verbs)

heater *n* **océti** n fireplace, hearth; stove, oven; heater

heaven *n* 1) **nağí makóce** cp heaven 2) **makóce owáštejaga** cp heaven

heavily *adv* **ktáyagen** adv heavily

heavy *adj* **ktá** (CTK) ; **tká** (PR, OM) vs s/he/it is heavy

heel *n* **siyéda** n heel; Achilles tendon

hello *interj* 1) **háu** interj Hello! (male speaker to another male) 2) **hą́** adv, interj yes; Hello! (female speaker) 3) **hahá'aha** interj Greetings! (as one opens the door)

helmet *n* **mázawapaha** n helmet

help *v n* **ógiyA** vt1-dat s/he helps sb ‣ **ógiciyabi** vi1-recip, vi3-refl they help one another, s/he helps himself/herself *Vrefl:* **ógi'įc'iyA**

helper *n* **ógiyabi** n helper

hemorrhage *n* **weȟáȟa** vs s/he has a hemorrhage, bleeds constantly

hen *n* **ąbáhotųwįyena** n hen

her *adj pro* 1) **-gu-** ; **-ju** suff-infix his, her, their (3rd person singular possessor; used with kinship and a few common nouns) 2) **-ktu** ; **-tku** suff his, her (3rd person singular possessor; used only with kinship nouns) 3) **Ø-** pref his, her, its (3rd person singular unmarked possessor) 4) **-Ø-** prefix-infix him, her, it (3rd person singular, unmarked form of an active verb) 5) **-gi-** ; **-ki-** ; **-k-** pref on one's own (marker of possessive verbs where the agent is acting on his/her own thing, body part, or relative; the resulting possessive verbs are of Class 1) 6) **táwa** pro; vs his/her; s/he owns it, it is his/her own

herd *n* 1) **optéya** n herd 2) **maštį́jabina** n-pl rabbit herd 3) **taȟcíjana** ; **táȟtíjana** n deer (generic), herd of deer; white-tailed deer 4) **tatágabina** n-pl buffalo herd

here *adv* 1) **nén** adv here (precise location near the speaker), in a place 2) **néci** adv over here, here 3) **nedáhą** adv from here, from a group ‣ **nedáhągeja** vs it is from around here 4) **nedápadahą** adv moving from here, behind, from the side; from the beginning, start 5) **nédu** ; **néduȟ** vimp, vimp it is here, this is the place, it is right here, this is exactly the place 6) **duktékten** ; **duktékte** adv-redup here and there; occasionally 7) **én** post in, into, on, onto, at, to; here, there 8) **wįnwįda** adv-redup here and there

heron *n* **hoká** n heron

hers *pro* **táwa** pro, vs his/her; s/he owns it, it is his/her own

herself *pro* **iyé** pro, vs himself, herself, themselves, itself (emphasizes the subject or object); s/he/it/they is/are the one ‣ **iyéš** pro him, himself, her, herself as opposed to someone else; him/her on the other hand ‣ **iyégeȟ** pro him/her/it/themselves specifically ‣ **iyégeȟtįyA** ; **iyéȟtįyA** vs it is him/her/it/themselves specifically

hey *interj* **dó** interj hey

hiccups *n* **mnogáskA** vi1 s/he has hiccups

Hidatsa *nprop* **Ȟewáktųkta** nprop Hidatsa people, person of Hidatsa descent

hide₁ *n* 1) **há** n skin, hide, bag, pouch, any type of container ‣ **ptehá** n buffalo hide ‣ **tahá** n deer, moose, elk hide **·** **tatágaha** n buffalo hide 2) **teȟpí** n raw hide, buckskin

hide₂ *v* 1) **bustágA** vi1 s/he/it hides 2) **naȟmÁ** vt1 s/he hides sb, smth **·** **nagíjiȟmA** vt1-benef s/he hides sb, smth from him/her **·** **nagíȟmA** vt1-pos s/he hides his/her own thing 3) **įnáȟmA** vi1 s/he hides, elopes **·** **įnáȟmegiciyabi** vi3-recip they hide from one another **·** **įnáȟmekiyA** vt1 s/he hides from sb, smth 4) **mahéyįgA** vi3 s/he/it hides under 5) **įnám** adv hiding behind smth

high *adj adv n* 1) **wągáduwa** vs, adv it is high, highly placed, of value; way above, way up there, high up) **·** **cąwągąduȟ** adv high up in a tree 2) **wagą́n** adv up 3) **nehą́gejA** vs s/he/it is about this high, tall, or far **·** **nehą́hągejA** vs-redup they are about this high, tall, or far

high heels *cp* **siyéda wagádu** cp high heels

high school *cp* **owáyawatąga** n high school

highway *n* **ocągutąga** n highway

hill *n* 1) **bahá** n hill, mound **·** **abáha, abáhana** n knoll, small hill, mound **·** **bahádahą** adv from the hill **·** **bahágan** adv on a mound, hilltop **·** **bahátakiya** adv toward the hill 2) **hebíya** adv halfway up a hill 3) **ȟeyátakiya** adv toward the hill 4) **a'íbazija** n row of hills

hillside *n* **naȟ'ámya** adv on the hillside

hilly *adj* **ȟoškíškina** n sandy, hilly terrain

him *pro* 1) **-Ø-** prefix-infix him, her, it (3rd person singular, unmarked form of an active verb) 2) **iyé** pro, vs himself, herself, themselves, itself (emphasizes the subject or object); s/he/it/they is/are the one **·** **iyéȟ** pro specifically, really him, himself, she, her, herself, they, them, themselves, it, itself **·** **iyéš** pro him, himself, her, herself as opposed to someone else; him/her on the other hand

himself *pro* **iyé** pro, vs himself, herself, themselves, itself (emphasizes the subject or object); s/he/it/they is/are the one(s) **·** **iyéȟ** pro specifically, really him, himself, she, her, herself, they, them, themselves, it, itself **·** **iyégeȟ** pro him/

her/it/themselves specifically **·** **iyégeȟtįyA** ; **iyéȟtįyA** vs it is him/her/it/themselves specifically

hip *n* **nįdé** n lower part of the back, above the rump; hip

hip bone *n* **nįséhu** n hip bone

hire *v n* 1) **wówašikiyA** vt1-caus s/he hires sb; makes sb work 2) **wówaši okíyA** vt1-caus s/he hires sb 2) **wówaši ecúkiyA** vt1-caus s/he puts sb to work; hires sb

his *adj* 1) **-gu- ; -ju** suff-infix his, her, their (3rd person singular possessor; used with kinship and a few common nouns) 2) **-ktu ; -tku** suff his, her (3rd person singular possessor; used only with kinship nouns) 3) **Ø-** pref his, her, its (3rd person singular unmarked possessor) 4) **-Ø-** prefix-infix him, her, it (3rd person singular, unmarked form of an active verb) 5) **-gi- ; -ki- ; -k-** pref on one's own (marker of possessive verbs where the agent is acting on his/her own thing, body part or relative; the resulting possessive verbs are of Class 1) 6) **táwa** pro; vs his/her; s/he owns it, it is his/her own

hit *v n* 1) **apÁ** vt1, vi1 s/he hits, strikes, knocks sb, smth; it is X hour **·** **tam'ápA** vi1 s/he hits a ball 2) **į'ápA** vt1 s/he hits sb, smth with it 3) **badín iyéyA** vt1 s/he nudges sb, hits sb slightly 4) **ga-** pref by striking, hitting with an intrument; by the blowing wind; by the heat of the sun; by itself **·** **gaptáyA** vt1 ; vi1 s/he/it knocks, hits smth down; the wind knocks, hits smth down; s/he has a car accident 5) **mokógA** vt1 s/he makes a tapping sound by hitting with a projectile, or a stick on smth; s/he plays pool **·** **mokók** vcont making a tapping sound; playing pool

hitch *n v See:* **load**

hobble *v n* 1) **hugáškA** vt1 s/he ties its leg; hobbles a horse 2a) **įhúpaȟtA** vt1 s/he ties its leg; hobbles a horse 2b) **įhúpaȟte** n hobble

hockey *n* 1) **caȟkázo ecúbina** n hockey team,

game 2) **gazógic'u** vi-irr s/he skates; plays hockey 3) **gazógic'u skádA** vi1 s/he plays hockey 4) **cá ús apábi** np wooden stick (baseball, hockey stick)

hoe *n* **maká ijápte** cp hoe

hog *n* **gugúšamnoga** n hog

hog-nosed snake *cp* **paknážutka** n hog-nosed snake

hold *v* 1) **yúzA** vt2 s/he holds, pulls grabs, nabs, catches sb, smth; s/he marries sb ‣ **yuskíyA** vt1 s/he makes sb hold sb, smth ‣ **yús** vcont holding sb, smth ‣ **knuzÁ** vt1-pos s/he holds his/her own thing ‣ **oyúze síjA** vs it is difficult to hold 2) **yús náyuzA** vt2 s/he holds, grasps, clinches on smth 3) **nąbáda yúzA** vt2 s/he holds sb's hand (not used for greetings) 4) **teȟína** vt1 s/he loves, holds on to smth, cherishes sb (like a relative), prizes smth and does not want to part with it 5) **yuhÁ** vt2, adv s/he has, possesses smth; s/he carries sb, smth; s/he gave birth to a child; s/he holds smth (meeting, ceremony); s/he keeps, looks after, treats sb, smth; carry, hold, have with one (precedes verbs of traveling) 6) **hokšíknuhA** adv holding one's baby

holder *n* **iyáyuza** n holder, anything that holds

hole *n* 1) **oȟnógA** n, vs hole; it is a hole in smth ‣ **oȟnóȟnogA** vimp-redup it is full of holes 2) **wa'óȟnoga** n hole, cave 3) **bis'óȟnoga** n gopher hole 4) **mayá'oȟnoǧa** n hole in a rock ‣ **ti'óȟnoga** n smoke hole of a tipi 5) **núǧe oȟnóga** cp ear holes 5) **baȟnógA** vt1 s/he pierces, makes a hole with a sharp tool 6) **gaȟnógA** vt1 s/he makes a hole by striking with a tool ‣ **gaȟnóȟnogA** vt1-redup s/he makes holes by striking with a tool 7) **maȟnógA** vt1 s/he pierces a hole in smth with a knife, saw, or punch 8) **naȟnógA** vt1 s/he makes a hole by stepping on, kicking smth, with one's body weight 9) **yaȟnógA** vt2 s/he/it gnaws a hole in smth, chews smth up (like a mouse chewing on clothes) 10) **yuȟnógA** vt2 s/he makes a

hole in smth with an instrument or manually 11) **ticéda** n smoke hole

hollow *adj* 1) **ȟnogéja** vs it is hollow 2) **škokpá** vs it is hollow, caved in

holy *adj* **waką** vs, adv s/he/it is holy, spiritually powerful; s/he/it is mysterious, magical (occurs with words for European objects); medicine line; in holy manner ‣ **wakáya** adv in a holy way, spiritually correct way ‣ **wakákiyA** vt1-caus s/he considers sb, smth as holy ‣ **wakáką** vs-redup s/he/it is kind of holy, very holy

Holy Mary *nprop* **Iná waką** cp Holy Mary

home *n* 1) **tída, cída** adv home, at home, homewards (often used with going/returning verbs) 2) **tiyáda** adv toward home ‣ **tiyám** adv-cont toward home; at home ‣ **tiyápkiya** adv toward home 4) **ti'ánagidą** vt1-pos s/he flees, runs to his/her home

homeland *n* **tó'u** n homeland

homeless *adj* **ticóna** vs s/he is homeless

homerun *n* **tiyám kní** cp homerun

homework *n* **wayáwa wókmA** vi1-abs s/he writes, does his/her homework

homosexual *n* **waǧínuba ; wanáǧi núba** n homosexual person

honest *adj* 1) **cóǧA** vs, n s/he is honest; truth, honesty ‣ **cóǧeȟ** adv honestly, in an honest manner 2) **cóȟtiyA** vs, n s/he/it is very honest; it is the truth; truth

honestly *adv* 1) **cóȟ** adv-cont absolutely, truely, honestly, for sure, really (puts emphasis on the verb) 2) **cóǧeȟ** adv honestly, in an honest manner 3) **wijákeya** adv truthfully, honestly

honey *n* **tuȟmáǧa cesní** cp honey

honor *n v* 1) **iyódą** n honor 2) **iyódągina** vt1-pos s/he honors his/her own ‣ **iyódąkiyA** vt1-caus s/he honors sb, smth 3) **wógidą** vi1 s/he gains honors ‣ **wógidąya** adv gaining honor 4) **ya'ónihą** vt2 s/he congratulates, honors sb by speech; s/he brags about smth 5) **yu'ónihą** vt2 s/he honors, respects, defers to him/her/

it 6) **yupíbiga** vs-pass s/he is honored 7) **catkú** n honor place

hoof *n* 1a) **šagé** n nail, hoof, claw 1b) **tašáge** n ruminant's hoof 2) **šuknábe** n paw with claws, hoof 3) **šukšáge** n hoof of a horse

hoop *n* **magé** n hoop

hoop dance *np* **cạ'ómįmạ owáci** cp hoop dance

hop *n* **iyópsije** n hop, jump

horn *n* 1) **hé** n horn ▸ **tahé** n horns of a ruminant 2) **heyúkạ** vs s/he/it has horns 3) **šųkhéyuke** n sheep

horny *adj* **įškạ́** vs s/he/it is horny

horse *n* 1a) **šúgatạga ; šųktága** n horse ▸ **šúgatạgana** n little horse 1b) **šúga** n dog, canine; horse (in possessed forms only) ▸ **šųk-** cont dog, horse, sheep (used as the first member of compounds) 2) **šųgána** n old horse 3) **šųkmnóga** n stallion

TYPES OF HORSES

4) **įwátape** n horse used in buffalo hunting 5) **šųkháhana** n spirited, lively forse 6) **šųk'įkceya** n Cayuse, horse or pony of little value 7) **šųkskúsku** n mangy horse 8) **šųksídeksa** n bobtail horse 9) **šųktúske** n stunt horse 10) **šųkwówaši** n work horse 11) **šųk'ókuwasije** n bronc 12) **šųkpámnina** n bucking horse 13) **šųkwį́caȟtiyaną** n old stallion 14) **šųkyúhųhųza** n pacer (horse that lifts the front and back leg on the same side, and rocks or "shakes" side to side as it moves forward) 15) **šųkwáyaȟtages'a** n bitting horse

COLORS OF HORSES

16) **šųkhį́ša** n bay horse, reddish horse 17) **šųkhį́to** n blueish, gray horse 18) **šųkhį́tokneška** n straight-eyed horse, blue roan horse 19) **šųkknékneǧa** n pinto horse 20) **šųknį́deska** n Appaloosa 21) **šųksába ; šúgasaba** n black horse 22) **šųkská** n white horse 23) **šųkzí** n buckskin horse; sorrel horse 24) **ak'į́šúgatạga** cp pack horse

ACTIVITIES AROUND HORSES

25) **agányįgA, agányạgA** vt3 s/he rides a horse (short form for šúgatạga agányạga 's/he sits on a horse') 26) **šųk'áktakkiyA** vt1-caus s/he rides a horse, makes a horse run 27) **ak'įtųga** vt1 s/he saddles a horse, harnesses a dog 28) **gadónawạkkiyA** vt1-caus s/he makes a horse gallop 29) **hugáškA** vt1 s/he ties its leg; hobbles a horse 30) **nawạ́kwạga** vi1-redup it (horse) trots 31) **šųk'ášpạyA** vi1 s/he brands horses 32) **šųkhį́ȟpạyA** vs s/he falls from a horse 33) **šųkhótųtų, hotų́tų** vi1 it (wolf, coyote, dog) howls; it (horse) neighs 34) **šųk'įkiyA** vi1 s/he gallops a horse 35) **šųk'įkoyakyA** vi1 s/he harnesses a horse, ties a horse to a wagon 36) **šųkkúwa** vi1 s/he chases, handles, pursues horses 37) **wak'įtáwa** vi3 it (horse) is saddled 38) **šųkmínik'u** vi1 s/he waters horses 39) **šųk'ówode** n place where horses feed

Horse dance *np* **Šųkwácibi** n horse dance

horsefly *n* **tažúškatạga** n horsefly

horseshoe *n* 1) **šųksíhamaza** n horseshoe 2) **šųkšágemaza** n horseshoe

hospital *n* **wįcóyazạ tíbi** cp hospital

hot *adj* 1) **kádA** vimp, vs it is hot (weather, food, objects), spicy; s/he is feverish ▸ **katkádA** vs-redup they are hot 2) **okádA** vimp it is hot inside ▸ **okánya** adv being hot inside ▸ **ti'ókadA** vimp it is a hot dwelling 3) **nạkádA** vi it becomes hot by itself, internal force 4) **maštá** vimp it is hot weather ▸ **maštášta** vimp it is very hot 5) **makádA** vimp it is hot weather (contraction of maštá káda)

hot dog *cp* **šúga káda** cp hotdog

hotel *n* **o'į́štima tíbi** cp hotel, motel

Hotomani *nprop* **Hotų́mani** nprop Hotomani (surname in Carry The Kettle)

hound *n* **šųkpúdehạska** n hound

hour *n* 1) **o'ápe** n hour 2) **wạží ehạ́'i** cp hour

house *n* 1a) **tí** vi1, n s/he lives somewhere (house, place, area); house, place (used in mostly in compounds, or with a demonstrative) ‣ **tín** adv inside a house ‣ **ti'ókšą ; tiwókšą** adv around the house, camp ‣ **ti'íyaza** adv from house to house; all throughout camp 1b) **tíbi** n house, dwelling, any type of structure ‣ **wašíju tíbi ; wašíjuti** cp house, framed house 1c) **tóhe ; tíhe** n his/her place, house, bed 2a) **cą'óti** n log cabin 2b) **cątíbi** n log house 3) **íyą wašíjuti** cp brick house 4) **opšíje tíbi** cp mud house 5) **tiyúžaža** vi1 s/he cleans a house 6) **ti'óšijámna** vimp it is a smelly house, dwelling 7) **ti'ókadA** vimp it is a hot dwelling, house 8) **ti'ósni** vimp it is a cold dwelling, house 9) **ti'ókšą** adv around the house

household n **tiwáhe** n family, household

how adv conj 1) **dóken** adv how, what; in some way, whichever way or manner (not used as interrogation) 2) **dóna** pro, quant how many, what number; how much; several ‣ **dónągeja** pro how many, much

howl v 1) **hó** n, vi1 voice; it (canine) howls 2) **šųkhótųtų** vi1 it (wolf, coyote, dog) howls; it (horse) neighs 3) **mohóya** vt1 s/he makes smth howl, cry (dog) by shooting

hug n v 1) **póskin** adv hugging, embracing; around the neck 2) **póskin yúzA** vt2 s/he hugs, embraces sb ‣ **póskin knúzA** vt1-pos s/he hugs, embraces his/her own

human n **wįca- ; wįc-** cont human (in compounds only)

humbly adj 1a) **ųšiya** adv pitifully, humbly 1b) **ųšigiya** adv pitifully, humbly 2) **įknúhokunyena** adv humbly

humility n **ahé** interj expression of humility said at the beginning of a prayer or song

hummingbird n **ziktána wakmúha ; zitkána wakmúha** cp hummingbird

hunchbacked adj **túǧa** vs, n s/he is hunchbacked; hunchback

hunched adj 1a) **pšųkáyenaȟ** adv hunched, crouched down, lying in a spherical shape 1b) **pšųkáya** adv hunched, crouched down, lying in a spherical shape

hundred adj n **obáwįǧe** num hundred

hungry adj 1) **įdúka** vs s/he is hungry 2) **nodín t'A** vs s/he/it is hungry, starving

hunt v n 1a) **iyáme í** vi1 s/he went hunting 1b) **iyáme yÁ** vi2 s/he goes hunting 2) **oné** vt1 s/he looks for smth; hunts ‣ **ogíjine** vt1-benef vt1-benef s/he hunts for sb ‣ **wóne** vi1-abs s/he hunts, looks for things 3) **kuwá** vt1 s/he/it chases, hunts, goes after sb, smth 4) **capkúwa** vi1 s/he hunts beaver 5) **watápA** vi1-abs s/he follows, pursues; hunts buffalo

hunter n 1) **owįcanebi** n hunter 2) **watápe** n buffalo hunter, hunter; elderly man, ancestor

hunting n **wakúdebi** n shooting, hunting

hurry v n 1) **húȟni** vi1 s/he hurries in ‣ **húȟniya ; húȟniyena** adv hurriedly, in a rush ‣ **húȟniyA** vt1-caus s/he hurries sb 2) **įnáȟni** vi1 s/he hurries; is in a rush ‣ **įnáȟniyA** vt1 s/he hurries sb ‣ **įnáȟnigen** adv kind of in a hurry; sort of hastily ‣ **įnáȟniyą** adv hurriedly ‣ **įnáȟniyena** adv hurriedly, in a rush (more intense than įnáȟniyą)

hurt v 1) **ksuyÁ** vt1 s/he/it hurts sb ‣ **ksugíyA** vt1-pos s/he/it hurts his/her own (mental or physical pain) ‣ **ksu'íc'iyA** vi3-refl s/he hurts, injures himself/herself 2) **yazá** vs s/he is sick; s/he is hurt; feels pain in a body part (always preceded by a body part)

husband n 1a) **-hįkna- ; -hįkną-** root husband 1b) **hįknáyA** vt1 she marries sb; has sb for husband 2) **wįcáȟca** n my husband (from of address; archaic) 3) **hįknátų** vt1 she has a husband; is married ‣ **hįknátųkiyA** vt1-caus s/he makes her marry, take a husband

I

I *pro* 1) **-wa-** prefix-infix I (1st person singular, agent/subject of active verbs of Class 1) 2) **-mn-** prefix-infix I (1st person singular; agent/subject of active verbs of Class 2) 3) **-m-** prefix-infix I (1st person singular; agent/subject of active verbs of Class 3) 4) **-ma-** prefix-infix I (1st person singular; subject of stative verbs); me (patient of transitive verbs); my (used with nouns for body parts) *See:* **myself**

ice *n* 1) **cáǧa** n ice ‣ **caȟ-** cont ice ‣ **mnicáǧa** n frozen water 2) **caȟmáhen** adv under ice 3) **caȟ'ópA** vi1 s/he falls in the ice

ice cream *n* **caȟyúkpạbi** n ice cream

ice house *cp* **caȟtí** n house, building to store ice

ice tops *n* **caȟkáhomni** vi1 s/he spins ice tops

iced *adj* **agácaǧa** vs it is iced, frozen over

iced tea *cp* **waȟpécaǧa ; waȟpé acáǧa** n iced tea

identical *adj* **akíye** adv same, identical

idiot *n* 1) **pe'óȟnoga** n idiot, person that is not smart 2) **snúga** n foreskin; idiot, a person who is pretending not to know anything

if *conj* 1) **štén** conj if when, if then; when, whenever, in, at, on, next; equals (in arithmetic) 2) **ųkáš** part, conj if, if only (marker of optative modality)

ill *adj* **ktúšya ų** vi1 s/he is mentally ill *See:* **sick**

illegitimate *adj* **duwéni aktúguyeší** cp illegitimate child

illness *n* 1) **wįcóyazạ** n, vs-coll illness, epidemic disease; people are sick from an epidemic disease 2) **dogíš ų** vi1 s/he/it is weak from an illness 3) **asní** vs s/he has recovered from an illness, is well again ‣ **agísni** vt1-dat s/he recovers from smth (illness) 4) **gisníyA** vt1 s/he saves, heals sb from an illness

imitate *v* **úca** vt1 s/he imitates sb

immediately *adv See:* **right away**

in *prep adj adv* 1) **én** post, adv in, into, on, onto, at, to; here, there 2) **ektá** post at, in, to a location or destination ‣ **ektáktaš** post-redup at, in, to various locations or destinations; wherever ‣ **ektám** post there, in a place (often used with cardinal directions) 3) **o-** pref inside, in, into (occurs on nouns of place; derives a verb into a noun or a simple verb into a more specified verb)

in spite of *prep ph See:* **despite**

incense *n* **įzínyabi** n incense

incorrect *adj* **žéceduší** vs, adv it is incorrect; it is not in that way; incorrectly

index *n* 1) **wa'ébazo** n index finger 2) **nạbáwạge įjíwaží** cp index finger

indeed *adv* 1) **-š** suff serves to put emphasis on nouns, adverbs and verbs and is translated as "indeed") 2) **éš** vs it is it; it is indeed (expresses a contrast between an expected event and what actually occurs)

Indian bridle *cp* **įštípaȟte** n Indian bridle

Indian corn *cp* **wakmúhazạkneǧe** n Indian corn

Indian Head (SK) *ngeo* **Įštágitụ tí** ngeo Indian Head (Saskatchewan)

indicate *v See:* **mean**

Indigenous *n* **Įkcé wįcášta** cp Indigenous person

industrious *adj* **wanítA** vs s/he is vigourous, industrious, ambitious

infant *n See:* **baby**

insect *n* **wamnúška** n insect (generic), ant, bug, worm

insert *v* 1) **obázạ** vt1 s/he sticks, inserts smth in it ‣ **ogíjibazạ** vt1-benef s/he sticks, inserts smth in it for him/her 2) **bamáhen iyéyA** vt1 s/he pushes, inserts smth inside

inside *prep adj adv n* 1) **mahédu** vimp it is deep inside ‣ **mahéduȟ** adv deeper, deep down inside ‣ **mahén** adv-cont, post inside, in, within; under, underneath ‣ **mahé- ; mahét-** cont under, down 2) **bamáhen** adv pushing smth inside 3) **o-** pref inside, in, into; outside (occurs in nouns of place; derives a verb into a noun or a simple verb into a more specified verb) 4) **ti'ágasam** n entrance, inside of a building 5) **tín** adv inside a house (often pronounced cín) 6) **timáhen** adv inside smth, in (building, car) ‣ **timáhentahą** adv from indoors, from the inside ‣ **įtímahen** adv-post inside of, within an area, enclosure, pasture, field 7) **hocógam** adv inside a camp circle

insist v **gidą** vt1 s/he insists on smth ‣ **wagídą** vi1-abs s/he is determined, insistent

insistent adj **wagídą** vi1-abs s/he is determined, insistent

instantly adv See: **suddenly**

instead adv **kéš** conj but, but invariably, but instead 2) **piyéniš** adv instead, still, notwithstanding

intelligent adj **wasnókyeja** vi1-abs s/he is intelligent, knowledgeable

intensively adv **nína** adv very; really, a lot, intense, intensively; always; not at all, not really (followed by a negative verb in -šį)

interpret v **iyéska** vi1 s/he interprets, translates, converses ‣ **iyégijiska** vt1-benef s/he interprets, translates for sb

interpreter n **iyéska** ; **iyéskabi** n interpreter, translator; announcer

into prep See: **in**

Inuit nprop **Wazíyam wįcášta** cp Inuit tribe, person of Inuit descent

invite v n **gicó** vt1-dat s/he invites sb; calls sb ‣ **gicícobi** vi1-recip, n they invite one another; gathering (where everyone is welcome)

iris n **įštásu** n iris, eyeball

iron n v 1) **máza** n iron, metal; money ‣ **mas-** cont iron, metal; money 2) **įbámnaye** ; **įwábamnaya** n iron (electrical device) 3a) **bamnáyA** vt1 s/he irons smth; s/he presses smth down by pushing ‣ **wabámnayA** vi1-abs s/he irons clothes 3b) **abámnayA** vt1 s/he irons smth

Ironstar nprop **Wįcáȟpimaza** nprop Ironstar (surname in Carry The Kettle)

island n 1) **wída** n island ‣ **wídana** n small island, islet 2) **cogánwida** adv island in the middle of a lake

it pro 1a) **-Ø-** prefix-infix he, she, it (3rd person singuler, unmarked form of an active verb) 1b) **-Ø-** prefix-infix he, she, it (3rd person singular, unmarked form of a stative verb) 2) **né** dem, pro this, these (near the speaker); this, he, she, it 3) **žé** dem, art, comp, pro he, she, it

itchy adj **yašpúya** vs s/he is itchy

item n **wógağe** n product; crafted item, object

its adj **Ø-** pref his, her, its (3rd person singular unmarked possessor)

itself pro 1) **iyé** pro, vs himself, herself, themselves, itself (emphasizes the subject or object); s/he/it/they is/are the one ‣ **iyéȟ** pro specifically, really him, himself, she, her, herself, they, them, themselves, it, itself ‣ **iyécįga** adv on his/her/its own, by himself/herself/itself 2) **įšnána** adv, vs3 by himself/herself/itself, alone; s/he is alone, by himself/herself 3) **na-** pref by kicking, stepping; by internal force, heat; by itself 4) **ga-** pref by striking, hitting with an instrument; by the blowing wind; by the heat of the sun; by itself 5) **na-** ; **ną-** pref by kicking, stepping, walking (forms active verbs); by internal force, heat; by itself (forms impersonal or stative verbs)

Į

Įktomi nprop **Įktomi** nprop Įktomi (name of a trickster)

J

jackrabbit n **maštíjatąga** n jackrabbit

janitor n **tiyúžaža wįcášta** cp janitor

January n **witéȟi wí** ; **witéȟi hąwí** cp January

Japanese nprop **Įštámaškida** nprop Japanese

jar n **wahíyoknąga** ; **wahí'oknąga** n bottle, glass; jar, cooking pot

jaw *n* 1) **cehú** n jaw 2) **cehúba** n chin and jaw area 3) **tacéhuba** n ruminant's jaw

jealous *adj* 1) **nawízi** vs1 s/he is jealous 2) **kibážį** vt1 s/he is against, jealous of sb ▸ **nawís** vcont jealous

jeans *n* **hųskáto** n jeans, denims

jerk *v n* 1) **yudą́** vt2 s/he pulls smth with a jerk 2) **yušnógA** vt2 s/he jerks, pulls smth out from another object; takes, removes smth off (cork, tooth, root, clothes) 3) **hoyúpsicA** vi2 s/he jerks fish out of water with a line

Jesus Christ *nprop* 1) **Waką́tąga cįhį́ktu** (CTK) ; **Waką́tąga cįhį́tku** (OM, PR) nprop Jesus Christ 2) **Hokšítogapa** ▸ nprop Jesus Christ ▸ **Waką́tąga hokšítogapa** nprop Jesus Christ

jingle *v n* 1) **šną́** vs it rings, jingles ▸ **šnašnáyena** adv jingling 2) **gasná** vt1 s/he makes smth ring, jingle by striking

job *n See:* **work**

join *v* **ópA** vt1 s/he is part of smth; joins, qualifies for smth (games, contest)

joke *n v* 1) **ya'įškade** n joke ▸ **wayá'įškadA** vi-abs s/he teases people, plays jokes on people 2) **wayá'įškada síje** cp dirty joke 3) **'h** encl joke (joking enclitic; used to turn a statement into a counterfactual one, and is used in teasing or joking [Cumberland 2005:339])

joker *n* 1) **wayú'įhes'a** n joker, buffoon 2) **wayá'įškades'a** n joker, teaser

judge *n* **wayáco** n judge ▸ **wayáco wįcá** n male judge ▸ **wayáco wíyą** n female judge

juice *n* 1) **hąbí** n juice, sap ▸ **taspą́hąbi** n apple juice 2) **waskúya ; wóskuya** n berries, fruit; juice

July *n* 1) **wašáša wí** cp July 2) **mnogén cogą́du wí** np July (midsummer moon)

jump *v n* 1) **iyópsijA** vi1 s/he/it jumps ▸ **iyópsikiyA** vt1-caus s/he makes sb, smth jump ▸ **šųk'íyopsikiyA** vt1-caus s/he makes a horse prance, jump 2) **a'íyopsijA** vt1 s/he jumps on, over sb, smth 3) **iyópsije** n hop, jump

jumping rope *cp* **a'íyopsijac škáda** vi1 s/he is jumping rope

June *n* 1) **wíbazuką hąwí** cp June 2) **wahpé wóšma wí** np June

juniper *n* **hąté** n juniper

junk *n* 1) **wašíjahpą** n junk, trash 2) **owógana** n trash pile

just *adv* 1) **įdú** adv just, simply, only 2) **ejé'ena ; ejéna** adv only, simply, alone, just

K

keep *v* 1) **yuhÁ** vt2; adv s/he has, possesses smth; s/he carries sb, smth; s/he gave birth to a child; s/he holds smth (meeting, ceremony); s/he keeps, looks after, treats sb, smth; carry, hold, have with one (precedes verbs of traveling) ▸ **yuhákiyA** vt1-caus s/he makes sb have, carry, keep smth 2) **gicíyuhabi** vi1-recip they keep smth for one another; share with one another 3) **įknúhA** vi3-refl s/he keeps himself/herself in a certain state; cares for himself/herself 4) **kuwá** vt1-aux s/he keeps on doing smth 5) **-cuna** encl all the time; keep on doing (marks a frequent action or event)

keeper *n* **cą́ceǧa awą́yaga** cp drumkeeper

kernel *n* **aǧúyabisu** n wheat kernel

ketchup *n* **ozį́kta hą́bi ; ozį́tka hą́bi** cp ketchup

kettle *n* **céǧa** n kettle, pot; bucket, pail ▸ **ceȟ-** cont kettle, pot; bucket, pail ▸ **ceȟšá** n copper kettle ▸ **wahpé céǧa** cp teapot

key *n* **įyúšpe** n key

kick *v n* 1) **na- ; ną-** pref by kicking, stepping, walking (forms active verbs); by internal force, heat; by itself (forms impersonal or stative verbs) 2) **napsíjA** vt1 s/he/it kicks, propels smth ▸ **napsín** vcont kicking, propelling 3) **napsínyeyA** vt1 s/he kicks smth 4) **nahókšu** vt1 s/he dismantles, kicks smth apart 5) **naȟnógA** vt1 s/he makes a hole by stepping, kicking on smth, with one's body weight 6) **naȟtágA** vt1 s/

he kicks sb, smth 7) **napsú** vt1 s/he spills smth by kicking, by pushing with the foot 8) **nat'Á** vt1 s/he kicks, tramples sb to death

kid *n* **gitézi** n boy, lad, kid, brat (pejorative connotation)

kidney *n* **ažúkta ; ažútka** n kidney ▸ **tažúkta ; tažútka** n ruminant's kidney

kidney stone *cp* **ažúkta íyą, ažútka íyą** cp kidney stones

kill *v n* 1) **kté** vt1 s/he/it kills sb, smth ▸ **gikté** vt1-dat ; vt1-pos s/he kills sb, smth for him/her; s/he kills his/her own ▸ **gicíktebi** vi1-recip they kill one another ▸ **įc'íkte** vi3-refl s/he commits suicide 2) **ó** vt1 s/he shoots and wounds sb, smth; kills sb, smth ▸ **gíji'o** vt1-benef s/he shoots and hits sb, smth for him/her; kills sb, smth for him/her 3) **bat'Á** vt1 s/he/it kills by pressing on sb, smth 4) **gat'Á** vt1 s/he kills, knocks sb by striking with a club ▸ **gigát'A** vt1-dat s/he kills, knocks by striking with a club sb in relation to him/her 5) **mot'Á** vt1 s/he kills, stuns smth by shooting 6) **yat'Á** vt2 s/he/it bites sb to death; kills sb by ingesting poison 7) **yut'Á** vt2 s/he kills sb by strangulation *See:* **shoot**

killdeer *n* 1) **juwíjijina** n killdeer 2) **sihújijina** n killdeer

killer *n* **wįcákte** n killer, assassin

kind₁ *n* 1) **žéca** vs s/he/it is of a certain kind (nationality, tribe, trade, behavior, condition) 2) **ocáže** n kind, sort, species 3) **dókejaga** vs it is what kind 4) **-gA ; a- . . . -gA ; -gejA ; -jA** suff rather, somewhat, kind of (attenuator of gradable expressions) 5) **-yagen** suff kind of, somewhat, rather 6) **-bas** suff in that way, manner; of that kind, like that kind

kind₂ *adj n* 1) **cądéwašte** vs s/he is kind, goodhearted 2) **waštéjaga** vs s/he is kind, goodnatured, pleasant to live with 3) **wa'úšina** vi1-abs s/he pities people, is kind to people ▸

wawá'úšįgina vi1 s/he is kind, good-natured, likes people

king *n See:* **chief**

kingbird *n* **wasnásnąheja** n-redup kingbird; catbird

kingfisher *n* 1) **žós'a** n kingfisher 2) **wakpógiya** n kingfisher

kinnikinnick *n* **wahpé cąní** cp kinnikinnick

kiss *v n* 1) **íbutagA** vt1 s/he kisses sb, smth ▸ **ígijibutagA** vt-benef s/he kisses sb for him/her ▸ **ígicibutagabi** vi1-recip they kissed one another 2) **íbutakuwa** vt1 s/he is always seeking a kiss from sb 3) **íyabiza** vt2 s/he smooches sb; kisses by producing a loud sucking sound

kitchen *n* 1) **owášpąyąbi** n kitchen 2) **owášpąye** n kitchen

kitten *n* 1) **buscíjana** n kitten 2) **búzana** n kitten

knead *v* 1) **yuská** vt2 s/he kneads smth (dough, powder) into shape ▸ **yuskáska** vt2-redup s/he clenches smth in the hand 2) **baská** vt1 s/he kneads smth by exerting pressure

knee *n* 1) **taháge** n knee 2) **taháge kné yįgÁ** vi3 s/he is sitting on his/her knees

kneecap *n* **tahágena** n kneecap

kneel *v* **taháge kné** vi1 s/he kneels down ▸ **taháge kné yįgÁ** vi3 s/he is sitting on his/her knees

knife *n* 1) **mína** n knife 2) **mįpšúbina** n pocket knife 3) **minkáš'į** n boning knife 4) **mísaba** n knife used for bloodletting

knock *v n* 1) **apÁ** vt1, vi1 s/he hits, strikes, knocks sb, smth; it is X hour ▸ **apápA** vt1-redup s/he knocks lightly on sb, smth 2) **bušpá** vt1 s/he knocks smth open with force, pressure 3) **gahómni** vt1 s/he knocks, spins sb, smth around 4) **yuwága** vt2 s/he knocks sb, smth down manually; takes smth down 5) **gaptáyA** vt1 ; vi1 s/he/it knocks, hits smth down; the wind knocks, hits smth down; s/he has a car accident 6) **gaštágA** vt1 s/he knocks, hits, beats sb (with a tool, stick); s/he clubs sb, smth to death 7) **gat'Á** vt1 s/he kills, knocks sb by striking with a club ‣ **gigát'A** vt1-dat s/he kills, knocks by striking with a club sb in relation to him/her 8) **moȟpÁ** vt1 s/he knocks sb, smth down by shooting

knoll *n* **abáha ; abáhana** n knoll, small hill, mound

know *v* 1) **snokyÁ; snohyÁ** vt1, vi1 s/he knows sb, smth; s/he understands ‣ **snokkíciyabi** vi1-recip they know one another ‣ **snokyékiyA** vt1-caus s/he lets sb know smth; lets smth be known 2) **osnókyA; osnóhyA** vt1 s/he understands smth; is knowledgeable about smth

know-it-all *vp* **wasnókye įc'ína** cp know-it-all

knowledge *n* **wasnókyabi** n knowledge

knowledgeable *adj* **wasnókyA, wasnóhyA** vi1-abs, n s/he is clever, knowledgeable; wisdom ‣ **wasnókkiyA** vt1-caus vt1-caus s/he teaches smth to sb ‣ **wasnókya-įc'ina, wasnóhya-įc'ina** vi3-refl s/he thinks himself/ herself as clever, knowledgeable

L

laxative *n* **įcésnibi** n laxative

labor *n v adj* 1) **wówaši ecú** vi3 s/he works, does his/her work; she is in labor 2) **hokšíyuhA** vi2 she gives birth, is in labor

Labor Day *cp* **Wówaši ába** cp Labor Day

lace *n* **ijáškA ; įgáškA** vt1, n s/he ties a knot, ties smth to it; lace, laces

lack *v n* 1) **níjA** vs s/he lacks smth (needed); it is lacking ‣ **waníjA** vs s/he/it lacks; there is none; s/he passed away; is dead 2) **cóna** post; suff without, lacking, deprived of 3) **įgážąga** vs s/he is anxious, worried, bothered because of the lack of smth

ladder *n* **į'áni** n ladder

ladle *n* 1) **wahąbi éyagu** cp ladle 2) **kiškána tą́ga** cp ladle

lake *n* 1) **minítąga** n lake ‣ **minítąktąga** n-redup lakes 2) **mné** n lake (archaic)

Lake Superior *ngeo* **Mniwą́ži** ngeo Lake Superior

Lakota *nprop* **Lakóta** nprop Lakota people, person of Lakota descent *See:* **Oglala**

lamb *n* **šųkhéyuke cįjá** cp lamb

lame *adj* **hušté** vs s/he/it is lame ‣ **mohúšte** vt1 s/he makes smth (animal) lame by shooting

lamp *n* **įktúyąbi** n light, lamp

land *n v* 1) **makóce** n land, territory, earth, ground; homeland 2) **makómnaya** n prairies, flat land 3) **maštámakoce** n land to the south 4) **iyáhĄ** vi1 s/he/it lands

language *n* 1) **i'ábi** n language ‣ **to'í'ebi** n one's language; his/her/their language ‣ **wįcó'i'abi** n language, word; letter ‣ **wįcó'i'e** n language, word 2) **Nakón'iyabi ; Nakón'i'e** n Nakoda language ‣ **Nakón-wįcó'i'e** n Nakoda language, words 3) **Wašín'i'abi** n English language 4) **iyásije** n foreign language

lantern *n* 1) **a'óžąžą yuhá'ųbi** ph lantern 2) **pedížaža ; wíkni pedížąžą** cp oil lantern

lap *n* **įkpí** n lap

lap dog *cp* **šúgagana** n-redup lap dog

larb *n* **abá'e ; abáye** n larb (psychoactive plant often mixed with red willow bark and used in ceremonies)

lard *n* **wíkniskana ; wíkniska** n lard, shortening

large *adj* 1) **tą́gA** vs s/he/it is big, large ‣ **tąktą́gA** vs-redup they are big, large 2) **ogípi** vs-dat s/he fits in there; is large enough (shoes, pants)

last *adj n v adv* **aháge** adv, vs ‣ **ahágeȟ** adv finally, at last

last *adj adv n v* 1) **aháge** adv last, last one; behind ‣ **ahágeȟ** adv finally, at last one ‣ **ahágeȟtįyĄ** vs s/he/it is the very last one 2) **gídąȟ** adv finally, at last 3) **įháge** vs, n it is the end, the last one; the end of smth 4) **hągéya** adv finally, at last ‣ **hągéyadahą** adv and then finally, at last 5) **hąhébic'ehą** adv last night 6) **-hą** encl at a particular time; last ‣ **ptį́hą** adv last fall ‣ **waníhą** adv last winter ‣ **wéhą** adv last spring 7) **žehą́** adv then, at that time, at a certain point in time (used to express English past tense); last (with days of the week)

late *adj* 1) **aškádu** vs s/he/it is late 2) **téhą** adv late; long time ‣ **hątéhą ; ahą́tehąga** adv late at night 3) **waná iyáyabi né**

lately *adv* **aškán** adv lately, recently ‣ **aškáduň** adv lately, recently

later *adv* **togáda** adv ahead, in front, in the lead, in the first place; in the future, later

laudromat *n* **tíbi owáyužažabi** cp laundromat

laugh *n v* 1) **įȟÁ** vi1, vt2 s/he laughs; s/he laughs at sb, smth ‣ **įȟé'įc'iyA** vi3-refl s/he grins, laughs at himself/herself unpleasantly ‣ **a'įȟąbi įc'íyA** vi3-refl s/he makes a fool, laughing stock of himself/herself 2) **įȟát'A** vs s/he laughs hard ‣ **įȟát'eyA** vt1-caus s/he/it makes sb laugh to death ‣ **įȟát'at'A** vs-redup s/he laughs loudly; laughs to death 3) **ya'įȟA** vt2 s/he makes sb laugh by speech 4) **yu'įȟA** vt2 s/he makes smb laugh (by speaking, tickling, goofing around) ‣ **įknú'įȟA** vi3-refl s/he laughs at himself/herself, about one's own behavior

laughter *n* **įȟát'at'ana** n-redup laughter; magpie

laundry *n* **owáyužažabi** n laundry

law *n* **wó'ope** n law

lawnmower *n* **peží'įjašta** n lawnmower

lay *v* 1) **a'ų́** vi1 s/he lays on smth 2) **tú** vt1; vs-pass she bears a child, gives birth to sb; lays an egg; s/he/it is born

lazy *adj* **ecų́ gabį́** vi1 s/he is lazy

lead *n* **mą́za sú** cp lead (metal)

lead₁ *v n* 1) **gašká ayÁ** vt2 s/he leads an animal with a rope 2) **gašká yúzA** vt2 s/he leads sb, smth (as a dog, horse) on a rope 3) **togáhe** adv, num, vs first, the first, one in the first place; the very first one; s/he/it is the first; is in the

lead 4) **togágihĄ** vs ; n s/he is in the lead; s/he is the first; leader

leader *n* 1) **įtą́ca** n leader, boss 2) **togágihĄ** vs ; n s/he is in the lead; s/he is the first; leader

leaf *n* **waȟpé** n leaf; tea

leak *v n* 1) **šmú** vs it leaks, drips 2) **šmúwąga** vs it is dripping (as a faucet) 3) **moskébA** vt1 it drains by leaking, dripping out

learn *v* **ųspé** vs s/he learns on his/her own, acquires a skill ‣ **ųspé'įc'iyA** vi3-refl s/he learns smth on his/her own ‣ **wa'ų́spe** vi1-abs s/he is learned, knowledgeable

leather *n* **wįc'į** n leather

leave *v n* 1) **kiknÁ** vi1 s/he leaves home 2) **knijú** vi1 s/he departs, leaves to come back here 3) **áyA** vt2 s/he leaves, takes, goes with sb, smth there 4) **įȟpéyA** vt1 s/he discards, throws sb, smth away; s/he leaves sb, smth behind, alone; s/he/it is left behind; s/he divorces from him/her; s/he banishes sb ‣ **įȟpékiyA** vt1-dat s/he throw smth at sb; s/he deals the cards; s/he leaves smth for sb

ledge *n* **amádaba** n ledge

leech *n* **wé yazóges'a** cp leech

left₁ *adj* 1) **caktám ; catkám** adv left side, on the left side 2) **caktápadahą** adv from the left side

left₂ *adj* 1) **neną́knana** adv only these, this is all, just a bit left; less than expected (as something that is left over) 2) **aháge** adv, vs last, last one; behind; s/he/it is the last

left-handed *adj* **caktá** vs s/he is left-handed ‣ **nąbé caktána ; nąbé catkána** cp left hand

leftover *adj n* **oyáptA** vt2 s/he has leftovers after eating ‣ **oyáptabi** n leftovers

leg *n* 1) **hú** n leg, stem, stalk, wheel ‣ **hucíyadahą** adv from the leg on the other side 2) **hucą́** n pipestem; stem, leg of an object (like a chair, table) 3) **cejá** n thigh; leg of smth (chair, table) 4) **gamnáš** adv with the legs spread apart, open ‣ **gamnámnaš** adv-redup with the legs spread apart 5) **nasų́** vi1 s/he/it stretches out the feet and legs

legend *n* 1) **ohúgagą** n legend, fable 2) **owóknage** n story, legend, fable 3) **įwóknagA** vt1 s/he tells a story about smth; legend

legging *n* **teȟpí hųská** cp deerhide leggings

lemon *n* **taspą́ ǧí tutá** cp lemon

lend *v* **ok'ú** vt1 s/he lends smth to sb; s/he shares smth with sb ‣ **ogícic'ubi** vi3-recip they pass, lend sb, smth to one another

lengthen *v* 1) **yuhą́skA** vt2 s/he lengthens smth 2) **yahą́skA** vt2 s/he lengthens a story ‣ **knahą́skA** vt1-pos s/he lengthens his/her own story

lesson *n* **wó'ųspe** n lesson

let *v* 1) **yuštą́** vt2 s/he releases, lets sb, smth go 2) **-yA** suff s/he causes, makes, lets sb do smth; causes, lets sb be in a state or condition 3) **-kiyA** suff s/he makes, allows, lets sb do smth (triggers e-ablaut and attaches to contracted verbs) 4) **-s** suff let us do smth ‣ **-siye** suff let us do smth (archaic form of the exhortative -s) 5) **-ktA** encl will, 'll, would (marks a potential event that is not yet realized; when used in the past it indicates a counterfactual event); expresses a suggestion, let us (when occurring with verbs in the 1st person plural ų(g)- -bi or dual ų(g)-)

letter *n* 1) **wa'ókmabi** n letter, written word, drawing 2) **wa'óyabi ; wa'ówabi** n paper, letter, book

lettuce *n* **waȟpé tą́ga** cp cabbage, lettuce

liar *n* 1) **įtų́šįs'a** vi1, n s/he is a liar; liar 2) **Įktómi** nprop, vs name of a trickster; s/he is a liar

lice *n-pl* **hé'a** n louse, lice

license *n* **įbási** n driver's license

lick *v n* 1) **sníbA** vt1 s/he/it licks sb, smth ‣ **snísniba** vt1-redup s/he/it licks sb, smth 2) **yasníbA** vt2 s/he/it licks sb, smth ‣ **knasníbA** vt1-pos s/he/it licks his/her own

lid *n* **įyágaȟpa ; įyágaȟpe ; agáȟpe ; įyágaȟpena** n lid, cover

lie₁ *v n* 1) **įtų́šį** vi1, n s/he lies, does not tell the truth; lie ‣ **įtų́šįkiyA** vt1-caus s/he makes, convinces sb to lie ‣ **igíjitųšį** vt1-benef s/he lies for sb 2) **a'į́tųšį** vt1 they lie to one another about smth

lie₂ *v* 1) **yųgÁ, wųgÁ** vi3 s/he/it lies down; lays in a reclining position ‣ **yųgáya** adv in a lying, reclining position 2) **kniyų́gA** vi1/3 s/he arrives back here and lies down ‣ **kiyų́gA** vi1/3 s/he arrives back there and lies down ‣ **hiyų́gA, hiwų́gA** vi1/3 s/he arrives here and lies down 3) **bastó yųgÁ** vi3 s/he lies down tuckered out, exhausted 4) **iyápe** vt1 s/he lies waiting for sb; ambushes sb

life *n* 1) **oní** n life 2) **wįcóni** n human life, health, ways, spirit; ghost 3) **giní** vi1 s/he comes back to life, wakes up (from hibernation) 4) **niyá** vs, n s/he/it breathes, is alive; breath of life ‣ **niyą́ya** vt1-caus s/he heals sb, brings sb back to life 5) **wįcóȟ'age** n way of life, culture, tradition

lift *v n* **yuǧą́** vt2 s/he lifts up a cover

light₁ *n v* 1) **a'óžąžą** vimp, n it is sunny, lightened up; light 2) **įktúyabi** n light, lamp 3) **įktúyA** vt1-caus s/he makes smth burn; lights smth in fire 4) **ną'į́tkųyA** vt1 it lights it up 5) **yu'į́ktų, yu'į́tkų** vt1 s/he/it lights, turns smth on (light, stove, fire) ‣ **a'į́ktųkiyA, a'į́tkųkiyA** vt1-caus s/he lights up sb, smth; gives sb a light 6) **owádA** vs, n it is lit; lights 7) **yu'ówadA** vt2, n s/he lights smth up; flashlight, car headlights

light₂ *adj* 1) **gap'óǧena** vs s/he/it is light 2) **są́** vs indicates a lighter color tone when occurring as a suffix on color verbs 3) **-na** suff indicates a lighter color tone on color verbs

lightning *n* **owán-hįknA ; ową́hįknA** vimp, n there is lightning; lightning, electricity, flashlight

like₁ *v* **wašténa** vt1 s/he likes, loves sb, smth

like₂ *conj prep* 1) **stéyA** part it seems like; like 2) **steȟ** part like, in the manner of, somewhat, -ish, as if

limp *adj n v* **huštéyagen** adv with a limp

line *n* 1) **gazó** vt1 s/he draws a line 2a) **įjázo** n, vt1 line; yardstick, ruler; s/he draws a line on, in smth 2b) **įjážobi** n line 3) **ho'įcuwa** n fishhook; fishing pole and line

lining *n* **wi'óząbi** n tipi lining

lip *n* 1) **įští** n lower lip, lips 2) **ihá** (WB) n lips, both lips

lipstick *n* 1) **įštíšage** n lipstick 2) **íšagiya** n lipstick

liquid *n* **mni-** cont water, liquid, alcohol

liquor store *n* **omní owópetų** cp liquor store

listen *v* 1) **anáǧoptą** vt1 s/he listens to sb, smth ‣ **wa'ánaǧoptą** vi1-abs s/he listens to things ‣ **wa'ánagijiǧoptą** vt1-benef s/he listens to what sb has to say 2) **naȟ'ų** vt1 s/he hears, listens to sb, smth; s/he obeys sb

lit *v* 1) **įktú, įtkú** vs s/he/it is lit, in flames 2) **owádA** vs it is lit; lights

little *adj adv n* 1) **jónana** quant few, little, small amount 2) **gitána** adv a little bit, barely 3) **júsisibina** n-pl children, little children 4) **mayáwašiju ; mayášiju** n little people, cave dwellers (mythic being) 5) **-na** encl small, little, cute, dear

Little Chief *nprop* **Hųgájuk'a** nprop Little chief (1839–1973); Nakoda chief killed during the Cypress Hills massacre of 1873

Little girls people *nprop* **Wakáȟežabina** nprop Little girls people (band of Nakoda living in Fort Peck, Montana)

Little Rockies (Montana) *ngeo* **Įyaȟe wídana** ngeo Little Rockies (Montana)

live *v* 1) **tí** vi1, n s/he lives somewhere (house, place, area); house, place (used mostly in compounds, or with a demonstrative) 2) **otí** n, vi1 dwelling; s/he lives in a dwelling ‣ **wí'oti** vi1 s/

he lives in a tent 3) **ų** vi1, vi1-aux s/he/it is, lives, exists; s/he/it stays somewhere; s/he feels; exists, is in a certain way; s/he does continuously; goes around doing smth ‣ **tašną ų** vi1 s/he lives alone 4) **ní** vi1 s/he/it is alive, lives ‣ **niyÁ** vt1-caus s/he/it makes sb live; spares, allows sb to live

lively *adj* **hahána** vs s/he is lively, frisky, excited ‣ **haháyena** adv lively

liver *n* 1) **pí** n liver 2) **tapí** n ruminant's liver

living room *cp* **én yągábi** ph living room

lizard *n* **aknéška ; aknéškana** n lizard, salamander

load *v n* 1) **k'įkíyA** vt1-caus s/he causes sb to carry smth; s/he hitches, loads smth on sb 2) **ok'į** n ton, a full load

locate *v* **yįgÁ, yągÁ** vi3 s/he is sitting on, in smth; it is, it is located (used for broad-based objects)

lock *v n* **a'ónatagA** vt1-dit s/he locks sb in, out

lodge *n* 1) **wí** n lodge, tent 2) **wi'óti ; wiyóti** n tipi, dwelling, lodge 3) **agícida wi'óti** cp warrior lodge 4) **makóti** n earth lodge 5) **mazóti** n iron lodge

Lodge Pole (Montana) *ngeo* **Wasé wakpá** ngeo Lodge Pole (Montana)

log *n* **cągáǧa** n log

lonely *adj* 1) **osákkna** vi1 s/he feels lonely 2) **oȟpáyA** vs s/he is sad, lonely

lonesome *adj* 1) **osągaga ; o'ósągaga** vs-redup s/he is lonesome after sb leaves ‣ **o'ósąkya ; osákya** adv lonely, in a lonesome way 2) **osákkta** vi1 s/he is lonesome 3) **įšnánagen** adv alone, in a lonesome manner

long *adj* 1) **háskA** vs s/he is tall, it is long 2) **iyóhi** vt1, vs s/he reaches smth; s/he counts coup; it is long enough 3) **žehágeja** vs, adv, n it is that long, far, size; since then; distance, destination 4) **gahágeja** vs, adv it is about that long, high, far (used with remote objects or when guessing roughly)

long johns *n-pl* **mahén húska** cp long johns, thermal underwear

Long lodge *nprop* **Tíbi háska** nprop Long lodge (Nakoda chief and signatory of Treaty 4)

look *v n* 1) **akídA** vt1 s/he looks at sb, smth ‣ **agíjidA** vt1-benef s/he looks at sb, smth for him/her ‣ **akín** vcont looking, watching ‣ **agícidA** vt1-pos s/he looks after his/her own ‣ **a'íc'icidA** vi3-refl s/he looks at himself/herself) 2) **awáyagA** vt2 s/he cares, watches, looks after sb, smth ‣ **wa'áwayagA** vi1-abs s/he looks, watches things 3) **owáyak** vcont looking a certain way ‣ **owáyak wašté** ph s/he/it nice to look at ‣ **owáyage síja** vs s/he/it is bad-looking; looks bad ‣ **owáyage wašté** vs s/he/it is good-looking; looks good 3) **édųwą ; éduwą** vi1 s/he looks, faces in a direction ‣ **ahídųwą** vi1 s/he looks here (in the direction of the speaker) 4) **gikmá** vt-irr s/he/it resembles sb; looks like sb 5) **oné** vt1 s/he looks for smth; hunts ‣ **wóne ; wa'óne** vi1-abs s/he looks, hunts for things ‣ **ogíjine** vt1-benef s/he hunts for sb ‣ **ogíne** vt1-pos s/he looks for his/her own ‣ **o'íc'ine** vi3-refl s/he looks for, seeks smth for himself/herself 6) **šųk'óne** vi1 s/he looks for a horse, or horses ‣ **šųk'ógine** vt1-pos s/he looks for his/her own horse, horses ‣ **šųk'ógijine** vt1-benef s/he looks for sb else's horse, or horses 7) **pte'óne** vi1 s/he looks for a cow, or herd ‣ **pte'ógine** vt1-pos s/he looks for his/her cow, or herd ‣ **pte'ógijine** vt1-benef s/he looks for a cow or cattle for sb else 8) **ti'óne** vi1 s/he looks for a home to buy, room to rent ‣ **ti'ógine** vt1-pos s/he looks for his/her own house, room ‣ **ti'ógijine** vt1-benef s/he looks for a house, room for sb else 9) **wį'óne** vi1 he looks for a girl, woman ‣ **wį'ógine** vt1-pos he looks for his wife 10) **hokší oné** vi1 s/he looks for a child ‣ **hokší ogíne** vt1-pos s/he looks for his/her own child 11) **wįc'óne** vi1-coll s/he looks for people 12) **cąné** vi1 s/he looks for wood 13) **hagíkta** vt1-pos s/he looks back 14) **yuhÁ** vt2, adv s/he has, possesses smth; s/he carries sb, smth; s/he gave birth to a child; s/he holds smth (meeting, ceremony); s/he keeps, looks after, treats sb, smth; carry, hold, have with one (precedes verbs of traveling)

loose *adj* 1) **owáȟna'į** vs it is loose, not steady 2) **wįktówį ; wįtkówį** n foolish, loose woman

Loose dance *np* **Knoknók wací** cp Loose dance (when one's limbs go in all directions, as a clown)

loosely *adv* **knoknók** adv loose, loosely

lose *v* 1) **ayúštą** vt2 s/he loses sb, smth ‣ **aknúštą** vt1-pos s/he loses his/her own thing 2) **t'a'íȟpayA** vs s/he faints, loses consciousness

lost *adj* 1) **núni** vi1 s/he/it is lost 2) **hanúni** vi1 s/he gets lost at night

lot *pro adv* 1) **ódA** quant, vs a lot, many, much; it is a lot; there are many (used with 3rd person subjects only) 2) **wįcódabi** vs-coll there a lot of people, it is crowded 3) **nína** adv very, really, a lot, intense, intensively; always; not at all, not really (followed by a negative verb in -šį) 4) **baháyena ; baháya** quant plenty of smth, a lot

lotion *n* **sná** n lotion, oil ‣ **snayÁ** vt1-caus s/he rubs sb, smth with grease, oil, lotion

loud *adj* 1) **piȟyá** vimp it is a loud sound 2) **kpá** vs it is a loud, resonant metallic, sound 3) **namú** vi1 s/he/it makes a loud sound with the foot 4) **hónisko** vs s/he has a loud voice; has a voice as loud as this 5) **hótągA** vs s/he has a loud voice 6) **-niyą** suff loudly, with a loud voice, audibly (mostly used with verbs for singing, crying, speaking, etc.)

loudly *adv* **-niyą** suff loudly, with a loud voice, audibly (mostly used with verbs for singing, crying, speaking, etc.)

love *v n* 1) **teȟína** vt1 s/he loves, holds on to smth, cherishes sb (like a relative), prizes smth and does not want to part with it ‣ **wóteȟina** n value, object of love or admiration ‣ **tegícihinabi** vt1-recip they love one another 2) **wašténa** vt1 s/he likes, loves sb, smth ‣ **waštégina** vt1-dat s/he enjoys, loves, is pleased with smth ‣ **waštégicinabi** vi1-recip they like, love one another 3) **kišnéyA** vt1 s/ he loves sb romantically, steadily; s/he has a lover ‣ **kišnégiciyabi** vi1-recip they love one another 4) **nahmą́ kuwága** vt1 s/he has a love affair with sb 5) **wį'į́nową** n love song (usually about what the couple would do if they got together) 6) **wįnówą** vi1 he sings a love song

lover n **akíšne** n beau, lover

low adj **kúdina ; kúdiyena** adv low, down, near the ground

lower v adj **yuhókuda** vt2 s/he lowers smth by pulling ‣ **yuhókun** vcont lowering smth by pulling

luck n **sijá akípa** vi1 s/he encounters, is afflicted with bad luck; it is bad luck ‣ **šin'ákipa** vt1, vi1 s/he encounters smth bad; is afflicted with bad luck ‣ **wósija akípa** vi1 s/he encounters, is afflicted with bad luck; it is bad luck

lucky adj 1a) **wacą́hyA** vs s/he is lucky ‣ **wacą́h'ic'iyA** vi3-refl s/he is lucky 1b) **wacą́hyeja** vs s/he is lucky, fortunate

lung n **cağú** n lung

Lustful dance np **Įšką́ wacíbi** cp Lustful dance

lynx n See: **wildcat**

M

mad adj **šikná** vi1 s/he/it is mad, angry ‣ **šiknákiyA** vt1-caus s/he is mad at sb ‣ **šiknáyA** vt1-caus s/he makes sb mad

maggot n **honáğina cįjábi** cp-pl maggots

magpie n 1) **ųkcékiğa** n magpie 2) **įhát'at'ana** n-redup laughter; magpie (Denig (2000[1930]:189)

make v n 1) **gáğA** vt1, vi1 s/he makes smth; s/ he makes money ‣ **gáh** vcont making smth ‣ **gíjağA** vt1-benef s/he makes smth for

him/her ‣ **gíjah** vcont making smth for sb ‣ **gahkiyA** vt1-caus s/he makes, lets sb make, do it ‣ **įc'íjağA** vi3-refl s/he makes smth for himself/herself; s/he turns himself/herself into sb, smth ‣ **wagíjijağA** vt1-abs-benef s/ he makes things for sb ‣ **gahpíja** vs, it is possible to make, to do ‣ **gahší** vt1-dit s/he orders sb to make it ‣ **gáh iyéyA** vt1 s/he makes smth quickly ‣ **gíjah iyéyA** vt1-benef s/he makes it quickly for sb 2) **agáğA** vt1-dit s/he makes smth on it 3) **ogáh** vcont making ‣ **ogáhtąyą** vs it is easy to make ‣ **ogáh síjA** vs it is hard to make ‣ **ogáh wašté** vs it is easy to make 4) **ogáğe** n make of smth, manner, style 5) **-kiyA** suff s/ he makes, allows, lets sb to do smth (triggers e-ablaut and attaches to contracted verbs) 6) **-yA** suff s/he causes, makes, lets sb do smth; causes, lets sb be in a state or condition

male n adj **mnóga** n male animal (occurs mostly in compounds)

mallard n **tahúto** n mallard duck

Malta (Montana) ngeo **Oyúweğa** ngeo Malta (Montana)

man n 1) **wįcá** n, vs man; he is a man 2) **wįcáwaką** n Holy man 3) **wįcáhtįyąna, wįcáhtįyą** n ; vs elderly man, senior; he is an elderly man, senior) 4) **wįcášta** n man, adult male; person (of both sexes), people (both in the singular and plural); tribe (collective plural) 5) **wįcáteja** n new, young man 6) **wįcá'įc'ina** vs3-refl, n she thinks she is a man; tomboy 7) **košká** n, vs young man; he is a young man ‣ **koška'įc'ina** vi3-refl he thinks of himself as a young man

Man who took the coat nprop **Cuwíknąga žé éyagu** nprop Man who took the coat (Nakoda chief and signatory of Treaty 4)

mane n **apéhį ; apéhą** n mane

mangy adj 1) **skuskú** vs s/he/it (dog, wolf, coyote, horse) is mangy; is missing spots of fur 2) **šųkháskusku** n mangy dog, coyote, wolf; unkept dog 3) **šųkskúsku** n mangy horse

Manitou Beach (Saskatchewan) *ngeo* **Miníwakạ** ngeo Manitou Beach (Saskatchewan)

manly *adj adv* **wịcáktA** vi1 she becomes manly

manner *n* 1) **ogáğe** n make of smth, manner, style 2) **o'écụ** n manner, style of doing smth 3) **oȟ'ạ́** n action, behavior, habit, manner 4) **-gen ; -yagen** suff in the manner of (derives adverbs of manner from verbs and adverbs)

manually *adv* **yu-** pref manually (with the hand, fingers), by pulling; (derives transitive verbs of Class 2 from stative or intransitive verbs); causes sb, smth to be; derives instrumental adverbs

manure *n* **tacésni** n manure

many *adj pro n* 1) **ódA** quant, vs a lot, many, much; it is a lot; there are many (used with 3rd person subjects only) 2) **dóna** pro, quant, vs how many, what number; how much; several; s/he/it is so many ‣ **dónaca** vs s/he/it a certain number 4) **dáguwiyeknaš** vs it is numerous, there are many more 5) **dónạgeja** pro how many, much 6a) **nenạ́geja** vs it is this many; it is such amount (when showing an amount close to the speaker, at the present time) 6b) **ženạ́geja** vs it is some; it is an unspecified amount 6c) **ganạ́geja** vs it is that many; it is such an amount

Maple Creek (Saskatchewan) *ngeo* **Cạsúska wakpá** ngeo Maple Creek (Saskatchewan)

March *n* 1) **wịcị́šta yazạ́ hạwí** np March 2) **wamnónija hạwí** cp March

mare *n* **šụkwíyena** n mare

marijuana *n* **peží wịtkó** cp marijuana, cannabis

mark *n v* 1) **mağó** vt1 s/he marks, carves smth with a sharp tool 2) **omáğe** vt1, n s/he marks smth into it (with a sharp instrument, knife or pencil); mark (made with a knife or pencil)

marriage *n* 1) **hịknátụbi** n marriage 2) **wịk'ú** vt1 s/he gives him a wife, daughter in marriage

marrow *n* **tacúba** n animal marrow

marry *v* 1) **hịknáyA** vt1-caus she marries sb; has sb for husband 2) **hịknátụ** vt1 she has a husband; is married ‣ **hịknátụkiyA** vt1-caus s/he makes her marry, take a husband 3) **tawíjutụ** vi1, n he has sb for wife, he is married; married man 4) **yúzA** vt2 s/he holds, pulls, grabs, nabs, catches sb, smth; s/he marries sb 5) **gicíknuzabi** n ; vi1-recip wedding; they marry within their own (people, kind)

marsh *n See:* swamp

mascara *n* **ịštá ogíkma** cp mascara

mask *n* **ịdéha** n mask

massacre *n v* 1) **wịcágasodabi** n massacre 2) **gasódA** vi, vt1 it (sky) cleared up; s/he massacres, wipes out sb

masturbate *v* **ịc'íškadA** vi3-refl s/he plays with himself/herself; masturbates

match *n* 1) **péda** n fire, match 2) **gak'óȟcạka**; n match

matter *n* 1) **dókejašị** vs there is nothing wrong with him/her/it; it is all good; it does not matter 2) **dókeduš** adv no matter what, at any rate 3) **-ga kóšta** part any, no matter which/who/ what (lack of interest)

mature *adj* **wịtága** vs, n she is a mature woman

May *n* 1) **waȟpétoto hạwí** cp May 2) **ịdú wiğá hạwí** np May

may *modal See:* might

maybe *adv* 1) **wanúȟ** adv maybe, might 2) **dókaš** adv maybe, perhaps; in time, in a while, eventually 3) **ịtó** adv; interj now, well; maybe, I guess

meadowlark *n* **tašiyapopobena** n meadowlark

mean₁ *adj* 1) **hịnígA** vs s/he/it is mean 2) **owéšijA** vs s/he/it is mean, vicious

mean₂ *v* **kÁ** vt1 s/he/it means smth, indicates sb, smth; s/he chooses smth, sb

meantime *n adv* **žécan** adv in the meantime, during that time, then

meanwhile *n adv* 1) **ecána** adv during that time, meanwhile 2) **kohạ́** adv meanwhile, while

measles *n-pl* **šayá hiyúbi** cp measles

measurement *n* **iyútabi** n unit of measurement (centimeter, inch, foot, yard)

meat *n* 1) **tanó** n meat, flesh 2) **wacónice ; coníca** n dried meat 3) **ptecónica** n dried buffalo meat 4) **wakní** vi1-abs s/he returns, arrives home bringing meat ‣ **wáknibi** n game, meat brought back from a hunt

medal *n* **a'óbazo** n medal, pin

medicine *n* 1) **pežúda** n medicinal plant, medicine in general ‣ **hoȟpá pežúda** cp cough medicine ‣ **Pežúda éyagu ecúbi** ph Medicine Ceremony 2) **iwágaškeca** n love medicine 3) **snohéna pežúda** cp snake medicine

medicine bag *cp* **wótuye** n medicine bag

Medicine ceremony *np* **Pežúda éyagu ecúbi** ph Medicine Ceremony

meet *v* 1) **akípa** vt1 s/he meets sb; encounters, experiences smth ‣ **wa'ákipa** vi1-abs s/he meets someone, people ‣ **agícicipabi** vi1-recip they meet one another 2) **écipa** vi1-recip they (things, people) meet one another 3) **ecíbağa** vt1 s/he collides with sb, smth; s/he joins the two ends together; meets sb

meeting *n* **omníjiye** n meeting, gathering

Mexican *nprop* **Špe'óna; Špe'úna** nprop person of Mexican or Spanish descent

melt *v* 1) **ská** vimp it is thawing, melting ‣ **skayÁ** vt1-caus s/he/it melts smth 2) **waská** n melting snow 3) **baská** vt1 s/he melts smth by sitting, pressing smth down 4) **gaská** vt1, vi s/he/it melts the snow; it (heat) melts the snow ‣ **ijáská** vt1 s/he melts smth by heating 5) **šnó** vi s/he/it melts ‣ **šnoyÁ** vt1-caus s/he melts, renders fat; fries smth 6) **wašmú** n melted snow 7) **gisápsabA** vimp-redup, n-redup there are spots of bare ground where the snow has melted; spots of bare ground where the snow has melted

mend *v* **wabásisA** vi1-abs s/he sews, mends things

menses *n* 1) **išnáti, išnána tí** vi1 she has her menses 2) **hawí žehá ecéya** ph she has her menses

mentor *n* **wicá ógiyes'a** cp mentor

merchant *n* **wópetu** vi1-abs, n s/he buys things; merchant

messy *adj* **tutú** vs s/he/it has a messy behind

metal *n* **máza** n iron, metal; money ‣ **mas-** cont iron, metal, money ‣ **mázakada** n hot metal ‣ **mázasni** n cold metal

Metis *nprop* **Sakná** nprop person of Metis descent; mixed blood

mix *v n* 1) **ijáhi** vs it is mixed, blended with smth else ‣ **ijáhiyA** vt1-caus s/he blends, mixes smth together, with it 2) **iknúhi** vt1-pos s/he mixes his/her own 3) **ijášoša** vt1-dit s/he mixes smth into it to thicken it

microwave *n* **océti waká** cp microwave

midday *n* 1) **wiyódahą** n south; noon, midday 2) **amcógadu** adv noon, midday

middle *n* 1) **cogán** adv-cont in the middle, center ‣ **cogádu** adv in the middle, center ‣ **cogáduȟ** adv right in the center, middle ‣ **hácogadu** adv midnight, middle of the night 2) **ocógan** adv in the center, middle 3) **wacógadu** vs it is in the middle of the snow ‣ **wacógan** adv in the middle of the snow 4) **cuwícogan** adv in the middle of the chest, breast 5) **óhą** post among, in the middle, in it 6) **ki-** pref two, in two; separated in the middle; evenly

middle-aged *adj* **wicátagaga** n middle-aged man

midmorning *adv* **hayákena cogádu** adv midmorning

midnight *n* **hácogadu** adv midnight, middle of the night

midwife *n* **hokšíyuza** n midwife

midwinter *n* **waníyedu cogána** adv midwinter

might *modal* **ca** part must, might (deontic and epistemic modality; conveys the idea that an event is likely to occur)

milk *n v* 1) **asą́bi** n milk 2) **yusní** vt2 s/he squeezes
the liquid out; milks a cow

Milk River (Montana) *ngeo* 1) **Wakpá juk'ána**
ngeo Milk River (Montana) 2) **Asą́bi wakpá**
ngeo Milk River (Montana)

Milky Way *cp* **wanáǧi ocą́gu** cp Milky Way

million *n adj* **wóyawa tą́ga** num million

mince *v* **makpą́** vt1 s/he minces smth fine

mind *n v* 1) **wacį́** vi3, n, part s/he feels like doing
smth; mind, plan, goodwill; it is about to hap-
pen; intentive, prospective, or imminent event
2) **tawácį** n, vs mind; his/her mind, mindset,
goal; s/he thinks thus ‣ **tawácį síja** vs, n s/he
has a wicked mind; bad habits ‣ **tawácį waští**
vs, n s/he has a good mind 3) **awácį** vt3, vs s/
he feels, thinks about smth, has smth on the
mind; it is a purpose 4) **įknį́gA** vt1 s/he minds,
wonders, has regards for, pays attention to sb,
smth; obeys sb ‣ **įknį́k** vcont mind, observe,
pay attention to sb, smth

mine *n v* **mas'ók'e** n mine for digging metal

minister *n* **wócegiya wįcášta** cp church minister

mink *n* **įkusąna** n mink

minnow *n* **hoǧą́ǧana** n-redup minnow

minute *n* **omą́ǧo** n minute

minute hand *cp* **nąpsíhu hąwí akída** ph minute
hand on a clock

mirror *n* 1) **įwą́knage** n mirror; window, glass
2) **a'į́c'icidabi** n mirror

misbehave *v* **wįktókto, wįtkótko** vs-redup s/he
is bad, crazy; misbehaves

miscarriage *n* 1a) **gíji'į́hpayA** vi-benef she/it has
a miscarriage 1b) **hokší gíji'į́hpayA** vi-benef
she/it has a miscarriage

mischievous *adj* 1a) **zakté** vs s/he is mischievous ‣ **zaktébi** n person who fools around;
who is mischievous ‣ **zaktéwįyą** n mischievous woman 1b) **žakté** vs s/he/it is overtly mischievous (intensifying sound symbolism z>ž)

miss *v* 1) **gašná** vt1 s/he misses smth (target, date)
‣ **gašnášna** vt1-redup s/he misses smth over

and over ‣ **gicíjašnabi** vi1-recip they miss one
another (as with a phone call) 2) **mošną́** vt1 s/
he shoots and misses smth

Missouri dog penis people *nprop* **Miníšoše**
šųkcébi wįcášta nprop Missouri dog penis
people

Missouri River *cp* **Miníšoše wakpá** ngeo Missouri River

mist *n* 1) **p'ó** n mist, vapor, steam 2) **p'oyáhą** vimp
it is misty, foggy

mistakenly *adv* **ektášįšį** adv-redup mistakenly

mistreat *v* **yužáǧA** vt2 s/he mistreats, bullies sb;
picks on sb ‣ **yužą́k** vcont mistreating, bullying sb; picking on sb ‣ **knužą́gA** vt1 s/he mistreats, bullies his/her own; picks on his/her
own (as sibling)

mitten *n See:* **glove**

mnitácągu *n* stream

moan *v* **cąyága** vi2 s/he moans ‣ **cąyák** vcont
moaning

moccasin *n* **hą́ba** n moccasins, shoes ‣ **hą́pa**
kšúbi cp decorated moccasins ‣ **hąbóska** n
quilted moccasins ‣ **tehpíhąba** n hide, buckskin moccasins ‣ **hą́ba oskábi ; hąbóska** cp ; n
quilted moccasins ‣ **hąm- ; hąp-** cont shoe, pertaining to shoes ‣ **hąmcóna** adv without moccasins, shoeless ‣ **hąm'áyazabi** n beaded moccasins 2) **hąpkáǧA** vi1 s/he makes moccasins

moist *adj* **nó** vi it is moist, fresh (as meat)

molar *n* **hítąga** n molar

moldy *adj* **a'á** vs it is moldy ‣ **a'ámna** vs it is a
moldy smell

mole *n* 1) **wahį́heya** n mole 2) **wahé'aǧa** n mole

Monday *n* 1) **ába įwą́žį** cp Monday 2) **ábawaką**
gicúni cp Monday

money *n* 1) **mázaska** n money; dollar (usually
followed by a number) ‣ **mas-** cont iron, metal;
money ‣ **maskámna** vi1 s/he earns money ‣
maskásodA vi1 s/he wastes money ‣ **mask'ú**
vt1-dat s/he gives money to sb ‣ **mas'ónoda**
vi1 s/he borrows money ‣ **masyúhA** vi2 s/he

has money ‣ **masyúhešį** vi2 s/he does not have money; is poor 2) **mázaska wążí** cp one dollar; loony 3) **wiyáwašóga** n nickel 4) **mázaša** n penny, cent 5) **wiyą́ša** n penny, cent 6) **gašpábi** n 25 cents, quarter 7) **wa'ówabitoto** n paper money

monkey n 1) **iyúnena** n monkey 2) **wa'úcana** n monkey

monster n 1) **šiħ'ą** n beast, monster ‣ **ptešíħ'ą** n buffalo monster 2) **ħuħúna** n ghost, monster (invoked to scare off children) 3) **mnową́ga** n water monster

Montmartre (Saskatchewan) ngeo **Wómnapta** ngeo Montmartre (Saskatchewan)

moody adj **tawáci dąyą́šį** vs s/he is moody; feels bad

moon n 1) **hąwí ; wí** n moon; sun; month 2) **hąwí bapsú** cp wet moon, Cheshire moon 3) **hąwí cogą́du ; hąwí okíse** cp half moon 4) **hąwí ožúna** cp full moon 5a) **hąwí togáhe oyášpe** ph quarter moon 5b) **wí yašpábi** ph last quarter of the moon 6) **hąwí úšį** vimp it is a period with no moon; it is a night without a moon 7) **hąwísaba** n lunar eclipse 8) **hąwácibi** n women's dance, night dance, moon dance

moonlight n **hąwíyąba** n moonlight

moose n **tá** n moose ‣ **táwiyena** n female moose

Moose Jaw (Saskatchewan) ngeo **Tácehubana** ngeo Moose Jaw (Saskatchewan)

Moose Mountain (Saskatchewan) ngeo 1) **Ħépa** ngeo Moose mountain (Saskatchewan) 2) **Taħé** ngeo Moose mountain (Saskatchewan)

mop n **ti'íyužaža** n mop

more adv 1) **nągú ; nakú** conj, adv and, and also, in addition; more, anymore (has the latter meaning when followed by a negated verb in -šį) 2) **aké** adv again; another one, one more (usually followed by one); plus 3) **kapéya** vt1-caus s/he/it is more than, goes beyond sb, smth ‣ **kapéyena** adv more

morning n adv 1) **hąyáke** adv late morning (8–9 am) ‣ **hąyákesą** adv throughout the morning, all morning 2) **hąyákena** adv, vimp early morning; it is early morning ‣ **hąyákenaħ** adv very early in the morning

mosquito n **capúga** n mosquito

Mosquito/Grizzly Bear's Head/Leanman reservation (Saskatchewan) ngeo **Capúga/Matópa/Hústaga** ngeo Mosquito/Grizzly Bear's Head/Leanman reservation (Saskatchewan)

moss n 1) **matánijoħ** n moss 2) **watánijoǧa** n moss growing in sloughs

mother n 1) **iná** voc, n Mother! (address form); my mother (reference) 2) **-hų-** root mother ‣ **húguyA** vt1-caus s/he has her as a mother

Mother Earth nprop **Iná maká** nprop Mother Earth

mother-in-law n **-kų-** root mother-in-law

Mother's Day cp **Iná ába** cp Mother's Day

mount v n **agán iyé'ic'iyA** vi3-refl s/he mounts on smth (horse)

mountain n 1) **íyaħe ; íyahe** n mountain, stony hill 2) **iħé** n mountain, gravel 3) **mayátąga** n mountain 4) **gaħé** n ravine, coulee, cut bank; mountain, hill

mountain goat cp 1) **hékiška ; kíška; įkú háska** n, cp bighorn sheep, mountain goat, mountain goat

Mountain village people nprop **Ħénatųwąbina** nprop Mountain village people (band of Nakoda living in the Little Rocky Mountains and Fort Belknap)

mourn v **wašíkna** vi1-abs, n s/he mourns; is bereaved by the death of a relative; sacrifice

mourner n **wašíknabi** n mourner

mouse n 1) **bispízena** n-redup mouse 2) **įtúpsipsijana** n-redup kangaroo mouse

mouth n 1) **í** n mouth 2) **íkmuza** vii s/he/it has his/her/its mouth closed 3) **iyóknągA** vt1 s/he puts smth in his/her own mouth

mouthful *n* **i'óžuna** vs s/he/it has a mouthful ‣ **i'óžunyapa ; i'óžuyapa** vi2 s/he gets a mouthful

mouthy *adj* **íwašiju** vs s/he is mouthy

move *v n* 1) **šką́** vt1, vi1 s/he tries to do smth; s/he is busy; s/he moves, behaves; s/he feels thus ‣ **škąšką́** vs-redup s/he/it moves, shakes; it shakes, moves by inner force ‣ **šką́hįknA** vi it moves suddenly; it is a sudden movement 2) **yuškąšką́** vt2 s/he moves smth back and forth ‣ **įknúškąšką** vi3-refl s/he/it moves himself/herself/itself around 3) **pi'įc'iyA** vi3-refl s/he/it moves around 4) **o'ų́knaga** vi1-coll they (family, group) move camp ‣ **o'ų́knak** vcont-coll moving camp

movie *n* **wašką́škąyabi** n movie, movies, cinema

mow *v* **gašná** vt1 s/he cuts smth short with a tool (hair, grass); mows the lawn

much *adj adv n* 1) **dónągeja** pro how many, much 2) **nísko** vs it is this size, much; it is as big as this ‣ **nískoga** vs it is about this size, much 3) **dóna** pro, quant, vs how many, what number; how much; several; s/he/it is so many

mud *n* 1) **opšíja** n mud 2) **ktába ; tkába** vi it is thick, mud-like, adhesive

mule *n* **nų́ǧe hąskáska** cp-redup mule *See:* **donkey**

muscle *n* **ką́** n muscle; gristle; tendon, vein, artery

mushroom *n* **tabéh'ana táwode** cp mushroom

muskrat *n* **sųkpé** n muskrat

muslin *n* **zizíbenaskana** n muslin

Musselshell River *ngeo* **Tugíska wakpá** ngeo Musselshell River (Montana)

must *v n* 1) **cá** part must, might (deontic and epistemic modality; conveys the idea that an event is likely to occur) 2) **céyagA** part should, must, ought to, might as well (marker of deontic modality) ‣ **céyagešį** part should not, must not, cannot possibly (negative deontic modality) 3)

cen encl must be, I guess, or what (expresses uncertainty)

mustache *n* **pudéhįšmą** n mustache

mute *adj n v* **i'éšį** vi1, n s/he is mute; mute

muzzle *n* **máza'i** n gun muzzle

my *adj* 1a) **ma-** pref my (1s person singular possessor) 1b) **mi-** pref my (1s person singular possessor) 2) **mitáwa** pro my; mine; I own it, it is my own 3) **-gi- ; -ki- ; -k-** pref on one's own (marker of possessive verbs where the agent is acting on his/her own thing, body part or relative; the resulting possessive verbs are always of Class 1)

myself *pro* **miyé** pro, vs myself (emphasizes the subject or object); I am the one

mysterious *adj* **waką́** vs, adv s/he/it is holy, spiritually powerful; s/he/it is mysterious, magical (occurs with words for European objects); medicine line; in a holy manner

N

nail *v n* 1) **ogádą** vt1 s/he nails smth; pounds a nail in ‣ **a'ógadą** vt1, n s/he nails smth on it; nail 2) **šagé** n nail, hoof, claw ‣ **wamní šagé** cp eagle claw

naked *adj* 1) **tącócona** vs s/he is naked 2) **šnišníyena** adv naked, with no clothes on

Naked dance *np* **Tącówaci, Tącó wacíbi** n Naked dance

Nakoda *n adj* 1) **Nakóda** nprop, vs Nakoda person; s/he is Nakoda ‣ **Nakón-** cont related to the Nakoda, or Nakoda way of life ‣ **Nakón-wįcóh'ąge** cp Nakoda custom, tradition, way of life ‣ **Nakón'įc'ina** vi3-refl s/he behaves like a Nakoda 2) **Nakón'i'A, Nakón'iyA** vi1 s/he speaks Nakoda; s/he speaks Nakoda to sb 3a) **Nakón'iyabi, Nakón'i'e** n Nakoda language 3b) **Nakón-wįcó'i'e** n Nakoda language, words

name *n v* 1) **cažé** n name ‣ **caš-** cont name ‣ **Nakón-cažé** n traditional Nakoda name ‣ **cažé ópekiyA** vt1-caus s/he puts his/her name down to become a member; enrolls in an organization ‣ **cažé ótągaga** vs-redup s/he/it has a great, famous name 2) **wįcácaže** n name, personal name 3) **caštų** vt1 s/he names sb, smth ‣ **acáštų** vt1 s/he names sb after another person 4) **cažéyadA** vt2 s/he calls sb's name 5) **egíyabi** vs-pass s/he/it is called (by a name)

Naming ceremony *np* **Acáštųbi ecúbi** cp Naming ceremony

nape *n* 1) **nažúde** n nape of the neck, occiput (hollow part) 2) **tahú** n neck, nape of the neck 3) **pahú** n nape of the neck

nation *n* **oyáde** n tribe, people, nation

navel *n* **cekpá** n navel

near *adv adj prep v* 1) **kiyána** adv close, nearby ‣ **tikíyana** adv near a tent 2) **gaktá** adv near that yonder 3) **néduna** adv near, close ‣ **nédunaȟ** adv very near, close to here 4) **édunaȟ** adv close by, near 5) **penkákna** adv near the fire 6) **penkáyena** adv near the fire

necklace *n* 1) **wanáp'į** n necklace 2) **huhúwanap'į** n breastplate, necklace

needle *n* 1) **tahį́špa juk'ána** cp sewing needle 2) **įbásise ; įbásisa** n needle, security pin 3) ** įjáȟtage** n tattooing or vaccination needle

neglect *v* **a'íc'iktašį** vi3 s/he neglects himself/herself

neigh *v* **hotų́tų** vi1-redup it (horse) neighs, cackles; it (cattle) whines ‣ **šųkhótųtų** vi1 it (wolf, coyote, dog) howls; it (horse) neighs

nephew *n* 1) **-tųška-** root nephew (sister's son; male speaker) 2) **-toška-** root nephew (brother's son; female speaker) 3) **-cįkšina- ; -cįhįktuna-** root nephew (brother's son for a male speaker; sister's son for a female speaker)

nest *n v* 1) **hoȟpí** n nest 2) **wahóȟpi** n nest 3) **gihí** vi1-pos s/he/it leaves the nest, is fledged

next *n prep adv adj* 1) **įjíma** adv next time, next 2) **štén** conj if when, if then; when, whenever, in, at, on, next

never *adv* **dóhani** adv never

new *adj* **téjana ; téja** vs s/he/it is young (humans, animals); it is new (things) ‣ **watéjana** vs s/he/it is new ‣ **tektéjana** vs-redup they are new

New Year's Day *cp* **ómakateja ; omákateja** n New Year's Day

Nez Perce *nprop* **Póǧe oȟnóga ; Póȟnoga ; Pasú oȟnóga** nprop Nez Perce people, person of Nez Perce descent

nibble *v* **yašpášpA** vt2-redup s/he nibbles, bites a piece off sb, smth

nice *adj* 1) **wašté** vs it is good, nice (event, temperature, object); s/he is pretty, handsome, nice 2) **yuwášte** vt2 s/he makes smth nice manually; redoes smth in a better way ‣ **knuwášte** vt1-pos s/he improves, makes his/her own in a better, good way

nicely *adv* 1) **waštéya** adv nicely, in a good manner, well 2) **yupíya** vs, adv, adv-redup it is valuable; well, in a good skillful manner; nicely, very well *Redup:* **yupípiya**

nicest *adj* **waštéȟtiyĄ** vs it is very good, the best, nicest

nickel *n* **wįyąwašóga** n nickel

niece *n* 1) **-tųžą-** root niece (sister's daughter; male speaker) 2) **-tožą- ; -tožąna-** root niece (brother's daughter; female speaker) 3) **-cųkšina-** root niece (brother daughter's for a male speaker; sister's daugther for a female speaker)

night *n adj* 1) **hąhébi** n, vimp night; it is nighttime ‣ **hąhébic'ehą** adv last night 2) **hą-** cont night ‣ **hącogądu** adv midnight, middle of the night ‣ **hą'éyasą** adv throughout the night, all night ‣ **hątéhą ; ahátehąga** adv, adv late at night, late at night ‣ **hąmáni** vi1 s/he walks at night ‣ **hą'ómani** vi1 s/he/it walks around, travels at night 3) **a'ókpazą** vimp it is a dark night; in the darkness

nighthawk *n* **bíško** n nighthawk

nine *adj n* **napcúwąga** num nine ‣ **napcúwągana** quant only nine

nineteen *num* **agénapcuwąga** num nineteen

ninety *num* **wikcémna napcúwąga** num ninety

ninth *adj n* **ijínapcuwąga** num ninth

nipple *n* **azépįkpa** n nipple, teat

no *adv adj n* 1) **hiyá** adv no 2) **-ni** ; **-na** suff not, no (negator used with indefinite pronouns)

No retreat dance *np* **Napéšį wacíbi** cp No retreat dance

No retreat society *np* **Napéšį** nprop No retreat society

nobody *pro n* 1a) **duwéni** ; **duwéna** pro nobody, no one, none (always followed by a negated verb) ‣ **duwéniȟ** pro absolutely nobody, no one 1b) **duwénišį** vs s/he/it is nobody ‣ **duwénišį įc'ína** vi3-refl s/he considers himself/herself as nobody

noise *n* 1) **wot'į** vi1 s/he/it is noisy 2) **piȟyá kné** vt1 s/he/it makes noise

none *pro adj adv* 1) **wanįjA** vs s/he/it lacks; there is none; s/he passed away; is dead 2) **dágu** pro, quant, vs thing, something; what; any, none; it is something ‣ **dáguni** pro none, nothing (refers to objects only; requires a negated verb) ‣ **dágunišį** pro, num it is nothing, there is none; zero 3) **duwé** quant nobody (followed by a negated verb) ‣ **duwéni** ; **duwéna** pro nobody, no one, none (followed by a negated verb) ‣ **duwénišį** vs s/he/it is nobody 4) **iyúha** quant all, every (has a distributive meaning, one after the other); none (followed by a negated verb)

noon *n* 1) **wiyódahą** n south; noon, midday 2) **ąmcógądu** adv noon, midday

north *adv n* 1) **wazíyada** adv north; in, to the north 2) **wazíyam** adv in, to the north 3) **wihíyayešį** n north

Northern lights *n-pl* **Wanáǧi wacíbi** n 1) Northern Lights; aurora borealis; 2) Ghost dance

northward *adv* **wazíyatakiya** ; **wazíyakiya** adv northward, toward the north

nose *n* 1) **póǧe** n nose ‣ **poȟ-** cont nose 2) **pasú** n beak; tip of the nose 3) **paȟnáda** n bridge of the nose

nosebleed *n* **páwe** vs s/he has a nosebleed

nostril *n* **poȟ'óȟnoga** n nostril

nosy *adj* **wasnókye wacį** cp nosy person

not *adv* 1) **-šį** encl not, in- (expresses the negation of verbs, adverbs, particles, and pronouns) 2) **-gen** encl not (expresses the negation of verbs but adds strong disagreement or contradiction often accompanied by a touch of sarcasm or carelessness; it is translated as "did not ... anyway" or "did not ... for what I care") 3) **-ni** ; **-na** suff not, no (negator used with indefinite pronouns)

nothing *pro adv n adj* 1) **dáguni** pro none, nothing (refers to objects only; requires a negated verb) ‣ **dáguniȟ** pro nothing at all ‣ **dágunišį** vs, num it is nothing, there is none; zero 2) **dágugen** vs it is nothing; it is nothing to worry about 3) **dókejašį** vs there is nothing wrong with him/her/it; it is all good; it doesn't matter 4) **įdúȟtayena** ; **įdútahena** adv for nothing 5) **įdúya** adv for no reason, for nothing 6) **dágecųšį** vs nothing is done; it is a waste of time

notwithstanding *adv prep* **piyéniš** adv instead, still, notwithstanding

November *n* 1) **cuȟéwąga wí** cp November 2) **wįcógądu sųgágu wí** ph November 3) **caȟ'ótka hąwí** cp November

now *adv* 1) **waná** adv now, already 2) **nągáhą** adv now ‣ **nągáhąȟ** ; **nągáȟ** adv just now, right away ‣ **nągáhąš** ; **nągáš** adv now as compared to before; but now 3) **néhą** adv at this time; now, today ‣ **nehądu** vs it is now; it took place

at this time ▸ **nehą́duȟ** adv now, at this time
4) **nahą́n ; nahą́** adv now, about now 5) **žehą́š**
adv but now

nowadays adv **wanéhadu** vimp at this time, in
time

nowhere adv **duktḗni** adv nowhere ▸ **duktḗniȟ**
adv nowhere at all ▸ **duktḗnišį** vs it is nowhere

nudge v 1) **baní** vt1 s/he nudges at sb with the
elbow to get his/her attention 2) **badį́n iyéyA**
vt1 s/he nudges sb, hits sb slightly 3) **nadą́dą**
vt1 s/he nudges sb with the foot

numb adj 1) **t'at'Á** vs-redup s/he/it is numb, paralyzed 2) **sit'át'Á** vs-redup s/he has a numb foot
3) **nąbé t'at'Á** vs-redup s/he has a numb hand

number n 1) **wóyawabi** n number 2) **yawábi** n
number 2) **į-** pref cardinal numbers in -th

numerous adj **dáguwiyeknaš** vs it is numerous,
there are many more

nurse n v 1) **wíyą omnéza** cp nurse 2) **pežúda
wíyą** cp nurse 3) **azį́kiyA** vt1-caus s/he nurses
sb

nut n See: **peanut**

O

ox n **ptewówaši** n ox

oats n-pl **wayáhoda** n oats

obey v 1) **naȟ'ų́** vt1 s/he hears, listens to sb, smth;
s/he obeys sb ▸ **wanáȟ'ų** vi1-abs s/he obeys 2)
įknígA vt1 s/he minds, wonders, has regard
for, pays attention to sb, smth; obeys sb

oblong adj 1a) **stó** vs it is rectangular, oblong 1b)
stohą́skA vs it has a long oblong shape

occasionally adv 1) **įknúhahana ; įknúhąhąna**
adv-redup now and then, occasionally 2)
duktḗkten ; duktḗkte adv-redup here and
there; occasionally

occupation n **wówaši** n job, work, occupation;
workplace; servant, worker See: **wówaši**

Ocean man nprop **Ų́šiya máni** nprop Ocean man
(Nakoda chief)

Ocean Man (Saskatchewan) ngeo **Ų́šiya máni**
ngeo Ocean Man reservation (Saskatchewan)

ochre n **wasé** n clay, ochre, paint of any color

o'clock adv **ehą́'i** vii s/he/it reaches, arrives at a
certain point; it is such hour, day of the week,
year

October n 1) **tašnáheja ȟóda hagíkta wí** ph
October 2) **tašnáheja akída wí** ph October 3)
anų́k'ope n October

octagon n **o'ípa šaknóǧą**, cp octagon

odd adj **oštéga** vs s/he/it is peculiar, odd, weird

of prep **į-** pref this preposition has no single word
equivalent in Nakoda as it is part of the verb
meaning or the prefix **į-**, because of, with a tool

off prep this preposition has no single word
equivalent in Nakoda as it part of the verb
meaning

offend v **iyógipišįyA** vt1-caus s/he offends sb

offering n 1) **knegíyabi ; kneyábi** n offering 2)
wó'įye n cloth offering used in Sun dances 3)
waȟéyaga n cloth offering

offspring n 1) **cįjána** n calf, offspring, cub 2)
cįhį́ktuna n human offspring

off-white adj **są́** vs it is beige, faded, off-white

often adv 1) **jé ; jé'e** part always, often 2) **-s'a**
encl often, usually, habitually (used on verbs;
triggers e-ablaut); agent, one who does smth
(derives agentive nouns with or without pejorative connotations)

Oglala nprop **Ókalala** nprop Oglala Lakota people

oil n 1) **wíkni** n fat, grease; gas, oil ▸ **mąkwíkni**
n, skunk oil 2) **sná** n lotion, oil ▸ **snayÁ** vt1-
caus s/he rubs sb, smth with grease, oil, lotion

old adj 1) **gánA ; gą́nA** vs s/he/it is old, elderly,
aged 2) **gą́bina** n-pl elders, old people 3)
wagą́gana ; wagą́ga n-redup elderly woman 4)
wįcáȟtiyana ; wįcáȟtiyą n elderly man, senior
5) **ga'į́t'eyA** vs s/he/it died of old age

Omaha dance *np* **Omáha wacíbi** cp Omaha dance

omasum *n* **tiȟáha** n omasum

on *prep adv adj* 1) **én** post in, into, on, onto, at, to; here, there 2) **agán ; agám** post on top of smth, on smth ▸ **bahágan** adv on a mound, hilltop ▸ **makágan** adv on the ground, on earth 3) **agánya** adv on, upon, on top of smth 4) **ha'ágam** adv on the skin 5) **agányįgA, agányagA** vt3 s/he rides a horse 6) **a-** pref on, onto, over, at 7) **-n** suff on smth 8) **age-** pref on top of (ten) (used with teen numerals)

once *adv, n* 1) **wąjaȟ** adv one time, one time specifically; once (used in introducing a tale, or story) ▸ **wąjanaȟ** adv only once; one more time ▸ **wąjanaȟtįyA** vs it is only once; it is one more time 2) **wąžíȟtįyą** adv once again 3) **įknúhana ; įknúhąnaȟ** adv suddenly, instantly, all at once

one *adj n pro* 1) **wąží** num, det one; a, an ▸ **wąžíȟ** num, det one in particular, a certain one (marker of focus); any, a single one (nonspecific, hypothetical referent) ▸ **wąžíkšina** adv-redup one by one, one after the other ▸ **wąžína** num only one ▸ **wąžínaȟ** adv only one, just one of a group ▸ **wąžíni** adv no one, not one, neither of them 2) **wája** adv single (archaic); one (the meaning "one" is found only in White Bear and Fort Peck) ▸ **wąjaȟ** adv one time, one time specifically; once (used in introducing a tale, or story) ▸ **wąjanaȟ** adv only once; one more time ▸ **wąjanaȟtįyA** vs it is only once; it is one more time 3) **omá ; ųmá** pro one of two; the others ▸ **omána** pro just, only one ▸ **omáȟ** pro either one ▸ **omáȟtįyą** pro this one specifically 4) **įšnąnaȟtįyA** vs s/he/it is the only one 5) **sąní** adv single, one side ▸ **sąnína** adv on one side only

onion *n* 1a) **cąm'úzįkta, cąm'úzįtka** n wild onion, onion 1b) **cąm'úzįkta įkcéya ; cąm'úzįtka įkcéya** cp wild onion

onlooker *n* **wópaȟte** n onlooker

only *adj adv conj* 1) **ejé'ena ; ejéna** adv only, simply, alone, just 2) **ejé ; ecé** adv only, nothing but, exclusively ▸ **éceyen** adv only 3) **įdú** adv just, simply, only 4) **-na** suff expresses "only" with numerals and adverbs ▸ **wąžína** adv only one ▸ **omána** adv just, only one ▸ **sąnína** adv on one side only

onto *prep See:* **on**

onward *adv* **kosán** adv beyond, onward

ooze *v* **a'ú** vimp it flows, comes, oozes out

open *v* 1) **bašpá** vt1 s/he pushes, pries smth open 2) **gašpá** vt1 s/he opens smth with an axe, tool; it opens by itself ▸ **gíjašpa** vt1-benef s/he opens smth with an axe, tool for him/her 3) **nąšpá** vt1 s/he opens smth with the foot 4) **yušpá** vt2, vs s/he opens smth by pulling, to open with an instrument; it is opened ▸ **gíjiyušpa** vt1/2-benef s/he opens smth for him/her ▸ **knušpá** vt1-pos s/he opens his/her own 5) **įjábA** vi1 s/he opens his/her mouth ▸ **įjáp- ; įjám** vcont opening one's mouth ▸ **įjáptągA** vi1 s/he opens his/her mouth wide 6) **nacágu** vt1 s/he opens a trail, path by walking in it 7) **dųwá** vi1 s/he opens his/her eyes 8) **yuzámni** vt2 s/he spreads smth open; opens a book 9) **gazába** vt1 s/he opens smth ▸ **gazám** vcont opening smth 10) **įǧúȟkiyaga** adv barely opened

opening *n* **o'óna** n opening

opposed *adj* **-š** suff as opposed to, on the other hand (adversative suffix; with pronouns it indicates a contrast between two referents)

or *conj* **eštá** conj or, either; whether it is the case or not

orange *adj n* 1) **šašána** vs-redup, n s/he/it is orange; candies (archaic) 2a) **taspą ǧí** cp orange 2b) **taspą́ǧiǧi** n-redup orange

order *v* 1) **-ši** vt1-dit-aux s/he tells, asks, orders, commands sb (attaches or follows a preceding verb) 2) **iyógiši** vt1 s/he sends sb away; orders sb to stop doing smth

ordinary *adj n* **įkcéya** adv in a common, ordinary, usual way ‣ **įkcéyagen** adv in an ordinary way

organ *n* **įcábahotų ; įcámahotų** n organ, piano

orphan *n* **wamnónįja** n orphan

other *adj pro n* **omá ; ųmá** pro the other of two, the others ‣ **omágakiyadahą** adv from the other side

otter *n* **ptá** n otter

ought *v* **céyagA** part should, must, ought to, might as well (marker of deontic modality)

our *adj* 1a) **ųgí-...-bi** circumfix our (1st person plural possessor) 1b) **ųgí-** pref our (1st person dual possessor) 2) **-gi- ; -ki- ; -k-** pref on one's own (marker of possessive verbs; agent is acting on his/her own thing, body part, or relative; the resulting possessive verbs are of Class 1) 3a) **ųgítawabi** pro; vs our; we own it, it is our own 3b) **ųgítawa** pro; vs our; we two own it, it is our own

ours *pro* **ųgítawabi** pro; vs our; we own it, it is our own

ourselves *pro* **ųgíye** pro, vs ourselves (emphasizes the subject or object); we are the ones

out *prep* See: **outside**

out of sight *idiom* **įsá'į** adv out of sight

outfit *n* 1) **wokóyage** n clothes, fancy clothes, outfit 2) **įwáci** n dance outfit

outhouse *n* 1) **owįduka ; owįduka tíbi** n toilet, bathroom, outhouse 2) **océsni tíbi** cp outhouse

outside *n adj adv prep* **tągán ; tągáda** adv outside ‣ **tągápadahą ; tągápada** adv from the outside

oven *n* See: **stove**

over *prep adv adj* 1) **sám ; sąm** post beyond, over, across 2) **į'ágam** adv, conj over it; than 3) **sápana** adv further on, over 4) **amníjiya** adv all over, all around 5) **ówąja** adv everywhere, all over ‣ **į'ówąja** adv all over (more intense than ówąja) ‣ **makówąja** n all over the world 6) **a-** pref on, onto, over, at 7) **-ki ; -ci** suff over, around (indicates a general or approximative location)

overshoe *n* **osníhąba** n overshoes

overturn *v* **baptáyĄ** vt1 s/he overturns sb, smth by pushing, or with a tool

O'watch *nprop* **Wówaši** nprop O'Watch (surname in Carry The Kettle, Saskatchewan)

owl *n* 1) **hįhą** n owl (generic); dove 2) **hįhą ohňóga otís'a** np burrowing owl 3) **hįhą tága** cp great gray owl 4) **hįhąhana** n-redup pigmy owl 5) **hįháwapapana** n short-eared owl 6) **hįhąsą** n snowy owl

own *adj v pro* 1) **táwa** pro; vs his/her; s/he owns it, it is his/her own 2) **-gi- ; -ki- ; -k-** prefix-infix on one's own (marker of possessive verbs; agent is acting on his/her own thing, body part or relative; possessive verbs are of Class 1) 3) **-giyA ; -kiyA** suff cause one's own to do smth (possessive form of the causative -yA; creates transitive verbs from stative ones; -kiyA is used after a consonant)

P

pacer *n* **šųkyúhųhųza** n pacer (horse that lifts the front and back leg on the same side, and rocks or "shakes" side to side as it moves forward)

pack *v n* 2) 1) **opáhtA** vt1 s/he ties, packs smth into a bundle; ties smth in it ‣ **opágihtA** vt1-pos s/he ties, packs his/her own thing into a bundle 2) **wagíc'į** vii-abs s/he packs things, packs a horse 3) **wahéc'ų** vii-abs s/he packs things in bundles, breaks camp for traveling ‣ **wahégic'ų** vii-abs-pos s/he packs his/her things in bundles, breaks his/her camp for traveling 4) **wóšma** n, vs brush, thick bush; it is dense, tightly packed 5) **šųkwágic'į** n pack animal (horse or dog)

paddle *v n* 1a) **wadópa** vii s/he paddles ‣ **watóm** vcont paddling 1b) **wan'įdopa** n paddle, oar 2) **wadóptom** vcont-redup paddling

Paddler *nprop* **Wadópena ; Wadópana** nprop Paddler people (band of Nakoda living in

Fort Peck, Montana and Pheasant Rump, Saskatchewan)

pail *n* **céǧa tą́ga** cp pail

pain *n* 1) **cąyák ų́** vi1 s/he/it agonizes in pain 2) **bahówayA** vt1 s/he makes sb scream in pain by bumping, pushing, sitting on him/her/it; squeal as when bumping onto smth 3) **nahówayayA** vt1-redup s/he makes sb scream in pain by stepping (on one's foot or tail) 4) **yuhówayA** vt2 s/he makes sb scream in pain by pinching, or pressing on a body part 5) **oyázą** n pain

paint *v n* 1) **į̇'ų́** vt1-dit s/he paints, rubs, applies smth on it ‣ **įgíji'ų** vt1-benef s/he paints, rubs, applies smth on him/her for sb ‣ **įgí'ų** vt1-pos s/he paints, rubs, applies smth on his/her own ‣ **įc'į́'ų** vi3-refl s/he paints, rubs, applies smth on himself/herself 2) **į̇'útų** vt1 s/he paints smth 3) **ša'į́'ų** vt1-dit s/he paints, applies red paint on sb, smth 4) **okmÁ** vt1 s/he writes, draws smth; paints, sketches sb, smth 5) **wasé** n clay, ochre, paint of any color ‣ **waséǧina** n yellow paint

paintbrush *n* **į̇'útų įwókma** cp crayon, paintbrush

painter *n See:* **writer**

palate *n* **cagá** n palate

palm *n* **nąpcóga** n palm of the hand

palomino *n* **šųk'ápeskana** n palomino

pan *n* 1) **įwáco'ųba** ; **įwáco'ųbe** n frying pan 2) **wį̇kni owáco'ųba** cp frying pan 3) **iyógapte sába** cp frying pan 4) **įwóbaska** n bread pan

pandemic *adj n See:* **epidemic**

pants *n* 1) **hųská** n pants, leggings ‣ **hųskógit'ų** vi1 s/he wears pants 2) **ųzóžuha** n pants

paralyzed *adj See:* **numb**

parents *n-pl* **hųgágebi** n-pl parents

parfleche *n* **tahásaga** n rawhide bag; parfleche

parsnip *n* **pąǧí hą́ska** cp parsnip

part *n* **ošpáye** n divisions, parts of smth

particles *n-pl* **špušpúna** n particles

partridge *n* **tįknámųmųna** n partridge, grouse

Pasap *nprop* **Pásaba** nprop Pasap (surname in White Bear, Saskatchewan)

pass *v n* 1) **iyékiyA** vt1 s/he passes smth to sb ‣ **kosán yegíyA** vt1-pos s/he passes, gives away his/her own position to sb 2) **ogícic'ubi** vt1-recip they pass, lend sb, smth to one another 3) **hiyáyA; wanį́jA** vi2, vs s/he goes, passes by 4, s/he/it lacks; there is none; s/he passed away; is dead

pass out *v* **ktųšį́ȟpayA** vs s/he passes out

past *n* 1) **-c'eȟą** encl back then, in the past, last (attaches to adverbs, verbs, and interrogative pronouns) 2) **eȟą́** adv then, as it happened, at a specific point in the past (often translates the English past tense) 3) **žeȟą́ ; žéȟą** adv then, at that time, at a certain point in time (often translates the English past tense) ‣ **žéȟąc'eȟą** adv at that time in the past 4) **hékta** adv back then, in the past

pasture *n* **ocą́baza** n pasture

patch *v n* 1) **iyóbatA** vt1 s/he patches smth 2) **buspÁ** vt1 s/he daubs, patches smth ‣ **kpúspA** vt1-pos s/he daubs, patches his/her own

path *n* 1) **ocą́guna** n path, trail 2) **cągú** n path, trail 3) **amánibi** n path

patient *adj* **tawácį hą́skA** vs s/he is patient

patrol *n* **ocą́gu ceskámaza** cp highway patrol

paw *n* **šųkną́be** n paw with claws, hoof

pay *v n* **gažúžu** vt1 s/he pays smth off (debt), pays for smth ‣ **knažúžu** vt1-pos s/he pays for his/her own ‣ **gíjažužu** vt1-benef s/he pays for smth for sb ‣ **gicíjažužubi** vi1-recip they pay for one another

paycheck *n* **įjážužu** n fare, paycheck

peace *n* 1a) **onákoda** n peace 1b) **onákodagiciyabi** vi1-redup they are in peace with one another 2) **gicízabišį** n peace, ceasefire

peach *n* 1) **taspą́ ǧí hįšmą ; taspą́ hįšmą** cp peach 2) **taspáhįtųtų** n-redup peach peanut *n* **yahúgabi** n peanut, any kind of nut

pear *n* **taspą pestóstona** cp pear

pearl *n See:* **shell**

peck *v n* **gadódo** vt1 s/he shakes, brushes, sweeps, dusts smth off; s/he/it pecks sb, smth (tree, ground)

peek *v* 1) **a'ógas'į** vt1 s/he peeks in at sb, smth 2) **tiyógas'į** vi1 s/he peeks inside a tent

peel *v n* 1) **gaȟ'ú** vt1 s/he scrapes, peels, shaves, chips smth 2) **maȟ'ú** vt1 s/he peels smth with a sharp tool (fruit, vegetable) 3) **yaȟ'ú** vt2 s/he peels smth with the teeth 4) **yuȟ'ú** vt2 s/he scrapes, peels smth manually 5) **yuȟná'į**, vt2 s/he peels smth off

peg *n v* 1) **įbáspe** n peg, stake 2) **wa'įbaspa** n tent peg 3) **húpe** n picket, tipi peg ‣ **húpepena** n-redup pickets, tipi pegs

pelican *n* **mnóza** n pelican

pemmican *n* 1) **wíjaskabi ; wíjaska** n pemmican, dried meat with crushed chokecherries 2) **wašną** n pemmican, dried goods; fat, grease, lard 3) **wagápabi** n pemmican

pen *n* **įwá'okma ; įwó'okma ; įwókma ; owá'okma ; owó'okma** n pen, pencil, chalk, any writing instrument

penis *n* 1) **cé** n penis ‣ **šųkcé** n dog penis 2) **cetápą** n male genitalia (penis and testicles)

penny *n* 1) **mázaša** n penny, cent; copper 2) **wįyą́ša** n penny, cent

pension *n* **gábina maswįcak'ubi** cp old age pension

people *n* 1) **oyáde ; oyádebi** n tribe, people, nation 2) **wįcášta** n man, adult male; person (of both sexes), people (both in the singular and plural); tribe (collective plural) ‣ **waną́gaš wįcášta** cp people from long ago

People of the cold *nprop* **Osníbi wįcášta** nprop People of the cold (Stoney band)

pepper *n* 1) **cąpásusuna ; cąpásu** n-redup, n

pepper 2) **štušténasapsaba ; štušténa sába** n-redup, cp pepper

peppermint *n* 1) **waȟpé ce'ága** cp peppermint 2) **ceyágadaga ; cayágadaga** n wild mint, peppermint

perch *n* **hopépe** n perch, pike, pickerel

perfume *n* 1) **a'įkpoǧa** vi3-refl, n s/he blows smth (medicine, perfume) on himself/herself; cedar; Indian perfume (sweet pine, cedar) 2) **a'įkpapsų** n perfume ‣ **a'įkpapsųpsųbi** n-redup spray perfume

perish *v* **sódA** vs s/he is extinct, gone; perishes

person *n* 1) **duwé** pro, n who; person 2) **tágaga** n mature person 3) **wįcát'a** n human corpse, dead person 4) **t'ábi** n deceased person

perverse *adj* **ašínwokcą** vt1 s/he has perverse thoughts about sb, smth

pet *n v* 1) **iyústo** n pet 2) **ayústo** vt2 s/he smooths, pets, pats smth with the hand (hair, fur of an animal) ‣ **ayústoto** vt2-redup s/he pets smth repeatedly ‣ **agíciyustobi** vi1-recip they pet one another ‣ **agíjiyusto** vt1-benef s/he pets sb, smth for him/her ‣ **agíknusto** vt1-pos s/he pets his/her own 3) **gastó** vt1 s/he pets an animal

pharmacy *n* **pežúda tíbi** n pharmacy

pheasant *n* **šiyó** n prairie chicken, pheasant, grouse; domestic chicken

Pheasant Rump *nprop* **Šiyónide** nprop Pheasant's Rump (Nakoda chief and signatory of Treaty 4, in 1876)

Pheasant Rump (Saskatchewan) *ngeo* **Šiyónide** ngeo Pheasant Rump reservation (Saskatchewan)

phlegm *n* **ijášpe** n phlegm

photograph *v n* 1) **wįcíde éyagu** vt2, n s/he photographs, takes a picture of sb; makes a footage of sb; camera 2) **įdé okmÁ** vt1 s/he photographs, takes a picture of sb 3) **wįcíde oyábi** ph picture, painting, photograph 4) **owákma** n photograph

Piapot Cree people *np* **Šahíyeskạbi** nprop Piapot Cree people, person of Piapot Cree descent

pick *v n* 1) **yušpí** vt2 s/he picks smth (small things, beads, berries) ‣ **gíjiyušpi** vt1/2 s/he picks berries for sb manually 2) **wóšpi** vii-abs s/he picks berries, things ‣ **wógijišpi** vt1-benef s/he picks berries for sb 3) **yušpú** vt2 s/he picks, plucks a piece off smth ‣ **knušpú** vt1-pos s/he picks, plucks a piece off from his/her own; s/he picks, plucks his/her own off from smth 4) **bahí** vt1 s/he gathers, picks up smth ‣ **gíjibahi** vt1-benef s/he gathers, picks up smth for him/her 5) **yuzé** vt2 s/he picks smth manually (as a piece of meat) 6) **yuzặga** vt2 s/he mistreats, bullies sb; picks on sb ‣ **yuzặk** vcont mistreating, bullying sb; picking on sb

pickaxe *n* **anúkpesto** n pickaxe

picket *n* **húpe** n picket, tipi stake ‣ **húpepena** n-redup pickets, tipi stakes

pickle *n* 1) **gụgúma** n wild cucumber, cucumber; pickle 2) **gụgúbi** n cucumber, pickle

picnic *n* **oškáde** n picnic; festival; arena

picture *n v See:* **photograph**

pie *n* 1) **oȟnáte co'ụ́babi** ph pie ‣ **cíkta oȟnáte co'ụ́babi** ph raisin pie ‣ **tanó oȟnáte co'ụ́babi** ph meat pie ‣ **taspạ́ oȟnáte co'ụ́babi** ph apple pie ‣ **taspạ́ cogạ́du co'ụ́babi** (WB) ph apple pie

piece *n* 1) **ogápsija** n piece struck off 2) **mašpé** n piece cut off

Piegan *nprop* **Bigána** nprop Piegan people, person of Piegan descent

pierce *v* 1) **baȟnógA** vt1 s/he pierces, makes a hole by pressure ‣ **ịkpáȟnogA** vi3-refl s/he pierces himself/herself 2) **maȟnógA** vt1 s/he pierces a hole in smth with a knife, saw, or punch

piercing *n* **cawịcapabi** n piercing ritual in ceremonies

pig *n* **gugúša** n pig

piglet *n* 1) **gugúša cịjána** cp piglet 2) **gugúšana** n piglet, or little pig

pigsty *n* **gugúša tí** cp pigsty

pike *n See:* **perch**

pile *n* 1) **žubína** n pile 2) **cạgáȟni** n pile of wood 3a) **ị'ógana** n pile, place where substances (such as ashes) are poured 3b) **owógana** n trash pile 4) **nağé** vt1 s/he pushes smth into a pile (sand, snow) with the foot 5) **oyúğe** vt2 s/he rakes smth into a pile manually 6) **cạ́bağe** n pile of wood 7) **ocạ́gaksaksa** n-redup pile of wood

pillow *n* **ịbáhị** n pillow

pilot *n* **gịyạ́ ụ́s'a** cp airborne pilot

pin *n v* 1) **ị'íjaška** n pin 2) **ịjáše** n button, safety pin 3) **ịbásise ; ịbásisa** n needle, security pin 4) **abáȟnadA** vt1, n s/he stitches, pins smth on it; ribbon; silk, silk cloth ‣ **abáȟnan** cont silk, ribbon, smth pinned or stitched ‣ **abáȟnadekiyA** vt1-caus s/he lets sb pin smth on it

pin cherry *cp* **cạpájuk'a** n pin cherry

pinch *v n* **yužíba** vt2 s/he pinches sb, smth with the fingers ‣ **knužíba** vt1-pos s/he pinches his/her own (as skin) with the fingers ‣ **gicíknužibabi** vii-recip they pinch one another with the fingers ‣ **ịknúžiba** vi3-refl s/he pinches himself/herself with the fingers

pine *n* 1) **cạwába** n evergreen tree, pine 2) **wazícạ** n pine tree

pink *adj* **ša'ị́mna** vs s/he/it is pink

pinkie *n* **šašté** n pinkie

pinto *n* **šụkknékneğa** n pinto horse

pipe *n* 1) **cạnúba** n, vs pipe; s/he smokes pipe ‣ **cạnúbaha** n pipe pouch ‣ **cạnúba ịbáȟage ; ịbáȟage** cp pipe tamper ‣ **cạnúba ịhúcạ; hucạ́** cp pipe stem ‣ **cạnúba oȟpáğa ecụ́bi** ph Pipe ceremony ‣ **cạnúba wakạ́** cp sacred pipe 2) **obáğe** n filled pipe ‣ **ogíbağe** vt1-dat s/he fills a pipe for sb; gives sb a smoke 3) **yağú** vt2 s/he finishes up a pipe ‣ **gíjiyağu** vt1-benef s/he finishes up a pipe for sb ‣ **knağú** vt1-pos s/he finishes up his/her own pipe

pistol *n* **ịšákpe** num, n sixth; pistol, handgun

pitch₁ *v* **wi'ógiziba** vi1-pos s/he pitches, puts up his/her own tent

pitch₂ *n adj* 1) **sapsábA** vs-redup, n it is black-spotted, black here and there; pitch, tar 2) **sáben̄t̄iyA̧** vs it is pitch black

pitchfork *n* **ocápe** n pitchfork

pitiful *adj* 1) **úši** vs s/he/it is pitiful ‣ **úšigiya** adv pitifully, humbly ‣ **úšiya** adv pitifully, humbly 2) **úšiga** vs s/he/it is poor, pitiful 3) **wišíjena** n pitiful tent

pity *v n* 1) **úšina** vt1 s/he pities sb ‣ **wa'úšina** vi1-abs s/he pities people, is kind to people ‣ **wawá'úšigina** vi1 s/he is kind, good-natured, likes people

place *n* 1) **tóhe ; t̄íhe** n his/her place, house, bed 2) **a'ómnina** n place sheltered from the wind 3) **tušúda** n place near the entrance of a tipi 4) **catkú** n honor place 5) **édu** vimp it is there, it is the place, time 6) **tokámpadaḩa** adv from a different place 7) **oķá** n aisle, narrow path; vacant place 8) **ųwá̧ži** n one place 9) **šųk'ówode** n place where horses feed *See:* **put**

placenta *n* **tamní** n placenta

plan *v n* **wókça** vi1 s/he thinks, plans on doing smth

plane *v n* 1) **gažíba** vt1 s/he planes smth 2) **çagážiba** vi1, n s/he planes wood (as to make wood shavings for kindling); wood shavings 3) **įçágažibe** n wood plane

plant *v n* 1) **okšú** vt1 s/he plants smth (seed, plant, crop) ‣ **wókšu** vi1-abs s/he plants things (garden, crops) ‣ **ogíjikšu** vt1-benef s/he plants smth (plants, garden) for sb ‣ **ogíkšu** vt1-pos s/he plants his/her own (garden) 2) **basnádA** vt1 s/he pushes, plants smth straight into the ground ‣ **kpasnádA** vt1-pos s/he pushes, plants his/her own straight into the ground

plaster *v n See:* **daub**

plate *n* **iyógapte ; ogápte** n plate, dish, dipper

play *v n* 1) **škádA** vi1, vt1 s/he plays; s/he plays a musical instrument ‣ **škat- ; škan-** vcont playing ‣ **škatkíyA** vt1-caus s/he lets sb play ‣ **įc'íškadA** vi3-refl s/he plays with himself/herself; masturbates 2) **aškádA** vt1, s/he plays on smth 3) **oškádA** vi1; n s/he plays inside of smth; playground ‣ **tiyóškadA** vi1 s/he plays in a lodge, house 4) **įškádA** vt1 s/he plays with smth ‣ **pen'íškadA** vi1 s/he plays with fire; pokes a fire 5) **škanwáyupiya** vt2 s/he is skilled at playing games 6) **yu'íškadA** vt2 s/he teases, plays jokes on sb; s/he plays with sb sexually 7) **bahóţu** vt1 s/he makes a sound by pushing on smth; plays a musical instrument (trumpet, accordion) 8) **yuhóţu** vt2 s/he makes smth sound manually; plays a musical instrument with the hands 9) **gazógic'ų** vi-irr s/he skates; plays hockey 10) **mokógA** vt1 s/he hits smth with a stick; plays pool ‣ **mokók** vcont making a tapping sound; playing pool 11) **t'egúza** vi1 s/he plays dead

player *n* 1) **togáhe įná̧žibi** cp first base player 2) **įnúm-na̧ži** n second base player 3) **įyámni-na̧ži** n third base player *See:* **gambler**

playground *n* **oškádA** vi1; n s/he plays inside of smth; playground

pleased *adj* **įçádewašte** vs s/he is pleased with smth; happy about smth

plenty *adj* **baháyena ; baháya** quant plenty of smth, a lot

plow *n v* 1) **įmá̧kayupte** n plow 2) **yuptÁ** vt2 s/he breaks, turns over, plows smth ‣ **ayúptA** vt2 s/he plows smth (field, garden) 3) **ma̧káyuptA** vi2 s/he plows a field

pluck *v* 1) **yudúgA** vt2 s/he plucks, pulls smth out (as the feathers of a bird) ‣ **knudúgA** vt1-pos s/he plucks, pulls his/her own out (eyebrow, hair) 2) **yušpú** vt2 s/he picks, plucks a piece off smth ‣ **knušpú** vt1-pos s/he picks, plucks a piece off from his/her own; s/he picks, plucks his/her own off from smth

plum *n* 1) **ķáda** n plum 2) **ķasú** n plum seed

plural *adj* the notion of plurality is expressed by suffixes on demonstratives, nouns, and verbs 1) **-na** suff plural of demonstratives 2) **-bi** encl plural marker of nouns and verbs (used with animate referents (human, animal)

plus *prep adj n* **aké** adv again; another one, one more (usually followed by one); plus

pneumonia *n* **cağú nądáboğa** cp pneumonia

pocket *n* **owópiye ; o'ópiyeda** n pocket

point₁ *n* 1) **įkpá** n tip, point 2) **o'įpa** n tip, point of a shape 3) **wągámneȟ** adv highest point, top, highest part of smth 4) **wągáduwaȟ** adv way up there, at the highest point ‣ **wągáduwaȟtįyĄ** vs s/he/it is the highest, at the highest point 5) **žecíyo** adv at destination, at an end point 6) **pésto** vs it is a sharp point

point₂ *v* 1) **bazó** vt1 s/he shows, points at smth ‣ **gibázo** vt1-dat s/he shows, points, reveals smth to him/her 2) **abázo** vt1 s/he points at sb, smth 3) **ébazo** vt1 s/he points his/her finger, gun at sb, smth

pointed *adj* 1) **péstona** vs it is pointed 2) **tipésto** n pointed tipi

poke *v* 1) **pen'įškadA** vi1 s/he plays in the fire; pokes a fire 2) **bažíba** vt1 s/he pokes, touches sb, smth lightly ‣ **gicíbažibabi** vi1-recip they poke one another

pole *n* 1) **tušú** n tipi pole, lodge pole 2a) **ho'įcuwa** n fishhook; fishing pole and line 2b) **įhókuwa** n fishing pole

police *n* 1) **agícida** n warrior, soldier, police; army; military uniform 2) **agícida įtáca** cp policeman 3) **ceškámaza** (CTK) n council, alliance (refers to council members to whom a badge was given); police officer (used in Carry The Kettle) 4) **aȟcómaza** n police constable in a Nakoda reservation 5) **tiyóbaska** (PR) n police, police car

polish *n v* **cáhąba įsámye** cp shoe polish

pond *n* **mniyák'iba** n pond

pool₁ *n* **onúwą** n pool, swimming pool

pool₂ *n* 1) **mokógA** vt1 s/he hits smth with a stick; plays pool ‣ **mokók** vcont using a stick to hit smth; play pool 2) **mokógabi** n pool game

poolroom *n* **omókoge** n poolroom

poor *adj n* 1) **úšiga** vs s/he/it is poor, pitiful 2) **masyúhešį** vi2 s/he does not have money; is poor

poorly *adv* 1) **teȟíya** adv with difficulty, poorly 2) **sijáya** adv badly, poorly 3a) **dogįš** adv poorly, weakly 3b) **dogįšyagen** adv poorly

pop *v n* **našnógA** vi it pops out ‣ **našnókyA** vt1-caus s/he makes smth pop out

popcorn *n* 1) **nąpópomyabi** n-redup popcorn 2) **wacóğuğu** n Indian popcorn

poplar *n* 1) **cąská** n white poplar 2) **waȟníca** n white poplar

Poplar (Montana) *ngeo* **Waȟníca wakpá** ngeo Poplar (Montana)

porcupine *n* **pahį** n porcupine; porcupine quill

portage *n* **wadó k'į** vt1 s/he does a portage

possess *v See*: **own**

possession *n* **-ta-** pref marker of alienable possession (friend, object, animal)

post *n* **cąbásnadabi** n post

post office *cp* **wa'óyabi oyúȟpe** ph post office

pot *n* 1) **céğa** n kettle, pot; bucket, pail ‣ **huȟnáȟyabi céğa** cp coffee pot 2) **céğanuğe yukákana** cp-redup pot with handles 3) **įwóhe** n cooking pot

potato *n* 1) **pağí** n potato 2) **pağí gakúkabi** cp mashed potatoes 3) **pağíska** n Irish potato 4) **pağískuya** n sweet potato

pound *v* 1) **gapá** vt1 s/he pounds smth with a tool ‣ **gapápą** vt1-redup s/he pounds smth fine with a tool 2) **gaškí** vt1 s/he crushes, pounds, grinds smth; pulverizes berries with the seeds using a stone ‣ **cągáški** vi1 s/he pounds chokecherries 3) **amóskijA** vt1 s/he pounds smth smooth with an instrument 4) **maskádo** vt1 s/he pounds metal; blacksmith

pounder *n* **įgáški** n pounder

pour *v* 1a) **agánA** vt1 s/he pours liquid on sb, smth; spreads, sprinkles smth on it ‣ **aknánA** vt1-pos s/he pours smth on his/her own; powders his/her own ‣ **agíci'įknanabi** vii-recip they pour smth (water, sand) on one another ‣ **a'įknanA** vi3-refl s/he pours smth over himself/herself (powder, dirt) 1b) **ogánA** vt1 s/he empties, pours smth (like ashes) down there 2a) **bapsú** vt1 s/he pours, spills a liquid out; empties 2b) **abápsu** vt1 s/he pours, sprinkles a liquid on sb, smth; waters smth 2c) **obápšu** vt1 s/he pours smth (a liquid) into a container 3a) **gaštá** vt1 s/he pours smth out 3b) **agáštą** vt1 s/he pours smth on it ‣ **aknáštą** vt1-pos s/he pours smth on his/her own 3c) **ogáštą** vt1 s/he pours smth in it 4) **gastágA** vt1 s/he daubs, pastes, throws, pours out a gooey substance (as to make it stick); s/he glues smth ‣ **gastástak** vcont-redup pouring out ‣ **agástagA** vt1 s/he daubs, pastes, throws, pours out a gooey substance (as to make it stick)

pout *v n* **wóȟįyą** vii s/he pouts

powder *n* 1) **a'įknanabi** n powder, bath powder 2) **aknána** vt1-pos s/he pours smth on his/her own; powders his/her own 3) **mnuyéna** vs it is in powder

Powder River (Montana) *ngeo* **Caȟní wakpá** ngeo Powder River (Montana)

power *n* 1) **wówaš'age** n energy, strength, power 2) **k'úbi** n power given to sb (as in a vision)

powerful *adj* 1) **waką́** vs, adv s/he/it is holy, spiritually powerful; s/he/it is mysterious, magical (occurs with words for European objects); in holy manner 2) **mnihą́** vs s/he/it is strong, powerful

powwow *n* 1) **ogáge wacíbi** cp powwow 2) **o'étibi** n powwow

practice *v n* **įknúta** vi3-refl s/he tries for, practices at smth (activity, sport); rehearses smth (speech, play)

prairie *n* 1) **makómnaya** n prairie, flat land 2) **makóce mnaská** cp prairie, flat land 3) **otį́da** n clearing, opening without trees, prairies

prairie chicken *cp* **šiyó** n prairie chicken, pheasant, grouse; domestic chicken

prairie dog *cp* **bistą́ga** n prairie dog

praise *v* 1) **yadá** vt2 s/he praises sb, smth ‣ **yadą́biga** participle s/he is one who is highly praised 2) **ahótą'į** vt1 s/he respects, praises sb

pray *v* 1) **cégiyA** vt1-dat s/he blesses sb, smth; s/he supplicates, prays to sb ‣ **wacégiyA** vii-abs s/he prays ‣ **įcégiyA** vt1-dit s/he prays to sb for smth 2) **awácegiyA** vt1 s/he prays over, blesses sb, smth

prayer *n* 1) **wacégiyabi** n prayer, ceremony 2) **wócegiye** n religion, spirituality; prayer

pregnant *adj* 1) **įknúš'agA** vs she is pregnant ‣ **įknúš'akyA** vt1-caus he makes her pregnant 2) **wį'įknuš'age** n pregnant woman

prepare *v* **ecá'įc'ų** vi3-refl s/he prepares, does smth to himself/herself

president *n* **tugášina ; tugášina** n Grandfather!; creator; president

press *v n* 1) **ba-** pref by pushing smth away, poking, sitting on smth to exert pressure 2) **bu-** pref by pressure (obsolete; occurs only in a handful of verbs)

pressure *n* **ba-** pref by pushing smth away, poking, sitting on smth to exert pressure ‣ **bawéga** vt1 s/he breaks smth by pressure ‣ **kpawéga** vt1-pos s/he breaks his/her own by pressure

pretend *v* **gų́za** vii-aux s/he pretends (attaches to a verb and triggers e-ablaut) ‣ **huštégųza** vii s/he pretends to be lame ‣ **t'egų́za** vii s/he plays dead

Prettyshield *nprop* **Tawáhacąga wašté** nprop Prettyshield (surname in Carry The Kettle, Saskatchewan)

prick *v See:* **stab**

prickly *adj* **pepéna** vs-redup it is prickly, sharp

prison *n* 1) **owį́cagaške** n jail, prison 2) **yuštą́**

vt2 s/he loosens, lets sb, smth go; releases sb from jail

prisoner *n* **wąyák'eyagubi** n prisoner

privately *adv* **naȟmáȟman** adv-redup secretly, privately

prize *v n* 1a) **wo'óhiya** n prize 1b) **ohíyabi** n prize 2) **teȟína** vt1 s/he loves, holds on to smth, cherishes sb (like a relative), prizes smth and does not want to part with it

problem *n* **otéȟigA** vs, adv it is difficult, hard, problematic, sad; problem, trouble

producer *n* **wagáǧas'a** n producer

product *n* **wógaǧe** n product; crafted item, object

progress *v n* **maní ; máni** vi1 s/he walks; s/he progresses, behaves as such in life (used after an adverb); s/he accompanies, walks with sb (used with gicí and óm)

promise *v n* **wahóyA ; įwáhoyA** vt1-dit s/he promises sb to do smth

promote *v* **wągáduwa éknągA** vt1 s/he promotes sb to a higher position

propel *v* 1) **yeyÁ** vt1, vi-aux s/he sends sb, smth away; propel ‣ **ye'įc'iyA** vi3-refl s/he propels himself/herself, gets himself/herself going ‣ **napsín ye'įc'iyA** vi3-refl s/he propels himself/herself (as in a race) 2) **kį'íyeyA** vt1 s/he throws, casts, propels smth

prostitute *n* **maskúwa wíyą** cp female prostitute

protection *n* **anágipA** vt1 s/he seeks for his/her own for refuge, protection

proud *adj* 1) **įdą́** vs s/he is proud 2) **agísaza** vs s/he is proud (with negative connotations) ‣ **asásyA** vt1-caus s/he is proud of him/her; makes sb proud ‣ **a'įc'isaza** vi3-refl s/he it proud of himself/herself

proudly *adv* **agísas** vcont proudly

provision *n* **wą'éya** n provisions

puff *v n* See: **swell**

pull *v n* 1) **yu-** pref manually (with the hand, fingers), by pulling; (derives transitive verbs of Class 2 from stative or intransitive verbs); causes sb, smth to be; derives instrumental adverbs 2) **yuhį́ȟpayA** vt2 s/he pulls smth down 3) **yahį́ȟpayA** vt2 s/he pulls smth with the teeth 4) **yadída** vt2 s/he pulls smth with the teeth 5) **yudída**, vt2 s/he pulls sb, smth toward himself/herself 6) **yukmį́kmA** vt2 s/he/it (horse) is pulling smth (wagon) 7) **yusnóȟĄ** vt2 s/he drags, pulls smth along ‣ **knusnóȟĄ** vt1-pos s/he drags, pulls his/her own 8) **yasnóȟĄ** vt2 s/he pulls sb, smth with the mouth 9) **yušpá** vt2, vs s/he opens smth by pulling, to open with an instrument; it is opened 10) **yúzA** vt2 s/he holds, pulls, grabs, nabs, catches sb, smth; s/he marries sb 11) **hubákšija** vi1 s/he pulls his/her legs pulled to the side 12) **yukmíja** vt2 s/he pulls sb's hair ‣ **yukmín** vcont pulling sb's hair 13) **yuǧábA** vt2 s/he pulls the skin or the bark off smth; skins an animal ‣ **gíjiyuǧabA** vt1-benef s/he pulls the skin or bark off smth for him/her; skins an animal 14) **yumáhen** adv pulled in, tucked in, under

pull out *v* 1) **yudúgA** vt2 s/he plucks, pulls smth out (as the feathers of a bird) ‣ **knudúgA** vt1-pos s/he plucks, pulls his/her own out (eyebrow, hair) 2) **yusnúda** vt2 s/he pulls smth out (plant) ‣ **yusnún** vcont pulling smth out 3) **yušnógA** vt2 s/he jerks, pulls smth out from another object; takes, removes smth off (cork, tooth, root, clothes) ‣ **yušnóšnogA** vt1 s/he dismantles smth by pulling ‣ **įc'íyušnogA** vi3-refl s/he has smth pulled out 4) **yašnógA** vt2 s/he/it pulls smth out of it with the teeth 5) **yužú** vt2 s/he pulls it out manually 6) **yukmí** vt2 s/he pulls out plants from the ground; weeds smth

pulse *n* **iyápabi** n pulse

pump *n* **įbóȟkiya** n pump

pumpkin *n* **wįcánuȟnuǧena** n pumpkin

punch *n* **įbáȟnoge** n punch (for making holes)

puncture *v* 1) **baȟnéjA** vt1 s/he tears, punctures smth with a sharp tool ‣ **kpaȟnéjA** vt1 s/he tears, punctures his/her own by pushing 2)

mapóbA vt1 s/he bursts, punctures smth with a sharp tool

puppy *n* 1) **šų̃kcį́jana** n puppy 2) **šóšobina** n-pl puppies

Puppy soup ceremony *np* **Šų̃kcį́jana wóhạbi ecų́bi** ph Puppy soup ceremony

purple *adj* 1) **tošá** vs s/he/it is purple 2) **tóȟtịyÁ** vs s/he/it is purple

purpose *n* **dagúȟtịyÁ** vs, adv it is the real reason, purpose; for a reason, purpose

pursue *v* *See:* **follow**

pus *n* **tų́** n pus ▸ **tų̃yÁ** vs it (sore) suppurates, emits pus ▸ **otų́yÁ** vs it (sore) has pus inside

push *v n* 1) **ba-** pref by pushing smth away, poking, sitting on smth to exert pressure (many verbs are formed with this instrumental prefix, we give below only the most common ones) 2) **badį́da** vt1 s/he pushes, forces smth (with the hands or body) ▸ **badį́n** vcont 3) **baȟpÁ** vt1 s/he throws, pushes smth off 4) **bamáhen iyéyA** vt1 s/he pushes, inserts smth inside ▸ **bamáhen** adv pushing smth inside 5) **banáži̧** vt1 s/he pushes smth upwards; makes smth stand by pushing on it 6) **basnóhА̧** vt1 s/he pushes sb, smth along 7) **basnádA** vt1 s/he pushes, plants smth straight into the ground ▸ **kpasnádA** vt1-pos s/he pushes, plants his/her own straight into the ground 8) **bašpá** vt1 s/he pushes, pries smth open 9) **bawą́ga** vt1 s/he pushes sb, smth over ▸ **bawą́k** vcont pushing over ▸ **nawą́ga** vt1 s/he pushes sb, smth with the foot 10) **bažúžu** vt1 s/he erases smth by pushing; s/he demolishes, make smth fall apart by putting pressure 11) **obáǧe** vt1 s/he pushes smth into it; fills smth with it ▸ **naǧé** vt1 s/he pushes smth into a pile (sand, snow) with the foot 12) **bacáknekne yeyÁ** vt1 s/he makes sb stagger by pushing, shoving 13) **ba'éknekiyA** vt1 s/he pushes smth together 14) **batógam** adv pushed aside

put *v* 1) **kné** vt1 s/he sets, puts smth into place 2) **ékne** vt1 s/he puts, places smth somewhere

▸ **égijikne** vt1-benef s/he puts, places smth ready for sb 3) **won'ékne** vi1 s/he sets the table ▸ **won'égijikne** vt1-benef s/he sets the table for sb 4) **knágA** vt1 s/he puts smth ready; stores smth (food, wood); has smth on hand ▸ **gíjiknagA** vt1-benef s/he puts smth ready for sb; stores smth (food, wood) for sb to have on hand 5) **éknagA** vt1 s/he/it puts, places smth down, away ▸ **égijiknaga** vt1-benef s/he puts, places smth down for him/her ▸ **égiknagA** vt1-pos s/he puts, places his/her own thing down (feet, bag) 6) **oknágA** vt1 s/he puts, stores smth away in it ▸ **ogíknagA** vt1-pos ; n s/he puts, stores his/her own thing away in it; bag ▸ **ogíjiknagA** vt1-benef s/he puts, stores smth away in it for sb ▸ **iyóknagA** vt1 s/he puts smth in his/her own mouth 7) **yapÁ** vt2 s/he carries, puts smth in the mouth ▸ **knapá** vt1-pos s/he carries, puts smth in his/her mouth 8) **yusákiba** vt2 s/he puts smth together manually ▸ **yusákim** vcont putting together manually ▸ **knusákiba** vt1-pos s/he puts his/her own together manually (shoes, books) ▸ **knusákim** vcont putting one's own together

put on *v* **koyágA** vt2 s/he puts on clothes, fine garment, outfit ▸ **koyákyA** vt1-caus s/he makes sb put on clothes, fine garment, outfit

put out *v* 1) **ayúsni** vt1 s/he dims, reduces smth in force; put smth out (light, flame) 2) **basní ; bosní** vt1 s/he puts a light, fire out by smothering it, putting smth on it 3) **gasní** vt1, vi s/he smothers, puts out a fire, light; the rain puts out a fire ▸ **knasní** vt1-pos s/he smothers, puts out his/her own fire, light

put up *v* 1) **ozíba** vt1 s/he puts up a tent ▸ **ogíjiziba** vt1-benef s/he puts up a tent for sb ▸ **ogíziba** vt1-pos s/he puts up his/her own tent 2) **cạbáza** vii s/he puts up a fence

Q

quail *n* **šiyójusina** n quail

qualify *v* **ópA** vt1 s/he is part of smth; joins, qualifies for smth (games, contest)

quarter *n* **gašpábi** n 25 cents, quarter

queen *n* **hųkwíyą** n queen; queen in playing cards

question *n v* **he** part question marker (male and female speakers)

quickly *adv* 1) **kohą́na** adv quickly 2) **iyéyA** aux s/he does smth quickly or suddenly 3) **núzahą** vi1 s/he/it is fast, quick ▸ **nús** vcont fast, quickly 4) **éstestena** adv-redup very early, soon, quickly

quicksand *n* **wiwí** n swamp, marsh; quicksand

Quiet people *cp* **Inína ųbi** nprop Quiet people (band of Nakoda that lived near Cypress Hills, Saskatchewan)

quietly *adv* **a'ínina ; ánina ; inína** adv quietly, in silence ▸ **Áninah hą́'.** It is really quiet. (Cumberland 2005:236)

quill *n* 1) **pahį́** n porcupine; porcupine quill 2) **óska** vt1 s/he decorates smth (outfit, rawhide) with porcupine quills

quillwork *n* **wóska** vi1-abs s/he does quillwork

quilt *n v* 1) **owį́ža** n quilt, bedding sheet, blanket 2) **owį́ža basísA** vi1 vi1 s/he quilts

quilted *adj* 1) **óskabi** vs-pass it is quilted 2) **hąbóska** n quilted moccasins

quit *v* **gicúni** vt1-irr s/he quits an activity; it is finished

quite *adv* **ehą́š** adv too much, exceedingly; surely, quite

quiver *n* **wą́žu** n quiver; bag for powder and balls

R

rabbit *n* **maštíja** n rabbit ▸ **maštín ; maštį́** cont rabbit ▸ **maštín mnóga** cp male rabbit ▸ **maštín wįyéna** cp female rabbit ▸ **maštį́tapA** vi1 s/he follows, pursues, tracks rabbits

Rabbit dance *np* **Maštín wacíbi** cp rabbit dance

raccoon *n* 1) **wįcá** n raccoon 2) **ištásabA** vs, n s/ he has a black eye; raccoon

race *n v* 1a) **ki'íyągA** vi1 s/he races ▸ **ki'íyąk** vcont racing 1b) **ki'íyągena ; kíyągena** n, vi1 race; s/he races 2) **íyągA** vi3 įs/he runs, speeds up, races 3) **šųk'áktagabi** n horse race

rack *n* **cąknágiyą** n yoke; drying rack made of two poles and a transversal bar

radio *n* 1) **wahíkiyabi** n Yuwipi, Tie up or calling of the spirits ceremony; radio (object); radio broadcast 2) **owánah'ųbi** n radio

ragged *adj* 1) **ȟciná** vs it is ragged, tattered 2) **ȟneȟnéjA** vs-redup it is ragged

raid *n v* 1) **anádą** vt1 s/he raids an enemy 2) **nadą́i** vi1 s/he went on a raid, to war

rain *n v* 1) **mağážu** n, vimp rain; it rains ▸ **amáğažu** vs it rains on smth 2) **amáȟpiya naȟnéjA** vimp there is a cloudburst, a sudden heavy rainfall

Rain dance *np* **Mağážu wacíbi** cp rain dance

rainbow *n* **mağážu įkmúǧa ; mağážu kmúǧa** cp rainbow

raise *v n* **įcáȟyA; pte'įcáȟyA** vt1-caus, vi1-caus s/he grows, breeds smth; raises sb, s/he raises cattle

raisin *n* **cįkta, cįtka** n raisin ▸ **cįkta oȟnáte co'úbabi** ph raisin pie

rake *n v* 1) **peží ogáǧe** cp rake 2) **gaǧé** vt1 s/he rakes, gathers, sweeps smth together (leaves, snow) 3) **peží įyúǧe** cp rake 4) **yuǧé** vt2 s/he rakes smth manually ▸ **oyúǧe** vt2 s/he rakes smth into a pile manually

rancher *n* **pteyúhA** vi2, n s/he is a rancher; rancher

rape *v n* **iyáȟpayA** vt1 s/he attacks, rapes sb; grabs sb, smth with force

rash *n* **ȟniȟní** vs-redup s/he/it has rashes, scabies

rasp *n* **įcą́wabamna** n rasp, file

raspberry *n* **taką́heja** n raspberry

rat *n* **bisbístąga** n-redup rat

rate *v* **-na** vt1-aux s/he considers, rates, has regard for sb, smth (attaches to stative verbs and e-triggers ablaut)

rather *adv* 1) **-gA ; a- . . .-gA ; -gejA ; -jA** suff rather, somewhat, kind of (attenuator of gradable expressions) 2) **-gen** suff rather, sort of, fairly, somehow (derives adverbs from verbs and adds an attenuative meaning) ‣ **-yagen** suff kind of, somewhat, rather (creates adverbs of manner from stative and active verbs, but also from adverbs; in some cases there is no attenuative meaning)

rations *n* **wówįcak'u** n rations

rattle *n v* 1) **wakmúha ; wakmúha** n gourd rattle 2) **gaȟnáȟnabina** n-redup baby rattle 3) **ȟmúyahą** vi1, n s/he/it buzzes, rumbles, emits a buzzing sound (motor, airplane, bee); rattle, maraca, band instrument 4) **ȟná** vi it is a rattling sound; it rattles 5) **ȟnáȟna** vi-redup it rattles 6) **hóȟna** vs s/he has a coarse, rattling voice 7) **gaȟná** vt1 s/he makes a rattling sound 8) **yušná** vt2 s/he rattles, rings a bell by pulling, by the force of the wind 9) **yukógA** vt2 s/he makes a rattling sound manually

rattlesnake *n* 1) **sįdéȟna** n rattlesnake 2) **wó'ošija** n rattlesnake

rattling *adj* 1) **yuȟná** vt2 s/he makes smth rattle, ring by pulling; shakes a rattle 2) **gaȟná** vt1 s/he makes a rattling sound

raven *n* **kaǧí ; kaǧí** n raven

raw *adj* **špášį** vs it is raw, not cooked

rawhide *n* **tahásaga** n rawhide bag; parfleche

reach *v n* 1) **ehą'i; eháki** vi1, vi1 s/he/it reaches, arrives at a certain point; it is such hour, day of the week, year, s/he reaches, arrives at a certain point; ‣ **eháki** vi1-pos, s/he is of a certain age (used after the numbers of winters/years) 2) **iyóhi** vt1, vs s/he reaches smth; s/he counts a coup; it extends, is long enough ‣ **iyóhiyA** vt1-caus s/he causes sb to reach it; extends, reaches

toward 3) **égihųni** vt1-pos s/he reaches the end of his/her own (studies, work)

read *v n* **yawá** vt2 s/he counts smth; s/he reads smth ‣ **giyáwa** vt1-dat s/he reads smth to sb ‣ **wayáwa** vi2-abs s/he counts things; s/he reads things, has the ability to read; s/he studies, goes to school, is a student

ready *adj* 1) **wíyeya** adv ready 2) **yuwíyeyA** vt2 s/he makes smth ready ‣ **įknúwįyeyA** vi3-refl s/he gets himself/herself ready 3) **o'íc'icuwa** vi3-refl s/he gets himself/herself ready

real *adj adv* **-ȟtįyA** suff, encl very, really, real, genuine, -est (intensifier of stative verbs of quality and colors and some kinship verbs; also expresses superlative meaning)

really *adv* 1) **nína** adv very; really, a lot, always, intense, intensively; not at all, not really (followed by a negative verb) 2) **žecéya** adv really, actually 3) **-ȟ** suff absolutely, the very X, exactly, specifically, at all (marks focus on demonstratives, nouns, pronouns and negative interrogative pronouns); very, really (intensifer of gradable expressions such as manner and time adverbs; occurs obligatory with the degree adverb nína 'very' in negative clauses) 4) **-ȟtįyA** suff, encl very, really, real, genuine, -est (intensifier of stative verbs of quality and colors and some kinship verbs; also expresses superlative meaning)

realm *n See:* **dimension**

reason *n* 1) **dókedu** vs, adv s/he/it happened as such; for whatever reason, whatever happens; somehow 2) **dagúȟtįyA** vs, adv it is the real reason, purpose; for a reason, purpose 3) **įdúya** adv for no reason, for nothing

recently *adv* 1) **aškán** adv recently, lately 2) **wanągažašį** vs it is not too long ago; recently

reclined *adj* **yųgÁ** vi3 s/he/it lies down; lays in a reclined position ‣ **yųgáya** adv in a lying, reclined position

recognize *v* **iyégiyA** vt1-pos s/he recognizes,

finds his/her own ‣ **ho'íyegiyA** vt1-pos s/he recognizes sb's voice

recorder *n* **wįcóho éyagu** ph recorder, recording device

recover *v* **asní** vs s/he is healed, has recovered from an illness; is well again ‣ **agísni** vs-dat s/he heals, recovers from smth (wound, illness)

rectangular *adj* **stó** vs it is rectangular, oblong

red *adj* 1) **šá** vs s/he/it is red ‣ **šašá** vs-redup-pl they are red (inanimate plural) ‣ **šagíjiyA** vt1-benef s/he paints, colors sb, smth in red for sb ‣ **šagíyA** vt1-pos s/he reddens, paints, colors, dyes his/her own in red ‣ **ša'íc'iyA** vi3-refl s/he reddens, paints himself/herself in red ‣ **šayéna** adv red condition ‣ **šayÁ** adv red condition ‣ **šágeja** vs s/he/it is kind of red 2) **ša'į'ų** vt1-dit s/he paints, applies red paint on sb, smth 3) **ošá** vs it is red inside ‣ **ošágiyA** vt1-pos s/he paints his/her own red inside ‣ **ošáša** vs-redup-pl they are red inside 4) **núda** vs s/he/it is red, scarlet (mostly used in compounds)

Red bottom *nprop* **Húdeša** ; **Húdešana** ; **Húdešabina** nprop Red bottom people (band of Nakoda living in Fort Peck, Montana)

Red dog *nprop* **Šúga núda** nprop Red dog (1855–1925); Nakoda chief

Red Pheasant (Saskatchewan) *ngeo* **Šiyóša** ngeo Red Pheasant reservation (Saskatchewan)

Red River (Manitoba) *ngeo* **Miníša** ngeo Red River (Manitoba)

Red River people *nprop* **Miníšatųwąbi** nprop Red River people (band of Nakoda living near the Red River and later Winnipeg [Manitoba])

red willow *cp* 1) **cašáša** ; **cašášana** n red willow 2) **iyúhibi** n tobacco mixed with red willow (used in ceremonies)

redden *v* **šayÁ** vt1-caus s/he reddens, paints sb, smth in red ‣ **šagíyA** vt1-pos s/he reddens, paints his/her own in red ‣ **ša'íc'iyA** vi3-refl s/he reddens, paints himself/herself in red

red-wing blackbird *cp* **wa'ámnoša** n red-wing blackbird

refuge *n* 1) **anágipA** vt1-pos s/he seeks for his/her own for refuge, protection 2) **ti'ónapA** vii s/he takes refuge, shelter inside

refuse *v* **cígešį** vt1 s/he objects against, refuses sb, smth

regalia *n* **wa'ážutųbi** n regalia, decorated outfit

regard *v n* 1) **-na** suff s/he considers, rates, has regard for sb, smth (attaches to stative verbs and triggers e-ablaut) 2) **-kiyA** suff s/he considers, regards sb, smth as (attaches to stative verbs)

regardless *adv* **wógitahą** adv regardless, in spite of

Regina (Saskatchewan) *ngeo* **Huhúžubina** ngeo Regina (Saskatchewan)

regret *v n* 1) **įcádešijA** vs s/he regrets smth 2) **ogíjihįyą** vt1-benef s/he regrets smth; is sorry about smth

rehearse *v See:* **practice**

reins *n* 1) **iyúdįda** (CTK) n reins 2) **įká** (PR) n reins

reject *v* **aktášį** vt1 s/he rejects, does not want, disowns sb

relative *n* 1a) **dagúye** ; **dagúyabi** n relative, kinsman 1b) **dagúyA** vt1 s/he has sb as a relative; s/he is related to sb ‣ **wadáguyA** vii-abs s/he has relatives ‣ **dagúgiciyabi** vii-recip they are related to one another ‣ **wódaguya** n kinship, relatives

release *v* **yuštá** vt2 s/he releases, lets sb, smth go; s/he finishes smth ‣ **gíjiknuštą** vt1-benef s/he finishes smth for sb (work, meal); s/he decides smth for sb ‣ **knuštą** vt1-pos s/he finishes his/her own thing (meal, work); s/he decides regarding his/her own thing

relieve *v* **asní'íc'iyA** vi3-refl s/he heals, relieves himself/herself

religion *n* **wócegiye** n religion, spirituality; prayer

reluctant *adj* 1) **tayúkašį** vt3 s/he is reluctant to, dreads smth 2) **gabį** vi1-aux s/he is reluctant, hates doing smth (follows a verb)

remember *v* 1) **giksúyA** vt1-irr s/he remembers sb, smth ‣ **gicíksuyabi** vi1-recip they remember one another 2) **hokšígiksuyA** vi1 s/he remembers, thinks of his/her child

Remembrance Day *np* **Ạbédu wéksuya** *cp* Remembrance Day

renew *v* **piyá ecų́** vt3 s/he does smth again; renews, remodels, renovates smth

renovate *v See:* **renew**

rent *v n* 1) **onóda** vt1 s/he borrows, rents smth ‣ **ogíjinoda** vt1-benef s/he borrows, rents smth for sb else ‣ **ogínoda** vt1-dat s/he borrows, rents smth from sb 2) **ti'ónoda** vi1 s/he rents a house ‣ **ti'ógijinoda** vt1-benef s/he rents a house for sb else

repair *v n* 1) **pi'écų** vt3 s/he repairs, fixes smth 2) **yudáyą** vt2 s/he does a good job, makes it better, repairs smth

repetitive *adj* 1) **-ga** encl marker of durative aspect (marks a repetitive or continuous action or event that occurs within a definite period of time; lengthens a preceeding vowel) 2) **wą́ga** vi-aux again and again, one after the other, repetitively (marks a repetitive action that occurs in a short time frame)

reputation *n* **cažé wašté** vs s/he has a good reputation

rescue *v* 1) **nigíyA** vt1-pos s/he heals, saves, rescues his/her own 2) **nikíyA** vt1-caus s/he saves, rescues, causes sb to live

reservation *n* 1) **Nakón-makoce** n Nakoda reservation 2) **oyą́ge** n reservation

resin *n* 1) **cąšį́** n resin, gum; chewing gum; rubber 2) **cąwába cąšį́** cp pine resin

respect *v n* 1) **ahópA** vt1 s/he respects, honors, reveres sb ‣ **wa'áhopA** vi1-abs s/he shows respect for people, things ‣ **ahógipA** vt1-pos s/he has a deep, religious respect for sb,

smth ‣ **ahópe'įc'iyA** vi3-refl s/he has self-respect, honors himself/herself ‣ **wó'ahope** n respect, observance for customs, social rules ‣ **wa'áhopabi** n respect 2) **ohóna** vt1 s/he respects, honors sb ‣ **ohógicinabi** vi1-recip they respect one another 3) **ahótạ'į** vt1 s/he respects, praises sb 4) **bagą́** vt1 s/he respects sb ‣ **wóbagą** vs-abs s/he/it is respected

respectable *adj* **ótạna** adv straight, in a straight manner, in a respectable way

rest *n* **asnígiya** vi1-pos s/he rests, takes a break from his/her activity

restaurant *n* **owóde tíbi** ; **owóde** cp restaurant

retarded *adj* **awį́ktogejA** ; **awį́tkogejA** vs s/he is slightly retarded

retirement home *cp* **gábina tíbi** cp retirement home

return *v n See:* **arrive**

rhubarb *n* 1) **cahnóǧa** n wild rhubarb, rhubarb 2) **cahnóħhu** n rhubarb stem

rib *n* 1) **cucúšte** n ribs 2) **niǧúde** n flank, part below the ribs

ribbon *n* **abáħnadA** vt1, n s/he stitches, pins smth on it; ribbon; silk, silk cloth ‣ **abáħnan** cont silk, ribbon, smth pinned or stitched

rice *n* **psį́** n wild rice, rice

rich *adj See:* **wealthy**

ride *n* 1) **agą́nyįgA, agą́nyągA** vt3 s/he rides a horse (short form for šúgatạga agą́n-yįgA 's/he sits on a horse') ‣ **agą́nyįgakiyA, agą́nyągakiyA** vt1-caus s/he makes him/her ride on a horse 2) **šųk'áktakkiyA** vt1-caus s/he rides a horse, makes a horse run

ridge *n* **įštáħe** n ridge of the eyebrow

ridicule *v* **kíǧe** interj word used to ridicule sb

right *ad adj n v exclamation* **hį́n** part isn't it so?; right?

right away *adv* 1) **nạgáhąħ** ; **nạgáħ** adv just now, right away, immediately 2) **nạgénuna** adv right away, immediately; temporarily 3) **éstestena** adv-redup very early, soon, quickly

rim *n* i̧céte n rim

ring₁ *n* napsų́ i̧ňnáye cp ring

ring₂ *v n* 1) šná vs it rings, jingles ▸ **mošná** vt1 s/he makes smth ring by shooting ▸ **yušná** vt2 s/he rattles, rings a bell by pulling, by the force of the wind 2) **yuňná** vt2 s/he makes smth rattle, ring by pulling; shakes a rattle 3) **gasná** vt1 s/he makes smth ring, jingle by striking

rinse *v n* gažáža vt1 s/he rinses sb, smth

river *n* wakpá n river ▸ **wakpádahą** adv from the river

road *n* 1) ocágu n road, street 2) **ocáguňe** n gravel road 3) **ocágusaba** n paved road; drunkenness 4) **makóškiška** n, vs rough, bumpy road; it is a rough, bumpy road

road builder *cp* ocágugağa n road builder

robe *n* 1) šiná n blanket, robe 2a) **tatągašina** n buffalo robe 2b) **ptešína** n buffalo robe 3) **teňpíšina** n deerskin robe 4) **wahį́tųšina** n robe with hair

Rock mountain people *nprop* Ȟébina nprop Rock mountain people (band of Stoney living in Morley, Alberta)

Rocky Mountains *ngeo* Íyąȟe tága ngeo Rocky Mountains

rodent *n* bis- cont, vcont rodent (such as gopher, prairie dog, mouse, rat); squealing

rodeo *n* šųkpámnikiyabi n rodeo

roll *v n* 1) babéhą vt1 s/he rolls smth up by pushing ▸ **gíjibabehą** vt1-benef s/he rolls smth up for him/her ▸ **kpabéhą** vt1-pos s/he rolls up his/her own thing 2) **yubéhą** vt2 s/he twists, rolls smth (rope, tobacco) 3) **bakmíkma** vt1 s/he rolls smth by pushing forward ▸ **abákmįkma** vt1 s/he rolls smth by pushing on it 4) **bamíma** vt1 s/he rolls smth forward (dough, snow) 5) **bapšų́ka** vt1 s/he rolls smth into a ball by pushing 6) **ptąptą́yA** vii-redup s/he/it rolls over and over 7) **i̧knúptąyA** vii-refl s/he rolls, turns himself/herself over 8) **gakšá** vt1 s/he coils, rolls smth up

roof *n* 1) ti'ágam n roof 2) **ti'ágaȟpa** n roof

rookery *n* wahóȟpiya n rookery

room *n* 1) ti'ų́ma n room 2) **ticáktu** n separate part of a building; private room 3) **ticógam** adv in the center of a camp circle, room ▸ **ti'ócogamkiya** adv toward the center of a camp circle, room 4) **yuká** vi2 s/he makes room ▸ **giyúką** vt1-dat s/he makes room for sb

rooster *n* abáhotųnamnoga n rooster

root *n* 1) húda n root 2) **hutką** n root 3) **psá** n cattail root

rope *n v* 1) ȟaȟúda n thread, rope 2) **toȟmísu** n rope, leather rope 3) **wasóbi** n rope from raw hide 4) **pakóyakyA** vt1 s/he ropes an animal by the head (steer, horse)

rosehip *n* ozį́kta ; ozį́tka n rosehip

rotten *adj adv* 1) ȟųwį́ vs it has a rotten smell 2) **kuká** vs it is worn out, tattered; it is rotten 3) **cąbúbu** vs, n it is rotten wood; rotten wood

rouge *n* tapúšage n rouge for the cheeks

rough *adj* okšíkša ; oškíša vs it is rough, bumpy ▸ **makóškiška** n, vs rough, bumpy road; it is a rough, bumpy road

round *adj* 1) mįmÁ vs it is round ▸ **mįméya** adv roundly, circularly, in circles 2) **pšųká** vs s/he is round, spherical ▸ **pšųkáya** adv hunched, crouched down, lying in a spherical shape ▸ **pšųkáyenaȟ** adv hunched, crouched down, lying in a spherical shape ▸ **pšųkáka** vs-redup it is round, spherical

round dance *np* 1) gahómni wacíbi np round dance, courting dance 2) **mįméya wacíbi** np round dance

Royal Canadian Mounted Police *np* 1) ókneša n Royal Canadian Mounted Police, mounties 2) **cuwíknąga šašábi** cp-pl Royal Canadian Mounted Police, mounties

rub *v* 1) i̧'ú vt1-dit s/he paints, rubs, applies smth on it ▸ **igíji'ų** vt1-benef s/he paints, rubs, applies smth on him/her for sb ▸ **i̧gí'ų** vt1-pos s/he paints, rubs, applies smth on his/her own

‣ **įc'į'ų** vi3-refl s/he paints, rubs, applies smth on himself/herself 2) **gahtáyĄ** vt1 s/he rubs smth against it 3) **snayÁ** vt1-caus s/he rubs sb, smth with grease, oil, lotion ‣ **snagíyA** vt1-pos s/he rubs, oints his/her own with grease, oil, lotion ‣ **sna'įc'iyA** vi3-refl s/he rubs himself/herself with grease, oil, lotion 4) **asnáyA** vt1-caus s/he rubs sb, smth with grease 5) **bawįda** vt1 s/he rubs smth ‣ **gíjibawįda** vt1-benef s/he rubs smth for him/her (like a body part) 6) **bamną** vt1 s/he files, rubs smth against it (like a piece of metal)

rubber n **cąšį** n resin, gum; chewing gum; rubber See: **gum**

ruin v n 1) **basíjA** vt1 s/he ruins smth by sitting on it ‣ **gíjibasijA** vt1-benef s/he ruins sb's thing by sitting on it 2) **gasíjA** vt1 s/he ruins, breaks smth by hitting 3) **yasíjA** vt2 s/he bad-mouths sb, ruins smth by speech 4) **yusíjA** vt2 s/he destroys, ruins smth manually

rule v n **wóšuye** n rule

ruler n 1) **į'íyute** n ruler 2) **ijázo** n, vt1 line; yardstick, ruler; s/he draws a line on, in smth

ruminant n **ta-** n ruminant (generic meaning; moose, deer, elk, buffalo, antelope; occurs in compounds)

rummage v **wagáhi** vi1-abs s/he rummages around, ransacks ‣ **wagíjahi** vt1-pos s/he rummages through his/her own

rump n 1) **nįdé** n lower part of the back, above the rump; hip 2) **šųk'ųze** n dog rump 3) **ųzéšį** n rump fat

run v n 1) **aktágA** vi1 s/he/it runs ‣ **aktákkiyA** vt1-caus s/he makes sb, smth run ‣ **akták** vcont running ‣ **aktáktak** vcont-redup running along ‣ **agíktagA** vt1-dat ; vt1-pos s/he runs to sb, smth; s/he runs to his/her own ‣ **kapéyaktagA** vi1 s/he runs faster ‣ **šųk'áktakkiyA** vt1-caus s/he rides a horse, makes a horse run 2) **ga'áktagA** vt1 s/he hits sb, smth while running ‣ **ga'áktak** vcont hitting sb, smth while running 3) **íyągA** vi3 s/he runs, speeds up, races ‣ **íyąk** vcont running ‣ **íyąkyąk** vcont-redup running around 4) **napÁ** vi1 s/he flees, runs away, retreats ‣ **nagípA** vt1-pos s/he flees for his/her own safety, runs away toward home 5) **nawąkkiyA** vt1-caus s/he/it makes it trot, run off 6) **ti'ánagidą** vt1-pos s/he flees, runs to his/her home

runner n 1) **atkáges'a, aktáges'a** n runner 2) **íyąges'a** n runner

runt n **dušké** vs, n s/he/it is a runt; runt

rush v n See: **hurry**

Russian nprop See: **German**

S

sacrifice v n **wašíkna** vi1-abs, n s/he mourns; is bereaved by the death of a relative; sacrifice ‣ **wašíkna įc'íya** vi3-refl s/he sacrifices himself/herself

sad adj 1) **cądésijA ; cądéšijA** vs s/he/it is sad, broken hearted ‣ **cądéšinya** vt1 s/he makes sb sad, breaks sb's heart 2) **otéhigA** vs, n it is difficult, hard, problematic, sad; problem, trouble 3) **įcómni** vs s/he is lonely, sad 4) **sijáyekna** vs s/he feels sad, badly 5) **iyógipisijA** vs s/he is sick, bad, sad, grieving ‣ **iyógipisinyA** vt1-caus s/he saddens sb; makes sb feel bad, sorry 6) **ohpáyA** vs s/he is sad, lonely

saddle n v 1) **ak'į** n saddle ‣ **ak'įsų** n pad saddle 2) **ak'įtųga** vt1 s/he saddles a horse, harnesses a dog ‣ **ak'įgijitų** vt1-benef s/he saddles a horse for him/her ‣ **šųk'ák'įgitų** vi1 s/he saddles a horse 3) **wak'įtáwa** vi3 it (horse) is saddled

saddle blanket n **ak'įmaheda** n saddle blanket

saddle horn n **ak'įpasu** n saddle horn

saddlebag n **ak'įha** n saddlebag

sagebrush n **pežíhoda** n sagebrush

sake n **awáciyą** adv for the sake of it, in a contemplative manner; heading for a place

salad n **wahpé ijáhibi** cp salad

salamander *n See:* **lizard**

sale *n* **wíyopeyabi** n sale ‣ **wagáhi wíyopeyabi** cp garage sale

saliva *n* **tažó** n saliva, spit

saloon *n See:* **bar**

salt *n v* 1) **štušténa** n, vs salt; it is salty ‣ **štušténagijiyA** vt1-benef s/he salts sb's food ‣ **štušténagiyA** vt1-pos s/he salts his/her own food 2) **štuštéyA** vt1-caus s/he salts smth

salty *adj* 1) **štušténa** n, vs salt; it is salty 2) **štuštá** vs it is salty

same *adj pro adv* 1) **akí'ecen** adv-cont equally, the same, alike 2) **akí-** pref same, alike, both, joined ‣ **akíye** adv same, identical

sand *n* 1) **wiyáska** n sand 2) **mąkázi** n sand

sandhill crane *cp* **pehą́ǧina** n sandhill crane

Sandhill crane dance *np* **Pehą́ǧina wací** cp sandhill crane dance

sandpiper *n* **juwína** n sandpiper

sandwich *n* **tanó yažímkiya** cp sandwich

sandy *adj* **ȟoškíškina** n sandy, hilly terrain

Santa Claus *nprop* **Wazíya** nprop Santa Claus

sap *n* **cąhą́bi** n tree sap

Saskatoon berry *cp* **wíbazuką** n Saskatoon berry

Saskatoon (Saskatchewan) *ngeo* **Wíbazuką wakpá** cp Saskatoon

Sasquatch *n See:* **Bigfoot**

sate *v* **ipí'įc'íyA** vi3-refl s/he sates, fills himself/ herself up

satisfy *v* 1) **cądéwašteyA** vt1-caus s/he satisfies sb 2) **iyógipiyA** vt1-caus s/he/it makes sb happy, satisfied

Saturday *n* 1) **ą́ba yužą́ža** ; **ą́ba tiyúžaža** ; **otíyužaže** ; **otíyužaža ą́ba** cp Saturday 2) **wowícak'u ą́ba** cp Saturday

Saulteaux *nprop* **I'ášijana** ; **I'ášija** ; **I'ásija** ; **Iyášija** ; **Iyásija** nprop person of Dakota, Chippewa, Saulteaux, French, German, Ukrainian, or Russian descent

sausage *n* **tanó obáząbi** cp sausage

save *v n See:* **store; rescue**

saw *n* 1) **įcáyukse** n saw 2) **cą'ímaksa** n wood saw

sawdust *n* **cą'ókpa** n sawdust

sawmill *n* 1) **ocánakseyabi** n sawmill 2) **ocá'įyukse** n sawmill

say *v* 1) **eyÁ** vt-irr s/he says smth ‣ **ejíyakiyA** vt1-caus s/he makes sb say it ‣ **eyéši** vt1-dit s/he orders sb to say it ‣ **neyÁ** vt-irr s/he says this (precedes or follows a quote) ‣ **žeyÁ** vt-irr s/he says that (precedes or follows a quote) ‣ **gáyA** ; **gáyabi** vii s/he says, said; they say, it is said; third-hand source when used after eyá 's/he says' 2) **dágeyešį̌ȟ** adv saying nothing 3) **hųštÁ** part people say, they say, it is said (marker of reported speech) 4) **yawášte** vt2 s/he makes smth sound nice; says nice things about sb, smth

scab *n* **ȟą́** n scab

scaffold *n* 1) **piyábi** n scaffold 2) **wócakne** n scaffold (archaic)

scalp *v n* 1) **pahá éyagu** ; **wįcápaha éyagu** vt2 s/he scalps sb, an enemy 2) **wįcápaha** n human scalp

Scalp dance *np* **Wakté wacíbi** cp scalp, victory dance

scaly *adj* **ȟpuȟpú** vs s/he/it is chapped, scaly, rough

scar *n* **o'óye** n scar

scare *v* 1) **tąsákt'A** vs s/he is frightened, scared ‣ **tąsákt'ekiyA** vt1-caus s/he frightens, scares sb ‣ **tąsákt'eyA** vt1-caus s/he frightens, scares sb to death 2) **yuš'íyeya** vt2-caus; vs s/he/it frightens, startles sb; s/he is frightened, scared, afraid 3) **ȟamyÁ** vt1-caus s/he scares, chases smth (animal) away

scatter *v* 1) **bamnéja** vt1 s/he scatters smth by sitting, or putting pressure 2) **gamnéja** vt1 s/he/ it destroys, shatters smth by hitting; the wind scatters, spreads smth out 3) **namnéja** vt1 s/he scatters smth with the foot 4) **yumnéja** vt2 s/he scatters smth manually ‣ **yumnén** vcont scattering smth manually ‣ **yumnémneja** vt2-redup s/he scatters smth manually (something small as beads) 5) **bóhiya** vs it is scattered 6) **iyámnigiya** adv in all directions, scattered

school *n v* 1) **owáyawa ; wayáwa tíbi** cp, n school (building) ‣ **owáyawatąga** n high school 2) **wayáwabi** n schooling, studying, school (as a learning process) 3) **wayáwa** vi2-abs s/he reads things, has the ability to read; s/he studies, goes to school, is a student

schoolbus *cp* **owáyawa otókšu** cp schoolbus

scissors *n-pl* **ijášna** n scissors

scold *v n* **iyópeya** vt1 s/he scolds, reproves sb ‣ **wawíyopegiya** vi1-abs s/he scolds people ‣ **iyópegiciyabi** vi1-recip they quarrel, scold, attack one another

scorch *v* 1) **ǧuyá** vt1 s/he scorches, burns smth 2) **aǧúmna** vs it smells scorched, burnt 3) **yutíba** vt2 s/he scorches, burns smth

scout *v n* 1) **dųwé hí** vi1 s/he arrives scouting 2) **dųwé'i** vi1 s/he went scouting 3) **dųwé'u** vi1 s/he comes scouting 4) **dųwéyA** vi2 s/he goes scouting

scrap *n v* **wóyapte** n table scraps

scrape *v* 1) **naȟ'ú** vt1 s/he scrapes smth with the foot 2) yuȟ'ú, vt1 s/he scrapes, peels smth manually 3) **gaȟ'ú** vt1 s/he scrapes, peels, shaves, chips smth 4) **nakį́dA** vt1 s/he scrapes smth clean with the foot ‣ **nagíkįdA** vt1-pos s/he scrapes, cleans, wipes his/her own feet 5) **wahį́baȟpa** vi1 s/he scrapes the hair off a hide 6) **baȟpú** vt1 s/he scrapes smth off by pushing

scraper *n* 1) **į'íbaȟpa** n scraper 2) **wahį́tka** n scraper ‣ **wahį́tkatkana** n-redup hide scrapers

scratch *v n* 1) **yuk'éǧA** vt2 s/he/it scratches sb, smth manually ‣ **knuk'éǧA** vt1-pos s/he scratches his/her own ‣ **knuk'ék'eǧA** vt1-pos-redup s/he scratches his/her own repeatedly ‣ **įknúk'eǧA** vi3-refl s/he scratches himself/herself ‣ **įknúk'eȟ** vcont scratching oneself ‣

įknúk'ek'eǧA vi3-refl-redup s/he scratches himself/herself continuously 2) **bak'éǧA** vt1 s/he scratches smth by pushing, rubbing against smth else ‣ **įkpák'eǧA** vi3-refl s/he scratches himself/herself by pushing, rubbing against smth 3) **igáǧo** vt1 s/he scratches, makes a notch on smth, marks a line on smth

scream *v n* 1) **bahówayA** vt1 s/he makes sb scream in pain by bumping, pushing, sitting on him/her/it; squeals as when bumping onto smth 2) **gahówayA** vt1 s/he makes sb scream, cry by hitting on him/her/it 3) **yuhówayA** vt2 s/he makes sb scream in pain by pinching, pressing on a body part

scrutinize *v See:* **examine**

scythe *n* **mínaškoba** n short scythe

sea *n* **mniwája** n sea, ocean

seamstress *n* **wagáǧeǧe wíyena** cp seamstress

seat *n* **amógiyą én yįgábi** ph car seat *See:* **chair**

second *adj adv n* **ijínųba ; įnúba** num ; n second; double-barreled shotgun

secret *n* 1) **onáȟmą** n secret 2) **anáȟmA** vt1 s/he keeps a secret

secretly *adv* 1) **naȟmána ; naȟmÁ** adv secretly, inwardly 2) **naȟmáyena** adv secretly, furtively, quietly 1) **anągiȟmą** adv secretly 2) **anáȟmaya** adv secretly

see *v* **wąyágA** vt2, vi2 s/he/it sees sb, smth; s/he/it sees; s/he has sight ‣ **wąyák** vcont seeing ‣ **wągíknagA** vt1-pos s/he sees his/her own (relative) ‣ **wągíciknagabi** vi1-recip they see one another ‣ **wą'íc'iknagA** vi3-refl s/he sees himself/herself

seed *n* **sú** n seed, pellet; bullet ‣ **kąsú** n plum seed

seem *v* 1) **epcá** vi1 I think, it seems, apparently (used only with 1st person singular) 2) **otí'įgA ; otį́gA ; otą́'įgA** part it seems, I think, apparently (this particle can occur with the negative enclitic -šį) 3) **stéyA** part it seems like; like

sell *v* **wíyopeya** vt1 s/he sells smth ‣ **wíyopegiya** vt1-pos s/he sells his/her own thing

send *v* 1) **yeyÁ** vt1-caus, vi-aux s/he sends sb, smth away; propel ‣ **yegíjiciyA** vt1-benef s/he sends sb, smth away for sb ‣ **yekíyA** vt1-dat s/he sends sb, smth away to sb; s/he starts, turns smth on (car, engine) ‣ **yegíciyabi** vi1-recip they send smth to one another ‣ **ye'íc'iyA** vi3-refl s/he propels himself/herself 2) **iyéyA** vt1 s/he sends smth, sb there from here (away from speaker) 3) **hóyekiyA** vt1-dat s/he sends a message to sb 4) **hiyúkiyA** vt1-dat s/he tosses, sends sb, smth here to him/her; sends sb here 5) **iyógiši** vt1 s/he sends sb away; orders sb to stop doing smth

senior *n* **wįcáȟtįyąna** ; **wįcáȟtįyą** n ; vs elderly man, senior; he is an elderly man, senior)

September *n* 1) **waȟpézizi hąwí** cp September 2) **waȟpé ǧí wí** np September

servant *n* 1) **ógiyes'a** n servant, assistant 2) **wówaši** n job, work, occupation; workplace; servant, worker

serve *v* **kpamní** vt1 s/he serves sb; passes smth around (as food in a ceremony) ‣ **wakpámni** vi1-abs s/he serves

servery *n* **owákpamni ti'úma** cp servery

set *v n See:* **put**

settle *v* **hiyódągA** vi1/2 s/he arrives here and sits down; s/he arrives here and settles down

seven *adj n* 1) **iyúšna** (CTK) num, vs seven; s/he/it is seven; there are seven 2) **šagówį** (PR, OM, WB) num, vs seven; s/he/it is seven; there are seven

Seven council fires *cp* **Šągówį océti** nprop Seven council fires

seventeen *num* 1) **agé'iyušna** (CTK) num seventeen 2) **agéšagowį** (PR, OM) num seventeen

seventh *adj n* **įjíšagowį** num seventh

seventy *n* 1) **wikcémna iyúšna** (CTK) num seventy 2) **wikcémna šagówį** (PR, OM) num seventy

several *adj* 1) **dóna** pro, quant, vs how many, what number; how much; several; s/he/it is so many 2) **dónacą** adv several days; how many days

sew *v* 1) **basísA** vt1 s/he sews, stitches smth ‣ **gíjibasisA** vt1-benef s/he sews smth for sb ‣ **wabásisA** vi1-abs s/he sews, mends things ‣ **hábasisA** vi1 s/he sews skins together 2) **abásisA ; obásisA** vt1 s/he sews smth on it 3) **gaǧéǧe** vt1-redup s/he sews smth ‣ **wagáǧeǧe** vi1-abs s/he sews things 4) **agáǧeǧe** vdit1 s/he sews, stitches smth onto it (ribbon, patch)

sewing machine *cp* 1) **ús įbásisa** ph sewing machine 2) **įwábasisa** n sewing machine

sex *v n* **hú** vt1 he has sex with her

sexual disease *cp* **ceȟníbi** n syphilis, sexual disease

sexually *adv* this adverb has no direct equivalence, but is part of the verb meaning 1) **yu'íškada** vt2 s/he teases, plays jokes on sb; s/he plays with sb sexually 2) **iškádabi** n woman that is teased sexually

shade *n v* 1) **a'óhązi** vimp it is cloudy, overcast; shade 2) **cą'ówahązi** n shade in front of a house, tent

shaggy *adj* 1) **hįȟcá** vs s/he/it is shaggy 2) **šųkhíȟca** n shaggy dog

shake *v n* 1) **bahúhųza** vt1 s/he shakes, rocks, moves smth by pushing on it 2) **gahúhųza** vt1 it shakes by itself, or by the force of the wind 3) **yuhúhųza** vt2 s/he jerks, shakes smth manually 4) **škąšką** vs-redup s/he/it moves, shakes; it shakes, moves by inner force ‣ **škąškáyą** adv with a moving motion 5) **yuškášką** vt2 s/he shakes smth manually back and forth 6) **sinápsą yįgÁ** vi3 s/he/it is sitting shaking his foot ‣ **sinápsąpsą** vi1-redup s/he/it shakes his/her foot 7) **nąbéyuzA** vi2 s/he shakes hands with sb ‣ **nąbéyus** vcont shaking hands 8) **yucącą** vt2 s/he/it shakes smth back and forth 9) **bacącą** vt1 s/he shakes sb, smth by pushing with the arms

shame *v n* **įšténya** vt1-caus s/he embarrasses, shames sb

shameful *adj* 1) **wo'įštéjaga** vs s/he/it is shameful 2) **wó'įštenyagen** adv shamefully

shamelessly *adv* **įštéješį** adv shamelessly

shape *v n* **yuská** vt2 s/he kneads smth (dough, powder) into shape

share *v n* **ok'ú** vt1 s/he lends smth to sb; s/he shares smth with sb

sharp *adj* **péna** vs it is sharp ‣ **pepéna** vs-redup it is prickly, sharp

sharpen *v* 1) **yumá** vt2 s/he sharpens smth (knife, axe) ‣ **knumá** vt1-pos s/he sharpens, files his/her thing 2) **gapéna** vt1 s/he sharpens smth 3) **gapésto** vt1 s/he shaves, sharpens a point with a tool

sharpener *n* **iyúmą** n sharpener, file

shatter *v* 1) **gaktú** vt1 s/he shatters smth with a projectile (like a window) 2) **gamnéja** vt1 s/he/it destroys, shatters smth by hitting; the wind scatters, spreads smth out

shavings *n* **cagážiba** vi1, n s/he planes wood (as to make wood shavings for kindling); wood shavings

shawl *n* **šinágaȟci** n fringed shawl ‣ **šinágaȟciȟcibi** n-redup fringed shawl

she *pro* 1a) **-Ø-** prefix-infix he, she, it (3rd person singuler, unmarked form of an active verb) 1b) **-Ø-** prefix-infix he, she, it (3rd person singular, unmarked form of a stative verb) 2) **né** dem, pro this, these (near the speaker); this, he, she, it 3) **žé** dem, art, comp, pro he, she, it

sheath *n* **mínaha** n sheath

sheep *n* 1) **šųkhéwąga** n sheep 2) **šųkhéyuke ; šųkhéyuką** n sheep

Sheho (Saskatchewan) *ngeo* **Šiyó** ngeo Sheho (Saskatchewan)

shell *n* 1) **tugí** n shell, seashell, pearl 2) **tugískana** n white shell

shelter *n v* 1) **wókeya** n manmade shelter 2)

a'ókeyabi n shelter 3) **ti'ónapA** vi1 s/he takes refuge, shelter inside

shield *n* **wahácąga** n shield

shin *n* 1) **cąkpé ; cąkpéhu** n, shin, shinbone 2) **sicą́** n shin 3) **humnó** n shinbone

shine *v* 1) **smiyáyą** vs it shines 2) **bawíyakpa** vt1 s/he shines, polishes smth 3) **wiyákpakpa** vs-redup it is shiny; it shines brightly

shiny *adj* 1) **wiyákpa** vs it is shiny ‣ **wiyákpaya** adv shining, sparkling, reflective ‣ **wiyákpakpa** vs-redup it is shiny; it shines brightly 2) **kokní** vimp it is shiny, glassy, bright, translucent ‣ **kokníyą** adv shinily, brightly

ship *n See:* **boat**

shirt *n* **cuwíknaga** n coat, shirt

shiver *v n* 1a) **cącą́** vs s/he/it shivers 1b) **cącána** n shiver 2) **ȟníyąyą** vs-redup s/he shivers (from cold or a fever)

shoe *n* 1a) **hába** n moccasins, shoes ‣ **hąm- ; hąp-** cont shoe, pertaining to shoes 1b) **cą́hąba** n shoes

shoeless *adj* **hąmcóna** adv without moccasins, shoeless

shoestore *cp* **cą́hąba owópetų tíbi** np shoestore

shoot *v* 1) **kudé** vt1 s/he shoots at sb, smth 2) **ó** vt1 s/he shoots and wounds sb, smth; kills sb, smth 3) **utá ; a'úta** vt1, vt1 s/he fires, shoots, discharges a weapon, s/he shoots at sb, smth ‣ **a'úgijitA** vt1-benef s/he shoots at sb, smth for him/her 4) **mosódA** vt1 s/he shoots smth, sb down; s/he uses all of the bullets on sb, smth ‣ **wamósodA** vi1-abs s/he shoots down, kills all the game ‣ **mosónyA** vt1-caus s/he has smth, sb killed by shooting ‣ **mosón** vcont shooting smth, sb down 5) **moȟpÁ** vt1 s/he knocks sb, smth down by shooting 6) **mo-** pref by an impact from a distance (by shooting, hitting with a projectile, poking with a stick)

shooting *n* **wakúdebi** n shooting, hunting

shop *n v* **wópetų** vi1-abs s/he buys things; shops *See:* **store**

shore *n* 1) **mnihúde** n shore 2) **mnigákna** adv beside the water, at the shore 3) **buzáda** adv on the shore, away from the water ‣ **buzádakiya** adv toward the shore

short *adj* **ptéjena** vs s/he/it is short

short-eared owl *cp* **hįhą́wapapana** n short-eared owl

shorten *v* **iyúksA** vt1 s/he shortens smth, to make designs on smth; measures and cuts smth

shorter *adj* **yuptéjena** vt2 s/he cuts smth shorter (with scissors)

Shoshone *nprop* **Snohéna wįcášta** nprop Shoshone people, person of Shoshone descent

shotgun *n* **iyókšu** n cartridge; shotgun

should *v* 1a) **céyagA** part should, must, ought to, might as well (marker of deontic modality) 1b) **céyagešį** part should not, must not, cannot possibly (negative deontic modality)

shoulder *n* 1) **hiyéde** n top of the shoulder 2) **aňcó** n shoulder (below the shoulder joint)

shoulder blade *cp* **amnó** n shoulder blade

shout *v n* **bą́** vi1 s/he shouts, yells ‣ **bąyą́** adv loudly, while shouting ‣ **gíjibą** vt1-benef s/he shouts for, on behalf of him/her ‣ **gibą́** vt1-dat s/he yells, shouts at sb; calls sb's attention

shove *v* **bacáknekne yeyÁ** vt1 s/he to make sb stagger by pushing, shoving

shovel *n* 1) **iwábadįja** n shovel 2) **mas'íbadįda** ; **maswíbadįde** n metal shovel 3) **maká ogápte** cp shovel

show *v n* 1) **bazó** vt1 s/he shows, points at smth ‣ **gibázo** vt1-dat s/he shows, points, reveals smth to him/her ‣ **kpazó** vt1-pos s/he shows his/her own ‣ **įkpázo** vi3-refl s/he shows, reveals himself/herself 2) **šnayá** vi it shows; is visible, uncovered, bare

shower *v n* See: **bathe**

shrew *n* **wíyašpuna** n shrew

shrink *v* 1) **yuškí** vi it shrinks ‣ **yuškíya** vt1-caus s/he causes smth to shrink 2) **nąjúsina** vi it sits in the sun and shrinks

shrub *n* **cąňéňe** n shrub

shut *v* 1) **natága** vt1 s/he closes, locks, shuts smth; it (wind) closes it; turns it off ‣ **nagítaga** vt1-pos s/he closes, shuts his/her own 2) **dágeyešį** interj Shh! Shut up!

shy *adj* 1) **įtų́pa** vt1 s/he avoids sb out of embarrassment; s/he is shy 2) **įštéjA** vs s/he is bashful, shy, easily embarrassed, ashamed

six *adj n* **šákpe** num, vs six; s/he/it is six; there are six ‣ **šakpéň** adv six times ‣ **šákpena** quant only six

sick *adj* 1) **yazą́** vs s/he is sick; s/he is hurt; feels pain in a body part (always preceded by a body part) 2) **iyógipisija** vs s/he is sick, sad, grieving 3) **kúža** vs s/he is weak, sick ‣ **kušyá** adv sickly

sickly *adj* **kušyá ų́** vi1 s/he is sickly

side *n v adj* 1) **omáktam** adv other side 2) **omą́gakiyadahą** adv from the other side 3) **sąní** adv single, one side ‣ **sąnína** adv on one side only 4) **anų́k** adv both sides, ways ‣ **anų́kadahą** adv on each side, end, both ways 5) **catkám** adv left side, on the left side ‣ **caktápadahą** adv from the left side 6) **nąkéya** adv on one's side 7) **nedápa** adv on this side ‣ **nedápadahą** adv moving from here, behind, from this side; from the beginning, start

sideways *adv* 1) **knągíyą** adv sideways 2) **cuwíknagįyą** adv sideways

sight *n* **a'íšį'įyayA** vi2 s/he/it goes out of sight

sign *n v* 1) **ogíkmA** vt1-pos; vt1-dat s/he writes, signs his/her own (book, name); s/he writes smth to, for sb 2) **įkpážiba** vi3 s/he makes the sign of the cross

sign language *cp* **wíyuta** vi2-abs s/he talks in sign language, makes signs ‣ **wígiyuta** vt1-dat s/he talks in sign language to sb, makes signs to sb

silence *n v* **a'ínina** ; **ánina** ; **inína** adv quietly, in silence

silk *n* **abáňnadA** vt1, n s/he stitches, pins smth

on it; ribbon; silk, silk cloth ‣ **abáȟnan** cont silk, ribbon, smth pinned or stitched

silver *n* **mázaskana** n silver

simply *adv* **ejé'ena ; ejéna** adv only, simply, alone, just

sin *n v* 1) **wówaȟtani** n sin 2) **waȟtáni** vi1-abs s/he sins

since *adv* 1) **ehą́dahą** adv since 2) **žehą́dahą** adv from then on, and so now, since then 3) **žehą́geja** adv about that long (measurement); since then

sinew *n* **taką́** n sinew; deer, moose gristle

sing *v* 1) **nową́** vi1 s/he/it sings ‣ **gíjinową** vt1-benef s/he sings for sb; sings in his/her honor ‣ **ginówą** vi1-refl s/he sings to himself/herself 2) **anówą** vt1 s/he sings over sb (as a cure) 3) **inówą** vt1 s/he sings about smth 4) **winówą** vi1 he sings a love song 5) **ahíyayA** vi1, vi1/2 s/he sings a song 6) **ȟ'oká** vi1; n s/he sings with a drum group; beats the drum in a powwow or dance; singer 7) **aknáda** vt1 s/he accompanies sb singing (as in a chair)

singe *v* 1) **hiknú** vt1 s/he singes off an animal 2) **ǧuǧúya** vt1-redup s/he chars, singes smth

singer *n* 1) **nową́s'a** n singer 2a) **ȟ'oká yįgábi** cp drum singer, member of a drum group 2b) **ȟ'oká** vi1; n s/he sings with a drum group; beats the drum in a powwow or dance; singer

singing *v n* 1) **anówąbi ; wótijaǧa anówąbi** n, np quarterly singing, Sun dance singing

single *adj quant* 1) **wąžíȟ** num, det one in particular, a certain one (marker of focus); any, a single one (used with nonspecific, hypothetical referent) 2) **wą́ja** num single (archaic); one (the meaning "one" is found only in White Bear and Fort Peck) 3) **tašną́ ú** vi1 s/he is single; he is a bachelor

sink *n* **o'íknužaža** n bathroom; washbasin, sink

sinner *n* **waȟtánis'a** n sinner

Sintaluta (Saskatchewan) *ngeo* **Kį'íbi** ngeo Sintaluta (Saskatchewan)

sip *v n* **yaǧóba** vt2 s/he sips a beverage

sister *n* 1) **-cųna-** root older sister (female speaker); older female parallel cousin (female speaker) 2) **-tąga- ; -tą-** root younger sister (female speaker); female parallel cousin (female speaker) 3) **-tągena ; -tąguna** root older sister (male speaker); older female parallel cousin (male speaker) 4) **-tąkši-** root younger sister (male speaker) ‣ **tąkšíjuyA** vt1-caus he has her as a younger sister

sister-in-law *n* 1) **-šijepą-** root sister-in-law (female speaker) 2) **-hąga-** root sister-in-law (male speaker) ‣ **hągáguyA** vt1-caus he has her as a sister-in-law

sit *v* 1) **iyódągA** vi2 s/he sits down ‣ **iyódąkkiyA** vt1-caus s/he makes sb sit down ‣ **iyódąk** vcont sitting down ‣ **éyodągA** vi1-coll they sit down 2) **ga'íyodągA** vi1 s/he/it sits down heavily ‣ **ga'íyodąk** vcont sitting down heavily 3) **kniyódągA** vi1/2 s/he arrives back here and sits down ‣ **kiyódągA** vi1/3 s/he arrives back there and sits down ‣ **hiyódągA** vi1/2 s/he arrives here and sits down; s/he arrives here and settles down 4) **yįgÁ, yągÁ** vi3 s/he is sitting on, in smth; it is, it is located (used for broad-based objects) ‣ **yįgékiyA, yągékiyA** vt1-caus s/he makes sb sit ‣ **taȟą́ge kné yįgÁ** vi3 s/he is sitting on his/her knees 5) **owóda** n, vs feast; s/he sits down to eat 6) **ba-** pref by pushing, poking, sitting on smth

sixteen *num* **agéšakpe** num sixteen

sixth *adj n* **įjíšakpe ; įšákpe** num, n sixth; pistol, handgun

sixty *n* **wikcémna šákpe** num sixty

size *n v* 1) **nísko** vs it is this size, much; it is as big as this ‣ **nískoga** vs it is about this size, much ‣ **nískogaga** vs-redup it is about this small size 2) **žįskoga** vs it is about that size 2) **žehą́geja** adv about that size (measurement, distance); since then

skate *n v* 1) įgázogic'ų ; įgázo n skates 2) gazógic'ų vi-irr s/he skates; plays hockey

Skeleton Hill (Saskatchewan) *nprop* Wįcápaȟe nprop Skeleton Hill or Skull Mountain (burial site near Sintaluta (Saskatchewan) and one of the former names for Carry The Kettle reservation)

skill *n* ųspé vs s/he learns on his/her own, acquires a skill

skilled *adj* 1) wayúpi vi2-abs s/he is skilled, good at smth ‣ škanwáyupiya vt2 s/he is skilled at playing games 2) wayápi vi2-abs s/he is skilled at speaking

skillful *adj* 1) yupíya vs, adv, adv-redup it is valuable; well, in a good skillful manner; yupípiya adv-redup very well 2) wawáyupi vi1-abs s/he is skillful 3) wayúpiyagen adv in a skillful manner 4) yapíyagen adv in a verbally skillful manner

skillfully *adv* yupí vt2 s/he does smth skillfully

skin *n v* 1) há n skin, hide, bag, pouch, any type of container ‣ ha'ágam adv on the skin 2) há okmábi cp birthmark, tattoo 3) hásuda vs s/he/it has a hard skin 3) yuǧábA vt2 s/he pulls the skin or the bark off smth; skins an animal ‣ gíjiyuǧabA vt1-benef s/he pulls the skin or bark off smth for him/her; skins an animal

skinny *adj* hústaga vs s/he/it is skinny

skull *n* 1) wįcápa n human skull 2) pašéja n dried-up skull 3) ptepá n buffalo skull

skunk *n* mągá n skunk ‣ mąk cont skunk

sky *n* maȟpíya n sky, heaven; cloud ‣ maȟpíyam adv in the sky

slash *v* naǧóǧo vt1 s/he slashes sb, smth (as with a knife) ‣ įknáǧoǧo vi3-refl s/he slashes himself/herself

sled *n* 1) cuwįsnohą n sleigh, sled 2) iyúsnohą n sleigh 3) cą'íyusnohą n wooden sleigh, sled

sledgehammer *n* mas'íyapa tága cp sledgehammer

sleep *v n* 1) įštíma vi3 s/he sleeps, is asleep ‣ a'įštima vt1 s/he sleeps over at someone's place ‣ ąbé'įštima vi3 s/he sleeps during daytime; has a catnap ‣ o'íštime síja vs it (bed, camp) is bad to sleep in ‣ o'íštime wašté vs it (bed, camp) is good to sleep in ‣ yu'íštima vt2 s/he soothes sb to sleep manually 2) iyúga ; iwúga (PR) vi3 s/he goes to bed, sleeps; sleeps on smth

sleepy *adj* 1) ȟmá vs s/he is sleepy 2) įštímat'a n sleepyhead; someone that is hard to wake up

sleet *n* cáǧa amáǧažu cp sleet

slice *v n* 1) gamná vt1, vi1 s/he slices smth (like meat for drying); s/he earns money ‣ wagámna vi1-abs s/he slices, makes slices (like meat) 2) gaktú vt1, vi1 s/he slices meat for drying; s/he earns money 3) modá vt1 s/he slices smth (bread, bannock) 4) modápta n slice 5) omáksabi n slice

slide *v* 1) osnóhA vs s/he/it slides 2) o'ósnohągic'ų n slide 3) snohądugen adv sliding

slimy *adj* šnušnúda vs-redup it is slippery, slimy

sling *n v* cudóȟpeya vi1 s/he has smth slung over the shoulder ‣ knudóȟpeya vt1-pos s/he has his/her thing (blanket) slung over the shoulder

slip *v n* 1) našnúda vi1 s/he slips while walking on it 2) i'éknašna vi1 s/he had a slip of the tongue, misspoke

slipper *n* timáhen ųbi cp slipper

slippery *adj* šnušnúda vs-redup it is slippery, slimy

slit *v n* 1) gaȟcí vt1 s/he slits smth; cuts a fringe ‣ wagáȟci vi1-abs s/he slits things; cuts fringes 2) masnéjA vt1 s/he splits, slits smth in the middle

slobbering *adv* ítutuya adv in a slobering manner

slough *n* ptéǧa n slough, lake ‣ pteptéǧana n-pl-redup little sloughs

slow *adj v* 1) húgešį vs s/he/it is slow 2) t'ejá vs s/he is slow at moving

slowly *adv* įwáštena ; owáštena adv slowly, carefully, softly ‣ įwášteȟ adv very slowly ‣

owášteȟ adv slowly, gently ‣ owáštenagen adv rather slowly

slushy adj gaspą́ vi1 it (grease, snow, ice) is slushy

sly adj įnáȟmeya vi1 s/he is sly

small adj 1) júsina vs s/he/it is small (size or age) ‣ júsinana vs-redup s/he/it is very small 2) juk'ána vs it is small, narrow 3) jiškína ; júskina vs s/he/it is small 4) yuwídana quant small amount 5) nískogaga vs-redup it is about this small size 6) -na encl small, little, cute, dear (with nouns and verbs it indicates the small size of an entity, or the endearment/sympathy of the speaker for the person or object)

smallest adj júsinaȟtįyą vs s/he/it is the smallest (of a group)

smallpox n wįcáȟniȟni n smallpox

smear v ijáȟni vt1 s/he smears smth with it

smell n v 1) ómna vt1, n s/he/it smells, sniffs sb, smth; smell 2) mná vs s/he/it smells like 3) -mna suff s/he/it smells like (used in compounds; triggers e-ablaut) ‣ a'ámna vs it is a moldy smell ‣ aǧúmna vs it smells scorched, burnt ‣ cąmná vs s/he/it smells like wood ‣ dagúmna vs it is the smell of something ‣ ecámna vi1 it has a smell, odor; it smells ‣ ǧúmna vs it has a smell of burnt (hair), scolding ‣ hámna vs s/he/it smells; has a body odor ‣ hoǧámna vs s/he/it smells like fish ‣ ȟųwímna vs s/he/it smells rank, putrid ‣ izį́mna vs it is the smell of smth burning (like incense, sweetgrass) ‣ matómna vs s/he/it smells like bear ‣ nežémna vs s/he/it smells urine ‣ ošódemna vs s/he/it smells like smoke ‣ sewímna vs it has a rancid, sour smell ‣ skúyemna vs it has a sweet smell ‣ šųgámna vs s/he/it smells like a dog ‣ ti'óšijámna vimp it is a smelly house, dwelling ‣ ųkcémna vs it smells like feces ‣ waštémna vs s/he/it smells good ‣ pédamna vs s/he/it smells like fire, smoke 4) ȟųwí vs it has a rotten smell

smile v n įȟá'įc'iyA vi3-refl s/he smiles

smoke n v 1a) šóda n smoke ‣ šon- cont smoke 1b) šonyÁ vt1-caus s/he smokes smth (such as meat) 2) ošódA n; vs smoke from a chimney; it is smoky (room, atmosphere) 3) ošódemna vs s/he/it smells like smoke 4) zinyÁ vt1-caus s/he smokes smth 5) įjú vi1 s/he smokes ‣ įgíju vt1-dat s/he smokes for sb ‣ įgíju vt1-pos s/he smokes his/her own thing; s/he smokes for sb 6) cąnúba n, vi1 pipe; s/he smokes a pipe 7) oȟónageje interj holy smokes (expression of surprise for someone who has accomplished a great deed)

smoky adj ošódA n ; vs smoke from a chimney; it is smoky (room, atmosphere)

smooch v n íyabiza vt2 s/he smooches sb; kisses by producing a loud sucking sound

smooth adj 1) smuyá vs it is smooth 2) mnaská vs it is flat, plain, smooth 3) yastó vt2 s/he/it smooths smth down by licking (as a candy) ‣ įknásto vi3-refl s/he smoothes himself/herself by licking (as fur) 4) ayústo vt2 s/he smooths, pets, pads smth with the hand (hair, fur of an animal) 5) nastó vt1 s/he straightens, smoothes smth with the foot

smother v 1) basní vt1 s/he puts a light, fire out by smothering it, putting smth on it 2) gasní vt1, vi s/he smothers, puts out a fire, light; the rain puts out a fire ‣ knasní vt1-pos s/he smothers, puts out his/her own fire, light

smudge v n azínyA vt1-caus s/he smudges sb, smth ritually ‣ wa'ázinyA vi1-abs s/he smudges things ritually ‣ azíngijiyA vt1-benef s/he smudges sb for him/her ritually ‣ azíngiciyabi vi1-recip they smudge one another ritually ‣ azín'įc'iyA vi3-refl s/he smudges himself/herself ritually

snail n tugígina n snail

snake n snohéna n snake (generic); garter snake

Snake Butte (Montana) ngeo Įǧúǧa wídana ngeo Snake Butte (Montana)

snare *v n* 1) **kmúgA** vt1 s/he snares smth ›
gíjikmụgA vt1-benef s/he snares smth for him/
her 2) **wakmúga ; ịkmúge** n snare › **maštín
wakmúga ; maštín ịkmúge** n rabbit snare

sneak *v* 1) **nasnádA** vt1 s/he sneaks, crawls up
to sb › **nasnán** vcont sneaking, crawling up
to sb 2) **anásnadA** vt1 s/he sneaks up on sb,
stalks smth (prey)

sneeze *v n* 1) **pšÁ** vi1 s/he sneezes › **pšayÁ** vt1-
caus s/he/it causes sb to sneeze › **pšakíyA** vt1-
caus s/he makes sb sneeze 2) **apšÁ** vt1 s/he
sneezes on smth

snipe *n* **sikázina** n snipe

snore *v* **ǧóbA** vi1 s/he snores

snorer *n* **ǧóbes'a** n snorer

snort *v* **poȟžó** vi1 s/he/it snorts

snot *n* **paȟní** n snot, mucus

snow *n v* 1) **wá** n, vs snow; s/he/it is snowy ›
wamáhen adv under the snow › **wa'ágan**
adv on the snow 2) **wáhịhẠ** vimp it snows ›
awáhịhẠ vs it snows on it; s/he/it is covered in
deep snow 3) **wámini** n snow water 4) **waskạ́** n
melting snow 5) **wašmá** vimp it is deep snow 6)
wašmú n melted snow 7) **wamnúmnu** vi there
are fine snow particles blowing 8) **wacógạdu**
vs it is in the middle of the snow

snowball *n* **wá yupšúkabi** cp snowball

snowfall *n* **wáhịȟpa** vimp it is a snowfall

snowmobile *n* **wa'ániya hiyáya** cp snowmobile

snowplow *n* **wa'ịbadịda** n snowplow › **ịwátokšu
wa'ịbadịda** cp snowplow truck

snowshoe *n* **wahába** n snowshoe(s)

snowy owl *cp* **hịháska** (OM) n snowy owl

so *adj conj adv* 1) **žécen** conj; adv so, thus, then;
in this way, as such 2) **cén** conj then, so, thus,
therefore, because, that is why

soak *v n* **ȟpayẠ́** vt1-caus s/he soaks smth in water

soaked *adj* **ogáȟnogA** vs s/he/it is soaked in
water; is wet › **ogáȟnok** vcont soaked in water

soap *n* 1) **ịyúžaža** n soap, laundry soap 2) **yužáže**
n soap

soar *v* **ogíyẠ** vi1 s/he/it soars, flies about ›
ogíyạgen adv flying about; flying around

sober *adj* **imnézA** vs s/he sobers up; lifts his/
her spirit up

sobriety *n* **ocáguša** n sobriety

socialize *v* **imáǧaǧa** vs s/he is amused, entertained by sb, smth; socializes

society *n* 1a) **okónagiciyabi** vi1-recip; n they are
friendly, associate with one another; society,
union, association 1b) **okónagiciye** n society

sock *n* **oyáku** n socks, stockings

soda pop *cp* **mínískuya** n soda pop

soft *adj* 1) **pạpạ́** vs it is soft (like suede) ›
teȟpípạpạ n soft hide (like deer hide) 2)
pạžéna vs it is soft › **pạšpạ́žena** vs-redup it is
soft and small (like down feathers) 3) **skúyageȟ**
adv in a sweet, soft manner 4) **šnošnóna** vs it
is soft (like butter or mud) 5) **wakána** vi1 it
(meat) is tender, soft › **wakákana** vi1-redup
they (meat) are tender, soft

soil *n See:* **earth**

solder *n v* 1) **mázašnoyabi** n solder 2) **ašnóya**
vt1-caus s/he solders smth › **wa'ášnoya** vi1-
abs s/he solders things

soldier *n* 1) **agícida** n warrior, soldier, police ›
agícida ịtáca cp policeman › **agícida wi'óti
hụgá** np chief of the warrior lodge › **maȟpíya
agícida** cp airborne soldier › **makóce agícida**
cp foot soldier › **miní agícida** cp navy soldier
2) **zuyéska** n soldier

Soldier dance *np* **Agícida wacíbi** cp soldier
dance

sole *n* 1) **sicúha** n foot, sole 2) **hábasicu** n moccasin soles

solid *adj See:* **hard**

some *adj pro adv* 1) **abá** quant some, some of
a group (used with count and mass nouns)
2) **edáhạ** quant ; vs some of that (used with
mass nouns); some of a larger group (used with
countable nouns); s/he/it is from (a place or

tribe); is a member of a group ‣ **gadáhą** quant some (unspecified amount)

someone *pro* **duwé** pro n quant vs who; person; nobody (followed by a negated verb); s/he is someone

something *pro* 1) **dagúȟ** pro something, anything (unspecified referent) 2) **dágu** pro, quant, vs thing, something; what; any, none; it is something 3) **dágukiya** vt1 s/he thinks it is something

somewhat *pro adv* 1) **-gA ; a-…-gA ; -gejA ; -jA** suff rather, somewhat, kind of (attenuator of gradable expressions) 2) **steȟ** part like, in the manner of, somewhat, -ish, as if

somewhere *adv* 1) **duktéȟ** adv somewhere 2) **duktám** adv away from a place; to somewhere 3) **togámpadahą** adv from somewhere else

son *n* 1) **-cįkši- ; -cįhį-** root son 2) **cįhį́ktuya ; cįhį́tkuya** vt1-caus s/he adopts a son 3) **hųcį́hįtku** n chief's son

song *n* 1) **onówą** n song ‣ **hųgóȟ'ą onówą** cp giveaway song ‣ **ogícuni onówą** cp closing song ‣ **ticówaknąga onówą** cp flag song ‣ **wópina onówą** cp Thanksgiving song ‣ **zuyé onówą** cp war song ‣ **zuyéska onówą** cp soldier song 2) **wį'į́nową** n love song (usually about what the couple would do if they got together) 3) **wįgų́nową** n love song 4) **hąnówąbi** n night song 5) **Nakón-nowąbi** n Nakoda song 6) **ahíyaya** vi1, vi2 s/he sings a song 7) **įcinową** n brave song

son-in-law *n* **wįcáwoȟa** n son-in-law

soon *adv* **éstena** adv early, soon, right away ‣ **éstestena** adv-redup very early, soon, quickly

soothe *v* **yu'į́štima** vt2 s/he soothes sb to sleep manually

sore *n adj* 1a) **ȟní** vs s/he has a sore 1b) **ȟní ; ȟníbi** n sore

sorry *adj excl* **ogíjiȟįyą** vt1-benef s/he regrets smth; is sorry about smth

sort *n v* **ocáže** n kind, sort, species

sound *n v adj adv* 1) **hotų́** vi1 it produces a sound (refers to cries of animals) ‣ **yuhótų** vt2 s/he makes smth sound manually; plays a musical instrument with the hands ‣ **bahótų** vt1 s/he makes a sound by pushing on smth; plays a musical instrument (trumpet, accordion) 2) **gamú** vt1, s/he beats on smth; makes a drumming sound 3) **namú** vt1 s/he/it makes a loud sound with the foot 4) **muyákne** vt1 s/he makes a drumming sound, a drumbeat ‣ **muyáknebi** n drumbeat, drumming sound 5) **kokyÁ** vt1-caus s/he/it produces a clattering, clicking sound ‣ **kókhįknA** vs s/he/it is a sudden clicking sound ‣ **gakókyA** vt1-caus s/he/it makes a sound by hitting things together ‣ **yukógA** vt2 s/he makes a rattling sound manually 6) **kpá** vs it is a loud, resonant, metallic sound 7) **bamnúǧa** vt1 s/he makes a crunching sound with the hands or a tool 8) **ȟmúyahą** vi1, n s/he/it buzzes, rumbles, emits a buzzing sound (motor, airplane, bee); rattle, band instrument 9) **gaȟná** vt1 s/he makes a rattling sound 10) **yawášte** vt2 s/he makes smth sound good; says nice things about sb, smth 11) **nakpákpa** vimp-redup there is a repetitive crackling, popping sound 12) **cúú** interj imitation of the sound of a bullet

soup *n* 1) **wahą́bi** n soup, broth 2) **wóžabi** n Saskatoon soup, berry soup; gravy, stew

sour *adj* 1) **sewí** vs it is sour ‣ **sewímna** vs it has a rancid, sour smell 2) **tutÁ** vs it is sour, bitter, astringent

south *n adv adj* 1) **wiyódahą** n, adv south; noon, midday, afternoon ‣ **wiyódahąm** adv in, to the south ‣ **wiyódahątakiya** adv southward, toward the south 2) **maštámakoce** n land to the south

southward *adv* **wiyódahątakiya** adv southward, toward the south

spank *v n* **gabé** vt1 s/he spanks sb

spare *v adj n* **niyÁ** vt1-caus s/he/it makes sb live; spares, allows sb to live

sparkling *v* **wiyákpaya** adv shining, sparkling, reflective

sparrow *n* **sįdéžada** n sparrow

speak *v* 1) **i'á ; iyá** vt1, vi1 s/he speaks, talks to sb, with sb; s/he speaks; speaks a language ‣ **i'ékiya** vt1-caus s/he makes sb speak ‣ **igíji'a** vt1-benef s/he speaks for, on behalf of sb 2) **ya-** pref action done with the mouth, teeth, or by speech 3) **knaštá** vt1-pos s/he finishes his/her own speech 4) **įkná'ušįga** vi3-refl s/he speaks pitifully of himself/herself 5) **knašná** vt1-pos s/he omits smth while speaking 6) **wayápi** vi2-abs s/he is skilled at speaking 7) **wįtkótkoga i'á** vi1 s/he speaks backward as in a Clown ceremony 8) **wót'į** vi1 s/he makes noises when speaking 9) **yapíja** vt2 s/he memorizes, mentions smth; speaks highly of smth, sb

spear *n v* **wahúkeza ; wahų́keza** n spear

species *n See:* **sort, kind**

specifically *adv See:* **exactly**

spectator *n* **wópaȟtes'a** n spectator

spend *v* 1) **yusódA** vt2 s/he wastes, spends, uses smth up (money, supplies) 2) **masyúsodA** vi2 s/he spends money ‣ **masknúsodA** vt1-pos s/he spends his/her own money 3) **waní'ų** vi1 s/he spends the winter somewhere

spherical *adj See:* **round**

spicy *adj* **kádA** vimp, vs it is hot (weather, food, objects), spicy; s/he is feverish

spider *n* **ȟeȟágana ; ȟeȟágagana** n spider

spill *v* 1) **bapsú** vt1 s/he pours, spills a liquid out; empties a container ‣ **okpápsų** vt1-pos s/he spills his/her liquid on himself/herself 2) **gapsų́** vt1 s/he hits smth accidently, and it spills ‣ **agápsų** vt1-dit s/he/it spills a liquid on smth 3) **napsú** vt1 s/he spills smth by kicking, by pushing with the foot 4) **yapsų́** vt2 s/he spills smth from his/her mouth 5) **yupsú** vt2 s/he spills smth from a container manually

spin *v n* 1) **nahómni** vt1 s/he spins smth with the feet; pedals ‣ **knahómni** vt1-pos s/he spins his/her own 2) **gahómni** vt1 s/he knocks, spins sb, smth around

spine *n* **cąkáhu** n spine, dorsal bone

spirit *n* 1) **naǧí** n spirit of a person or thing (stone, tree) ‣ **wįcánaǧi** n human spirit ‣ **naǧítaga** n Great spirit 2) **wanáǧi** n spirit, soul, ghost (of an unknown referent) ‣ **kúši wanáǧi oyáde** np grandmother nation spirit ‣ **wanáǧi nų́ba** cp homosexual ‣ **wanáǧi wacíbi** cp Northern Lights; aurora borealis; ghost dance ‣ **ȟaȟébi wanáǧi wówįcak'ubi** ph feed the night spirits ceremony 3) **wįcóni** n human life, human ways, spirit, ghost 4) **Wašíju** n minor spirit, deity; White man 5) **adé** voc Father!; my father, dad; Father, paternal spirit

spirituality *n* **waką awókcą** cp spirituality

spit *n v* 1) **tažó** n saliva, spit 2) **tažóšA** vi1 s/he spits ‣ **atážošA** vt1 s/he spits on smth ‣ **otážošA** vt1 s/he spits into smth

splint *n v* **cągáksaksąbi** n-redup splints

split *v n* 1) **gasnéjA** vt1 s/he chops smth in two, splits smth in two by hitting 2) **masnéjA** vt1 s/he splits, slits smth in the middle ‣ **magísnejA** vt1-pos s/he cuts, slits his/her own 3) **mosnéjA** vt1 s/he splits smth open by shooting or colliding into it

spoke *n* **cą'óhuhuna** n wagonspoke

spoon *n* 1) **kiškána** n spoon 2) **tahékiškana** n horn spoon

spot *v n* **gisába** n spot of bare ground where the snow has melted ‣ **gisápsabA** vimp, n there are spots of bare ground where the snow has melted; spots of bare ground where the snow has melted

spotted *adj* 1) **kneknéǧa** vs-redup s/he/it is spotted 2) **knešká** vs s/he/it is spotted 3) **sapsábA**

vs-redup it is black-spotted, black here and there

spotted eagle *cp* **wamníkneška** n spotted eagle

spouse *n* **gicí'ų** n spouse

sprain *v n* 1) **anákokkiyA** vt1-pos s/he sprains his/her own (foot, thumb) 2) **napšų́** vt1 s/he dislocates, sprains smth with the foot or by kicking ‣ **nagípšų** vi1-pos s/he dislocates, sprains his/her own (knee, foot, ankle)

spread *v n* 1) **agánA** vt1 s/he pours liquid on sb, smth; spreads, sprinkles smth on it 2) **yumnáyA** vt2 s/he spreads smth out flat (paper, rug, sheet) ‣ **yumnáyayA** vt2-redup s/he spreads them out ‣ **ayúmnayA** vt2 s/he spreads smth over it (like a blanket over a horse, cloth on a table) 3) **gamnáyA** vt1 s/he throws, spreads smth out flat (fishnet) 4) **gamnéja** vt1 s/he/it destroys, shatters smth by hitting; the wind scatters, spreads smth out 5) **yuzámni** vt2 s/he spreads smth open; opens a book 6) **yumnú** vt2 s/he spreads, crumbles smth around manually; spreads smth fine

spring *n* 1) **wédu** n, vs spring; it is spring ‣ **wéhą** adv last spring ‣ **owédu** adv in the springtime 2) **wahpétoya hą́** adv in the spring-time

sprinkle *v* 1) **agánA** vt1 s/he pours liquid on sb, smth; spreads, sprinkles smth on it 2) **abápsų** vt1 s/he pours a liquid on sb, smth; waters smth ‣ **abápsųpsų** vt1-redup s/he sprinkles smth (with water)

sprout *v n* **ahínąpA** vi it (plant) sprouts

spur *n-pl* **mas'į́nahtage** n spur

square *n adj v* 1) **omnétų** n; vs square; it is square 2) **o'į́pa dóba** cp square

squash *n* **wįcánuȟnuǧe** n squash

squeak *v* 1) **gíza** vs it creaks, squeaks ‣ **gíza wága** vs it is a creaky, squeaky sound 2) **bagíza** vt1 s/he makes smth squeak by putting pressure, by

rubbing 3) **nągíza** vt1 s/he/it makes sb, smth squeak by stepping on him/her/it

squeal *v* 1) **bizÁ** vi1 s/he/it squeals ‣ **bis-** cont cont ‣ **bispízA** vi1-redup s/he/it squeals 2) **yubízA** vt2 s/he makes smth (gopher) squeal when picking it up 3) **bahówayA** vt1 s/he makes sb scream in pain by bumping, pushing, sitting on him/her/it; squeals as when bumping onto smth 4) **nahówayayA** vt1 s/he makes sb squeal, cry in pain by stepping (on one's foot or tail)

squeeze *v* 1) **yusní** vt2 s/he squeezes the liquid out; milks a cow 2) **yusníza** vt2 s/he squeezes the air out; s/he produces a small, silent fart 3) **baskíjA** vt1 s/he squeezes smth down by pushing, by pressing on it with the hands open 4) **yuskíjA** vt2 s/he squeezes smth manually

squirrel *n* 1) **cąyúpina** n squirrel 2) **tašnáheja ȟóda** cp grey squirrel 3) **bízena** n gopher, ground squirrel 4) **bisknékneǧa** n-redup spotted gopher, thirteen-lined ground squirrel

St. Paul's Mission (Montana) *ngeo* **Waką́ tíbi** ngeo St. Paul's Mission (Montana)

stab *v* **capÁ** vt1 s/he stabs sb; pricks smth ‣ **wacápA** vi1-abs s/he stabs people ‣ **cagípA** vt1-pos s/he stabs, pricks his/her own ‣ **capápA** vt1-redup s/he stabs sb, pricks smth repeatedly ‣ **cą'íc'ipA** vi3-refl s/he stabs himself/herself ‣ **cą'íc'ipapA** vi3-refl-redup s/he stabs himself/herself repeatedly

Stabbed many times *nprop* **Wacápe óda** nprop Stabbed many times (woman from Carry The Kettle who had been stabbed many times by Blackfeet warriors)

stable *n* **šųktí** n stable, barn

staff *n* **wábaha** n eagle staff, banner

stag *n* **taȟcámnoga** n stag

staggering *adj* 1) **anósnos maní** vi1 s/he walks staggeringly 2) **mnakápkąpa** adv unsteadily, staggering 3) **bacáknekne yeyÁ** vt1 s/he makes sb stagger by pushing, shoving

stain *n v* **gaȟnáda** vs s/he/it is stained ‣
  gíjaȟnada vs3-pos s/he has a stain on his/
  her own (clothes)

stake *n See:* **peg**

stalk *v* 1) **anásnadA** vt1 s/he sneaks up on sb,
  stalks smth (prey) 2) **wį'íyape** vi1 he is waiting for her, stalking her

stallion *n* **šųkmnóga** n stallion

stamp *n v* 1) **iyáskapa** vs s/he/it is glued, sealed,
  stamped ‣ **iyáskamyA** vt1-caus s/he glues,
  seals, stamps smth on it 2) **iyáskamye** n stamp,
  tape, something that is glued on ‣ **wa'óyabi**
  iyáskamye cp stamp

stand *v n* 1) **nážį** vi1 s/he/it stands; s/he is, exists
  in a certain condition (used after an adverb
  or a postposition); it is, it is located (used for
  objects) ‣ **nagíjižį** vt1-benef s/he defends,
  stands for sb ‣ **nagícižįbi** vi1-recip they defend,
  stand for one another ‣ **na'íc'ižį** vi3-refl s/he
  defends, stands for himself/herself ‣ **énažį**
  vi1-coll they (collectively) stand up 2) **inážį** vi1
  s/he stands up 3) **banážį** vt1 s/he pushes smth
  upwards; makes smth stand by pushing on it
  4) **ijínažį** vi1 s/he/it stands above 5) **inážį** vi1 s/
  he/it stops, halts, stands still 6) **kninážį** vi1 s/
  he arrives back here and stands 7) **hinážį** vi1 s/
  he arrives here and stands 8) **nasnéjA** vt1 s/he
  stands on smth and breaks; breaks smth with
  body weight 9) **hą** vs it stands, is; it is placed
  (used with inanimate referent only)

star *n* **wįcáȟpi** n star

Star people *cp* **Wįcášta wįcáȟpi** cp Star people

starblanket *n* **owįža wįcáȟpi** cp starblanket

start *v n* 1) **naȟmúyą** vt1 s/he starts an engine 2)
  inída vs s/he is anxious to start smth)

startle *v* **yuš'íyeya** vt2-caus, vs s/he/it frightens,
  startles sb; s/he is frightened, scared, afraid

starve *v* **nodį t'a** vs s/he/it is hungry, starving

stay *v n* 1) **ų** vi1, vi1-aux s/he/it is, lives, exists;
  s/he/it stays somewhere; s/he feels; exists, is

in a certain way; s/he does continuously; goes
around doing smth 2) **išnána ų** vi1 s/he is, stays
alone; is a bachelor, is a bachelor (some speakers also inflect **įšnána**) 3) **yįgÁ ; yągÁ** vi3-aux
s/he remains doing, does continuously; stays)

steal *v* 1) **manú** vt1 s/he steals smth ‣ **wamánu**
  vi1-abs s/he steals things ‣ **magíjinu** vt1-benef
  s/he steals smth for sb ‣ **magínu** vt1-dat s/he
  steals smth from sb ‣ **magícinubi** vi1-recip
  they steal from one another 2) **šųkmánu** vi1
  s/he steals a horse, horses

steam *n v* 1) **p'ó** n, vimp mist, vapor, steam; it
  is steam; it steams 2) **nap'óyA** vi1 it produces
  steam

steep *adv* **knihéya** adv steep

steering wheel *cp* **iyúhomni** n steering wheel

stench *n* **amná** n stench

step *n v* 1) **ahá** vt2 s/he steps on sb, smth 2) **įhá**
  n ; vi1 step; s/he steps, takes a step 3) **aní** vt1 s/
  he steps, climbs, walks over smth ‣ **aníni** vt1-
  redup s/he steps, climbs, walks over smth here
  and there 4) **mánini** vi1-redup s/he takes small
  steps (like a baby or an elder) 5) **na- ; ną-** pref
  by kicking, stepping, walking (forms active
  verbs); by internal force, heat; by itself (forms
  impersonal or stative verbs)

stepfather *n* **aktúguna** n his/her uncle (father's
  brother); stepfather)

sternum *n* **makúhuhu** n sternum

stick *v n* 1) **ayáskamyA** vt1 s/he glues, sticks,
  pastes smth onto it 2) **obázą** vt1 s/he sticks,
  inserts smth in it ‣ **ogíjibazą** vt1-benef s/he
  sticks, inserts smth in it for him/her 3) **moȟcá**
  vs s/he/it is tangled; sticks up 4) **ayútita** vt2
  s/he trims smth (edges of a piece of cloth);
  sticks different pieces on smth 5) **cą** n tree;
  wood; stick ‣ **cą gahómni** np stick used in a
  round dance ‣ **cą ús apábi** np wooden stick
  such as baseball bat, a hockey stick 6) **pedísto**
  n roasting stick

sticky *adj* 1) **gigídA** vs it is sticky 2) **niní** vs it thickens, coagulates; it is sticky

stiff *adj* 1) **badį́** vs s/he/it is stiff 2) **modį́** vs it is stiff, inflexible; stands straight

stiffly *adv* **modį́ya** adv stiffly

still *adv* 1) **naháȟ** adv still, yet 2) **škáši** adv calm, still, quiet ‣ **škáši yįgA** vi3 s/he is sitting still 3) **ínáži** vi1 s/he/it stops, halts, stands still 4) **ųwą́ši** adv still, quiet 5) **amnágena** vimp it is still, peaceful

stillborn *adj* **tanín waníje** cp stillborn infant

stingy *adj* 1) **oȟ'ą́sija** vs s/he is stingy 2) **watéȟina** vi1-abs s/he is stingy

stink *v* **s'ámna** vs s/he/it stinks

stir *v* **agásosa** vt1 s/he stirs up smth

stitch *v n* 1) **basísA** vt1 s/he sews, stitches smth ‣ **nųbáȟ basísA** vt1 s/he double stitches smth 2) **abáȟnadA** vt1, n s/he stitches, pins smth on it; ribbon; silk, silk cloth ‣ **abáȟnan** cont silk, ribbon, smth pinned or stitched 3) **agágeǧe** vt1 s/he sews, stitches smth onto it (ribbon, patch)

stocking *n* 1) **oyáků** n socks, stockings 2) **hųskána** n stockings

stomach *n* 1) **niǧé ; niǧá** n stomach, tripe, abdomen ‣ **niǧé įhókun** cp lower part of the stomach below the navel ‣ **niǧé húde** cp lower part of the stomach below the navel (less common) 2) **tatézi** n ruminant's stomach 3) **oknápšiya oknápši yįgÁ** adv, vi3 on the stomach; upside down, s/he lays on the stomach

stone *n* 1) **íya** n stone 2) **agáškibi** n flat, round stone with a groove used to pound chokecherries 3) **ažúkta íya** cp kidney stones

Stoney *nprop* 1) **Íyaȟe wįcášta** nprop Stoney Nakoda people, person of Stoney Nakoda descent 2) **Téȟan Nakóda** nprop Stoney Nakoda people, person of Stoney Nakoda descent

stool *n* **cešnóšno** vi1-redup s/he has soft stool, diarrhea

stoop *v* **batúža** vi1 s/he bends over; stoops down

stop *v n* 1) **asní** vi1 s/he stops, quits 2) **aną́ptA** vt1 s/he stops, blocks sb, smth ‣ **wa'áną ptA** vii-abs s/he stops, blocks, forbids things 3) **ínáži** vi1 s/he/it stops, halts, stands still 4) **yu'ínáži** vt2 s/he stops sb, smth; cuts the motor off (car, engine) 5) **yaštą́** vt2 s/he stops talking about smth

store *v, n* 1) **knágA** vt1 s/he puts smth ready; stores smth (food, wood); has smth on hand ‣ **gíjiknagA** vt1-benef s/he puts smth ready for sb; stores smth (food, wood) for sb to have on hand ‣ **giknágA** vt1-pos s/he stores, saves, caches smth for himself/herself 2) **eknágA** vt1 s/he/it puts, places smth down, away ‣ **egíknagA** vt1-pos s/he puts, places his/her own thing down (feet, bag) 3) **oknágA** vt1 s/he puts, stores smth away in it ‣ **ogíknagA** vt1-pos s/he puts, stores his/her own thing away in it; bag ‣ **ogíjiknagA** vt1-benef s/he puts, stores smth away in it for sb 4) **owópetų tíbi ; owópetų ; o'ópetų** cp, n store ‣ **hayábi owópetų** cp clothing store ‣ **cąní o'ópetų** cp tobacco, smoke shop ‣ **máza o'ópetų** cp hardware store ‣ **omní owópetų** cp liquor store, bar ‣ **wóyude owopetų** cp grocery store

stormy *adj* 1) **ošíjejA** vimp there is a storm; it is stormy weather ‣ **ąpšíjejA** vimp it is a stormy day; a day with bad weather 2) **opšíja gamóta** vimp there is a dust storm

story *n* 1) **owóknage** n story, legend, fable 2) **wóknagA** vii-abs, vii-abs-pos s/he tells stories; s/he tells his/her own story ‣ **wógiknagA** vt1-dat s/he tells sb a story

storytelling *n* **wóknagabi** n storytelling

stove *n* 1) **océti** n, vii fireplace, hearth; stove, oven; heater; s/he lights up a stove; cooks on top of a stove ‣ **caȟóda océti** cp coal stove ‣ **cą́ océti** cp woodstove 2) **cetí** vii s/he starts a stove

straddle *v* **agámnaza** vt1 s/he/it straddles above smth ‣ **agámnas** adv straddling above

straight *adv adj v n* 1) **ótąna** adv straight, in a straight manner, in a respectable way 2a) **gadíyą ; ganíyą** adv straight, directly; in a bee-line, straight line

straighten *v* 1) **yu'ótą** vt2 s/he straightens sb, smth ‣ **įknú'otą** vi3-refl s/he straightens him/her up (figuratively "puts one's life back on track") 2) **ya'ótą** vt2 s/he straightens smth with the teeth 3) **nastó** vt1 s/he straightens, smoothes smth with the foot

strainer *n* **įbúskeba** n strainer

strait *n* **makóce wídaya** ph strait

strange *adj* 1) **wóšteja** vs s/he/it is strange 2) **tawáci otóką** vs s/he is strange

strangely *adv* **oštéšte** adv strangely

Strangers people *nprop* **Tokąbi** nprop Strangers people

straw *n* **pežíšeja** n straw

strawberry *n* **wažúšteja** n strawberry

strawberry roan *cp* **šųkpáša** n strawberry roan horse

stream *n* **mnitácągu** n stream

strengthen *v* **mnihé'įc'iya** vi3-ref s/he strengthens himself/herself; has courage in himself/herself

stretch *v n* 1) **yugádį** vt1 s/he stretches smth out ‣ **knugádį** vt1-pos s/he stretches his/her own out ‣ **gíjiyugadį** vt1/2-benef s/he stretches out smth for sb 2) **nasų́** vii s/he/it stretches out the feet and legs 3) **yuzíjA** vt2 s/he stretches smth manually ‣ **įknúzijA** vi3-refl s/he stretches himself/herself 4) **yut'ízA** vt2 s/he tightens smth up by stretching

string *n v* **wíbaȟte** n string

stringy *adj* **zązą́** vs it is stringy, long and thin

strip *n* 1) **wógamna** n flat strips of meat prepared for drying 2) **masó** vt1 s/he cuts a strip ‣ **masóso** vt1-redup s/he cuts smth in strips

stripper *n* 1) **yužúžu wacíbi** cp stripper 2) **yužúžu wíyą** cp female stripper

strong *adj* 1a) **mnihéja** vs s/he/it is strong 1b) **mnihą́** vs s/he/it is strong, powerful ‣ **mnihé** vcont strong 2a) **š'ágA** vs s/he/it is strong 2b) **waš'ágA** vs s/he/it is strong ‣ **waš'akyA** vt1-caus s/he makes smth strong ‣ **awáš'ageja** vii s/he/it is kind of strong 3) **sudá** vs it is hard, solid; it is strong, tough

Strong wood people *nprop* **Cą́ȟnada** nprop Strong wood (band of Nakoda, Saskatchewan)

Strongeagle *nprop* **Wamníwaš'aga** nprop Strongeagle (surname)

stuck *adj* 1) **gaȟní** vs s/he/it is stuck ‣ **agáȟni** vs s/he/it is stuck on smth 2) **ayáskaba ; ayáskama** vt1, vs s/he/it is stuck on sb, smth; infatuated with smth ‣ **ayáskamyA** vt1-caus s/he glues, sticks, pastes smth onto it 3) **oyátaga** vs s/he/it is stuck after being inserted; gets stuck while going out

student *n* **wayáwa wįcášta** cp student

stuff *v n* **obúȟni** vt1 s/he stuffs smth into it

stumble *v* 1) **hugáše** vs s/he stumbles, trips over 2) **ȟijáhą** vs s/he trips, stumbles on smth and falls ‣ **ȟijáheyA** vt1-caus s/he makes sb trip, stumble

stump *n* 1) **cąbáksa** n tree stump 2) **cąhúde** n tree stump, base of a tree

stupid *adj* 1) **tawáci ecéduši** vs s/he is stupid 2) **įknúdąši** vi3-refl s/he disrespects, brags about himself/herself; is stupid 3) **pat'á** n dumb, stupid person

submarine *n* **mnimáhen wáda** cp submarine

submissive *adj* **onįkte wací** vii s/he is meek, submissive; s/he is a coward

succession *n* **iyáza** adv in succession, one after the other ‣ **iyázagen** adv in succession, one after the other; wandering

such *adj pro adv* 1) **cá** det such a person, such a kind, at such a time; a, an, the 2) **duktéduȟ** adv exactly as such

suck *v* 1) **azį** vi1 s/he sucks on his/her mother's breast 2) **yazóga** vt1 s/he/it (baby) sucks on smth ‣ **yazók** vcont sucking ‣ **yazókkiyA** vt1-caus s/he makes him/her suck on smth 3) **yadą́** vt2 s/he extracts smth by sucking 4) **íyabiza** vt2 s/he smooches sb; kisses by producing a loud sucking sound 5) **yaskíja** vt2 s/he sucks the juice out of smth

suddenly *n* 1) **įknúhana ; įknúhąnaȟ** adv suddenly, instantly, all at once 2) **hįknA** aux suddenly happens, begins; sudden and sharp ‣ **múhįknA** vi1 it is a heavy and sudden boom ‣ **ot'į́hįknA** vimp there is a clap of thunder ‣ **škáȟįknA** vi it moves suddenly; it is a sudden movement 3) **iyéyA** aux s/he causes smth to be done quickly or suddenly

sue *v* **yacó** vt2 s/he sues, summons, takes sb to court

suet *n* **wasną́** n suet; tallow, grease

sugar *n* **cąšmúyabi** n maple syrup; sugar, refined sugar

suggest *v* **-ktA** encl will, 'll, would (marks a potential event that is not yet realized; when used in the past it indicates a counterfactual event); expresses a suggestion, let us (when occurring with verbs in the 1st person plural ų(g)- ... -bi or dual ų(g)-)

suicidal *adj* **įc'íkte tawáci** vi s/he has suicidal tendencies

suicide *n v adj* **įc'íkte** vi3-refl s/he commits suicide

suitcase *n* **hayábi opíye** cp suitcase

sulk *v* **cąníyą ; cąníya** vi1 s/he sulks

summer *n* 1) **mnogédu** n summer; it is summer ‣ **mnogén** vcont summer 2) **omnédu** adv in the summertime 3) **mnogésą ; mnogéyasą** adv throughout the summer, all summer 4) **mnogéhą** adv last summer

sun *n* **hąwí ; wí** n sun; moon; month

Sun dance *np* **tijáȟ wacíbi** cp Sun dance

Sun dance arbor *np* 1) **wótijaǧa** n medicine lodge, Sun dance arbor 2) **tíbi tą́ga** cp Sun dance arbor 3) **tijáǧabi** n Sun dance arbor

Sun dance tree *np* **cąwáką** n Sun dance tree, center pole; wood cross

sun dog *n* **penyúza** n sun dog, parhelion

sunburned *adj* **maštį́špą** vs s/he is sunburned

Sunday *n* **ą́bawaką** n Sunday

sunflower *n* **hąwí waȟcá** cp sunflower (calque from English)

sunglasses *n* 1) **įštáštana sába** cp-redup sunglasses 2) **įštáyabi sába** cp sunglasses

sunrise *n* **hąwí hįną́pa** vimp it is sunrise; it dawns

sunset *n* 1) **wiyóȟpeya, wiyóȟpaye** n west; sunset 2) **wí'įšį'įyaya** vimp the sun sets; it is the sunset

superhero *n* **hokšína ohídiga** cp superhero

supper *n* **hąhébi wódabi** cp supper

suppurate *v See:* **pus**

surely *adv* **eháš** adv too much, exceedingly; surely, quite

surprise *n* 1) **hį́į** interj expression of surprise (female speaker) 2) **ohá** interj expression of surprise (used in storytelling; female speaker) 3) **hukwáá, húk** interj expression of surprise or disinterest, discontent (male speaker) 4) **kó** part intensifier; expresses irony, amazement, surprise (occurs after the verb) 5) **namóo** interj expression of surprise for unexpected news (female speaker) 6) **hąhą́** interj expression of surprise for unexpected news (male speaker) 7) **įhú** interj exclamation of surprise

surround *v* **a'ókšąyA** vt1-caus s/he encircles, surrounds sb, smth

surveyor *n* **makáyutą** n land surveyor

suspend *v* **oktéyA ; otkéyA** vt1-caus s/he hangs up, suspends smth ‣ **oktégiyA, otkégiyA** vt1-pos s/he hangs, suspends her/his own (clothes, meat) ‣ **okté'įc'iyA, otké'įc'iyA** vi1-refl s/he hangs, suspends himself/herself

swallow₁ *n* 1) **įjápsįpsįdana** n swallow 2) **ubížade** n barn swallow

swallow₂ *v* **napcá** vt1 s/he swallows smth

swamp *n* **wiwí** n swamp, marsh; quicksand

Swamp people *nprop* **Pteğábina** nprop Swamp people (band of Stoney)

swampy *adj* **wiwína** vi it is swampy

sweat *v* 1) **temní** vs; n s/he/it sweats; sweat ‣ **temnímna** vs s/he/it smells of sweat ‣ **temníyA** vt1-caus s/he/it causes sb to sweat ‣ **temní'įc'iyA** vi3-refl s/he causes himself/herself to sweat 2) **temníšmu** n sweat drop 3) **otémni** vt1 s/he sweats on sb, smth ‣ **otémni'įc'iyA** vi3-refl s/he makes himself/herself sweat in smth (as in a heavy coat) 4) **įtémnit'A** vs s/he/it is sweating profusely because of smth

sweatlodge *n* 1) **įníbi** n sweatlodge (structure or ceremony) ‣ **įnítíbi** ; **įníbi gáğabi** cp sweat lodge (structure) ‣ **įníbi ecúbi** cp sweatlodge ceremony 2) **įní** vi1 s/he does a sweatlodge ceremony, goes into a sweatlodge 3) **įnígağA** vi1 s/he builds a sweatlodge

sweep *v* 1) **gadódo** vt1 s/he shakes, brushes, sweeps, dusts smth off; s/he/it pecks sb, smth (tree, ground) ‣ **tigádodo** vi1 s/he sweeps the floor of the house 2) **gağé** vt1 s/he rakes, gathers, sweeps smth together (leaves, snow)

sweet *adj adv* 1) **skúyA** vs it is sweet ‣ **skúyemna** vs it has a sweet smell 2) **nąbímna** vs it is delicious, sweet 3) **giknã** vt1 s/he cuddles, sweet talks to sb

Sweet Grass Hills (Montana) *ngeo* 1) **Pežískuya bahá** ngeo Sweet Grass hills (Montana) 2) **A'íkpoğą oyúze** ngeo Sweet Grass Hills (Montana)

sweetcorn *n* **wakmúhazaskuya** n sweetcorn

sweeten *v* 1) **skuyéyA** vt1-caus s/he sweetens smth 2) **gaskúyA** vt1 s/he stirs and sweetens smth

sweetgrass *n* 1) **wacáğa** n sweetgrass 2) **pežískuya** n sweetgrass

swell *v* 1) **bó** vs s/he/it swells ‣ **knabó** vs-pos his/her foot (lower body part) is swollen 2) **nąbó** vs it (hand) is swollen; it swells by itself 3) **nąknábo** vi it swells, puffs up on its own (beans, injury) 4) **yubó** vt2 s/he/it makes smth, sb swell by the action of the hands ‣ **knubó** vt1-pos, vi1-pos s/he/it makes his/her own swell by the action of the hands; his/her becomes swollen 5) **wįcábo** n human swelling 6) **nądáboğA** vs vs s/he/it is bloated, swollen, puffed up ‣ **nądáboh'įc'iyA** vi3-refl s/he/it bloats, swells himself/herself/itself up (frog)

swift *adj See:* **fast**

Swift Current River (Saskatchewan) *ngeo* 1) **Wakpé núzahą** ngeo Swift Current River (Saskatchewan) 2) **Minínuzahą** ngeo Swift Current river; Swift Current (Saskatchewan)

Swift Current (Saskatchewan) *ngeo* **Minínuzahą** ngeo Swift Current river; Swift Current (Saskatchewan)

swim *v n* 1) **nųwÁ** vii1 s/he/it swims, bathes, showers ‣ **nųwékiyA** vt1-caus s/he lets sb swim 2) **anúwÁ** vt1 s/he swims after sb, smth; goes after sb, smth while swimming

swine *n* **gugúšawįyena** n swine

swing *n v* 1) **hódodo** n baby swing 2) **įhódodogic'ų** n swing 3) **gapsápsą** vt1 s/he swings, shakes smth that is hanging by hitting, pushing; it (wind) makes smth swing 4) **mohúshųza** vt1 s/he makes smth swing (branch) by shooting 5) **goskóza** vt1-redup s/he/it waves, swings, flaps smth (as bird) ‣ **goskós** vcont waving, swinging, flapping smth

swollen *adj See:* **swell**

swoop *v* **s'ás'a** vi it is a swooping sound (as of wings)

sword *n* **mínahąska** n sword, sabre

syphilis *n* **ceȟníbi** n syphilis, sexual disease

syrup *n* ‣ **cąšmúyabi** n maple syrup; sugar, refined sugar ‣ **cąšmúyabi gigída** cp syrup

T

table *n* 1) **awódabi** n table 2) **won'ékne** vii s/he sets the table ‣ **won'égijikne** vt1-benef s/he sets the table for sb

tack *v n* **abúspA** vt1 s/he daubs, glues, tacks smth onto it

tail *n* 1) **sįdé** n tail ‣ **tasįde** n ruminant's tail ‣ **šųksįde** n horse tail 2) **ubí** n tail of bird

tailbone *n* **sįdéhuhu** n tailbone, coccyx

take *v* 1) **éyagu** vt2 s/he takes, seizes, grasps sb, smth ‣ **égijiyagu** vt1-benef s/he takes, holds sb, smth for/from him/her ‣ **éknagu** vt1 s/he takes smth back 2) **áyA** vt2 s/he leaves, takes, goes with sb, smth there ‣ **gíjayA** vt1-benef s/he takes sb, smth there for him/her 3) **éyayA** vt2 s/he takes, sets to go with sb, smth there 4) **akná** vt1 s/he takes sb, smth back there ‣ **aknékiyA** vt1-caus s/he lets, makes sb take sb, smth back ‣ **wa'ákna** vii-abs s/he takes things back there 5) **hįknátųkiyA** vt1-caus s/he makes her take a husband 6) **įdé okmÁ** vt1 s/he takes a picture of sb 7) **hiyó-** pref gets, takes sb, smth (prefixed to verbs of movement) ‣ **kniyó-** pref gets, takes his/her own (prefixed to verbs of movement)

take down *ph* 1) **yuȟpÁ** vt2 s/he unloads smth; throws smth down ‣ **knuȟpÁ** vt1-pos s/he unloads his/her own; throws his/her own down 2) **gaȟpÁ** vt1 s/he takes smth down (as a tent) ‣ **knaȟpÁ** vt1-pos s/he takes down his/her own (as a tent) 3) **yuwága** vt2 s/he knocks sb, smth down manually; takes smth down ‣ **tiyúwąga** vi2 s/he takes a lodge down

take off *v* 1) **bašnógA** vt1 s/he takes smth off 2) **yušnógA** vt2 s/he jerks, pulls smth out from another object; takes, removes smth off (cork,

tooth, root, clothes) ‣ **įknúšnogA** vi3-refl s/he undresses himself/herself; takes off his/her clothes ‣ **knušnógA** vt1-pos s/he takes his/her own thing off (hat, coat) ‣ **knušnók** vcont taking his/her own thing off (hat, coat)

take turns *ph* **omįtokto** adv back and forth; taking turns

tale *n* 1) **hųgága** vii s/he tells a fairy tale 2) **hųgágabi** n fairy tale 3) **o'óknage** n fable, tale

talented *adj* **ówecoga** vs s/he is talented

talk *v n* 1) **i'Á ; iyÁ** vt1, vii s/he speaks, talks to sb, with sb; s/he speaks; speaks a language ‣ **i'átoką** vii s/he talks differently ‣ **i'égicuni** vii-irr s/he is done talking ‣ **i'égabį** vii s/he is reluctant to talk 2) **oyágA** vt2 s/he announces, tells, talks about smth ‣ **oknágA** vi3-refl s/he talks about himself/herself; s/he confesses himself/herself 3) **awóknagA** vt1 s/he talks, discusses smth 4) **gikną** vt1 s/he pampers, cuddles, sweet talks to sb 5) **ya-** pref action done with the mouth, teeth (biting, chewing, speaking; derives a stative verb into a transitive verb) 6) **yaktúžA** vt2 s/he makes sb crazy by talking ‣ **yaktúš** vcont talking crazily 7) **yaštá** vt2 s/he stops talking about smth 8) **gikną** vt1 s/he pampers, cuddles, caresses, sweet talks to sb

tall *adj* 1) **háskA** vs s/he/it is tall, long ‣ **háskaskA** vs-redup s/he/it is very tall, long 2) **nehágejA** vs s/he/it is about this high, tall, or far ‣ **neháhągejA** vs-redup they are about this high, tall, or far

Tall man *nprop* **Wįcášta háska** nprop Tall man (Armand McArthur's traditional name)

tallow *n* 1) **wasną** n suet; tallow, grease 2) **wacéğuğu** n-redup pieces of tallow 3) **ptéšį** n buffalo tallow

tamed *adj* **okúwawašte ; okúwašte** vs it (animal) is tamed

tan *v n* **kpąyą** vt1 s/he tans a hide ‣ **wakpáyą** vii-abs s/he tans

tangled *adj* **moȟcá** vs s/he/it is tangled; sticks up

tank *n* **ogícize maká agą́n wáda** ph tank

tape recorder *cp* **hó'ewįcayagubi** n tape recorder

taste *v n* **oyún wašté** vs it is good to eat; tastes good *See:* **try**

tasteful *adj* **yunwášteya** adv in a tasteful manner

tattered *adj* 1) **kuká** vs it is worn out, tattered 2) **ȟciná** vs it is ragged, tattered *See:* **raggy**

tattoo *n v* 1) **há okmábi** cp birthmark, tattoo 2) **agíto** vs s/he is tattooed ‣ **agíto'įc'iyA** vi3-refl s/he tattooed himself/herself

tavern *n See:* **bar**

tea *n* **waȟpé** n leaf; tea ‣ **waȟpésaba** n black tea ‣ **waȟpéto** n green tea

teach *v* 1) **ųspékiyA** vt1-caus s/he teaches smth to sb ‣ **wa'ų́spekiyA, wó'ųspekiyA** n, vt1-abs-caus teacher; s/he teaches sb things 2) **wasnókkiyA** vt1-caus s/he teaches smth to sb

teacher *n* 1) **wayáwawįcakiye ; wayáwawįcakiya** cp school teacher 2) **wa'ų́spekiyA ; wó'ųspekiyA** n, vt1-abs-caus teacher; s/he teaches sb things ‣ **wa'ų́spewįcakiya** n male teacher ‣ **wa'ų́spewįyąkiya** n female teacher

teal *n* **amnóto ; amnótona** n blue-winged teal

teapot *n* **waȟpé céǧa** cp teapot

tear₁ *n* 1) **įštámniǧe** n tear 2) **ocą́gu įštámniǧe** cp trail of tears

tear₂ *v n* 1) **yuȟnéjA** vt2 s/he tears smth manually (paper, cloth) ‣ **yuȟnéȟnejA** vt2-redup s/he tears smth in strips manually 2) **yaȟnéjA** vt2 s/he tears smth with the teeth 3) **gaȟnéjA** vt1 s/he tears, rips smth open by pressure, or with his/her own weight 4) **baȟnéjA** vt1 s/he tears, punctures smth with a sharp tool ‣ **kpaȟnéjA** **vt1** s/he tears, punctures his/her own by pushing 5) **naȟnéjA** vi it tears, bursts open by inner force) 6) **yuȟcína** vt2 s/he/it tears, frays smth (cloth, blanket, coat) 7) **yumnázA** vt2 s/he tears, rips smth open manually 8) **oyábodA** vt2 s/he tears smth with the teeth

tease *v* 1) **ya'į́škadA** vt2 s/he teases sb verbally ‣ **ya'į́škan** vcont teasing verbally ‣ **wayá'įškadA** vi2-abs s/he teases, plays jokes on people ‣ **gicíkna'įškadabi** vi1-redup they tease one another ‣ **gicíya'įškadabi** vi1-recip they tease one another verbally ‣ **įkná'įškadA** vi3-refl s/he teases himself/herself 2) **įškádabi** n woman that is teased sexually 3) **yu'į́škadA** vt2 s/he teases, plays jokes on sb; s/he plays with sb sexually 4) **į́kuwa** vt1 s/he tempts, teases sb

teat *n See:* **nipple**

teddy bear *cp* **wó'įškada ; wó'įškade** n toy, teddy bear

teething *adj n* **hí įcáǧA** vs s/he (baby) is teething

telegraph *n See:* **telephone**

telephone *v n* 1a) **mas'ápA** vi1, n s/he makes a telephone call; telephone, telephone call ‣ **mas'ágijipA** vt1-benef s/he telephones sb on behalf of him/her ‣ **mas'ágipA** vt1-dat, vi1-recip s/he telephones sb, they telephone one another 1b) **mas'ápabi** n telegraph, telephone 2) **mas'ó'i'abi** n telephone 3) **omás'ape ; omás'apa** n telegraph, telephone office

telescope *n See:* **binoculars**

tell *v* 1) **egíyA ; ejíyA** vt1-dat s/he tells sb smth ‣ **ejíyakiyA** vt1-caus s/he makes sb say it 2) **hųgágą** vi1 s/he tells a fairy tale 3) **oyágA** vt2 s/he announces, tells, talks about smth ‣ **ogíjiyagA** vt1-benef s/he tells smth to sb; tells smth for sb else ‣ **ogíyagA** vt1-dat s/he tells smth to sb ‣ **ogíyak** vcont-dat telling smth to sb ‣ **oknágA** vt1-pos s/he tells his/her own (story, news); s/he confesses ‣ **ogíciyagabi** vi1-recip they tell smth about one another ‣ **o'į́knagA** vi3-refl s/he tells of himself/herself; makes himself/herself known 4) **wįjákA** vi1, vs s/he tells the truth; it is true 5) **wóknagA** vi1-abs, vi1-pos s/he tells stories; s/he tells his/her own story ‣ **wóknakkiyA** vt1-caus-pos s/he makes sb tell his/her story ‣ **wóknak** vcont telling sto-

ries ‣ **wógiknagA** vt1-dat s/he tells sb a story ‣
wógiciknagA vi1-recip they tell stories to one
another ‣ **wógiciknak** vcont-recip telling stories to one another ‣ **įwóknagA** vt1, n s/he tells
a story about smth; legend 6) **ya'ótạ'į** vi2 s/he
announces smth, tells the news 7) **-ši** aux s/he
tells, asks, orders, commands sb (attaches or
follows a preceding verb)

ten *n adj* **wikcémna** num, vs ten; it is ten, there
are ten ‣ **wikcémnana** num only ten

tent *n* 1) **wí** n lodge, tent ‣ **wíwina** n-redup small
tent ‣ **wišíjena** n pitiful tent 2) **wistó** n tent
(with walls), prospector tent ‣ **įkcé wistó** n
tent (with walls), prospector tent 3) **wi'óziba**
vi1 s/he erects a tent 4) **titóką** n different tent

tenth *n* **įjíwikcemna** n tenth

testicle *n* **susú ; susúna** n-redup testicle

than *conj* **į'ágam** adv, conj over it; than

thank *v* 1) **wópina** n thanks, gratitude 2) **pináyA**
vt1-caus s/he pleases sb, makes sb be grateful;
s/he thanks sb

thankful *adj* 1) **piná** vt1 s/he is thankful for smth
‣ **pináyA** vt1-caus, vs s/he pleases sb, makes sb
be grateful (used to express "Thank you!") 2)
wópina n gratitude, thanks ‣ **wópinayA** vt1-
caus s/he makes sb thankful ‣ **owópina** vs s/
he is thankful, grateful

Thanksgiving *n* 1) **wópina ạba** cp Thanksgiving
day 2) **wópina onówạ** cp Thanksgiving song

that *pro conj adv* 1) **žé** dem, art that (near the listener), general reference demonstrative; the
(definite topic marker); that (marker of complement and relative clauses) ‣ **žecéš** adv only that
(contrary to one's expectation) ‣ **žé'įš** adv that,
those too; that one, those ones too ‣ **žekžéš**
pro-redup only that one ‣ **ženíyuha** adv all of
that 2) **gá** dem that one over there

thaw *v n* 1) **ská** vimp it thaws, melts 2) **štúda** vs
it is thawed, defrosted, soft ‣ **štunyÁ** vt1 s/he
thaws, defrosts smth

the *art* 1) **žé** dem, art that (near the listener),
general reference demonstrative; the (definite
topic marker); that (marker of complement and
relative clauses) 2) **cá** det such a person, such
a kind, at such a time; a, an, the

theater *n* **owábazoti** n theater

their *adj* 1) **-bi** encl their (3rd person plural possessor) 2) **-gu- ; -ju** suff-infix his, her, their (3rd
person singular possessor; used with kinship
and a few common nouns) 3) **-gi- ; -ki- ; -k-**
affix on one's own (marker of possessive verbs
where the agent is acting on his/her own thing,
body part or relative; the resulting possessive
verbs are of Class 1) 4) **táwabi** pro; vs their;
they own it, it is their own

theirs *pro* **táwabi** pro; vs their; they own it, it
is their own

them *pro* 1) **-wįca-** pref them (3rd person plural;
animate patient of transitive verbs) 2) **žékžena**
dem-redup each of them, those

themselves *pro* **iyé** pro, vs himself, herself, themselves, itself (emphasizes the subject or object);
s/he/it/they is/are the one ‣ **iyégeȟ** pro him-
self/herself/itself/themselves specifically ‣
iyégeȟtįyĄ ; iyéȟtįyĄ vs it is himself/herself/
itselfthemselves specifically

then *adv adj n* 1) **ga'éca** conj and then 2) **cén** conj
then, so, thus, because, that is why ‣ **ecén** adv,
conj in the right, original way; accordingly;
thus; then, and then, so ‣ **žécen** conj, adv thus,
then; in this manner, as such 3) **štén** conj if
when, if then; when, whenever, in, at, on, next
4) **žecán** adv in the meantime, during that time,
then 5a) **ehá** adv then, as it happened, at a specific point in the past (often used to express
English past tense) ‣ **c'ehạ** encl back then, in
the past, last (attaches to adverbs, verbs and
interrogative pronouns) ‣ **žehá ; žéhạ** adv
then, at that time, at a certain point in time
(often translates the English past tense); last

(with days of the week) 5b) **eháṇ** adv then 6) **žehágeja** adv about that long (measurement); since then 7) **hékta** adv back then, in the past 8) **hagéyadaháṇ** adv and then finally, at last

there *adv* 1) **žén** adv there 2) **žéci** adv around there, over there, there ‣ **žéciya** adv over there, over that way ‣ **žecíyadaháṇ** adv from that direction, from over there ‣ **žécipadaháṇ** adv from over there 3) **žedáháṇ, žedáháṇ** adv, vs from there, from it; s/he/it is from there 4) **žedápadaháṇ** adv moving from there, that way 5) **žédu** vs it is there, that is the place ‣ **žéduȟ** vs it is right there, that is exactly the place ‣ **žédunaȟ** adv exactly there 6) **éciyadaháṇ** adv from there 7) **ektám** post there, in a place (often used with cardinal directions) 8) **gáṇ** adv over there 9) **gakí** adv way over there, yonder, in a distant area ‣ **gákiya** adv over there ‣ **gákiyadaháṇ** adv from over there, yonder 10) **édu** vimp it is there, it is the place, time 11) **wíṇwida** adv-redup here and there

therefore *adv* 1) **cén** conj then, so, thus, therefore, because, that is why 2) **né'ṵs ; né'ṵ** conj because of this, on account of this, therefore 3) **žé'ṵs** conj that is why, because of that, on account of this, therefore

these *pro adj adv* 1) **nená** dem these here (close to the speaker) 2) **newós** pro these two 3) **nówa** pro all of these (people, animals, things, ideas) 4) **né'ṵš** dem this, these too; this one, these ones too

they *pro* 1) **-bi** encl they (plural marker of verbs with an animate referent; human, animal) 2) **é-** pref to, at, there, toward, in this direction; they (marks the collective plural form of some intransitive verbs)

They carry their own wood people *nprop* **Cáknúhabi wicášta** nprop They carry their own wood people (band of Nakoda)

They clean bones people *nprop* **Huhúmasmibi** nprop They clean bones people

They have sharp knives people *nprop* **Tamínapebina** nprop They have knives people (band of Nakoda)

thick *adj* 1) **šóga** vs it is thick 2) **ktába ; tkába** vi it is thick, mud-like, adhesive

thicken *v* 1) **ktamyÁ** vt1-caus s/he thickens smth (soup, broth) 2) **niní** vs it thickens, coagulates

thicket *n* **cútaga** n thicket

thickly *adv* **šokyá** adv thickly, extensively

thief *n* **wamánṵs'a** vi1, n s/he is a thief; thief

thigh *n* 1) **cejá** n thigh; leg of smth (chair, table) 2) **onúde** n thigh 3) **niséhu** n thigh

thimble *n* **nabó'ṵšna** n thimble

thin *adj* 1) **zibéna** vs it is thin ‣ **zipzíbena** vs-redup it is thin ‣ **zizímyenaȟ ; zipzímyenaȟ** adv thinly 2) **zizímnana** vs it is thin 3) **zázá** vs it is thin, transparent

thing *n* 1) **dágu** pro, quant, vs thing, something; what; any, none; it is something 2) **ijíyuha** adv entire, whole thing (archaic) 3) **taník'e** vs it is an old thing 4) **omémega** n-redup different things; a variety of things 5) **núske** n, vs thing, thingy; it is so, as such

think *v* 1) **iyúkca** vt2 s/he thinks, has an opinion about sb, smth ‣ **wíyukca** vi2-abs s/he thinks, ponders things; forms his/her opinion about smth ‣ **iknúkca** vt3-pos s/he thinks of his/her own thing ‣ **iyúkcakca** vt2-redup s/he thinks long and hard about sb, smth 2) **ecí** vt1, vt3 s/he thinks, wonders about smth (used with a preceding quote) ‣ **gecí** vt1 s/he thought smth (used to report thoughts, ideas, or opinions, but not quotes) 3) **wókca** vi1 s/he thinks, plans on doing smth ‣ **šinwókca** vi1 s/he thinks it is bad ‣ **awókca** vt1 s/he has thoughts about sb, smth ‣ **ašínwokca** vt1 s/he has perverse thoughts about sb, smth 4) **tawáci** n, vs mind; his/her mind, mindset, goal; s/he thinks thus ‣ **awáci** vt3, vs s/he feels, thinks about smth, has smth on the mind; it is a purpose ‣ **agíwaci** vt1-pos s/he thinks about his/her own 5) **wacímnezA**

vs s/he thinks clearly 6) **ecákiyA** vt1 s/he considers, thinks sb is as such 7) **epcá** vi1 I think, it seems, apparently (used with 1st person only) ▸ **gepcá** vi1 I thought that, it seems like (used with 1st person only) ▸ **žepcá** vi1 I think that, I thought that (used with 1st person only) 8) **otí'igA ; otígA ; otá'igA** part it seems, I think, apparently (this particle can occur with the negative enclitic -šį) 9) **duwé'ic'ina** vi3-refl s/he thinks of himself/herself as such a person 10) **wadágu'ic'ina** vi3-refl s/he feels, thinks greatly of himself/herself

thinly adv **zizímyena; zizímyenaȟ ; zipzímyenaȟ** adv, adv **zizímyena**, thinly

third adj n **iyámni** num third

thirsty adj **mni'it'a áyA** vs s/he/it is thirsty

thirteen num **agéyamni** num thirteen

thirty n **wikcémna yámni** cp thirty

this pro adv adj **né** dem, pro this, these (near the speaker); this, he, she, it ▸ **né'iš** adv this, these too; this one, these ones too ▸ **néš** pro this one indeed, this one unlike the other

thistle n **cápépena** n-redup thistle, prickly plant

thorn n **wapépe** n thistle

thoroughly adv 1) **dayáȟ** adv easily; very well, thoroughly 2) **adáyaȟ** adv thoroughly

those pro conj adj 1) **žená** dem those (not far from speaker) ▸ **žékžena ženáwa; ženáknana** dem-redup, dem, adv each of them, those, all of those, only those 2) **žewós** pro, dem those two 3) **ganá** dem those over there 4) **gawós** pro those two yonder 5) **žé'iš** adv that, those too; that one, those ones too

thought n **owókca** n thought

thoughtless adj 1) **wókcašį wicášta** cp thoughtless person 2) **wacítušį** vi1 s/he is thoughtless

thousand n adj **koktóbawige** num thousand

thread n **ȟahúda** n thread, rope

threaten v **wacógu** vi1-abs s/he threatens people

three adj n **yámni** num, vs three; s/he/it is three; there are three ▸ **yámnigiya** adv three by three, in three ways, in three different directions, locations ▸ **yámniȟ** adv three times ▸ **yámnina** num only three

Three Buttes (Montana) ngeo **Bahá tága yamní** ngeo Three Buttes (Montana)

thresher n 1) **owáyušnoge** n thresher 2) **iwánakaya** n thresher

thrift store cp 1) **waȟpáya o'ópetu** cp thrift store 2) **inúba wiyópeyabi tíbi** np thrift store, second-hand store

through prep adv adj 1) **okná** post in, through ▸ **nókna** post through this 2) **opáya** adv through, along, following the course of smth; in, through a valley, coulee

throughout prep adv 1) **-eyasa ; -e'asa ; -(e)sa** suff throughout, during ▸ **ha'éyasa** adv throughout the night, all night ▸ **hayákesa** adv throughout the morning, all morning ▸ **mnogésa** adv throughout the summer, all summer ▸ **omáka'esa** adv throughout the year, all year ▸ **ptayésa** adv throughout the fall, all fall ▸ **wanéyasa** adv throughout the winter ▸ **wiyó'esa** adv throughout the afternoon, all afternoon 2) **ti'íyaza** adv from house to house; all throughout camp

throw v n 1) **iȟpéyA** vt1 s/he discards, throws sb, smth away; s/he leaves sb, smth behind, alone; s/he/it is left behind; s/he divorces from him/her; s/he banishes sb ▸ **wa'íȟpeyA** vi1-abs s/he throws things away ▸ **iȟpékiyA** vt1-dat s/he throws smth at sb; s/he deals the cards; s/he leaves smth for sb ▸ **iȟpé'ic'iyA** vi3-refl s/he throws himself/herself on the ground 2) **oȟpéyA** vt1 s/he throws smth in it 3) **hiyú'ic'iyA** vi3-refl s/he throws himself/herself down 4) **iyóȟpeyA** vt1 s/he throws, drops smth into it ▸ **o'íyoȟpeyA** vt1-caus s/he throws smth in it 5) **ki'í** vt1 s/he throws, casts smth at sb; stones sb ▸ **ki'íyeyA** vt1 s/he throws, casts, propels smth ▸ **ki'íyegiciyA** vi1-recip they throw smth to one another 6) **agástagA** vt1 s/he daubs, pastes, throws, pours out a gooey substance (as to make it stick) 7) **gamnáyA** vt1 s/he throws, spreads smth out flat (fishnet) 8) **baȟpÁ** vt1 s/he throws, pushes smth off

thumb *n* **nąbáwąhųge tága** cp thumb

thunder *n* **ot'į** vimp, n it is thundering; thunder

thunderbird *n* 1) **wagíyą** n thunderbird 2) **wagíyą ȟubáhu máza** np iron-winged thunderbird 3) **waȟúbagoza** n thunderbird

thunderclap *n* **ot'į apÁ** vimp it is a thunderclap

Thursday *n* **ába įdóba** cp Thursday

tibia *n* See: **shin**

tickle *v* **yuš'íš'į** vt2 s/he tickles sb ‣ **įknúš'įš'į** vi3-refl s/he tickles himself/herself

tie *v n* 1) **paȟtÁ** vt1 s/he ties smth up 2) **apáȟtA** vt1-dit s/he ties smth onto it 3) **opáȟtA** vt1 s/he ties, packs smth into a bundle; ties smth in it ‣ **opágiȟtA** vt1-pos s/he ties, packs his/her own thing into a bundle 4) **gaškÁ** vt1 s/he ties smth fast as to hold ‣ **ícigaška** vt1 s/he ties sb, smth together 5) **įjáškA** vt1 s/he ties sb, smth to it; ties a knot; lace, laces ‣ **a'íjaškA** vt1 s/he ties it on sb, smth 6) **įgáškena** n tie

tighten *v* 1) **yut'ízA** vt2 s/he tightens smth up by stretching ‣ **yut'ís** adv tightly 2) **yuzípaȟtA** vt1 s/he tightens smth up

tightly *adv* 1) **t'įsyá** adv tightly 2) **yut'ís** adv tightly

time *n* 1) **wihíyaye** n time 2) **-hą** encl at a particular time; last 3) **nehádu** vs it is now; it took place at this time ‣ **neháduȟ** adv now, at this time ‣ **nehán ; neháduȟtiyА** adv-cont, vs at this time; now, today, it is now specifically; it is at this time ‣ **wanéhadu** vimp at this time, in time; s/he/it is of this age 4) **gahádu** vs it will be around that time (in the future); s/he/it is right there ‣ **gahán** adv-cont around that time (used when guessing roughly) ‣ **gaháduȟ** adv around that time (not sure exactly when) ‣ **gaháduȟtiyА** vs it will be at that time exactly (in the future) 5) **žehádu** vs it was at that time, then ‣ **žehán** adv-cont at that time; just when ‣ **žeháduga** vs it took/it will take place at about that time ‣ **žeháduȟ** adv at that time specifically, right at that time 6) **žehá ; žéhą** adv then, at that time, at a certain point in time (often translates the English past tense); last (with days of the week) ‣ **žéhac'ehą** adv at that time in the past 7) **dóhądu** vimp it is at such time 8) **doháyą** adv for a certain time, distance, length 9) **iyéhądu** vs it is now the time 10) **dágecųšį** vs nothing is done; it is a waste of time 11) **naháȟtįšį** vs, adv it is not time yet; before time 12) **piyáhąšį** adv in no time 13) **žíyasą** adv all that time 14) **wájaȟ** adv one time, one time specifically; once (used in introducing a tale, or story) ‣ **wájanaȟ** adv only once; one more time ‣ **wájanaȟtiyА** vs it is only once; it is one more time 15) **-du** suff at a particular point in time or space (as seen above this suffix creates impersonal verbs or nouns from adverbs, some of which are based on édu 'it is there, it is the place') ‣ **-n** suff at a particular point in time or space (contracted and adverbial form of -du)

times *prep* **-ȟ** suff derives numerals or verbs into adverbs of time or manner (indicates multiplication when used with numerals)

tip *n* **cą'íkpa** n treetop; end, tip of a stick

tipi *n* 1) **wi'óti ; wiyóti** n tipi, dwelling, lodge 2) **tipésto** n pointed tipi 3) **ticé** n top part of a tipi where the poles are tied up 4) **wi'ówa** n painted tipi 5) **witága** n large tipi

tire *n* **amógiyą hú** cp car tire, wheel

tired *adj v* 1) **stustÁ** vs s/he/it is tired ‣ **stustéyA** vt1 s/he tires sb 2) **astústagA** vs s/he/it is rather tired ‣ **astústagen** adv kind of tired 3) **ǧa'ít'eyA** vt1-caus s/he exhausts, tires sb out, make sb be out of breath

to *prep adv* 1) **ektá** post at, in, to a location or destination ‣ **ektáktaš** post-redup at, in, to various locations or destinations; wherever 2) **én** post in, into, on, onto, at, to; here, there

3) **é-** pref to, at, there, toward, in this direction; they (marks the collective plural form of some intransitive verbs) 4) **-bi** encl marker of a subordinate clause (like English to in "I like to swim") 5) **-kiyA** suff to, for 6) **-gi-** prefix-infix to, for, of (marker of dative verbs; used when the action is directed to or intended for somebody else)

toast *n* **aǧúyabisaga** n toast

tobacco *n* 1) **cąní** n tobacco ‣ **cąní sudá** cp twisted tobacco 2) **cąníyatabi** n chewing tobacco 3) **wahpé cąní** cp kinnikinnick 4) **iyúhibi** n tobacco mixed with red willow (used in ceremonies)

tobacco plant *cp* **cąníhu** n tobacco plant

tobacco tie *cp* **cąnípahta** n tobacco tie

today *adv* 1) **ąba nén ; ąba né** adv today; this day 2) **ąbédu nén** adv today; this day

toe *n* 1) **sipá** n toe, toes 2) **sipátąga** n big toe, big toes

toenail *n* **sipášage** n toenail *Syn:* **sišáge**

together *adv adj* 1) **bağé** adv together, bunched up, as a group 2) **sakím** adv together, joined 3) **iyúha** adv as a group, together 4) **iyákne** post together with 5) **íci-** pref together ‣ **ícigaška** vt1 s/he ties sb, smth together ‣ **íciyuhana** adv everybody, all the people together

toilet paper *cp* **uzíkpakįdA** vi1-pos, n s/he wipes his/her own buttocks; toilet paper

tomato *n* **ozíkta ; ozíkta tága ; ozítka ; ozítka tága** n rosehip; tomato

tomboy *n* **wįcá'įc'ina** vs3-refl, n she thinks she is a man; tomboy

tomorrow *n adv* **hąyákeji** adv tomorrow

ton *n* **ok'į** n ton, a full load

tongue *n* 1) **ceží** n tongue; gun trigger 2) **i'éknašna** vi1 s/he had a slip of the tongue, misspoke

too *adv* 1) **eháš** adv too much, exceedingly; surely, quite 2) **kó** conj also, too, even ‣ **kóko** conj-redup even them; they too 3) **íš** pro s/he, it, they too, as well ‣ **né'įš** adv this, these too; this one, these ones too ‣ **žé'įš** adv that, those too; that one, those ones too

tooth *n* 1) **hí** n tooth ‣ **hímaza** n gold tooth ‣ **hícona** vs s/he/it is toothless 2) **ya-** pref indicates that the action is done with the teeth or mouth, and by extension by speech

toothless *adj* **hícona** vs s/he/it is toothless

top *n* **agán ; agám** post on top of smth, on smth ‣ **agánya** adv on, upon, on the top of smth ‣ **agámpadaha** adv from, on the top of it

toss *v* **hiyúkiyA** vt1-caus s/he tosses, sends sb, smth here to him/her; sends sb here

touch *v n* **bažíba** vt1 s/he pokes, touches sb, smth lightly

touchy *adj* **wasáza** vs s/he/it is touchy, ill-tempered

toward *prep adj* 1) **iyóptaya** adv toward; in the right way, properly 2a) **-giya** suff toward; X by X, in a number of ways, directions, locations 2b) **-takiya ; -kiya** suff toward 3) **é-** pref to, at, there, toward, in this direction

towel *n* **idé'įbakįda ; idébakįde** n towel

town *n* 1) **ti'óda** n town, village 2) **o'énaží** n town, station 3) **otúwe** n city

toy *n* **wó'įškada ; wó'įškade** n toy, teddy bear

track *n v* 1) **oyé** n track, animal tracks ‣ **oyébi** n-pl tracks ‣ **bis'óye** n mouse, gopher tracks ‣ **maštín oyé** cp rabbit tracks ‣ **pte'óye** n buffalo tracks ‣ **šųk'óye** n horse, dog tracks ‣ **táhca oyé** cp deer tracks ‣ **ziktán oyé** cp bird tracks 2) **máza ocágu** cp train track 3) **tapÁ** vt1 s/he follows, pursues, tracks sb, smth ‣ **maštítapA** vi1 s/he follows, pursues, tracks rabbits 4) **oyé'opA** vi1 s/he tracking sb, smth; follows the tracks of sb, smth

tractor *n* 1) **wádapa** n tractor 2) **makóce įkúwa** cp tractor

trade *v n* 1a) **íciyopeyA** vt1 s/he trades, exchanges smth ‣ **íciyopegiciyabi** vi1-recip they barter, trade with one another ‣ **íciyopekiyA** vt1 s/he trades smth for it 1b) **íciyopeyabi** n exchange, trade

trading post *cp* 1a) **opégitu̜ tíbi** cp trading post 1b) **Wašíju opégitu̜bi** cp trading post

trail *n* 1) **cągú** n path, trail ‣ **ocągúna** n path, trail 2) **cąwóhocągu** n trail in the woods 3) **ocágu i̜štámniğe** cp trail of tears (refers to the hardships that occurred during the relocation of the Western Nakoda in eastern Saskatchewan after the Cypress Hills massacre of 1873)

Trailblazer *nprop* **Cągúgağe** nprop Trailblazer or Pathmaker (traditional name of Chief Dan Kennedy, father-in-law of Wilma Kennedy)

trailblazer *n* **cągúgağe** n trailblazer

trailer *n* **cągáȟage** n trailer of a warbonnet

trailer house *cp* **tíbi tokšú** cp trailer house

train₁ *v* 1) **iyáksamkiyA** vt1-caus s/he trains an animal (horse, dog) 2) **ga'úspe** vt1 s/he trains an animal with a tool, stick

train₂ *n* 1) **wáda** n canoe, boat, ship; train, engine 2) **mázawada** n train

train station *cp* **wadó'i̜naži̜** n train station

transparent *adj* 1) **žąžą́** vs s/he/it is transparent 2) **kosąc ną'í̜** vi1 it is transparent, sheer

translate *v* **iyéska** vi1 s/he interprets, translates, converses ‣ **iyégijiska** vt1-benef s/he interprets, translates for sb

transparent *adj* 1) **kosąc ną'í** vi1 it is transparent, sheer 2) **mnézA** vs it is clear, pure, transparent 3) **zązą́** vs it is thin, transparent

trap *v n* 1a) **yaȟtákyA** vt1-caus s/he traps 1b) **i̜yáȟtage, i̜yáȟtakiya** n trap

trapper *n* **wakmúges'a** n trapper

trash *n v* **owógana** n trash pile See: **junk**

travois *n* **cuwíc'iba** n travois

treat *v n* 1) **kuwá** vt1 s/he/it chases, hunts, goes after sb, smth; s/he treats, acts toward, cares for sb, smth ‣ **gicúwa** vt1-pos s/he treats, acts toward, cares for his/her own 2) **yuhÁ ; i̜knúhA** vt2; adv, vi3-refl s/he has, possesses smth; s/he carries sb, smth; s/he gave birth to a child;

s/he holds smth (meeting, ceremony); s/he keeps, looks after, treats sb, smth; carry, hold, have with one (precedes verbs of traveling), s/he keeps himself/herself in a certain state; cares for himself/herself

Treaty Day *cp* **Maswí̜cak'ubi ą́ba** cp Treaty Day

tree *n* 1) **cą́** n tree; wood; stick ‣ **cąwą́gan** adv up in a tree 2) **cą́šeja** n dead tree 3) **cąpáhu** n cherry tree

Tree dweller *cp* **Cą́'ótina** nprop Tree dweller (dwarf that lives in the forest)

treetop *n* **cą́'i̜kpa** n treetop; end, tip of a stick

triangle *n adj* **o'í̜pa yámni** cp triangle

tribal agency *cp* **owákpamni ; owókpamni** n tribal agency, rations house

tribe *n* 1) **wi̜cášta** n man, adult male; person (of both sexes), people (both in the singular and plural); tribe (collective plural) 2) **oyáde** n tribe, people, nation

trigger *n* **ceží** n tongue; gun trigger

trill *v n* **cehúbaknakna** vi1-redup s/he trills

trim *v* 1) **ayútita** vt2 s/he trims smth (edges of a piece of cloth); sticks different pieces on smth 2) **yuksÁ** vt1 s/he cuts, trims smth off with a tool (like scissors)

trip *v* 1) **hugáše** vs s/he stumbles, trips over ‣ **hugášeyA** vt1-caus s/he trips sb 2) **ȟijáhą** vs s/he trips, stumbles on smth and falls ‣ **ȟijáheyA** vt1-caus s/he make sb trip, stumble

tripe *n* **taníğa** n tripe of an animal

triplets *n* **cekpá yámni** cp triplets

trot *v* 1) **nawą́kwąga** vi1-redup it (horse) trots ‣ **nawą́kkiyA** vt1-caus s/he/it makes it trot, run off 2) **yucába** vi2 it (horse) trots ‣ **yucápcaba** vi2-redup it (horse) trots along

trouble *v n* 1) **wósijA** vi1-abs, n s/he causes trouble, does bad things; something bad, evil, disastrous ‣ **wósijeya** adv acting problematically, troublesome 2) **wa'í̜ksamkiyA** vi1-abs s/he pesters, causes trouble; is bothersome

truck *n* **i̧wátokšu** (CTK) ; **otókšu** ; **tokšú** (PR, OM) n truck, pickup truck, large vehicle ‣ **i̧wátokšu tága** cp large truck (like a trailer van)

true *adj* 1) **wi̧jákA** vi1, vs s/he tells the truth; it is true 2) **có** n truth, true

truth *n* 1a) **wi̧jákA; coh̃wíjakA** vi1, vs, vi1 s/he tells the truth; it is true, s/he tells the real truth 1b) **wi̧jákabi** n truth 2a) **có** n truth, true 2b) **cógA** vs, n s/he is honest; truth, honesty 2c) **cóh̃ti̧yA** vs, n s/he/it is very honest; it is the truth; truth

truthfully *adv* **wi̧jákeya** adv truthfully, honestly, truly

try *v n* 1) **i̧yútA** vt2 s/he tests, tries, measures smth (food, drink, clothes, task) ‣ **i̧gíjiyutA** vt1-benef s/he tries, measures, tastes sb else's ‣ **i̧knútA** vi3-refl s/he tries for, practices at smth (activity, sport); rehearses smth (speech, play) 2) **šką́** vt1, vi1 s/he tries to do smth; s/he is busy 3) **adą́ka** vi1 s/he tries hard

T-shirt *cp* **zizíbena cuwíknąga** cp T-shirt

tuberculosis *n* 1) **cağúsija** n tuberculosis 2) **cağúyazą** n tuberculosis

Tuesday *n* **ába i̧núba** cp Tuesday

turkey *n* 1) **pah̃ní agástaga** ; **pasú agástaga** cp turkey 2) **tahúša** n turkey 3) **pah̃núda** n turkey

turkey vulture *cp* **hejá** n buzzard, turkey vulture

turn *v n* 1) **ptąyÁ** vi1 s/he turns over 2) **aptáyÁ** vs s/he/it turns over, capsizes; is upside 3) **naptáyÁ** vt1 s/he turns smth over with the foot 4) **yuptáyÁ** vt2 s/he turns smth over manually ‣ **i̧knúptąyÁ** vi1-refl s/he rolls, turns himself/herself over 5) **yuhómni** vt2 s/he rotates, turns sb, smth around ‣ **i̧knúhomni** vi3-refl s/he turns himself/herself around 6) **i̧knáhomni** vi3-refl s/he turns himself/herself around 7) **yu'ót'i̧za** vt2 s/he twists, turns in smth tightly (like a lid)

turn into *ph* 1) **i̧c'íjağA** vi3-refl s/he makes smth for himself/herself; s/he turns himself/herself into sb, smth 2) **hiyú** vi1, vs s/he departs,

is setting to come here from there; it begins, appears, arises, turns into smth

turn off *v* 1) **natága** vt1 s/he closes, locks, shuts smth; it (wind) closes it; turns it off 2) **yusní** vt2 s/he turns, dims smth off manually (heat, gas)

turn on *v* 1) **yu'í̧ktų, yu'í̧tkų** vt1 s/he/it lights, turns smth on (light, stove, fire) 2) **yekíyA** vt1-dat, vt1 s/he sends sb, smth away to sb; s/he starts, turns smth on (car, engine)

turnip *n* **típšina** ; **típsina** n wild turnip, turnip

turtle *n* 1) **keyá** n snapping turtle 2) **patką́šana** ; **patkášina** n slough turtle

tusk *n* **hiské** n tusk

twelve *adj n* **agénuba** num twelve

twenty *num* **wikcémna núba** num twenty

twice *adv* **númnubanah̃** *adv-redup* only twice

twig *n* **cąsága** n twig

twin *n adj* 1) **cekpábina** n-pl twins 2) **gicí kpą́bi** cp twins 3) **núbabina** ; **núbabi** n-pl twins 4) **wi̧cátuga** vt1 she bears twins, triplets

twist *v n* 1) **bemní** vs s/he/it is twisted, crooked 2) **yubémni** vt2 s/he twists smth manually 3) **yubéhą** vt2 s/he twists, rolls smth (rope, tobacco) 4) **yu'ót'i̧za** vt2 s/he twists, turns in smth tightly (like a lid)

two *adj pron n* 1) **núba** num, vs two; s/he/it is two; there are two ‣ **núm-** cont two ‣ **númnana** num only two ‣ **númnanah̃** adv only two ‣ **núbagiya** adv two by two; in two ways, in two different directions, locations 2) **newós** pro, dem these two 3) **žewós** pro, dem those two 4) **gawós** pro, dem those two yonder 5) **sakípa** adv two of something 6) **ki-** pref two, in two; separated in the middle; evenly

two by two *ph* **núbagiya** adv two by two, in two ways, in two different directions, locations

two-legged *adj* **wahú núba** cp two-legged creature

U

udder *n* **azé** n breast, udder

ugly *adj* 1) **síjA** vs s/he/it is bad, hard, difficult, harmful, unpleasant; s/he/it is ugly ‣ **sin- ; šin- ; sij-** vcont bad 2) **síjena** n, vs ugly person; s/he is ugly 3) **wihíniknaga** vs s/he/it is ugly

uh *interj* **núške** interj uh (hesitation marker)

Ukrainian *nprop See:* **German**

unbearably *adj* **waš'áke** adv unbearably

uncle *n* 1) **adéna** n my uncle (father's brother; mother's sister's husband; father's sister's husband) 2) **-nekši-** root uncle (mother's brother; father's sister's husband) 3) **aktúguna** n his/her uncle (father's brother); stepfather

uncoil *v* **yukcá** vt2 s/he uncoils, unravels smth manually ‣ **knukcá** vt1-pos s/he undoes his/her own braids ‣ **yukcákca** vt2-redup s/he keeps on uncoiling, unraveling smth manually

uncomfortable *adj* **oškášijA** vs s/he feels uneasy, uncomfortable

uncovered *adj* **šnayá** vi it shows; is visible, uncovered, bare

undecided *adj* **tawácį núba** vs s/he is undecided

under *prep* 1) **íhokun** adv under, underneath smth 2) **mahén** adv-cont, post inside, in, within; under, underneath ‣ **caȟmáhen** adv under ice ‣ **wamáhen** adv under the snow ‣ **mąkámahen** adv underground; under the ground; below the surface of the earth 3) **mahéyįgA** vi3 s/he/it hides under

underground *adj adv* **mąkámahen** adv underground; under the ground; below the surface of the earth

underneath *prep adv See:* **under**

understand *v* 1) **ogáȟniğA** vt1 s/he understands sb, smth 2) **osnóhyA** vt1 s/he understands smth; be knowledgeable about smth 3) **nagíciȟ'ųbi** vi1-recip they hear, understand one another 4) **gaspéya** vt1-caus s/he understands sb, smth (archaic)

underwear *n* 1) **mahén ǫ́bi** cp underwear 2) **mahén huská** cp long johns, thermal underwear

undress *v* 1) **įknúšnogA** vi3-refl s/he undresses himself/herself; takes off his/her clothes 2) **yužúžu ; įknúžužu** vt2, vi3-refl s/he undresses sb, takes smth apart, s/he undresses himself/herself

uneasy *adj* 1) **oškášijA** vs s/he feels uneasy, uncomfortable ‣ **oškášinyA** vt1-caus s/he makes sb feel uneasy, uncomfortable 2) **watókąkna** vii-abs s/he feels uneasy around strangers

unexpectedly *adv* **awánuȟ** adv unexpectedly, as it happens

United States of America *ngeo* 1) **Cągúsam** ngeo United States of America; Canada 2) **Tųgášina makóce** ngeo United States of America

universe *n* **iyúhana ówąja** cp universe

university *n* **wayáwa tágaȟtįyą** cp university

untie *v* **yušká** vt2 s/he unties, detaches smth ‣ **gíjiyuška** vt1-benef s/he unties, detaches sb, smth for him/her

up *prep* 1) **wągám** adv up high, above, upright ‣ **cawągan** adv up in a tree 2) **wągáduwa** adv way above, way up there 3) **giktá** vii s/he gets up (from bed)

uphill *adv* **wągámkiya** adv uphill, upward

upright *adj* 1) **mosnádA** vs s/he/it is upright ‣ **mosnán** adv upright, straight 2) **yuwągan** adv pulled up, upright

upside down *adv* **oknápšįyą** adv on the stomach; upside down

urinate *v* 1) **nédžA** vii, n s/he/it urinates; urine (occurs mostly in compounds) 2) **anédžA** vt1 s/he urinates on smth 3) **onédžA** vt1 s/he urinates in smth; pees in bed 4) **wíduka** vs s/he relieves himself/herself (urinate, defecate); uses the bathroom

urine *n* 1) **nédžA** vii, n s/he urinates; urine (occurs mostly in compounds) ‣ **onédžA** vt1 s/he urinates on/in smth; pees in bed 2) **nežémna** vs s/he/it smells urine

us *pro* 1a) -**ų̇**- . . .-**bi** ; -**ųg**- . . .-**bi** circumfix we (1st person plural; subject of active and stative verbs); us (1st person plural, patient of transitive verbs) 1b) -**ų̇**- ; -**ųg**- prefix-infix we two (1st person dual; subject of active and stative verbs); us two (1st person dual, patient of transitive verbs)

use *v n* 1) **wíyų** vt1 s/he uses smth 2) **ų̇** vt3 s/he uses smth ‣ **ų́na** vt3 s/he uses smth small; s/he/it (baby, child) wears smth ‣ **gíji'ų** vt1-benef s/he wears sb else's own; s/he uses sb else's own 3) **ús** ; **ų̇** post using it, with it, because of it (occurs after the word for the thing or body part used) 4) **yusódA** vt2 s/he uses smth up

using *v* **ús** ; **ų̇** post using it, with it, because of it (occurs after the word for the thing or body part used)

uvula *n* **cežížina** n-redup uvula

V

vacant *adj* **oká̇** n aisle, narrow path; vacant place

vagina *n* **šá̇** n vagina ‣ **šahí̇** n woman's pubic hair ‣ **šamná** vs her vagina smells

Valentine's Day *cp* **Cą́déwašte á̇ba** cp Valentine's Day

valuable *adj* **yupíya** vs, adv it is valuable; well, in a good skillful manner; nicely ‣ **yupípiya** adv-redup very well

value *n v* **wótehina** n value, object of love or admiration

vegetation *n* **wó'ı̇cağe** n vegetation

vein *n* 1) **ká̇** n vein, tendon, artery; muscle; gristle ‣ **namká́** n vein of the wrist 2) **kątá̇ga** n large artery 3) **ká̇jusina** small vein 4) **wé'opta** n vein, artery 5) **ká̇gakpa** vi1 s/he taps on a vein

venison *n* **táhcitano** n venison

Venus *nprop* 1) **wı̇cáȟpi éstenaȟ** ph Venus 2) **á̇ba ú wı̇cáȟpi** cp morning star, Venus

very *adj adv* 1) **nína** adv very; really, a lot, intense, intensively; always; not at all, not really (followed by a negative verb) 3) **wiyéknaši̇** adv very, a lot 2) -**ȟ** suff absolutely, the very X, exactly, specifically, at all (marks focus on demonstratives, nouns, pronouns, and negative interrogative pronouns); very, really (intensifer of gradable expressions such as manner and time adverbs; occurs obligatory with the degree adverb nína 'very' in negative clauses)

vest *n* **oknécona** n sleeveless vest

vicious *adj* 1) **wó'išijA** vs s/he/it is vicious, terrible 2) **owéšijA** vs s/he/it is mean, vicious

Victoria Day *cp* **Hų̇kwíyą ta'á̇ba** cp Victoria Day

vigorous *adj* **wanítA** vs s/he is vigorous, industrious, ambitious

village *n* **wı̇cóti** n village

vinegar *n* **miní tutá** cp vinegar

violin *n* 1) **ı̇wábagı̇za** ; **cą̇wábazije** n violin 2) **ı̇bágı̇za** ; **ı̇bázije** n violin, fiddle

visible *adj* 1) **tą'í̇** vs s/he/it is visible, apparent; famous ‣ **tą'íyą** adv in sight, visible 2) **šnayá** vi it shows; is visible, uncovered, bare

vision *n* 1a) **wíhamnA** vi1-abs s/he dreams about things; has a vision 1b) **wı̇hámne, ı̇hámnabi** n dream, vision 2) **wı̇hámnas'a** n someone who has visions; dreamer 3) **waká̇ í** vi1 s/he went for a vision quest

visit *v n* **timáni** vi1 s/he visits ‣ **timágini** vt1-pos s/he visits his/her relative, or sb else's relatives

voice *n* 1) **hó** n, vi1 voice; it (canine) howls ‣ **wı̇cóho** n human voice ‣ **hócącą** vs s/he has a trembling voice ‣ **hóȟna** vs s/he has a coarse, rattling voice ‣ **hónisko** vs s/he has a loud voice; has a voice as loud as this ‣ **hótąga** vs s/he has a loud voice ‣ **hoyáȟnana** vi2 s/he has a raspy voice ‣ **hóyapsąpsą** vi1 s/he talks with a trembling voice 2) **hotų̇** vi1 it (animal) makes a distinctive cry 3) **hóyegiyA** vt1 s/he sends a message to sb; sends a voice to sb (as in a prayer) 4) **ho'íyegiyA** vt1-pos s/he recognizes sb's voice 5) **-niyą** suff loudly, with a loud voice, audibly (mostly used with verbs for singing, crying, speaking, etc.)

vomit *v n* **knébA** vi1 s/he vomits ‣ **knem-** vcont vomiting ‣ **knemkíyA** vt1-caus s/he/it makes sb vomit ‣ **knem'íc'iyA** vi3-refl s/he made himself/herself vomit ‣ **įknúknebA** vi3-refl s/he makes himself/herself vomit

vote *v n* 1) **gahníǧA** vt1 s/he selects, chooses sb, smth; elects, votes for sb 2) **cažé k'ú** vt1 s/he votes for sb 3) **cažé ópegiyA** vi1-pos s/he votes, puts his/her name down to become a member; enrolls in an organization 4) **cažé iyóhpegiyA** vi1-pos s/he votes

W

waggle *v n* 1) **nąpsápsą** vi1-redup s/he/it waggles smth 2) **sijúpsąpsą** vi1-redup it (dog) waggles its tail

wagon *n* **cąbákmįkma** n wagon ‣ **cąbákmįkma įyóknąga** cp wagon box ‣ **cąbákmįkma okíyabi** cp covered wagon

waist *n* **cuwí** n waist, chest; body (animals and humans)

wait *v n* 1) **iyápe; iyágipe** vt1, vt1-dat, vt1-pos s/he lies waiting for sb; ambushes sb, s/he waits for sb, smth; s/he waits for his/her own ‣ **iyágicipebi** vi1-recip they wait for one another 2) **apéya** adv in a waiting manner 3) **wa'ápe** vi1-abs s/he waits for things, people 4) **wį'íyape** vi1 he is waiting for her, stalking her 5) **hinąga** vimper Wait! Hold on!

wake₁ *n* **a'ábayabi** vi1-pass, n it is a funeral wake after the death of sb; funeral wake after a death

wake₂ *v* 1) **oǧúǧA** vs s/he/it is awake; wakes up 2) **yumnézA** vt2 s/he rouses, wakes sb up ‣ **knumnézA** vt1-pos s/he wakes up his/her own out of a drowsing, nap 3) **yuhíja** vt2 s/he wakes sb up by pushing or shaking 4) **yugíkta** vt2 s/he gets sb up manually; wakes sb up 5) **giní**

vi1 s/he comes back to life, wakes up (from hibernation)

walk *v n* 1) **maní ; máni** vi1 s/he walks; s/he progresses, behaves as such in life (used after an adverb); s/he accompanies, walks with sb ‣ **knuhá máni** vi1 s/he walks carrying his/her own ‣ **yuhá máni** vi1 s/he walks carrying smth ‣ **hąmáni** vi1 s/he walks at night ‣ **hą'ómani** vi1 s/he/it walks around, travels at night ‣ **ąm'ómani** vi1 s/he/it walks around, travels during the day ‣ **ųzímani** vi1 s/he walks backward 2) **amáni** vt1 s/he walks on smth 3) **ománi** vi1 s/he goes for a walk, travels, wanders ‣ **ománini** vi1-redup s/he walks around 4) **na- ; ną-** pref by kicking, stepping, walking (forms active verbs); by internal force, heat; by itself (forms impersonal or stative verbs)

wander *v* **iyázagen** adv in succession, one after the other; wandering

want *v* 1) **cįgÁ ; cígA** vt1 s/he wants, desires smth; is inclined to smth ‣ **gicígA** vt1-pos s/he wants his/her own thing 2) **aktášį** vt1 s/he rejects, does not want, disowns sb

war *n* 1) **zuyÁ** vi1, adv s/he goes on the warpath; going on the warpath (used before verbs of going) 2) **zuyé í** vi1 s/he went to war 3) **zuyéyabi** n war party 4) **nadą́ í** vi1 s/he went on a raid, to war 5) **ogíciza, ogícizabi, ogícize** n war, battle

warbonnet *n* 1) **wíyaga wapáha** cp feather hat, warbonnet 2) **wíyaga wapáha sįdé yuké** ph warbonnet with trailer

warehouse *n* **dágu giknąga tíbi** cp warehouse

warm *adj v* 1) **cóza** vs s/he/it is warm ‣ **cosyÁ** vt1-caus s/he warms up smth ‣ **coskíyA** vt1-pos s/he warms his/her own (feet, hand) ‣ **cos'íc'iyA** vi3-refl s/he warms himself/herself 2) **akádeja** vs it is kind of warm 3) **kádagen** adv kind of warm 4) **amáštagejA** vs it is kind of warm

warmly *adj* **cosyá** adv warmly

warrior *n* **zuyés'a** n warrior ‣ **zuyés'a tíbi** cp warrior lodge society

wart *n* **hucéšpu** n, vs wart, growth; s/he/it has a wart

wash *v* 1) **bažáža** vt1 s/he washes sb, smth by rubbing ‣ **įkpážaža** vi3-refl s/he washes himself/herself by rubbing 2) **yužáža** vt2 s/he washes sb, smth by scrubbing ‣ **wayúžaža** vi2-abs s/he washes things by scrubbing, does laundry ‣ **gíjiyužaža** vt1-benef s/he washes sb, smth for him/her ‣ **yužážakiyA** vt1-caus s/he makes sb wash smth ‣ **knužáža** vt1-pos s/he washes his/her own thing ‣ **įknúžaža** vi3-refl s/he washes, bathes himself/herself 3) **wóžaža** vi1-abs s/he washes things

washbasin *n* **o'įknužaža** n bathroom; washbasin, sink

washboard *n* 1) **įwábažáža** n washboard 2) **įbáskije** n washboard

washed away *ph* **įžáža** vi it is washed away

washtub *n* **owážaža** n washtub

wasp *n* See: **bumblebee**

waste *v n* 1) **maskásodA** vi1 s/he wastes money 2) **yusódA** vt2 s/he wastes, spends, uses smth up (money, supplies) 3) **dágecųšį** vs nothing is done, it is a waste of time

watch *v n* 1) **awáyagA** vt2 s/he cares, watches, looks after sb, smth ‣ **awágijiknagA** vt1-benef s/he watches, cares for sb, smth for him/her ‣ **awįcawąyagA** vt1-coll s/he watches over people, babysits children ‣ **awáknagA** vt1-pos s/he cares, watches over his/her own ‣ **awágiciyagabi** vi1-recip they watch, care for one another 2) **wópaȟtA** vi1-abs s/he watches people, things, a game

water *n v* 1) **miní** n water ‣ **mni-** cont water, liquid, alcohol ‣ **mnicáǧa** n frozen water ‣ **mnicógan** adv in the water ‣ **mnigákna** adv beside the water, at the shore ‣ **miníkta** adv in, to the water ‣ **miníkada** n hot water ‣ **mnísni** n cold water ‣ **wámini** n snow water

2) **miníwaką** n Holy water; whisky 3) **miník'u** vt1 s/he waters an animal ‣ **šųkmínik'u** vi1 s/he waters horses 4) **abápsų** vt1 s/he pours a liquid on sb, smth; waters smth

water blister *cp* **miní ožúna** vs it is a water blister

water willow *cp* **cąságena** n water willow

waterfall *n* 1) **šošéna** n waterfall 2) **miníȟaȟa** n waterfall

watering hole *cp* 1) **ošųkminik'u** n watering hole for horses, cattle 2) **omníhiyohi** n watering place

watermelon *n* **špášį yúdabi** cp watermelon

watersnake *n* **minísnohena** n watersnake

wave *v* 1) **góza** vt1 s/he waves, swings sb, smth ‣ **goskós** vcont waving, swinging, flapping smth ‣ **goskóza** vt1-redup s/he/it waves, swings, flaps smth (as bird) 2) **napkáwįwį** vi1-redup s/he waves at sb ‣ **namgícigawįwįbi** vi1-recip they wave at one another ‣ **namgíjawįwį** vt1-dat s/he waves at sb

way *n*

METHOD, STYLE, MANNER

1a) **ecén** adv, conj in the right, original way; accordingly; thus then, and then, so 1b) **nécen** adv in this way, like this, as such 1c) **gáken** adv in that way 1d) **žécen** conj, adv so, thus, then; in this way, as such, in a given style ‣ **žéceȟ** adv exactly in that way ‣ **žéceduȟ** adv exactly in that way 2) **-bas** suff in that way, manner; of that kind, like that kind

IT IS SOME/WHAT WAY

3a) **ecédu** vs, adv s/he/it is like this, it happens as such, it is the right way; equally, the same way, the right way ‣ **ecédušį** vs ; adv it is an uncommon way, not the way it is supposed to be; in an uncommon way, not the way it is supposed to be 3b) **nécedu** adv, vs in this way; s/he/it is like this 3c) **žécedu** adv, vs in the correct way, thus, like that; it is like that, it happened like that

DIRECTION

4a) **nedám** *adv* this way (toward the speaker)
4b) **žedám** *adv* that way (away from speaker) 5)
žéciyota *adv* that way 6) **-giya** *suff* toward; X
by X, in a number of ways, directions, locations

way of life *np* **wįcóȟ'aǧe** n way of life, culture,
tradition

we *pro* 1a) **-ų- . . .-bi ; -ųg- . . .-bi** circumfix we
(1st person plural; subject of active and sta-
tive verbs); us (1st person plural, patient of
transitive verbs) 1b) **-ų- ; -ųg-** prefix-infix we
two (1st person dual; subject of active and stative verbs); us two (1st person dual, patient of
transitive verbs)

weak *v adj* 1) **mnihášį** vs s/he/it is weak 2) **dogíš
ú** vi1 s/he/it is weak from an illness 3) **cǎdé
ogíhišį** vii s/he has a weak heart; s/he cannot make it

wealthy *adj* 1a) **mastúǧa** vs s/he is rich, wealthy
1b) **mastúbiga** n-pl wealthy, rich people 2a)
masyúheja vs s/he has money; is wealthy 2b)
wayúheja vi2-abs s/he is wealthy 3) **ohídiga**
vii, vs s/he is brave, fearless; s/he is a wealthy,
prosperous person

wean *adj* **azíǧicuni** vs1 s/he is weaned ›
azíǧicunikiyA ; azíkiyagicuni vt1-caus she
weans a baby

weapon *n* 1) **įkúde** n weapon, something one
shoots with (bow, crossbow, gun) 2) **wípena**
n weapon

wear *v* 1) **ú** vt3 s/he wears smth › **gic'ú** vt1-pos s/
he wears his/her own (clothes, jewelry) › **ųkíyA**
vt1-caus s/he makes sb wear smth 2) **úna** vt3 s/
he uses smth small; s/he/it (baby, child) wears
smth 3) **į** vt1 s/he wears smth on the shoulder
› **įkíyA** vt1-caus s/he makes him/her wear it
on the shoulders 4) **nap'í** vt1 s/he wears smth
on the neck › **nap'íkiyA** vt1-caus s/he makes
sb wear it around the neck; puts smth around
sb's neck 5) **ohǍ** vt1 s/he wears a shoe › **ogíhǍ**
vt1-pos s/he wears his/her own footwear 6) **tú**

vt1 s/he wears, puts smth on; s/he bears smth
(is in a relation); she bears a child, gives birth ›
gítų vt1-pos s/he wears smth his/her clothes or
smth over the upper body part (shawl, glasses,
mask) 7) **coknákkitų** vt1-pos s/he wears his/
her breechcloth 8) **babódA** vt1 s/he wears out
a piece of clothing 9) **mokúka** vt1 s/he shoots
and makes holes in smth; s/he wears smth out
10) **nagíkuka** vt1-pos s/he wears out his/her
thing by walking (like shoes) 11) **nazúda** vt1 s/
he wears smth down 12) **yutéba** vt2 s/he wears
smth out (as a knife blade) 13) **nąbóda** vt1 s/he
wears smth out with the feet

weasel *n* 1) **įtúgasą** n weasel › **įtúgasąskana** n
white weasel (winter time) › **įtúgasązina** n
brown weasel (summer time)

wedding *n* **gicíknuzabi** n, vii-recip wedding;
they marry within their own (people, kind)

Wednesday *n* **ába įyámni** cp Wednesday

weed *v n* 1) **yukmí** vt2 s/he pulls out plants from
the ground; weeds smth 2) **peží wįtkó** cp marijuana, cannabis

week *n* **ábawaką wąží** cp week

weird *adj* See: **odd**

weld *v* See: **solder**

well₁ *adj* **dąyá ; dayá** vs s/he/it is well, good,
all right; is in good health (after an illness)
› **dąyána** vs s/he/it (small thing, baby, child)
is well

well₂ *n* **mnik'ábi** n well

west *n adv* 1) **wiyóȟpaye, wiyóȟpeya** n west;
sunset 2) **wiyóȟpeyam** adv in, to the west 3)
wiyóȟpeyada adv at, in the west

westward *adv* **wiyóȟpeyatakiya** adv westward,
toward the west

wet *adj* 1) **ogáȟnogA** vs s/he/it is soaked in
water; is wet › **ogáȟnok** vcont soaked in water
› **ogáȟnokyA** vt1-caus s/he gets smth wet (as
shoes in a puddle) › **ogáȟnokkiyA** vt1-pos
s/he wets his/her own (boots, shoes, coat) ›

ogáȟnok'įc'iyA vi3-refl s/he gets himself/herself wet 2) **totóba** vs it is damp, wet

what *pro adv adj* 1) **dágu** pro, quant, vs thing, something; what; any, none; it is something 2) **dóka'ų ; dókų** vi3-irr s/he/it does what? 3a) **dukté** pro what, which one (of a set) 3b) **duktén** adv where, at what place 4) **dókeduš** adv no matter what, at any rate 5) **dókeja** vs it is a matter, way, kind, concern; what is it like? ▸ **dókejaga** adv what kind

whatever *pro adj adv* 1) **dágugaš** pro whatever, whichever one 2) **dáguga kóšta** pro anything, just anything, whatever, whichever one

wheat *n* **aǧúyabisu** n wheat kernel

wheat binder *cp* **aǧúyabisu įjášna** cp wheat binder

wheel *n* 1) **hú mįmámina ; hú** n wheel ▸ **amógiya hú** cp car tire, wheel 2) **įbákmįkma** n wheel, tire; wheelbarrow

wheelbarrow *n* **įbákmįkma** n wheelbarrow

when *adv conj* 1) **dóhaŋ ; dóhąda** adv when (used with future and hypothetical events) 2) **dóhągeja** adv when, at what time (used with future events) 3) **dóhąc'ehą** adv when (used with past events)

whenever *conj adv* 1) **hádahą** adv whenever, when, when it is the case 2) **štén** conj if when, if then; when, whenever, in, at, on, next

where *adv conj n* 1) **dóki** adv where, where to (used with verbs of coming and going); anywhere, somewhere, to some place (often used with negated verbs) ▸ **dókiya** adv where to (functions like an interrogative stative verb and occurs in sentence-final position) ▸ **dókiyapadahą** adv from where 2) **duktén** adv where, at what place ▸ **duktédahą** adv from where, where ▸ **duktépadahą** adv from where 3) **éduȟ** adv where exactly

wherever *adv conj* 1) **dókiya** adv wherever (followed by a positive verb of movement); anywhere (followed by a negated verb of move-

ment); where to (functions like an interrogative stative verb and occurs in sentence-final position) 2) **duktédugaš** adv wherever, anywhere 3) **ektáktaš** post-redup at, in, to various locations or destinations; wherever

whether *conj pro* **eštá** conj or, either; whether it is the case or not

which *adj pro* 1) **dukté** pro what, which one (of a set) 2) **dukté'ega kóšta** pro any which one, whichever one 3) **dókiyo** adv in which direction, direction, course

whichever *pro adj* 1) **dáguga ; dágugaš** pro whatever, whichever one (usually followed by kóšta) 2) **dukté'ega kóšta** pro any which one, whichever one 3) **duktéyaš** pro whichever one

while *n conj prep* 1) **ecúhą** adv while ▸ **žécuhą** adv while 2) **dókaš** adv maybe, perhaps; in time, in a while, eventually 3) **dohágeȟ** adv after a while ▸ **dohágeȟtiyA** vs it is a while, whenever 4) **otéhągeȟ** adv a while longer 5) **kohą** adv meanwhile, while

whine *v* **zągÁ** vii s/he /it whines ▸ **ząkzágA** vi-redup s/he/it whines

whip *n v* 1) **įjáȟabe** n whip 2) **gapsíde ; įjápsįdena ; įjápsįde** n whip 3) **šųk'įjapšíde** n horse whip 4) **gapsídA** vt1 s/he whips sb, smth ▸ **gapsípsįdA** vt1-redup s/he whips sb, smth repeatedly ▸ **gapsípsįn** vcont whipping sb, smth repeatedly 5) **gasága** vt1 s/he whips sb, smth

whipman *n* **įjáȟabe wįcá** cp whipman

whirlwind *n* 1) **wi'ómni** n twister wind, whirlwind, dust devil 2) **tadé omní tága** ph whirlwind

whiskey *n* **miníwaką** n Holy water; whisky

whisper *v* 1) **ožíži** vii s/he whispers 2) **naȟmána i'á ; naȟmą́ i'á** vii s/he whispers

whistle *n v* 1) **žó** vii, n s/he whistles; whistle ▸ **gíjižo** vt1-benef s/he whistles for him/her ▸ **gižó** vt1-dat s/he whistles at sb ▸ **gicížobi** vii-recip they whistle at one another ▸ **žožó** vi1-

redup s/he/it whistles repeatedly 2) **gažó** vt1, vi, vi1 s/he makes it whistle by spinning; it whistles because of the wind; s/he has diarrhea ‣ **gažóya** adv with a whistling sound 3) **yažó** vi1 s/he/it blows into smth (whistle, instrument) 4) **iyážo** n whistle, eagle bone whistle

whistling *n* **gažóya** adv with a whistling sound

white *adj n* **skána ; ská** vs s/he/it is white ‣ **skaská** vs-redup-pl they are white (inanimate plural) ‣ **skaskána** vs-redup s/he/it is pure white) ‣ **skayÁ** vt1-caus s/he whitens sb, smth; paints, colors, dyes smth in white ‣ **skagíjiyA** vt1-benef s/he paints, colors sb, smth in white for sb ‣ **skagíyA** vt1-pos s/he whiten, paints, colors, dyes his/her own in white ‣ **ska'íc'iyA** vi3-refl s/he whitens, paints himself/herself in white ‣ **skayéna** adv white condition

White Bear *nprop* **Matóska** nprop White Bear (Nakoda chief and signatory of Treaty 4)

White Bear people *nprop* **Įdúgah wįcášta** nprop White Bear people

White Bear reservation (Saskatchewan) *ngeo* **Matóska** n White Bear reservation (Saskatchewan)

Whiteman *nprop* 1) **Wašíju** nprop, vs minor spirit, deity; European people, person of European descent, Caucasian, White man; s/he is of European descent ‣ **Wašín** cont in a White man, European manner; pertaining to White people ‣ **Wašín'įc'ina** vi3-refl s/he behaves like a White person 2) **Haskána ; Haská** nprop person of European or Euro-Canadian descent; White man 3) **Sna'ót'e** nprop half-breed, White man (archaic) 4) **Wasképana** nprop person of European, Euro-Canadian descent, White man (idiolectal)

whiten *v* 1) **skayÁ** vt1 s/he whitens sb, smth ‣ **skagíyA** vt1-pos s/he whitens his/her own white 2) **gaská** vt1 s/he whitens smth by rubbing

who *pro* **duwé** pro, n, vs who; person; s/he is someone ‣ **duwéň** pro who (presupposed by the speaker); somebody (known to the speaker); whoever (unknown to the speaker)

whoever *pro* 1) **duwéň** pro who (presupposed by the speaker); somebody (known to the speaker); whoever (unknown to the speaker) 2) **duwégaš** pro, vs whoever, anybody; whoever s/he is

whooping cough *cp* 1) **hohpábi hą́ska** cp whooping cough 2) **hohpábi téhą** cp whooping cough

why *adv conj n interj* 1) **cén** conj then, so, thus, therefore, because, that is why 2) **dágucen** pro why 3) **žé'ųs** conj that is why, because of that, on account of this, therefore

wide *adj* **otą́gA** vs it is broad, wide

widow *n* **wįwázija** n widow

widower *n* **wįcáwiza ; wįcáwizija** n widower

wife *n* 1) **-tawįju- ; -tawį-** root wife 2) **tawíjutų** vi1, n he has sb for a wife, he is married; married man 3) **tawíyą** vt1 he has her as a wife 4) **wagą́gana, wagą́ga** n-redup elderly woman; my wife (form of address; archaic)

wig *n* **wįcápahagağabi** n wig

wild *adj* **watókna** vs it (animal) is wild, untamed

wild mint *cp* **ceyágadaga ; cayágadaga** n wild mint, peppermint

wild onion *cp* **cąm'ų́zitka ; cąm'ų́zitka įkcéya** n, cp wild onion, onion, wild onion

wildcat *n* **įkmú** n wildcat (generic), lynx

will *modal* **-ktA** encl will, 'll, would (marks a potential event that is not yet realized; when used in the past it indicates a counterfactual event); expresses a suggestion, let us (when occurring with verbs in the 1st person plural **ų**[g]- -bi or dual **ų**[g]-)

willow *n* 1) **cąšáša ; cąšášana** n-redup red willow 2) **cąságena** n water willow 3) **coğážija** n, diamond willow

win *v* **ohíyA** vt1 s/he wins smth (game, contest, battle)

wind *n* 1) **ganúza** vimp, n it is windy; wind ‣ **maštá ganúza** vimp it is a hot wind, like a Chinook wind 2) **ijánuza** vimp there is gust of wind (as when a car passes by) 3) **tadé** n wind 4) **tadéwam** adv facing the wind 5) **gaȟmógA** vs the wind is blowing smth off 6) **waspá** n Chinook wind 9) **uyá** vimp the wind blows this way

windmill *n* **mnijáhomni** n windmill

window *n* **iwáknage** n mirror; window, glass

windy *adj* 1) **ganúza** vimp, n it is windy; wind 2) **tadéyaba ; tadé'aba** vimp it is a windy day

wine *n* **miníšaša** n-redup wine

wing *n* **ȟubáhu** n wing

winner *n* **ohíyes'a** n winner

winter *n v* 1) **waníyedu** n, vimp winter; year (used only in counting the age of someone); it is winter ‣ **wani-** cont winter ‣ **waníȟa** adv last winter ‣ **wanéyasa** adv throughout the winter, all winter 2) **wicógadu** n midwinter 3) **waní ú** vi1 s/he spends the winter somewhere 4) **awédu'ic'iyA** vi3-refl s/he survives winter; s/he stays somewhere during the winter

wipe *v n* 1) **bakídA** vt1 s/he wipes, brushes sb, smth off; cleans the surface of smth ‣ **gíjibakídA** vt1-benef s/he wipes, cleans sb else's (body part) ‣ **kpakídA** vt1-pos s/he wipes his/her own ‣ **uzíkpakídA** vi1-pos, n s/he wipes his/her own buttocks; toilet paper 2) **nagíkídA** vt1-pos s/he scrapes, cleans, wipes his/her own feet

wire *n* **masyúwibi** n metal wire

wisdom *n* **wasnókyA, wasnóhyA** vi1, n s/he is clever, knowledgeable; wisdom

wise *adj* **ksábA** vs s/he is wise, intelligent, prudent ‣ **ksamyágen** adv rather wisely, prudently

wish *v n* 1) **as'í** vt1 s/he wishes for sb, smth ‣ **wa'ás'í** vi1-abs s/he wishes 2) **gú** vt1 s/he desires sb; wishes for sb

with *prep* 1) **gicí** post with sb, smth (single person or object) 2) **óm** post with them 3) **ús ; ú** post using it, with it, because of it (occurs after the word for the thing or body part used)

within *adv prep* **itímahen** adv-post inside of, within an area, enclosure, pasture, field

without *prep adv conj n* 1) **cóna** post; suff without, lacking, deprived of 2) **wódešiya** adv without eating

witness *n* **wayáge** n witness

wolf *n* 1) **šuktógeja** n wolf 2) **šuktógena ; šuktóga** n wolf

Wolf Point (Montana) *ngeo* **Šuktógeja Ébazo** ngeo Wolf Point (Montana)

Wolseley (Saskatchewan) *ngeo* **Ktusyá** ngeo Wolseley (Saskatchewan)

wolverine *n* 1) **mnáza** n wolverine 2) **wíkcena** n wolverine

woman *n* 1) **wíya** n, vs woman; she is a woman ‣ **wi-** cont woman ‣ **-wi** suff woman (in personal names); female (animals) 2) **hukwíya** n queen; queen in playing cards 3) **wiyáteja** n young (new) woman 4) **widáyaga** vs she is a fine woman, lady 5) **wa'úspewiyakiya** n female teacher 6) **Hásaba wíya, Wašíjusaba wíya** cp woman of African or African-American descent 7) **wikóške** n, vs teenage girl, young woman 8) **wikúwa** vi1 he chases, courts, flirts with a woman 9) **witága** vs, n she is a mature woman 10) **wagágana, wagága** n-redup elderly woman; my wife 11a) **wogúgana** n pretty woman 11b) **wiwóguga** n beautiful woman 12) **wiwáštega** n beautiful woman 13) **iškádabi** n woman that is teased sexually 14) **wiȟíknatu** n married woman 15) **watápe wíya** cp elderly woman

womb *n* **tamní** n womb

wonder *n v* 1) **ecí** vt1, vt3 s/he thinks, wonders about smth (used with a preceding quote) 2) **iknígA** vt1 s/he minds, wonders, has regard

for, pays attention to sb, smth; obeys sb 3) **hų́n**
encl I wonder (marker of modality; used when
the speaker does not know the likeliness of
an event) 4) **nahą́nįštaš** part I wonder, I wish
5) **céwąna** encl I wonder ‣ **céwąna:ga** encl I
wondered, I thought

wood *n* 1) **cą́** n tree; wood; stick ‣ **cąbų́bų** vs, n it
is rotten wood; rotten wood ‣ **cątóto, cą́teja** n
green wood 2) **cąné** vii s/he looks for wood ‣
cągíjine vt1-benef s/he gathers firewood for sb
3) **cábağe** n pile of wood 4) **cąk'į́** vii s/he carries wood on the back 5) **cą́ktam** adv toward
the wood 6) **cąmná** vs s/he/it smells like wood

Wood Mountain people *np* **Cą́ȟe wįcášta** nprop
Wood Mountain people (band of Nakoda,
Saskatchewan)

wood tick *cp* 1) **taskákpa** n wood tick 2)
cąwámnuška n wood tick

woodpecker *n* **cągádodona** n woodpecker

woods *n-pl* **cągákna** adv along the woods, on the
edge of the woods

wood stove *n* **cą́ océti** cp wood stove

wool *n* **šųkhį́** n wool

word *n* 1) **wa'ókmabi** n letter, written word,
drawing 2a) **wįcó'i'e** n language, word ‣
Nakón-wįcó'i'e n Nakoda language, word
2b) **wįcó'i'abi** n language, word; letter 3)
wócažeyada n words of a song 4) **woksÁ** vt1
s/he breaks his/her word; betrays sb

work *n v* 1) **wówaši** n job, work, occupation;
workplace; servant, worker ‣ **wówašikiyA** vt1-
caus s/he hires sb; makes sb work 2) **wówaši**
ecų́ vi3 s/he works, does his/her work; she is in
labor ‣ **wówaši ecágiji'ų** vt1-benef s/he works
for sb ‣ **wówaši ecų́kiyA** vt1-caus s/he puts sb
to work; hires sb 4) **wówaši įc'íkni** vi3 s/he
arrives back here looking for work 5) **wó'ecų**
n work, occupation, ceremony

worker *n* **wówaši** n job, work, occupation; workplace; servant, worker

workplace *n* **wówaši** n job, work, occupation;
workplace; servant, worker

world *n* 1) **makówąja** adv all over the world 2)
tadé'ųya n cardinal directions, world quarters

worry *v n* 1) **įníhą** vs s/he fears; is worried ‣
įníhąyĄ vt1-caus s/he/it makes sb worry 2)
įgáği vs s/he is anxious, worried about smth
3) **įgážąga** vs s/he is anxious, worried, bothered because of the lack of smth

worst *adj adv n* **síjeȟtįyĄ** vs s/he/it is the worst,
wildest, meanest, ugliest (used to describe
behavior and appearance)

worth *adj* **-pija** aux it is easy, worth it, feasible,
good to do, -able

worthless *adj* **waȟtéšį** vs s/he/it is worthless

would *modal* **-ktA** encl will, 'll, would (marks a
potential event that is not yet realized; when
used in the past it indicates a counterfactual
event)

wound *v n* 1) **ta'ó** vt1 s/he/it wounds sb, smth 2)
ta'óbi n wound

woven *v* **yuwíbi** n something woven (wire, rope)

wrap *v n* 1) **obémni** vt1 s/he wraps sb, smth in
it ‣ **ogíjibemni** vt1-benef s/he wraps sb, smth
for sb in it ‣ **ogíbemni** vt1-pos s/he wraps his/
her own with it ‣ **o'íc'ibemni; o'íkpemni** vi3-
refl s/he wraps himself/herself in smth 2)
óğe vt1 s/he wraps, covers up smth up with
it 3) **wópiya** vii-abs s/he wraps up things; it is
wrapped 4) **iyápehą** vt1-dit s/he binds, wraps
smth around it

wreck *v n* See: **ruin, destroy**

wren *n* **cayágagana** n wren

wrench *n* **įyúšnoge** n wrench, pliers

wrestle *v* 1a) **kiȟpé ecúbi** vt3-pl they wrestle 1b)
n **kiȟpé ecúbina** cp wrestling match

wretch *n* **waȟtéšį** vs, interj s/he/it is worthless;
Oh the wretch! (uttered when one is ready to
spank a kid)

wrinkled *adj* **bižá** vs s/he/it is wrinkled ‣ **bišpíža** vs-redup s/he/it is wrinkled

wrist *n* **nąkpá** n wrist ‣ **nąkpáhuhu** n wrist bone

write *v* 1) **okmÁ** vt1 s/he writes smth ‣ **ogíjikmA** vt1-benef s/he writes smth for sb ‣ **ogíkmA** vt1-pos, vt1-dat s/he writes, signs his/her own (book, name); s/he writes smth to, for sb 2) **wa'ókmA, wókmA** vi1-abs s/he writes things; s/he has debts, has credit in a store ‣ **wógijikmA** vt1-benef s/he writes to or for him/her

writer *n* **wa'ókmas'a** n writer, author, painter, scribe

wrong *adj* **sijáyA** vi it is wrong

wrongly *adv* **ektášį** adv wrongly

Y

yank *v n* **gazám įȟpéyA** ph s/he yanks smth

yawn *v* **į'óyA ; i'óyayA** vi1-redup, vs s/he yawns

year *n* 1) **ómaka ; omáka** n year ‣ **omáka'esą** adv throughout the year, all year 2) **waníyedu** n winter; year (used only in counting the age of someone) 3) **osní nųba** cp person or animal that is two years old

yearling *n* **osní wąžína** cp yearling (calf)

yeast *n See:* **baking powder**

yellow *adj* 1) **ǧí** vs s/he/it is light yellow ‣ **ǧiǧí** vs-redup-pl they are light brown (inanimate plural) ‣ **ǧiyÁ** vt1-caus s/he paints, colors, dyes smth in brown ‣ **ǧigíjiyA** vt1-benef s/he paints, colors sb, smth in brown for sb ‣ **ǧigíyA** vt1-pos s/he paints, colors, dyes his/her own brown ‣ **ǧi'íc'iyA** vi3-refl s/he paints himself/herself in brown ‣ **ǧiyéna** adv brown condition 2) **ǧíȟtiyĄ** vs s/he/it is deep yellow 3) **zí** vs s/he/it is golden, dark yellow, tan, brown ‣ **zizí** vs-redup they are golden, dark yellow, tan, brown (inanimate plural) ‣ **ziyÁ** vt1 s/he paints, colors, dyes smth in yellow ‣ **zigíjiyA** vt1-benef s/he paints, colors sb, smth in yellow for sb ‣ **zigíyA** vt1-pos s/he paints, colors, dyes his/her own yellow ‣ **zi'íc'iyA** vi3-refl s/he paints himself/herself in yellow, brown, blond ‣ **ziyéna** adv yellow condition

yellow-hooded blackbird *cp* **wapáǧi** n yellow-hooded blackbird

yelp *v* **howáyayA** vi1-redup it (dog) yelps

yes *interj* 1) **hą́** adv, interj yes (both male and female speaker); Hello! (female speaker) 2) **hóka he** adv yes, exclamation when one is eager to do smth (male speaker) 3) **hón** adv, interj yes, all right

yesterday *adv n* **ȟtánihą** adv yesterday

yet *adv conj* 1) **naháĥ** adv still, yet 2) **naháȟtįšį** vs, adv it is not time yet; before time 3) **éyaš** conj but, and yet

yoke *n* **cąknáǧiyą** n neck yoke; drying rack made of two poles and a transversal bar

yolk *n* **wíktaǧi** n yolk

you *pro* 1a) **-ya-** prefix-infix you (2nd person singular, agent/subject of active verbs of Class 1) 1b) **-ya-. . .-bi** circumfix you all (2nd person plural, agent/subject of active verbs of Class 1) 2a) **-n-** prefix-infix you (2nd person singular; agent/subject of active verbs of Class 2 or 3) 2b) **-n-. . .-bi** circumfix you all (2nd person plural, agent/subject of active verbs of Class 1) 3a) **-ni-** prefix-infix you (2nd person singular; subject of stative verbs); you (patient of transitive verbs); your (2nd person singular possessor; body parts and kinship nouns) 3b) **-ni-. . .-bi** circumfix you (2nd person plural, subject of stative verbs); you (patient of transitive verbs); your (2nd person plural possessor; body parts and kinship nouns) 4a) **-ci-** prefix I . . . you (marker of 1st person singular agent acting on 2nd person patient of transitive verbs) 4b) **-ci-. . .-bi** circumfix I . . . you all

(marker of 1st person singular agent acting on 2nd person plural patient of transitive verbs)

young *adj* 1) **téjana ; téja** vs s/he/it is young (humans, animals); it is new (things) 2) **watéjaga** vs s/he is young and strong *See:* **man; woman**

younger *adj* **įhágapa** vs s/he/it is younger than sb

your *adj* 1a) **-ni-** prefix-infix you (2nd person singular; subject of stative verbs); you (patient of transitive verbs); your (2nd person singular possessor; body parts and kinship nouns) 1b) **-ni- . . .-bi** circumfix you (2nd person plural, subject of stative verbs); you (patient of transitive verbs); your (2nd person plural possessor; body parts and kinship nouns) 2a) **nitáwa** pro your; yours; you own it, it is your own 2b) **nitáwabi** pro your; yours; you all own it, it is your own 3) **-gi- ; -ki- ; -k-** pref on one's own (marker of possessive verbs where the agent is acting on his/her own thing, body part, or relative; the resulting possessive verbs are always of Class 1)

yours *pro* 1a) **nitáwa** pro your; yours; you own it, it is your own 1b) **nitáwabi** pro your; yours; you all own it, it is your own

yourself *pro* **niyé** pro, vs yourself (emphasizes the subject or object); you are one

Yuwipi ceremony *np* **Wahíkiyabi** n Yuwipi, Tie up, Calling of the spirits ceremony; shaking tent; radio (object); radio broadcast ▸ **Wahíkiyabi ecúbi** cp Yuwipi, Tie up, Calling of the spirits ceremony; shaking tent

Z

zero *num* **dáguniši** pro, num it is nothing, there is none; zero

zigzag *n v* **gaksíksi** adv in a zigzag manner

Zortman (Montana) *ngeo* **Máza Ok'á** ngeo Zortman (Montana)

Zurich (Montana) *ngeo* **Gaȟé núba** ngeo Zurich (Montana)

References

Andersen, Raoul, and Alberta Stoney. 1970. "(Assiniboin) Origins and Adaptations: A Case for Reappraisal." *Ethnohistory* 17, no. 1–2: 49–61.

Bellam, Ernest Jay. 1975. *Studies in Stoney Morphology and Phonology*. Master's thesis, University of Calgary.

BigEagle, Bronte. 2017. *The Legend of the T-Rex's Short Arms*. Saskatoon: Saskatchewan Indian Cultural Center.

———. 2018. *Legend of the Duck-Billed Dinosaur*. Saskatoon: Saskatchewan Indian Cultural Center.

———. 2019. *The Legend of the Ankylosaurus*. Saskatoon: Saskatchewan Indian Cultural Center.

Collette, Vincent. "Comparative and Historical Aspects of Nakoda Dialectology." *International Journal of American Linguistics*. 88, no. 4: 441–67.

Collette, Vincent, Armand McArthur, and Wilma Kennedy. 2019. *Nakón-i'a wo! Beginning Nakoda*. Regina: University of Regina Press.

Cumberland, Linda, A. 2005. *A Grammar of Assiniboine: A Siouan Language of the Northern Plains*. PhD diss., Indiana University.

DeMallie, Robert, and David Miller. 2001. "Assiniboine." In *Handbook of North American Indians, vol. 13, part 1*. Edited by Raymond DeMallie. Washington DC: Smithsonian Institution.

Denig, Edwin T. 1854. "Assiniboine Vocabulary." *Historical and Statistical Information Respecting the History, Condition and Prospects of the Indian Tribes of the United States: Collected and Prepared under the Direction of the Bureau of Indian Affairs per Act of Congress of March 3rd 1847*. Vol. 4. Edited by Henry R. Schoolcraft. Washington DC: Historical American Indian Press.

Drummond, Valerie E. 1976. *Carry-The-Kettle Assiniboine Texts*. Master's thesis. Toronto: University of Toronto.

Erdman, Rhyasen, and Corrie Lee. 1997. *Stress in Stoney*. Calgary: University of Calgary.

Farnell, Brenda. 1995. *Do You See What I Mean? Plains Indian Sign Talk and the Embodiment of Action*. Austin: University of Texas Press.

Fourstar, Jerome. 1978. *Assiniboine Dictionary*. Self-published, Wolf Point MT.

Haywahe, John. 1992. *Four Seasons-Four Languages, Five year calendar* (Nakoda section). Edited by Jean Bellegarde and Marian Dinwoodie. Handbook. Fort Qu'Appelle: Touchwood File Hills' Qu'Appelle Tribal Council.

Hewitt, J. N. B., ed. 2000 [1930]. *The Assiniboine*. Introduction by David R. Miller. Norman: University of Oklahoma Press.

Hollow, C. Robert, Jr. 1970. "A Note on Assiniboine Phonology." *International Journal of American Linguistics* 36, 4. 296–98.

Levin, Norman B. 1964. *The Assiniboine Language*. Bloomington: Indiana University Press and Mouton.

Lowie, Robert H. The Trustees of Indiana University. 1960. "A Few Assiniboine Texts." *Anthropological Linguistics* 2, no. 8: 1–30.

Lowie, Robert H. 1910. *The Assiniboine, Vol. 1*. New York: Published by order of the Trustees.

McLeod, Neal. 2000. "Plains Cree Identity: Borderlands, Ambiguous Genealogies and Narrative Irony." *Canadian Journal of Native Studies* 20, no. 2: 437–54.

Parks, Douglas R. 2002 *English-Nakoda, Nakoda-English Student Dictionary*. Bloomington: Hoteja Project and Indiana University Press.

Parks, Douglas R., and Raymond J. DeMallie. 1992. "Sioux, Assiniboine, and Stoney Dialects: A Classification." *Anthropological Linguistics* 34, no. 1–4: 233–55.

———, eds. 2002. *Nakoda Stories from Fort Belknap Reservation, Montana*. Fort Belknap MT: Hoteja Project and Indiana University American Indian Studies Research Institute.

Parks, Douglas R., Raymond J. DeMallie, Brenda Farnell, and Erik Gooding. 1994. Assiniboine Alphabet Workshop, Fort Belknap College, July 26, 1994.

Parks, Douglas, Selena Ditmar, and Mindy Morgan. 1999. "Nakoda Language Lessons." Fort Belknap MT: Indiana University Nakoda Language Project.

Parks, Douglas R., and Robert L. Rankin. 2001. "Siouan Languages." *Handbook of North American Indians vol. 13, part 1.*. Edited by Raymond DeMallie. Washington DC: Smithsonian Institution.

Rankin, Robert L., Richard T. Carter, A. Wesley Jones, John E. Koontz, David S. Rood, and Iren Hartmann Eds. 2015. *Comparative Siouan Dictionary*. Leipzig: Max Planck Institute for Evolutionary Anthropology. http://csd.clld.org.

Ray, Arthur J. 1974. *Indians in the Fur Trade: Their Role as Trappers, Hunters, and Middlemen in the Lands Southwest of Hudson Bay, 1660–1870*. Toronto: University of Toronto Press.

Riggs, Stephen Return. 1992 [1890]. *A Dakota-English Dictionary*. Edited by James Owen Dorsey. Washington DC: Government Printing Office.

Rodnick, David. 1938. "The Fort Belknap Assiniboine of Montana." 1938. PhD diss., A Study for the Applied Anthropology Unit of the United States Indian Service, University of Pennsylvania.

Rodnick, Dennis. 1937. "Political Structure and Status among the Assiniboine Indians." *American Anthropologist, New Series* 39: 408–16.

Russell, Dale, R. 1990. "The 18th Century Western Cree and Their Neighbours: Identity and Territory." Master's thesis, University of Saskatchewan.

Ryan, Kenny. 1998. *Nakona Language*. Fort Peck MT: Fort Peck Community College.

Schudel, Emily K. 1997. "Elicitation and Analysis of Nakoda Texts from Southern Saskatchewan." Master's thesis, University of Regina.

Shields, George, Sr. 2012. *2012a Assiniboine Narratives from Fort Belknap, Montana. Stories told by George Shields Sr., part 1: Interlinear Texts*. Bloomington: Indiana University American Indian Research Institute.

Taylor, Allan R. 1981. "Variations in Canadian Assiniboine." *Siouan and Caddoan Linguistics Newsletter* (July). 9–16.

———. 1983. "Old Vocabularies and Linguistic Research: The Case of Assiniboine Napao." *Saskatchewan Anthropology Journal* 13: 31–44.

Thwaites, Reuben Gold. 1904–7. *Early Western Travels, 1748–1846: A Series of Annotated Reprints of Some of the Best and Rarest Contemporary Volumes of Travel, Descriptive of the Aborigines and Social and Economic Conditions in the Middle and Far West, during the Period of Early American Settlement.* Vol. 24. Cleveland: A. H. Clark.

Trudgill, Peter, and J. K. Chambers. 1988. *Dialectology.* Cambridge: Cambridge University Press.

Ullrich, Jan F., ed. 2008. *New Lakota Dictionary: Lakȟótiyapi-English, English-Lakȟótiyapi & Incorporating the Dakota Dialects of Yankton-Yanktonai & Santee — Sisseton.* 2nd ed. Bloomington: Lakota Language Consortium.

Walde, Dale. 2010. "Ethnicity, the Archaeological Record, and Mortlach." *Plains Anthropologist* 55, no. 214: 153–68.

Weasel, Rose. 2012b. *Assiniboine Narratives from Fort Belknap, Montana, part 1: Interlinear Texts.* Stories Told by Rose Weasel. Bloomington: Indiana University American Indian Research Institute.

West, Shannon L. 2003. "Subjects and Objects in Assiniboine Nakoda." Master's thesis, University of Victoria.

In Studies in the Native Languages of the Americas

To order or obtain more information
on these or other University
of Nebraska Press titles, visit
nebraskapress.unl.edu.

Printed in the USA
CPSIA information can be obtained
at www.ICGtesting.com
LVHW082341281023
762437LV00007B/141

9 781496 229724